Criminal Procedure II:
From Bail to Jail

Criminal Procedure II: From Bail to Jail

Fourth Edition

Richard G. Singer

Distinguished Professor of Law Emeritus
Rutgers, The State University of
New Jersey School of Law

Kenneth Williams

Professor of Law
South Texas College of Law Houston
Houston, Texas

Wolters Kluwer

Published by Wolters Kluwer in New York.

Wolters Kluwer Legal & Regulatory U.S. serves customers worldwide with CCH, Aspen Publishers, and Kluwer Law International products. (www.WKLegaledu.com)

To contact Customer Service, e-mail customer.service@wolterskluwer.com, call 1-800-234-1660, fax 1-800-901-9075, or mail correspondence to:

Wolters Kluwer
Attn: Order Department
PO Box 990
Frederick, MD 21705

Printed in the United States of America.

1 2 3 4 5 6 7 8 9 0

ISBN 978-1-4548-4812-7

Library of Congress Cataloging-in-Publication Data

Names: Singer, Richard G., author. | Williams, Kenneth (Kenneth A.), 1961-, author.
Title: Criminal procedure II : from bail to jail / Richard G. Singer, Distinguished Professor of Law Emeritus, Rutgers, The State University of New Jersey School of Law; Kenneth Williams, Professor of Law, South Texas College of Law Houston, Houston, Texas.
Description: Fourth edition. | New York : Wolters Kluwer, [2018] | Includes bibliographical references and index.
Identifiers: LCCN 2017052572 | ISBN 9781454848127 (hardcover : alk. paper)
Subjects: LCSH: Criminal procedure — United States.
Classification: LCC KF9619.85 .S56 2018 | DDC 345.73/05—dc23
LC record available at https://lccn.loc.gov/2017052572

About Wolters Kluwer Legal & Regulatory U.S.

Wolters Kluwer Legal & Regulatory U.S. delivers expert content and solutions in the areas of law, corporate compliance, health compliance, reimbursement, and legal education. Its practical solutions help customers successfully navigate the demands of a changing environment to drive their daily activities, enhance decision quality and inspire confident outcomes.

Serving customers worldwide, its legal and regulatory portfolio includes products under the Aspen Publishers, CCH Incorporated, Kluwer Law International, ftwilliam .com, and MediRegs names. They are regarded as exceptional and trusted resources for general legal and practice-specific knowledge, compliance and risk management, dynamic workflow solutions, and expert commentary.

To Daniel and Hana —
Twins definitely different in temperament,
but firmly alike in love, fun, and soccer.

Summary of Contents

Contents

Contents

Contents

Contents

A (Very) Short Preface and Request

Although students may not believe it, academics rarely write for the purpose of owning Ferraris. I wrote this book in the hope that it may bring to students both clarity of doctrine and some insight of theory in one of the less illuminated corners of criminal practice. The book cannot succeed in that goal unless I actually learn what students have found helpful and unhelpful. I implore all readers, therefore, to take the time to write me at *rsinger@crab.rutgers.edu* and tell me what they liked, and didn't, in the work. Future readers will reap the benefit of those comments. Several major changes in the third edition — including some new chapters — were a result of student response to the second edition.

Richard Singer

I also implore readers to contact me at kwilliams@stcl.edu to tell me what you liked or didn't like about the book, and also with suggestions on improvements you'd like to see in future editions.

Kenneth Williams

December 2017

A (Very) Short
Preface and Request

December 2012

Acknowledgments

This edition — like those before it — has been worked on and improved by many people. To Debbie Carr, who worked graciously and patiently on earlier drafts of these materials, and Debi Leak, who filled in marvelously after Debbie received a well-deserved promotion, I owe more thanks than I can pen. My editor at Wolters Kluwer, Sue McClung, was extremely generous in comments and in providing extensions on deadlines. My wife, Karen Garfing, again sacrificed much time to read drafts and contributed many of the new comments. Daniel and Hana, who were growing up during the first edition and were headlong into soccer during the creation of the second edition, have now completed two years (each) at college. Astute readers will find them throughout these pages. Finally, I thank those readers who wrote to correct errors or add observations or suggestions. Only through those e-mails can this work be enhanced as the editions grow.

Criminal Procedure II:
From Bail to Jail

CHAPTER 1

Introduction

The police cars come to a screeching halt. Defendant Dan Dastardly emerges from his car, hands in the air. The police conduct a warrantless search authorized by the exigency of the moment, and give Dastardly his Miranda warnings. Dan, in handcuffs, sneers at Steve McGarrett, who utters those infamous words: "Book 'im, Danno."

Now what? What does it mean to "book him"? And what happens after that, during the long interval between arrest and trial?

The major steps in the process are shown on the next page in Figure 1.1. This book will explore each of these steps in turn. As we do so, keep in mind that each of the actors in the system is well aware of the powers (and restrictions on the powers) of people in other parts of the system. That is critical to understanding many of the things that lawyers do during this process. Here we go, Danno.

A. SOURCES

Students who have studied the materials on police investigative techniques, canvassed thoroughly in Bloom and Brodin, Constitutional Criminal Procedure: Examples and Explanations, know that many questions of searches and seizures, police interrogation techniques, lineups, and other such areas, have been subjected to detailed scrutiny by the United States Supreme Court.

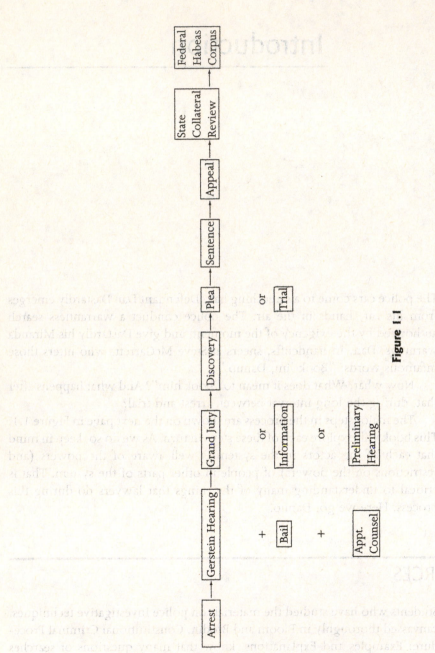

Figure 1.1

I. Introduction

It was not always so. Fifty years ago, before the "Warren Revolution" in the Supreme Court, it was the rare decision which held any part of the Bill of Rights applicable to the states at all. Even then, the standards established for assessing the validity of police conduct tended to be fairly flexible and open-ended (for example, the due process clause was said to proscribe only conduct that exceeded the "conscience of the court").

In the activities discussed in this book, the law is much more in the status it was in the pre-Warren days. Although in several key areas — for example, the selection of juries — the United States Supreme Court appears to have established meaningful standards of conduct, in the main the Court has been far less "active" in these areas than in those of police (mis)conduct. That means that state governments are left to supervise these arenas more carefully and thoroughly. In this regard, there are two main actors — (1) state courts as case-deciders; (2) state courts as administrative agencies. Two other forces, far less active, are (3) the legislature; (4) executive agencies, such as the prosecutor's office. A brief excursus on this situation may be helpful here.

Students are familiar with state courts as deciders — indeed creators — of common law and statutory questions. As courts decide an individual's plea for justice, they may — and often do — set out rules which are to be followed by other parties in later similar cases. But courts are more than deciders of individual cases. Supreme Courts are the highest authority in a state (judicial) agency. As such, those courts must establish rules for all manner of questions arising during judicial proceedings. To take an extreme example, courts must decide whether briefs should be limited to a specific number of pages. It would be unlikely that a litigant would raise that question in a justiciable fashion; yet a court might well wish to create such an administrative rule.

In the past 50 years, courts have established a panoply of regulations that affect areas of the conduct of litigation. In civil procedure, states have tended to adopt, almost verbatim, the federal rules enunciated to control federal procedure by the United States Supreme Court. In the area of criminal procedure, however, states have often elected not to follow the federal lead, but to promulgate their own regulations, many of which are in sharp contrast to the federal rules. Here, therefore, there is a wide range of rules on almost every subject. In adopting such rules the state Supreme Court acts essentially as a legislature for lower courts. These rules, however, are subject to change and reassessment even in the absence of a case or controversy that arises in a judicial setting.

The point here is that the adjudication of criminal charges is subject to regulation by a number of distinct processes and institutions. A lawyer (and hence a student) must often determine whether there is a state court decision governing the question. And even if there is no "decision," there may well be a rule of procedure established by the state supreme court in its "legislative" capacity. Indeed, many of the areas discussed in this book *are* so governed. This means that there is less uniformity in the law governing this subject area than there is in many subjects to which students may have been exposed.

And there is another layer. Courts sometimes resolve actual cases not by relying on either the state or federal constitution, or statutes, or court-enunciated and adopted "rules," but on their "supervisory" power,[1] a residual authority over courts and attorneys to make sure that "the waters of justice are not polluted."

Various agencies — the police, the prosecutor's office — may establish internal "rules," or "guidelines." While these will not create legally enforceable rights for defendants, courts may use them to suggest the parameters of "proper" behavior. And even within these systems there may be more decentralization. Federal Rule of Criminal Procedure 57, for example, allows each district court to fill in interstices with specifically local rules applicable only to that district, and the federal statute governing jury selection similarly allows some leeway to each federal district in carrying out the general aims of the statute.

Finally, because many of the issues covered in this book involve the conduct of lawyers — prosecutors and defense counsel — the rules of ethics of a particular state governing lawyers' conduct are likely to apply even if there are no court rules or decisions that cover the question. For example, even if a state does not require disclosure of particular items generally (see Chapter 6), the failure to disclose in a specific case might violate the state's rules of ethics. Of course, violation of rules established by the constitution or state decisional law is likely automatically to constitute an ethical infraction. Ethics should guide discretion in ways that the law does not — and perhaps cannot — purport to reach.

In the absence of some controlling regulation, such as a constitutional decision, or a state court-created rule of court, judges are more apt to look for guidance in other sources. One such group of sources, to which we will refer frequently, are sets of rules proposed by impartial arbiters and include the American Bar Association's various standards,[2] the American Law

---

1. For discussions of the supervisory power generally, see Beale, Reconsidering Supervisory Power in Criminal Cases: Constitutional and Statutory Limits on the Authority of the Federal Courts, 84 Colum. L. Rev. 143 (1984); Brady, A Separation of Powers Approach to the Supervisory Power of the Federal Courts, 34 Stan. L. Rev. 427 (1982).

2. Several separate sets of "standards" promulgated by the American Bar Association will have some bearing on at least some topics in this book: The "Standards for Criminal Justice," the "Standards of Professional Conduct," and the "Model Rules of Professional Conduct." The first set of standards consists of 23 volumes, relating specifically to "Defense Counsel," "Prosecutorial Conduct," "Sentencing," etc., and, more recently, specific standards relating to defense counsel conduct in capital cases, as well as mental health issues in criminal law, (http://www.americanbar.org/groups/criminal_justice/policy/standards.html). The second and third set of rules is meant to govern the conduct of all lawyers, in all litigation, although some rules are limited to governing the conduct of prosecutors. When one set of standards appears to conflict with another set of standards, some sense of the specialization

Institute's Model Code of Pre-Arraignment Procedure (hereafter ALI); and the National Conference of Commissioners on Uniform State Laws' Uniform Rules of Criminal Procedure (hereafter URCP).

This hierarchy may be illustrated as follows:

United States Constitution — Binding on all courts, federal and state

Federal Rules of Criminal Procedure — Binding on all federal courts; occasionally used as persuasive authority by state courts

State Constitutions — Binding on all courts in that state

State Rules of Criminal Procedure — Binding on all courts in that state

American Bar Association Standards or Model Rules — Persuasive authority only. Note: some ABA standards or rules are written to deal with all lawyers in all litigation other standards are restricted to the criminal process, and others are limited to specific actors in the criminal process. Some state courts have adopted some or all of these standards, either as a matter of case law or rule promulgation (see below)

Rules of Ethics/Conduct adopted by a state supreme court — binding on all attorneys licensed in that state (or on attorneys representing the U.S. government during litigation in that state)

American Law Institute Model Codes — Persuasive authority; binding on no one

Other "National" Standards — Persuasive authority; binding on no one

Prosecutorial guidelines — Regulate conduct of employees in that office, but are usually interpreted not to convey legal rights upon others (e.g., defendants) who might be affected thereby

One further caveat: As every law student knows, the procedural posture of the case may be crucial to determining the precise reach of the precedent — in a civil case, for example, the standard of review of a grant of summary judgment is different from that used by a court reviewing a jury verdict. The same holds true in the criminal process. Indeed, as detailed in Chapter 13, whether the decision is one on direct appeal, or during a petition for federal habeas corpus, or whether defense counsel objected

---

(or lack thereof) of the committee which proposed these standards may be helpful in assessing their impact. The United States Supreme Court has vacillated on the importance of some of these standards, on occasion appearing to embrace specific guidelines, and on other occasions spurning the notion that any set of standards or "checklist" could be of much assistance in determining constitutional (or even non-constitutional) questions. Indeed, in *Cone v. Bell*, 556 U.S. 449 (2009) Chief Justice Roberts concurred especially to reject the relevance of ABA Standards at all: "the lower courts should analyze the issue under the constitutional standards we have set forth, not under whatever standards the American Bar Association may have established. The ABA standards are wholly irrelevant to the disposition of this case, and the majority's passing citation of them should not be taken to suggest otherwise."

at the time, courts will use different standards in assessing a defendant's claim. In this book, however, case holdings will be treated as relatively interchangeable: we will not explicitly differentiate whether a case was on direct appeal or habeas, or whether it is being assessed on "harmless error" or "plain error." But those factors may make a difference in the ultimate importance of the decision.

B. AN OVERVIEW — THE IMPORTANCE OF DISCRETION

This book deals with events that occur after a defendant is arrested. For this reason, the course is sometimes referred to as "from bail to jail," and is distinguished from the "investigative" part of the process — search and seizure of materials, interrogation — which usually occurs before arrest in so-called street crimes. There, the defense attorney must act retrospectively, challenging what the state (police officers, etc.) has already done. In "white collar cases," on the other hand, the defense attorney may well become involved *before* the defendant is arrested, and well before an indictment. There is often much more leeway for lawyering skills in some cases. Although we will use the "street crime" as the paradigm case (as in the Dan Dastardly example above), the processes involved may occur in slightly different order and, therefore, provide more avenues for lawyering skills.

Perhaps the single most important thing to remember about this arena is that, like all systems, there are a significant number of points at which discretionary decisions either allow the process to continue, or halt the process. Thus: (1) a police officer may decide not to arrest a defendant, even if there is good evidence he has committed a crime; (2) a prosecutor may decide not to prosecute at all, or to prosecute on a lesser charge; (3) the grand jury, or a preliminary hearing, may determine that there is not sufficient cause to continue the prosecution; (4) juries may acquit the defendant, even if he is obviously guilty; and (5) judges, in their sentencing capacity, may impose a sentence substantially above or below the norm imposed in such cases. Moreover, any actor in this vast administrative process may attempt to influence, or even substantially constrain, later actors. A police officer who does not report key details in his report may well have precluded a prosecutor from seeking certain charges from the grand jury. A jury may substantially reduce a judge's sentencing power by acquitting the defendant of the most serious charges against her. And a parole board may ignore a judge's letter that it release the defendant "as soon as possible" or deny him parole "until he has served his maximum sentence." (Similarly, the judge may attempt to control a later actor's discretion, perhaps by imposing a sentence of $19\frac{1}{2}$-20 years, rather than one of 5-20.)

I. Introduction

Many analogize discretion to squeezing an inflated balloon: When one seeks to restrict the discretion in one part of the system, it will emerge at another point (the "hydraulic theory"). For example, if the legislature mandates specific sentences for all crimes, judicial discretion in sentencing is removed. But someone — the prosecutor, the jury, prison officials — will now have more power (discretion) to affect the ultimate fate of the defendant. Thus, wherever discretion appears, the question will be not whether it can be eliminated, but rather whether it can be regulated in such a way so that others in the system are not more empowered than before.

Justice Brandeis once extolled the states as "laboratories of democracy." By refusing to "constitutionalize" most of these trigger points, and only marginally impinging on the discretion within the system, the United States Supreme Court has enhanced that view. This book will, sometimes directly, but always indirectly, explore the strengths and weaknesses of those laboratories.

Early Decisions About the Newly Arrested Defendant

A. THE PROBABLE CAUSE HEARING AND THE INITIAL APPEARANCE

McGarrett told Danno to "book" Dan. "Booking" is an administrative process, occurring at a police station, at which the police identify the defendant, indicate the charges upon which he is arrested, and fingerprint and photograph him. But wait—maybe we're getting ahead of ourselves. First things first. Should the police even have seized Dan at all? Assume that the police arrested Dan, as they arrest most offenders, without an arrest warrant. While they believed they had probable cause for their actions, the Fourth Amendment requires the police to bring Dan to an impartial fact finder, usually a judge-magistrate, who will ascertain, based almost entirely on the evidence provided by the police, whether they had probable cause to seize Dan and to hold him for the alleged crime. In *Gerstein v. Pugh*, 420 U.S. 103 (1975), the United States Supreme Court held that such a "probable cause" hearing must be held within a "reasonable time." In a later decision, *County of Riverside v. McLaughlin*, 500 U.S. 44 (1991), the Court appeared to set the outside limit on such a hearing at no more than 48 hours after the arrest, although a careful reading of the decision suggests that the hour limit was only a presumptive guideline. These decisions were based on the Fourth rather than the Fifth Amendment, and do not directly address the issues of due process involved in such hearings.

This "probable cause" hearing need not be elaborate. After all, if the police had had the time to appear before a magistrate before the arrest, they would have obtained a warrant *ex parte*, on the basis of hearsay, informer's information, etc. That kind of *ex parte* procedure is clearly constitutional. The fact that the police now have Dan in custody does not affect the level of proof needed to "seize" him. Moreover, as students of the "investigation" part of the criminal process know, defining "probable cause" is difficult, but all agree that, because it is simply a means of initiating the process, it is a relatively low standard of proof. (See Bloom and Brodin, Constitutional Criminal Procedure, Ch. 4.)

Even if Dan is not constitutionally entitled to a *Gerstein* hearing (for example, if there had been an arrest warrant), all jurisdictions, either as a matter of statute or court rule, require that he be brought before a judicial officer to be apprised of the charges against him, and of his constitutional rights, such as the right to counsel, which will be available for the rest of the criminal proceeding. This is purely an informational event — the defendant need not (and usually is advised not to) speak, much less enter a plea to the charges. These charges are likely to be conveyed by means of a *complaint* — an informal paper that summarizes the facts (as then known and alleged) sworn to before a magistrate. This complaint will quickly be supplanted by more official papers filed by the prosecutor.

The *Gerstein* probable cause issue is often combined with an "initial appearance." For administrative convenience, a determination of bail may be made at this same proceeding. *CAVEAT:* Jurisdictions sometimes refer to this very first hearing as a "preliminary hearing," rather than a "probable cause" hearing or "initial appearance." That may cause confusion later when we examine a true "preliminary examination" in contrast to a grand jury proceeding (see Chapter 5). Thus, it is best to refer to this proceeding as either a *Gerstein* or "probable cause" hearing. There are, then, three terms which you should not confuse, even if the courts sometimes do:

- *Gerstein or "probable cause" hearing* — must be held within 48 hours of a warrantless arrest; its sole purpose is to determine whether the police had probable cause to arrest the defendant.
- *Initial appearance* — before a magistrate who (a) informs the defendant of the charges in the complaint; (b) sets bail; (c) determines whether defendant is entitled to appointed counsel. Held even if the defendant was arrested pursuant to a warrant. Often combined with a *Gerstein* hearing if the arrest was without a warrant.
- *Preliminary hearing or examination* — a term denoting a proceeding before a magistrate (or sometimes a nonjudicial officer) at which the defendant is represented by counsel, and may present evidence and cross witnesses. The term is often used improperly to describe either a "probable cause" hearing or "initial appearance."

B. BAIL

1. The Mechanics of Bail

Assume that the magistrate finds that there was probable cause to arrest Dan. What should the police do with him now? Should they throw him in jail and hold him there until trial? Let him return to his house for afternoon tea? Race down to the courthouse and try him that afternoon?

a. Bail Before the 1960s

Dan, of course, wants to be released now. He wants to get out of jail, where conditions are often hideous, and return to his family and his job, and to seek evidence rebutting the charges against him. But the problem is that he may skip town. On the other hand, if all defendants were detained pending trial, the jails would be overcrowded quickly. English and American law, therefore, established the idea of "bail" *as an attempt to assure the defendant's return for trial, but to avoid his incarceration pretrial.* Initially, defendants were required to obtain a surety who, should the defendant abscond, would be tried (and punished) in his place.[1] Over several centuries, this notion changed to simply having the defendant, or the surety, proffer an amount of money, or real property, which would be forfeited if the defendant did not return for trial.

Since most defendants are relatively poor, any amount of money bail set by a judge might well be prohibitive. These defendants go to *bail bondsmen* to whom they give a percentage (usually 10 percent) of the bail amount. The bail bondsmen then submit to the court the entire bail amount. If the defendant appears for trial, the bondsman gets his money back — but the defendant does not get the 10 percent which he has placed with the bondsman. If the defendant absconds, the bondsman is theoretically liable to forfeit the entire bail amount, though this rarely happens. On the other hand, the bondsman is authorized to hire "bounty hunters" to pursue the defendant and obtain his return, unrestrained by the Constitution[2] (because the bounty hunters are merely enforcing a contract between the defendant and the bondsman).[3] While bail bondsmen and bounty hunters obviously

---

1. Several centuries later, the courts took a polar view. In a New York case, a trial judge refused to allow a stranger to post a defendant's bail, arguing that the defendant would have no incentive to return to court if strangers were allowed to post bail. *New York Times*, May 4, 2001, at B3.

2. See, e.g., *United States v. Rose*, 731 F.2d 1337 (8th Cir. 1984). See generally Andrew Patrick, Running from the Law: Should Bounty Hunters Be Considered State Actors and Thus Subject to Constitutional Restraints?, 52 Vand. L. Rev. 171 (1999).

3. See *Taylor v. Taintor*, 83 U.S. (16 Wall.) 366 (1872).

perform an important role in enforcing bail conditions and pursuing "bail jumpers," there has always been a tension surrounding their work. Thus, for example, in *Schilb v. Kuebel*, 404 U.S. 357 (1971), Justice Blackmun, speaking for the Court, referred to the "professional bail bondsman system with all its abuses . . . in full and odorous bloom. . .".

b. Bail Reform in the 1960s and Later

By the 1960s, a distaste for bail bondsmen, as well as a recognition that requiring money bail from many indigent defendants was tantamount to precluding release on bail, led courts and legislatures to experiment with new approaches to bail. These critiques were complemented by studies which seemed to demonstrate that persons incarcerated prior to trial were more likely to be convicted, and, when convicted, likely to receive a harsher sentence than those who had secured their release on bail. Some of this disparity was thought to be attributable to the ability of released defendants to find witnesses and other evidence which would support their claims of innocence (or reduced culpability).[4] Initially, on an experimental basis, the VERA Foundation in New York attempted to establish methods by which facts surrounding the defendant's character and his ties to the community could be quickly verified. Personnel, many of whom were law students, were placed in police stations or jails and interviewed the defendant almost immediately after arrest, obtaining facts that might be verified by calls to family members, or employers, even prior to the first setting of bail. Such bail agencies are now a fixed part of the pre-trial firmament in most urban jurisdictions.

The experimental programs proved successful — defendants whose ties to the community and/or character could be quickly established were released on bail, and overwhelmingly returned for later court appearances.[5] Based in part upon these felicitous results, the entire paradigm shifted. In 1966 Congress enacted the Federal Bail Reform Act of 1966, which established a presumption that all (federal) defendants should be released without any money bail at all; i.e., released on their own recognizance (ROR). The statute

---

4. At least one court found that, in the particular circumstances in that case, a white attorney representing a black defendant would have great difficulty in finding witnesses and persuading them to testify for the defendant. This, said the court, required release. See *Kinney v. Lenon*, 425 F.2d 209 (9th Cir. 1970). Recent figures indicate that two-thirds of detained defendants were convicted of a felony, compared to 46 percent of released defendants. See Bureau of Justice Statistics, Felony Defendants in Large Urban Counties, 1998, p.24 (NCJ Report # 187232 2001). These data, however, do not reflect whether those detained were already more likely to have committed felonies, and therefore, were more likely to be detained.
5. Although statistics are always somewhat suspect, it appears that 76 percent of released defendants make all scheduled appearances, and 95 percent return for trial. See Bureau of Justice Statistics, *supra*, n.4, p.21. Most of the failures to appear seem to be because of poor notice; only 5 percent remained a fugitive after a year.

expressly provides, for example, that "the judicial officer may not impose a financial condition that results in the pre-trial detention of the person." For instances where the court was doubtful about pre-trial release, judges were instructed to set increasingly stern conditions for release. States followed the same reform path, either by abolishing money bail, or by providing the same kind of service, at a 10 percent rate, that bondsmen had previously provided. The significant distinction, however, was that if the defendant came to trial he would receive his 10 percent surety amount back (less a small administrative fee). This system, known as "cash bail," has been replicated in most states. The dramatic leap from surety-money bail as the primary means of detaining defendants to these other systems has been swift and full.

Although far less common than pre-1960, money bail may still be required in many states for at least some offenses. Courts have consistently rejected the argument that indigent defendants unable to make bail, even of a small amount, are denied equal protection of the laws. Cf. *Schilb v. Kuebel*, 404 U.S. 357 (1971) (upholding as not unconstitutional Illinois' state bail system, by which defendant was required to forfeit 1 percent of his bail, to cover administrative costs). See, however, Justice Douglas's opinion in *Bandy v. United States*, 81 S. Ct. 197 (1960): "To continue to demand a substantial bond which the defendant is unable to secure raises considerable problems for the equal administration of the law . . . Can an indigent be denied freedom, where a wealthy man would not, because he does not happen to have enough property to pledge for his freedom?" See also *Pugh v. Rainwater*, 557 F.2d 1189 (5th Cir. 1977).

c. Determining Bail

In theory, the amount of bail — or the conditions attached to pretrial release — should be a result of the weighing of several factors, of which the most important are:

1. *The seriousness of the crime charged.* All crime is serious; but some crimes are more serious than others. The more serious the crime, the higher the penalty, and the less likely, all other things being equal, the defendant will return voluntarily.
2. *The evidence against the defendant.* If the evidence is overwhelming, and the defendant knows that, voluntary return becomes less likely. Remember, however, that this determination can be made only on the evidence that the police or prosecution believe they have at the time the determination is made. Facts uncovered at a later time during the investigation may change the assessment here.

3. *The defendant's ties to the community.* A defendant who has lived in, or has other ties to, the community is assumed less likely to leave than one who is a transient passing through.

4. *The character of the defendant.* The defendant's past criminal record may be considered here: a transient religious leader may be deemed more likely to return for trial than a three-time convicted felon even if he has a family in the community.

Assessing the facts in each case may be extremely difficult. Of the four factors cited above, only the first is both relatively unchangeable and not subject to subjective evaluation: The legislatively set maximum penalty for robbery does not alter with the facts of the specific case. For that reason, among others, courts setting bail are likely to look at the charge as the most important criteria. Thus, many jurisdictions have established a "bail schedule," under which a specific charge generates a specific presumed bail unless there is overwhelming reason to vary from that presumption. It is *possible* (but unlikely) that reliance on such a schedule would now be held unconstitutional. In *Stack v. Boyle*, 342 U.S. 1 (1951), the Supreme Court intimated — but did not need to *hold* — that every bail determination must be made on the particular facts of the case, including those related to the defendant.

As to the second factor, police are unlikely to suggest that their evidence is weak. Until the processes of ROR described above, the third and fourth factors almost always depended, at least at the initial appearance, solely upon the defendant's statements. It would have been unusual, at least at the first setting of bail, that that information could be validated.

d. Determining the Conditions of Release

Even if a defendant is released without bail, the judge may impose conditions on that release. As a general matter, the conditions must be shaped to the individual, not as the result of a fixed rule. Thus, several federal courts have declared unconstitutional a provision in the "Adam Walsh" amendment to the Bail Reform Act (18 U.S.C. §3142(c)(1)(B)) that required electronic monitoring and restriction on travel for all persons charged with specific sexual offenses, because the provision precluded any individualized consideration of the defendant's likelihood of flight. See, e.g., *U.S. v. Merritt*, 612 F. Supp. 2d 1074 (D. Neb. 2009); *U.S. v. Polouizzi*, 697 F. Supp. 2d 381 (E.D.N.Y. 2010). Contra: *United States v. Stephens*, 594 F.3d 1033 (8th Cir. 2010) (holding that a facial challenge to the Amendment fails because there must be "some" defendants to whom the conditions could constitutionally apply). See 54 A.L.R. F.2d 1195 (2011).

2. The Procedures of Bail

Because the most important immediate concern of an arrested defendant is obtaining release, initial bail determinations are often made in informal settings, without counsel, and often without any set procedures. This is not surprising; defendants are not anxious to delay the moment of the first determination of bail, hoping that the decision will allow them to go home. And for persons charged with minor offenses, many states allow the setting of bail (or release on a summons or citation) to be done by the police in the police station. Moreover, initial bail decisions are made on the basis of what may be very skimpy evidence — almost always hearsay evidence of some sort. Again, however, waiting for evidence which would be admissible under the rules of evidence, and for the defendant to obtain evidence supporting his desire for no (or low) bail might result in delaying the defendant's release.

Surprisingly, there appears to be no definitive answer as to whether the defendant or the prosecutor has the burden on the flight risk question, or what the standard of proof is. Obviously, the prosecutor must rely on whatever information she has at the time to carry that burden.

In at least some states the victim may appear and present evidence.[6] This practice seems undesirable, however, since the victim is unlikely to be able to speak to the defendant's flight risk, and is more likely to simply ask for some kind of protection from the defendant.

While states do not preclude attorneys from representing defendants at the first determination, requiring an appointed counsel be present at that first determination would be extremely difficult. The United States Supreme Court in *Coleman v. Alabama*, 399 U.S. 1 (1970), appeared to lean in the direction of seeing this proceeding as a Sixth Amendment "criminal prosecution," where there would be a right to appointed counsel. In *Rothgery v. Gillespie County*, 554 U.S. 191 (2008), the Court held that a defendant was entitled to have counsel present at the "first judicial proceeding."[7] The Court was reluctant to say that this suggested a right to *appointed* counsel, although

---

6. See, e.g., Mo. Const. art. I, §32.

7. After Rothgery's initial appearance, he was released on bail, but then indicted and rearrested. He was unable to make bail, and was sent to jail. When he finally obtained appointed counsel, that attorney quickly demonstrated to the state that he had been wrongly identified, and the indictment was quashed. Thereafter he sued the state under §1983 for deprivation of civil rights, in particular his being jailed after the (wrongful) indictment. He argued that if he had counsel present at his initial appearance, the mistake would have been discovered, and he never would have been indicted and jailed. The Court held that the suit would lie. Even though this was a civil suit, there is little doubt that the holding applies directly to criminal cases, though the remedy for not allowing (or providing) the lawyer is obscure.

Rothgery had specifically asked for appointed counsel at his appearance. Many commentators believe that the Court will issue a positive, clarifying opinion. In light of his desire for a speedy resolution (and hopefully, release), however, a defendant might well waive that right (if it were so established) at that hearing. Of course, whether at the initial bail hearing or at any later proceeding, if the defendant has counsel, the counsel will be allowed to participate in that proceeding.

Suppose, at his initial appearance, at which bail is being set, the defendant, attempting to avoid liability, says to the magistrate: "I shot him, your honor, but only after he lunged at me with that knife." The defendant does not know (particularly, if he has not been so informed by a lawyer) that his claim of self-defense does not go to undermine the probable cause basis of the prosecution — at least not at this point of the proceedings. If the defendant later wishes to deny that he shot the victim, can the statement made at the bail hearing be used against him? The case law is unclear as to whether a defendant's statements at a bail hearing, usually made without the presence of counsel, are "coerced" within the meaning of the Fifth Amendment, and therefore barred from trial. On the one hand, no one actually compels the defendant to speak; indeed, magistrates often caution the defendant that he need say nothing at the proceeding. On the other, a defendant who does not speak is unlikely to obtain (or at least fears that he will not obtain) a "favorable" bail. Is that pressure sufficient to make any statement "involuntary" under the Fifth Amendment? See *State v. Fenner*, 381 Md. 1, 846 A.2d 1020 (2004) (statement is admissible).

This discussion of the initial determination of bail suggests one very important point: the decision on bail is always fluid. Because bail as initially established is based upon fragmentary facts, the amount of bail, or the other conditions of release, imposed upon a defendant are always subject to reassessment. The amount of bail may be revised upward or downward whenever the factors above are perceived to change. Thus, if the leading witness against the defendant recants his statements to the police, the court may perceive that the likelihood of conviction has sufficiently decreased so as to warrant a change of the conditions of release. Conversely, if the victim emerges from a coma to identify the defendant as the perpetrator, the amount of bail may be increased, or the conditions of community release made more restrictive. And while most bail is set initially in the absence of counsel, once counsel is obtained (either privately or through appointment), facts may be garnered which will support the defendant's earlier naked assertions, whether relating to the crime, or to his eligibility for bail. Thus, motions for reduction (or removal) of bail are quite common.

3. Preventive Detention — Security of the Community as a Criterion of Bail

a. The "Capital" Exception to Bail

The Eighth Amendment to the Constitution provides that "excessive bail shall not be required . . ." Some writers have argued that this means that all defendants must be constitutionally entitled to some level of bail. After all, if jurisdictions could assure that the bail set was not "excessive" by simply not allowing bail at all, the provision would become relatively meaningless. Notwithstanding this rather straightforward interpretation of the provision, the Supreme Court has never held that bail is constitutionally guaranteed, and has in fact strongly intimated that it is not. The prime explanation for this is historical; both before and after the Revolution, defendants charged with capital offenses were not afforded the opportunity for bail. Thus, the Court has said, there must be "some" exceptions to the otherwise plain meaning of the provision, and the exceptions would be established pragmatically. Today, at least 40 states preclude bail in "capital offenses, where the proof is evident or the presumption great." See, e.g., Vt. Const. chapter II, §40. It has been held that placing the burden on the defendant to show that the proof of his guilt is not "evident" is unconstitutional, *State v. Purcell*, 778 N.E.2d 695 (Ill. 2002) (applying state constitution), although other courts allow the state to place the burden on the defendant. See *Commonwealth v. Baker*, 343 Mass. 162, 177 N.E.2d 783 (1961); *State v. Arthur*, 390 So.2d 717 (Fla. 1980), aff'g *Arthur v. Harper*, 371 So.2d 96 (Fla. Dist. Ct. App. 1978).

b. Non-Capital Felonies

The "capital" exception was established when many, indeed most, felonies were subject to capital punishment. It seems commonsensical that a defendant facing death, particularly if the evidence is strong, might decide to see his aunt in Rio if allowed out on bail, and never return. But suppose the defendant is charged with offenses that could — or must — result in imprisonment of 150 years? Or life imprisonment without the possibility of parole? Some states extend the "capital exception" to these situations as well, on the ground that the punishment threatened is "the equivalent" of death, and, therefore, just as likely to result in the defendant's absconding.

A majority of states allow preventive detention of non-capital felons in some situations, either explicitly, or by interpretation of clauses not unlike those of the Eighth Amendment. Indeed, recent legislation in a number of states has made bail either unavailable, or difficult to obtain, for defendants charged with, among other crimes, stalking or domestic violence. Such statutes *precluding* bail in cases involving non-capital charges have been viewed warily, and on occasion held unconstitutional. See, e.g., *Hunt v.*

Roth, 648 F.2d 1148 (8th Cir.), judgment vacated for mootness, 455 U.S. 478 (1981) (Nebraska statute prohibiting bail in sexual offenses involving penetration by force where the proof is evident or the presumption great violates the excessiveness clause of the Eighth Amendment). But see *State ex rel. Romley v. Rayes*, 206 Ariz. 58 (Ariz. App. Div. 1, 2003) (upholding a state constitutional provision, adopted by voters, precluding bail for certain sexual offenses if the case is "evident" and the "presumption of guilt" "great"). The European Court of Human Rights has held that a similar practice of automatically denying bail, at least based solely on the fact that defendant had a prior record, violated the European Convention of Human Rights. See *Caballero v. United Kingdom* (Application No. 32819/96, Decided Feb. 8, 2000). On the other hand, at least since the *Salerno* case, discussed below, there is no *a priori* reason to believe that these statutes are *per se* unconstitutional.

c. Preventive Detention — Locking the Barn While the Horse Is Still There

Even if a magistrate concludes that a defendant charged with eight separate incidences of commercial burglaries is not a flight risk, she might be concerned that, if released pending trial, he may continue his life of crime — or that he would intimidate witnesses against him. Until *United States v. Salerno*, 481 U.S. 739 (1987), the magistrate could not overtly consider those fears — the attempt to assure the defendant's return to trial was the only acceptable *articulated* basis for setting the amount of bail. In the real world, however, judges faced with defendants whom they deemed likely to commit further crimes if released pending trial (even if they would return) would simply raise bail to a level they thought impossible for the defendant to reach. The magistrate would argue (if pressed) that, while a single burglary might not warrant a high bail, the cumulative penalty which the defendant faced necessitated what would otherwise be an "excessive" bail because of flight risks. Thus, community safety was an ever-present, if unstated, concern in setting bail.

Salerno removed the need for judicial subterfuge and endorsed, at least in limited circumstances, denial of bail based upon an assessment that the defendant would commit more crimes if released. The case involved the federal 1984 Bail Reform Act, which amended the 1966 Act referred to above. As noted above, under the earlier statute:

- there was a presumption that the defendant was to be released on his or her own recognizance;
- if the judge found that such release was problematic, she or he was still to release the defendant on a series of increasingly severe conditions;
- if those conditions were still not sufficient, money bail could be set.

2. Early Decisions About the Newly Arrested Defendant

Critics pointed to data showing a sizable percentage of those released pending trial were arrested for another felony.[8] These data, however, were less probative than they would first appear, since they did not include figures on how many of those charges resulted in conviction. (On the other hand, there may well have been released defendants who committed offenses but were not arrested for them. Thus, the data were truly unhelpful in deciding this matter.) Nevertheless, Congress amended the 1966 statute explicitly to provide, for the first time in American history, for "preventive detention" of individuals charged with certain enumerated felonies, if a judge, after a hearing, were persuaded by clear and convincing evidence that "no condition or combination of conditions will reasonably assure the appearance of the person as required and the safety of any other person and the community."

Although the challenge in *Salerno* to the statute was facial, and not as applied, the facts of the case are not unimportant. Anthony ("Fat Tony") Salerno, charged with a number of racketeering offenses, including murder, was alleged to be the "capo" of one of the most important organized crime families in the United States. His co-defendant, Vincent ("The Fish") Cafaro was a major figure in that organization. It is difficult to imagine two defendants for whom the statute was enacted, if not these two. Moreover, because the challenge *was* facial, the statute would be upheld if the Court could imagine *any* set of facts which would allow such detention. Suppose, for example, that a defendant were to say unequivocally "If I am released, the first thing I will do is kill the 50 people who informed on me." Only if that statement would not warrant preventive detention could the Court invalidate the statute.

The Court ultimately held that the statute was narrow enough, and sufficiently difficult to invoke[9] that it was not unconstitutional *on its face*. The Court first decided that the detention did not violate the Eighth Amendment because the detention was "regulatory" and not "punitive."[10] It then pointed out that the statute:

---

8. In 1998, 84 percent of persons released pending trial were not rearrested, while 10 percent were rearrested for charged felonies. See NCJ report, *supra*, n.4 at p.22.

9. This premise of the opinion may no longer obtain. By 2002, 48 percent of federal defendants were preventively detained pending trial under the Bail Reform Act provisions. See Bureau of Justice Statistics, U.S. Dep't of Justice, Compendium of Federal Justice Statistics, 2002, p.44, Table 3.4 (2004).

10. In a wide variety of instances, the courts have been faced with attempting to decide whether a particular governmental action is punitive, and hence activates the procedural protections of the Bill of Rights, or "regulatory" and is governed, if at all, only by a sense of balance under the due process clause. That dilemma will be ignored here, except to note that the Court relied primarily on legislative intent — if the legislature defined the action as "regulatory," only grossly excessive processes would then allow the Court to override that definition.

- provided for a full hearing, complete with counsel, cross-examination, and presentation of witnesses in front of an impartial judicial officer, who had to issue written findings of fact before detention could be ordered;
- placed upon the prosecution the burden of proof by clear and convincing evidence that *no* set of conditions could be established that would satisfy the goals of the statute (appearance and non-crime);
- provided that a detained defendant should be tried as promptly as possible, and given priority before others;
- provided that detainees should, as much as possible, be housed in facilities other than those used to house convicted offenders.

Salerno also appears to have settled that:

- the Eighth Amendment does *not* guarantee the possibility of bail to all defendants, even those charged with a non-capital offense;
- the presumption of innocence has no effect upon a pre-trial detainee's status; the presumption is merely a procedural device for allocating the burden of proof at trial. In other words, between arrest and trial the "presumption" has no effect, and the defendant is not "presumed" to be either innocent or guilty.

The right to bail is often defended on the "presumption of innocence" — that it is better that ten true offenders go free than to falsely punish an actually innocent person. In Deadly Dilemmas II: Bail and Crime, 85 Chi. Kent L. Rev. 21 (2010), Larry Laudan and Ronald J. Allen argued that unwarranted release of persons on bail resulted in substantial injury to innocent citizens, who became victims of crime. The authors strongly urged at least a minor alteration in bail practices, establishing a presumption against release of persons who had two or more criminal convictions. They contended that this would "likely reduce violent criminal victimization levels from 140,000 annually to about 53,000." *Id.* at 37.

While it is possible to read *Salerno* extremely narrowly, both because it was a facial challenge, and because the Court emphasized these statutory limitations upon preventive detention, that has not been the case. Nearly 20 states have statutorily authorized such detention based upon *Salerno*. Moreover, subsequent decisions by the lower federal courts (and state courts drawing sustenance from the opinion) have not narrowed *Salerno*.

One aspect of the 1984 Act, not involved in *Salerno*, is the statute's (rebuttable) presumption that there is no set of conditions that will assure the safety of the community from persons charged with (a) capital or life imprisonment offenses; (b) some drug offenses; (c) a "crime of violence"; or (d) any felony, if the defendant has twice before been convicted of any of the offenses mentioned in (a) through (c). Lower courts have upheld this presumption on the ground that it shifts only the burden of production, and not the burden of proof (remember that in the federal statute, the prosecutor's burden is clear and convincing evidence). Equally unclear is what "community safety" entails. Obviously, it includes possible crimes against the person. But suppose the judge concludes that the defendant will, if released, (continue to) sell drugs, or obstruct justice? Aren't *all* criminal acts by definition a danger to the community?

One other aspect of preventive detention may be troubling: it asks the fact finder to make explicit predictions about future (criminal) behavior. Yet scores of studies, conducted with varying methodologies, have concluded that the ability to predict future behavior, much less future *criminal* behavior, much less future criminal *violent* behavior, is very weak. Nonetheless, this inability has not troubled the courts. Assuming proper procedural protections, the courts, including the United States Supreme Court, have upheld judgments based upon such predictions. See, e.g., *Schall v. Martin*, 467 U.S. 253 (1984) (juveniles); *Kansas v. Hendricks*, 521 U.S. 346 (1997) (sexual predators). Moreover, *every* bail decision involves the judge's prediction about the defendant's potential to flee. Of course, it is impossible to determine whether a decision, based upon future dangerousness, not to grant bail, was accurate, since the defendant never had an opportunity to commit (or not to commit) another crime.

Salerno may suggest that bail decisions must be made on an individual, case-by-case basis rather than based on the crime charged.[11] *Salerno's* declaration that bail decisions must be made on an individual, case-by-case basis again suggests the invalidity of a "bail schedule," but that was not the holding of the case, and the determination to *detain* a person may be seen as different from a decision *not to detain* him.

It is not easy to determine whether the approbation given by the *Salerno* decision to preventive detention has resulted in more or less pre-trial detention. As one Department of Justice report acknowledged, "pre-trial detention has largely been substituted for bail as a means of detaining defendants." The data from the states seem to indicate that preventive detention is infrequently imposed: Although approximately 36 percent of state defendants were detained until disposition of their case, about 80 percent of those were actually allowed release on money bail, but were detained because they were unable to make the amount. Thus, only 20 percent of that group, or 7 percent of all state defendants, appeared to be held preventively.[12]

---

11. In *Demore v. Kim*, 538 U.S. 510 (2003), the Court decided that such individualized bail decisions were not constitutionally mandated, at least with respect to non-citizen permanent resident aliens, who could be incarcerated while they were awaiting proceedings to deport them.

12. See NCJ report, *supra* n.4 at p.18.

The concern that gave rise to these preventive detention statutes — that at least some pre-trial releasees would commit more crime — cannot be gainsaid, even if the data are unhelpful. But many states have chosen another (sometimes supplemental) way of confronting this issue by increasing the defendant's sentence for committing a crime while on bail. While this does not prevent the second crime directly, as preventive detention would, the hope is that the threat of increased punishment will deter the second crime, without requiring the government to rely on somewhat shaky inferences about character and future behavior.

Finally, suppose the defendant is released on bail and then charged with a new crime, or with a violation of a condition of bail — for example, to report to the probation office once a month. If the only issue on bail is possible flight, one might suggest that even these acts do not affect that determination. (If Dan refused to turn in his passport, on the other hand, the inference that he intends to flee might be substantial.) On the other hand, if possible danger to the community is a consideration, even an alleged violation might be sufficient to warrant reconsideration of the bail set earlier. Some courts have suggested that this is erroneous — that disregard, even disrespect, of the judiciary or the government generally, is not grounds for denying or revoking bail.

C. PRE-TRIAL DIVERSION

Beyond bail, or conditional release, many jurisdictions provide other methods by which a defendant can avoid pre-trial incarceration. The most important of these, because it can often mean the defendant entirely avoids trial, and a criminal record, is pre-trial diversion (often referred to as PTI (Pre-trial Intervention)). Essentially, a defendant is placed in the community, sometimes under intense supervision, rather than tried; if he does not commit another crime for a specific period of time, the record of his arrest and charge may be either sealed or destroyed. Since these programs often involve disputes about prosecutorial discretion, we will postpone that discussion until the next chapter.

Examples

1. In a small town in rural South Dakota, Karen is arrested (without a warrant) on Friday evening and taken to the police station, where she is told that she is charged with insurance fraud. She is placed in a jail cell. She demands to be brought to a magistrate, but the magistrate is sick, and the local judge is at a conference several hundred miles away. On Monday afternoon, she is finally brought before the magistrate, now recovered, some 69 hours after being arrested. What remedies does she have?

2. Early Decisions About the Newly Arrested Defendant

2. Jack, CEO of Outron Corp., was arrested after a grand jury returned a 78-count indictment for fraudulent practices. At the initial appearance before a magistrate, the magistrate relied upon hearsay testimony before the grand jury, testimony which (as we shall see in Chapter 6) is not discoverable by the defendant in many jurisdictions. The magistrate thereupon set bail at $5,000,000, declaring that she believed Jack to be a flight risk. May the magistrate properly consider such testimony?

3. Carol works for a top secret federal agency. They come to suspect her of trading secrets to another country, but indict her, instead, for several felonies dealing with misuse of a government computer. The government then seeks preventive detention under the Federal Bail Act of 1984. Testimony at the detention hearing involves hearsay that the secrets are critical to the defense of the United States. The judge finds, by clear and convincing evidence, that the defendant is a flight risk. She is turned over to the custody of the Department of Justice, which then places her in solitary confinement in a nearby federal prison, asserting that there is a great danger that she may communicate governmental secrets to any visitor. What likelihood is there that Carol will prevail if she appeals her preventive detention?

4. Rick has been harassing his ex-wife, Helen, and was charged with burglary, unlawful mischief, and trespass for entering her house. He was released on bail, including a condition that he neither associate with nor harass her, nor enter her premises without being accompanied by a police officer. Prior to that date, Helen had allowed Rick to sleep on a sofa on her back porch because he was homeless. When Rick, contrary to the bail conditions, reappeared on the porch and refused to leave, he was arrested and charged with trespass and alcoholic beverage violations. The judge revoked his bail on the old charges, and refused bail on the new charges, based upon Rick's conduct. Is this valid?

5. Dick Chainkey was arrested for placing a fake bomb in a mailbox in a community postal box in his own neighborhood. The "bomb" was actually comprised of three road flares taped together to simulate dynamite with a commercial-grade dynamite fuse inserted. On one of the flares the words "NEXT TIME — BACK OFF" were written. The state has a preventive detention statute based on the federal one. Is the government likely to win if it moves for his detention?

6. You are the clerk to a judge in a jurisdiction which has legislatively adopted a preventive detention statute like the federal Bail Reform Act. The government seeks preventive detention of the following three defendants. What is your advice to the judge on these three?
   a. Julia, 29 years old, is a first offender who is charged with 35 counts of conspiracy, mail fraud, and money laundering. She has lived in the area for more than six years and has family ties in the United States. She has

significant monies abroad. Although the sentences on all 35 counts would, if set consecutively, reach past her lifetime, it is "likely" that she faces about 10 years in prison if convicted on all counts.

b. Stoyan has been indicted for corruptly obstructing, impeding, and impairing the due administration of the Internal Revenue Laws, and with evasion of federal income taxes, all in relation to his alleged execution of a sophisticated scheme to avoid payment of federal taxes on nearly half a billion dollars of investment income earned over a five-year period. A search of his house revealed a passport with a false identity; Stoyan claims that he used it to obtain utility services at no cost. And defendant offers no explanation for the blank forms for the creation of a United Nations–issued "International Driving Permit" and "private investigator" identification cards, or for the blank "certificate of baptism" from the Military Ordinariate of the United States of America found in his residence. Again, the combined sentences, if imposed at the maximum and consecutively, would be very long, but the best estimate of a likely sentence is about 23 years, if Stoyan were found guilty on all counts. Stoyan also explains that he is "intrigued" by books about persons living underground and that he reads books on identity theft and "the games people play with foreign corporations" because he wants to protect himself from the activities of such persons. There is some evidence, though inconclusive, that Stoyan has over $20 million in overseas bank accounts.

c. Herve, a 21-year-old student at an Ivy League university, runs a hedge fund (on the side) and controls bank accounts in Connecticut and Switzerland. He deposited fake checks for nearly $42 million in those two accounts, and sought to withdraw nearly $2 million from the Connecticut bank. The investigating agents found 15 credit cards in his name in the house. The prosecution argues that the defendant is a "shrewd and manipulative financial whiz kid who poses an economic danger to the community."

Explanations

1. It is often said that there is no right without a remedy. But this may prove the exception to that saying. Karen has clearly been held in excess of the 48-hour standard enunciated in *McLaughlin*. The burden therefore would fall upon the government to demonstrate that its failure to bring her to an initial appearance was unavoidable. The difficulty is that the courts have yet to create a remedy for that violation. Of course, one possible remedy might be to require the police to release her, but one assumes that she would only be rearrested immediately as she left the police station or court house. If Karen had confessed during her incarceration, her statement might be suppressed, under *McNabb v. United States*, 318 U.S. 332

(1943), and *Mallory v. United States*, 354 U.S. 449 (1957). See Bloom and Brodin, *supra* p.1, at p.267. Other than this, Karen might have a civil suit against the police, but if they in fact had probable cause to detain her, it is unlikely that she would succeed, for reasons that are beyond the scope of this book. Moreover, while Karen might seek her "release" as soon as she is brought to the magistrate, it is more likely that this issue would not be litigated until a later date, perhaps even after her trial. At that point, of course, the issue is really moot.

2. Yes. There is nothing wrong with the magistrate's use of, or reliance upon, such testimony. The rules of evidence do not apply at bail hearings, and the reasons for grand jury secrecy would outweigh the defendant's need to see the evidence. See, e.g., *State v. Campisi*, 64 N.J. 120 (1973).

3. For several reasons, Carol should win her appeal and be released. She is not charged with a crime of violence, and she is not a likely flight risk. Moreover, flight risk can be minimized by intensive surveillance and control of passport.

   Nevertheless, in a real case involving similar, but not identical facts, the result, at least initially, was different. This problem tracks the case of Dr. Wen Ho Lee, which graphically illustrated the problematic aspects of bail determinations generally, and of preventive detention decisions specifically. Lee, a Chinese American, had worked as a physicist at Los Alamos National Laboratory for over 20 years when, in 1999, he was arrested and charged with a variety of offenses relating to national defense information. The government believed he had stolen, and delivered to the Chinese government, information on how to construct a nuclear weapon, and on deployment of those weapons in the United States. The government, using the Bail Reform Act involved in *Salerno*, sought Lee's preventive detention on the basis that, if Lee had not communicated with the Chinese government, he should be totally precluded from doing so pending trial. At the detention hearing, FBI agents and others testified that the information in question constituted the "crown jewels" of American security. On the basis of that (and other) testimony, the court ordered Lee detained without bail pending trial. The Justice Department, fearful of some leak, then placed Dr. Lee in solitary confinement, often chained to his bed.

   Almost immediately thereafter, however, the government's case began to undergo serious questioning. Persons who until then had not been vocal about the charges came forward, and Lee's attorneys received much new information about the charges. The "crown jewels," they learned, were vastly overstated—if not paste, they were certainly not material for the Tower of London. Despite several motions between December and September to reconsider the detention order, Lee was unable to persuade the judge to grant him bail. Only after nine months of solitary confinement was he able to amass sufficient information and expert testimony to persuade the judge that the initial bail determination, made under the strictures imposed by *Salerno*, had not merely been wrong, but the result of misleading evidence and testimony, which could not have been seriously challenged at the first hearing.

As described more in Chapter 6, on discovery, Lee also won a motion to obtain discovery of numerous Justice Department files. Within days, the government agreed to a plea bargain to one count of a minor felony of misusing a computer. At the hearing on his plea, the district court judge excoriated the government, accusing some of the witnesses at the December hearing of lying, and apologizing to the defendant, saying: "I feel I was led astray last December . . . I sincerely apologize to you, Dr. Lee, for the unfair manner you were held in custody." *U.S. v. Lee*, No. 99-1417-JC (D.N. Mex. Sept. 14, 2000) (transcript, p.60-64).

The *Lee* case shows, again, the difficulties that defendants can face if there is some doubt as to whether they should be allowed release on bail and, if so, what the amount should be. The government had had months to prepare its case against him. Even though Lee was aware that he was being scrutinized over that time, he had not obtained attorneys until just before the indictment. Thus, even his counsel at the bail hearing was unable to present any persuasive information to counter the government's case. Moreover, the facts as alleged in the December hearing constantly changed, and Lee's view of the case, and of the proofs, (as well as the government's), had constantly altered. Bail is the first decision, but it is certainly not final.

For more on the case, see Wen Ho Lee, My Country versus Me: The First-Hand Account by the Los Alamos Scientist Who Was Falsely Accused of Being a Spy, Hachette Books, USA (2002).

4. No. This is a real case, in which the court held that only interference with the criminal process would warrant a refusal of bail. Noting that the defendant was never charged with abuse, or with assaulting or threatening his wife, the court declared that there must be a nexus between the defendant's violations and disruption of the prosecution, and that "[F]lagrant disregard of conditions may show disrespect for the judicial system, but . . . do[es] not necessarily threaten the integrity of the judicial system." *State v. Sauve*, 159 Vt. 566, 621 A.2d 1296 (1993). Clearly, the preference for liberty pending trial was a major consideration in this court's determination.

5. No. The federal Bail Reform Act declares that all defendants should be released, preferably on their own recognizance, and there is no *prima facie* reason to believe that the presumption is not relevant in this case. On the other hand, the Act establishes a rebuttable presumption in favor of detention in certain cases, including those of possible violence. However,

because a court should consider all possible alternatives, including house arrest, or other methods of reducing the risk, "detention can be ordered only in certain designated and limited circumstances, irrespective of whether the defendant's release may jeopardize public safety . . . a defendant's threat to the safety of other persons or to the community, standing alone, will not justify pre-trial detention." *United States v. Byrd*, 969 F.2d 106, 109 (5th Cir. 1992). See *United States v. Montoya*, 2007 WL 841577 (D. Ariz.), upon which this example is based.

6. Each of these defendants is charged with a serious economic crime, and faces substantial prison time. Unless these crimes are considered "crimes of violence," however, the only relevant consideration is flight risk. The critical issues there are (1) whether the defendant is facing such serious punishment that he will attempt to flee; (2) whether he has the ability to flee and remain at large if he does *and* whether there are ways, short of full incarceration, to prevent him from fleeing. (Don't think only of giving up his passport; at least until 2008, one didn't need a passport to cross the border into Canada or Mexico.)

   a. Given the presumption in favor of non-bail release, the court in a similar case put the defendant on $1 million bond, and imposed house arrest and electronic monitoring. *United States v. Giordano*, 370 F. Supp. 2d 1256 (S.D. Fla. 2005).

   b. This one took the court only four pages. Motion for bail denied. The defendant was too great a flight risk. But why wouldn't house arrest, as in *Giordano*, work here? Was the $20 million just too much? See *United States v. Anderson*, 382 F. Supp. 2d 13 (D.D.C. 2005).

   c. The trial court denied bail on this one. The defendant later spent almost two years incarcerated before trial. He was ultimately sentenced to four years, including credit for pre-trial detention. He was then given bail pending appeal.

CHAPTER

3

Charging Decisions

> The prosecutor has more control over life, liberty, and reputation than any other person in America.
>
> Robert Jackson, United States Attorney General and Justice of the United States Supreme Court, and Chief United States Prosecutor at the Nuremberg Trials[1]

A. INTRODUCTION

Although the bail decision is somewhat discretionary, we are now ready to see discretion in its grandeur. As we move through this chapter, keep in mind the "hydraulic theory" of discretion — that however we restrain discretion in one area, it will reappear in another. Thus, for example, if Hana, the prosecutor, had to prosecute every person arrested on every charge the police brought, the police would have the discretion not merely to arrest, but effectively to resolve charging questions as well. Similarly, as we will see in Chapter 12, many criticize sentencing guideline systems, which limit judicial discretion in sentencing, because they believe the sentencing power has effectively been given to prosecutors.

The first instance where this discretion becomes apparent is in the actual charges which the state, represented by the prosecutor, will bring against Dan. (From this point on, we will talk of the prosecutor "bringing charges."

---

1. Robert Jackson, The Federal Prosecutor, 24 Am. Jud. Soc'y J. 18 (1940).

However, in many states, only the grand jury can actually "bring charges" (and even in the remaining states, where the prosecutor can indeed "bring charges" by filing an "information," there may be other procedures for keeping the case moving)). Remember — the "initial appearance" was held quickly after Dan's arrest, and quite possibly relied only upon the police testimony as to what they were told (and saw) about the basic crime.[2] There may have been no prosecutor (as well as no defense attorney) present. In the next days and weeks, however, lawyers on both sides will become involved.

Thus begins an intricate dance between prosecutor and defense. In this book, we will approach the process as though the prosecutor "controls" the timing. But that may be a fiction — defense attorneys may well bring motions, initiate negotiations, etc., on their own. And certainly a good lawyer — whichever side she represents — will try to "outguess" the other, thereby maneuvering to thwart the other's actions. As we move through these materials, keep asking yourself (if we do not): "What would I do now if I were (defender; prosecutor)?" "How would I respond to (the other side's) actions?" Good lawyering is "proactive" — attempting to assess the other side's strengths and weaknesses and probing them early and often.

Remember also that while the scenario we have painted involves the typical process of an arrest without a warrant, and before an indictment, many indictments, particularly in white collar crimes, precede arrest. In these instances, defense counsel who learn of the grand jury inquiry may be even more aggressive, attempting to preclude an indictment entirely (for example, by seeking immunity by helping the state prove its case against other defendants), or to dilute any charges which the prosecutor might be contemplating.

B. THE DECISION TO PROSECUTE

I. The Public Prosecutor[3]

Although most criminal prosecutions in England had been litigated by the victim in tandem with tort suits against the perpetrator of the harm,

---

2. "[A] prosecutor's decision making would be maximized if she had access to all relevant evidence gathered by the police prior to making the initial charging decision. . . . [But] police agencies act independently of prosecutors' offices in most jurisdictions [and] prosecutors have no guarantee that police will give them the information they need to make a fully informed evaluation of a case." Alafair S. Burke, Improving Prosecutorial Decision Making: Some Lessons of Cognitive Science, 47 Wm. & Mary L. Rev. 1587, 1615 (2006). In some other systems, prosecutors often interview a suspect before proceeding. See, e.g., A. Didrick Castberg, Prosecutorial Independence in Japan, 16 UCLA Pacific Basin L.J. 38, 52 (1997).
3. Carolyn B. Ramsey, The Discretionary Power of Public Prosecutors in Historical Perspective, 39 Am. Crim. L. Rev. 1309 (2003).

American colonies, almost from their establishment, relied upon publicly elected prosecutors to bring most of the criminal prosecutions. Public prosecution is essentially an American invention. Today, although many states provide for some participation by the victim (and perhaps his counsel) in a prosecution so long as the proceeding is "controlled" by the prosecutor, only a few states allow a victim to proceed against a defendant if the prosecutor has decided against criminal sanctions; even then a court appoints the counsel.

A system of prosecution by public prosecutors rather than by the victim has many virtues. For example, it avoids blackmail by the victim, who in early England could, and often did, threaten criminal prosecution unless the defendant "compromised" (settled) the tort suit. It also bars unreasonable, vengeance-seeking victims (or their survivors) who are incapable of neutrally assessing the defendant's criminal responsibility from the courts' perspective. It also assures that poor victims will have their rights protected even if they could not afford the costs of prosecution. Finally, it encourages fiscal responsibility by assuring that public monies are spent on prosecuting types of crime, and individual instances of crime, deemed "important" by the public.[4]

But there are also pitfalls. Prosecutors are elected in all but a handful of states (Delaware, Rhode Island, Connecticut, and New Jersey). Many aspire to higher office[5] and may decline to prosecute defendants who are politically well-connected or favored by the public; or to proceed against persons disfavored by the public. Finally, remember that while we talk of "the prosecutor," it is important to distinguish between the chief prosecutor in a particular office, who sets general policy, and the many "line prosecutors" who handle the cases day by day. The extent of supervision of those line prosecutors by their superiors determines how much discretion each has individually, and the degree of discretion generally exercised by the office.[6]

---

4. Again, however, there is a double edge here. Because "street" crimes are said to be easier to prosecute and prove than complex white collar offenses, well-placed offenders are less likely to be targets of prosecution. The prosecution of high-level officials in a number of major corporations often occurs only after their exploits result in economic and psychological injury to literally millions of employees and investors who demand action. There are, as well, possibilities of racial or ethnic bias lurking behind indecisions to prosecute street, but not "suite," crime.

5. As examples, consider Earl Warren, who was attorney general and governor of California, and who sought the Republican nomination for president, or Thomas Dewey, former prosecutor and then governor of New York, who ran for president against Harry Truman.

6. "Imposing a prosecutorial duty of seeking, and providing, supervisory review of significant decisions should help avoid the occasional warped judgment of the single isolated prosecutor." Rory K. Little, Proportionality as an Ethical Precept for Prosecutors in Their Investigative Role, 68 Fordham. L. Rev. 723, 733 (1999).

2. The Basic Decision — Whether to Charge

It is extremely unlikely that Hana will decide not to prosecute Dan Dastardly, if the crime which the police assert Dastardly committed is a relatively important one, such as bank robbery. But suppose the charge were jaywalking? Shoplifting? Or possession of one marijuana cigarette? Police officers may have incentives — personal advancement or institutional loyalty — to arrest defendants whom even they know will not be prosecuted. But prosecutors have different criteria; for them, each case, even if it ends before trial, may consume significant resources.[7] And big cases will consume big resources — the homicide prosecution of O.J. Simpson, for example, is estimated to have cost the Los Angeles prosecutor's office several million dollars. While few would suggest that murders should not be prosecuted, the hard reality is that the resources used on that single prosecution could have been equally used to prosecute hundreds, perhaps even thousands, of other crimes. One might object that it is not the prosecutor's job to weigh such factors, but to bring every legitimate case, allowing others (judges, juries, etc.) to decide the individual defendant's guilt or innocence, and the social harm done by the crime. Indeed, it is often argued that in other systems, in particular those in Europe, virtually every crime is prosecuted, and that prosecutors do not perceive their job to weigh the kinds of factors listed above. But American prosecutors see these decisions as a major part of their power and of their job. Moreover, a system of mandatory prosecutorial charging would dramatically shift more power to the police, who already have the power, at least in nonserious offenses, simply to fail to arrest or charge.

Further, it is at least possible that the legislature purposely "overcriminalizes" the law and underfunds the prosecutor, establishing a "bark and bite" system in which the prosecutor is expected intelligently to exercise discretion. Less cynically, observers beginning with Aristotle have noted that legislatures must enact "universal" statutes that do not, and cannot, consider potentially important facts of a specific case. Even the most carefully drafted statutes are bound to be not fully determinative when a specific case is weighed. Someone, it is argued, must decide whether the legislature, if apprised of the precise act of which Dan stands accused, would have wanted the prosecution to continue. As Dean Roscoe Pound wrote:

---

7. Although the bulk of crime occurs in major cities, the overwhelming majority of local prosecutors function in rural communities or small towns. Thus, proposals which envision large offices, with many prosecutors and a sizable hierarchical bureaucracy, may strain most prosecutorial offices. This is surely one reason why the courts — particularly the U.S. Supreme Court — have been reluctant to impose restrictive constitutional regulations upon such offices.

No legislative omniscience can predict and appoint consequences for the infinite variety of detailed facts which human conduct continually presents . . . [8]

Discretion, therefore, is essential not only to efficient justice, but to effective justice as well. Once again, the public prosecutor is the repository of that discretion — American notions of "individualized justice" are critical. Even severe critics of prosecutorial discretion concede this point: "A system without discretion in which police, judges and prosecutors were not permitted to take into account the individual facts, circumstances, and characteristics of each case would undoubtedly produce unjust results . . . . The goal should be to establish practices that promote the goals of individualized justice without producing unfair disparities among similarly situated defendants." A. Davis, Arbitrary Justice 6 (2007).

Using the slight amount of information contained in the original complaint, and whatever information she may glean from discussions with the police, other investigators, the victim, and others, Hana has two decisions to make: (a) *Whether* to charge Dan with a crime at all; and (b) with *what crime* to charge him.

What, then, should a prosecutor consider in deciding whether to prosecute at all? Although many prosecutorial offices do not make their policies public, others have revealed their guidelines. The most common factors given for deciding whether to prosecute include:[9]

- The kind of crime. Is it "serious"?
- *Punishment goals.* Will prosecution deter others? Is there a need for retribution? Does this defendant appear dangerous?
- The *severity* of this particular crime. Shoplifting may be relatively "innocuous," but shoplifting the Hope Diamond is (or may be) another matter.
- The *evidence.* Even recognizing that this is an early stage of the investigation, is there sufficient evidence, or the likelihood of obtaining sufficient evidence, not merely to bring the case, but to win it?[10]

---

8. Roscoe Pound, Criminal Justice in America 36 (1945). See also: "Prosecutors are mediators between phenomenally broad legislative pronouncements and the equities of individual cases." Richard S. Frase, The Decision to File Federal Criminal Charges: A Quantitative Study of Prosecutorial Discretion, 47 U. Chi. L. Rev. 246, 246-247 (1980).

9. For another set of proposals, see ABA Standards Relating to the Prosecution and Defense Function 3-3.9 (1993). However vague and fluid these factors may seem, it should be remembered that it is only within recent decades that these factors have been officially acknowledged by prosecutors at all. Prior to the 1980s, virtually no prosecutor would have published, much less adopted, even a list of such factors.

10. The ABA's Criminal Justice Standards provide that a prosecutor should not initiate, cause to be initiated, or permit the continued pendency of criminal charges "in the absence of sufficient admissible evidence to support a conviction." (This Standard, the commentary

- The *individual defendant*. Does this defendant have a criminal record? Is he or she likely to be "rehabilitated" in a probation setting? Is a prosecution necessary to deter his or her actions in the future?
- *Alternative, civil paths* available either to the government or the individual victim, such as a tort suit, *qui tam* action, or collateral proceedings (such as professional disciplinary sanctions).
- The *defendant's cooperation* in bringing other actors to justice.
- The *prosecutor's caseload*, and the amount of resources prosecution of this case will require.

In addition, the prosecutor will consider—whether rightly or wrongly—the relationships with the arresting officer or agency, the judge assigned the case, the defense counsel, and, in some instances, the victim. (The role of the victim is discussed in more detail in Chapter 15.)

There is a debate as to whether the prosecutor is ethically, or practically, required to consider, either at the initial charging stage or later, evidence negating the defendant's guilt, or raising possible defenses. While some argue that the prosecutor is intended to be an advocate for the state, others contend that failure to take such claims into account is both unethical (because even an accusation can harm a defendant) and wasteful (because if the defendant ultimately prevails, resources will have been unsuccessfully, if not needlessly, expended).[11]

Cooperation figures significantly in plea bargains and will be discussed in Chapter 7 as well. Here the question is whether the defendant will cooperate sufficiently so as to avoid prosecution at all.

In the early 2000s, the Department of Justice (DOJ) established "guidelines" for determining whether it would prosecute corporations, and for what charges. Among the factors it declared it would consider was whether a company was paying the legal fees of its employees both before and after they were indicted. The DOJ then began investigation of KPMG in what was widely considered to be the most far-ranging tax and accounting fraud case ever brought. The employees sued to preclude consideration of this fact, arguing that it interfered with their right to counsel. The government argued that the company's cooperation was a legitimate consideration in determining whether the company was being "rehabilitated." The district court agreed with the employees: "KPMG refused to pay because the government

---

emphasizes, is substantially higher than probable cause.) If the evidence *now* is insufficient, the prosecutor has to decide whether to allocate further resources to look for more evidence; if the decision is made to terminate investigation, it is likely that the defendant will never be charged.

11. See, e.g., the California Standards, cited at note 14 *infra*, which argue that "whenever the accused makes a statement that . . . negates criminal liability the statement should be investigated, if possible, no matter how implausible it may seem," but that affirmative defenses are different because "the data necessary to establish them is [sic] usually unavailable to the prosecutor at the charging stage." *Id.* at p.7, 15.

held the proverbial gun to its head. Had that pressure not been brought to bear, KPMG would have paid these defendants' legal expenses" and ordered the DOJ to not consider the company's coverage of fees as a factor as to whether to indict KPMG. *United States v. Stein*, 435 F. Supp. 2d 330 (S.D.N.Y. 2006), aff'd, 541 F.3d 130 (2d Cir. 2008).

3. Deciding *Not* to Prosecute

a. The Victim Without a Remedy

If Hana decides to prosecute Dan, that decision will be reviewed by many others in the course of the criminal process — the grand jury, the presiding judge, and ultimately the petit jury. But a decision *not* to prosecute is not reviewable, even for an abuse of discretion — as a result of the separation of powers doctrine most state courts will not review a decision not to prosecute. Courts believe that prosecutorial judgments as to the weight of the evidence, the need for deterrence, the allocation of executive resource, etc., are virtually beyond the power of the judiciary to assess.

While we tend to think of prosecution of alleged crime as the norm, the data will not support that assumption. Federal prosecutors decline as much as 63 percent of the cases brought to them,[12] perhaps because many federal crimes are also state offenses, and can be prosecuted in state court. While state prosecutors are unlikely to decline as frequently — in part because there is no "other" agency which can prosecute if the state (county) refuses to do so — it is still likely that a substantial percentage of all reported (alleged) crimes are not prosecuted at all.[13] Some of this is undoubtedly due to good lawyering by defense counsel, who act quickly and decisively before the prosecutor is committed to prosecuting.

Many prosecutorial offices have established in-house guidelines for the declination decision. Washington, for example, has adopted such guidelines by statute. See Rev. C. of Wash., sec. 9.94A.440(1).[14] Among the factors listed there are:

1. whether the statute is antiquated;
2. whether the violation is de minimus;

---

12. See Statement of Assistant Attorney General Phillip Heymann before the Committee on the Judiciary of the United States Senate (April 23, 1980).

13. In 1970, it was estimated that Los Angeles County prosecutors declined 50 percent of all felony arrests. See Donald McIntyre and David Lippman, Prosecutors and Early Disposition of Felony Cases, 56 A.B.A.J. 1154 (1970).

14. See also California Crime Charging Standards (1996), a relatively dense (53 pages) compilation of standards and commentary on how and when to charge, published by the California District Attorneys Association.

3. whether the victim's motives are improper;
4. the request of the victim.

Declining to provide some review against unreasoned declination of prosecution is hard to rationalize. Prosecutors may decide not to prosecute domestic violence or date rape cases not because they are difficult to win, but because they believe this to be a private matter, or because they think the law is wrong.[15] They may not bring murder prosecutions against members of mobs that lynch minority victims because they empathize with the lynching. In such situations, the prosecutor is not "really" using discretion to protect the (entire) public's interest; to preclude any judicial (or other) review seems anomalous. Thirty years ago, the National Advisory Commission on Criminal Justice Standards and Goals recommended judicial review of decisions not to prosecute, but that has not come to fruition.

Again, the problem is discerning the "real" reason for nonprosecution. Many of the cases mentioned above, for example, are extremely difficult to prove. Witnesses (and victims) recant their testimony in domestic abuse cases; the paper trail on stock market transactions may be incredibly slippery; prosecutors may argue that local juries will acquit lynchers, and that public funds should not be expended in futility. Some states provide for the appointment of a special prosecutor when the local prosecutor has declined to proceed. Thus, Pennsylvania allows a disenchanted victim to ask a court to appoint a special prosecutor for that case. Pa. Stat. Title 16, §1409.[16] See, generally, Annot., 84 A.L.R.3d 29 (1978). In the aftermath of Watergate, concern that prosecutors might not pursue defendants within the federal executive branch, or who were politically well situated, led to the creation of an "Independent Counsel" law, by which a specially appointed federal prosecutor would investigate allegations that members of the federal executive had committed crimes. By the late 1990s, however, Congress decided that this system, too, had its flaws, and failed to renew the legislation.[17]

---

15. Studies of prosecutional action have demonstrated that prosecutors consider the "level of previous intimacy" in determining whether to charge defendants with statutory rape. See Kay L. Levine, The Intimacy Discount: Prosecutional Discretion, Privacy, and Equality in the Statutory Rape Caseload, 55 Emory L.J. 691 (2006). Should that be a relevant fact?

16. See also Wash. Rev. Code §10.27.170-190; Mich. Rev. Stat. 767.41; Neb. Rev. Stat. §29-1606.

17. In *Young v. United States ex rel. Vuitton et Fils S.A.*, 481 U.S. 787 (1987), the Supreme Court, in a supervisory power opinion, held that district courts have the authority to appoint a private attorney to prosecute a criminal contempt case, but should do so only as a last resort. It is not clear, however, whether *Young* is restricted to contempt cases, in which the appointment serves to protect the judiciary (not a private victim) against a possible overturning of a contempt citation. Moreover, Justice Blackmun, in a lone concurrence, would have held that appointing an interested party's counsel to prosecute for criminal contempt is a violation of due process. Several state courts have so held. See *State v. Harrington*, 534 S.W.2d 44 (Mo. 1976); *Cantrell v. Virginia*, 329 S.E.2d 22 (Va. 1985).

3. Charging Decisions

Once the defendant has been indicted, however, the situation is arguably different. A number of jurisdictions provide, either legislatively or by court rule, for judicial review of a prosecutorial motion to *nol pros* (cease a prosecution) but courts are exceptionally deferential to the executive's decision. Rule 48(a) of the Federal Rules of Criminal Procedure, for example, calls for granting a motion to dismiss unless the motion is clearly contrary to the public interest. See *State ex rel. Unnamed Petitioners v. Connors*, 136 Wis.2d 118 (1987), holding unconstitutional a statute allowing a judge to permit the filing of a private complaint after the prosecutor declines to prosecute.

Judicial reluctance to allow or provide any oversight of prosecutorial discretion not to charge has led many to argue for a victim's bill of rights, included in which would be the victim's right, in one way or another, to proceed in some way even if the prosecutor declines the case (see Chapter 15). Moreover, some states have sought to mandate prosecution of certain crimes — among them domestic abuse,[18] drunken driving, possession of firearms — but in virtually all instances prosecutors (often with the help and instigation of defense counsel) have found ways to avoid these mandates. Many continental systems allow persons unhappy about a decision not to charge to obtain internal office review by a prosecutor's superior.[19]

Where the prosecutor *wants* the assistance of the private party, the courts are likely to be more agreeable to private participation. Indeed, many states provide for private assistance, *so long as* the prosecutor still "controls" the proceedings. See, e.g., Tenn. Code Ann. sec. 8-7-401. See also *State v. Boykin*, 298 N.C. 687 (1979) (private prosecutor in a capital case). On the other hand, in *People v. Eubanks*, 14 Cal. 4th 580 (1996), a corporation charged that several of its employees had conducted industrial espionage against it. The prosecution claimed that the case would take months to investigate and prepare, and that none of its lawyers were sufficiently proficient in computer crime successfully to try the case. The corporation offered to pay these expenses, and to provide computer experts to train the prosecutorial staff, or even to provide computer-trained lawyers to try the case. The California Supreme Court held that the prosecutor's office was barred from accepting such assistance, because private prosecution, or even possible private influence of the decision to prosecute, violated the state constitution.

---

18. E.g., Fl. Stat. §741.2901; Wis. Stat. §968.075 (both "encouraging" prosecution in such cases).

19. In Japan, an 11 person committee, serving for six months and consisting of lay citizens, reviews all decisions not to prosecute. Eight votes are necessary to override a prosecutor's decision to suspend prosecution. See Castberg, *supra* note 2, at 61.. Mark D. West, Prosecution Review Commissions: Japan's Answer to the Problem of Prosecutorial Discretion, 92 Colum. L. Rev. 684 (1992).

Of course, the individual victim may seek damages in a typical civil proceeding, for tort or breach of contract. In some instances, a *qui tam* action will be available, in which the victim sues for himself as well as for the state. But the *qui tam* is a civil action, subject to specific statutory limitations. In some instances, if the state "takes over" the *qui tam* action, the plaintiff is entitled to a specified portion of whatever civil damages the government obtains.

b. Agreeing Not to Prosecute — Waiver of Civil Claims

When Dan was arrested, the police "trashed" his car, and then his apartment, causing thousands of dollars of damage. Whereupon Dan filed a civil suit against the police. The prosecutor thereafter agreed not to prosecute Dan's peccadillos, if he would sign a written agreement not to pursue his civil rights claim.

Most courts, recognizing that prosecutors want to discourage civil suits, even if they are otherwise valid, because they require resources to defend, or because they might chill the police in effectuating an arrest or search, have upheld such agreements not to prosecute. In *Town of Newton v. Rumery*, 480 U.S. 386 (1987), the First Circuit had held all such agreements invalid, but the Supreme Court reversed, holding that at least some of these agreements would be valid, assuming it could be shown that they were truly voluntary. The balance is a tenuous one: If the police have violated Dan's rights, those rights should be vindicated, even if Dan is a scumbag robber. On the other hand, if Dan wants to waive his rights, both constitutional and civil, there is no *a priori* reason to preclude him from doing so. Moreover, in most instances, whether the police violated Dan's rights will be murky at best, and would require a substantial trial.

4. *WHAT* to Charge

Once a prosecutor has decided to proceed against a defendant, there is still the all-important question as to what crimes should be charged. The prosecutor is not bound by the charge contained in the original police complaint — information gleaned from a number of sources may tell her or him that the police were either over (or under) aggressive in their assessment of the facts as she now understands them to be. This judgment must be made *de novo*.

In some instances, which we explore in Chapter 9, the Double Jeopardy Clause, or rules as to aggregation and severance, might compel, or at least strongly induce, particular charges. Thus, if Eloise is found with 10 bags of heroin, each containing 1 gram, she might be charged with 10 possessions of one gram each, or with one possession of 10 grams. Similarly, she might be charged with possession with intent to distribute (particularly if the amount is aggregated), as well as attempted sale (depending on how the jurisdiction defines attempt). As we will see later, constraints on punishment and on sentencing might make the charging decision relatively straightforward.

But many decisions are more complex. Even a simple robbery of a convenience store might confront the prosecution with choosing to charge one, or all, of these various possible charges: (1) robbery; (2) armed robbery; (3) possession of a gun; (4) possession of a gun while committing a felony; (5) possession of a gun by an ex-felon; (6) theft of the getaway car; (7) etc., etc., etc. Again keeping in mind that the facts known about the case are likely to change from day to day and that the initial charge will affect at least the bail decision, if not others, how should the prosecutor select the "initial" charge?

Prosecutors are often afforded the luxury of choosing between two statutes that punish the same offense but with different penalties. In *State v. Caskey*, 539 N.W.2d 176 (Iowa 1995), for example, defendant's behavior could have been charged as either an aggravated misdemeanor or a Class C felony. Convicted of the latter crime, she appealed on the ground that she should have been prosecuted for the lesser offense, but to no avail — the level of charge, said the court, was solely in the hands of the prosecutor. There are no federal constitutional prohibitions to such a statutory scheme. See *United States v. Batchelder*, 442 U.S. 114 (1979).

As one might suspect, courts have been loathe to oversee charging decisions for much the same reasons they give for not overseeing the prosecution decision itself. If there are any "guides," they tend to be found in statements promulgated by prosecutorial offices themselves. Typical is that of the United States Attorney's Manual, which provides that the attorney should charge "the most serious offense that is consistent with the nature of the defendant's conduct and that is likely to result in a sustainable conviction."

These criteria are perhaps unavoidably vague. After all, if discretion is to remain discretion, particularly since the information upon which it is based may change daily, even other prosecutors must rely on the good judgment of the person actually involved in the decision. But other questions can be raised. For example: Why should the highest, and not the lowest, possible crime be charged? A significant charge will almost certainly affect the amount of bail (or the severity of conditions of release), possibly leading to the continued confinement of the defendant. On the other hand, if the guideline adopted the lowest possible crime as the criterion, we might release a defendant who is a true flight risk, since he fears the greater charge will be brought as more facts appear.

One of the most recent notorious examples of the way in which perception of the "facts" change — and defendants can be affected by even an arrest and charge — is the case involving the Head of the International

Monetary Fund, Dominique Strauss-Kahn, who was widely considered to be a major contender for the Presidency of France in the next election. Arrested only moments before flying to France, he was charged with sexual assault and other similar crimes. He was initially denied bail, but then put on house arrest. He resigned his position with the IMF within days. As the investigation continued, prosecutors concluded that the victim's credibility was so suspect that the charges were ultimately dropped entirely. Strauss-Kahn's position at the IMF, however, was terminated, and his political future problematic. The case demonstrates both the impact of a charge, and the way in which evidence discovered after that initial charge may alter one's perception of the case.[20]

Fifty years ago, any such guidelines would have been tightly held, and there is good reason to believe that not even these guidelines constitute "all" the culture of the prosecutor's office.[21] Moreover, every published set of guidelines expressly declares that it does not create "rights" for defendants, and courts have uniformly upheld such statements. Even with all these caveats, however, the mere fact that such guidelines are now public reflects a major change in prosecutorial perspective.[22]

Just as clear are the court holdings that the decision to prosecute in one jurisdiction, rather than another, based primarily, if not exclusively, on the punishments available, is beyond judicial review. *Hutcherson v. United States*, 345 F.2d 964 (D.C. Cir. 1965). A(n) (in)famous example occurred in New York City, where then United States Attorney Rudolph Giuliani proclaimed that on "federal" day, chosen randomly once a week, many drug offenders arrested by state or city police would be prosecuted in the federal system, which had much harsher penalties than the state system. Although this was never challenged in litigation, even assuming that the challenge survived the usual litany about prosecutorial discretion, a general deterrence rationale would clearly support such a policy.

---

20. On the other hand, the alleged victim's lawyer contended that the prosecutor had deprived her of the opportunity to prove she had in fact been raped. See Chapter 15.
21. In 1982, the Department of Justice refused to disclose to Congress its strategy for prosecuting persons who failed to register for the draft, lest disclosure affect the behavior of potential nonregistrants.
22. Complete skeptics will argue that these guidelines are intended merely to placate public (and defense attorney) clamor, and bear no resemblance to real life.

C. ATTACKING THE DECISION TO PROSECUTE — THE DEFENDANT WITHOUT AN IMMEDIATE REMEDY

1. Generally

Defendants who seek to have the charge against them dismissed on the grounds that the prosecution is "unfair" are almost certain to lose. The speeping driver (speeder) who concedes he was speeding, but complains that others were going faster than he, even while he was being ticketed, is raising a sterile claim. Unless the prosecution has grossly abused its discretion, courts have consistently held these judgments to be within the total power of the executive and, as a matter of separation of powers,[23] they will not interfere. Even if the improperly charged defendant will be (or is likely to be) acquitted, the defendant will suffer extraordinary financial and emotional costs attendant simply upon a charge being laid — loss of reputation, job, marriage, friends, etc., may all follow once a charge has been made, and not even an acquittal is likely to undo all the damage. Still, judicial review of a decision to prosecute is highly proscribed. In *United States v. Armstrong,* 517 U.S. 456 (1996), the Court called the charging decision a "core executive constitutional function." And in *Wayte v. United States,* 470 U.S. 598, 607 (1985), it used these words:

> [T]he decision to prosecute is particularly ill-suited to judicial review. Such factors as the strength of the case, the prosecution's general deterrence value, the Government's enforcement priorities and the case's relationship to the government's overall enforcement plan are not readily susceptible to the kind of analysis the courts are competent to undertake.

2. "Selective Enforcement"

Every decision to prosecute is, in some sense, "selective." But if the selection is "improperly" based, it is subject to some judicial scrutiny. In *Yick Wo v. Hopkins,* 118 U.S. 356 (1886), the Court held that a prosecutor who prosecutes only members of a specific ethnic or religious group has violated the equal protection clause. In *Hopkins,* the local government prosecuted only Chinese owners of laundries operating without a permit; the Court found such prosecution unconstitutional. But such claims have rarely been successful, in part because none of the possible remedies for selective prosecution is particularly palatable. If the Court concludes that the prosecutor has

---

23. This refusal is ironic — from early colonial days until the mid-nineteenth century, the prosecutor was thought to be a judicial, rather than an executive, officer.

singled out the defendant because of the defendant's gender (or religion, or race, or political unpopularity), it is faced with the dilemma of either (a) allowing the prosecution to proceed, notwithstanding that the prosecutor was improperly motivated, or (b) preventing the prosecution of a possibly guilty defendant.[24]

The defendant, for purposes of the motion, must concede his guilt at least arguendo. In attempting to negotiate a balance where a defendant alleges such discrimination, courts have therefore, not surprisingly, established an extremely high barrier. Viewing these challenges as sounding in equal protection ("The prosecution chose me out of the hundreds of alleged violators only because of my [race, religion, etc.]"), the decisions apply the usual equal protection calculus, requiring the defendant to show both

1. discriminatory impact and
2. discriminatory intent.

In *Wayte v. United States*, 470 U.S. 598 (1985), defendant alleged that, of several hundred thousand persons who had not registered for the military draft, the United States prosecuted only those who notified the government of their refusal to register on political grounds. The district court required the Justice Department to open its files to the defendants, to allow them access to the information available to the department, but the Supreme Court reversed, imposing a "rigorous standard for discovery in aid of" a selective prosecution claim. Similarly, in *United States v. Armstrong, supra,* the defendants alleged that federal officials in Los Angeles were prosecuting only black sellers of cocaine. The defendants put forward several newspaper clippings, and an affidavit from a paralegal in a public defender's office supporting this claim. The Supreme Court held that the defendants had failed to proffer sufficient evidence to warrant discovery into the files of the federal prosecutor. There must be, said the Court, "a credible showing of different treatment of similarly situated persons."

This, of course, is a Catch 22. An allegation that the prosecution knows of, but is failing to prosecute, members of other groups who are violating the law almost always requires some scrutiny of the prosecutor's files. When courts deny discovery of those files, they are virtually assuring that the defendant will be unable to raise even a *prima facie* case of selective prosecution.[25]

---

24. The court might allow the prosecuting office to appoint an "outside" prosecutor to evaluate the cases against the current defendant and the "other" putative defendants. See *Bragan v. Poindexter*, 249 F.3d 476 (6th Cir. 2001).

25. "*Armstrong* effectively requires proof of an equal protection violation before a court could allow the defendant to engage in discovery of the prosecution's motive. Such discovery would then be used to establish the equal protection violation." Peter Henning, Prosecutorial Misconduct and Constitutional Remedies, 77 Wash. U.L.Q. 713, 750 (1999).

Even where the defendant can produce some such evidence — in one case, for example, the defendant store hired a private detective to show that other stores were also selling banned items on a Sunday, but were not prosecuted[26] — the burden is extremely high, and only rarely will be sufficient to support the inferences required.

a. Discriminatory Impact

Assuming that he has some facts upon which a claim may be predicated, the defendant must first show that he is the object of (unconstitutional) discrimination. It is insufficient for him to show that Episcopalians such as he are being prosecuted; he must also demonstrate that other persons with other religious affiliations (a) commit the same crime; and (b) are not being prosecuted or (c) are not being prosecuted to the same degree as Episcopalians. *Ah Sin v. Wittman*, 198 U.S. 500 (1905).

Thus, prosecuting (usually female) prostitutes, but not their (usually male) customers might not be suspect, because the two groups (prostitutes and customers) are not arguably similarly situated. But a showing that there was no prosecution of male prostitutes might meet the first step, because "prostitutes" are similarly situated. Logically, showing that the two groups — the one to which the prosecuted defendant belongs and the nonprosecuted group — commit similar offenses would seem to be part of the proof of impact, but the courts have usually seen it as a separate criterion the defendant must prove. Thus, the defendant who cannot show that there are others violating the statute, will be unable to succeed, despite convincing the court that the prosecutor is pursuing him or her and other defendants because of race, politics, religion, etc. For example, the inability of the defendants in *Armstrong* to show that there were other (nonminority) offenders who were not prosecuted was fatal to their claim for discovery.

It will be difficult for defendants (or even the prosecution) to show how many more people are committing the offenses than are arrested and charged, since most crimes are notoriously underreported. But even if the defendant somehow leaps that hurdle, defining those who are "similarly situated" is extremely difficult. Assume, for example, that Josh is charged with "selling cocaine." Are sellers of other drugs (heroin, crack, marijuana) "similarly situated"? What about "manufacturers" of cocaine? What about persons who sell in larger amounts? Smaller amounts? May defendants who sell primarily to children use statistics relating to those who sell only to adults? Recently, the United

---

26. *People v. Utica Daw's Drug Co.*, 16 A.D.2d 12, 225 N.Y.S.2d 128 (N.Y. App. Div. 1962).

States Supreme Court underscored how hard it will be to demonstrate that the defendants are "similarly situated" with another group. In a one-page per curiam opinion, the Court rejected an attempt to seek discovery of the files of the Department of Justice based upon allegations that the federal death penalty was invoked against blacks at a disproportionate rate. The Court noted tersely that the allegations had not argued that the aggravating factors in the defendant's group and the control group were similar. *United States v. Bass*, 536 U.S. 862 (2003) ("[R]aw statistics regarding overall charges say nothing about charges brought against *similarly situated defendants*"[27]) (emphasis added).

b. Discriminatory Intent[28]

The second step in proving selective enforcement, also a usual criterion in equal protection cases, requires a defendant to show that this discrimination is *purposeful* — that the state has purposely singled out this "protected" group, and intended to prosecute only its members. See *Oyler v. Boles*, 368 U.S. 448 (1962). If the problems of proof and data are difficult at the first step, this second step is virtually impossible to fulfill. After all, prosecutors are unlikely to announce, even in internal memoranda, that their office will only prosecute Episcopalians, or women, etc. Instead, as in virtually all cases where mental state is relevant, the party carrying the burden (in this case the defendant) must rely on inferences — that there appears to be no bona fide reason for prosecuting only Episcopalians and, therefore, the explanation "must" be animus toward Episcopalians. Statistical evidence comparing the percentage of blacks in the population with the percentage of prosecutions for certain kinds of offenses involving black defendants has been held insufficient because it shows nothing about the number of minority and majority group members who in fact have committed the particular crimes. Moreover, even if those data were available, the defendant would have to show that the prosecutor *knew* about those other possible criminals, *and* had jurisdiction to prosecute them, before any inference of discriminatory intent could be drawn. Finally, courts may be reluctant to dismiss a prosecutor's nondiscriminatory explanation for what appears to be blatantly obvious bigotry: A judicial finding that the prosecutor *did* intend to discriminate against a minority group is likely to severely damage the prosecutor's career for years. While such a result may not be unwarranted for a truly bigoted prosecutor, unless the court is convinced that this was not a momentary

---

27. See, e.g., *United States v. Tuitt*, 68 F. Supp. 2d 4 (D. Mass. 1999). See *United States v. Smith*, 207 F.3d 662 (11th Cir. 2000) (defendants, charged with violating absentee voter laws by having written false information or forged names on absentee applications were not similarly situated with other, noncharged, persons who merely harassed potential voters, or took pictures of persons voting).

28. See generally Peter Henning, supra, note 25.

aberration, the judge may well accept — with whatever inward reservations — the prosecutor's explanation.

Because proving the actual intent of any actor, whether a criminal defendant, a prosecutor, or a legislative body, is always problematic,[29] courts sometimes employ an objective standard to infer intent. Fourth Amendment analysis employs an objective ("reasonableness") standard (though the police's good faith but misplaced reliance on a warrant may save an unreasonable search).[30] As you go through this book, look for instances in which the courts have either demanded proof of bad intent, or used an objective standard, not dependent on intent. Consider, as well, what would happen if the "intent" requirement in these areas were either objectivized (or eliminated). This would not resolve the other question in these cases, however; the barrier of demonstrating that other "similarly situated" persons were not prosecuted because of their race, gender, etc., would still be very high.

c. Prosecutorial "Defenses" to Selective Enforcement

Virtually no cases alleging selective enforcement have survived the first barriers to discovery and, therefore, to proof. But even if a criminal defendant successfully cleared those hurdles, prosecutors would raise a number of plausible explanations for the "proved" discrimination. Even invidious discrimination may be warranted. Thus, for example, if only *young* speeders were being prosecuted, the prosecutor might argue that statistical evidence demonstrates that young speeders are more dangerous, or more common, than older speeders. Or that *white* CEOs of companies with more than $5 billion in assets are more visible than other inside traders, and therefore more likely to be deterred than other such criminals. Or that *female* prostitutes were more likely to engage in street solicitation, while male prostitutes were more likely to be employed by agencies, which would require greater expenditure of funds to ferret out. While some of these arguments may be more plausible than others, given the general deference which courts have given to prosecutors in reviewing their charging practices generally, it might be expected that most of these explanations would be accepted without stringent oversight. (We will reach this same problem several times in this course; see especially Chapter 8, discussing *Batson v. Kentucky* and peremptory challenges.) Indeed, the federal prosecutors in

---

29. But see *Oregon v. Kennedy*, 456 U.S. 667, 675 (1982): "A standard that examines the intent of the prosecutor, though certainly not free from practical difficulties, is a manageable standard to apply. It merely calls for the court to make a finding of fact. Inferring the existence or nonexistence of intent from objective facts and circumstances is a familiar process in our criminal justice system."

30. *United States v. Leon*, 468 U.S. 897 (1984).

Armstrong might argue that they were prosecuting only (or disproportionately) black crack dealers because (a) the state prosecutor's office was handing over crack dealers because of the harsher penalties in federal court; (b) while any crack user is obviously hurt, the injury caused to young blacks (the majority of customers of black dealers) was, on the whole, more socially devastating. Indeed, federal prosecutors might have pointed out that the ratio of whites to blacks among federal drug prisoners is about 3-2, while the ratio among state and local drug prisoners is closer to 2-3.

This is not to say that the selective prosecution claim has never been successful. In *People v. Walker*, 14 N.Y.2d 901, 200 N.E.2d 779 (1964), a landlord who had concededly violated certain housing regulations was allowed to show that, of all such violators, she was singled out for prosecution of housing code violations because she had exposed corrupt practices in the Department of Buildings. In *People v. Utica Daw's Drug Co., supra*, 225 N.Y.S.2d 128, the court allowed the defendant to argue that, of all stores selling certain banned items on Sundays, only it was being prosecuted. And in *United States v. Steele*, 461 F.2d 1148 (9th Cir. 1972), the defendant prevailed when he showed that all four persons prosecuted for refusing to answer questions on the census form were members of the census resistance movement.

3. Vindictive Prosecution

The second exception to the general rule that courts will not monitor charging decisions occurs when the defendant alleges that the prosecutor has selected a specific charge out of a sense of vindictiveness. The initial decision on vindictiveness, *North Carolina v. Pearce*, 395 U.S. 711 (1969), involved a defendant who successfully appealed a conviction and was sentenced, on reconviction, to a harsher term for the same crime. The Court there applied a rebuttable presumption of *judicial* vindictiveness that the harsher sentence was imposed because the judge was irked that he had been reversed. In *United States v. Goodwin*, 457 U.S. 368, 381-2 and note 14 (1982), the Court declined to impose a presumption of vindictiveness in pre-trial prosecutorial actions, declaring:

> There is good reason to be cautious before adopting an inflexible presumption of prosecutorial vindictiveness in a pre-trial setting. In the course of preparing a case for trial, the prosecutor may uncover additional information that suggests a basis for further prosecution or he simply may come to realize that information possessed by the State has a broader significance. At this stage of the proceedings, the prosecutor's assessment of the proper extent of prosecution may not have crystallized. . . . Thus, a change in the charging decision made after an initial trial is completed is much more likely to be improperly motivated than is a pre-trial decision . . . . A prosecutor should remain free before

trial to exercise the broad discretion entrusted to him to determine the extent of the societal interest in prosecution. An initial decision should not freeze future conduct. . . . To presume that every case is complete at the time an initial charge is filed, however, is to presume that every prosecutor is infallible, an assumption that would ignore the practical restraints imposed by often limited prosecutorial resources.

It may be true that first impressions are likely to last, but the importance of not clinging to one's early perceptions is obviously critical. Recent psychological studies have discerned "cognitive bias," the psychological phenomenon, well established outside of the criminal justice arena, by which persons adhere to their earlier views, even when confronted with virtually irrefutable evidence that they are wrong. There are four aspects to this notion: (1) confirmation bias; (2) selective information processing; (3) belief perseverance; and (4) avoidance of cognitive dissonance. Those conclusions may suggest that prosecutors (or defense counsel, or judges, or even law professors) who "refuse" to alter their views, even when new evidence seems compelling, are not malevolent; it is simply that, having invested in one "truth," they are ill-disposed to concede its falsity and therefore their fallibility. Alafair S. Burke, Improving Prosecutorial Decision Making: Some Lessons of Cognitive Science, 47 Wm. & Mary L. Rev. 1587 (2006).

Where a defendant argues that he is being *vindictively* prosecuted, the courts do not look at the prosecutor's actual intent, but use an objective standard to assess whether the prosecutor's motives were vindictive.

D. DECIDING NOT TO DECIDE — PRE-CHARGE OR PRE-TRIAL OPTIONS

Probably since the beginning of time, prosecutors who did not wish to prosecute, but were loathe to simply release the defendant, found informal ways of assuring that the defendant provided restitution to the victim, sought rehabilitative help, performed community service, etc. Such "pre-trial diversion" programs have now become institutionalized.[31] Defendants who meet criteria defined by statute or court rule (usually limited to first offenders and excluding at least some kinds of serious felonies) may avoid trial for a "test period" in the community, but on a number of conditions, such as those above. Success may result in sealing, or total erasure, of the charge and Dan's criminal record.

---

31. For a recommended statutory scheme for diversion, see Model Pre-Arraignment Code §§320.5-320.9.

Suppose, however, that while Dan meets the basic criteria of the program, Hana either refuses to recommend such placement, or actively argues against it? Consistent with the deference shown prosecutors, courts typically refuse to overrule prosecutorial refusal to seek or allow such placement. In at least one state, however, where the pre-trial program was established by the judiciary pursuant to its rule-making power, the courts have been far more willing to reverse a prosecutorial decision not to permit such placement. See *State v. Caliguiri*, 158 N.J. 28, 726 A.2d 912 (1999).

Prosecutors often promise pre-indictment or pre-trial leniency not only to individuals, but to corporations as well. Federal prosecutors, for example, have established a "leniency" program relating to antitrust violations, in which the first conspiring company to self-incriminate may obtain a non-prosecution agreement from the office, in return for cooperation against the other co-conspirators. (For those who know the philosophical problem dubbed "the prisoner's dilemma," this will be familiar territory.) Disputes may arise as to whether the defendant has complied with the agreement. If the Department of Justice then proceeds to prosecute, using information which the defendant provided pursuant to the agreement, the putative defendant has been held not to be entitled to a pre-indictment judicial review of the *bona fides* of the government's position. *Stolt-Nielsen, S.A. v. United States*, 442 F.3d 177 (3d Cir.), *cert. denied*, 549 U.S. 1015 (2006).[32]

Examples

1. Marsha, the prosecuting attorney in Los Angeles County, receives a phone call from the Police Captain in Precinct 9 that Winona, a famous movie actress, has been arrested on suspicion of shoplifting in a well-known luxury department store. The captain says that the store indicates there is a surveillance tape, but no one has seen it yet. The police report indicates that the manager says Winona had $5,000 worth of merchandise under her coat. State law divides the felony of larceny into two "degrees" (petit and grand), depending on the value of the goods involved: The dividing line is $1,000. Shoplifting is defined by state law as removing any item of sale from a store without paying for it; shoplifting is a misdemeanor. Burglary is defined by state law as entering

---

32. In *Stolt-Nielsen*, defendant corporation (S-N) entered into such an agreement, but when the Department of Justice declared that it believed S-N had violated the agreement, and sought to indict S-N, the corporation moved to enjoin the prosecution. The court held that the written agreement only promised not to try if S-N carried out its agreement, rather than promising not to *indict*, and thus the motion was not ripe for adjudication. The impact of the actual decision is likely to be short-lived; attorneys for future clients will almost certainly draft their agreements with more precision. Nevertheless, the opinion demonstrates that courts rarely see the harm visited upon a defendant by indictment as being severe. See M. Ryan Williams, Recent Development: The Devil They Know: The Department of Justice's Flawed Antitrust Leniency Program and Its Curious Pursuit of Stolt-Nielsen, 85 N.C.L. Rev. 974 (2007).

(without breaking) any building with the intent to commit a felony therein. (a) Should Marsha prosecute Winona at all? (b) If so, on what charge(s) should she seek an indictment? (c) Can Winona successfully challenge this prosecution on selective enforcement grounds?

2. You are the chief prosecutor in Shropshire County. Dennis Rogers, the Dean of Shropshire Law School, has just called to tell you that the school's disciplinary committee has suspended Roscoe Pound, a student at the school, for becoming involved in a physical encounter with another student over ownership of a criminal procedure casebook. Pound broke the other student's hand. Rogers declares that it is the law school's policy to inform the prosecutor's office whenever a student is officially sanctioned for conduct that could be considered criminal. Pound has compensated the injured student, and covered all medical fees, and has agreed to work pro bono in the local small business tax program. Rogers is sure that a criminal conviction would make Pound unable to pass the Character Committee's criterion, and Pound would therefore be unable to take the bar examination. He urges you not to prosecute Pound. What should you do?

3. As the federal prosecutor in the case of Dr. Lee (see example 3, Chapter 2, pp. 25-26), you have received a motion to discover the Department of Justice files alleging selective prosecution. The defendants bolster their claim by arguing that (1) Dr. Lee is the only person ever charged for mishandling government materials that had not been formally classified; (2) numerous people who have transgressed similar regulations relating to high security documents have been internally sanctioned or not sanctioned at all including (a) a CIA director who used an unsecured personal computer to access top secret files; (b) an employee who removed "highly sensitive details and gave other sensitive information to the Japanese"; and (c) others who mishandled secret documents; (3) a former counterintelligence official who participated in the investigation of Dr. Lee declares, in an affidavit, that Dr. Lee was targeted because he was "ethnic Chinese"; (4) a posting to the Los Alamos Employees Forum by one of its employees charges that he personally observed that the Department of Energy engaged in racial profiling of Asian Americans at Los Alamos during these investigations. How would you respond?

4. You have been retained by an executive of a bank. He is charged with insider trading. You note that all of the defendants, like your client, have been white, male, and over 50. What is the likelihood that you could successfully bring a claim of selective discrimination? What evidence would you look for before even making such a claim?

5. Police arrested Roderigo, who was clearly intoxicated, driving his car at 2:30 A.M., half a mile from the Memorial Hospital. Roderigo was bleeding badly, and told the officers that he had been assaulted in the parking lot of the Nearby Inn, by three men. He had crawled to his car and was on his way to the hospital. You are the prosecutor. Do you charge Roderigo with driving under the influence? What facts might you wish to determine even before charging him?

6. George, age 45, was dying from cancer when he robbed the First National Bank, in an attempt to obtain funds to support his children before his death. The penalty for robbery is 5-20 years. As defense counsel, what arguments do you make to the prosecutor about the possible charges?

7. A state statute provides that any attempt to commit a misdemeanor is punishable by a fine or by imprisonment for not more than 160 days. The statute prohibiting *making threats*, however, carries a penalty of six months, which has been interpreted by the courts to mean *more* than 180 days. During a heated argument in a Boston bar, Jawahl screams at Mikhail, "I'll kill you, you Yankee lover." Tom Collins, the prosecutor, knows that the statutory (and constitutional) line for having a jury trial is more than 180 days (see Chapter 8). Concerned that a Boston jury might acquit Jawahl (or at least fail to convict him), Collins charges Jawahl with "attempting to make a threat." Jawahl moves for a jury trial, arguing that Collins has unconstitutionally deprived him of that right. What result?

Explanations

1. (a) Marsha might well not prosecute Winona, allowing the store to settle the matter civilly. But there are other considerations:

(1) The fact that the press may know of the story might lead Marsha to fear that, if she did not bring charges, there would be allegations that her office "coddled" celebrities. Marsha *could* see that as undermining respect both for her office and for criminal law generally.

(2) While the fact that this case could generate a great deal of publicity and thereby enhance Marsha's career is obviously an unacceptable basis for decision, it is certainly permissible for Marsha to consider that publicity might be seen as a deterrent to anyone thinking about committing this kind of crime. See, e.g., *Moog Industries, Inc. v. FTC*, 355 U.S. 411 (1958). Indeed, in a very similar, real case, critics argued that if the defendant had been poor, she would not have been prosecuted, and therefore argued selective enforcement. But that misses the major point here — prosecutors often selectively enforce cases that are likely

to give a "big bang" for the resources used: "singling out" a notorious defendant might well be justified precisely on the grounds of that defendant's notoriety.

(3) The possibility of a tape suggests that this case could be easily won — otherwise, it might be difficult to prove intent, a critical factor in the larceny or burglary charges. Marsha should get her hands on the tape posthaste.

(b) Marsha is considering a larceny charge (grand or petit), two possible shoplifting charges, or a burglary charge. The shoplifting seems obvious, whether or not there is a surveillance tape. Winona's (likely) claim that she intended to pay for the items before she left the store, but simply forgot, would be more plausible if the items were in a shopping bag. On the other hand, larceny and burglary require intent; attempting to prove that Winona entered the store with the intent to take the items may be very difficult, unless she has a past record for such acts. It will be easy for her to assert that she did not enter the store intending to shoplift but simply "got carried away." At this point, Marsha could follow the advice in the federal prosecutor's manual, and charge the burglary, or she could now bring the lesser crimes, hoping that further investigation (remember that charging doesn't end the game) would allow her to prove the pre-existing intent. Bringing the higher charge now, if it later turned out that there was no such proof so that the charge would have to be dropped, might be more embarrassing. On the other hand, as we will see in the double jeopardy chapter, Marsha may want to consider that if Winona quickly offers to plead to the shoplifting, and Marsha agrees, Marsha may later be barred from charging burglary, even if there is strong proof of intent. One more point — the hypo leaves purposely unstated what the item was. Consider the difference between a small diamond earring and a substantial-size belt or golf club. Even if the values were the same, would the ease of hiding the item be relevant to the likelihood of conviction?

(c) Winona will surely not win this. Aside from the fact that "celebrities" are not a suspect class, the prosecutor, if forced to explain the decision to charge, could use Winona's very celebrity against her, as indicated above.

2. Dean Rogers has really put it to you. The evidence is fairly convincing that Pound committed an assault; there is certainly "probable cause" to believe this, and a conviction is likely. But the conviction will have severe consequences for Pound. Those aren't criminal consequences, and it's not punishment (see Singer and Lafond, Criminal Law Examples and Explanations, Chapter 2, for a discussion of why not all suffering is punishment). This does not violate double jeopardy. See Chapter 9. But did the legislature really expect such assaults to be prosecuted, when the results of a

conviction would be so enduring? On the other hand, would you hesitate to prosecute a nonlawyer (to-be) under the same circumstances? Can you really consider the "collateral consequences" of Pound's conviction? Should the law tolerate such consideration? And why should your weighing of those factors be any more important than other persons — such as the victim, or the jury? Does Pound's willingness to make restitution persuade you? Or is it simply an attempt to avoid prosecution? Did any of your legal training give you greater ability to make these kinds of moral and ethical decisions? Should you even be making them? Why didn't you go to medical school, as your parents wanted?

In short, there is no "law" here. And even if this prosecutor's office has issued guidelines, they are unlikely to help answer the question in the specific factual setting which this, or any other individual case, presents. A guideline which cautions against "unnecessarily harsh" results, for example, must be interpreted to determine whether that caution includes noncriminal results, such as Pound's possible loss of a livelihood as a lawyer.

3. Things don't look so good, do they? The government doesn't really want to counter with affidavits rebutting the inferences and conclusions drawn by Lee's supporters that would raise an issue of fact and implicitly concede the need for discovery. The best approach is not to attack the veracity of these statements, but to suggest that Dr. Lee is unique — that while the statutory (and administrative) charges against him may use the same words as used in dealing with other employees, no one else has allegedly stolen "the crown jewels" (see the example in Chapter 2). Even if the terms used by defendant to describe what other employees mishandled ("secret documents," "top secret files," etc.) were accurate — the materials stolen (and possibly given to the Chinese) were much more critical to national security. Thus, while admitting the surface similarity of the charges, you would want to provide the court with distinguishing underlying facts. In the actual case, the trial judge found that Lee had established a *prima facie* case, and ordered discovery. Two weeks later, the government reached a plea agreement with Dr. Lee, dismissing all but one count, and agreeing to time served (in solitary confinement).

4. Don't even try. The only possible arguments here would deal with equal protection and "suspect" or "quasi suspect" classes — gender and race. In order to make even a *prima facie* case of discrimination, you must show that there are "similarly situated" persons of the other race, gender, etc., committing the same offenses but who are not being prosecuted. That of course will be hard to do; most executives of these firms were, in fact, white males. You might be able to point to Martha Stewart, but she *was* prosecuted (although not for insider trading). Perhaps you could make the case that she was guilty of insider trading, but how would you get the facts

to show that? (Perhaps from the SEC proceedings, which were not criminal.) It is highly unlikely that you could even meet the first hurdle. But assuming that you did, you would still have to show that the prosecutor did not pursue Stewart, but did pursue your client (and others like him) *because* they were male. Finally, if you succeeded in both those ventures, the prosecutor would argue that since most CEOs are white males, prosecuting your client and others like him is more likely to deter those CEOs than if blacks or females were prosecuted. Indeed, a prescient prosecutor might even suggest that to prosecute too many black or female CEOs might lull the white males into thinking they were less likely to be prosecuted.

5. The New Jersey prosecutor in this case did. *State v. Romano*, 355 N.J. Super. 21, 809 A.2d 158 (N.J. Super. Ct. 2002). The real issue here is whether a prosecutor should ever consider not prosecuting a defendant who is clearly guilty, and on what basis that decision might be predicated. If you believe, as American prosecutors and courts clearly do, that prosecutors have discretion not to charge even clearly guilty defendants, you might want to know whether Roderigo could have gone back into the bar (and if he could have, why he did not — e.g., whether he was afraid of the customers there). You might also check whether Roderigo has a history of drunk driving. In the real case, the facts were actually more extreme: The defendant was arrested only two-three hundred feet outside the parking lot. His conviction was reversed on appeal, because the trial court did not consider the possibility of the defense of necessity.

6. Obviously, for George this prison sentence — indeed any prison sentence — will mean that he will never live with his family again. You could state it more dramatically — "the five-year sentence is a death sentence" — and the legislature didn't establish death as the penalty. On the other hand (a) he committed a serious crime; and (b) any prisoner might die in prison. Should terminally ill people be given a "pass" on such factors? You know that a failure to prosecute will not be judicially reviewable; but the prosecutor would like to be a judge someday. Perhaps you should suggest that she charge George with a crime which does not carry a mandatory minimum, and hope that the judge would take that avenue. Indeed you might even urge the prosecutor to press that sentence upon the court. We will revisit these issues in Chapter 12 on sentencing.

7. Jawahl is right about the spirit of the law, but not the letter. Prosecutorial charging discretion is unreviewable, and Tom could have charged Jawahl with even a lesser offense with a sentence not even close to 180 days. Indeed, Tom could have chosen not to prosecute Jawahl at all. While the Supreme Court has said that if a prosecutor selects defendants in order to punish them for exercising constitutional rights, or uses an

unconstitutional basis such as race or speech for the charge (*Armstrong*), there is no rule prohibiting the prosecutor from exercising discretion to prevent a defendant from obtaining a right he does not automatically have. See *Evans v. U.S.*, 779 A.2d 891(D.C. App. 2001).

The Grand Jury: Gathering Information and Overseeing the Prosecutor's Charging

Historically, (the grand jury) has been regarded as a primary security to the innocent against hasty, malicious and oppressive persecution . . . standing between the accuser and the accused . . . to determine whether a charge is founded upon reason or was dictated by an intimidating power or by malice and personal ill will.

Wood v. Georgia, 370 U.S. 375 (1962)

The grand jury would indict a sandwich.

Courthouse lore

A. INTRODUCTION

The grand jury has an estimable history. The early Norman conquerors of England, who had no local law enforcement agencies, simply asked the local citizenry (1) what crimes had occurred and (2) who had committed them. This body, known as the presentment jury, provided the King's agents with facts about local crime and criminals. Thus began our grand jury.

The framers of the Constitution perceived the grand jury not only as an investigative institution, but as a protection for a citizen against an overzealous king. In a famous incident involving John Peter Zenger, a newspaper editor whose prosecution generated much of the heat for rebellion, three separate colonial grand juries refused to indict Zenger.[1]

The Fifth Amendment of the Constitution guarantees that:

> No person shall be held to answer for a . . . crime, unless on a presentment or indictment of a grand jury.

The Supreme Court has held that this part of the amendment does not apply to the states. *Hurtado v. California*, 110 U.S. 516 (1884).[2] Strikingly, it may well be the only "substantive" part of the Bill of Rights not so incorporated in the due process clause of the Fourteenth Amendment. Nevertheless, at least 18 states and the federal system require Hana to bring the case to a grand jury.

Although the grand jury is convened by a judge at the request of a prosecutor, once it begins to sit, it is, in theory, totally independent of each. The prosecutor is deemed to be only a "legal advisor" to the grand jury, not entitled to be present at its deliberations; no judge is present at any time.

There is no constitutionally required method of selecting those who will serve on the grand jury; the only requirement is that the process not discriminate against a specific "cognizable" or "protected" group. *Vasquez v. Hillery*, 474 U.S. 254 (1986). As of 1990, 31 states provided for some form of "random selection," while 19 states adhered to a much older process known as the "key man" system, in which judges, or jury commissioners, personally selected members of the grand jury. Historically, a grand jury consisted of 23 citizens who decided matters by a majority vote (the number 12 still retains magic in many ways), but today the number varies widely. Unanimity, however, is still not required—a majority can take action. Unlike petit juries, which decide only one case, grand juries may decide hundreds of cases, and many sit for months (usually, however, only one day a week or even less frequently).

---

1. The king then proceeded by information (see Chapter 5), but the petit jury refused to convict. See Chapter 8.

2. Although both *Lem Woon v. Oregon*, 229 U.S. 586 (1913), and *Hurtado* were decided long before the current interpretations of due process and selective incorporation were established, the Supreme Court has shown no desire to revisit those issues. Thus, as a federal constitutional matter, no state *must* provide the defendant with any hearing, before any private or public tribunal, before trial. While a handful of states allow a prosecutor to simply file an "information" with a judicial officer, most states that do not have grand juries provide for a preliminary hearing to assess the prosecutor's evidence. See Chapter 5.

B. THE GRAND JURY AS AN INVESTIGATIVE BODY

In most "street" crimes, arrest precedes investigation, and the investigation is primarily conducted by police. In contrast, however, are complicated criminal offenses in which it may be very difficult to determine whether a crime has been committed at all, much less who committed it. (Can you say AIG?) To ascertain whether a bank customer who claims to have lost $3,000 over five years has been the victim of a computer mistake or an embezzling bank teller may take years. Usually that investigation will be managed by the grand jury.

1. Subpoena Power

Originally, grand jurors were selected because they knew everything that went on in their small vicinage. In a metropolis, however, that is no longer possible. Today, grand jurors rely almost exclusively on prosecutors, who themselves rely on police, victims, and a few others, to bring to them at least the hints of a crime. To further explore this evidence, however, grand juries are armed with incredibly broad subpoena power, allowing them to investigate virtually anyone, anywhere, to determine whether a crime has been committed. The common phrase is that the grand jury is entitled "to every man's evidence." Although these subpoenas are signed by a judge, the judge's signature is pro forma: The grand jury is an independent body whose investigation may be impeded by no official, including a judge. In R. Enterprises, Inc. v. United States, 498 U.S. 292 (1991), the Supreme Court essentially held that a grand jury's investigative powers were unlimited:

> [T]he grand jury . . . can investigate merely on suspicion that the law is being violated, or even just because it wants assurance that it is not. . . . The function of the grand jury is to inquire into all information that might possibly bear on its investigation until it has identified an offense or has satisfied itself that none has occurred. . . . A grand jury investigation is not fully carried out until every available clue has been run down and all witnesses examined in every proper way to find if a crime has been committed.

Given this breadth, said the Court, a subpoena will stand "unless the district court determines that there is no reasonable possibility that the category of materials the Government seeks will produce information relevant to the general subject of the grand jury's investigation."[3]

---

3. We will not discuss here the Fifth Amendment questions raised when a subpoena is used to obtain individual or corporate files; suffice to say that there is much law — and some

Because a subpoena is issued by a grand jury through a court, it is much more powerful than other investigatory techniques. Dan must answer or plead a relevant privilege. If he pleads a relevant privilege then, as discussed below, he may receive immunity; if he has no privilege, he must either provide the information requested or be found in contempt of court (which he may then appeal). Moreover, the Court has held that the prosecutor need not inform Dan that he has the right to refuse to answer. *United States v. Mandujano*, 425 U.S. 564 (1976). Nor must he inform the witness that he is a "target" of the grand jury and may well be indicted. *United States v. Washington*, 431 U.S. 181 (1977). Although in theory it is the grand jury that asks that the subpoena be issued, the prosecutor is the impetus behind the request. Many states now recognize that fact, giving the prosecutor the authority to either ask the court clerk to issue a subpoena or to simply issue it herself without even consulting the grand jury. FRCP 17, which provides for the issuance of a subpoena upon application of a "party," has been construed to include the prosecutor as a "party," thus allowing her to bypass the grand jury.

2. Secrecy of Grand Jury Proceedings

The grand jury's sweeping subpoena power is permissible in large part because the proceedings in the grand jury are entitled to absolute confidentiality. Any person divulging any information given to the grand jury is subject to contempt of court — except that a witness appearing before the grand jury may disclose what questions the grand jury asked her.

The bounds of secrecy are rigorously observed. In *United States v. Sells Engineering, Inc.*, 463 U.S. 418 (1983), the United States Supreme Court held that, under the Federal Rules of Criminal Procedure, a United States Attorney involved in a criminal investigation could not provide grand jury evidence to another United States Attorney, involved in a civil proceeding against the same defendant, unless a court approved. This requires the construction, within the prosecutor's office, of a "firewall" around the grand jury's testimony.[4] For example, the court quashed a murder indictment because the prosecutor had provided the state's arson expert access to a transcript of a witness's grand jury testimony. *State v. Gutweiler*, 940 So.2d 160 (La. App. 2006).

---

confusion — as to the limits of the subpoena power here, but that resistance to a subpoena is unlikely to be successful.

4. A "firewall" seeks to assure that no one working on (a) a civil complaint against Smith (for example, a civil tax claim); or (b) another criminal case involving Smith learns of what has transpired at a grand jury proceeding. For example, the Court of Appeals for the Third Circuit has held that disclosure to another federal district pursuing a criminal prosecution against the same defendant was not covered by *Sells*. *Impounded*, 277 F.3d 407 (3d Cir. 2002).

The secrecy of grand jury records does not cease once the criminal case has ended. Even then, any person seeking those records must show a "particularized need" that outweighs the interest in continued grand jury secrecy. *Douglas Oil Co. of California v. Petrol Stops Northwest*, 441 U.S. 211 (1979).

Nor may the grand jurors disclose, even after the term has ended, what occurred during those proceedings. In *In re Special Grand Jury 89-2*, 2004 U.S. Dist. LEXIS 3942 (D. Colo.), former members of a grand jury sought permission to release information and be free to speak publicly about what they had learned about the (mis)operation of a facility which manufactured plutonium and nuclear bombs. The court dismissed the petition, holding that "adjudicat[ing] and balanc[ing] the competing interests of grand jury secrecy and the interests of the petitioners in public disclosure" was a political question, and that any decision would be advisory only. On the other hand, in *In re Grand Jury Subpoena*, 438 F.3d 1138 (D.C. Cir. 2006), the court, prior to the indictment of the defendant, J. Lewis ("Scooter") Libby, had issued a sealed opinion that two reporters could not be relieved of their "obligation as citizens to give the grand jury evidence." *After* the indictment was made public, the court unsealed the opinion.

3. Conferring Immunity

a. Judicially Authorized Immunity

One of the hotly debated powers of the grand jury, exercised through a judicial order to a witness which requires him to testify, grants that witness immunity from (some) criminal prosecution. This immunity overrides the witness's Fifth Amendment rights against self-incrimination, and the witness must testify or be held in contempt of court. Generally, immunity is either "*use*" or "*transactional*." The former prevents any prosecutor, in any jurisdiction, from using the testimony of the immunized witness, or *anything derived from that testimony*, against the witness in a later proceeding. Transactional immunity, however, forbids any later prosecution based upon any information, whether related to the testimony or not.

Use immunity is subject to the "independent discovery" exception. If the prosecutor can demonstrate that a later prosecution is not based on or even influenced by the evidence obtained as a result of the immunity grant, the prosecution may proceed. However, courts have been extremely rigorous in restraining this exception, establishing a "heavy burden" which the prosecutor must carry by "clear and convincing evidence" that the evidence has not been tainted by the immunized testimony. In one of the most notorious of these instances, Congress had granted immunity to Oliver North, a marine major who worked for the National Security Council, who then testified before Congress concerning criminal events involving NSC shipments of weapons to "freedom fighters." Prior to North's testimony, prosecutors sealed the evidence they intended to use against him in a later criminal proceeding, but his conviction was reversed because the prosecution could not show that witnesses against him at the trial had not heard, or been influenced by, his congressional testimony. *North v. United States*, 910 F.2d 843 (D.C. Cir. 1990).

Transactional immunity is much broader. Even if the government *has* independent evidence against the witness, it is still barred from prosecuting him. In the typical classroom example, even if the government, prior to John's testimony, had a video tape of John committing the crime, if John has been given transactional immunity, he is free from prosecution.

Until *Kastigar v. United States*, 406 U.S. 472 (1972), it was believed that the Fifth Amendment required all immunity to be "transactional," but *Kastigar* held that only "use" immunity was constitutionally required.

Whether to grant immunity to a witness is within the prosecutor's discretion, and his refusal to grant such immunity to a witness who might be helpful to the defendant usually does not violate due process. *Woods v. Adams*, 631 F. Supp. 2d 1261 (C.D. Cal. 2009). However, a judge may confer immunity if it appears that failure to do so would distort the trial process. *United States v. Straub*, 538 F.3d 1147 (9th Cir. 2008).[5]

b. "Pocket" Immunity

Immunity conferred pursuant to statute by a court subsequent to a grand jury request should be distinguished from so-called pocket immunity. In the former instance, the court is ordering the defendant to waive her Fifth Amendment rights; such an order is binding everywhere in the United States, and no other prosecutor, state or federal, may use any information obtained pursuant to such a grant. "Pocket immunity," on the other hand, occurs when the prosecutor, on her own, agrees not to prosecute the witness for any crimes to which he may admit during his testimony. This form of immunity, not sanctioned by a court, is really only a variation of prosecutorial discretion not to prosecute, and binds no one other than the individual prosecutor's office.

4. "Runaway" Investigative Grand Juries

As a practical matter, members of the grand jury are unlikely to know what to investigate, and they rely heavily upon the prosecutor to decide whom, and what papers, to subpoena. Thus, while the prosecutor is theoretically merely a "legal advisor" to the grand jury, in fact she provides the evidence,

---

5. *Straub* involved the granting of immunity during a trial but would seem applicable to grand juries as well, assuming that the defendant (or the witness) were able to present the issue to a judge.

as well as the names of targets, subjects, and witnesses, to whom subpoenas should be directed. On occasion, however, sparked by information obtained from these sources, grand jurors may seek to go beyond the parameters which the prosecutor has set. When this occurs, the pejorative term "runaway" grand jury is employed, although the grand jury is merely carrying out its basic task — to ferret out crime and bring criminals to justice.

Runaway juries are not new — in 1872, a grand jury, without the prosecutor's concurrence, issued an indictment against members of Boss Tweed's followers.[6] A more recent notorious example occurred in the Rocky Flats Nuclear Weapons Plant in Colorado. In 1989, after the facility had been operating for nearly 40 years, FBI and EPA investigators conducted several raids on the facility. A grand jury was convened, which returned indictments against several individuals, and also prepared a report excoriating those who managed the place, but the prosecutor refused to sign the indictments, and the court would not release the report. Much litigation ensued to disclose the reports and other information, but in 2004, a district court refused to allow the former grand jury members to disclose any such information.[7]

Disaffection with "runaway" grand juries has also led courts to conclude, as they have with petit juries (see Chapter 8), that there is no right to "nullify" the law, and that instructions to the grand jurors that it was their duty to indict if they believed the accused was probably guilty of the charged offense were proper. *United States v. Navarro-Vargas*, 408 F.3d 1184 (9th Cir. 2005) (*en banc*, divided 6-5).

5. Evidence in the Grand Jury

a. Rules of Evidence

The rules of evidence that would obtain at trial do not apply to grand juries, in large part because the investigative power — particularly the subpoena — is so broad. Thus, hearsay, improperly seized evidence, possibly even coerced confessions are admissible. *Costello v. United States*, 350 U.S. 359 (1956); *United States v. Calandra*, 414 U.S. 338 (1974).[8] Moreover, since it is controlled by the prosecutor, the grand jury is likely to hear only evidence

---

6. Roger Roots, If It's Not a Runaway, It's Not a Real Grand Jury, 3 Creighton L. Rev. 821, 833 (2000).

7. *In Re Special Grand Jury 89-2*, 2004 U.S. Dist. LEXIS 3942 (D. Colo.). See L. Ackland, Making a Real Killing: Rocky Flats and the Nuclear West (2d ed. 2002). Rachel Lettow, Reviving Grand Jury Presentments, 103 Yale L.J. 1333 (1994). Congress also held hearings on the Rocky Flats incident, but no legislation ensued.

8. *Calandra* was explained by pointing out that the purpose of the exclusionary rule (deterrence of police conduct) would not be enhanced by precluding the use of evidence at the grand jury stage. This explanation is, at best, problematic, since police know that few cases actually get to trial. To the extent, therefore, that the evidence can be used to obtain an indictment to which the defendant might plead, police might be encouraged to obtain "illegal" evidence.

that demonstrates that a crime has occurred and that the soon-to-be defendant ("target") committed it.

b. Exculpatory Evidence

Because the issue before the grand jury is whether there is a *prima facie* case of probable cause, the early law was that the prosecutor need not present any evidence favorable to the defendant. The United States Supreme Court has agreed that there is no constitutional requirement that she do so. *Williams v. United States*, 504 U.S. 36 (1992). Nevertheless, the U.S. Attorneys' Manual instructs federal prosecutors to inform the grand jury of "substantially exculpatory evidence that directly negates" the guilt of the target. The Manual explicitly declares that "appellate courts may refer violations" of the policy to the DOJ's Office of Professional Responsibility. U.S. Attorneys' Manual 9-11.233. The American Bar Association provides that "No prosecutor shall knowingly fail to disclose to the grand jury evidence which tends to negate or mitigate the offense. . . ." A growing number of states, either by court rule or decision, have taken a similar approach, although the language varies. For example, New Mexico requires that prosecutors must present evidence that "directly negates the guilt of the accused." N.M. Stat. Ann. §31-6-11(b). New Jersey adds that the evidence must also be "clearly exculpatory." *New Jersey v. Hogan*, 144 N.J. 216, 676 A.2d 533 (1996). Alaska requires presentation of evidence that is "substantially favorable to the accused" (*Lipscomb v. State*, 700 P.2d 1298 (Alaska Ct. App. 1985)), while the District of Columbia speaks of evidence that "might reasonably be expected to lead the grand jury not to indict."

Of course, determining whether evidence is "clearly exculpatory" is extremely difficult, and is even more difficult when the decider is the prosecutor. Courts have held that the following are "clearly exculpatory"[9]:

1. the credible testimony of a reliable unbiased alibi witness;
2. physical evidence of unquestioned reliability demonstrating that the defendant did not commit the alleged crime.

On the other hand, *not* "clearly exculpatory" are:

1. a defendant's self-serving statement denying involvement in a crime;

---

9. See Annot., Duty of Prosecutor to Present Exculpatory Evidence to State Grand Jury, 49 A.L.R.5th 639 (1997); Suzanne Roe Neely, Preserving Justice and Preventing Prejudice: Requiring Disclosure of Substantial Exculpatory Evidence to the Grand Jury, 39 Am. Crim. L. Rev. 171 (2002); Ali Lombardo, The Grand Jury and Exculpatory Evidence: Should the Prosecutor Be Required to Disclose Exculpatory Evidence to the Grand Jury, 48 Clev. St. L. Rev. 829 (2000).

2. recantation evidence, by the victim or others;
3. testimony of defense experts;
4. identification of a person other than the defendant by two witnesses, where others identified defendant;
5. a co-defendant's written statement which claims complete responsibility for a crime to the exclusion of another co-defendant.

These cases reflect the fact that the standard which the courts have set, however articulated,[10] has generally been so high that few decisions have actually invalidated an indictment because the prosecutor failed to disclose information to the grand jury.

6. Inapplicability of the Sixth Amendment

Because the Sixth Amendment, by its terms, only applies to "criminal proceedings," none of the protections guaranteed by that amendment apply to grand jury proceedings, because the criminal process does not begin until after the grand jury has completed its work. *United States v. Mandujano*, 425 U.S. 564 (1976). Thus, the defendant is not entitled to be present to confront witnesses against him, nor to present evidence to the grand jury, nor to have counsel present at the grand jury proceedings. Indeed, when a witness (including target) is interrogated by the grand jury, his counsel must wait outside the grand jury door, and the witness must request permission to consult with counsel (often after every question) before he may leave the room.

C. THE GRAND JURY AS A SCREENING DEVICE

Once it has obtained the information it (or the prosecutor) thinks important, the grand jury has three options: (1) it may issue a "presentment"; (2) it may indict persons it believes have committed crimes; (3) it may refuse to indict any person. Whichever of these steps it takes, the grand jury, in this

---

10. For example, New Mexico requires that prosecutors must present evidence that "directly negates the guilt of the accused" (N.M. Stat. Ann. sec. 31-6-11(B)). Similarly worded tests require presentation of evidence "substantially favorable to the accused" (*Lipscomb v. States*, 700 P.2d 1298 (Alaska Ct. App. 1985)); or which is "clearly exculpatory" (*State v. Coconino County Superior Court*, 139 Ariz. 422, 678 P.2d 1386 (1984)); or which "might reasonably be expected to lead the grand jury not to indict" (*Miles v. United States*, 483 A.2d 649 (D.C. 1984)) or "would materially affect grand jury proceedings" (*State v. Moore*, 438 N.W.2d 101 (Minn. 1989)); or which "implicates a complete legal defense or could eliminate needless or unfounded prosecution" or which "directly negates guilt and is clearly exculpatory" (*New Jersey v. Hogan*, 144 N.J. 216, 676 A.2d 533 (1996)).

view, is essentially screening the prosecutor's decision to charge specific defendants with specific crimes.

1. Presentments

A **presentment** is essentially a report, and while it may name persons the grand jury thinks have committed crimes, it does not officially "charge" them with the crime, and leaves that to other institutions. At common law, the "presentment function was at least as important as the indictment; and its inclusion in the Constitution shows its significance to the framers." Rachel Lettow, Reviving Federal Grand Jury Presentments, 103 Yale L.J. 1333 (1994). Indeed, colonial grand juries "had become multipurpose administrative bodies in a frontier culture. They were monitoring public officials, administering public affairs themselves, and even initiating legislative policy." Ronald F. Wright, Why Not Administrative Grand Juries?, 44 Admin. L. Rev. 465, 468 (1992). Today, however, few "presentments" are issued. The Federal Rules of Criminal Procedure effectively preclude them by allowing a district judge to seal them. This reflects, in part, a fear of "runaway" grand juries (see section B4, *supra*), and in part the concern that naming people as "malefactors" without indicting them (and thus giving them a chance to demonstrate at trial the inaccuracy of the charges) is unfair.[11] Moreover, since an indictment becomes effective only if the prosecutor signs it, the prosecutor also has final control over the actions of the grand jury. On the other hand, as part of the Racketeer Influenced and Corrupt Organizations (RICO) Act, Congress authorized "special grand juries" that conduct the lengthy investigations required to fully explore these events and may submit reports summarizing their findings. Indeed, the "Rocky Flats" grand jury, discussed *supra*, section B4, was just such a "special" grand jury.

2. Indictments

In most instances, the grand jury does charge someone with a crime; this charging document is known as an *indictment*. Although "(b)y the time of the United States Constitution, the grand jury had evolved to its purest form:

---

11. See, e.g., *Application of Jordan*, 439 F. Supp. 199 (D. W.Va. 1977). Annot., Authority of Federal Grand Jury to Issue Indictment or Report Charging Unindicted Person with Crime or Misconduct, 28 A.L.R. Fed. 851; Barry Jeffrey Stern, Revealing Misconduct by Public Officials Through Grand Jury Reports, 136 U. Pa. L. Rev. 73 (1987).

A citizen's tribunal set resolutely between the state and the individual,"[12] the grand jury is now portrayed by many as a "rubber stamp" of the prosecutor. In 1984, federal grand juries indicted defendants in 99.6 percent of the cases brought to them by the prosecutor.[13] Of course, prosecutors may be screening the cases before they are brought to the grand jury, but most observers attribute this high indictment rate to several factors: (1) the secrecy of grand jury proceedings; (2) the evidence they obtain and the absence of any countervailing voice;[14] (3) the low level of proof needed for an indictment; (4) the refusal of many courts to oversee the actions of prosecutors in grand jury proceedings.

The grand jury should indict a defendant if it finds that there is *probable cause* to believe that a crime has been committed by the named defendant. This standard, which uses the same words but is slightly different from the one used in assessing police searches and seizures,[15] is seen as very low, and as requiring only a bare minimum of evidence of a crime connected to the defendant:

> [P]robable cause is a flexible, common-sense standard. It merely requires that the facts available to the officer would "warrant a man of reasonable caution in the belief," [that a crime has been committed, and by defendant]. . . . [I]t does not demand any showing that such a belief be correct or more likely true than false. A "practical, nontechnical" probability that incriminating evidence is involved is all that is required. *Texas v. Brown*, 460 U.S. 730, 742 (1983) (internal citations omitted).

This is not necessarily surprising. From the prosecutor's viewpoint, the point of the indictment is to (1) obtain (or retain) custody over the

---

12. Justice Mosk, in *Johnson v. Superior Court of San Joaquin County*, 15 Cal.3d 248, 539 P.2d 792, 124 Cal. Rptr. 32 (1975).

13. Judith M. Beall, Note, What Do You Do with a Runaway Grand Jury? A Discussion of the Problems and Possibilities Opened Up by the Rocky Flats Grand Jury Investigation, 71 S. Cal. L. Rev. 617, 631 (1998).

14. As noted above, prosecutors are the "legal advisors" to the grand jury. They thereby dominate the grand jury, usually "suggesting" whom to subpoena, whom to indict, and for what. They also provide instructions to the grand jury on the law. Hawaii, in an attempt to overcome the dominance of the prosecutor, has actually provided in section 11 of Article I of its Constitution for a nonprosecutorial counsel to the grand jury to give it legal advice.

15. Many argue that the "probable cause" needed to indict (or file an information, see the next chapter) should be "greater" than that needed to authorize an arrest, particularly when the arrest is made on the spot, without any opportunity for police coolly to assess facts. The common hypothetical is that the police may have "probable cause" to arrest two defendants, only one of whom committed the crime, rather than having to choose to release one on the street. When the issue, however, is whether the prosecution should proceed, and the state has been unable to obtain further proof against either, the balance might then swing against the state. Contrarily, however, few would contend that "probable cause" means "preponderance of the evidence." As we have said frequently already, the process of investigation of crime is a continuing one; the possibility of finding new evidence should not be forgotten.

defendant and possibly deny him bail; (2) begin the process which will culminate in trial, where the defendant will have counsel and the rules of evidence (as well as other protections) to challenge the charge. From the defendant's perspective, however, the standard is far too low — as one court put it, a wrongful presentment (or indictment):

> . . . is no laughing matter. Often it works a grievous irreparable injury to the person indicted. The stigma cannot be easily erased. In the public mind, the blot on a man's escutcheon, resulting from such a public accusation of wrong doing is seldom wiped out by a subsequent judgment of not guilty. Frequently the public remembers the accusation, and still suspects guilt, even after an acquittal.

In re Fried, 161 F.2d 453, 458-59 (2d Cir. 1947) (Frank, J., concurring).

Courts are reluctant to review grand jury processes. In part, this reticence is institutional in nature. The grand jury is said to be sui generis — neither judicial nor executive; courts view their power to supervise the grand jury as exceptionally limited. Thus, in *Williams v. United States*, 504 U.S. 36 (1992), the Court declared that the grand jury "belongs to no branch of the institutional government." The Court thereupon concluded that the courts could not exercise supervisory power over whatever happened inside that room.[16] The Court would act only if Congress had established a rule of criminal procedure, or the Constitution prohibited specific aspects of the grand jury. There are few such rules in the Federal Rules of Criminal Procedure, and the only clear constitutional prohibition appears to ban discrimination in the selection of the grand jurors. *Vasquez v. Hillery*, 474 U.S. 254 (1986). Thus, as one commentator has observed: "[T]he Supreme Court has placed the prosecutor's conduct before the grand jury almost completely off-limits to any contemporaneous judicial review." Peter Henning, Prosecutorial Misconduct in Grand Jury Investigations, S1 S.C.L. Rev. 1 (1999).

It may well be that it is better that courts not supervise the grand jury too rigorously. But the argument articulated in *Williams* for eschewing supervisory power seems weak indeed. Leaving aside the premise that the grand jury must fit within one of the three branches, and is ultimately governed by a judge, the rationale ignores the state courts that do oversee the grand jury. Moreover, the explanation is subject to challenge as mere semantics: If the Court were to establish a "supervisory" rule that no district court could try a case in which the grand jury process had not met certain standards the

---

16. For commentary on both sides of the question of the existence of Supreme Court supervisory power with regard to grand juries, see Douglas P. Currier, The Exercise of Supervisory Powers to Dismiss a Grand Jury Indictment — A Basis for Curbing Prosecutorial Misconduct, 45 Ohio St. L.J. 1077 (1984); Susan M. Schiappa, Preserving the Autonomy and Function of the Grand Jury: *United States v. Williams*, 43 Cath. U.L. Rev. 311 (1993).

4. Gathering Information and Overseeing the Prosecutor's Charging

argument might dissipate quickly. The "judicial integrity" explanation for the exclusionary rule, for example, takes precisely that position (though it has never commanded more than four of the nine Justices). In addition, courts clearly have "supervisory" power over attorneys, and could control prosecutorial excesses under that theory. (For more on this, see Chapter 14).

Courts also hesitate to oversee grand jury processes because they fear (1) creating too many rules would turn the process into a "mini-trial," and (2) allowing challenges to grand jury processes will delay the adjudicatory process.

In *United States v. Mechanik*, 475 U.S. 66 (1986), the Court held that a petit jury conviction rendered harmless virtually any error committed by the prosecutor in grand jury proceedings (in *Mechanik*, it was allowing two witnesses to testify in tandem, in violation of the Federal Rules of Criminal Procedure[17]). A year later, in *Bank of Nova Scotia v. United States*, 487 U.S. 250 (1988) it held that even a pre-trial challenge to errors in the grand jury was insufficient to warrant dismissal of the indictment, absent clear evidence that the error "substantially influenced" the grand jury. *Mechanik* may actually induce trial courts to delay acting on motions involving alleged misconduct in the grand jury room, because either a conviction or acquittal will effectively render the motion moot. The combined holdings of *Mechanik* and *Nova Scotia* essentially insulate from judicial oversight most prosecutorial misconduct in the grand jury. The only likely successful path to invalidating an indictment now lies in an attack on the composition of the grand jury itself under the equal protection clause. All other challengers need not apply.[18]

The reluctance to encourage challenges to an indictment is understandable. Overturning a conviction and requiring a new trial seems an excessive remedy, even if the grand jury's reaction was taken in response to intentional prosecutorial error. *United States v. Hasting*, 461 U.S. 499 (1983). Overturning the conviction and disallowing a new trial would seem even more excessive. Even pre-trial relief may seem both futile and disproportionate, since in most instances the prosecutor will simply reindict the defendant (assuming the statute of limitations has not run out). But this "realistic"

---

17. Other "errors" might include leaks of materials before the grand jury, (unknowingly) presenting false evidence, operating under a conflict of interest, and misinforming witnesses that they could not reveal to others the substance of their own testimony.

18. Prior to *Mechanik* and *Williams*, many federal courts had expressly invoked their supervisory power to regulate grand jury investigations. See, e.g., *United States v. Serubo*, 604 F.2d 807 (3d Cir. 1979), declaring that "the federal courts have an institutional interest, independent of their concern for the rights of the particular defendant, in preserving and protecting the appearance and the reality of fair practice before the grand jury." Contrary to *Mechanik*, some states, such as New York, allow a defendant to challenge the indictment even after the defendant has been convicted. If *Mechanik* treats the grand jury as an obstacle, these states believe it is important to comport with due process even in the grand jury.

view means that there is essentially nothing to deter overzealous prosecutors from abusing the grand jury process.

Even a pretrial challenge based upon some infirmity in the proceedings, or in the indictment itself, is often a Pyrrhic victory since most jurisdictions allow the prosecutor to resubmit the application to either the same grand jury or another one. See *United States v. Thompson*, 251 U.S. 407 (1920). Some jurisdictions impose various limitations (including about one-fourth that require authorization from a court), but many of these are states where the grand jury is not mandated in the first instance. Further, the Supreme Court has held that a "defect" in the indictment does not deprive a trial court of jurisdiction to try the case. *United States v. Cotton*, 535 U.S. 625 (2002).

D. REFORM? OR ABOLISH?

As the quotation at the beginning of this chapter suggests,[19] there are many who believe the grand jury has ceased to be a "bulwark" between the prosecutor and the citizen. Although there are instances of "no bills,"[20] data demonstrate that the grand juries indict more than 95% of the time. This has led to two separate approaches: (1) abolishing the grand jury, and (2) reforming it. The literature is voluminous—only a few of the many articles are cited below.[21]

England, the birthplace of the grand jury, abolished it in 1933. In 1973, the National Advisory Commission on Criminal Justice Standards and Goals recommended that states do the same thing. Where the grand jury has been removed, it is almost always replaced by a "preliminary examination" (discussed in Chapter 5) which provides much more procedural protection to a

---

19. Although the "ham sandwich" line is perhaps best known, other descriptions include "fifth wheel," "tool of the executive," "prosecution lapdog," and "ignominious prosecutorial puppet." Niki Kuckes, Delusion of Grand Juries: Everyone Knows that a Grand Jury Would Indict a Ham Sandwich. So Why Do We Bother to Use Them? Legal Affairs, November–December (2003) at 38, 39 (compiling such descriptions).

20. One instance of a "no bill" occurred following Hurricane Katrina, where the attorney general of Louisiana prosecuted a surgeon who had provided care for four days in a "sweltering hospital." Though prosecutors accused the surgeon of administering lethal doses of painkillers and sedatives, the grand jury refused to issue indictments and instead returned a "no true bill" decision. Kevin K. Washburn, Restoring the Grand Jury, 76 Fordham L. Rev. 2333, 2338 (2008) at 2338, citing Gwen Filosa and John Pope, Grand Jury Refuses to Indict Anna Pou, Times-Picayune New Orleans, July 25, 2007, at A-1.

21. John F. Decker, Legislating New Federalism: The Call for Grand Jury Reform in the States, 58 Okla. L. Rev. 341 (2005); Thomas J. Farrell, An Overview of How Grand Juries Operate, 30-JUL Champion 26 (2007); Niki Kuckes, The Democratic Prosecutor: Explaining the Constitutional Function of the Federal Grand Jury, 94 Geo. L.J. 1265 (2006); Andrew Leipold, Why Grand Juries Do Not (and Cannot) Protect the Accused, 80 Cornell L. Rev. 260 (1995).

witness or defendant. But since the clause is in the federal (and many state) constitutions, abolition is not likely. Reform, therefore, seems the only viable path in those jurisdictions.[22]

The following changes have occurred in grand juries over the past 30 years:

- At least 24 states have created a statutory right to counsel, and 13 states provide that counsel may be present in the grand jury room but may not participate in the proceedings.
- Ten states require the prosecutor to present "exculpatory" evidence (see Section B5b).
- Twenty-three states mandate particular admonishments be given to grand jury witnesses.
- Only three states recognize a target's *right* to appear before a grand jury, but several others expressly permit the prosecutor to allow the target to appear.
- One state — Hawaii — established (in its constitution) an office of counsel to the grand jury so that the grand jury may hear a more objective view of "the law" they must apply.
- Four jurisdictions apply the rules of evidence to grand jury proceedings, and three others apply the rule with only a few specific exceptions.[23]
- A few states allow the grand jury to obtain outside assistance, such as accountants, investigators, and other experts.

Many of these procedures are, in fact, in place in the preliminary examination (see Chapter 5), a public hearing at which evidence is adduced against the accused.

The real dilemma is that grand juries suffer from "institutionalized schizophrenia"[24] — attempting to be both an investigator of crime and an accusatory institution.[25] Secrecy, for example, may be crucial to the

---

22. The American Bar Association has listed 25 "principles" that should apply to the grand jury. The National Association of Criminal Defense Lawyers (NACDL) has issued a "bill of rights" it would apply to the grand jury, available at http://www.nacdl.org/public.nsf/freefrom/grandjuryreform. None of these, of course, has any binding effect, but may be persuasive in a particular jurisdiction.

23. Ric Simmons, Re-Examining the Grand Jury: Is There Room for Democracy in the Criminal Justice System, 82 B.U.L. Rev. 1, 22 (2002).

24. *Hawkins v. the Superior Court of the City and County of San Francisco*, 22 Cal.3d 584, 586 P.2d 916, 150 Cal. Rptr. 435 (1978).

25. In a strange case demonstrating this tension, the New Jersey Supreme Court held that a prosecutor could ask witnesses before the grand jury questions relating to (adverse) information concerning the defendant's childhood, substance abuse, history of violence, and psychological background that the defendant might seek to proffer at the penalty phase of his murder case, *should he be convicted*. *State v. Francis*, 191 N.J. 571, 926 A.2d 305 (2007).

investigative process, but it is hardly necessary once an indictment has been issued. Similarly, secrecy may be important while numerous witnesses are being interviewed, but why that witness cannot have counsel present must be related to secrecy, which could easily be remedied by binding both the witness and counsel to confidentiality. Several states have actually abolished the grand jury as an indicting body while preserving its role in investigations. See Niki Kuckes, The Useful, Dangerous Fiction of Grand Jury Independence, 41 Am. Crim. L. Rev. 1, n.307 (2004).

Examples

1. Your client, Belinda, has just received a subpoena requiring her to appear before the grand jury in one week. What do you do?

2. Billy Ray and Jimmy Bob were arrested in Billy Ray's car. The police found 500 grams of cocaine under the front seat. Billy Ray has sent Hana (the prosecutor) from jail, a notarized letter stating that the cocaine was his and only his, and that Jimmy Bob was unaware of the drugs. Must she disclose this letter to the grand jury? Should she?

3. During the grand jury proceedings, Sam, the prosecutor, called three separate witnesses to the alleged crime, each of whom testified that Justin (1) warned witnesses not to say anything to the police until Justin's lawyer arrived, and (2) refused to speak to the police before his lawyer arrived, even though he was not under arrest. Moreover, Sam referred to silence during his legal advice to the grand jury. He further told them that they could draw an inference about Justin's guilt from his silence. Can Justin successfully challenge the indictment on the basis of such conduct?

4. Kim, a prosecutor, has presented photo arrays to six witnesses, three of whom identified the defendant, two of whom were unable to identify any of the persons, and one of whom expressly declared that the defendant was not the person he saw. She also has (a) the rap sheet of a witness who identifies the defendant as the perpetrator, and (b) a police report that there was extremely poor visibility that evening. Which, if any of these pieces of information, must Kim present to the grand jury?

5. Called as a witness before the grand jury, and appearing without counsel, George, Nick's best buddy, responds, in an answer to a question from the grand jury foreman, "I gave Nick the gun, but I told him it wasn't really

---

The Court, relying on the "investigative powers" of the grand jury, found that the questioning did not invalidate the indictment. The Court also found that under New Jersey's "open files" discovery rules, the defendant would be "duty-bound" to present the evidence at the penalty phase, and therefore, the only issue was one of timing.

the best weapon to use in a bank robbery." The prosecutor thereupon indicts George as a co-conspirator and facilitator. If George attacks the indictment because he was not given Miranda warnings before his answer, what result?

6. You represent Reynaldo, who has already been indicted for mail fraud. You learn that his former secretary, Frank, has been subpoenaed by the grand jury. You are concerned that Frank will provide more information, under oath, against Reynaldo. He may also provide subpoenaed papers which the prosecutor would be able to obtain under the state discovery rules. What can you do, and will you be successful?

7. Christine Donnel was arrested for stabbing her best friend, Sarah Whitin, to death.

(a) In preparing the case for the grand jury, prosecutor Eric Holding discovers that Donnel was released from a mental hospital only two days before the event and yelled, as she stabbed Sarah, "I am not a witch. You are not Sarah. You are the devil incarnate come to pollute the earth." In a state that requires the prosecutor to present "exculpatory" evidence to the grand jury, is Eric required to give them that information?

(b) There is nothing in the police report about such a statement or about Christine's mental status. However, one of the grand jurors states to his fellow jurors that he read such material in the paper. Eric objects, saying that this is not relevant to the issue before the grand jury. Should the jury be allowed to consider this material?

8. Ed Johnson is a mid-level executive with Gold Bags, a major banking institution. He reads in a newspaper that the district attorney is investigating Gold Bags and calls you as his defense counsel. He tells you he will spill the beans if he gets immunity. You and the prosecutor agree and sign a document in which the prosecutor promises "full immunity as required by the United States Constitution and protected by the Fifth Amendment." Johnson provides excruciatingly detailed information that results in massive criminal penalties for Gold Bags. Two years later, Johnson calls you — he's just been indicted for some of the very things he testified about. When you call the DA, he says that he obtained the information from Rom Mittney well before he ever spoke to you or Johnson. You argue that he's breached the agreement, to which he responds "See you in court, counselor." When you get there, will you (and Johnson) win?

Explanations

1. Pick up the phone and call the prosecutor. You need to know whether the prosecutor merely wants to talk to Belinda as a witness, or whether Belinda is a "target" (possible defendant) of the investigation. If so, you will want to schedule a "pre-appearance" conference with the prosecutor. If Belinda has any information at all which is relevant to the investigation, you will negotiate for immunity. Transactional is better, but use immunity is a good start. Note that the granting of immunity usually benefits persons of relatively low status within an organization (criminal or otherwise), because organizational crimes require substantial investigation before charges can be brought against anyone.

2. This example is based upon *United States v. Short*, 777 F. Supp. 40 (D.D.C. 1991). In many jurisdictions, this would not even pose a problem, since they refuse to impose any duty on a prosecutor to disclose any information to the grand jury. But even in those jurisdictions that do require some disclosure, the issue is complicated. In *Short* itself, the court dismissed the indictment because the co-defendant's letter, which it characterized as "substantial exculpatory evidence," had not been presented to the grand jury. The opposite result was reached in *State v. Evans*, 352 N.J. Super. 178, 799 A.2d 708 (N.J. Super. Law Div. 2001). Although the New Jersey Supreme Court had held in an earlier decision that "clearly exculpatory" materials must be presented to the grand jury, the trial court in *Evans* determined that the letter did not meet that standard. Thus, there are two questions — one legal and the other ethical — which Hana must face. As a legal matter, and assuming that there is no controlling authority in Hana's jurisdiction, the fact that two courts, employing tests using virtually the same words, have reached different results, would seem to protect a decision not to disclose the letter to the grand jury. Moreover, as we will see in Chapter 6, whether the letter would be discoverable after indictment might be a relevant consideration. The *Evans* court was also concerned that deciding credibility factors would "require the grand jurors to engage in . . . extensive weighing of factors . . . that . . . would . . . transform it from an accusative to an adjudicative body." Further, the grand jury might disbelieve the letter, and it was therefore not "clearly" exculpatory. But if the grand jury might — even most likely will — reach that conclusion, what is the harm to the prosecutor's case of presenting the letter? The ethical question, however, is harder.

3. This is (possibly) a trick question. The first issue is whether the prosecutor has violated any rule, constitutional or otherwise. While a comment about the silence would clearly violate constitutional limits if done at trial, the Court has indicated doubts whether those rules apply

at the grand jury level. See *United States v. Hasting*, 461 U.S. 499 (1983), where the Court assumed that this would be constitutionally impermissible, but concluded that the misconduct would be subject to the harmless error rule (see Chapter 12). Moreover, even if a prosecutor cannot comment at trial on defendant's silence, courts that allow grand juries to consider evidence which cannot be admitted at trial would almost certainly find no "prejudicial" error in the prosecutor's actions here.

The second question is whether, even assuming a violation of rule or constitution, there is any remedy for any possible violation. Here, the answer might depend on whether the challenge occurs before or after conviction. As the text indicates, the *Mechanik* Court held that a conviction essentially negates any error that occurred in the grand jury, at least unless the defendant can demonstrate "prejudice." The only "prejudice" which might have occurred here is the indictment itself. For example, no witness was "locked into" testimony which might be used at trial (since that evidence could not be admitted at trial).

4. The general rule is that the prosecutor need not present any potentially exculpatory evidence to the grand jury. However, in a number of states, various standards are used to require such disclosure. In cases involving at least some of these items, a New Jersey court, using a standard that required disclosure only if the evidence "negated guilt" and was also "clearly exculpatory," held that failure to disclose contrary identifications did not violate that standard. *State v. Cook*, 330 N.J.Super. 395, 750 A.2d 91 (N.J. Super. Ct. 2000). While much of the evidence in question might go to impeaching the witnesses (and hence might be discoverable before trial — see Chapter 6), it is unlikely that even states requiring presentation to the grand jury of favorable evidence would find any (reversible) error if Kim keeps all this information in her file during the grand jury procedures. The line between information which is "helpful" to the defendant, as opposed to that which is "exculpatory" versus "clearly exculpatory," is gossamer thin. In the infamous Duke lacrosse case, discussed in Chapter 14, for example, the prosecutor argued that findings that the DNA found on the clothes and person of an alleged rape victim matched no possible suspects, including three who had already been indicted, was not "exculpatory" of the three but merely "not inculpatory." While such an interpretation may be seen as simply malevolent, it may also be another example of that "cognitive bias" discussed in Chapter 3.

5. Surprise. This is a frequently litigated question, and the answer is mixed. As a matter of constitutional law, George is (probably) not entitled to *Miranda* (or similar) warnings, because he is not in custody (and he could have refused to answer on Fifth Amendment grounds). See, e.g.,

Mandujano v. United States, 425 U.S. 564 (1976); *United States v. Wong*, 431 U.S. 174 (1977). Many states, however, require such a warning at least as to "targets" of an investigation, but only as a matter of judicial decision or statute. On the facts given here, it is not clear whether George was a "target" before the grand juror asked the question; if not, fewer states would require a warning.

6. If this were post-trial, *Mechanik* would probably preclude any complaint at all. Even so, you are unlikely to be successful in preventing Frank's appearance, or his production of the records. The "black letter" law is that once Reynaldo has been indicted, the prosecutor cannot use the grand jury as an investigative body. But courts have generally looked to the prosecutor's intent in determining whether the prosecutor is abusing the grand jury's powers. If the investigation is ongoing, the fact that Frank may provide some further information against Reynaldo will be insufficient to stop the process. If, however, the court concludes that the prosecutor's only reason for calling Frank is to obtain information which Frank could otherwise now refuse to provide, the court may be sympathetic. See *United States v. Dardi*, 330 F.2d 316 (2d Cir. 1964). Some courts require that the defendant also show prejudice. See *United States v. Sellaro*, 514 F.2d 114 (8th Cir. 1973).

7. (a) This, of course, goes to the substantive criminal law question of whether excuses, or justifications, "negate" the defendant's *mens rea*. Some have argued that these "affirmative defenses" do not negate the *prima facie* case of the prosecutor and hence are not covered even in those states which might require evidence of claims that DO go to the *prima facie* case (e.g., an alibi that says that it was not the defendant who committed the act). The decisions on this matter have not, as a general rule, parsed the issue that carefully and have required prosecutors to present evidence that would mean the defendant was "not guilty." But Eric can easily argue that "explanations" of the defendant's act — self-defense, necessity, and so on — are "defenses" that do not go to the issue of whether the defendant is *prima facie* guilty of "the crime." See, generally, Singer and LaFond, Criminal Law: Examples and Explanations, Chapters 15-17 (5th ed. 2009). So even in a state that requires "exculpatory" evidence to be disclosed, this may not fit the bill.

(b) This is a difficult question. First, there is the question of whether the juror may even read, much less tell others of, the article. In a *petit* jury setting, of course, this might be grounds for questioning the juror. But grand juries are not bound by the rules of evidence, and they do not convict, so it is not clear that the juror has done anything wrong. Moreover, the information, in this case, might be helpful to Christine. But there is still the issue, as in (a) above, as to whether the information is relevant. Even if one decides that the information is not "legally relevant" because it does not rebut the prosecutor's case in chief, there is yet a third issue here: whether the grand jury may seek information beyond that which the prosecutor thinks they should have. The juror here is in "danger" of becoming a "runaway" — but Eric should probably simply let it pass. It may hurt his case, but he can argue in summation to the jurors that her (in)sanity is not a question for them, but only for the trial jury. See *State v. Wollan*, 303 N.W.2d 253 (Minn. 1981).

8. No. The difference here is that the Fifth Amendment only provides "use" and not "transactional" immunity. You (and Johnson) should have held out for transactional immunity. It's true that the prosecutor will have to persuade the court that the evidence on which he relies is not "tainted" or "fruit of the (immunized) tree" and that this is a relatively heavy burden to carry. But you won't walk out in three minutes, as you would have if you had obtained "transactional" protection. Next time, read the case law before you have your client sign an agreement like this. (Don't be too concerned about malpractice, but it may be looming out there.)

5 CHAPTER

Alternatives to the Grand Jury: Informations and Preliminary Hearings

Once Hana has decided to prosecute Dan, and on what charges, that decision must become formalized, and Dan must be notified, so that he (and his attorney) can begin to prepare for trial. Grand juries are required in 19 states. But in the others, Hana can proceed:

1. by information and/or
2. through a preliminary hearing which will result in a binding over.

A. "INFORMATION"

In a small minority of jurisdictions, Hana need only file with the appropriate court an "information" — a piece of paper which simply recites (some of) the evidence (information) against Dan, and the charges. The information will be forwarded to Dan, and criminal proceedings will begin. This procedure, allowing the state to proceed against Dan without any intervening review of the prosecutor's charging decision, has been upheld against a constitutional challenge.[1] When the prosecution files an information, many states require a more formal procedure — the preliminary hearing.

---

1. Lem Woon v. Oregon, 229 U.S. 586 (1913) (murder charge could be instituted by prosecutor filing a complaint). See Gerstein v. Pugh, 420 U.S. 103 (1975) (affirming, in dictum, the rule of Lem Woon).

B. PRELIMINARY HEARING

In slightly more than 20 states, Hana may refuse to call a grand jury, but if so, she must ask for a *preliminary hearing* before a judicial officer to determine whether there is *probable cause* to believe that Dan has committed a crime (usually, but not always, the precise crime Hana has sought to charge). *CAVEAT:* This is *not* the same question posed at the *Gerstein v. Pugh* hearing (see Chapter 2) — there, the question was whether, under the Fourth Amendment seizure clause, the police at the time of arrest had sufficient evidence to seize him. Here, the question is whether, in light of the accumulated evidence, there is reason to proceed with the criminal prosecution. To the extent that it goes beyond setting bail and apprising the defendant of the charges the police have raised, the initial hearing looks backward to the arrest; in contrast, the preliminary hearing looks forward to the possible trial.

Preliminary hearings are conducted by an impartial judicial officer (usually a magistrate, although some magistrates need not be lawyers); there is no jury. Most critically, this is an adversary proceeding. Defendant is present. Although the Supreme Court has held that the confrontation clause of the Sixth Amendment does not apply at a preliminary hearing, *Goldsby v. United States*, 160 U.S. 70 (1895), the Court has also held that, as a matter of due process, if counsel is present, she should be able to perform lawyerlike acts, such as: (a) cross-examining state's witnesses; (b) presenting evidence on behalf of the defendant; and (c) "marshaling" the evidence in an attempt to persuade the magistrate not to allow an information to be filed. *Coleman v. Alabama*, 399 U.S. 1 (1970). The degree to which any of these roles is allowed, however, varies among jurisdictions, and the extent of cross-examination is limited to substantive matters. When the magistrate believes the defendant's questions are primarily for discovery, she may stop the questioning. Some states appear to apply the rules of evidence, but in the vast majority, nonadmissible evidence may be introduced by the prosecution, while a few states require a "residuum" of probative (admissible) evidence upon which the fact finder may rely.

Defense counsel rarely expects to "win" a preliminary hearing[2] — the standard of probable cause is seen as too low, and defense counsel is often unwilling to disclose any defenses he may have, thus making it difficult for the magistrate to determine the validity, for example, of a possible alibi. Defense counsel, however, may try to use the preliminary hearing as a discovery tool. In using this tool, however, defense counsel must be careful.

---

2. Percentage of dismissals range from 2 to 30 percent, but many of the dismissals at the high end probably occur in jurisdictions where prosecutors do little screening before bringing cases to such a hearing.

5. Alternatives to the Grand Jury: Informations and Preliminary Hearings

On the one hand, examining a witness for the prosecution may provide information or ammunition for impeachment, should that witness testify at trial. The United States Supreme Court has held that a witness's testimony at a preliminary hearing may be admitted at the trial, if the witness thereafter becomes unavailable, so long as defense counsel has a meaningful opportunity to cross-examine a witness, whether or not cross-examination occurred. *California v. Green*, 399 U.S. 149 (1970); *Ohio v. Roberts*, 448 U.S. 56 (1980). On the other hand, attorneys on both sides are aware that a witness who repeats a story, particularly under cross-examination, may become more entrenched with that view than if there had been no such examination. Thus, heatedly challenging an eyewitness's testimony at the preliminary hearing may "lock in" that witness to what otherwise might have been a weak identification.[3] While defense counsel must consider these concerns, he must also remember that over 90 percent of all cases do not get to trial (see Chapter 7).

Since the purpose of a preliminary hearing is to determine whether there is probable cause to proceed against the defendant, if a grand jury has indicted the defendant, a preliminary hearing is deemed unnecessary. Thus, where the grand jury has conducted the investigation and issued an indictment (and arrest warrant) before the defendant was arrested, there will be no preliminary hearing.[4] Prosecutors who wish to avoid a preliminary hearing may present evidence to a grand jury before a preliminary hearing is held, thereby mooting the preliminary hearing. *State v. Edmonson*, 113 Idaho 230, 742 P.2d 459 (1987). In some instances, the prosecutor's purpose may be to protect the victim (for example, in a sexual assault case, to avoid requiring frequent public testimony) or other legitimate purposes (to reduce the number of hearings necessary to proceed against several linked defendants). But often the prosecutor may simply wish to preclude even the minimal amount of discovery the defense might glean. Because a prosecutor can usually convene a grand jury, the decision whether to have a public or private hearing at which the defendant's rights are so dramatically different is purely within the prosecutor's discretion.

Although the following chart does not consider specific states or jurisdictions, it does outline the pertinent differences between grand jury and preliminary hearing processes as a general matter. Ironically, a defendant has more procedural protection and rights at a preliminary hearing than at a grand jury, even though that institution was established to prevent reckless prosecution.

---

3. This, of course, is another aspect of "cognitive bias," discussed in Chapter 3 — people tend to adhere to their early opinions, even when presented with overwhelming contrary evidence.
4. A few states require an adversary preliminary hearing even after a grand jury. See, e.g., *People v. Duncan*, 388 Mich. 489, 201 N.W.2d 629 (1972); *State v. Freeland*, 295 Or. 367, 667 P.2d 509 (Or. 1983).

5.1

	Grand Jury	Preliminary Hearing
Evidence	Can be only hearsay	Similar, but often requires residuum of admissible evidence
Does D have right to be present?	No	Yes
Does D have right to present witnesses?	No	Yes
Does D have right to testify?	No	Yes
Right to counsel in room?	No	Yes
Right to appointed counsel?	No	Yes
Right to cross-examination?	No	Yes
Right to transcript?	No[5]	Yes
Presiding officer	Prosecutor; foreman; citizens	Magistrate; judicial officer of some sort; no citizens
Standard of proof	Probable cause	Probable cause

Examples

1. You are the public defender in Claritin County. Your client, Bill, was arrested yesterday (Wednesday) for bank robbery. You are about to appear at his *Gerstein v. Pugh* hearing. You know that the grand jury meets only on Tuesdays. Besides seeking Bill's release (on his own recognizance or bail), what other motions will you make?

2. You represent Esmerelda, whom Eager Beaver, the prosecutor, charged with conspiring to sell amphetamines. After a preliminary hearing, at which the defendant testified, the magistrate dismissed the complaint. Thereafter, Beaver presented the same facts to the grand jury, but did not inform them of either (1) Esmerelda's testimony at the hearing; or

---

5. An increasing number of states provide transcripts of grand jury testimony, including prosecutorial instructions to the grand jury; to an indicted defendant. None of these, or other changes, has been held to be constitutionally required, however, and the federal system continues to provide for neither any pre-trial disclosure nor defendant participation, as a right, even as a matter of criminal rule. (See Chapter 6.)

(2) the results of the hearing. You learned of these events three days before trial. What will you do, and what are your chances of success?

3. Eduardo is charged with the second degree murder of Ramon. At a preliminary hearing, defense counsel asks an eyewitness to the shooting whether she heard Ramon threaten Eduardo with death. The prosecution objects. How should the magistrate rule?

Explanations

1. You should certainly move for an immediate preliminary hearing to be held no later than next Monday. If the prosecutor seeks a continuance (as she is likely to do), be prepared with arguments — both practical and legal — against it. You may wish to suggest that the prosecutor is seeking to deprive the defendant of his right to a public hearing. But be careful. As we will keep reminding ourselves throughout this book, your relationship with the prosecutor is a continuing one, even in this case, and you don't want to antagonize someone with whom you will be dealing for the next few months. And — just in case your motion is denied — you should move (at least verbally and preferably with papers) for whatever discovery the jurisdiction allows. (See Chapter 6.)

2. In *Johnson v. Superior Court of San Joaquin County*, 15 Cal.3d 248, 539 P.2d 792, 124 Cal. Rptr. 32 (1975), the case upon which this example is based, the defense counsel sought a *writ of prohibition* restraining the court from proceeding to trial. (It's often helpful to know those antiquated writs.) But even if that kind of proceeding is available, remember that most jurisdictions have no requirements about what the prosecutor must present to the grand jury, and that even where there are such requirements, they speak in terms of evidence which is "clearly exculpatory" and "directly negativing guilt." While the defendant's testimony would almost surely negate guilt, it might not be clearly exculpatory. Fortunately for Mr. Johnson, the test in California at the time required the prosecutor to present evidence "reasonably tending" to negate guilt, a much lower standard, and Mr. Johnson obtained his writ of prohibition. If you're lucky, you and Esmerelda live in California. And remember, if you had learned of Eager's conduct after the trial, *Mechanik*, and its progeny, would probably mean you were out of luck. Timing really is everything.

3. Since the only issue at the preliminary hearing is whether there is probable cause that Eduardo intentionally killed Ramon, this question, which apparently attempts to raise a self-defense issue, is irrelevant. (Even though all jurisdictions, save one, require the prosecution to disprove self-defense, once properly raised by the defendant (see John Q. LaFond and Richard G. Singer, *Criminal Law: Examples and Explanations*,

Chapter 16 (1997)); this is not part of the *prima facie* case. Thus, the magistrate should sustain the objection. On the other hand, if the witness were to become unavailable at trial, the magistrate's decision to preclude this question might mean that the entire testimony would be barred as substantive evidence, because the defense was precluded from effective cross-examination. Thus, the magistrate will have to weigh these two factors before she makes her decision.

Evidence Disclosure (Discovery)

CHAPTER 6

Under our criminal procedure, the accused has every advantage. While the prosecutor is held rigidly to the charge, he need not disclose the barest outline of his defense. He is immune from question or comment on his silence; he cannot be convicted when there is the least fair doubt in the minds of any one of the twelve. Why, in addition, he should in advance have the whole evidence against him to pick over at his leisure, and make his defense, fairly or foully, I have never been able to see.

Judge Learned Hand, in United States v. Garsson,
291 F. 646, 649 (S.D.N.Y. 1923)

The anachronistic apprehension that liberal discovery, if extended to criminal causes, will "inevitably" bring the serious and sinister dangers of perjury in its wake will seem strange to many when coming from this court which has been generally commended for its aggressive sponsorship of liberal discovery. . . . [W]e ought not in criminal causes, where even life itself may be at stake, forswear in the absence of clearly established danger, a tool useful in guarding against the chance that a trial will be a lottery or mere game of wits and the result at the mercy of the mischiefs of surprise. We must remember that society's interest is equally that the innocent shall not suffer and not alone that the guilty shall not escape. Discovery, basically a tool for truth, is the most effective device yet devised for the reduction of the aspect of adversary element to a minimum.

State Supreme Court Justice William Brennan, State v. Tune,
13 N.J. 203, 228, 98 A.2d 881 (1953) (dissenting)

OVERVIEW

Back in the good old days, lawyers practiced "trial by ambush" — each side had to guess what evidence the other side would present, and hope there would be no surprises, such as a secret witness. Civil discovery, whatever its weakness, has mitigated at least that vice of litigation[1] but criminal discovery has not gone so far. The most salient explanation for this reticence is that criminal defendants are not (seen as) civil defendants. The concern is that persons facing severe punishments may take drastic steps to prevent conviction, including destruction of evidence and intimidation (or even extermination) of witnesses.[2] Moreover, there is the concern, voiced by Judge Hand, that defendants may shape their own evidence to fit within the prosecutor's case.[3]

The United States Supreme Court has edged slightly toward discovery. The Federal Rules of Criminal Procedure — followed by approximately 12 states — are seen as among the most restrictive court rules,[4] while another 12 or so states have adopted essentially an "open file" approach, under which defense counsel may see everything in the prosecutor's file (subject to the prosecutor seeking a judicially issued protective order, either totally hiding the information from the defense counsel or limiting the use of the evidence). The remaining states (roughly 50%) have taken "intermediate positions."

A. "BRADY" EVIDENCE — THE CONSTITUTIONAL MINIMUM

The United States Supreme Court has held that the due process clause requires the state to disclose to a defendant evidence that is *material* and *favorable* to the accused. *Brady v. Maryland*, 373 U.S. 83 (1963). In *Brady* itself, the Court appeared to use the word "material" in the normal evidentiary sense. In more recent decisions, however, the Court has redefined the term

---

1. W. Glannon, Civil Procedure: Examples and Explanations, Chapters 19, 20.
2. This claim is frequently made, for example, by those dealing with "organized crime." Indeed, even though those defendants could also be prosecuted in state courts, where discovery may be more readily obtainable, state prosecutors on occasion will "turn over" state-indicted defendants for federal prosecution for the obvious purpose of precluding discovery. A study of threats generally (not limited to organized crime figures) indicated 26 percent of witnesses said they had been threatened by the defendant, or his family, or friends. Michael H. Graham, Witness Intimidation 4 (1985).
3. Justice Brennan labeled this a "hobgoblin" and a "complete fallacy." William Brennan, The Criminal Prosecution: Sporting Event or Quest for Truth, 1963 Wash. U. L.Q. 279, 291.
4. Although the Department of Justice continues to oppose a broadening of the Rules, it has urged federal prosecutors to "err on the side of disclosure" in light of the aftermath of the *Stevens* and other cases, discussed *infra*, pp.107ff.

narrowly to require disclosure only if there is a "reasonable probability" that the verdict would have been different had defense counsel received the evidence. *Kyles v. Whitley*, 514 U.S. 419 (1995).[5] The result is that the nature of the prosecutor's constitutional duty to disclose has shifted from: (a) an evidentiary test of "materiality" that can be applied rather easily to any item of evidence (Would this evidence have some tendency to undermine proof of guilt?) to (b) a result-affecting test that obliges a prosecutor or an appellate court to make a counterfactual, retrospective prediction.

Thus, today *Brady* "does not require the prosecution to disclose all exculpatory and impeachment materials; it need only disclose material that, if suppressed, would deprive the defendant of a fair trial." *United States v. Coppa*, 267 F.3d 132 (2d Cir. 2001). Favorable "nonmaterial" information apparently may remain undisclosed, as may all nonfavorable "material" information.

Several things should be noted about this approach. First, it focuses retrospectively on the evidence's impact at defendant's trial; yet 90 percent or more of all cases never reach trial (see Chapter 7). Second, the rule focuses not on the prosecutor's motives in failing to disclose, but on the potential impact of the evidence. Questions of the prosecutor's ethics appear to be irrelevant in determining whether the failure to disclose has violated the Constitution. As one writer has put it, "The Court is indifferent to the moral culpability of the prosecutor as long as the defendant receives a fair trial."[6] Third, the burden is on the defendant to show prejudice, not on the state to show the lack of prejudice.[7] Moreover, the "prejudice" test puts the burden on the defendant to show, retrospectively, that his trial was significantly affected. Yet the prosecutor deciding whether to disclose evidence must act *prospectively* — before trial, she must ask whether this information is "material" in the *Brady* sense — a very difficult task in the abstract, and one made even more difficult because the prosecutor is at the time of decision an advocate attempting to show that the defendant is guilty. Fourth, the test is highly subjective. In determining whether there is a "reasonable probability" that the result would have been different, judges must attempt to guess at how a lawyer (the best? average? experienced?) would have acted had the evidence been disclosed. This counterfactual approach is extraordinarily complex.

---

5. And, the Court emphasized, "the adjective [reasonable — ED.] is important." Some have criticized the *Brady-Kyles* test on the ground that it tolerates even intentional discovery violations if the defendant's guilt is "overwhelming."

6. Leslie Griffin, The Prudent Prosecutor, 14 Geo. J. Legal Ethics 259, 261 (2001).

7. Two commentators have noted that, if the evidence *had* been disclosed, an appellate court on review of the conviction would view all the evidence as well as any inference that could be drawn therefrom, in a light favorable to the government. By requiring the defendant to show prejudice where the evidence is *not* disclosed, the appellate courts effectively view even undisclosed evidence in a light favorable to the government. "Where, then," ask the authors, "is the incentive to disclose it?" Brian Serr and Mark Osler, Fifth Circuit Survey, June 2001-May 2002: Survey Article: Criminal Procedure, 34 Tex. Tech. L. Rev. 649, 690 (2003). Compare the "harmless error" test discussed in Chapter 13.

6. Evidence Disclosure (Discovery)

In *Kyles*, for example, the majority and dissenters spent pages attempting to guess at how a good attorney would have used the nondisclosed evidence.[8]

Brady clearly held that the state must disclose information relevant to *guilt or sentence*. Beyond that, however, the law is murky. For example, it has been held that *Brady* does not apply to (1) preliminary hearings,[9] probation proceedings,[10] or probation revocation proceedings.[11] In states where judges have broad discretion in sentencing to consider virtually all information (see Chapter 12), it is arguable that a broad view of *Brady* would require the prosecutor to disclose much more information than has normally been thought to be covered. See Andrew Weismann and Katya Jestin, Brady and Sentencing, National L.J., Oct. 27, p.12 (2008). Disclosure is automatically required — it does not depend on whether the defendant had made a generalized, or even a specific, request for exculpatory evidence.[12]

Brady thus requires the following analysis:

- Is the information "material" as that word has been defined, i.e., is it favorable to the accused?
- Did "the prosecution" suppress it?
- Was this discovery the only, or the most reasonable, way defendant could have found this information?
- Must the defendant have been prejudiced — i.e., must there be a "reasonable probability" that the result would have been different had the information been disclosed to the defendant (and the fact finder)?

---

8. In *Wong v. Belmontes*, 558 U.S. 15 (2009), the Justices debated not only how a (good?) defense counsel might have dealt with the (nondisclosed) evidence, but then considered the counter-counter-factual of what the prosecutor would have done had the defense counsel taken that approach. See also *Wood v. Allen*, 558 U.S. 290 (2010) (evidence about defendant's mental deficiencies "may have led to rebuttal testimony about the capabilities he demonstrated through his extensive criminal history"). For a different approach, see Christopher Deal, Brady Materiality Before Trial: The Scope of the Duty to Disclose the Right to a Trial by Jury, 82 N.Y.U. L. Rev 1780 (2007).

9. *State v. Schaefe*, 308 Wis.2d 279, 746 N.W.2d 457 (2008).

10. *State v. Hemmes*, 2007 N.D. 161, 740 N.W.2d 81 (2007).

11. *State v. Hill*, 368 S.C. 649, 630 S.E.2d 274 (2006).

12. Initially, the United States Supreme Court appeared to differentiate between instances where the defendant had made a request for specific (or at least general) information, and those in which there had been no request. The theory was that a defense counsel who had made a specific request, but who had been told that there was no evidence meeting that request, would be lulled into a sense of false confidence. The Court, however, has now moved away from that position. Some state courts, however, require the prosecutor to carry the burden of showing (if the defendant has made a specific request) that undisclosed evidence "would not have affected the verdict," while placing on the defendant who has not made a request the burden of showing prejudice. *State v. Laurie*, 39 N.H. 325, 653 A.2d 549 (1995); *Commw. v. Gallarelli*, 399 Mass. 17, 502 N.E.2d 516 (1987).

I. Defining "Materiality"

The *Brady* rule is easy to articulate, but difficult to implement. First, there is the matter of definition — what evidence is "material"? Since the definition is retrospective, information that could be "material" in one case need not be in another. In *Giglio v. United States*, 405 U.S. 150 (1972), the Court held that evidence which could be used to impeach a witness was sufficiently "favorable" as to fall within the *Brady* disclosure requirement. But under such a rule, if the prosecutor is not going to ask a witness to testify, his statement may not be "material" within the meaning of *Brady*.

The same kind of problem arises with inadmissible evidence. The Supreme Court has held that *Brady* does not require disclosure of inadmissible evidence (there a polygraph test) even though a defendant might be able to "use" even inadmissible evidence, perhaps to find admissible evidence.[13] *Wood v. Bartholomew*, 516 U.S. 1 (1995).

Brady's approach requires the prosecutor — who has concluded the defendant is guilty — to determine whether the evidence is "*Brady* material." Even the most even-handed prosecutor is likely to want to avoid disclosure, particularly if the evidence weighs strongly in the defendant's interest. As Professor Sundby has demonstrated,[14] the prosecutor contemplating whether to disclose a particular item must think:

> This piece of evidence is so exculpatory in nature that it actually undermines my belief that a guilty verdict would be worthy of confidence. Under *Brady*, therefore, I need to turn this evidence over to the defense. Then, once I turn the evidence over and satisfy my constitutional obligation, I can resume my zealous efforts to obtain a guilty verdict that I have just concluded will not be worthy of confidence.

Moreover, as we have already mentioned, human beings, including prosecutors, are subject to "cognitive bias" — once they are convinced of a certain thesis (defendant did it), they are likely to read all information as confirming, or at least not disaffirming, that thesis.

If the prosecutor can persuade herself that the evidence does not meet the *Brady* test, her decision not to disclose, even if determined at a later date to be wrong, is not subject to ethical criticism. In *Agurs v. United States*, 427 U.S. 97 (1976), the Court refused to *mandate* disclosure except in extreme circumstances, but urged disclosure by indicating that the "prudent

---

13. See *Robinson v. Cain*, 510 F. Supp. 2d 399 (E.D. La. 2007); Brian D. Ginsberg, Always Be Disclosing: The Prosecutor's Constitutional Duty to Disclose Inadmissible Evidence, 110 W. Va. L. Rev. 611 (2008).

14. Scott E. Sundby, Fallen Superheroes and Constitutional Mirages: The Tale of Brady v. Maryland, 33 McGeorge L. Rev. 643, 651 (2002).

prosecutor" would always disclose where the evidence was ambiguous. The Court's approach, however, pulls against this salutary admonition — a standard encouraging (though not mandating) disclosure would put the burden on the prosecution to demonstrate (perhaps by a very high standard such as clear and convincing evidence or beyond a reasonable doubt) that the absence of the evidence did not affect the verdict, rather than putting the burden on the defendant.

2. Aggregating the Nondisclosed Evidence

In determining whether evidence should have been disclosed, the court should count *all* evidence which can meet the *Brady* test and use it *cumulatively*. In *Kyles v. Whitley*, 514 U.S. 419 (1995), Kyles was charged with a homicide in a convenience store theft, and escaping in the victim's car. The police had taken the license numbers of all cars in the parking lot shortly after the robbery. Moreover, the police received much of their information about Kyles (including the possible hiding spot of the robbery loot) from "Beanie," an informant. Among the items which the police did not disclose to the defendant were:

1. Kyles's license plate was not among the license plates in the parking lot;
2. Beanie's initial call to the police;
3. A tape recording of Beanie's later conversations with the police in which he increasingly pointed to Kyles;
4. Evidence linking Beanie with other robberies of a similar nature;
5. Evidence linking Beanie to another homicide;
6. Conflicts in the eyewitness testimony; some described someone similar to the defendant, others did not, and some suggested someone like Beanie;
7. An internal police memorandum regarding a search of Kyles' trash.

The Court held that even if, individually, none of these items would undermine confidence in the verdict, *Brady* was violated if, considered cumulatively, they met the "reasonable probability" test. The dissenting Justices argued that each piece of evidence must be assessed separately, rather than cumulatively. The majority approach would seem to be sensible, lest the prosecutor seek to "pick and choose" which items to disclose based upon its individual impact. See, e.g., *Monroe v. Angelone*, 323 F.3d 286 (4th Cir. 2003).

The decision to "accumulate" nondisclosed evidence, however, raises its own problems. First, the prosecutor may decide that Evidence #1 is not "material" within *Brady*, and he may reach that same conclusion with regard to Evidence #2. If these judgments are made at different times, he may never "cumulate" them in his own mind. Similarly, if he decides that, together, they *are* "material," he may decide to disclose #2, thereby keeping #1 hidden. Second, the "accumulation doctrine" requires the reviewing court to determine both what a good defense counsel might have done with those pieces of evidence *and* how the jury might have reacted to that information. That problem was sharply demonstrated by the various opinions in *Kyles* itself, as well as in a subsequent case, *Strickler v. Green*, 527 U.S. 263 (1999), in which the Court appeared much more deferential to the trial outcome.

These difficulties merely reflect the problems of any retrospective rule. (See, for example, the discussion of the "harmless error" rule in Chapter 13.)[15] Courts are reluctant to overturn a conviction even if, had nondisclosure been challenged prior to trial, they would have been willing to grant some kind of relief. See *United States v. Sudikoff*, 36 F. Supp. 2d 1196 (C.D. Cal. 1999), where the court, explicitly relying on the premise that the pretrial standard for discovery should be broader and less restrictive than the post-trial standards of *Brady*, employed a standard of whether the evidence "might reasonably be held to be favorable" to the defense. The prejudice prong can also cut the other way — where a witness's testimony is "clearly untruthful," failure of the government to reveal a "deal" with him was not "material." *Mataya v. Kingston*, 371 F.3d 353 (7th Cir. 2004).

3. Did the "Government" Suppress the Evidence?

We often casually speak of "the" "government" or "the" "prosecution" as though these were a single entity. But even while many governmental agencies are involved in one aspect or another of the criminal justice system, they may not constitute the "government" for purposes of discovery. Realistically, prosecutors do not "control" police departments or offices. Moreover, different agencies have different agendas — police departments, and individual police officers, may often be at odds with prosecutorial offices and individual prosecutors, and may purposely not inform the prosecutor of information. In *Kyles*, the Court rejected the contention that information known to the state police who were actually in charge of the case was not imputable to the prosecutor's office. ("The individual prosecutor has a duty to learn of any favorable evidence known to the other acting on the government's behalf in the case, including the police.") As the court said in *Moldowan v. City of Warren*, 578 F.3d 351, 378 (6th Cir. 2009): "*Brady* would be largely ineffective if those other members of the prosecution

---

15. Some courts state that *Brady* errors are not subject to a harmless error analysis — but that is because the *Brady* test itself requires a showing that the nondisclosure was not "harmless."

team had no responsibility to inform the prosecutor about evidence that undermined the state's preferred theory of the crime." The *Kyles* rule both prevents collusion between the prosecutor and other investigative agencies *not* to give him copies of documents for the purpose of preventing their discovery, and encourages the prosecutor to maintain very good relations with the police.

Prosecutors do not need to "forage far and wide" to find documents in the hands of other "governmental" agencies. In *United States v. Chalmers*, 410 F. Supp. 2d 278 (S.D.N.Y. 2006), involving defendants charged with conspiracy while involved in the United Nations' oil-for-food program for Iraq, the court ruled that defendants were not entitled to discovery of all "material" documents within the control of all government departments and agencies, including Congress, that investigated or oversaw the program, because those documents were not in the "possession, custody or control" of the prosecutor's team. On the other hand, in *United States v. Libby*, 429 F. Supp. 2d 1 (D.C. Cir. 2006), the Court held that the "government" included the Central Intelligence Agency and (notwithstanding later protestations that he was a member of the legislature), the Office of the Vice President.

Courts are divided on less overarching questions. Thus, at one end of the spectrum, the following are typically held to be persons on the "prosecutorial team" for discovery purposes:[16]

- all persons within the prosecutor's office;
- the investigating agency or agencies (most obviously the police);
- assisting agencies, even if not employed directly by the prosecutor's office.

On the other hand, the following have been held *not* to be part of a federal prosecutorial team for purposes of discovery:

- Bureau of Prisons;
- FBI agents involved in a case unrelated to defendants' prosecution;
- parole officers.

More difficult questions arise when the information is controlled by another jurisdiction — either a different county within a state, or by another state, or by the federal government (in a state prosecution) or vice versa. Courts have

---

16. Under the new Department of Justice guidelines (see *infra*, p.108-109), prosecutors trying to determine whether another agency is part of the "prosecution team" should consider whether (1) the agency jointly conducted the investigation; (2) the agency played an active role in the prosecution; (3) the prosecutor knew of *and* had access to discoverable information held by the other agency; and (4) the degree to which decisions have been made jointly.

generally held that defense counsel do not need to "search the wilderness" for materials. E.g., *State v. Fukusaku*, 85 Haw. 462, 946 P.2d 32 (1997).

Items held by third, private, parties are usually not considered within the control of the government—if defense counsel desires them, he can try to subpoena those documents, without forcing the prosecutor to do so.

CAVEAT: If any of these persons or offices had been directly involved in a cooperative venture with the federal government (e.g., a joint federal-state task force on drugs), the result might well be different, or if the prosecutor's office physically possesses reports from those sources, they are discoverable. *United States v. Gatto*, 763 F.2d 1040 (9th Cir. 1985).[17]

Finally, an agency of the "government" which may constitute part of the government's "team" may not be sufficiently aware of its obligations. In *United States v. Bin Laden*, 397 F. Supp. 2d 465 (S.D.N.Y. 2005), members of the United States Marshal's Service interrogated for 28 hours on videotape a suspected terrorist who turned out to be a key government witness against an important member of Al Qaeda. The Service never informed the Department of Justice about the tapes, which contained significant evidence with which to impeach the witness. After conviction, the defense learned of the tapes' existence, and moved for a new trial, based upon the violation of *Brady*, the Jencks Act, and Rule 16. The district judge bemoaned the "rampant ignorance about disclosure obligations within the Marshal's Service," and opined that one important official "had, and likely still has, no idea that videotapes like the ones he created are extremely likely to contain material discoverable. . . . This [innocent] mixture of inaction, incompetence and stonewalling to cover up their mistakes . . . ha[s] seriously jeopardized the convictions. . . ."[18]

4. Did the Government "Suppress" the Evidence?

Some courts hold that a prosecutor's failure to comply with *Brady* or discovery rules is not reversible error if defense counsel did not exercise "due diligence" in seeking to obtain that information. The view is that such a requirement serves "to weed out incredible claims of ignorance, to prevent sandbagging, . . . consistent with a focus on actual knowledge. . . ." *United*

---

17. Where police gave tape of defendant's interrogation to a television station for a program on police, the tape, though not under the prosecution's "control," was discoverable. The court suggested that this might have been a ploy by police to avoid discovery of the tape. *People v. Combest*, 4 N.Y.3d 341, 828 N.E.2d 583, 795 N.Y.S.2d 481 (2005).

18. Nevertheless, the trial court found that there was insufficient prejudice to warrant a new trial, and the convictions were upheld on appeal. In *Re Terrorist Bombings of U.S. Embassies in East Africa*, 552 F.3d 93 (2d Cir. 2008). The Second Circuit therefore refused to decide whether the Marshal's Service was part of the "prosecution team."

States v. Zagaari, 11 F.3d 307 (2d Cir. 1997). These courts explain that such evidence is not "suppressed" by the prosecutor. *Coleman v. Mitchell*, 286 F.3d 417 (6th Cir. 2001). This conclusion is really due to the fact that *Brady* incorporates prejudice as part of the violation. A better approach would be to conclude that a *Brady* violation *has* occurred, and then ask whether the defendant has been prejudiced, requiring the state to carry that burden, but allowing it to argue that the defendant could have "cured" the prejudice by reasonable diligence. Other courts are less tolerant of prosecutor nondisclosure. In *Boss*, n.31, *infra*, defense counsel had interviewed a witness once, who had later disclosed to the prosecutor exculpatory information which the prosecution had not thereafter disclosed to the defendant. The court declared that even an astute defense counsel would not have thought to ask that witness questions about the matter she disclosed to the prosecutor after the defense interview only days before trial:

> We regard as untenable, a broad rule that any information possessed by a defense witness must be considered available to the defense for *Brady* purposes . . . a defense witness may be uncooperative or reluctant. Or . . . may have forgotten or inadvertently omitted some important piece of evidence . . . Or . . . the defense witness [may have learned] of certain evidence in time between when she spoke with defense counsel and the prosecution. . . .

Boss, infra, 263 F.3d at 740.

B. NONCONSTITUTIONAL RULES OF DISCOVERY

All states, as well as the federal government, have court-written and promulgated "Rules of Criminal Procedure" that require disclosure of some types of information that would not have to be disclosed under *Brady*. (For example, most states require disclosure of some types of "inculpatory" evidence, such as defendant's confession, while *Brady* speaks exclusively of "exculpatory evidence.") We will discuss below each of the major kinds of information which are the target of discovery motions. As you read through these, keep in mind that many attorneys are still infused with the notion of "trial by ambush," and are extremely reluctant to part with any information. Just as a prosecutor may persuade himself that information is not "material" within *Brady*, both sides' reluctance to disclose will increase exponentially with the adverse implications to be drawn from the information. Each attorney will narrowly interpret the wording of each discovery provision, attempting to avoid including the information in that interpretation. As one example, consider a court rule allowing defendants to discover "statements" which witnesses have given to the police. If the paper must be signed in order to be the witness's "statement," the attorney[19] can avoid discovery by not having the witness sign it, or by simply taking "notes" of the conversation. The point is not that the rules are manipulable or that meretricious attorneys will manipulate them; the point is that to change the "culture" may require much more than a mere change in the written rules.

A second problem permeating many court rules turns on the precise wording of the rule. Some rules require that the attorney disclose any evidence which he "possesses"; other rules require disclosure only of items he "intends to offer" at trial. Two contrary issues arise here. If an attorney "possesses" a statement which would be harmful to his case, he will certainly not "intend to offer" it at trial. Yet in a search for truth, this is precisely the type of evidence we want the parties to disclose (subject to other limitations considered below). On the other hand, asking an attorney to determine — sometimes months in advance — what evidence she will use at trial is inherently problematic. More importantly, such provisions could lead to litigation, either before or after conviction. In 1991, an amendment to Federal Rule 16 discarded the "intended use" requirement as to a written record containing the substance of defendant's oral statements, but retained the "intended use" limitation for disclosing oral statements where there is no such writing.

Many of the more important types of information to which discovery rules in the United States may apply are discussed below. But two general observations may be in order. First, there is a broad range among the rules. Some states (about one-third) such as Arizona (R. Crim P. 15.1/15.2); Florida (Rule 3.220); Hawaii (R. Penal P. 16); and Illinois (Sup. Ct. R. 411-14) provide for very broad discovery. These are often referred to as *open file* states. At the other extreme, the federal rules, followed by a number of states such as New York, severely limit discovery beyond that which is mandated by *Brady*. Most jurisdictions fall in the middle. Second, even where the rule is essentially the same between jurisdictions, the rationale for the rule may differ widely, thus leading to possibly different outcomes in those jurisdictions, depending on the facts of the instant challenge. Third, these rules *supplement, rather than supplant, Brady*. In every instance, but particularly in those jurisdictions with narrowly written rules, defense counsel will attempt to assert that the information is "*Brady* evidence," thus avoiding any possible restrictive interpretation of the rules.

Since many casebooks discuss Federal Rule 16, and since almost a dozen states emulate it, we reproduce it here. Remember, however, that the majority of states are much more generous in one or more of the categories covered by the rule.

---

19. Most of the questions of discovery involve what the defendant may require the prosecutor to disclose. But a number of jurisdictions allow the prosecutor to discover at least some documents that defense counsel controls. See pp.111-112, *infra*. We use the term *attorney*, although most of the time the issue really relates to *prosecutor*.

6. Evidence Disclosure (Discovery)

(a) Government's Disclosure

(1) *Information Subject to Disclosure.*

(A) *Defendant's Oral Statement.* Upon a defendant's request, the government must disclose to the defendant the substance of any relevant oral statement made by the defendant, before or after arrest, in response to interrogation by a person the defendant knew was a government agent if the government intends to use the statement at trial.

(B) *Defendant's Written or Recorded Statement.* Upon a defendant's request, the government must disclose to the defendant, and make available for inspection (copying or photographing) all of the following:

(i) any relevant written or recorded statement by the defendant if:

- the statement is within the government's possession, custody, or control; and
- the attorney for the government knows — or through due diligence could know — that the statement exists;

(ii) the portion of any written record containing the substance of any relevant oral statement made before or after arrest if the defendant made the statement in response to interrogation by a person the defendant knew was a government agent; and

(iii) the defendant's recorded testimony before a grand jury relating to the charged offense. . . .

(D) *Defendant's Prior Record.* Upon a defendant's request, the government must furnish the defendant with a copy of the defendant's prior criminal record that is within the government's possession, custody, or control if the attorney for the government knows — or through due diligence could know — that the record exists.

(E) *Documents and Objects.* Upon a defendant's request, the government must permit the defendant to inspect and to copy or photograph books, papers, documents, data, photographs, tangible objects, buildings or places, or copies or portions of any of these items, if the item is within the government's possession, custody, or control, and:

(i) the item is material to preparing the defense;

(ii) the government intends to use the item in its case-in-chief at trial; or

(iii) the item was obtained from or belongs to the defendant.

(F) *Reports of Examinations and Tests.* Upon a defendant's request, the government must permit a defendant to inspect and to copy or photograph the results or reports of any physical or mental examination and of any scientific test or experiment if:

(i) the item is within the government's possession, custody, or control;

(ii) the attorney for the government knows — or through due diligence could know — that the item exists; and

(iii) the item is material to preparing the defense or the government intends to use the item in its case-in-chief at trial.

(G) *Expert witnesses.* At the defendant's request, the government must give to the defendant a written summary of any testimony that the government intends to use under Rules 702, 703, or 705 of the Federal Rules of Evidence during its case-in-chief at trial. If the government requests discovery under subdivision (b)(1)(C)(ii) and the defendant complies, the government must, at the defendant's request, give to the defendant a written summary of testimony that the government intends to use under Rules 702, 703, or 705 of the Federal Rules of Evidence as evidence at trial on the issue of the defendant's mental condition. The summary provided under this subparagraph must describe the witness's opinions, the bases and reasons for those opinions, and the witness's qualifications.

(2) *Information Not Subject to Disclosure.* Except as Rule 16(a)(1) provides otherwise, this rule does not authorize the discovery or inspection of reports, memoranda, or other internal government documents made by an attorney for the government or other government agent in connection with investigating or prosecuting the case. Nor does this rule authorize the discovery or inspection of statements made by prospective government witnesses except as provided in 18 U.S.C. §3500.

(3) *Grand Jury Transcripts.* This rule does not apply to the discovery or inspection of a grand jury's recorded proceedings, except as provided in Rules 6, 12(h), 16(a)(1), and 26.2.

I. Defendant's Statements

Less than 50 years ago, courts refused to require the state to give a defendant a copy of his own confession. Although the apparent policy here was to prevent a defendant from molding his testimony to jibe with the statement, the explanations for nondisclosure were sometimes incredible. Thus, one court indicated that the police need not give a defendant "his" statement because, while the words were "his," the paper on which the words were written belonged to the state. Today, virtually all jurisdictions require disclosure of these statements. Even then, however, there are problems of interpretation.

A brief glance at Rule 16, for example, finds that the prosecution must disclose (a) "relevant" "statements," if they are written or recorded; (b) the portion of any written (but not recorded?) "record" containing the substance of an oral statement — if that statement was made to a person known to be a government agent;[20] (c) any other "relevant" "statement" made to a known government agent but only if the prosecutor intends (several months from now) to use it at trial. This apparently simple set of rules raises many questions: (1) what are "statements"; (2) what is a "recording"; (3) why are the records in (b) and (c) differentiated depending on whether the prosecutor intends to use them at trial? Etc., etc., etc.

Most state rules are not so restrictive. For example, California makes all defendant's statements discoverable, whether or not written or recorded. See Cal. Pen. Code §1054.1(b).

2. Information About Witnesses

a. Names and Addresses

It happens in every courtroom movie; the prosecution or defense calls a "surprise witness" whose testimony clinches the case one way or the other. As the twenty-first century begins, that image is still real in many states. While over half of the states provide for discovery of the names and addresses of all persons known to have relevant information, the federal rules do not make such information available.

In 1975, the Conference Committee of the Senate and House, rejecting a proposal to allow such disclosure, declared that

> A majority of the Conferees believe it is not in the interest of the effective administration of criminal justice to require that the government or the defendant be forced to reveal the names and addresses of its witnesses before trial. Discouragement of witnesses and improper contact directed at influencing their testimony were deemed paramount concerns in the formulating of this policy.

Other states require disclosure only of persons "intended" to be called at trial, thereby permitting an attorney to hide from an opponent a potentially favorable witness (assuming *Brady* is not activated). Again, the primary explanation is fear of witness intimidation. Federal courts put a heavy burden on defendants to show a need for witness list disclosure. See *United States. v. Alex*, 791 F. Supp. 723 (N.D. Ill. 1991). Those courts have considered, among other factors: (1) the type of crime charged; (2) defendant's history of violence or witness intimidation; (3) whether the evidence could be easily altered; (4) defendant's resources.

---

20. The obvious point here is to protect undercover agents.

b. Statements by Witnesses

A substantial number of states either totally preclude defense pre-trial access to statements made by interviewed witnesses,[21] or leave it to the discretion of the judge.[22] At least 14 follow the *Jencks Act* of the federal system, which does not require pre-trial disclosure of witness statements, requiring disclosure only after the witness has actually testified at trial.[23] As with disclosure of names and addresses, the policy supporting nondisclosure is clear: We wish to assure that the witness will not be harassed (or worse) before trial.[24]

c. Evidence to Impeach Witnesses

Spurred by a fear that witnesses will be intimidated, Rule 16 provides virtually no evidence about the witnesses. That a prosecution witness has a prior criminal record (perhaps even for perjury) is not discoverable under Rule 16. Neither is a "deal" that the witness has made with the government. That information is discoverable only under *Brady-Giglio*. The vast majority of states, however, would require disclosure of this evidence. E.g., *Commw. v. Strong*, 563 Pa. 455, 761 A.2d 1167 (2000) (prosecutor must disclose discussion of a possible deal, even if one has not been "reached" yet).[25] Other information, however, such as statements by co-defendants, are sometimes open to discovery (about one-third of the states), but these issues are sometimes expressly left to court rule or decision.

3. Police Reports

Some states explicitly provide for disclosure of every police report "in the possession, custody, or control of the prosecutor,"[26] but a large number do not directly address the issue, allowing discovery of parts of the report only if they fall under other provisions. (For example, in a prosecution based upon an automobile accident, police observation of road conditions might be

---

21. Approximately 20 states make pre-trial access to the statements of witnesses who have been interviewed a matter of right.

22. E.g., Mississippi and Alabama require further showings that the statements are "material" and "relevant" or "essential" for cross-examination.

23. For a summary of all states' rules, with an appendix comparing them, see Note, Defendant Access to Prosecution Witness Statements in Federal and State Cases, 61 Wash. U.L.Q. 471 (1983).

24. Ellen S. Podgor, Criminal Discovery of Jencks Witness Statements: Timing Makes a Difference, 15 Ga. St. U.L. Rev. 651 (1999).

25. *People v. Martinez*, 127 Cal. Rptr. 2d 305 (Cal. App. 4 Dist. 2002).

26. E.g., N.J. R. 3:13-3(c)(8).

exculpatory, but not "material" within *Brady*.) Under Federal Rule 16, the defendant is not entitled to the prosecutor's non-*Brady* investigative file, including the FBI 302 report, but in some states, any potentially exculpatory information in police reports, including information about alternate suspects, are discoverable. See *Harrington v. State*, 659 N.W.2d 509 (Iowa 2003). On the other hand, many states' codes explicitly include police reports in the work product exemption.[27]

4. Expert Reports and Witnesses

Most systems require early disgorgement, by both prosecutors and defense, of the names of experts and their reports. The reasons seem fairly clear — these reports may require rebuttal by other experts, who will require time to analyze both the general questions in the trial as well as the experts' reports. Federal Rule 16 requires disclosure of reports that the prosecutor intends to use in its "case-in-chief" (i.e., not in impeachment or rebuttal), or reports that are "material to preparing the defense." If the report of an expert employed by the prosecutor *disfavors* the prosecution's view, but does not directly favor that of the defendant, it is not clear that it is discoverable, since it may not be "material" to preparation of a defense. This rule does not differentiate expert witnesses and their reports from other witnesses, even though once the expert report is in, recantation by the expert is likely to seem suspect, so they are arguably less subject to intimidation. On the other hand, many jurisdictions hold that the prosecution must disclose information which casts doubt upon an expert witness's accuracy. Discovery relating to expert reports may also entail a right to discovery of the expert or laboratory's standard operating procedures, including its quality assurance manual. *Cole v. State*, 378 Md. 42, 835 A.2d 600 (2003).

5. Information About the Police

Sometimes defendants want to challenge the veracity of the police officers who arrested or interrogated them. These records are generally nondiscoverable. Some states, such as California, have established specific

---

27. Anne Shaver, *United States v. Fort and the Future of Work Product in Criminal Discovery*, 44 Cal. W.L. Rev. 127 (2007), citing, inter alia, Ariz. R. Crim. P. 15.4 (2007); S.D. Codified Laws §23A-13-5 (2007).

procedures for *in camera* judicial examination of police officer records. *Pitchess v. Superior Court*, 11 Cal.3d 531, 522 P.2d 305, 113 Cal. Rptr. 897 (1974). Others require disclosure if the records are "likely to contain information relevant to the officer's credibility."[28]

6. The Work Product Exception

Those familiar with the civil system of discovery know the difficulties caused by the concept of "work product" — the idea that documents prepared for trial, by the attorney or persons working directly under her direction, are not discoverable. That rule applies to prosecutors and defense counsel in the criminal sphere as well. *United States v. Nobles*, 422 U.S. 225 (1975). And it is no more transparent in criminal than in civil matters. But, as *Nobles* makes clear, the move toward restricting what qualifies as work product continues in the criminal area. There, the Court held that the prosecutor could discover a report relating to possible witnesses written by an investigator hired by the defense counsel. The Court declared: "[defendant] did not prepare the report, and there is no suggestion that the portions subject to the disclosure order reflect any information that he conveyed to the investigator." Thus, the Court held, these were not defendant's "statements," and hence was not work product, whose disclosure might otherwise violate the Fifth Amendment self-incrimination clause.

---

28. Although grand jury testimony is usually not available, the Court in *United States v. Hayes*, 376 F. Supp. 2d 736 (E.D. Mich. 2005), ordered the testimony unsealed where defendant, charged with illegal gun possession, sought to discover grand jury testimony concerning misconduct by his arresting officer. Canada allows discovery of the following information about police officers:

- statements of any individuals who have brought complaints against the arresting officer;
- the phone numbers and addresses of those individuals;
- statements made by the arresting officer in relation to any complaints;
- the disposition of any complaints and the criminal record of the arresting officer, including any discharges granted under the Criminal Code;
- police service records describing the nature of any misconduct found to have been committed by any of the officers and the penalty imposed;
- any outstanding formal allegations of misconduct before the police disciplinary tribunal.

R. v. Tomlinson (1998) 16 C.R. (5th) 333 (Ont. Prov. Div.). Training logs maintained by the handler of a "drug dog," and the dog's qualifications, were discoverable under Rule 16(a), but not as "statements" under the Jencks Act. *United States v. Cedano-Arellano*, 332 F.3d 568 (9th Cir. 2003). (The nondisclosure in this case, however, was held to be non-prejudicial.)

C. TIMING OF DISCOVERY

1. Pre-trial

Timing is everything. Neither *Brady* nor its progeny directly addressed a critical issue of discovery—*when* must the information be disclosed? The normal standard is that the disclosure must be made "in time for its efficient use at trial."

The American Bar Association provides that disclosure should be made at a "specified and reasonable time prior to trial." Rule 11/2.1 Standards for Criminal Justice: Discovery (3d ed. 1994). And many court rules actually specify a particular time period (15, 30, or 60 days) after a specific event (request by the defense; unsealing of an indictment, etc.). But others are vague on this matter, holding that *Brady* itself does not specifically address timing of discovery, and that so long as the defendant receives the evidence in time for its "effective" use at trial, *Brady* is met. See *United States v. Higgs*, 713 F.2d 39 (3d Cir. 1983). Where there is no statutory directive, courts often allow the prosecutor to delay disclosure, so long as the defendant has some opportunity to use the evidence during trial (should there be one). For example, the federal district court of the District of Massachusetts requires disclosure of "exculpatory information" at least 21 days before the trial date.

In *United States v. Gil*, 297 F.3d 933 (2d Cir. 2002), one or two business days before trial, the prosecutor turned over to the defendant two boxes of documents accompanied by a 41-page index designating over 600 exhibits. After trial, defense counsel found, among these documents, a memorandum which unquestionably supported his contention that defendant's conduct had been authorized by the government. The appellate court noted that "a conscientious defense lawyer would be preoccupied working on an opening statement and witness cross-examinations and all else," and that "[t]he defense [at that time] may be unable to divert resources from other initiatives and obligations that are or may seem more pressing." The court then noted "the government runs a certain risk when it turns over so late documents sought by the defense for so long," and held that the documents, even though disclosed, were "suppressed" within the meaning of *Brady*. In a similar case, the court held that there was no *Brady* violation because the documents given to defendant on the Friday before a Monday trial only totaled 290 pages and were sorted and indexed. *United States v. Douglas*, 525 F.3d 225 (2d Cir. 2008).[29]

---

29. One commentator has suggested that even if there is no *Fifth* Amendment violation here, late discovery could be seen as "state interference" with counsel, in violation of the *Sixth* Amendment (see Chapter 11, *infra*). Jenny Roberts, Too Little, Too Late: Ineffective Assistance

6. Evidence Disclosure (Discovery)

In the Duke lacrosse case, the relevant rule required the prosecutor to divulge information in a "timely" manner. The prosecutor contended that, although he had the relevant information months before he revealed it, the disclosure was "timely" because, even then, no trial date had been set. While the North Carolina Bar Association rejected that contention in light of all the facts (considered in more detail in Chapter 14), it is not facially implausible as a general matter.

In federal cases, the problem is made even more intricate by the so-called Jencks Act, incorporated in Federal Rule 26.2 and many states, which provides that:

> After a witness called by the United States has testified on direct examination, the court shall . . . order the United States to produce any statement . . . of the witness . . . which relates to the subject matter as to which the witness has testified.

The federal courts are divided over whether the *Brady* general rule — "in time for effective use" — is trumped by the more specific Jencks Act language.[30] Some require disclosure before trial, while others take a "balancing" approach, attempting to distinguish those statements which are merely for impeachment from those which contain some *Brady* evidence. See *United States v. Beckford*, 962 F. Supp. 780, 790-792 (E.D. Va. 1997) (collecting cases). In those remaining jurisdictions that follow the Jencks Act language, because disclosure occurs during trial, and after the witness has testified, the typical defense response is to ask for a continuance. But the time given by a trial court is almost bound to be shorter than that necessary both to read the statements and investigate not merely their substance, but any possible leads they might provide.[31] And if the statement is lengthy (imagine a declaration by an executive which attaches multiple documents relating to discussions with the company's accountants), the defense side may find itself wallowing in reams of arcane information. (This is sometimes referred to as "death by

---

of Counsel, the Duty to Investigate, and Pre-trial Discovery in Criminal Cases, 31 Fordham Urb. L.J. 1097 (2004).

30. At least five circuits hold that the Jencks Act controls the timing of disclosure. See, e.g., *United States v. Scott*, 424 F.2d 465 (5th Cir. 1975); *United States v. Jones*, 612 F.2d 453 (9th Cir. 1980) (Jencks Act dominates). Others require pre-trial disclosure, in the discretion of the judge. See, e.g., *United States v. Starusko*, 729 F.2d 256 (3d Cir. 1984). At least one court allowed the prosecution to obtain a mandamus overturning a discovery order which permitted discovery of materials prior to trial. See *In re United States*, 834 F.2d 283 (2d Cir. 1987).

31. In *Boss v. Pierce*, 263 F.3d 734 (7th Cir. 2001), cert. denied, *Pierce v. Boss*, 535 U.S. 1078 (2002), the prosecutor gave to the defense an investigative report summarizing an interview conducted four days before the trial began. Defense counsel was unable to conduct an investigation at that point. Only after the conviction did a new defense attorney obtain information, using the summary as a lead, that garnered information which eventually led to a reversal of the conviction. See also *Leka v. Portuondo*, 257 F.3d 89 (2d Cir. 2001).

discovery.") Even with a continuance (often unlikely in a jury trial), the defense will be put at a serious disadvantage.

Moreover, since most cases never get to trial, many defendants are unlikely ever to know that there was favorable, undisclosed evidence.[32] The United States Supreme Court appeared to endorse this result. In *United States v. Ruiz*, 536 U.S. 622 (2002), the Court held that a defendant considering pleading guilty was not entitled to discovery, prior to deciding whether to enter that plea, of *Giglio*-type impeachment evidence.[33] The Court indicated, but did not hold, that there might be a right to pre-plea disclosure of *Brady* exculpatory material going to actual guilt. Although the lower court had held that a plea could not be "knowing" unless made with complete knowledge of the government's *Brady* material (see Chapter 7 on plea bargaining for a more complete discussion of the knowledge requirement), the Supreme Court emphasized that *Brady* was intended to assist a defendant *at* trial, and not necessarily before.[34]

2. Post-trial

Before and during trial, the disclosure obligation is a "continuing" one—just because the prosecutor provided information three months before trial does not mean that she need not disclose evidence obtained at a later time. *Banks v. Dretke*, 540 U.S. 668 (2004).

Whether *Brady* requires disclosure of evidence obtained by the prosecutor *after* conviction is, surprisingly, unsettled and heavily debated. On the one hand, *Brady*'s focus is on requiring the defense to have whatever evidence is available so that a fair trial can be held. In the sense that the prosecution did not have an "advantage" because known evidence was not disclosed, the trial was "fair" to each side. And if the purpose of *Brady* is to control errant prosecutors, the prosecutor did not "fail" to disclose the evidence pre-trial. On the other hand, the defendant might be exonerated by the new evidence,

---

32. Many courts will be unsympathetic to a defendant who seeks to have a guilty plea, otherwise voluntarily entered, overturned because he has now learned that the prosecutor failed to disclose some evidence which, if disclosed, (1) would have persuaded him to go to trial; (2) might have resulted in an acquittal. The harmless error rule, discussed in Chapter 12, will frequently insulate such nondisclosure, even if it were purposeful.

33. The actual issue in *Ruiz* was the validity of a government demand that, to obtain a more lenient sentence in exchange for a plea, the defendant waive her right to discover any *Brady* information. The Ninth Circuit had held such a condition *per se* invalid; the Supreme Court reversed. Thus, the case could be construed as holding that a defendant has a right to impeachment evidence before trial, but can waive that right. Obviously, the government has an incentive to include such a waiver clause in every plea agreement.

34. Canada requires disclosure of "all relevant information" before a plea agreement, including witness statements, that the prosecution does not intend to introduce as evidence, and both inculpatory and exculpatory evidence. *R v. Stinchcombe* [1991] S.C.R. 326, 343; Quigley, Procedure in Canadian Criminal Law 275 (1997).

and *Brady* expressly held that where known information was not disclosed pretrial, the prosecutor's intent, or even actual knowledge, was irrelevant, thus suggesting that the focus is not on monitoring prosecutors, but on a fair trial of the defendant. See Fred C. Zacharias, The Role of Prosecutors in Serving Justice After Convictions, 58 Vand. L. Rev. 171 (2005); Todd E. Jaworsky, A Defendant's Right to Exculpatory Evidence: Does the Constitutional Duty to Disclose Exculpatory Evidence Extend to New Evidence Discovered Post-Conviction, 15 St. Thomas. L. Rev. 245 (2002). In 2008, the ABA amended its Model Rules of Professional Conduct Sec. 3.8 to affirm that a prosecutor had a post-conviction duty of disclosure, investigation, and rectification where she learns of "material" and "credible" evidence that establishes a "reasonable likelihood" that the defendant is innocent. Bruce Green and Ellen Yaroshefsky, Prosecutorial Discretion and Post-Conviction Evidence of Innocence, 6 Ohio St. J. Crim. L. 467 (2009).

The "discovery" of new methods of testing preexisting evidence has raised this question directly for purposes of DNA. Scores of convicted defendants have been proven innocent by DNA testing, and at least 46 states (one of the exceptions is Alaska, involved in the *Osborne* case discussed immediately below) now provide, in varying degrees, for post-conviction DNA analysis, particularly if the "newest" method of testing was not available at the time of trial. In *District Attorney's Office for the Third Judicial District v. Osborne*, 557 U.S. 52 (2009), a prisoner sought access, under 42 U.S.C. Sec. 1983, to evidence that the state had in order to subject it to a newer, more sophisticated form of DNA testing. The Court declared that "*Brady* is the wrong framework," explaining:

> Osborne's right to due process is not parallel to a trial right, but rather must be analyzed in light of the fact that he has already been found guilty at a fair trial, and has only a limited interest in postconviction relief.

In a later decision, *Skinner v. Switzer*, 2011 WL 767703, the (U.S.) Court gave two reasons for this position: (1) "*Brady* announced a constitutional requirement addressed first and foremost to the prosecution's conduct pre-trial"; and (2) "[A] *Brady* claim, when successful post-conviction, necessarily yields evidence undermining a conviction." The former statement suggests that *Brady* does not apply post-conviction, but the second reason would apply equally to a convicted felon who seeks to impose a duty upon a prosecutor to divulge potentially exculpatory evidence that has only been unearthed post-trial.[35]

Thus, on this question the law is unclear as the second decade of the twenty-first century opens.

---

35. In *Skinner*, the Court observed that while 42 U.S.C. Sec. 1983 was available for such a prisoner, *Osborne* "severely limits the federal action a state prisoner may bring for DNA testing (and) rejected the extension of substantive due process to this area."

D. NON-*BRADY* DISCOVERY: A RECAP

Table 6.1 summarizes the basic approach taken by "open file" jurisdictions (exemplified by the ABA proposals), by "narrow" jurisdictions (such as the federal rules), and by "intermediate" states. These summaries, however, cannot capture the nuances and possible differences among the various state rules; only a close parsing of a particular state's rules (as interpreted by its judiciary)

6.1

Type of Information	Federal Rule	Intermediate	ABA Proposals
Defendant's statements	Any relevant (not merely "material") written or recorded statements and the "substance" of any oral statement if the defendant knew he was talking to a government agent	Discoverable	Discoverable, if they relate to the "subject matter of the offense"
Defendant's prior criminal record	Discoverable	Discoverable	Discoverable
Witness statements	Not discoverable until witness testifies	Usually discoverable	All statements of all persons having information that *relates* to the subject matter of the offense
Police reports	Not discoverable unless specific matter is covered by other rules	Similar to Fed. Rule	Essentially the same as Fed. Rule; some "open file" states require full disclosure
Witness names and addresses	Not discoverable	Discoverable	All persons known to have information
Witness past criminal history	Not discoverable	Usually discoverable	Disclosure required of any witness "to be called by either party"

6.1 Continued

Type of Information	Federal Rule	Intermediate	ABA Proposals
Expert report	If intended to be used in chief or material to preparing defense case	Almost always discoverable	All reports are to be disclosed; if prosecution intends to call expert, must disclose qualifications and give a description of the proposed testimony
Grand jury transcripts	Not discoverable	Not discoverable	Full disclosure required
"Deals" for testimony	Not discoverable	Discoverable	Discoverable: Must disclose the relationship including the nature and circumstances of any agreement, understanding, or representation . . . that constitutes an inducement for the cooperation of testimony of the witness
Tangible objects	Books, papers, photos, etc., if intended to be used in case-in-chief or material to use in preparing defense	Anything relevant	Anything which "pertains to" the case or was obtained from or belongs to defendant
Timing	There is no specific time set by Federal Rule for discovery. Generally, "in time before trial to be useful." However, witness statements are discoverable only under the Jencks Act, and Rule 26.2, after the witness has testified	Times vary, but usually stated within 30-60 days of (a) a request; or (b) the date of indictment or information	"as early as practicable in the process"

can perform that function. Note carefully — *these summaries relate only to non-Brady/Giglio evidence — there is much that might be discoverable under those cases.*

E. ALTERNATIVE MEANS OF DISCOVERY

Thus far, we have spoken of how a defendant may obtain discovery under either court rules or the Constitution. Even when this discovery occurs, defendants are often required to pay for it (discovery rules frequently simply require the prosecutor to "make available" documents for copying). But there are other methods which may be more fruitful or less costly. First, of course, there is the preliminary hearing (see Chapter 5). Second, in many states, a defendant, acting in her capacity as a citizen (not a defendant), may seek information under the jurisdiction's Freedom of Information Act, or Sunshine Law. Other statutes dealing with specific information, such as reports of family violence for which the defendant has been arrested, may also be used. A defendant may also seek to subpoena records held by third parties, though specific rules may make this difficult in some jurisdictions. Finally, a defendant who could afford it might seek to depose a witness, but most court rules do not provide for depositions,[36] and they have been frowned upon as a means of discovery, although they are allowed if it appears that the witness would not be present at trial. In all other situations, ordering a deposition lies fully within the trial court's discretion.

F. DISCOVERY IN THE REAL WORLD

1. Frequency of Violations of Discovery Rules

a. The Data

Recent studies have demonstrated a distressingly high number of instances of prosecutors not disclosing information that later was held to be covered by *Brady-Giglio* or court rules. While the percentage of these cases among all cases is still low (leaving aside the question of how many nondisclosures were never revealed), the picture is not attractive. Among these studies:

- The Innocence Project reports that in 65 of 225 cases where DNA exonerated the defendant, there was also an allegation of a

---

36. E.g., Florida. Fla. R. Crim. Proc. 3.220.

6. Evidence Disclosure (Discovery)

Brady violation in 38 percent of those cases. The court overturned convictions in 6 of those cases. See http://www.innocenceproject.org/understand/Government-Misconduct.php.

- Perhaps the most serious study of death penalty cases ever conducted said that 68 percent of all death verdicts imposed and fully reviewed during the 1973-1995 study period were reversed by courts due to serious error. The suppression of evidence accounted for the second highest incidence of serious error.[37] James S. Liebman and Jeffrey Fagan, A Broken System Part II: Why There is So Much Error in Capital Cases and What Can Be Done About It, June 2002, available at http://www2.law.columbia.edu/brokensystem2/index2.html.
- A Chicago Tribune study found that of 381 homicide convictions that were reversed because the prosecution withheld evidence or used false testimony; only 3 of the involved prosecutors received serious discipline. See Ken Armstrong and Maurice Possley, The Verdict: Dishonor, Chi. Trib., Jan. 10, 1999, cited in Geoffrey Corn and Adam Gershowitz, Imputed Liability for Supervising Prosecutors: Applying the Military Doctrine of Command Responsibility to Reduce Prosecutorial Misconduct, 14 Berkeley U. Crim. L. 395, n.111 (2009).
- A detailed study of California state defense attorneys reported that 65 percent declared that withholding *Brady* evidence was a significant problem. See Laurence A. Benner, The Presumption of Guilt: Systemic Factors That Contribute to Ineffective Assistance of Counsel in California, 45 Cal. W. L. Rev. 265 (2009).

In addition, a number of recent, high-profile cases have demonstrated a continuing need for further enforcement of discovery requirements:

- *United States v. Stevens,* 593 F. Supp. 2d 177 (D.D.C. 2009). The Justice Department prosecuted Senator Ted Stevens of Alaska for bribery and misuse of funds, among other charges. After he was convicted, defense counsel uncovered hundreds of documents that had not been disclosed and that substantially questioned the veracity of the government's key witness. The Department, under a new Attorney General, moved to dismiss the conviction. The trial judge, excoriating the individual prosecutors, initially appointed a special counsel to investigate and possibly prosecute the federal prosecutors involved for criminal contempt, but ultimately urged the Office of Professional Conduct to investigate these violations. The Attorney General

---

37. These data replicate a 1987 study that found that in 35 of 350 cases in which defendants were wrongfully convicted of capital or potentially capital crimes, exculpatory evidence had been suppressed. Hugo Adam Bedeau and Michael L. Radelet, Miscarriages of Justice in Potentially Capital Cases, 40 Stan. L. Rev. 21, 57 (Table 6) (1987).

thereafter asked the Ninth Circuit to release two convicted lawmakers because federal prosecutors had failed to disclose exculpatory evidence in their cases as well. On January 4, 2010, in response to these and other cases in which courts found Department of Justice prosecutors to have committed serious violations, the Department issued a memorandum providing guidance to prosecutors with respect to their discovery and disclosure obligations. See Memorandum from David W. Ogden, Deputy Att'y Gen., to Dep't of Justice Prosecutors (Jan. 4, 2010), available at http://www .justice.gov/dag/dag-memo.html or www.justice.gov/dag/discovery-guidance.htm.

Subsequently, the department established and published new "guidelines" for discovery but adhered to the general restrictiveness of the Federal Rules of Criminal Procedure.[38] The DoJ appointed a new national coordinator for criminal discovery initiatives to oversee the educational efforts and other initiatives.

- *United States v. Jones*, 609 F. Supp. 2d 113 (D. Mass. 2009). A United States District Court judge summarized eight other cases which had occurred in that district alone that involved nondisclosure or belated disclosure of discovery information. In *Jones* itself, the prosecutor told the judge that she had turned over every piece of exculpatory evidence. She had withheld her notes, which disclosed that the principal eyewitness against the defendant (who identified him in court) had told the prosecution several times that he did not recognize the man.

In addition to considering specific sanctions against the federal prosecutor in the case, the judge wrote a letter to Attorney General Holder describing various instances of misconduct — mostly failure to disclose evidence — which he called "blatant," "deliberate," "outrageous," "extreme," and "intentional." He declared that the federal office had "enduring difficulty in discharging its duty to disclose material exculpatory information to defendants in a timely manner." He "arranged" a program on discovery in criminal cases and "invited" all federal prosecutors in the district to attend. He further ordered the Department of Justice to file additional affidavits, addressing whether their performance and progress have "obviated the need to impose sanctions." In a subsequent decision, the court

---

38. The Department revised its Attorneys' Manual to provide federal prosecutors with more specific guidance on the conduct of their disclosure duties. The Manual now instructs federal prosecutors to make broader disclosure than that required under *Brady*. U.S. Dep't of Justice, United States Attorneys' Manual §9-5.001-C (2006), available at http://www.usdoj.gov/ usao/foia_reading_room/usam/title9/5mcrm.htm ("This policy requires disclosure by prosecutors of information beyond that which is 'material' to guilt. . . .").

held that the particular prosecutor in that case was contrite and had furthered her education on the subject of discovery obligations and that sanctions against her were not necessary. *United States v. Jones*, 686 F. Supp. 2d 147 (D. Mass. 2010).

- *United States v. Shaygan*, 661 F. Supp.2d 1289 (S.D. Fla. 2009). The judge issued public reprimands of the prosecutors and recommended their actions be reviewed by the DOJ. The Office of Profession Responsibility imposed sanctions for a wide array of misconduct, including failure to disclose *Brady* evidence. The judge also awarded approximately $600,000 in attorney's fees.
- *United States v. Prince*, 1994 WL 992312 (E.D.N.Y.). The Court complained that "Time after time after time the government (fails) to turn over information it's obliged to turn over by law under either Rule 16, *Brady* or *Giglio*."

b. Reasons for Nondisclosure

Some prosecutors no doubt purposely hide the ball, attempting to gain any advantage and hoping for a return to "trial by ambush." They may wish to advance their careers by stacking up convictions, or they may believe so ardently that the defendant is guilty that they are willing to stretch — or even knowingly break — their ethical and legal obligations. Moreover, they may know that defendants are unlikely to ever stumble on the undisclosed evidence. But most prosecutors follow, or attempt to follow, their ethical, as well as legal, obligations. Why, then, are there so many instances of misconduct?

- Confirmation bias and the adversary system. Prosecutors must convince themselves that the people they indict are guilty. "Confirmation bias" allows a prosecutor to adhere to this view, even when confronted with "absolutely certain" evidence that the defendants are not guilty.[39]
- The vagueness of the standards employed by many courts — including, obviously, the Supreme Court — has certainly contributed to confusion about what is discoverable. Terms such as *favorable* or *material* or even *exculpatory* are empty vessels into which a prosecutor can pour his own personal views, even if he wishes to comply with the law.
- By definition, most discovery violations are never uncovered, and even those that are revealed remain hidden until after the trial (and conviction) of the defendant. Since most courts, including the United

---

39. Keith A. Findley and Michael S. Scott, The Multiple Dimensions of Tunnel Vision in Criminal Cases, 2006 Wis. L. Rev. 291, 329.

States Supreme Court, have placed the burden on the defendant to show prejudice from the nondisclosure, the retrospective inquiry, coming after the jury has convicted, places the reviewing court in a difficult position for reversal.

- Many convictions rely on the testimony of informants ("snitches") or codefendants who have "turned state's evidence," almost always for a plea bargain that reduces their sentence (or dismisses the charges entirely). Prosecutors tend not to make a final "deal" with the witness until after the trial so that the witness can "truthfully" answer, on cross-examination, that there "is no deal."

- The lack of disciplinary or other controls over prosecutors (see Chapter 14), even after a court decision has reversed a conviction, may persuade prosecutors that the decisions are "technical" and do not reflect the innocence of the defendant.

- Although *Brady* requires a court to "accumulate" the nondisclosed evidence, prosecutors are likely to examine each piece separately; unless the evidence is clearly controlled by *Brady*, it may be difficult for the prosecutor to decide to disclose. Moreover, even if she looks at the evidence "cumulatively," she may decide to release only "the least harmful" piece, concluding that there is no need to disclose "all" the evidence.

- Public pressure not to "look soft" on crime.

2. Broadening Discovery Beyond the Rules

Notwithstanding these alarming examples, most prosecutors do their best to comply with *Brady*. In fact, in some jurisdictions that do not provide for broad discovery, prosecutors nevertheless provide something often approaching "open file."

In 1984, 76 percent of responding Assistant U.S. Attorneys stated that they provided discovery beyond what was required by the Federal Rules, and 42 percent adopted an open-file policy. See W.B. Middlekauff, What Practitioners Say About Broad Criminal Discovery Practice, Crim. Just. Spring 1994, 14, 55. On the other hand, "with each individual Assistant United States Attorney at the Richard Russell (Federal) Building, you would find a series of opinions that vary widely." Comments of Art Leach, Assistant U.S. Attorney, and Chief of the Organized Crime Strike Force, Georgia, in Panel Discussion: Criminal Discovery in Practice, 15 Ga. St. U.L. Rev. 781, 805 (Spring 1999). See also Laurie L. Levenson, Working Outside the Rules, 26 Fordham Urb. L.J. 553, 554 n.5 (1999): "[I]t is standard practice in some [federal] jurisdictions to disclose witness statements before trial begins, even though the law only requires disclosure after the witness testifies."

Prosecutors may provide more discovery than restrictive rules require for several reasons: (1) a sense of fair play; (2) experience that more discovery will lead to plea bargains, and hence an avoidance of trial, where no one can be sure of the result; (3) a fear that if the case goes to trial, judges will allow the defendant significant time to assess newly disclosed information; and (4) husbanding of scarce resources, which can then be applied in instances where pleas are not desirable.

G. DISCOVERY FROM THE DEFENSE

Courts and legislatures were slow to require discovery from the prosecution in criminal cases in part because they believed that both the Fifth and Sixth Amendments protected defendants from "reciprocal" discovery. That view is now untenable. Beginning by upholding requirements that defendants notify the state if they planned to use an alibi or insanity plea, courts have now upheld rules requiring reciprocal discovery between the two parties. Except for *Brady*-required constitutional discovery, many states now make some, or all, prosecutorial disclosure conditional on reciprocal discovery by the prosecutor from the defense.

The Fifth Amendment wall cracked in *Williams v. Florida*, 399 U.S. 78 (1970), where the Court decided that the defense could be required pre-trial to disclose alibis. Two years later, the Court made clear that prosecutors could obtain discovery only if the state provided equal discovery by the defendant (although the defendant did not have to avail herself of the right in order to activate the prosecutorial right). *Wardius v. Oregon*, 412 U.S. 470 (1972).

The Court has relied upon several theories to support prosecutorial discovery. The most obvious reason for requiring disclosure of alibi or mental incompetence claims is simply practicality — a prosecutor suddenly confronted in the middle of a trial with such a claim would need a fairly lengthy continuance to garner evidence to rebut the claim. Rather than prolong an already commenced trial, courts were willing to tolerate requirements of pre-trial disclosure of those claims.

Second, courts agreed with Judge Hand that to allow the defendant to obtain information, while precluding the state from doing so was unfair. Reciprocity seemed a partial attempt at equilibrium. But this ignores the fact that thorough prosecutors use the grand jury (and its subpoena power) to obtain substantial evidence, to anticipate defenses, to "lock in" witnesses who (otherwise) might prove favorable to the defense, and to gather impeachment information for use in cross-examining defense witnesses at trial. Moreover, the prosecutor can make deals with other potential defendants, which is usually beyond the power of any defendant.

A third argument for allowing prosecutorial discovery, put forward in *Williams v. Florida*, is the notion of *acceleration*. Since the defendant will produce the evidence at trial, there is no ultimate harm to him — the question is one not of overcoming a Fifth Amendment (or other) right, but merely the timing of disclosure. The acceleration theory, however, ignores (1) the possibility a defendant may decide, after prosecutorial discovery, not to use a particular claim or witness and (2) most cases never get to trial. Moreover, the acceleration theory could be used to require disclosure, immediately after indictment, by both sides, thereby overcoming the Jencks Act (see *supra*, p.101) or other timing limitations on discovery by either side.

These critiques, however, do not necessarily undermine the general case for reciprocal, and early, discovery in criminal cases. More information is always better than less; early knowledge always trumps late discovery. If a trial, or even a plea negotiation, is to be a search for "the truth," both sides should be as informed as possible.

CAVEAT: Even if the defense refuses to disclose his evidence, the prosecutor *still* must disclose any *Brady* information — which makes defining that term critical to defense counsel who do not wish to disclose any part of their case to the prosecution. The broader the *Brady* rule, the less eager defense counsel will be to pursue discovery under state discovery rules.

H. PRESERVATION OF EVIDENCE

We all lose things, even the best of us. But what happens if the police, or another agency of the state, loses evidence which could be discoverable under *Brady*, or even under discovery rules? In *Arizona v. Youngblood*, 488 U.S. 51 (1988), police threw out semen samples which had been obtained from the victim of a sexual assault. It thereupon proved impossible for the defendant to perform blood group testing to see whether the sample matched his. Reversing a lower court finding that the impact upon the defendant's case violated his due process rights, regardless of the polices' intent, the Supreme Court held that only a bad faith failure to preserve this evidence would violate due process.[40] Moreover, the defendant carries the burden of showing that there was malevolent purpose; although the apparent exculpatory nature of

---

40. The *Youngblood* case had a particularly poignant ending. After serving more than 10 years, Youngblood was released from prison, but was soon rearrested for another crime. As the prosecutor prepared for the new trial, he discovered a cotton swab from the initial charge which had been misplaced. DNA testing proved that Youngblood had not committed the first offense.

the evidence may assist him in this, there is no presumption, rebuttable or otherwise, that the destruction or loss was malicious.

The *Youngblood* "bad faith" rule is followed by a majority of states, although a few focus only on the impact upon the defendant's case, rather than the prosecutor's or agent's state of mind.[41]

Even if bad faith is required before a court will find a due process violation where evidence is destroyed, a Jencks Act or Rule 16 violation does not necessarily require bad faith, at least where the evidence lost is absolutely critical to both the prosecution and the defense. In *Fisher v. Illinois*, 540 U.S. 544 (2004), the defendant was charged with possession of cocaine; 11 days later he moved for discovery of the powder seized. The police tested the powder four times, concluding each time that it was cocaine. Before the defendant could test the powder himself, however, he escaped, and was a fugitive for over 10 years. Before he was recaptured, but years after the arrest, the police, acting in accord with established procedures, destroyed the powder seized from him. Defendant argued that this evidence, unlike that in *Youngblood*, could fully exonerate (or inculpate) him, and that *Brady*, rather than *Youngblood*, applied. The Court's response was unclear. On the one hand, it firmly rejected the argument that *Brady* applied whenever the contested evidence provides a defendant's "only hope for exoneration and is . . . essential to and determinative of the outcome of the case." Immediately thereafter, however, the Court declared that the applicability of the bad-faith requirement in *Youngblood* depended "not on the centrality of the contested evidence to the prosecution's case or the defendant's defense, but on the distinction between 'material exculpatory' evidence and 'potentially useful' evidence. . . ." The *Fisher* Court concluded that "the substance destroyed here was, at best, 'potentially useful' evidence, and therefore *Youngblood*'s bad-faith requirement applies." Consider, then, a tape which clearly shows the perpetrator to be other than the defendant.

---

41. Thirty-six states follow *Youngblood*. Teresa N. Chen, The Youngblood Success Stories: Overcoming the "Bad Faith" Destruction of Evidence Standard, 109 W. Va. L. Rev. 421 (2007). That article unearthed 1,675 published opinions that cited *Youngblood*; in only seven had bad faith been found. The author declares that state and federal courts have adopted three different approaches after *Youngblood*:

- follow *Youngblood*'s bad faith and exculpatory requirements;
- apply *Youngblood* when the evidence is "potentially useful," reject bad-faith requirement when the evidence has "apparent exculpatory value";
- require bad faith for all claims, but not a showing that the evidence was apparently exculpatory.

As one commentator has put it: destruction of evidence does not violate *Youngblood* "(u)nless (it) screams 'Save me.'" Peter J. Henning, Prosecutorial Misconduct and Constitutional Remedies, 77 Wash. U.L.Q. 713, 776-790 (1999). See also Norman C. Bay, Old Blood, Bad Blood and Youngblood: Due Process, Lost Evidence, and the Limits of Bad Faith, 86 Wash. U.L. Rev. 241 (2008).

That evidence would seem *both* to be "exculpatory" and to be "essential and determinative of the outcome of the case." If the police inadvertently destroyed that tape, it is possible, under the later language in *Fisher*, that *Brady*, and not *Youngblood*, would control. A situation like that occurred in *Robinson v. United States*, 825 A.2d 318 (D.C. App. 2003). Defendant was charged with making threats over the telephone. The conversation had been tape-recorded (defendant was an inmate at a federal prison at the time), but the government destroyed the tape of that conversation, and relied exclusively on the testimony of the person called. Defendant argued that the tape recording would demonstrate that he had not threatened the party. The court held that the destruction alone, without any showing of bad faith, undermined defendant's rights and, since the testimony of the complaining witness could not be corroborated, ordered the trial court to dismiss the case. See generally Elizabeth A. Bawden, Here Today, Gone Tomorrow — Three Common Mistakes Courts Make When Police Lose or Destroy Evidence with Apparent Exculpatory Value, 48 Clev. St. L. Rev. 335 (2000).

Destruction of evidence, even when done according to internal police or prosecutorial regulations, still has dire effects. The Innocence Project, which has successfully overturned convictions (mostly by DNA testing), estimates that 75 percent of the cases it accepts cannot go forward because the (biological) evidence has been lost or destroyed.[42] Virtually all states now have "innocence protection" statutes providing paths by which prisoners may challenge, based upon DNA or other biological concerns, their convictions, since a federal statute, effective in 2004, provides for reduction of federal funds to states that do not have such a statute. These statutes, however, deal primarily or only with DNA and similar biological evidence, and almost half of the currently existing statutes do not *mandate* the preservation of evidence, merely assuring the right to obtain such evidence if it *exists*.[43]

I. SANCTIONS

Most discovery violations are only uncovered after the defendant has been convicted. The common remedy, then, is a new trial, in which the defendant will be aware of the previously undisclosed information.

---

42. Cynthia E. Jones, Evidence Destroyed, Innocence Lost: The Preservation of Biological Evidence Under Innocence Protection Statutes, 42 Am. Crim. L. Rev. 1239 (2005) (citing E. Connors et al., Convicted by Juries, Exonerated by Science: Case Studies in the Use of DNA Evidence to Establish Innocence After Trial, 19 U.S. Dept. of Justice (1996), available at http:www.ncjrs.org.pdffiles/dnaevid). See also Nathan Kipp, Preserving Due Process: Violations of the Wisconsin DNA Evidence Preservation Statutes as Per Se Violations of the Fourteenth Amendment, 2004 Wis. L. Rev. 1245 (2004).
43. Id. at 1252-1261.

6. Evidence Disclosure (Discovery)

On the other hand, if the violation is discovered before or during trial, the common remedies include:

- a continuance of the trial, allowing the affected party to read the material and perhaps to act upon it (by pursuing leads, etc.);
- exclusion of the nondisclosed evidence, or witness;
- a "curative instruction" that the jury assume certain facts that might have been established through the nondisclosed material;
- mistrial;
- contempt;
- dismissal of the entire prosecution or of specific charges;
- disciplinary action against the violator, or his office.

In *Taylor v. Illinois*, 484 U.S. 400 (1988), the Supreme Court upheld the preclusion of evidence when the defendant did not disclose the availability of a witness whom he intended to use. In *Taylor*, however, the trial court found, and the Supreme Court stressed in its opinion, that there was a strong suspicion that defendant's counsel acted intentionally or in bad faith. The Court has also overturned a state-court-established *per se* rule that the defendant could never be precluded from presenting evidence, however improper his counsel's actions. *Michigan v. Lucas*, 500 U.S. 145 (1991). *And see United States v. Davis*, 244 F.3d 666 (8th Cir. 2001) (where government failed to produce DNA tests promptly for defendant's examination, trial court's suppression of the evidence was not improper).

As a general rule, dismissal of counts is not a sanction readily endorsed by courts. Indeed, it has been held that even where the government has purposely refused to produce a defense witness whom it controls, dismissal of the indictment was too severe, at least absent prejudice to the defendant. *United States v. Lee*, 906 F.2d 117, 1120 (4th Cir. 1990).[44] A dramatic instance of such a sanction occurred in *United States v. Moussaoui*, 282 F. Supp. 2d 480 (E.D. Va. 2003). Moussaoui, the alleged "missing terrorist" in the 9/11 conspiracy, was representing himself, and had sought the right to interview several other persons being detained by the government, alleging that they could disprove the government's contention that he was part of that conspiracy. When the government refused to allow this discovery, the trial court precluded the government from seeking the death penalty in the case, since those charges were the only ones carrying that penalty. The Fourth Circuit,

---

44. In *United States v. Kohring*, 637 F.3d 895 (9th Cir. 2011) the court reversed a conviction of a state legislator because the same prosecutors who had handled the Stevens case (see p. 107, *supra*) had similarly withheld several thousand pages of documents containing *Brady* information. But the court refused to dismiss the indictment, over the vehement objection of one judge who argued that the violation was "flagrant, willful and in bad faith." For a rare case in which the indictment was dismissed after the defendant was convicted, see *United States v. Chapman*, 524 F.3d 1073 (9th Cir. 2008).

however, reversed this sanction, ordering the trial court to attempt to find compromise procedures that would both protect Moussaoui and allow the government to pursue the death penalty. *United States v. Moussaoui*, 365 F.3d 292 (4th Cir. 2004). For an argument that courts should preclude retrial where the *Brady* violation is highly reckless or intentional, on the grounds that this is analogous to a prosecutor "goading" a defense attorney into asking for a mistrial (see Chapter 9), see Adam M. Harris, Two Constitutional Wrongs Do Not Make A Right: Double Jeopardy and Prosecutorial Misconduct under the *Brady* Doctrine, 28 Cardozo L. Rev. 931 (2006).

Examples

1. Roxanne, the prosecutor, has written statements from three eyewitnesses identifying Norman as the perpetrator of the severe beating of Bridget. She has a fourth such statement from another witness, Roget, but she also has learned that Roget is myopic and did not have on his glasses when the beating took place. (a) If she presents Roget personally to the grand jury, must she disclose Roget's infirmity to the grand jury? (b) If she intends to call Roget to the stand at trial must she disclose Roget's myopia, and his glassesless state, to the defense counsel before trial? (c) If she does not disclose the evidence, calls all four witnesses, including Roget, to testify, and Norman is convicted, what is the likelihood that an appellate court will reverse the conviction?

2. Luke, charged with manslaughter, contends that he was at home the night of the killing. He is convicted. He later learns that Laura, the prosecutor, had obtained, through a search conducted pursuant to warrant, e-mails that had been sent from his home computer at the time the homicide was committed, but she had never disclosed the information to him. He argues that the e-mails would have verified his alibi, and that the nondisclosure violated *Brady* and requires a new trial. Does Luke have a case?

3. Summer is charged with perjury, based upon testimony she gave to the grand jury, concerning a beating in which she may have participated. After her conviction, she learns that Spring, one of the trial witnesses against her, had indicated during police interrogation uncertainty about her recollection of the incident, and had asked to be hypnotized in order to "truly recall" events. She never did so. The government never disclosed to the defendant the memo recounting that request. What result when defendant moves for a new trial?

4. Peter Prosecutor interviews Wanda Witness in Witness's office. (1) He takes two pages of written notes of Wanda's statements. Two days

later, in his office, he dictates (2) a memorandum based upon the notes and his memory; the memorandum runs six pages. A week later, Wanda calls Peter and adds several facts which she had forgotten during the interview. Peter (3) notes these, in writing, on the memorandum he had dictated. If Wanda testifies at trial, which of the above items is discoverable under the Jencks Act (Fed. Crim. Rule 26.2)?

5. (a) Ben and Jerry are charged with robbing a bank and with homicide of a bank teller. Pat, the prosecutor, hired Edward Expert to determine which gun generated the fatal shot. Expert concluded that it is not possible to determine which gun fired the shot. Pat decided not to use the report against either defendant. Must Pat disclose this report to Ben? To Jerry?

    (b) Suppose the state statute provides that while each defendant may be sentenced to life imprisonment, only the actual shooter may be subject to the death penalty?

6. Escobar, a federal prosecutor, interviews Guiliano, a potential witness. Guiliano declares that his friend, Doug, saw the drug deal in question, and that Doug said the defendant (Barry) was not involved, or even present. Escobar does not call Guiliano at trial. Six months later, the defendant learns of the interview and the statement, and seeks relief on the basis of Brady. The defendant also learns that Doug died two months after the trial ended. What result?

7. Johannes, on probation, has been accused by his probation officer of drinking alcoholic beverages, contrary to a probation condition. The probation officer has moved to have Johannes' probation revoked. The prosecutor has a lab report that clearly indicates that the beverage Johannes was imbibing was not scotch, but Diet Coke. Must the prosecutor disclose this report to Johannes?

8. (a) Raymond has been arrested by the police and charged with assault, based on the complaint of the victim. Priscilla Prosecutor, three days before the preliminary hearing, finds in the file a letter from the victim addressed to "the prosecutor" in which the victim recants her earlier statements to the police, and maintains that the injury was merely accidental. Priscilla attempts to contact the witness but cannot. At the preliminary hearing, Priscilla calls the police officer who took the original statement from the victim. The magistrate "binds over" Raymond for trial. Has Priscilla violated Brady?

    (b) Suppose that, instead of the letter, Priscilla had learned just before the preliminary examination that the victim had died (not from the assault). Would she have to disclose that?

(c) Now assume that after the preliminary examination, Priscilla offers a plea bargain to a lesser degree of assault and Raymond accepts it. He later moves to vacate his plea because he was unaware that the victim was dead, and argues that Priscilla had to inform him of that before he accepted the plea.

9. Frankie, operating undercover, had a discussion with Johnny in which Johnny acknowledged possessing cocaine. Frankie tells the district attorney of this conversation, and puts it in writing. Under what circumstances is this discussion discoverable by Johnny?

10. Phillip LeCarre is charged in state court with robbing a bank. The state district attorney, Moira, has statements from several witnesses describing a man very much like LeCarre. She learns that the FBI is also investigating the robbery (because the bank was federally insured) and that the FBI has statements from several other witnesses whose descriptions are very different and would never apply to LeCarre. Not surprisingly, she immediately decides that she will not ask for these statements and will not call these witnesses at trial. (a) Must she tell the defense counsel of this information? (b) If she does not, and LeCarre is convicted, is the conviction likely to be overturned if defense counsel learns of this information post-trial?

11. Claude Coke has been charged with homicide. He tells his attorney, Gene Hacker, that the killing was in self-defense, and gives Hacker (a) the names of five people who were present at the killing; (b) the names of two people who heard the victim threaten to kill Coke the next time they met; and (c) the names of two people who can assert that the victim had a reputation for violence. Under what conditions must Hacker disclose any or all of this information to the prosecutor?

12. (a) Police, searching an abandoned house, discover a sofa with a bullet hole in it. They take pictures of the sofa, examine the bullet hole, and then take the sofa into their control. Several months later, the sofa has begun to deteriorate, and they have not yet tied it with any crime. As a health matter, they destroy the sofa. Thereafter, a body is discovered elsewhere and it is linked to the sofa. Your client, Cal, is ultimately tried for the murder. He argues self-defense, but the prosecution expert will testify that the angle of the bullet, as examined prior to the destruction of the sofa, would suggest that is unlikely. If you move to exclude the testimony, what is the likely result?

(b) If the trial judge denies your motion to exclude the evidence, what can you do?

13. Dillinger is charged with possessing an unlicensed firearm. Ness, the state detective in charge, runs a gun trace through the Bureau of Alcohol, Tobacco and Firearms, and receives a report that contains the name of the gun's registered owner. There was no evidence that the gun had been stolen. Ness does not reveal this report to McCoy, the prosecutor, but at trial, upon cross-examination, admits that the gun actually was registered. The government argues that the information is not *Brady* material, and is exempt from discovery as "work product" under Rule 16(a)(2), as an "internal government document made in connection with the investigation or prosecution of the case." The trial court rejects the government's contention, and immediately dismisses the prosecution, with prejudice. The government appeals. What result?

14. Alice, Beatrice, and Catherine, all underage females, allege that they were taken at gunpoint by the defendant, Denver, to Earl's house, where he forced one of them to perform oral sex on him. The three girls then left the house, went to another house where they called 911 and only asked for directions home, and returned to Earl's house. All four then drove to another house, where further (allegedly involuntary) sexual acts were performed. At the trial, a police officer testified that he stopped Denver's car, and talked to both him and the three females for several minutes, in the presence of Denver's mother (who happened to be in another car, passing by). Denver claimed that the sex was consensual. Several months later, but prior to the trial, Earl's landlady found a handwritten note in the phonebook in the house that appeared to relate to the events of that evening, and which could easily be interpreted as suggesting that the sex was consensual. The landlady took the note to the police investigator, who looked at it, and told her to destroy it. She did not, and after Denver was convicted, brought it to the attention of the defense counsel, who moved for a new trial. What result?

15. Julio is prosecuted by the United States Attorney's Office in Miami for participating in a drug sale conspiracy with Peewee. He testifies in court that he is a rival of Peewee's and would never enter a conspiracy with him. Peewee is not indicted; he has fled the country. After Julio's conviction, Peewee is arrested and indicted in New York City. An employee of the Drug Enforcement Administration, going through that agency's records in preparation for Peewee's trial, finds many papers, all written before Julio's trial, that would strongly suggest that Peewee and Julio are indeed archenemies. (a) Must the DEA inform the U.S. Attorney's Office, and must the U.S. Attorney inform Julio's counsel? (b) Suppose all the papers refer to information obtained only *after* Julio's conviction?

16. You are defense counsel in a state which has essentially adopted Federal Rule 16. The defendant is Asian American. At trial, the prosecution calls

an eyewitness (of whom you were unaware) who is Caucasian and who identifies your client as the culprit. You move for a continuance to allow you to find an expert on eyewitness evidence to allow you to counter this testimony. The judge denies the continuance. What can you do?

17. Hermione has been arrested for drug possession after drugs were discovered by a drug-sniffing dog in the gas tank of her car. Her attorney moves to discover the training record of the dog who located the drugs. Must the prosecutor disclose those records?

18. Stefano is in prison for a second time. On the way to lunch, he is required to walk through a metal detector, which alerts. The guards remove his pants and find, in his boxer shorts, a "shank." They take the weapon and order Stefano on his way. He is later prosecuted for possession of a weapon while in penal custody. The guards testify that his boxer shorts were altered to have a pocket for the knife. When defense counsel asks them to show the pocket, they respond that they let Stefano keep the shorts and did not photograph them. Counsel then moves to strike the testimony, arguing that the state had a duty to preserve the shorts, or at least photograph them, to show that the boxers had been altered. The trial court denies the motion, Stefano is convicted, and sentenced to 25–life, as a third-strike law requires. What result if Stefano appeals?

Explanations

1. (a) As we saw in Chapter 4, prosecutors rarely need to present any exculpatory evidence, no matter how persuasive, to the grand jury. Even in jurisdictions that would require such disclosure, Roget's vision problems do not seem to be "clearly exculpatory" — indeed, if anything, they are merely the basis for impeaching his testimony. Therefore, it is highly improbable that Roxanne need disclose this to the grand jury. (b) In a federal jurisdiction, the federal courts are divided on whether Brady ("timely before trial") or the Jencks Act (after the witness testifies) would apply to Roget's statement to the police. As for Roget's myopia, Brady would apply since this is information that might impeach Roget's testimony. (c) If Roxanne decides not to disclose this Brady-Giglio material, she has violated Norman's constitutional rights. But given the strong testimony of the other three eyewitnesses, an appellate court will find it unlikely that the result of the trial would have been different had defense counsel been made aware of Roget's problems. It is also possible that the court might conclude that defense counsel's investigation should have unearthed Norman's

myopia. Again, timing is everything. If Norman's attorney had learned that Roxanne had specific information undercutting Roget's testimony, he most likely would have succeeded on a motion to force disclosure pre-trial, and the failure would, at the very least, have resulted in unfavorable remarks from the bench to the prosecutor. But if the information emerges only after the trial, the *Brady-Kyles* test of "prejudice" makes such a nondisclosure remediless.

2. No. For several reasons. First, the mere fact that e-mails were sent from his home computer does not demonstrate that Luke sent them. He could have arranged for someone else to do that, or he might have programmed his computer to send them at that time. Thus, the timing of the e-mails is not exculpatory. And under *Brady*'s retrospective test, it is hard to say that there is a "reasonable probability" their revelation would have led to a different verdict. Second, even assuming that the e-mails could have bolstered Luke's defense, and were *Brady* material, he had access to those e-mails himself. Courts generally hold that "Evidence is not suppressed if the defendant either knew, or should have known, of the essential facts permitting him to take advantage of any exculpatory evidence." *United States v. LeRoy*, 687 F.2d 610 (2d Cir. 1982). Luke's conviction stands. (See Chapter 14, *infra*.)

3. The memo clearly contained *Giglio* (impeachment) evidence against the witness, which could have been helpful to the defendant. On the other hand, at trial, the defense counsel had an opportunity to cross-examine Spring, and demonstrate any confusion she might have had about the incident. Imagine if counsel had known of this memo and asked Spring, "Isn't it true that you were so unsure of your memory of the incident that you asked to be hypnotized, but never were?" That might be a crucial piece of information for the jury. It is therefore a close question as to whether there is a "reasonable probability" that discovery and use of Spring's request for hypnosis would have resulted in a different verdict. As always, these are fact-specific decisions. In *Conley v. United States*, 415 F.3d 183 (1st Cir. 2005), the court found that the weakness of other parts of the government's case made this memo crucial, and hence its suppression was a *Brady* violation requiring a new trial.

4. Probably none of them. Under the Jencks Act, only statements "of a witness" are discoverable and then only after the witness has testified. Statements are defined as (1) "a written statement that the witness makes or signs, or otherwise adopts or approves; or (2) a substantially verbatim, contemporaneously recorded recital of the witness's oral statement. . . ." Peter's notes do not qualify; had they been very long, they might have met the second clause. Peter's memorandum, while

much longer, might be argued to be "substantially verbatim," but it is not "contemporaneously recorded." Peter's notes are not discoverable; they might even qualify as work product. However, if Wanda had written a letter with the same information, or if the telephone call had been tape recorded, the information might be discoverable, the first as a statement "adopted or approved" by Wanda, the latter as a "substantially verbatim contemporaneous record" of her declarations. Note that if this were exculpatory evidence, it would be discoverable under *Brady*, but the timing issue, discussed in the text, would still apply.

5. (a) No. This is not *Brady* evidence, since it is not "helpful," much less exculpatory, to either defendant; each would be responsible for the other's actions. Under many state statutes or criminal procedure rules, expert reports are discoverable, but many also require that the prosecutor disclose only reports she "intends to use." One might question this limitation, since defendants would be delighted to learn that an expert hired by the prosecutor has either failed to find inculpatory material or, even better, has found exculpatory material. The latter would be discoverable under *Brady*, but not necessarily under the rule.

(b) Now the answer may be different. The evidence in *Brady* itself went not to whether the defendant was guilty but to the degree of his punishment. In *that* sense, the report is "exculpatory." But what is the burden of proof at capital sentencing? If the defendant carried the burden of demonstrating that he did not actually kill the victim, the report would be unhelpful. But, since the prosecutor carries the burden of proof, unless Pat has some other information, this report may make it difficult, perhaps impossible, for him to persuade the jury to send either of these defendants to the gurney. And that would make the report discoverable by each. Again, however, timing would be an issue. Since the report only goes to eligibility for the death penalty, Patsy could keep it concealed until after the two were convicted.

6. This is a difficult legal case, even if it's an easy one ethically. The first question is whether Guiliano's statement is discoverable at all. Although it appears to be favorable, it is not admissible, since it is hearsay. Therefore, if Guiliano had been called, it is not obvious that, under the Jencks Act, the prosecutor would have had to disclose this particular piece of the interview, because neither the prosecutor nor the defendant could have asked Guiliano about the statement.

In *Wood v. Bartholomew*, 516 U.S. 1 (1995), the prosecutor failed to disclose that a polygraph showed that a witness had lied about whether he had assisted the defendant in the crime. Polygraph results were not admissible. The Supreme Court held that these were not *Brady* evidence.

The Court went on to say that defense counsel's argument that he could have used the results to persuade the witness to change his statement was "not reasonably likely." There is a possible implication that had the result been "more likely," disclosure of the inadmissible evidence would have been required. The federal circuits are split, although the majority hold that failure to disclose inadmissible evidence which might lead to admissible evidence violates *Brady*. *Ellswoth v. Warden*, 333 F.3d 1 (1st Cir. 2003). But see *Hoke v. Netherland*, 92 F.3d 1350, 1356 (4th Cir. 1996). Beyond this, suppose the defense had learned about Doug during the trial. Would the trial judge have allowed a continuance while they searched for Doug? If not, then the failure to comply with *Brady* (even assuming there was a *Brady* violation) did not prejudice the defendant. Finally, under the facts as given, the defense did not learn about Doug until well after the trial. Unless the defense can argue that (1) it could have interviewed Doug immediately after the trial; (2) Doug would have spoken to them; (3) he would have said what Guiliano said he said, it will be difficult to obtain a new trial, based either on a *Brady* violation, or on the more general question of newly discovered evidence.

7. No. The information would be clearly governed by Rule 16, as well as by *Brady* (since clearly exculpatory), if this were a criminal proceeding. But it's not. Therefore, the prosecutor need not disclose this information under either of those doctrines. See *State v. Hill*, 368 S.C. 649 (2006).

8. (a) The letter is certainly "material" as defined in *Brady-Giglio*, and does have to be disclosed. The question is "when?" *Brady* does not specify the timing, and courts have divided on the question. In the disciplinary decision upon which this example is based, the prosecution argued that *Brady* only required disclosure before trial, not before the preliminary hearing. The state also argued that the standard of proof at a preliminary hearing was so low (probable cause) that the defendant suffered no harm by the failure to provide the recanting letter until after the preliminary hearing. As seen in Chapter 4, in many states the prosecutor need not disclose to the grand jury information adverse to its case, which could arguably be seen as the equivalent of the preliminary hearing, even if the evidence is "clearly exculpatory" and "directly negates" guilt.

The court in the case pointed to the ABA Standards for Criminal Justice: Prosecution Function and Defense Function 3-3.11(a) (3d ed. 1993), which requires disclosure "at the earliest feasible opportunity," and concluded that the prosecutor had acted improperly both under that standard, and under the state rule, which required "timely" disclosure. The court therefore rejected the prosecution's argument. The court also found that the preliminary hearing (in contrast to the

123

grand jury proceeding) was a "critical stage" and that "when a prosecutor is aware of exculpatory evidence before *any* critical stage of the proceeding" she must disclose the evidence before the proceeding occurs. However, since the failure to disclose was not "intentional" and since the ABA had expressly added the word "intentionally" into the third edition, the court declined to discipline the prosecutor, whose conduct had not intended to injure the defendant. In *re Attorney C*, 47 P.3d 1167 (Colo. 2002). However, the decision was rendered prior to *Ruiz*, in which the Supreme Court held that a prosecutor need not disclose *Giglio* information to a defendant prior to entering into a plea bargain. It is therefore probable that a prosecutor does not have a duty to disclose prior to trial, or at least prior to the time that the plea negotiations stall. That argument was not (directly) open to the prosecutor in the *Attorney C* case.

(b) Unlikely. Although this *information* is likely to mean that Raymond won't be prosecuted successfully, it is not "*evidence*" in the case, nor is it "material" as that term is normally used in evidence law. Moreover, the information does not "directly negate" Raymond's guilt, nor is it "clearly exculpatory." Finally, it is possible this is not information which only Priscilla has — the defense counsel could and should be keeping an ear out for this information as well. We might want to explore whether this was public information, or whether Priscilla obtained it because of her position. See David Aaron, Note: Ethics, Law Enforcement and Fair Dealing: A Prosecutor's Duty to Disclose Non-evidentiary Information, 67 Fordham L. Rev. 3005 (1999).

(c) We will discuss the law as to plea bargains in Chapter 7. But here the question is whether Priscilla had to disclose the victim's death. The answer is no. It is not *Brady* information (it is not exculpatory). See *People v. Jones*, 44 N.Y.2d 76, 375 N.E.2d 41, 404 N.Y.S.2d 85 (N.Y. 1978). Particularly after *Ruiz* (see p.124), it would appear that the prosecutor can withhold any information — except perhaps *Brady* information — during plea negotiations.

9. (a) Julio may present the cocaine to the grand jury without ever mentioning the affidavit. See Chapter 4 (the grand jury may rely on suppressible evidence). And even in those jurisdictions requiring the prosecutor to inform the grand jury of evidence which "clearly exculpates" or "directly negates" the defendant's guilt, the weakness of the affidavit does not fit into either of those categories; the cocaine *was* there.

(b) After *Ruiz*, Julio can certainly discuss a plea with LeRoy's counsel without even mentioning the affidavit. And if there is no motion to suppress, there is no need *ever* to inform defense counsel — this is not even *Brady* material (exculpatory evidence).

10. (a) Under *Brady-Giglio*, these are not discoverable. They are not good for impeachment since the witnesses will not be called. As in many of the questions here, the answer may well turn upon the precise language of the state court rules. Even if this is an "open file" state, these statements are not in Moira's file (see *Taus v. Senkowski*, 293 F. Supp. 2d 238 (E.D.N.Y. 2003)). If she took notes during the conversation, they might be discoverable, unless they are work product. But if the rule requires that she disclose information of which she "knows," then she has violated the rule if she does not disclose. (b) If LeCarre is convicted, it is unlikely that Moira's nondisclosure, even if an error, will result in reversal — there were apparently enough "good" witnesses that the verdict is "trustworthy."

     This may suggest a weakness in the *Brady* test. While it might not be reasonable to ask Moira in most cases to scour the countryside to determine if other law enforcement agencies have information on a crime, in this instance, the crime is clearly also federal, and such a requirement would not be onerous in this situation.

11. If Coke intends to deny the killing entirely, and has requested only discovery of *Brady* information, there is no requirement of disclosure at all. Unless he intends to raise a claim of self-defense, in most states Coke need not disclose to the prosecutor that he killed the victim. Some jurisdictions, however, treat a claim of self-defense the same way they treat an alibi or mental incapacity claim, and require at least notice of the defense. Depending on the precise wording of the statute or court rule, Coke will have to disclose some or all of the witness's names.

12. (a) This is a real case — *State v. Osakalumi*, 194 W. Va. 758, 461 S.E.2d 504 (1995). The court held, consistent with *Youngblood*, that there was no sign of bad faith on the part of the prosecution, and therefore there was no violation of due process. You might suggest that the fact that the prosecution took pictures and examined the sofa before destroying it indicates that they expected to prosecute a criminal act at some point. But the health aspect of the issue is probably sufficient to undermine any argument about bad faith. Of course, since this is a state prosecution, you can argue that the court should take a position more protective of defendants' rights. About a dozen states have declared that bad faith is not a necessary part of the defendant's showing because the destruction of evidence reflects governmental negligence. If *Fisher* suggests a distinction between the destruction of "merely helpful" evidence and "totally exculpatory" evidence, where bad faith is irrelevant in the latter, it is possible to argue that the angle of the bullet going into the sofa might fit the second definition. But don't bet on it.

(b) This is a good example of how you can lose the battle, but still win the war. A good defense attorney would ask for an instruction to the jury that put upon the prosecution some onus for having destroyed the sofa. From the defense viewpoint, the "best" instruction would establish an "irrebuttable presumption" that the evidence would have favored the defendant. A lesser burden would be that the destruction would establish a (rebuttable) "presumption" or even an "inference" to that effect. In *Osakalumi* itself, the trial judge had instructed the jury that:

> you should scrutinize it with great care and caution. This destruction of evidence occurred before the defendant could examine it. This destruction of the couch may very well have deprived the defendant of evidence crucial to his defense and which may in fact have exculpated him.

But the appellate court said that even that instruction was insufficient. The court quoted Justice Stevens, concurring in *Youngblood*, who suggested this instruction: " 'you may infer that the true fact is against the State's interest.' As a result, the uncertainty as to what the evidence might have proved was turned to the defendant's advantage." 488 U.S. 59-60. Nevertheless, said the West Virginia court, "in the present case, even if such an instruction were given, it would not have sufficiently protected appellant's due process rights."

The moral: Just because the defense lost the battle, doesn't mean it had to lose the war. Consider, as well, what kind of instruction the prosecutor should have sought, and should seek in the next lost evidence case.

13. First, on the merits — this is *not* work product protected by 16(a)(2), because neither Ness nor McCoy prepared it. Work product is usually limited to items containing "mental impressions, conclusions, opinions or legal theories"; the ATF document was computer-generated, and had no such content. Moreover, since *Brady* trumps the rules, it would be a *Brady* violation, going to the heart of the government's case, even if 16(a)(2) were interpreted to support the government. The real question here is the remedy. Ness clearly intentionally withheld the information, and that intent is transferred to McCoy for purposes of finding a violation. But McCoy did not purposefully withhold the information. While dismissal with prejudice is a possible remedy for willful, and possibly even reckless, conduct by a prosecutor, it is the most drastic of all institutional remedies. (Remedies against the individual prosecutor, or in this case against Ness, will be explored in Chapter 14, *infra*.) The court in the case upon which this example is based found no such intent on the prosecutor's part, and suggested mistrial was a

sufficiently severe sanction. *Government of the Virgin Islands v. Fahie,* 419 F.3d 249 (3d Cir. 2005).

14. These are — believe it or not — real facts, far beyond the capacity of even a law professor to concoct. (For all the salacious details and wording of the note, see *State v. Youngblood,* 221 W. Va. 20, 650 S.E.2d 119 (2007).)[45] The issues here, however, are several. First, did the *prosecutor* "suppress" the note? Is the police investigator part of the "government" for purposes of *Brady?* The answer seems clear — yes, under *Kyles v. Whitley,* any police officer is covered (this could have been much more difficult if the note had been brought to a third party, or a member of the rape victims' unit of the state, which is not necessarily part of the police department). Second, this is *Giglio* impeachment evidence; and this note might well have impeached any or all three of the victims in this case. The really difficult question is whether this evidence is "material." Under the original wording of *Brady,* the answer seems clear — the evidence was favorable to Denver, and had to be disclosed. But under the more recent tests of *Bagley* and *Kyles,* which focus on the possible effect the suppressed evidence might have had upon the verdict, it is not so obvious. Of course the note could impeach any or all of the victims' testimony. But the jury did hear the testimony of the officer that none of the girls sought his help when he stopped Denver's car, and that none of them seemed frightened. Since the jury nevertheless found the acts nonconsensual, they must have discounted that testimony, or believed that the girls were under duress, notwithstanding the presence of the police, and Denver's mother. It is at least *possible* that they would have also rejected (or minimized) the note's potentially exculpatory impact. (In the actual opinion, the court was very severely divided over whether a *Brady* violation had occurred.)

15. (a) The DEA is an arm of the Department of Justice, as are the United States Attorneys Offices. Thus, the same "government entity" had the information before Julio's conviction and should have given it to him to support his claim. It makes no difference that the U.S. Attorney did not in fact know about the DEA papers because *Brady-Giglio* does not depend on the mental state of the prosecutor. *United States v. Aviles-Colon,* 536 F.3d 1 (1st Cir.).

(b) This is more difficult. As the text discusses, the courts are divided over whether *Brady* imposes a postconviction duty to disclose newly found information that is "favorable" or "exculpatory" to the now convicted defendant. Newly amended section 3.8 of the ABA Model

---

45. This is a totally different Youngblood than the defendant in *Youngblood v. Arizona.* Truth is stranger . . . etc.

Rules of Professional Conduct would require such disclosure, but they are not binding on the courts. And the U.S. Supreme Court's discussions in the *Osborne-Skinner* decisions would suggest that it is not *Brady*, per se, but general due process concerns that would govern this issue.

16. Get to the phone — fast. You're not entitled to a continuance, although mounting evidence demonstrates that eyewitness identification — particularly cross-ethnic identification — is very problematic. See, e.g., Arye Tattner, Convicted But Innocent, 12 Law & Hum. Beh. 283 (1988) (in 205 wrongful convictions, 52.3 percent were the result of mistaken eyewitness identification testimony). But under the court rule, you were not entitled to know the name (much less the ethnicity) of the witness until he was called to the stand. So there's no rule violation. Moreover, you may have been at fault for not at least considering the possibility of such an eyewitness and having "on call" such a witness. If, of course, you have one, you will have time to call and prepare him before your presentation of evidence (although it would have been very helpful for him to have actually seen the witness testify).

17. This is a real case. The training records are not *Brady* material (they are not, *per se*, exculpatory), but they may be *Giglio*-impeachment evidence (to impeach the officer, not the dog). Even if the constitution does not require disclosure, the court in *United States v. Cedano-Arellano*, 332 F.3d 568 (9th Cir. 2003) held that they were discoverable under federal Rule 16(a)(1)(E) and were not exempted from discovery under (a)(2) because the training records themselves were not made "in connection with investigating or prosecuting" this specific case. Some have argued that the decision is a real dog.

18. Again, a real case. *People v. Velasco*, 194 Cal. App. 4th 1258, 124 Cal. Rptr. 238 (Cal. Ct. App. (2011)). The court held that the state has no duty to gather or preserve evidence: "Defendant kept the shorts, the state never confiscated them, and nothing suggests that the prison guards ignored the shorts or perceived they would likely be exculpatory." Of course, had the defendant been able to show that the shorts had not been modified, it might have impeached the guards' testimony. But the court said the state never "had" the shorts and so the state never "lost" them. The court referred to *Northern Mariana Island v. Bowie*, 243 F.3d 1090, 1117 (9th Cir. 2001), which appeared to impose a duty to gather evidence in the first place, as an "aberration."

Pleas of Guilt
and Bargained Pleas

CHAPTER 7

Once Dan has learned whatever he can about the prosecutor's case, he must determine whether to proceed to trial. However, very few defendants actually go to trial; well over 90 percent of all verdicts are accomplished by pleas of guilty — and virtually all of those are the result of plea bargains. We will discuss plea *bargains* in the second section. But it is important to discuss the general concept of guilty pleas before we get to bargaining as such.

A. THE CONCEPT OF "PLEADING GUILTY"

If a person is innocent until *proven* guilty beyond a reasonable doubt, why allow a person who is unfamiliar with what "proof" the law requires to "admit" guilt? When the death penalty was the usual sanction for any felony, defendants could *not* plead guilty — the government was put to its burden (although out-of-court confessions were commonly obtained and admitted). Some reasons suggested as to why we would allow a defendant to waive a trial include: (1) to save the defendant's soul, because "confession is good for the soul."[1] If the defendant actually committed the crime, and wants to atone, there is no obvious reason to preclude him from doing so and put him through what the Supreme Court has referred to as the "cruel

---

1. Parents sometimes require their children to admit their culpability, on the theory that learning to take responsibility, and to admit it, builds character. Whether the law should be interested in building the character of adults may be problematic.

impact . . . upon those defendants who would greatly prefer not to contest their guilt" (*Jackson v. United States*, 390 U.S. 570, 583 (1968)); (2) to "spare themselves and their families the spectacle and expense of a protracted courtroom proceeding" (ibid); (3) to save state resources; (4) to avoid acquitting the truly guilty defendant, because of the serendipity of trial.

None of these reasons is particularly compelling. To save his soul, the defendant could confess elsewhere (in a religious institution, or to a philosophy professor), rather than waive a jury trial. Indeed, some jurisdictions would not permit a defendant to plead "guilty" to a murder charge[2] [although allowing a plea of *nolo contendere* ("I do not contest the charge")]. We could reduce the resources entailed in trials by other methods, such as "summary" trials, which replace many straight guilty pleas. Concerns that a jury might be deceived suggest mistrust of jury (or even judge) trials generally.

B. THE PREREQUISITES OF A VALID GUILTY PLEA

A guilty plea waives most nonjurisdictional constitutional rights, most obviously the rights which obtain at trial: (1) a jury; (2) cross-examination and confrontation; and (3) the requirement that the government meet the burden of proving guilt, using a reasonable doubt standard of proof (the "big three"). In addition, many "pre-trial" rights, discussed in more detail below, are also lost by a valid guilty plea. See *Tollett v. Henderson*, 411 U.S. 258 (1973) (a guilty plea "breaks the chain of events" which have occurred prior to trial). Before a court will allow a defendant to waive these rights, it must be convinced that the waiver is:

- voluntary; and
- knowing and intelligent.

Both state and federal court rules make clear that the judge must ascertain that the plea meets these criteria — Federal Rule 11, for example, explicitly states that the judge must "personally" question the defendant (and not merely his counsel) about his or her knowledge and the voluntariness of his or her plea. *McCarthy v. United States*, 394 U.S. 459 (1969).

Because the guilty plea is made in public and with the assistance of counsel, the standard for guilty pleas is much easier for the state to meet

---

2. See, e.g., N.J. Stat. Ann. 2A133-1 in *Corbitt v. New Jersey*, 439 U.S. 212 (1978). That provision has since been replaced.

than that for confessions under the Fifth Amendment.[3] While the Supreme Court has not fully defined "voluntariness" in the guilty plea context, it is clear that a threat which might, in the absence of counsel or in a police station, render a defendant's confession involuntary, would not automatically be deemed coercive of a guilty plea.

Because the rules are not constitutionally mandated, a judge's failure to meet one of the specific requirements of the rule is assessed by the harmless error rule. *United States v. Vonn*, 535 U.S. 55 (2002).

I. Voluntary

> [A] plea of guilty entered by one fully aware of the direct consequences, including the actual value of any commitments made to him by the Court, prosecutor or his own counsel must stand unless induced by threats (or promises to discontinue improper harassment), misrepresentation (including unfulfilled or unfulfillable promises) or perhaps by promises that are by their nature improper as having no proper relationship to the prosecutor's business.
>
> Brady v. United States, 397 U.S. 742 (1970)
> (quoting Shelton v. United States 246 F.2d 571, 572,
> n.2 (5th Cir. 1957))

No one (anymore) puts a gun to the defendant's head to obtain a plea. But suppose the government does the equivalent — threatens the defendant with death if he does not plead guilty, but assures him that the worst punishment he would receive upon such a plea would be life imprisonment? In *United States v. Jackson*, 390 U.S. 570 (1968), the Court declared unconstitutional a statute which did essentially that. But if the defendant pleads guilty under the same statute, the plea is not involuntary. See *Corbitt v. New Jersey*, 439 U.S. 212 (1978).

In *Bordenkircher v. Hayes*, 434 U.S. 357 (1978), the defendant was charged with a forged check in the amount of $88, punishable by a sentence of 5-10 years. The prosecutor offered to recommend a five-year sentence if defendant pleaded; if he did not, the prosecutor warned, he would charge defendant as an habitual offender, which subjected him to a mandatory life sentence. Defendant rejected the offer; after a jury conviction, he attacked the life sentence as vindictive. The Supreme Court did not have to decide directly whether a guilty plea under such circumstances would be constitutional, but in *dictum* strongly indicated that it would be valid. The Court found the defendant's refusal to plead noncoerced, and indicated

---

3. See Robert M. Bloom and Mark S. Brodin, Criminal Procedure: Examples and Explanations at 257-269 (4th ed. 2004).

that, had he pled and then attacked the plea, the result would have been the same.

These results are plausible; hard choices are, nevertheless, choices. And the defendant has placed himself in the situation. Moreover, the defendant receives the advice of counsel, both as to the likelihood of conviction, and the possibilities of punishment. But how far can this view of voluntariness be taken? In *North Carolina v. Alford*, 400 U.S. 25 (1970), the Court held that a defendant who believes he is innocent, either actually or legally, may still enter a valid guilty plea (Alford faced the death penalty if he were convicted of the greater charge). At first blush, these choices seem preposterous. An innocent defendant would never plead guilty, confident that the jury would exculpate her. But life is much more complicated. Even where the defendant is factually, as well as legally, innocent, the pressures to plead guilty (even without a bargain offered by the prosecutor) may be severe because:

- the law is very murky, and defendant's behavior, even if not "illegal," might alienate the fact finder;
- the defendant knows that there is a "sentencing discount" for a plea — judges tend to impose longer sentences on defendants who do not plead but are found guilty after a trial;
- the defendant seeks to protect or assuage family or friends;
- the conditions of pre-trial incarceration are dire;
- there is a concern that fuller inquiry at trial may disclose additional facts;
- the defendant simply desires to expedite the proceeding;
- ignorance, delusion, feelings of moral (even if not legal) guilt are present;
- there are self-destructive inclinations.

Alford essentially elevates the "knowing" leg of the doctrine over the "voluntary" prong; so long as defendant *knows* the chances of conviction, and their consequences, the choice will be deemed valid. States are divided on whether to allow *Alford* pleas. The *Alford* plea disturbingly (realistically?) recognizes that innocent defendants may be erroneously convicted at trial, and that a decision by a defendant to plead guilty (usually to a lesser charge) is not irrational or coerced. Moreover, if fear of trial is a factor which could make a plea involuntary, every plea would be subject to reassessment.

2. Intelligent

So long as the defendant is mentally competent, and able to understand his lawyer's advice, courts are reluctant to probe into the defendant's understanding. In *Godinez v. Moran*, 509 U.S. 389 (1993), the Court adopted as the measure of intelligence the standard of competence to stand trial — whether the defendant understood the proceedings and could assist his counsel. This relatively low standard is almost always met; if it is doubtful, the court should delay the plea and inquire as to the defendant's mental ability.

3. Knowing

a. Knowing the Charge — Factual Basis

Federal Rule 11(b)(3) (and most state rules) requires a *factual basis* for the plea. Thus, at a "plea colloquy" someone (not necessarily the defendant) must proffer evidence that all the elements of the crime were present. If the defendant acknowledges those facts to be true, there is a factual basis for the plea.[4] Indeed, even if the defendant is not aware of all the elements that must be proved, the plea is knowing if the element of which he or she is ignorant is not crucial.[5] See *Henderson v. Morgan*, 426 U.S. 637 (1976). Thirty-five years ago, one writer said of this requirement: "Nothing could be less clear from the decided cases than the appropriate scope of judicial inquiry into the factual basis of the plea where any inquiry at all is required. The ambiguity is between the view that the record must show the defendant committed the offenses and the view that all the record need show is that the defendant . . . was rational." J. Bond, Plea Bargaining §3.55 (1982).

The primary source for determining whether the defendant knows — or has been informed about — these and other rights is the transcript from the colloquy, but in determining whether defendant (or his counsel) knew these facts, the court may look to other circumstances. The ideal method to establish the factual basis for a guilty plea is for the court to ask the defendant to state, in the defendant's own words, what the defendant did that she believes constitutes the crime to which she is pleading guilty. Often, however, the defendant simply "agrees to" a part of a plea agreement entitled "Factual Basis." The Supreme Court has never spoken to the burden of proof involved in these proceedings; Rule 11(b)(3) requires merely that the court must be "satisf[ied] that a factual basis exists."

The record must affirmatively show that the defendant was informed of his trial rights. *Boykin v. Alabama*, 395 U.S. 238 (1969). However, *Parke v. Raley*,

---

4. There is no firm indication that even this is a constitutional requirement. *McCarthy v. United States*, 394 U.S. 459 (1969), was clearly a construal of Rule 11, not a constitutionally based opinion. *Alford* hinted that a "factual basis" might be a constitutional prerequisite, but it did not so hold.
5. The court must advise the defendant that the government has to prove every element of the offense including the quantity of drugs involved, before a plea can be knowing. *United States v. Villalobos*, 333 F.3d 1070 (9th Cir. 2003). See also *United States v. Reyes*, 300 F.3d 555 (5th Cir. 2002) (court must inform defendant about the sentencing range). But the defendant need not be informed that any refusal by the court to depart downward at sentencing is not appealable. *United States v. Rada*, 319 F.3d 1288 (11th Cir. 2003).

506 U.S. 20 (1992), permits a presumption, on collateral attack, that *Boykin* was satisfied during guilty plea proceedings, even where there was no record, so long as counsel was present. Still, the courts have divided over whether the presumption applies in a post-conviction proceeding brought almost immediately after trial. See, e.g., *Hall v. State*, 849 N.E.2d 466 (Ind. 2006) (presumption applies); *Byrd v. Shaffer*, 271 Ga. 691, 523 S.E.2d 875 (1999) (presumption does not apply).

The Supreme Court has adopted different standards of review for the different procedural contexts of violations of Rule 11. If the error was properly preserved, then on direct appeal the government has the burden to show harmlessness. *United States v. Dominguez Benitez*, 542 U.S. 74 (2004). If the error is raised for the first time on a direct appeal, then the plain error standard (see Chapter 13) governs. On collateral review, Rule 11 errors require the defendant to show that failure to grant relief would be "egregious. . . . [A] defendant will rarely, if ever, be able to obtain relief for Rule 11 violations [through collateral attack]."

b. Knowing the Impact — "Direct" and "Collateral" Consequences

Beyond knowing (most of) the elements of the crime, the defendant is entitled to know the effects of his plea. After *McCarthy v. United States*, 394 U.S. 459 (1969) and *Boykin v. Alabama*, 395 U.S. 238 (1969), it is clear that the Constitution requires the court to inform the defendant that he is waiving the "big three" constitutional rights:[6]

- the right against self-incrimination;
- the right to jury trial; and
- the right to confrontation.

Until 2010, the lower courts had concluded that the defendant also had to "know" the "direct," but not the "collateral," consequences of his plea. "Direct" consequences included: any mandatory loss of some benefits, and a mandatory listing as a sexually violent predator, which may require life-long registration, and lifetime supervision.[7]

In the majority of jurisdictions, the following have been held to be "collateral," and neither the court nor the prosecutor is thought to be

---

6. It could also be added that the defendant is waiving his right to issue compulsory process to obtain witnesses at trial, to testify in his own defense (or to remain silent), and present evidence. These must be separately discussed. Although informed of his right to "trial," defendant was not specifically informed of his right to confront witnesses and against self-incrimination. This negated his no contest plea. *People v. Christian*, 125 Cal. App. 4th 688, 22 Cal. Rptr. 3d 861 (Cal. App. 2 Dist.).

7. See, e.g., *State v. Bellamy*, 178 N.J. 127, 835 A.2d 1231 (2003); *Palmer v. State*, 118 Nev. 823, 59 P.3d 1192 (Nev. 2002).

required to tell the defendant about the effects the conviction might have upon[8]:

- probation revocation;
- discretionary judicial authority to impose a consecutive or concurrent sentence;
- good-time credits;
- civil service employment;
- federal benefits whose loss turns on facts not known at time of plea;
- right to vote;
- unencumbered foreign travel;
- possible appearance before a psychiatric panel before parole;
- unlikelihood of review of refusal to depart downward in sentence;
- potential immigration consequences;
- future sentencing implications (three-time-loser laws);
- loss of professional licenses (debarment, etc.);
- an order of restitution;
- registration (even life-long) as a sex offender.[9]

The line appeared to be between those events which are "sure" to happen, and those which "may," but need not, happen because they are discretionary. If the reason supporting that requirement is that the defendant's main concern is with the amount of time he will actually serve, one might think that at least some of the items above would also be required. There is, perhaps, a concern that the "possible" consequences are limitless, and that requiring a judge to inform the defendant of every possible consequence would be fruitless, and produce litigation. The apparent reasons for not providing a longer list of such information are (1) the assumption that defense counsel will tell the defendant of these possibilities (see discussion *infra*); (2) preservation of the court's time;[10] and (3) concerns that the list would become "endless."

---

8. Of course, individual jurisdictions may vary. See, e.g., *State v. Howard*, 110 N.J. 113, 539 A.2d 1203 (1988), requiring the trial court to inform the defendant of the possibility of parole consequences of a sentence to adult diagnostic and treatment center.

9. In most states, some crimes automatically result in the defendant being subjected to sexual offender status, while in others that determination, or the determination of the "level" or "tier," is discretionary, often reached after a hearing. Thus, most courts will determine that this is not a direct consequence, although the effects may be severe, and life-long. *State v. Moore*, 135 N.M. 210, 86 P.3d 635 (N.M. Ct. App. 2004). See also *Mitschke v. State*, 129 S.W.3d 130 (Tex. Crim. App. 2004), holding that such a registration requirement is a direct consequence but is nonpunitive and, therefore, failure to admonish the defendant does not render the plea involuntary.

10. One study found that the average court time per felony plea was 9.9 minutes while misdemeanors were timed at 5.2 minutes. William McDonald, Judicial Supervision of the Guilty Plea Process: A Study of Six Jurisdictions, 70 Judicature 203 (1987).

The distinction between "direct" and "collateral" consequences, which was never clear, has possibly been thrown into total disarray by the decision in *Padilla v. Kentucky*, 559 U.S. 356 (2010). Padilla, who had been a lawful permanent resident of the United States for more than 40 years, was charged by the state of Kentucky with transporting a large amount of marijuana. His counsel advised him — erroneously — that because he had been in the country so long, he "did not have to worry about immigration status." On the basis of his counsel's advice, Padilla pled guilty. As it turned out, federal law actually *required* the deportation of any person convicted of any drug offense *except* offenses involving a small amount of marijuana; only a discretionary decision by the Attorney General of the United States, limited by statute, would prevent his "removal." When Padilla discovered his actual immigration status, he argued this his counsel had provided ineffective assistance.[11] The Kentucky Supreme Court, however, held that the misadvice was on a "collateral" rather than a "direct" consequence and rejected Padilla's claim of ineffective assistance.[12]

The United States Supreme Court reversed. The Court declared that it had "never applied a distinction between direct and collateral consequence" to an ineffective assistance claim and that the dichotomy was "ill suited" to this claim. The Court further noted that over the past 20 years deportation had become "virtually mandatory" and "virtually inevitable" in drug cases and that Padilla's deportation was "nearly automatic." "Whether that distinction is appropriate is a question we need not consider because of the *unique nature* of deportation" (emphasis added).

It is possible that *Padilla* is limited to advice about deportation, or at least to matters which are "unique" or "virtually" "mandatory" or "inevitable" or "automatic."[13] It may be limited to effects which, as the Court characterized deportation, have a "close connection" to the criminal process. But it may expand far beyond its four corners. It seems clear that defense counsel now must at least investigate "some" possible collateral consequences — or be

---

11. Ineffective assistance is discussed in Chapter 11. As a technical matter, Padilla's argument was therefore not a claim that his plea was unknowing, but that he had not been provided the level of constitutionally required assistance he deserved. Nevertheless, the opinion clearly brings into question the entire panoply of "direct" and "collateral" analysis for the validity of guilty pleas as such.

12. The courts had been substantially divided on precisely this question. Twenty states, by court rule, required judges to inform defendants of the possible immigration and deportation consequences of their guilty plea. See Attila Bogdan, Guilty Pleas by Non-Citizens in Illinois: Immigration Consequences Reconsidered, 53 DePaul L. Rev. 19 (2003).

13. Two writers have argued that many consequences (hitherto deemed "collateral") may not be "as" immediate as deportation for drug crimes, but are "of similar magnitude." Gabriel J. Chin and Margaret Love, Status as Punishment, A Critical Guide to *Padilla v. Kentucky*, 25 Crim. Just. 21 (Fall 2010). Moreover the American Bar Association, which was already compiling a state-by-state compendium of collateral consequences, has created a task force to determine the reach of the decision.

prepared to advise their clients that they should consult a specialist attorney in a specific field (e.g., loss of pensions of public employees). Moreover, while the court "emphatically" rejected a "checklist" approach to determining effectiveness,[14] requiring counsel to advise on deportation consequences may be the first step toward requiring at least warnings about other similar areas.

Moreover, *Padilla* rejected the distinction — made by many lower courts in many cases — between an attorney who provided "no" advice on a "consequence" and one who provided "misadvice," expressly observing that "it would give counsel an incentive to remain silent on matters of great importance" and was "fundamentally at odds with the critical obligation of counsel." On this point, Justices Alito and Roberts, concurring in the judgment, disagreed: while actively giving misadvice might constitute ineffective assistance, "a criminal defense attorney who refrains from providing immigration advice does not violate prevailing professional norms." Justices Scalia and Thomas dissented even on this point, concluding that even affirmative misadvice about deportation consequences "(does not render) an attorney's assistance constitutionally inadequate."

Finally, *Padilla* did not put the burden *on the trial judge* to tell the defendant of these consequences, although trial judges may be much more aware of these facts than an attorney who occasionally represents criminal defendants. It is conceivable that this was solely due to the basis on which *Padilla* claimed relief — ineffective assistance — but it is more probable that the Court did not wish to place the onus on judges rather than on attorneys.[15]

---

14. The American Bar Association Standards for Pleas of Guilty 14-1.4 essentially provides such a list.

15. In *Henderson v. Morgan*, 426 U.S. 637, 647 (1976), the Court stated: "[I]t may be appropriate to presume that in most cases defense counsel routinely explained the nature of the offense in sufficient detail to give the accused notice of what he is being asked to admit." More recently, in *Bradshaw v. Stumpf*, 545 U.S. 175, 183 (2005), the Court expanded on this view:

> [W]e have never held that the judge must himself explain the elements of each charge to the defendant on the record. . . . Rather . . . a valid plea may be satisfied where the record accurately reflects that the nature of the charge and the elements . . . were explained . . . by his own, competent, counsel. . . . [T]he court usually may rely on that counsel's assurance that the defendant has been properly informed of the nature and elements of the charge to which he is pleading.

One commentator has concluded: "[T]oday if a court . . . fails to inform a defendant of an item, or two, or three . . . such judicial neglect can now be cured extra-judicially [by counsel]." Julian A. Cook, III, Crumbs from the Master's Table: The Supreme Court, Pro Se Defendants and the Federal Guilty Plea Process, 81 Notre Dame L. Rev. 1895, 1898 (2006).

If the presence and advice of counsel is the grease which makes the process work, what if the defendant is unrepresented? That question was raised in *Iowa v. Tovar*, 541 U.S. 77 (2004). There, the Court held that even without counsel, a defendant may enter a guilty plea which cannot be withdrawn later, when he realizes the full implications of the conviction.

This approach emphasizes again the role of defense counsel in making sure the guilty plea is "knowing."

Extraordinarily, one thing the defendant need not "know" before pleading guilty is the strength of the state's case. In *United States v. Ruiz*, 536 U.S. 622 (2002), the Court held that a guilty plea made before the prosecutor had turned over *Giglio* discovery material could be valid at least if the prosecutor had agreed to provide "any information establishing the factual innocence of the defendant." *Giglio v. United States*, 405 U.S. 150 (1972). Thus, the defendant need not know even the constitutionally minimal discoverable case against her before validly pleading guilty.

4. The "Conditional" Plea

Although a defendant pleading guilty essentially loses any complaints about pre-plea violations (constitutional or otherwise), a defendant may sometimes wish to plead guilty, but retain the right to challenge, on appeal, a prior judicial decision, such as one refusing to suppress evidence which the defendant claims was illegally obtained. Today, courts allow such a "conditional" plea—if the appellate court agrees with the defendant, the plea is vacated and the case moves forward without that evidence. If the appeal is unsuccessful, the plea (and the sentence) stands.

C. WITHDRAWING A GUILTY PLEA

Although we speak in one breath of a defendant (1) deciding to plead guilty, (2) pleading guilty, and then (3) being sentenced on that plea, these events may be separated by days or weeks. What happens if, after each of these events, the defendant changes his mind? Most states — and the federal system — provide three different standards for a defendant's "withdrawal" of a plea, depending on the time of the withdrawal. A defendant who has entered a plea which has not yet been accepted may withdraw it for "any reason or no reason." If she moves to withdraw the plea *after* the court has accepted it, but *before* sentence, she must show a "fair and just reason" for withdrawal. *United States v. Hyde*, 520 U.S. 670 (1997).[16]

---

16. As one court put it, "the terms 'fair and just' lack any pretense of scientific exactness . . . [creating] rough guidelines that have emerged in the appellate cases." *United States v. Barker*, 514 F.2d 208 (D.C. Cir. 1975). Kirke D. Weaver, A Change of Heart or a Change of Law?

If the defendant seeks to withdraw the plea *after* sentence has been imposed, however, a defendant will meet a "near presumption" against granting such motions, and must show that a "manifest injustice" will occur if the plea is not withdrawn. Federal Rule 11 was amended in 2002 and now precludes any attempt to withdraw a plea after sentence — the only avenues are appeal or collateral attack. In *United States v. Benitez*, 542 U.S. 74 (2004), where defendant sought to have his guilty plea vacated for a non-constitutional error of Rule 11, the Court applied the *Brady* prejudice test (see Chapter 6), requiring the defendant to show a "reasonable probability that, but for the error, he would not have entered the plea." The Court distinguished in dictum the case where a *constitutional* error had occurred during the plea colloquy.

If a defendant is allowed to withdraw a plea at any stage, most courts declare that whatever concessions a prosecutor might have made to induce the plea are no longer applicable; the parties are returned to square one, and trial (or a new series of negotiations) must occur. Thus, if Harry, charged with first degree murder, pleads to second degree and then successfully withdraws that plea, the prosecution may proceed with the first degree charge,[17] assuming no vindictiveness. *Blackledge v. Perry*, 417 U.S. 21 (1974).

Examples

1. Dwayne places in the "outgoing mail" bin in his office a clearly fraudulent letter. The letter is seized from the bin before it reaches the post office and Dwayne is arrested and charged with "mail fraud," an essential element of which is that there was "use of the mails." At his plea colloquy, Dwayne acknowledges that he sent a letter in the mail and that it was part of the fraudulent scheme. The judge accepts the plea. Before the sentence, Dwayne learns from a law student (who else?) that the law actually requires that the letter be "picked up" by a postal carrier, which

---

Withdrawing a Guilty Plea Under Federal Rule of Criminal Procedure 32(e), 92 J. Crim. L. & Criminology 273 (2002), suggests that federal courts consider the following factors:

- whether defendant asserts legal (not factual) innocence;
- how long defendant waited to seek to withdraw plea; and
- whether the government would be prejudiced

For example, in *Ortega-Ascanio*, 376 F.3d 879 (9th Cir. 2004), an intervening United States Supreme Court decision that overruled Ninth Circuit precedent gave defendant a plausible ground for arguing that he was *legally* innocent. *Accord Justus v. Commw.*, 274 Va. 143, 645 S.E.2d 284 (Va. 2007). Professor Weaver argues that this is the most important of the factors considered by the courts.

17. It is generally agreed that this does not violate double jeopardy, because the prosecutor's voluntary agreement not to proceed with the higher charge never put the defendant in jeopardy of that charge. See Chapter 9. See *Alabama v. Smith*, 490 U.S. 794 (1989). If, on the other hand, the prosecutor brings *greater* charges than originally brought, problems of vindictiveness and double jeopardy might arise.

did not happen here. Dwayne now wishes to withdraw his plea on the ground that it was not "intelligent" and "knowing." Will he succeed?

2. Your client, Toby, unable to make bail, has been incarcerated for six months. He has always maintained his innocence, but now he tells you he wants to plead guilty. His explanation is that the conditions in the jail are horrible; he is particularly distressed by the strip searches which all prisoners must undergo both randomly and before and after every visit. He knows that this does not occur in the state minimum custody facility, to which he is likely to be sent after conviction. Is this plea "voluntary"?

3. On April 1, Rudolph wanted Boris's Rolex watch. He grabbed the watch, and when Boris resisted, Rudolph hit him in the face, causing bleeding. The examining physician described the injuries as "cerebral contusion of a contrecoup type with evidence of contusion of both temporal tips. Also a small right subdural hematoma." The doctor's final recommendations included that the victim be "rescan[ned] . . . in two weeks" because he expected that the "contusions and the subdural hematoma will resolve spontaneously." On April 15, Rudolph, who had hired a lawyer, pled guilty to first degree robbery, which is defined by statute as robbery with serious physical injury. At the colloquy, the judge, to assure there was a factual basis for the plea, asked Rudolph whether he had inflicted serious bodily injury, and Rudolph acknowledged that he had. On May 26, at the sentencing hearing, the judge sentenced Rudolph to a minimum of 10 years, with a requirement that he must serve 85 percent of that time before parole and that there would be a five-year term of parole whenever he was released. Rudolph was aghast and attempted to persuade the judge to sentence him less severely. "Sorry, Rudy," said the judge. "There's a statutory minimum for first-degree robbery. There's nothing I can do." The statute defines "serious physical injury" as "bodily injury which creates a substantial risk of death or which causes serious, permanent disfigurement, or protracted loss or impairment of the function of any bodily member or organ." Boris's injuries are all healed, and he has no scars of any kind. What should Rudolph do?

4. Jacques is charged with distributing cocaine. Two relevant statutes provide as follows:

> 1. Any individual . . . convicted of (such an offense) shall
> (A) at the discretion of the court, upon the first conviction for such an offense be ineligible for any or all (governmental) benefits for up to 5 years after such conviction;
> (B) at the discretion of the court, upon a second conviction for such an offense be ineligible for any or all (governmental) benefits for up to 10 years . . . ; and

(C) upon a third or subsequent conviction . . . be permanently ineligible for all Federal benefits.

2. Any individual convicted (of drug distribution) . . . shall not be eligible for

(A) assistance under any governmental program funded under (another statute);

(B) benefits under the food stamp program. . . .

You are the judge accepting Jacques's plea. Of which of these provisions, if either, must you inform Jacques for the plea to be valid?

5. Richard Cantor, a public school teacher for 38 years, is arrested while protesting the governor's attempt to limit union bargaining rights and charged with disorderly conduct. He appears before a magistrate, without a lawyer, and pleads guilty, declaring, "I believe in unions. I'd do it again if I had to." Two weeks later, Cantor receives in the mail a notice that he must come to a hearing to determine whether he will lose his pension, pursuant to a state statute which provides that "any public employee convicted of a crime of moral turpitude may have his pension revoked, after a hearing" conducted by a public agency. Cantor now calls you, an attorney, and asks what he can do. What do you tell him?

Explanations

1. Probably not. In *Henderson v. Morgan*, 426 U.S. 637, n.18 (1976), the Court suggested that there was no constitutional requirement that the defendant be aware of, or be informed about, "every element of the offense." It is difficult, if not impossible, to deduce which elements meet that definition, however, since without all the elements, the state has not proved the crime. In this particular crime, both the fraudulent intent and an *actus reus* would seem to be "critical" elements; whether the mailing had in fact been part of the scheme might be thought of as "noncritical" in the sense that the defendant's moral (if not legal) culpability has been established. The courts have grappled with attempting to determine which elements are "noncritical." Thus, it is likely that Dwayne's plea will be deemed "knowing," particularly since he was represented by counsel. While counsel can't "replace" the judge, courts frequently indulge a presumption that counsel have (attempted to) inform defendants of the elements of the crime. *Henderson* was, as the Court itself said, "unique" because the trial court there explicitly found that the defendant did not know the critical element of *mens rea*.

On the other hand, if the court uses factors like those listed in Professor Weaver's article (see fn.16, *supra*), Dwayne may convince the court that he has a "fair and just" reason for withdrawal — he has not waited long to seek withdrawal, he is asserting legal innocence, and it is hard to see how the government would be prejudiced since he does not contest the fraudulent nature of the letter. Perhaps the prosecutor should consider "attempted" mail fraud.

2. Under *Alford* even innocent defendants can plead guilty, if their pleas are "knowing," "intelligent," and "voluntary." Toby's desire to avoid harsh conditions, while hardly irrational, could be seen as rendering his decision "involuntary," if the conditions of confinement were illegal. But strip searches of the kind mentioned have been upheld as constitutional, even in pretrial detention centers, see *Bell v. Wolfish*, 441 U.S. 520 (1979), so the state's use of them does not constitute unconstitutional pressure. The other conditions, however, might be illegal, and hence render the plea involuntary. Whether Toby's decision is "knowing" and "intelligent," however, may be open to more dispute. If there are litigational, or administrative, methods of dealing with these other conditions, and Toby is not aware of those avenues of relief, his plea might not be "intelligent" or "knowing." Moreover, there is no assurance that he will be imprisoned under easier conditions. If Toby assumes that conditions will be less severe in prison than in jail, he might be acting unknowingly. But since less severe conditions are not assured, the court has no duty to point that out to Toby. You may have the obligation to point that out to him. This example is based upon an actual case; the trial judge refused to accept the guilty plea. See *New York Times*, Oct. 25, 2000.

3. Rudolph may have thought that he inflicted serious bodily harm, but while Boris's pride may be seriously hurt, he doesn't fit within the statutory definition. The problem is that once the sentence has been imposed, in order to withdraw his plea, Rudolph must show, in most jurisdictions, that his sentence constituted a "manifest injustice." That may be hard, particularly since he is clearly guilty of robbery. But if the minimum sentence for first degree robbery is greater than the maximum for second degree robbery, Rudolph may have an argument.

4. Although each of these provisions declares that the individual "shall" be ineligible, Section (1) nevertheless makes ineligibility dependent on the discretion of the judge. Thus, the loss of these benefits is not automatic, and becomes collateral. The loss of benefits under Section (2), however, is automatic and is therefore "direct." You must tell Jacques that he'll lose food stamp eligibility. Of course, Jacques might care more about the first kind of government benefits, but his concerns are not relevant here. See *United States v. Littlejohn*, 224 F.3d 960 (9th Cir. 2000).

5. This example raises the question of the reach of *Padilla*. Cantor will want to withdraw his guilty plea, but the loss of a pension would have been considered "collateral" rather than "direct" under pre-*Padilla* case law, at least where, as here, it is discretionary with the agency. After *Padilla*, however, it is possible to argue that loss of a pension is so severe that it is "like" deportation. After all, Cantor had hoped to retire and write books, and most people would agree that given a choice between five days in jail or the loss of a lifelong pension, the former seems light. There are several problems here, however. First, *Padilla* might be restricted to those losses that are "inevitable" or "virtually automatic." Since there will be a hearing before an agency, which has discretion, the pension loss might not fit that characterization. Second, *Padilla* did not go to the question of whether the defendant's lack of knowledge invalidated the plea. Instead, it held that the failure of *Padilla's* lawyer to give him accurate information about deportation rendered the assistance "ineffective." But Cantor had no lawyer, and if *Padilla* does not extend to the validity of guilty pleas generally, Cantor will be singing the blues for a very long time.

D. PLEA BARGAINING — BANE OR SALVATION?

There is no glory in plea bargaining. In place of a noble clash for truth, plea bargaining gives us a skulking truce. Opposing lawyers shrink from battle, and the jury's empty box signals the system's disappointment. But though its victory merits no fanfare, plea bargaining has triumphed. Bloodlessly and clandestinely, it has swept across the penal landscape and driven our vanquished jury into small pockets of resistance. Plea bargaining may be, as some chroniclers claim, the invading barbarian. But it has won all the same.

George Fisher, Plea Bargaining's Triumph,
109 Yale L.J. 857, 859 (2000)

Whatever might be the situation in an ideal world, the fact is that the guilty plea and the often concomitant plea bargain are important components of this country's criminal justice system. Properly administered, they can benefit all concerned. The defendant avoids extended pre-trial incarceration and the anxieties and uncertainties of a trial; he gains a speedy disposition of his case, the chance to acknowledge his guilt, and a prompt start in realizing whatever potential there may be for rehabilitation. Judges and prosecutors conserve vital and scarce resources. The public is protected from the risks posed by those charged with criminal offense who are at large on bail while awaiting completion of criminal proceedings.

Blackledge v. Allison, 431 U.S. 63 (1977)

I. An Overview[18]

There is little neutral opinion on the question of the desirability of plea bargaining — you either hate it, or you tolerate it (few people actually love it). On its face, plea bargaining is in tension with the general test of voluntariness of confessions — that the confession "must not be extracted by any sort of threat or violence, or obtained by any direct or implied promises, however slight, nor by the exertion of any improper influence." *Bram v. United States*, 168 U.S. 532, 542-3 (1897). Applied literally, this standard would invalidate every plea bargain, for there is always a promise or inducement to the defendant to plead.

A century ago, plea bargaining was excoriated; attorneys who participated in discussions were threatened with disbarment, if not worse.[19] By the 1960s, however, there was grudging acceptance of the process. In the so-called "Brady trilogy," the lead opinion of which was *Brady v. United States*, 397 U.S. 742 (1970), the Court, in dictum, seemed to embrace the practice.[20] CAVEAT — This is *not* the *Brady* decision discussed in Chapter 6. A year later, in *Santobello v. New York*, 404 U.S. 257 (1971), the Court gave *de jure*, and not merely *de facto*, approbation to the process. Daniel P. Blank, Plea Bargain Waivers Reconsidered: A Legal Pragmatist's Guide to Loss, Abandonment and Alienation, 68 Fordham L. Rev. 2011, 2063 (2000), believes that, only a year or two prior to the *Brady* trilogy, the Supreme Court "appeared poised to invalidate the practice of plea bargaining under the doctrine of unconstitutional conditions." Indeed, several years ago a three-judge panel of the Tenth Circuit startled the legal world by holding that any promise by a federal prosecutor of leniency in exchange for a plea of guilty violated the federal bribery statute, 18 U.S.C. §201(C)(2), which makes it a crime "to directly or indirectly give, offer, or promise anything of value to any person for or because of the testimony . . . to be given by such person. . . ." *Singleton v. United States*, 144 F.3d 1343 (10th Cir. 1998). (After the furor died down, the entire court, *en banc*, reversed the panel, 165 F.3d 1297 (10th Cir. 1999).)

Shortly after *Santobello* the National Advisory Commission on Criminal Justice Standards and Goals called for an abolition to plea bargaining by

---

18. For a scathing critique of the Court's early plea bargaining jurisprudence, see Becker, Plea Bargaining and the Supreme Court, 21 Loy. L.A. L. Rev. 757 (1988), arguing that "[T]he . . . cases move irregularly in different directions, like drunks scattering from a bar. Principles announced in one case are forgotten or ignored in the next. The result has been law without reason" (at 760). *See also* Jacqueline E. Ross, The Entrenched Position of Plea Bargaining in United States Legal Practice, 54 Am. J. Comp. L. 717 (2006), which argues that "the adversarial nature of the U.S. criminal process . . . validates convictions as the outcome of a contest . . . rather than the search for truth by an actively inquiring (and at least nominally neutral) judiciary."

19. See, e.g., *State v. Conway*, 20 R.I. 270, 273, 38 A. 656 (1897).

20. As noted above, *Brady* involved a statute which the Court had determined to be unconstitutionally coercive, but to which the defendant had pled guilty prior to the Court's decision. The Court upheld the plea as knowing and intelligent.

1978.[21] Obviously, the call was unheeded: The practice has not merely survived; it has thrived and grown since that time. Today, plea bargaining is not merely acknowledged — it is seen as the glue which holds the criminal justice system together.[22]

Nearly 90 percent of all cases settle by guilty pleas, and virtually all pleas result from bargaining. The basis of the process is mutuality; the defendant receives a lower sentence than she otherwise would have received, and the state avoids both the burden, and the risk, of a trial.[23] If every case went to trial, the contention is, courts would immediately become clogged. Some critics endorse alternatives to pleas and negotiation, such as the Philadelphia practice, in which "summary trials," lasting an average of two hours, often replace bargaining,[24] while others argue that those criminals with the most to offer the prosecutor (information on other criminals) can obtain the greatest concessions: precisely the wrong utilitarian message to deliver to those involved in crime. Conversely, those who cannot offer much, or who decide to go to trial, will receive harsher sentences for the "same" crime, based upon a factor unrelated to culpability.[25] An even more Machiavellian view might argue that it is only plea bargaining which has allowed legislatures to increase statutory sentences, knowing that prosecutors and defense counsel will, in "deserving" cases, find methods to evade the harshness.

Various studies, and students, of the criminal justice system have found that of two similarly situated defendants (perhaps co-defendants in the same offense), one will often receive a harsher sentence because he went to trial. They argue that this chills the Sixth Amendment right to trial. While some of that increase may be because more details about the crime — and the defendant's culpability — may be revealed at trial, at least some of the differential is explained by the threat (sometimes actually made by trial court judges) —

---

21. Courts, Standard 3.1 (1973).

22. "In budget-starved urban criminal courts, the negotiated plea literally staves off collapse of the law enforcement system." *People v. Slikoff*, 35 N.Y.2d 227, 318 N.E.2d 784, 788, 360 N.Y.S.2d 623 (1974).

23. Another societal gain is that more defendants can be punished, since there is more judicial time available to try cases (or take pleas).

24. See Stephen J. Schulhofer, Is Plea Bargaining Inevitable?, 97 Harv. L. Rev. 1037 (1984). It is alleged that when Philadelphia went to summary trials, the parties debated over whether defendants would waive their right to a jury trial and elect a brief bench trial instead, a process that was facilitated by the fact that the judges who ran bench trials were considered "soft" sentencers. See C. Silberman, Criminal Violence, Criminal Justice 284 (1978).

25. There are no hard data on the "discount" which a plea attains. Ronald F. Wright, Trial Distortion and the End of Innocence in Federal Criminal Justice, 154 U. Pa. L. Rev. 79 (2005), estimates that the discount for pleas may be up to 50 percent. Id. note 96, at 12 n.96 (citing sources). Wilkins, Plea Negotiations, Acceptance of Responsibility, Role of the Offence, and Departures: Policy Decision in the Promulgation of Federal Sentencing Guidelines, 23 Wake Forest L. Rev. 181, 190 (1998), gives a figure of 30-40 percent. "There has always been a sentencing discount for those who plead guilty and turn state's evidence. In this district, that discount used to range from 33% to 45%." *Berthoff v. United States*, 140 F. Supp. 2d 50 (D. Mass. 2001).

7. Pleas of Guilt and Bargained Pleas

"You took some of my time, now I'll take some of yours." Consider, for example, the following comments made by judges:[26]

- "[T]his is a one time offer."
- "I'll make sure you get sentenced to the max if you don't plead guilty now."
- "For today only . . ."
- "I will up the sentence if you take it to trial, because you could have pleaded and saved us all this trouble."[27]
- "I strongly suggest that you ask your client to consider a plea, because, if the jury returns a verdict of guilty, I might be disposed to impose a substantial prison sentence. You know I am capable of doing that."[28]
- "If you'd have come in here, as you should have done in the first instance, to save the State the trouble of calling a jury, I would probably have sentenced you, as I indicated to you I would have sentenced you, to one to life in the penitentiary. It will cost you nine years additional, because the sentence now is ten to life in the penitentiary."[29]
- "We had the police and the prosecutor sitting down here for three days to convict you and impanel this jury and try it and for that you're going to be punished."[30]
- "All bets are off" if defendant goes to trial, and court indicates that it intends to sentence defendant to same term as co-defendant, if he pleads.[31]

There was a time when everyone believed that Europe, and particularly Germany, was the "land without plea bargaining." No longer. Canada,[32] Russia,[33] and Germany[34] have all succumbed. The BGH clearly and

26. Klein, Judicial Misconduct in Criminal Cases: It's Not Just the Counsel Who May Be Ineffective and Unprofessional, 4 Ohio St. J. Crim. L. 195, 207 (2006).
27. Id., citing ABA Juvenile Justice Center et al., Georgia: An Assessment of Access to Counsel and Quality of Representation in Delinquency Proceedings 31 (Patricia Puritz and Tammy Sun, eds., 2001).
28. Klein, ibid., citing Commw. v. Longval, 378 Mass. 246, 390 N.E.2d 1117 (Mass. 1979).
29. Klein, ibid., citing People v. Moriarity, 25 Ill. 2d 565, 185 N.E.2d 688 (Ill. 1962).
30. State v. Scalf, 126 Ohio App. 614, 710 N.E.2d 1206, 1212 (Ohio Ct. App. 1998).
31. United States v. Baker, 489 F.3d 366, (D.C. Cir. 2007).
32. Joseph DiLuca, Expedient McJustice or Principled Alternative Dispute Resolution? A Review of Plea Bargaining in Canada, 50 Crim. L.Q. 14 (2005).
33. Stanislaw Pomorski, Consensual Justice in Russia: Guilty Pleas under the 2001 Code of Criminal Procedure, in Public Policy and Law in Russia, 187 (Robert Sharlet and Ferdinand Feldbrugge, eds.) (2005); S. Pomorski, Modern Russian Criminal Procedure: The Adversarial Principle and Guilty Plea, 17 Crim. L.F. 129 (2006).
34. In Germany, judges act as both a party to and a supervisor of plea negotiations. Jenia Iontcheva Turner, Judicial Participation in Plea Negotiations: A Comparative View, 54 Am. J. Comp. L. 199, 214 (2006).

unequivocally accepts that the German criminal justice system would eventually break down if courts were not allowed to engage in "bargaining." In at least some of these countries, it is the court, and not the prosecutor, who takes the first steps in beginning discussions. See Jenia Iontcheva Turner, Judicial Participation in Plea Negotiations: A Comparative View, 54 Am. J. Comp. L. 199 (2006); Yue Ma, A Comparative View of Judicial Supervision of Prosecutorial Discretion, 44 Crim. L. Bull. 2 (2008).

2. Types of Bargains

Prosecutors have enormous power. As we saw in Chapter 3, they can simply refuse to charge the defendant at all, or they can charge (1) every possible offense, in a series of counts; (2) very serious offenses carrying substantial penalties. Particularly since these decisions are made when not even the prosecutor has all the facts, the tendency is to charge the most severe possible charge, lest the initial indictment needs to be superseded with higher charges. This truth, however, means that prosecutors have at least two methods by which they can induce defense agreement:

- *charge bargaining*, by which charges are either removed entirely from the indictment, or "downgraded" to lesser included offenses;
- *sentence bargaining*, in which the prosecutor agrees either to support a specific sentence (lower than the maximum sentence provided by statute) or not to oppose a sentence recommendation by the defense.

Some argue that charge bargaining leads to prosecutorial overcharging, in the expectation that the negotiations will then result in the defendant pleading to the "right" charge. Sentence bargaining, on the other hand, is often criticized as a direct impingement on judicial sentencing discretion. While judges retain the authority to ignore the specific sentence included in a plea agreement, or a specific recommendation by the prosecutor, the reality is that few judges will do that, in part because it would undermine future plea bargaining.

Fact bargaining is a relatively new phenomenon. Until 1980 or so, sentencing discretion was fully in the hands of the individual judge, who could focus on *any* fact in determining the exact sentence within very wide ranges (e.g., 5-20 years). (See Chapter 12.) In the past two decades, a number of states have moved to "structured sentencing" systems, in which sentences are set much more narrowly, and "enhanced" only if specific statutory circumstances are present (e.g., whether the defendant carried a gun). Because the enunciated duration will depend on these facts, the lawyers on both sides now negotiate about these facts as well; if they agree not to mention the gun in the indictment, the judge may never learn of it, and therefore, may never use that fact to increase the sentence. The plea agreement rarely indicates that there was negotiation about these facts — it simply states the facts to be "stipulated" as true.

3. Inducements — Or Threats?

One person's "inducement" is another's "threat." A promise to delete a charge in exchange for a plea is equally, at least, an implied threat not to delete that charge if there is no plea. But no "threat," not even that of seeking the death penalty, will necessarily invalidate a guilty plea, so long as that plea is knowingly and intelligently made. Since (by hypothesis) the penalty threatened by the legislature is constitutionally permissible, it is not the individual prosecutor, but the state government itself, which is positing the possibility of the penalty. Any offer by the prosecutor, then, may be seen as an offer to mitigate a permissible penalty — a merciful, ameliorative act.[35] As the Supreme Court declared in Brady, the plea may have been "caused" by the heavier penalty, but it was not "coerced" by that penalty.

Again, because the courts have focused on the defendant's mental state (voluntarism and knowledge), the following inducements by prosecutors if the defendant agrees to a negotiated plea have been held not to be "coercion":

- not to prosecute another person (usually a loved one);
- not to bring greater substantive charges (so long as it is not vindictive);
- not to bring a charge, particularly recidivist charges, which would result in significantly higher penalty (usually life imprisonment);[36]
- not to inform the court of a defendant's cooperation in finding and prosecuting others.

The most potent explanation for not disallowing these (and other) threats is that the defendant who bargains is represented by counsel — a

---

35. This may explain the different results in Jackson (supra, p.131), and an instance where the prosecutor offers to "take the death penalty off the table" in exchange for a plea. In Jackson, the statute did not individualize among defendants charged with capital offenses, whereas in the second instance, the prosecutor makes an individualized judgment about who should be given the benefit if constitutional rights are waived.
36. Bordenkircher v. Hayes, supra, p.131.

counseled plea is presumptively valid, because the defendant is fully informed by counsel of the real risks involved.[37]

4. Judicial Participation

Judicial "inducements" might seem even more coercive, more certain, than those from a prosecutor — while the prosecutor can merely "recommend" a sentence, if the judge participates in the process and "suggests" that a particular sentence "would likely" be accepted, the defendant is likely to believe he can take that to the bank. For this reason, the federal system (Rule 11) and many states (e.g., Pa. R. Crim. P. 319 B(1); Ga. Unif. Super. Ct. R. 33.5(a); Mass. R. Crim. P. 12 (b)) prohibit any participation by the court in negotiations. But other states allow such participation. See N.C. Gen. Stat. sec. 15A-1021(a). The United States Supreme Court has not addressed the issue.

The tension created by judicial participation is between the two prongs of the guilty plea liturgy: Judicial participation makes the plea much more knowing (because the judge essentially guarantees what the sentence will be if there is a plea) but arguably much less voluntary (because the defendant now fears a longer sentence if he rejects the judge's "offer"). Excluding the judge from the plea discussion serves several purposes:

- it minimizes the risk that the defendant will be judicially coerced into pleading guilty;
- it preserves the impartiality of the court;
- it avoids any appearance of impropriety;
- it prevents possible "retaliation" if the defendant is convicted after rejecting the judicial "offer."

On the other hand, excluding the judge also means that:

- the prosecutor has much more control over the sentence;
- the defendant is much less informed about the actual sentence the judge might impose;
- the parties may spend a significant amount of time negotiating, finally reaching a sentence or charge agreement, and then have the judge reject their efforts.

---

37. "[T]he mere presence of counsel creates a presumption that the defendant's choices are made knowingly and are free from coercion." Blank, *supra*, at 2020. If counsel does not adequately inform or advise the defendant, there may be a claim of inadequate representation. See Chapter 10.

It is also arguable that, particularly in "structured sentencing" systems (see Chapter 12), judicial participation in plea bargaining offsets the wide discretion afforded prosecutors to effectively set sentences. See Nancy J. King, Judicial Oversight of Negotiated Sentences in a World of Bargained Punishment, 58 Stan. L. Rev. 293, 308 (2005); Susan R. Klein, Enhancing the Judicial Role in Criminal Plea and Sentence Bargaining, 84 Tex. L. Rev. 2023 (2006).

There is, of course, a spectrum of "participation." At one end, the judge may never talk to the attorneys until they appear in front of her having reached a full agreement, while at the other end, she may discuss fully and vigorously what she feels is a "good" sentence, and urge each side to compromise on various positions. In between, a judge might indicate her (dis)approval of an agreement which the two parties have tentatively reached, or indicate a span of alternatives which might be acceptable, without pinpointing any one (for example, a judge might find either of the following acceptable in a given case: (1) x years incarceration with some restitution; (2) x + y years incarceration with no restitution; (3) no incarceration with full restitution. Alternatives might also include the location of confinement (although in most instances only the department of corrections would make that decision).[38]

These tensions are reflected in the history of the American Bar Association's grappling with this issue. The first edition of the Criminal Justice Standards provided that the trial judge "should not" participate. The second edition provided that if the parties were unable to reach a plea, they could meet with the judge to discuss a plea. The third, and most recent, edition provides that a "judge should not through word or demeanor, either directly or indirectly, communicate to the defendant or defense counsel that a plea agreement should be accepted or that a guilty plea should be entered." ABA Standards for Criminal Justice: Pleas of Guilty, Standard 14-3.3(c) (3d ed. 1999). Nevertheless, the standard then allows the judge to indicate her reaction to a proposed sentence (though not directly telling the parties she would impose that sentence).

An intriguing variation of this process was tried in Detroit, where a special "plea judge" would offer the defendant a maximum ceiling on his sentence in exchange for a guilty plea. If the defendant accepted, the plea would occur; if not, the defendant would be tried by a different judge. The same process appears to be working in Connecticut. See Turner, p. 146,

---

38. Judicial participation in plea bargaining was "not uncommon" in state prosecutions. A late 1970s study found that approximately one-third of criminal trial judges attended plea discussions, usually in an active role. John Paul Ryan and James J. Alfini, Trial Judges' Participation in Plea Bargaining: An Empirical Perspective, 13 Law & Soc'y Rev. 479 (Wtr. 1979). And Alschuler reported participation by 90 percent of judges. Albert Alschuler, The Trial Judge's Role in Plea Bargaining, Part I, 76 Colum. L. Rev. 1059, 1061-1062 (1976).

supra. See Comment, Pretrial Sentence Bargaining: A Cure for Crowded Court Dockets?, 30 Emory L.J. 853 (1981).

5. Waiving Rights

Certain constitutional and statutory claims are not waivable, even as part of a plea agreement:

- the right to effective assistance of counsel;[39]
- the right to be tried in a court with proper jurisdiction;
- the right to conflict-free representation (see Chapter 10);
- the right to nonracially discriminatory sentencing;[40]
- the right not to be subject to a statutorily excessive sentence;[41]
- the right against double jeopardy.

Any guilty plea, even without negotiation, involves waiving some rights — constitutional, statutory, or court created. But prosecutors, particularly since *Santobello's* endorsement of plea bargaining, have increasingly required defendants to waive a significant number of other rights before a plea bargain will be accepted. The law is unsettled here; in the words of one commentator, "The Supreme Court has lurched from one decision to the next without providing meaningful guidance . . . or maintaining any consistent theoretical approach regarding criminal waiver."[42] Thus, in *United States v. Mezzanatto*, 513 U.S. 196 (1995), the Court held that the defendant may waive the right not to have statements made during plea negotiations used against him if he later goes to trial. *Mezzanatto*, however, was a fairly narrow decision — the defendant had agreed to permit the government to use plea negotiation statements only to rebut any contradictory testimony by the defendant himself. In *United States v. Velez*, 354 F.3d 190 (2d Cir. 2004), the Second Circuit substantially broadened the point, upholding a waiver of all privileges under Fed. Rule Evid. 401, which would, absent waiver, prohibit the government from using, for any purpose, statements made during a plea negotiation.

In addition, courts have increasingly upheld prosecutorial requirements that defendant waive his right to appeal from a guilty plea (except for the structural defects noted above). Although some states hold such a waiver as void against public policy, Kevin S. Burke, *State v. Dettman*: The End of the Sentencing Revolution or Just the Beginning?, 33 Wm. Mitchell L. Rev. 1331

---

39. *United States v. Attar*, 38 F.3d 727 (4th Cir. 1994).
40. *United States v. Jacobson*, 15 F.3d 19 (2d Cir. 1994).
41. *United States v. Marin*, 961 F.2d 493 (4th Cir. 1992).
42. Blank, *supra*, p.144.

(2007). See Annot., 89 A.L.R.3d 864, Federal Rule 11 has now been amended to allow waiving of the right to appeal. In *United States v. Mabry*, 536 F.3d 231 (3d Cir. 2008), the court held that a waiver of the right to appeal precluded defendant from bringing a motion to vacate his sentence on grounds that his counsel was ineffective. The Supreme Court denied certiorari, 557 U.S. 903 (2009).

The Court held in *United States v. Ruiz*, 536 U.S. 622 (2002), that the defendant could waive his *Giglio* rights to discovery of materials which could be "useful" at trial (see Chapter 6). Although the prosecutor in *Ruiz* promised to produce any information which proved defendant's innocence (*Brady* evidence), the proffered agreement would require the defendant to forgo discovery of materials useful for impeachment of a prosecution witness.[43] The distinction that the *Ruiz* Court drew between directly exculpatory evidence and impeachment evidence, which also goes to reliability, may seem thin but the issues here are more complex than may first appear. Although the *Ruiz* decision may initially seem implausible, it may be helpful to separate two issues in the case. First, could the defendant, *without a plea bargain*, plead guilty before obtaining *Brady* disclosure? Surely the answer to this question, assuming the plea would be voluntary and knowing, would be yes. A defendant who knows he is guilty,[44] and simply wishes to atone for that act, without any bargain, surely should not be forced to wait until the prosecutor has obtained and disclosed all *Brady* information. If a plea would be valid if unilaterally entered by the defendant, the second question then arises: Does the prosecutor's threat to withdraw a bargained-for leniency, unless the defendant waives those same rights, unfairly alter the balance, or affect the *voluntariness* of the plea? In significant part, this may relate back to the timing of disclosure (see Chapter 6). Since, under *Brady* itself, the defendant has no "right" to disclosure until just before trial (or, in the case of a witness's statement, until after the witness testifies) whatever pressure the defendant feels from the prosecutor's withholding that information prior to trial appears not to be unconstitutional coercion. Where, under statute or court rule, disclosure must be much earlier, it is more plausible to argue that prosecutorial refusal to disclose is illegal coercion, and renders null any resulting plea agreement.

---

43. See Larry Kupers and John T. Phillipsborn, Mephistophelian Deals: The Newest in Standard Plea Agreements, 23-Aug. Champion 18 (Aug. 1999) ("The *Brady* waiver is really an appalling attempt by the government to set us back to another age in criminal procedure".)

44. Herein lies a possible flaw — the distinction between "factual" guilt and "legal" guilt. While a defendant may know his conduct, he may not know the legal ramifications of his conduct, or possible defenses to liability. But assuming that he is competently represented, he may be sufficiently apprised of these matters. And if he is not, he may attack his guilty plea on grounds of inadequate representation. See Chapter 10.

Finally, it may be hard to conceive of a defendant "knowingly waiving" a right to information he does not know about. But that may simply be a semantic problem — if the *Ruiz* case is recast in terms of forfeiture, rather than waiver, it may be more understandable.

A rule forbidding the defendant to plead guilty until *Brady* material had been disclosed might protect him from prosecutorial coercion, but it also denies him a potential bargaining chip in his plea negotiations. If, as we have suggested here, the key issue is knowledge, the defendant who cedes this right with regard to the state's evidence-in-chief will also nevertheless be held to have entered a valid plea agreement.[45]

6. Accepting and Enforcing the Bargain

In contrast to the practice half a century ago, when plea bargaining was done secretly and never mentioned, plea agreements are now contained in written, open documents signed by the parties and given to the court before the entering of the plea. The agreement recites both the defendant's willingness to plead, and the *quid pro quo* which the prosecutor cedes as consideration for the plea. The agreement must recognize that as to sentencing, the judge can reject any sentence understanding. But while judges may reject the bargain, they are loathe to do so: (1) if the agreement reflects a *charge* bargain, some courts will be reluctant to review what they deem prosecutorial discretion; (2) courts may believe the system needs such negotiation; (3) they have ongoing relationships with the attorneys.

Deciding whether a defendant has failed to perform her agreement to cooperate may be difficult. In *Ricketts v. Adamson*, 483 U.S. 1 (1987), defendant agreed to testify against his co-defendants, in exchange for being allowed to plead to a charge which did not carry the death penalty. At the co-defendants' trial, he testified as the key witness on direct, but on cross-examination he invoked the Fifth Amendment, which gave his co-defendants a clear confrontation clause claim guaranteeing that their convictions would be reversed (as they were). Thereafter, defendant was sentenced as agreed to under the plea arrangement. The government wished to retry the co-defendants, and to have Adamson testify once more, but Adamson, arguing that he had complied with the wording of the agreement to testify once, sought more benefits (including release immediately after the co-defendants' retrial, although the original agreement had called for a sentence of more than 20 years). The government then moved to have the plea agreement rescinded, and to have Adamson tried for the capital offense. On the question of whether defendant would have to

---

45. Defendants may also be required to waive their right to file a civil claim against the officers who arrested them (or the governmental unit for which they work). *Town of Newton v. Rumery*, 480 U.S. 386 (1987).

"retestify" against his co-defendants, the agreement was ambiguous, and one might have expected the Court to construe that ambiguity against the government. But Adamson was clearly manipulating the process (and had done so by invoking the Fifth Amendment) and the Court allowed the state to rescind the plea agreement. The real problem here is that the usual remedies available for a breach of an agreement seem either excessive or impotent. To require Adamson to testify (truthfully) at the second trial would visit upon him no adverse consequences for an apparent breach. On the other hand, to impose the death penalty for his less than forthright testimony seems disproportionate to his offense (he did, after all, testify).[46] This might argue for allowing a court to impose an "equitable" remedy for defendant breach, such as increasing the length of the sentence, but not totally rescinding the agreement. As a result of these concerns, a wily prosecutor will seek to postpone the defendant's sentencing until all opportunity to cooperate has occurred.

On the other hand, if the prosecutor[47] fails to perform, or the defendant has detrimentally relied, courts have seen several possible remedies. The most frequently used are: (1) requiring specific performance of the agreement; (2) allowing the defendant to withdraw and renegotiate. Defendants, of course, would choose specific performance rather than recission of their guilty plea. After all, who wants to start re-negotiating with the prosecutor whose actions at your instigation have just been judicially questioned? Nevertheless, the consensus is that the choice of remedy lies in the hands of the judge, not the defendant. See *State v. Munoz*, 305 Mont. 139, 23 P.3d 922 (Mont. 2001). Washington, and a few other states, sometimes place the control in the hands of the injured party. *State v. Miller*, 110 Wash.2d 528, 756 P.2d 122 (1988).

When either side alleges a breach of the plea agreement, courts may hold a hearing, at which the understanding of the parties will be assessed, and their subsequent actions measured. These hearings may be complex, and involve subtle issues. For example, the agreement may be breached by other state agents. In *State v. Matson*, 268 Wis. 2d 725, 674 N.W.2d 51 (Wis. App. 2003), the chief investigating officer wrote a detailed five-page letter to the judge with approval of the police department, recommending a maximum sentence. This was in direct conflict with the plea agreement that the prosecutor would not recommend a sentence, and the court allowed the defendant to withdraw the plea.

46. Indeed, the Ninth Circuit so held in a later opinion. *Adamson v. Ricketts*, 865 F.2d 1011, 1022 (9th Cir. 1988).

47. The defense counsel, or defendant, may also fail to perform, but the only sanctions then are (1) personal and professional steps against counsel; (2) rescinding the plea and remanding the defendant for trial.

In assessing whether there has been performance, it is irrelevant that the prosecutor's nonperformance was purely inadvertent; the defendant may still be entitled to either enforce the bargain or withdraw from it.

If the defendant has detrimentally relied, but the promise is "unfulfill-able," a court may create a remedy of whole cloth. Thus, suppose that Leona, relying on a bargain by a state prosecutor which includes a promise that there will be no federal prosecution, thereafter testifies against a co-conspirator, only to learn that the state prosecutor cannot bind the United States. What remedy should the defendant receive? Judges often appear to think themselves restricted, but the equity of the chancellor, which is surely what is being invoked here, is essentially boundless. Substantial reduction of the sentence, for example, might appear to be a more balanced approach in some instances; in others, perhaps, the court could simply order the prosecutor, as an officer of the court, to rescind all charges against a defendant.

Unmentioned in almost all of the cases is the possibility of ethical sanctions against the attorney, either prosecutor or defense counsel, who fails to perform a bargain. See Chapter 14, *infra*.

7. The Contract Analogy

As suggested by the language used above, many courts, and commentators, have used contract doctrines in determining not only the meaning, but the enforceability of plea agreements. Some argue that the analogy is inapt, on the grounds that the parties have unequal bargaining power. Nevertheless, if the prosecutor breaches the agreement, courts may order the government to "specifically perform" the contract. On the other hand, in obvious contrast to usual contract doctrine that an executory contract is enforceable from the time the parties exchange promises, until the court has accepted the agreement, the plea bargain is "in embryo," and either side may withdraw from the agreement without apparent sanction. *Mabry v. Johnson*, 467 U.S. 504 (1984), unless there has been detrimental reliance. (See Brian A. Blum, Contracts: Examples and Explanations (5th ed., 2011).) Partial nonperformance might require some sanction short of abrogating the entire plea bargain, but many courts employ an "all or nothing" approach. Reflecting the view that the bargaining power is unequal, one court has declared that "Courts construe plea agreements strictly against the Government for a variety of reasons, including the fact that the Government is usually the party that drafts the agreement, and the fact that the Government ordinarily has certain awesome advantages in bargaining power." *United States v. Ready*, 82 F.3d 551 (2d Cir. 1996). The Supreme Court recently reaffirmed the contact analogy. *Puckett v. United States*, 556 U.S. 129 (2009). Commentators have suggested drawing even further from contact law, including providing for "cooling off" periods. Indeed, some have argued that the inequality of bargaining power may make plausible an argument that, notwithstanding *Ruiz*, courts should require more disclosure before allowing a defendant to bargain at all. Professors Scott and Stuntz, for example, argue that "the contract principles of adhesion, duress, mistake, unconscionability, and public policy all suggest that . . . waivers of the right to disclosure of *Brady* material cannot (pass constitutional muster)." Robert E. Scott and William J. Stuntz, Plea Bargaining as Contract, 101 Yale L.J. 1909, 2074 (1992). In any event, both sides should attempt to make the agreement as clear and unambiguous as possible, so that there is no question whether there has been a breach and, perhaps, what each side contemplates as a sanction for any such breach.

8. Assessing Plea Bargaining

As the quotations at the beginning of this subsection indicate, plea bargaining may be the single-most controversial aspect of criminal justice as it is actually practiced. Opponents, such as Professor Fisher, argue that plea bargaining is immoral "justice for sale." Moreover, from a utilitarian viewpoint, bargaining, as immunity generally, appears to benefit those most deeply enmeshed in crime, whereas the "small fish" have insufficient information by which to obtain prosecutorial largesse. Critics further argue that the process undermines jury trials, and makes both defense and prosecution less exacting in their preparation, because they know that most cases will not get to trial. Finally, they argue that some crimes are so dangerous, or heinous, that any reduction in the threatened sentence is unwarranted.

It would be hard to call the opposing camp "advocates" of bargaining. Instead, they argue that bargaining is a necessary evil, mandated by the burgeoning number of arrests. Since 90 percent of convictions occur as a result of pleas, a decrease to 80 percent would double the number of trials, causing impossible log jams and unconscionable delays. A relapse to 0 percent pleas would be unthinkable. Moreover, while bargaining with the "middle fish" is not palatable, it is said to be the only way to obtain sufficient information to prosecute the true managers and leaders of organized criminal activity. Finally, a bargain avoids the possibility that some weakness in the proofs, or some bizarre jury machination, could let a guilty defendant go.

Many jurisdictions have attempted to eliminate plea bargaining, at least with regard to some crimes, by explicitly declaring that plea negotiations shall not be allowed with such charges and establishing mandatory sentences. Conspicuous among such legislation have been sexual offenses, gun offenses, some drug charges, drunk driving, and domestic abuse. Critics have argued that these statutes have been unsuccessful, merely driving bargaining "underground." Thus, prosecutors will bargain with defense counsel before the indictment or information is filed, agreeing to "remove" that part of the facts that makes the crime eligible for a plea bargaining ban.

Some commentators think that these are only half measures, and that all bargaining should be banned. In Alaska, during the 1970s, such a statewide ban was imposed on all prosecutors by the Attorney General. The data from this experiment are uncertain; some believe that most bargaining did in fact disappear, while others argue that defendants were simply charged with the crimes to which they "would have" pled, so that the prosecutor simply anticipated the result of hypothetical bargaining.

In an original and challenging approach to what it saw as disparity of plea bargaining results in drug cases, one state has established plea bargaining "guidelines," much like the sentencing guidelines used by the federal system and nearly 20 states (see Chapter 13 for a discussion on the sentencing guidelines). In fact, the court explained that its power to order the prosecutors to establish such guidelines stemmed from the fact that prosecutorial charging was dramatically affecting sentencing and thus "touching on" the judicial power. *State v. Brimage*, 153 N.J. 1, 706 A.2d 1096 (N.J. 1998); Ronald Wright, Prosecutorial Guidelines and the New Terrain in New Jersey, 109 Penn. St. L. Rev. 1087 (2005). No other state has yet followed suit.

Another suggestion is to establish a "plea jury" composed of citizens who would sit for some length of time (perhaps a month) and review plea bargains for "reasonableness" before the agreement was submitted to a judge. Laura Appleman, The Plea Jury, 85 Ind. L.J. 731 (2010).[48]

Plea bargaining is clearly part of the legal landscape as the twenty-first century begins, and is not likely to disappear in the foreseeable future.[49] The debate will continue.

Examples

1. Kim enters into a plea agreement which states, in part: "Defendant is aware that 18 U.S.C. §3742(a) affords her the right to appeal the sentence imposed. Knowing that, in exchange for the Government's concessions made herein, the defendant hereby waives to the full extent of the law, all right to appeal her conviction or sentence." At the sentencing, the trial judge declares: "Now, I am finding, as required by the guidelines, that

---

48. This is merely one manifestation of a growing movement to bring the community back into the criminal justice system. Other writers have recommended, for example, that grand juries be composed of members of a very small and distinctive subpart of a city so that the community norms can affect decisions to indict.
49. "Bargaining is like a garden weed—malleable, organic, and exceedingly hard to eradicate." Jennifer L. Mnookin, Uncertain Bargains: The Rise of Plea Bargaining in America, 57 Stan. L. Rev. 1721, 1727 (2005).

you stole more than $5,000, which requires me to impose at least a four-year sentence. And that is what I will do. Of course, you have the right to appeal that sentence." Kim, in fact, wishes to appeal. The prosecution argues that she has waived that right. Who wins?

2. (a) Kirk and Jean Luc are charged with armed robbery of the corner grocery store together. The maximum sentence is 10 years. Kirk enters into a plea bargain to a charge of possession of a weapon, and receives a three-year sentence. He also testifies against Jean Luc, describing in detail how the robbery occurred. The jury acquits Jean Luc. Kirk now moves to vacate his plea. May he?

(b) Assume that the police captured the two long before the robbery, and that the charge against each was conspiracy to rob. Again, Kirk pleads guilty. At Jean Luc's trial, a videotape shows Kirk and Jean Luc discussing some robbery. Kirk testifies that the target was the grocery store. Jean Luc is acquitted. May Kirk vacate his plea now?

3. Bert and the prosecutor of Marin County reached an agreement in which the prosecutor agreed to recommend a 10-month sentence for a street mugging. At the sentencing hearing, the victim, the probation officer of Marin County, an investigating officer for Marin County, and two probation officers from Marylu County (who had supervised Bert on his probation for earlier offenses) each testify, and each recommend the maximum (five years). The court imposes a three-year sentence. Is the breach of the plea agreement such that Bert may vacate the sentence?

4. Which of the following is a breach of a plea agreement to recommend a specific sentence?
(a) The prosecutor offers new information to the probation officer writing the pre-sentence report, resulting in a recommended sentence longer than that agreed to in the plea bargain;
(b) The prosecutor informs the court that she supports the bargained-for sentence "with reluctance";
(c) Where the state agreed to recommend sentence at the low end or midpoint of the standard range, but the deputy prosecutor, at sentencing, after assuring the trial court that the state stood by its agreement, began speaking "on behalf of the victims," commenting that the crimes were "so heinous and violent . . . it showed a complete disregard and respect for [the victims]."

5. Marmaduke was found with a kilo of cocaine (punishable by 10 years), but the prosecutor charges him with possession of 50 grams (maximum sentence 2 years). The judge refuses to accept the agreement. Marmaduke then declares his willingness to plead guilty to the one count. The court refuses to accept the plea. If Marmaduke appeals that decision, what result?

6. (a) On May 30, defendant Barbara and the prosecutor, after intense negotiations, agree that if Barbara "cooperates with the prosecutor's office in pursuing John Jorge, a known drug dealer," the prosecutor will ask the court to drop three of the four pending charges against Barbara and will recommend a probationary sentence. The plea colloquy is set for June 25. On June 18, the prosecutor informs you, as Barbara's counsel, by letter, that he is withdrawing from the agreement, because it appears that Barbara is not a "mule," but a significant participant in the drug trade. What do you do?

   (b) Same facts as (a) except that on June 6, the prosecutor had asked Barbara to wear a "wire" in a buy from Jorge and she had done so. What outcome now?

   (c) Barbara has worn a wire, and the prosecution learns of the "true" facts only after the plea has been accepted. The prosecutor seeks to vacate the plea and try her on all four charges. What do you do?

   (d) Same facts as (b) except that the prosecution, rather than moving to vacate the plea and conviction, now phones you and asks Barbara to testify against Jorge. Barbara — and you — believe that this will put her life in jeopardy. Now what?

7. (a) Reynaldo was charged with six counts of bank fraud, each of which carried a possible five-year maximum sentence. He agreed to plead to one of those counts, if the prosecutor dropped the other five; he saw this as avoiding the risk of 25 more years in prison. The judge sentenced him to the maximum five years. State statutes provide that a prisoner is eligible for parole after serving one-third of his term, less good time. In this case, Reynaldo is eligible for parole after 14 months. Soon after his arrival in prison, Reynaldo is told by his fellow inmates that the practice throughout the state is for judges to impose concurrent sentences in all but exceptional cases. Reynaldo feels he's been bamboozled. Can he successfully move — now — to vacate his guilty plea?

   (b) Suppose that the sentencing practice mentioned in (a) is mandated by state statute, which allows concurrent sentences only where the judge makes written findings explaining why concurrent sentences are inappropriate.

   (c) At his first parole hearing, one of the members of the Board tells Reynaldo: "You got your leniency when you got those other charges dropped. We never parole someone who has gone through charge bargaining. You'll be our guest for five years."

8. (a) Ken Lie, CEO of a major corporation, has heard that a number of his employees have been subpoenaed before a grand jury. Lie knows that there is great consternation over a missing $30 million. Lie has received no subpoena, nor has he been informed that he is a target of the grand

jury. He comes to you for advice. The state precludes plea bargaining of any crime involving fraud. What do you do?

   (b) Suppose Lie has indeed received a letter that he is a target of the grand jury investigation. What do you do now?

9. After being convicted of first degree murder, but successfully appealing that verdict, Cormac enters into a plea bargain for second degree murder. The agreement provides that the government may make whatever recommendation they want at sentencing, except for life imprisonment. At the sentencing, the prosecutor asks for a 70-100 year sentence. She also informs the court that the victim's family wants a life sentence. The trial judge then sentences Cormac to 35-55 years. What result on appeal?

10. Mahmuk, the prosecutor, and Susan, defense counsel, reach a tentative plea agreement that calls for the prosecutor to drop three of five charges, for the defendant, Elinor, to plead guilty to the remaining two counts, and for the two counsels to support a total sentence of 10 years. At the plea colloquy, the judge declares that she "cannot accept" the plea bargain.

   (a) The judge says nothing more.

   (b) The judge says to the prosecutor, "Have you really thought about whether 10 years is sufficient for what Elinor did?"

   (c) Assume that after each of these scenarios, Mahmuk and Susan work out an agreement of $13\frac{1}{2}$ years. Mahmuk calls the judge's clerk and tells him what is being proposed. The clerk, without contacting the judge, says: "I suspect that's all right." That is the ultimate sentence imposed after the court validates the plea deal. Is Elinor's plea "voluntary"?

   (d) Assume at the first colloquy, the judge declared, "I could see 15 years, but very little less." Mahmuk and Susan thereafter have more meetings, and appear with a plea bargain that supports a 15-year sentence. At a subsequent hearing, the trial judge accepts the plea, and Elinor receives the 15 years. Is Elinor's plea "voluntary"?

Explanations

1. The prosecutor. Although a few courts have held that a blanket judicial assurance of the right to appeal cancels a preexisting waiver of appellate rights, most courts disagree. See *United States v. Michelson*, 141 F.3d 867 (8th Cir. 1998). While such assurances as that given by the trial judge "muddy the waters," they do not effect a per se nullification of plea agreement waiver of appellate rights. Because this conclusion is fact-specific, if there is any information which would make this particular

assurance unduly powerful, Kim might have a chance. Otherwise, she'll miss one entire leap year cycle.

2. (a) No. Kirk gave a factual basis for his plea both at the plea colloquy and at Jean Luc's trial. His plea was knowing and intelligent, and there is no ground for vacating his plea now. There surely is no "manifest injustice" in holding Kirk to his plea. The fact that the jury acquitted Jean Luc is a risk Kirk took. When you roll the dice . . .

   (b) No. But the argument here is different. Kirk will argue that (1) if the jury acquitted Jean Luc, it must be because there was no conspiracy; (2) if there was no conspiracy, Kirk could not have been a co-conspirator. But that's insufficient. First, the jury's acquittal does not mean they didn't find an agreement; the jury may simply have "nullified." Second, at least under some modern statutes, including the Model Penal Code, the jury may find a defendant guilty of a "unilateral conspiracy." (See Richard G. Singer and John Q. Lafond, Criminal Law, Examples and Explanations, Chapter 13.) Finally, even if the jury found that there was no conspiracy (because the discussion hadn't gone far enough, or there was no overt act, etc.), and therefore Kirk could not "logically" have been a co-conspirator, Kirk's plea was voluntary, and he knew the risks he was taking. The issue is not whether, as a matter of logic, Kirk could not have been a co-conspirator; the issue is whether the plea was knowing and voluntary. It was. As Holmes said, the life of the law has been not logic, but experience.

3. It is not likely that the prosecutor could control the victims' testimony. Moreover, just as he knows that he takes a risk that the judge will not follow a sentencing recommendation, it is not unreasonable to conclude that the defendant knows the victim is likely to be unhappy, and may well urge a more severe penalty. As to the other governmental witnesses, however, the risk analysis is less clear. Probably, the "answer" depends. (Does that sound (too) familiar?) If Bert is in Florida, there has probably been a breach. Florida holds that a prosecutor's plea bargain binds all state agents. *Lee v. State*, 501 So. 2d 591 (Fla. 1987). Most courts, however, are not persuaded. A good example is *State v. Sanchez*, 146 Wash. 2d 339, 46 P.3d 774 (Wash. 2002). Two defendants, Sanchez and Harris, in consolidated sexual assault cases, had entered plea agreements which bound their respective prosecutors either to make no sentence recommendation, or to recommend a specific sentence. In each case, the prosecutor individually kept that bargain. But in each case, another governmental agent — Sanchez's investigating officer (a local, and not a "state" employee) and Harris's community corrections officer — urged higher sentences. The court held that these last two government agents were not bound by the plea agreement, and that the prosecutor had no statutory authority

over either, "explaining" that the agreement was between the prosecutor and the defense attorney. The court noted that while, statutorily,
the prosecutor was required to notify the *victim* of a proposed plea
agreement,[50] there was no duty to discuss the plea agreement with
an investigating officer. A concurring opinion distinguished between
the IO (a law enforcement officer) and the CCO (an employee of the
court). The dissent also looked at the statutory duties of each officer,
and concluded that each was an agent of the prosecutor.

The federal courts appear to agree with the Florida position. See,
e.g., *Margali-Olvera v. I.N.S.*, 43 F.3d 345 (8th Cir. 1994); see also *Giglio v.
United States*, 405 U.S. 150, 154 (1972), probably because there is a
"unitary" governmental structure in the federal system. Does it make
sense to look at the precise statutory structure? Should one look to the
defendant's reasonable expectation? Is there any analogy here with the
discovery cases as to whether the prosecutor must disclose evidence "in
the control of" another governmental agency? (See Chapter 6.) Even
assuming that there was no collusion between the prosecutor(s) and the
witnesses in *Sanchez*, and even agreeing that the prosecutor could not
control them, why is there not a duty on the part of the prosecutor to
inform the defendant of the (probable) views of these witnesses?
In *Sanchez* itself, it appears that the prosecutor affirmatively sought out
the investigating officer, and discussed the plea agreement. Does it take
much to infer that, at least tacitly, the prosecutor (as Sanchez alleged)
knew that the IO would testify, and would recommend a harsher term?
After *Sanchez*, would you expect the defendant to attempt to have the
bargain include either a bona fide effort by the prosecutor to control
such testimony, or at least impose a duty upon her to notify the
defendant that another state employee will take a different view? If
you were the defense counsel, and the prosecutor refused to agree to
such a clause, what inferences would you draw? What new clauses
would you include in any future plea agreements?

4. (a) Held — the prosecution did not violate the agreement. *United States v.
Levy*, 374 F.3d 1023 (11th Cir. 2004).

(b) Held — the defendant may withdraw his plea. *Herrera v. State*, 64
P.3d 724 (Wyo. 2003).

(c) These comments, held the court, breached the agreement, and
defendant was entitled to withdraw his plea. *State v. Carreno-Maldonado*,
135 Wash. App. 77, 143 P.3d 343 (2006).

---

50. The vast majority of states have enacted "victims rights" laws, some of which mandate
such notification; most statutes, however, simply admonish the prosecutor to do her best to
keep the victim informed. Prosecutors who are too much influenced by the victim's views
may find their actions monitored by a court. See *State v. McDonnell*, 313 Or. 478, 837 P.2d 941
(Or. 1992).

5. A court must accept an unconditional plea, so long as the Rule 11(b) requirements are met. The existence of a plea agreement is irrelevant. *Vasquez-Ramirez v. United States District Court of the Southern District of California,* 443 F.3d 692 (9th Cir. 2006). "By refusing to accept Vasquez's guilty plea, the district judge is trying to force the government to pursue a charge it does not wish to press ... this intrudes too far into the executive function."

6. (a) Wince. A plea agreement is not enforceable until the court has accepted it. Thus, the prosecutor would be able to walk away from this agreement. A motion to compel specific performance would be unavailing.

   (b) Now the facts have changed. Barbara has acted in reliance on the agreement; it is unlikely that she would have put herself at risk by wearing the wire had she not anticipated that the prosecutor would conform with the agreement. In such a situation, the courts are much more willing to enforce her expectations and require specific performance. But don't wait until the judicial hearing to raise your concerns. Immediately call the prosecutor and remind him of the law on the matter. If you have an ongoing relationship with the prosecutor, and represent many clients, you will probably stop there. If, however, this is a one-time appearance, you might in passing mention the prosecutor's superior, or the disciplinary review board. But prepare your papers to compel specific performance on June 25.

   (c) Although prosecutors may seek to vacate agreements on the basis of nonperformance, there is no reason to allow them to overturn the agreement because of a misapprehension of the underlying facts. Barbara has performed the contract, and it has now been accepted by the court. Finality requires no further inquiry.

   (d) This is really tricky. It's not a legal issue, but a practical one. If Barbara refuses to testify, the prosecution will argue that she did not "cooperate" as the agreement required, and that she is, therefore, in breach, and the sentence should be vacated. This will require the court to decide what the words "cooperate" and "pursue" meant, and the extent to which the obligation extended past the judgment. After all, the state *could* have used the term "including testifying." As a general position, courts in earlier times construed plea agreements against the state, who generally drafted them, and often proffered them on a "take it or leave it" basis. In recent times, however, when both sides negotiate not only about the shape of the undertakings, but the specific wordings, this may be less likely. You may lose this argument — unless you could persuade the court that the prosecutor's new request is merely a gambit intended to manipulate you to refuse to cooperate, so that it could move to vacate.

7. (a) Reynaldo may be right, but there is no relief for him. Nothing in current law requires the court, or anyone else, to tell Reynaldo of the sentencing policies in the state. While the court did inform Reynaldo of the maximum he faced on the one count, there is no legal duty to inform Reynaldo of the sentence he "might have" obtained had he not entered the charge bargain. The courts depend on defense counsel to be aware of these policies, and to tell clients of those policies. Unless counsel's failure to know about these policies — and to tell Reynaldo about them — is ineffective assistance of counsel (see Chapter 11), Reynaldo has learned a good lesson, but he'll still be in prison. Ironically, this is one instance where defendants with public defenders may be in a better situation than those with retained counsel — the latter, unless doing exclusively criminal practice, are likely to be less informed than the former about sentencing or parole board practices, just as they may be less informed about the sentencing proclivities of individual judges.

This problem is not limited to concurrency. In many sentencing systems, particularly those not using "guidelines" (see Chapter 12), many crimes have sentences that overlap. For example, robbery may be punished by 5-20 years, and larceny by 3-10 years. If the practice within the jurisdiction is to sentence "robbers" to six years, a defendant who obtains a charge bargain from a robbery to a larceny charge may still receive the same six-year sentence that he would have received without the reduced charge, and hence without the bargain. Again, nothing in decisions about plea bargains requires the prosecutor or the court to familiarize defendants, or their counsel, with these vagaries. (The problem can be even more exacerbated; in "individualized" sentencing schemes, individual judges may vary widely in their sentencing philosophies: Judge A may impose prison terms of five years for crimes for which Judge B typically imposes probation. See Chapter 11.) Again, there is no constitutional rule for disclosing these practices in order for a plea to be "knowing and intelligent."

(b) This strengthens the argument that counsel was ineffective; even if an attorney is not required to be aware of "practices," he might be required to know statutory law. But it is still unlikely that there is relief for Reynaldo for two reasons: (1) the statute does not *mandate* concurrent sentences, so Reynaldo *did* get some benefit — the elimination of the risk (however slight) of consecutive sentences; (2) even if the statute did mandate concurrency, this one failure of counsel, however important to Reynaldo, is unlikely to mean that the entire representation was inadequate. Again, see Chapter 11.

(c) Although the federal rule, and many state rules, require the court to inform the defendant about "special parole" policies, which generally attach *after* full service of a prison term, courts do not require information about parole *practices*, whether informal or statutory. Thus, for example, many states in the 1990s statutorily precluded parole eligibility for "violent offenders" until they had served more than 80 percent of their sentence. Defendants, or their attorneys, who were unaware of these changes, or who had served time under more lenient standards, were sometimes stunned to discover the new ineligibility rules. But that didn't make their pleas invalid, and rarely resulted in a finding of inadequacy of counsel.

8. (a) This question *really* belongs back in Chapter 3, but it is tied in to plea bargaining, as subsection (b) indicates. At this point, defense counsel is in a quandary. You could let sleeping prosecutors alone; it is *possible* that the prosecutor is not targeting Lie, but that an inquiry, however discreet, might alert the state to such an idea. On the other hand, particularly in light of the ban against plea bargaining, you want to cut the indictment off at the pass, minimize the harm it might do, or get a "non-fraud" count. You could call the prosecutor and offer your client's testimony — if he is a target, the prosecutor should tell you that. And Ken's willingness to present his side of the case may be appreciated. It is probably too early to begin asking for immunity, but you should be sensitive to that possibility as your discussion with the prosecution progresses.

   (b) Here's the bargaining issue. You know that once Lie is indicted, it will be extremely difficult to bargain with the prosecutor, whether over charge or sentence. Your job as counsel now is to bargain over the possible facts — and hence the likely charge — *before* the indictment is issued. You might, for example, seek to persuade the prosecutor that Lie was only negligent, or reckless, rather than purposeful with regard to the $30 million. This might avoid a charge of "fraud," and result in another charge, which could *then* be bargained, because it is not "fraud." Indeed, you might (with Lie's permission, of course) indicate a willingness to plea directly to such a charge, were that the limit of the indictment. There is often room for good lawyering, even in the most rigid of systems.

9. Be careful when you draft an agreement. The state appellate courts, as well as the federal courts, found the prosecutor's recommendation not in breach of the agreement. *Smith v. Stegall*, 385 F.3d 993 (6th Cir. 2004). The court cited Williston on Contracts, for the rule that the actual intent of the parties is irrelevant when the words of a contract are clear. (Note, also, that this was a federal *habeas corpus* case, in which the defendant succeeds only if he demonstrates that the actions of the state courts upholding the plea violated "clearly established federal law" (see Chapter 13, *infra*).)

10. In jurisdictions that allow judicial involvement in plea negotiations, there is probably no problem here. But in those that forbid, or restrict, such involvement, this is a close question. The balance is between "informing" the defendant (and the prosecutor) of the judge's views of the bargain, and "coercing" defendant into accepting a harsher agreement. Resolution of these issues can often turn on the precise words used by the judge. If, for example, she declares: "You've got to be kidding! There's no way I can let this scumbag out in 10 years," "restrictive" jurisdictions are likely to find this much too coercive, and even "permissive" ones might find the reaction too intense. But many judges in restrictive jurisdictions have learned not to be quite so obvious. The scenarios in this example demonstrate the tension. In (a), the judge has not indicated why the plea is unacceptable to her — it is *possible* that she views the 10 years as too harsh. In (b), it is clear that she thinks the 10-year proposal is questionable, but there is at least the possibility that, at a later time, one or both of the counsel might persuade her that 10 years is a reasonable time. In (c), the Seventh Circuit held although the judge had not actually become involved in the negotiations, the "appearance is one of a deliberate inquiry" by the prosecutor of the judge as to a "reasonable" sentence; the court vacated the guilty plea. *United States v. Kraus*, 137 F.3d 447 (7th Cir. 1998). In (d) the coercion is more blatant — the judge has not only indicated that 10 years is unacceptable, but has articulated a precise sentence she has in mind. In systems such as the federal system, which prohibit *all* involvement, all three are questionable, but the pleas in (b), (c), and (d) are likely to be overturned. In systems such as that endorsed by the ABA, where a judge can comment on a plea already reached and agreed upon, some judicial involvement is acceptable, and only the plea in (d) is likely to be held involuntary.

The Jury

[The jury is] at best . . . the apotheosis of the amateur. Why should anyone think that twelve persons brought in from the street, selected in various ways, for their lack of general ability, should have any special capacity for deciding controversies between persons?

> (Harvard Law School Dean) Irwin Griswold,
> *Harvard Law School Dean's Report* 5-6 (1962-1963)

[It] is a terrible business to mark a man out . . . But it is a thing to which a man can grow accustomed, as he can to other things . . . And the horrible thing about all legal officials, even the best, about all judges, magistrates, barristers, detectives and policemen, is not that they are wicked . . . not that they are stupid . . . it is simply that they have got used to it.

Our civilization has decided . . . that determining the guilt or innocence of men is a thing too important to be trusted to trained men. It wishes for light upon that awful matter, it asks men who know more law than I know . . . When it wants a library catalogued, or the solar system discovered, or any trifle of that kind, it uses up its specialists. But when it wishes anything done which is really serious, it collects twelve of the most ordinary men standing round.

> G. K. Chesterton, *The Twelve Men*, in *Tremendous Trifles* 80 (1922)

A. OVERVIEW

The common American image of a criminal proceeding is that of a jury trial — prosecuted by Jack McCoy and defended by Perry Mason. But, as Chapter 7 demonstrated, most criminal cases are settled by plea bargains;[1] only the rare case goes to trial, and even among those, nearly half are tried "to the bench" rather than by a jury. In England, where the jury originated, jury trials now comprise only 1 percent of all criminal proceedings. Juries are even rarer in the rest of the (non-Commonwealth) world — many European countries employ "mixed panels" consisting of professional judges and one or two laymen, and most countries use exclusively judges. Still, many argue that the most important contribution made by Anglo-American law to jurisprudential thought and practice is the jury, particularly the criminal jury.

The English "created" the jury trial by accident. Of earlier civilizations, only Greece (and to a lesser extent Rome) relied upon a jury system.[2] Pre-conquest England relied primarily on blood feuds to settle scores. As seen in Chapter 4, the Norman conquerors employed "presentment" juries to inform them of suspected crimes and criminals. But the defendant was usually "tried" by "ordeal," such as being submerged in water,[3] being required to carry an extremely hot piece of iron for a certain distance, etc. The ordeal depended on the participation of a priest (for example, to bless the water). When, in 1215, the Pope forbade priests to participate in the process, the King scampered to find a substitute method of assessing guilt. By default, the presentment jury was given that job. And after several centuries, the presentment jury (now known as the grand jury) was separated from the petit (trial) jury.

---

1. These general figures can be misleading. Larger percentages of "serious" offenses appear to be tried to juries. Moreover, even if only 5 percent of all criminal cases are tried to juries, this would still be approximately 45,000 trials per year, state and federal.

2. The change from blood feud to jury is dramatized by Aeschylus, in the Oresteia, when Athena herself establishes the jury to thwart vengeance by the Furies against Orestes.

3. In English jurisprudence, the water was blessed by a priest; and the defendant was thrown into the water, while tied. If the defendant sank, it indicated that the blessed water was willing to receive him, and that he was innocent. If the water rejected him and he floated, he was guilty. Of course, a declaration of innocence might not mean much to a defendant who sank to the bottom of a pond; he might drown before being rescued. Other cultures used water ordeals as well, but (perhaps because the water was not blessed) took the view that sinking meant guilt, while floating meant innocence. See H. Lea, The Ordeal (1866).

I. Jury — Size and Unanimity

The right to a jury trial appeared in all 12 of the written state constitutions predating the Declaration of Independence.[4] It is the only "right" protected in the Constitution itself, as well as in the Bill of Rights. We usually speak of the defendant's "right" to a jury trial. But the government may insist on a jury trial, even if the defendant tries to waive one. E.g., FRCP 23. This suggests that the right is really one of the community as well as one of the defendant. See Laura I. Appleman, The Lost Meaning of the Jury Trial Right, 84 Ind. L.J. 397 (2009). Today, every state constitution except one contains the guarantee. Although at least 10 states guarantee a jury trial for all offenses,[5] the Sixth Amendment[6] does not require juries if the potential sentence is less than six months. *Baldwin v. New York*, 399 U.S. 66 (1969). In *Baldwin*, the Court adopted a "bright line" rule — there is no Sixth Amendment right to a jury trial if the possible punishment is less than six months' imprisonment. Even if the defendant is charged with several minor offenses, whose punishment cumulatively could reach more than six months, the jury right is not activated. *Lewis v. United States*, 518 U.S. 322 (1996).[7] On the other hand, if a conviction carries a severe "collateral consequence" — such as required sexual offender registration — defendant may be entitled to a jury trial under state law. *Fushek v. State*, 183 P.3d 536 (Ariz. 2008).

The *Baldwin* six-month rule contrasts sharply with the rule relating to the right to counsel: Indigent defendants are entitled to appointed counsel if they *actually* face one day of loss of liberty.

Moreover, while we often think of a jury as composed of 12 people, that number is not constitutionally required, although there may be no fewer than six people on a jury.[8] Nor, as a Constitutional matter, must the vote be

---

4. See Alschuler and Deiss, A Brief History of the Criminal Jury in the United States, 61 U. Chi. L. Rev. 867 (1994).
5. For example, W. Va. Const. Art. 3, §14; Wyo. Const. Art. 1 §9. The ABA agrees. See ABA Trial By Jury §15-1.1 (3d ed. 1996).
6. It was only in 1968 that the Supreme Court held that the Sixth Amendment applied to the states. *Duncan v. Louisiana*, 391 U.S. 145 (1968).
7. Originally, juries were required whenever the offense was considered "nonpetty," which carried a connotation of immorality as well as illegality. In *District of Columbia v. Colts*, 282 U.S. 63 (1930), for example, the Court held that a defendant charged with automobile speeding was entitled to a jury trial because the offense would be seen by the community as "reckless" and an act "of such obvious depravity that to characterize it as a petty offense would be to shock the general moral sense."
8. In *Williams v. Florida*, 399 U.S. 78 (1970), the Supreme Court held that a criminal jury could be smaller than 12, calling that number a "historical accident," but most states still require that number in criminal trials. In *Ballew v. Georgia*, 435 U.S. 223 (1977), it drew the line at six, relying on later studies showing that smaller juries: (1) are less able to achieve accurate results; (2) will not be a cross-section; (3) are less likely to foster effective group deliberation; and (4) produce fewer hung juries. ABA Standards, Standard 15-1.1(a) and (b) (1996) recommend 12-person juries, unless the penalty is six months or less.

unanimous. *Apodaca v. Oregon*, 406 U.S. 356 (1972). The fear is that where unanimity is not required, the initial "majority" will simply ignore the "dissenters." Shari Seidman Diamond, Mary R. Rose, and Beth Murphy, Revisiting the Unanimity Requirement: The Behavior of the Non-Unanimous Civil Jury, 100 Nw. U. L. Rev. 201 (2006).

Courts have generally held that jurors need not agree on every fact constituting a crime. *Richardson v. United States*, 526 U.S. 813 (1999). For example, if a defendant is charged with possession of unauthorized credit cards, the jurors need not agree on each credit card, so long as they agree that he possessed some illegal credit cards. *United States v. Lee*, 317 F.3d 26 (1st Cir. 2003). Similarly, where a defendant is charged with "seizing, confining, inveigling, decoying, kidnapping, abducting or carrying away" a victim, the jury need not agree unanimously on which of those actions defendant took, so long as they all agree he took one of those actions. *United States v. Powell*, 226 F.3d 11181 (10th Cir. 2000).

Americans, confident that the "common man" has more "common sense" than any governmental official, see the jury as providing a "safeguard against the corrupt or overzealous prosecutor and against the compliant, biased or eccentric judge." *Duncan v. Louisiana*, 391 U.S. 145, 156 (1968). These words should not be lightly dismissed — judges who have "heard that song before" may be less inclined to listen to each defendant's tune. And prosecutors, perhaps touched by "cognitive bias," may move too hastily in prosecuting those they "know" are guilty. Juries, said Justice Scalia, serve as the "circuit breaker in the state's machinery of justice." *Blakely v. Washington*, 542 U.S. 296 (2004).

2. Jury Nullification

This trust in the criminal jury has historically been cemented by the concept of "nullification" — that the jury may ignore the law, and acquit the defendant regardless of the evidence. This power is confirmed by the inability of a prosecutor to appeal an acquittal (see Chapter 9). Over three hundred years ago, in *Bushell's Case*, Vaughn 125, 6 Howell's State Trials 999 (1670), the jury, sitting in a prosecution against William Penn for what was essentially political activism, refused to convict. The trial judge, obviously annoyed, "attainted" them by sending several of them (literally) "to the Tower," without food or water, where they could "reconsider" their verdict. On a writ of *habeas corpus*, they were released, and the power of the jury to render a verdict of acquittal on any grounds was affirmed. The doctrine of "nullification," however, has been eroded. While the jury retains that power in the twenty-first century, it is no longer instructed, as it was centuries ago, that it has that power. Indeed, the decisions are now clear that a juror who concedes, upon voir dire, that he will not follow the law, may be excused for cause;[9] if he is empaneled, but later refuses to deliberate because he opposes the law,[10] he may be removed from the jury.[11]

B. SELECTING A JURY

In a nonurban, agricultural society, finding impartial jurors would often be left to an official who relied upon his personal contacts around the area — a system known as the "key man" approach to selecting juries. That system, which was used by some federal courts as late as 1968,[12] persists today in a number of states and localities, and has never been declared unconstitutional. In most jurisdictions today, however, the process of jury selection is highly computerized.

The image of the jury as "representative" of the general populace has long permeated legal and popular literature. But it is misleading at best. At the time of the Revolution, jury service was restricted to white, property-owning males. For almost the next two centuries, that changed little (consider that the most famous film about juries, made in the mid-1950s, is titled Twelve Angry MEN).[13] Then, in the late 1960s, major changes occurred. Congress enacted the Jury Selection and Service Act of 1968, which abolished the key man system, and required a "cross section" of the community. Also in 1968, in Duncan v. Louisiana, 391 U.S. 1435 (1968), the Supreme Court held the Sixth Amendment criminal jury requirement applicable to the states, ushering in federal oversight of state jury processes. Ironically, as

---

9. United States v. Samat, 207 F. Supp. 2d 259 (S.D.N.Y. 2002).

10. In Bushell's Case, the jury opposed the law. And it is that kind of case where the power has been used most frequently — in Prohibition cases, and prosecutions brought under the Fugitive Slave Acts — juries rebelled. But there are other kinds of "nullifications"; for example, where the jury likes the law, but (a) disagrees with its application to this kind of case (euthanasia prosecutions); (b) disagrees with its application to this particular defendant; (c) wants to send a message to "the authorities"; or (d) thinks the punishment is too severe.

11. People v. Williams, 25 Cal. 4th 441, 21 P.3d 1209, 106 Cal. Rptr. 2d 295 (2001). A year later, a majority of the California Supreme Court held that a jury instruction requiring jurors to inform the judge if any juror refuses to deliberate or expresses an intention to disregard the law should no longer be given. People v. Engelman, 28 Cal. 4th 436, 49 P.3d 209 (2002). There is voluminous literature on nullification. For a beginning, see Nancy S. Marder, The Myth of the Nullifying Jury, 93 Nw. U.L. Rev. 877 (1999).

12. Note, 57 B.U.L. Rev. 198, 216 (1977) citing Sen. Rep. No. 891, 90th Cong., 1st Sess. (1968).

13. Until 1957, the federal jury criteria copied that of the state in which the district court was located. Since many states precluded minorities, or women, or many others, from jury service, that also obtained in the federal system. In addition, to the extent that jury service was based upon voting registration, devices used to prevent minorities from voting (the Nineteenth Amendment handled this problem for women) also precluded them from serving on juries.

the opportunity to serve on juries has increased, the number of jury trials has decreased almost everywhere.

1. Determining the "District"

Obtaining 12 people from a population of (hundreds of) thousands is a daunting task. First, the relevant area must be determined: Is it a "city area" (e.g., the "Village" in New York City), a "city," a "county," a "metropolitan area," or some other area? The Sixth Amendment requires that the jury be selected from the "district" in which the crime occurred, but does not define that term. Lines drawn for other (usually political) purposes are used as a default. But suppose a "district" consists of well-defined, different areas, in which different racial or class groups live, and the crime involves a white defendant accused of injuring a black victim, in a "white" area of the "district." Should the jury be drawn from the "white" area, or from the entire "district"? This question often arises in cases where a defendant seeks a change of venue, arguing that the "local" jury would be impassioned against him. Indeed, in the Rodney King case, discussed in Chapter 9, where several white Los Angeles police officers were charged with assault on a black driver, the change of venue from Los Angeles (where the jury would have been significantly racially diverse) to another locale (where the jury was virtually all white) was highly controversial, particularly after the officers were acquitted. A subsequent federal trial, which employed a jury from a (more or less) wider Los Angeles area, resulted in a conviction. Whether that was due to the jury composition, of course, was hotly debated.

2. Determining the "Pool"

Once the "district" has been determined, jurisdictions may rely on many "source lists" to locate persons living there to create a jury "pool" (also referred to as an "array," "master list," or "jury list"). Most states employ voting registration lists, often supplemented by motor vehicle registration lists. Challenges arguing that these lists are too narrow, because many persons either do not register or are not eligible to vote, and many do not own cars, particularly in inner-city areas, have been unsuccessful. See Nancy J. King, Racial Jurymandering: Cancer or Cure, 68 N.Y.U. L. Rev. 707 (1993).[14]

---

14. Many countries use voting lists, including Russia, Ireland, Scotland, and Spain. Stephen C. Thaman, Europe's New Jury Systems: The Cases of Spain and Russia, 62 Law & Contemp. Probs. 233, 239 (1999).

3. Constructing the Wheel

Once a pool is established, officials select the number of persons who will be needed within the next (month; year) to serve on juries in the vicinage, and contact them — "summoning" them to jury duty. This creates the "wheel" (or "venire").

Once summoned,[15] people in the wheel may avoid jury duty if they are (1) exempt; or (2) excused. *Exemptions* usually reflect legislative judgments that as a matter of public policy, whole classes of individuals — law enforcement officers, firefighters, teachers, doctors (military personnel are exempted by federal statute from serving in state juries) — perform sufficiently important public service that outweighs jury duty. Others (such as lawyers) are so likely to be challenged for cause or peremptorily (see below), it is sometimes thought it would waste everyone's time to summon them.[16] As a general matter, statutory exemptions have not been attacked as unduly political and hence non-policy based, although some of these (game wardens, for example) might be problematic.[17] In *Taylor v. Louisiana*, 419 U.S. 522 (1975), the Supreme Court invalidated a state process by which women who sought to serve on juries had to write expressly to the jury commissioners to be placed on the jury wheel, while men were automatically kept on the jury wheel. In effect, the statute exempted women, while requiring men to serve.[18]

In contrast to exemptions, *excuses* are usually temporary, and are individually based. If service would create hardship, either physical or economic, an individual may be excused from jury duty until the hardship ceases. Thus, if Darryl is currently tending an infant, and cannot afford a sitter, he may be excused until the infant reaches school age (or some similar point in time).[19] But he will not be forever excused, as would be a police officer.

---

15. Federal law provides for a possible fine of $1000, 3 days imprisonment and community service, any combination of these possible punishments, for failure to respond to a summons to serve on a federal jury.

16. Many states have now rejected this view, but it is not obviously so irrational as to invalidate a legislative decision to that effect.

17. An early case upheld, as against a general due process claim, the exemption of lawyers, doctors, preachers, and firemen, among others. *Rawlins v. Georgia*, 201 U.S. 638 (1906).

18. As of 2004, 25 states had no exemptions from jury service. Bureau of Justice Statistics, State Court Organization 2004 (2006), available at http:www.ojp.usdoj.gov/.bjs/pub/pdf/sco04.pdf.

19. In Iowa, a person "solely responsible for daily care of a permanently disabled person in their home" is exempt. In New Jersey, a person who has "obligations to care for a sick, aged, or infirm dependent or a minor child" is exempt.

4. Composing the Wheel

a. The Cross-Section Requirement

Although it is common to speak of a "jury of one's peers," that is not the language of the Sixth Amendment, which provides only that the jury must be "impartial." In *Taylor, supra,* the Court held that the term required a "*cross section of the community*" to be present on the wheel. Any procedure which results in the exclusion of any "cognizable" (also referred to as "distinctive") group, such as women, violated that right. This requirement seeks to assure that different perspectives, values, and norms, constitutive of the community, will be reflected in the jury's moral determination that the defendant should be criminally sanctioned and stigmatized for his act.

b. What Is the "Community"?

The term "community" is not used in the Sixth Amendment, and the issue of what constitutes "the community" has seldom been litigated. It has been said that it usually means a previously defined geographical area, as in the "district" specifically referred to in the text of the Sixth Amendment. *United States v. Grisham,* 63 F.3d 1074 (11th Cir. 1995). But, of course, that area may have been defined for other reasons, having nothing to do with a "community" as that term is used in casual conversation. See *Davis v. Warden,* 867 F.2d 1003 (7th Cir. 1989) ("county lines or federal district lines do not magically determine the parameters of a community").

c. Defining "Cognizable Groups"

Defining "cognizable groups" has consumed much judicial energy. In *Lockhart v. McCree,* 476 U.S. 162, 174 (1986), the Court expressly declared that it had "never attempted to precisely define the term 'distinctive group' and we do not undertake to do so today." In *Taylor,* the Court declared that the partial exclusion of women meant that "a flavor, a distinct quality" is lost from deliberations. Since there is no reason to think that men and women would disagree on finding facts (whether the light was red or green), the difference is experiential; that is, what is the meaning, the normative impact, of the determination that the light was (red/green) when the defendant ran it? Such normative assessments vary with life experiences, and it is assumed that members of cognizable groups, because of their homogeneity, have life experiences different than those not of that group.[20] Other courts have used different words, but aim at the same

---

20. The concept of a "cross section" underscores the entire notion of a jury — that all citizens, from whatever background, can properly sit in judgment of a specific defendant, even if

idea: e.g., *Barber v. Ponte*, 772 F.2d 982 (1st Cir. 1985) ("a common thread or basic similarity in attitude, ideas, or experience run through the group"). Clearly, women, men, racial groups, ethnic groups — all those referred to in equal protection cases as "suspect" classifications — readily fit within the notion of cognizable group. One commentator has used this definition:

> They share (1) an attribute that defines and limits the group; (2) a common attitude, idea, or experience that distinguishes the group from other segments of society; (3) a "community of interests" that the jury pool would not adequately reflect if it excluded members of the group.

Mitchell S. Zuklie, Rethinking the Fair-Cross Section Requirement, 84 Cal. L. Rev. 101, 102 (1996).

Finding groups whose members' outlooks and experiences are so unique that only they can represent those experiences is extraordinarily difficult. If different perspectives is the key to "cognizability," are card-carrying members of the ACLU sufficiently different from other civil rights organizations as to constitute a "unique" perspective? What about members of the NRA?[21] Arguably, their perspectives can be replicated by many others who do not belong to those organizations; hence they do not bring a "unique" set of values or experiences to the jury. Indeed, if pressed, this test seems unworkable. Assuming, for example, that one reason for defining groups as cognizable is that they have suffered discrimination, can one presume that blacks have suffered a "different" discrimination than "women," who have been discriminated against differently than Jews, or Baptists, or homosexuals?

In *Lockhart*, the Court suggested that the key was whether there was an "immutable characteristic" that was not "within the individual's control." This dictum, however, seems inconsistent with the Court's earlier emphasis on the different perspectives that a group might bring to the jury's determinative process. In *Thiel v. Southern Pacific Co.*, 328 U.S. 217 (1946), the Court, in its supervisory power, invalidated a process by which persons who earned daily wages, rather than fixed salaries, were excluded from the jury. Neither Italian Americans (*United States v. Bucci*, 839 F.2d 825 (1st Cir.

(perhaps, especially if) they are not familiar with his culture. This is in stark contrast to the early English practice, where there were "mixed juries" in which certain groups, including merchants, aliens, and Jews, were guaranteed to have peers on the jury. See Marianne Constable, The Law of the Other (U. of Chicago Press 1994). The Code of Military Justice allows an enlisted soldier to demand that at least one enlisted person serve on his jury for a court martial.

21. In *Robar v. LaBuda*, 2011 WL 584842 (N.Y.A.D. 3 Dept.), a trial judge had found that hunters were a protected group under the equal protection clause because they were exercising their Second Amendment rights. The appellate court rejected that proposition. While this is not quite the same as a "cognizable group," the decision is worth reading.

1988)); nor Irish Americans (Murchu (aka Murphy) v. United States, 916 F.2d 50 (1st Cir. 1991)) constitute a cognizable group.

There are some clear limits to *Taylor.* The Court declared there, and has reaffirmed since,[22] that the cross-section requirement reaches only the jury wheel, and not the specific petit jury that tries the defendant.[23] Thus, there is no constitutional duty that the state affirmatively provide methods to ensure a cross-section, on either the venire or the petit jury.[24]

d. Equal Protection versus the Sixth Amendment

The Court's reliance on the Sixth Amendment in *Taylor* is critical to understanding later decisions. Under Sixth Amendment doctrine, the only question is whether a specific group was adversely affected by the state's selection process: *There is no requirement that the defendant demonstrate a discriminatory intent.* In *Taylor,* no state official prevented women from volunteering for jury service, and there was no evidence that the legislature intended to exclude women from such service. In *Duren v. Missouri,* 439 U.S. 357 (1979), in which women were placed on the jury wheel, but could "opt out," the system was even less likely to deter female participation in the jury system. Nevertheless, the *Duren* Court declared: "[I]n Sixth Amendment fair cross-section cases, systematic disproportion itself demonstrates an infringement on the defendant's interest in a jury chosen from a fair cross-section."

A second distinction between equal protection and Sixth Amendment doctrine is that the notion of a "cognizable group" is (at least in theory) much broader than that in other legal areas, most importantly in equal protection law, where only "suspect classifications" are given special protection. Thus, a group may be "cognizable" and protected against exclusion under the Sixth Amendment, but not "suspect" and protected against intentional discrimination under the equal protection clause. One important area where this might make a difference is religion. Various religious sects, particularly cults, might well be "cognizable" and their preclusion from the jury wheel violative of the Sixth Amendment. But that same group might not be "suspect" under equal protection doctrine. In recent years, however, the courts seem to have merged the two definitions, such that only

---

22. See *Lockhart, supra; Buchanan v. Kentucky,* 483 U.S. 402 (1987).
23. The Court in *Lockhart, supra* at 183 said, albeit in a different context, that to apply *Taylor* to petit juries would involve what it called "the Sisyphean task of . . . making sure that each (petit jury) contains the proper number of Democrats and Republicans, young persons and old persons, white-collar executives and blue-collar laborers, and so on."
24. Some jurisdictions, however, have sought to establish such processes. Thus, DeKalb County, Georgia, divided its entire population into thirty-six categories (e.g., "white male 35-44," "black female, 18-24"). The computer fills the quotas by a random draw from the list of registered voters in the various categories.

groups who are "suspect" under the equal protection clause will be considered "cognizable" under the Sixth Amendment.

The distinction was the key to *Holland v. Illinois*, 493 U.S. 474 (1990). The Court had held in *Batson* (see p. 185) that the *equal protection clause* prohibited discriminatory use of a peremptory challenge at the trial level. Yet *Holland* resisted a Sixth Amendment challenge to peremptories, emphasizing that the Sixth Amendment went only to the venire and not to the actual trial jury.

e. Measuring Disproportionate Representation

Determining that a "cognizable group" is involved is only the beginning of the issue. The defendant must still demonstrate that the process used by the state resulted in a *disproportionate* underrepresentation of that group in the jury venire. There are two main methods to measure (dis)proportionality: absolutely and comparatively. Assume that women are 50 percent of the population, but only constitute 10 percent of the venire. There is an *absolute* disproportion of 40 percent (50 percent — 10 percent). But compared to the percentage they should constitute (50 percent), they are only 20 percent (10/50) represented. The *comparative disproportion* is thus 80 percent. The difference is critical in groups that form only small percentages of the relevant population. Suppose, for example, that dwarfs were considered a "cognizable group," but only constituted .5 percent of the population. Even a total exclusion would result in only .5 percent under representation under the first method, but a 100 percent under representation using the second approach. For this reason, some courts have suggested that a group must be "reasonably large" to be cognizable.

In *Berghuis v. Smith*, 559 U.S. 314 (2010), the Court reviewed the various tests of disparity and found that each was "imperfect" and that the Court "would have no cause to take sides today on the method or methods by which under representation is appropriately measured." The case involved a county where 7.28 percent of the eligible population but only 6 percent of the jury pool were African Americans. The absolute disparity was therefore 1.28 percent, but the comparative disparity was 18 percent. Neither was sufficient for relief.

f. State Response to a *Prima Facie* Case of Discrimination

To defeat a *prima facie* case, the state has to show a "significant state interest that is manifestly and primarily advanced" by the jury selection scheme. Thus, the state could have argued in *Taylor* that it was concerned with allowing mothers to remain home with their children. The problem, of course, is that even if one believed that was the real purpose of the statute, and that the goal was laudable, the statutory means was both under- and overinclusive.

Thus, non-mother females were still given preferential treatment, while child-caring fathers were "forced" to go on jury duty and others who were responsible for the care of the helpless were not similarly protected. (See n.19 for the current language used by some states to be more specific about the goal.) On the other hand, under the Sixth Amendment, even if the exclusion is done for a beneficent purpose, the impact, and not the intent, is the key. In *Thiel*, for example, the Court deemed it irrelevant that the jury commissioner was well intentioned in allowing persons who would lose daily wages if chosen as jurors to avoid jury duty.

5. The Venire — From Potential Service to Juror

Once the wheel is chosen, the number of persons necessary to serve in the next relevant period of time will be summoned to court. Two further and highly controversial steps are involved: (1) *challenges for cause*; and (2) *peremptory challenges*. Both these mechanisms, based upon perceived characteristics of individual jurors, depend on information which the attorneys glean from two sources: (1) voir dire; and (2) pre-trial questionnaires or similar items.

a. Voir Dire — Establishing Information for Challenges

Voir dire[25] is the public[26] process by which jurors are asked questions about themselves to assist the court and the attorneys in intelligently exercising both kinds of challenges. Voir dire was initially conducted by attorneys, but in many jurisdictions it is now conducted primarily by judges, because both sides used the process not only to ferret out information about the members of the jury panel, but also to "indoctrinate" them about their view

---

25. In England, Ireland, and several other countries, voir dire, and the concomitant challenge for cause, have been abolished; the first 12 people seated are the jury. This extreme animosity to "cause" strikes is exemplified by M. v. H.M. *Advocate*, 1974 S.L.T. (Notes) 25 (H.C.J), as discussed in Peter Duff, The Scottish Criminal Jury: A Very Peculiar Institution, 62 L. & Contemp. Probs. 173 (1999). The defendants were alleged terrorists. The trial judge, responding to a request by defense counsel, asked whether any juror had lost any near relatives in the religious and political disturbances in Northern Ireland. The appellate court chastised the judge, declaring, "[There] should be no general questioning of persons cited for possible jury service to ascertain whether any of them could or should be excused from jury service in a particular trial . . . The essence of the system of trial by jury is that it consists of 15 individuals chosen at random from amongst those who are cited for possible service . . . It is not a sufficient excuse for a juror to be excused that he . . . might or might not feel prejudice one way or the other towards the crime itself or the background against which the crime has been committed." But if the juror has a personal connection with one of the parties, or has personal knowledge of the facts, he will be excused by *the court clerk*, usually *before* he is called to the jury box.

26. The public may not be excluded during voir dire of the jury. Presley v. Georgia, 558 U.S. 209 (2010).

of the case.[27] Attorneys argue that judges, who are unfamiliar with the facts of the case, and who are interested in moving the case along, are too cursory in voir dire.[28]

There is virtually no law on the kind of questions which judges "must" or "may" ask; in the run-of-the-mill case, this is left virtually to the discretion of the judge. The sole exception to this rule occurs where there is a possibility of racial bias, usually in a case involving interracial violence, in which case the court's discretion is much more limited. In *Ham v. South Carolina*, 409 U.S. 524 (1973), a black civil rights activist, charged with possession of marijuana, asked the judge to inquire about the jurors' potential racial bias. On appeal of his conviction, the Supreme Court held that in such instances exploration of racial animosity was required. Not surprisingly, this was later applied to a murder case involving the murder of a white victim allegedly by the (black) defendant. *Turner v. Murray*, 476 U.S. 28 (1986).

In death penalty cases, the judge will ask a potential juror about his views of the death penalty. In *Witherspoon v. Illinois*, 391 U.S. 510 (1968), the Court seemed to say that a juror could be removed only if his opposition was "unmistakably clear," but *Wainwright v. Witt*, 469 U.S. 412 (1985), adopted a less demanding standard — whether the juror's views would "prevent or substantially impair the performance of his duties as a juror." In *Uttecht v. Brown*, 551 U.S. 1 (2007), the Court appeared to make it even easier for the state to remove a "problem" juror, when it emphasized that substantial deference had to be given to the trial judge's discretionary determination to bar a potential juror because of his potential inability to impose the death penalty.[29] The case, however, may be narrow, since it was on *habeas corpus*, rather than on direct review. (See Chapter 13.) Of course, the standard works both ways — the defendant may inquire whether the juror would automatically impose the death penalty upon a defendant found guilty of capitally eligible murder. *Morgan v. Illinois*, 504 U.S. 719 (1992). These decisions seem to assume that a person's position on the death penalty would carry over to her decision on the guilt-innocence question; indeed, many commentators believe that a "death-qualified" jury is more prone to finding

---

27. One of the leading studies of the jury, H. Zeisel, H. Kalven, Jr., and B. Buchhol, Delay in Court, 103 note 9 (2d ed. 1978), concluded that half the time allotted to voir dire was used to prepare the jury for the case.

28. Voir dire is not the only method by which the parties may obtain information on the potential jurors. If the names and addresses are given to the parties beforehand, each side may attempt to investigate the jurors' background. Rule 421 of the Uniform Rules of Criminal Procedure requires the prosecutor to share information on prospective jurors, subject to the work product rule. Those who have read John Grisham's *Runaway Jury*, or seen the movie, should be assured that it is fiction, not reality, not even in the most intense trial.

29. Observers have noted the irony that, as more jurors become skeptical about the death penalty, based in part upon DNA and other "scientifically founded" exonerations, *Uttecht* will narrow the death-qualified jury even more.

a defendant guilty, but the Court has held that even a conclusive showing that this were true would not be relevant. *Lockhart v. McCree*, 476 U.S. 162 (1986).

b. Voir Dire and Juror Privacy

Jurors are citizens who have been summarily required to disrupt their lives and appear in public. Answering any question may be embarrassing in the unfamiliar surroundings of a courtroom. Surveys of jurors find that even relatively typical questions — what kind of newspapers they read, what bumper stickers they have — may strike them as invasive of their privacy. A gambling addict will be loathe to admit in open court, or even *in camera*, that he has such an addiction; but if the case involves a defendant charged with embezzling funds to feed his gambling habit, may the defendant's "right to know" outweigh the juror's right to privacy? What about a questionnaire that asks whether the juror has ever had an abortion? In one instance, a potential juror called an attorney; she was concerned that if she told the truth (she had had an abortion as a teenager), her family would find out, and that if she lied, she could face perjury charges. Molly McDonouogh, Rogue Jurors, ABA J., Oct. 2006, pp. 39, 42. Some courts have answered that jurors have such a privacy right to resist such questions (*United States v. McDade*, 929 F. Supp. 815 (E.D. Pa. 1996)), but in most jurisdictions this is an unresolved issue.[30] See David Weinstein, Protecting a Juror's Right to Privacy: Constitutional Constraints and Policy Options, 70 Temp. L. Rev. 1 (1997).

New technology has invaded the selection process. Some lawyers now come to jury selection with a phalanx of paralegals to run each potential juror's name through a variety of social media searches in real time. See Stephanie West, Lawyer Uses Web to Sort Through Jury Pool, ABA J. July 1, 2010. In one recent (civil) case in New Jersey, defense counsel objected that opposing counsel was conducting Internet searches on the jurors during voir dire. Not wanting to afford the web-surfing lawyer an unfair advantage, the trial judge ordered the attorney to close his laptop. The New Jersey Appellate Division found that the trial judge had abused his discretion in preventing counsel's use of the Internet. *Carino v. Muenzen*, 2010 WL 3448071 (N.J. App. Div.).[31]

---

30. Georgia Code Ann. §59-125(b) (1996) expressly provides: "In the questionnaire and during voir dire, judges should ensure that the privacy of prospective jurors is reasonably protected."

31. There have been reports that lawyers vet jurors on Facebook, MySpace, and other such social media. Phillip Anthony and Christine Martin, Social Media go to Court, Nat'l. L.J. (Feb. 2, 2009).

c. Challenges for Cause

Challenges for cause, as the term suggests, allow either side to remove a potential juror whose background, familiarity with the defendant, the witnesses, or the attorneys involved, or who, for some other reason, creates an impression that he or she might be less than impartial. Because the Sixth Amendment guarantees an "impartial" jury, there is no limit to the number of challenges for cause either side may seek, and the judge may grant. There are two "kinds" of bias upon which a challenge for cause may be based — *implied bias* and *actual bias*. Whether to allow a challenge for cause is within the discretion of the trial judge, and will be overturned only for an abuse of that discretion. *Mu'Min v. Virginia*, 500 U.S. 415 (1991). Moreover, even when a potential juror appears to be subject to a cause challenge, trial judges will often "rehabilitate" him by asking whether, notwithstanding the problematic situation, the juror could try the case fairly. Thus, suppose that Eric, a potential juror, opines that he is inclined to disbelieve drug addicts (of whom the defendant or a witness is one). The judge may ask him, "But you could overcome that concern and give this defendant, in front of you, a fair trial, couldn't you?" When Eric, either genuinely, or because he fears judicial wrath if he responds negatively, acquiesces, he has been rehabilitated, and a subsequent appeal on the basis that he should have been removed for cause is very likely to be unsuccessful.

The presence of peremptory challenges, discussed below, has undermined any attempt to fully explicate the law regarding challenges for cause; if the "injured party" feels strongly enough about a dubious juror, the courts appear to reason, he can always use a peremptory challenge to remove him. Moreover, while some courts hold that the loss of one peremptory in order to strike a juror who should have been removed for cause is itself automatic grounds for reversal, others subject the loss to a harmless error analysis.[32]

What *should* be grounds for challenge? Grounds for cause are often listed by statute, which often include a "catch all" provision allowing a challenge if there is "reasonable ground to believe that a juror cannot render a fair and impartial verdict," Ariz. R. Crim. P. 18.4. It is under this last rubric that most issues about cause arise.

The most common sources of (nonstatutory) potential bias are: (1) relationship with one of the parties (or their attorneys);[33] (2) prior experiences (such as being a victim of crime, particularly if the crime was similar to the one at issue); (3) prior knowledge of the case. While

---

32. William T. Pizzi and Morris B. Hoffman, Jury Selection Errors on Appeal, 38 Am. Crim. L. Rev. 1391 (2001).

33. Florida Stat. §913.02 lists 12 grounds for cause. On the other hand, there are — believe it or not — instances where a juror related to the trial judge has served; all result in reversal. *State v. Tody*, 316 Wis.2d 689 (Wis. 2009) (judge's mother); *Elmore v. State*, 355 Ark. 620 (2004) (judge's spouse); *People v. Hartson*, 553 N.Y.S.2d 537 (1990) (same).

none of these is a *per se* disqualifier, it is likely that a court will probe more deeply here than elsewhere — although even here courts attempt to rehabilitate the juror.

The case law on what might constitute cause is very fact-specific and hopelessly confused, for several reasons. Most importantly, whether the trial judge has upheld or denied a challenge, her decision will be reversible only if there was an "abuse of discretion" and harm to the defendant. Thus, one judge may deny a challenge based upon a potential juror's prior law enforcement background, while a second would uphold the same challenge, and neither decision would be overturned on appeal.

Appellate judges are reluctant to overturn a verdict and require a new trial; even the presence of a juror who has mislead the court in answering a voir dire question will not result in a new trial. *McDonough Power Equipment, Inc. v. Greenwood*, 464 U.S. 548 (1984), even though intentionally false answers may result in a criminal conviction. *Clark v. United States*, 289 U.S. 1 (1933). For example, a juror in a sexual assault case did not mention that she had been "almost" assaulted by an uncle when she was young. The trial court's refusal to remove her when this was disclosed was upheld on appeal on the grounds that: (1) her nondisclosure was not intentional; (2) her past experience was not similar to the crime in question; (3) she conscientiously made her past experience known; (4) other jurors were not influenced by that event. *People v. Kelly*, 185 Cal. App. 3d 118, 229 Cal. Rptr. 184 (1986).

The fact that a juror is employed by the government is not automatic grounds for a cause challenge. *Dennis v. United States*, 339 U.S. 162 (1950). Nor is a juror who is seeking a job with the prosecutor's office barred solely for that reason. *Smith v. Phillips*, 455 U.S. 209 (1982). Similarly, appellate courts have upheld the decision of trial courts not to remove for cause (1) in a rape trial, a psychiatric social worker who counseled rape victims;[34] or (2) an acquaintance of the victim of the crime.[35] On the other hand, a Minnesota court has held that potential jurors who believe that police officers are more truthful than others should be removed for cause. *State v. Logan*, 535 N.W.2d 320 (Minn. 1995).[36]

---

34. *Tinsley v. Borg*, 895 F.2d 520 (9th Cir. 1990).

35. *Fleming v. State*, 269 Ga. 245, 497 S.E.2d 211 (1998); *Sander v. Commw.*, 801 S.W.2d 665 (Ky. 1990).

36. Far more numerous are those cases in which courts have refused to find bias. See, e.g., *Jones v. Cooper*, 311 F.3d 306 (4th Cir. 2002) (finding no implied bias where a juror stated that several of her relatives had been subjected to arrests or jury trials; that she had gone to the store at which the crime occurred the day after the murder and robbery; that she had strong, religiously motived views in favor of the death penalty; and that she knew that the defendant had previously received a death sentence); *United States v. Tucker*, 243 F.3d 499 (8th Cir. 2001) (rejecting the defendant's allegations that a juror was presumptively biased against him because the defendant, who had previously been governor of Arkansas, had denied clemency to the juror's husband, a prison inmate).

i. Pre-Trial Publicity as a Ground for Cause

In "high profile" cases, defendants will often seek a change of venue on the basis that the publicity has severely compromised local jurors' ability to decide impartially. If they lose that motion, they will nevertheless seek to challenge jurors individually. Initially, persons subjected to widespread news about a case, or a defendant's prior record, were *presumed* to be prejudiced. Cf. *Marshal v. United States*, 360 U.S. 310 (1959). That, however, has changed, at least where the defendant raises the issue as a constitutional (rather than a supervisory power) issue. See *Murphy v. Florida*, 421 U.S. 794 (1975) (distinguishing between a supervisory case, such as *Marshall*, and constitutional cases, such as *Murphy*).

In *Mu'Min v. Virginia*, 500 U.S. 415 (1991), eight of 12 jurors had learned about the case from media reports or other outside sources. All jurors said on voir dire that they could be impartial. The trial judge denied the defendant's motion to question the jurors *in camera*, and refused to ask about the content of the publicity. The Supreme Court upheld this determination, stressing that these issues were generally left to the discretion of the trial judge. Of course, it is true, as the Supreme Court declared in *Irwin v. Dowd*, 366 U.S. 717 (1961), that "[E]ven a juror who has a 'preconceived notion as to the guilt or innocence of an accused' as a result of pre-trial publicity need not necessarily be excluded from the jury panel . . . if the juror can lay aside his impression or opinion and render a verdict based on the evidence presented in court." But if there is any doubt about the ability of a juror to serve on a particular case, why not remove him? Assuming that he could serve on other cases without difficulty, shouldn't the presumption be in favor of removal, assuming that there are alternate jurors who could replace him?

Empirical research has suggested that voir dire usually cannot identify all of the potential jurors who have been prejudiced by pre-trial publicity; indeed, those jurors may not recognize their own bias. And *Mu'Min* does not require the trial court to question a juror individually about the extent of publicity he may have heard. In *Patton v. Young*, 467 U.S. 1025 (1984), where four years had passed between the publicity and the trial, the Court, in determining that there was no clear evidence of bias, found three factors relevant: (1) the strength of the voir dire responses; (2) the nature of the pre-trial publicity; (3) the time elapsed.

d. Peremptory Challenges

Once the jury venire has been winnowed down by cause challenges, there remains the final step in selecting a jury — *peremptory challenges* — which allows either side to strike potential jurors without assigning any reason. At common law, every felony defendant had 35 peremptory challenges, but today that number is far fewer in most cases, primarily because most felonies do not carry the death penalty. The number of peremptory challenges, in contrast to those for cause, is limited, and determined by statute in every jurisdiction.

When the judge has denied a challenge for cause to a juror, a party is likely to use a peremptory challenge to remove that juror. The parties indulge "hunches" about jurors, theoretically formed on the basis of the information gained during voir dire or through questionnaires. In high-profile cases, each side may hire "jury consultants" who use opinion polls, psychological profiles, body language, and other such information to assist counsel in using these strikes.

Peremptory challenges were originally premised on the belief that intuition and first impressions, which are hard to articulate and certainly do not constitute "cause," are nevertheless valid human reactions. But in the context of a trial, they are perfidious, allowing each party to rely upon stereotypes to remove potential jurors based upon their race, gender, religion, apparent political beliefs, etc. Clarence Darrow, among many other prominent attorneys, painstakingly delineated which jurors the defense should strike:

> You would be guilty of malpractice if you got rid of an Irishman . . . An Englishman is not so good as an Irishman, but still, he has come through a long tradition of individual rights, and is not afraid to stand alone . . . Baptists are more hopeless than the Presbyterians. The Methodists are worth considering; they are nearer the soil. Beware of the Lutherans, especially the Scandinavians; they are almost always sure to convict. As to Unitarians, Universalists, Congregationalists, Jews, and other agnostics, don't ask them too many questions; keep them anyhow, especially Jews and agnostics. Never take a wealthy man on a jury.

Clarence Darrow, Attorney for the Defense, Esquire Magazine, May 1936, pp.36-37.[37]

---

37. F. Lee Bailey and Henry B. Rothblatt, Successful Techniques for Criminal Trials, §§6:41-6:45 (2d Ed, Lawyers Coop. Pub. Co. 1985) states: "It has often been said that persons of Italian, Irish, Jewish, Latin American, and Southern European extraction are more desirable as jurors than people of British, Scandinavian, or German extraction. The latter are presumably more law-abiding, conservative, and strict, with more rigid standards of conduct. Blind adherence to these over-generalized stereotypes can prove dangerous . . . Generally, retired police officers, military men, and their wives are undesirable . . . Salesmen, actors, artists, and writers are highly desirable." Moreover, while attorneys boast that they "can often recognize deep-seated prejudices that remain unspoken and are illegible to others . . . The eyes of a trial lawyer skim over the faces of jurors the way a blind person's fingers glide over the Braille letters of some unfamiliar book, in search of sights that will help him or her make the right choice." Herald P. Fahringer, The Peremptory Challenge: An Endangered Species?, 31 Crim. L. Bull. 400, 404 (1995). See Lara White, The Nonverbal Behaviors in Jury Selection, 31 Crim. L. Bull. 414 (1995): "[S]tudies suggest that the average lawyer does a poor job of discriminating among jurors."

In 1986, the Supreme Court reined in the use of peremptories which appeared to be based solely upon the race of the potential juror. In *Batson v. Kentucky*, 476 U.S. 79 (1986), the Court held that a prosecutor who employed peremptories in such a manner violated the equal protection clause. Later cases have made clear that *Batson* is based on the Fourteenth Amendment and protects the right of the potential juror not to be discriminated against, rather than protecting the Sixth Amendment right of the defendant. *Batson*, therefore, makes no judgment, in the way that *Taylor* does,[38] that persons of one race will systematically have different perspectives or even different approaches than those of another race.

Batson's goal is unquestionably salutary — to remove discrimination in jury selection, in at least one corner of the criminal justice system.[39] Implementation of this goal, however, has created administrative difficulties, and perhaps worse. Had the *Batson* Court relied upon the Sixth Amendment, only the result would have been relevant: If a disproportionate number of a protected group were removed by one side, that would be sufficient to require a remedy. Since the *Batson* Court relied upon the equal protection clause, however, standard doctrine requires the complaining party (since this is usually the defendant, we will use that reference here, but defense counsel, too, are accused of using the race, or gender, card) to prove that the strikes were *intended* to be discriminatory.

The hurdles here are manifold. First, and perhaps not so obviously, how do we know that a given juror (stricken or not) is a member of a suspect class? Is Lucille (Ball) Arnaz (a redheaded white woman of Irish parents) "Latina" because of her last name?[40] Second, what percentage constitutes a "high enough" level to establish a *prima facie* case? Third, what constitutes a "neutral" explanation? Finally, assuming that the explanation is a "neutral" one, on what basis can the trial judge nevertheless disbelieve the attorney, and conclude that the strikes *were* gender-based — and how would that decision be reviewable on appeal?

In *Purkett v. Elem*, 514 U.S. 765, 768 (1995), the Court endorsed a "three-step" procedure by which this proof is to be made:

---

38. Because the premise of *Batson* is equal protection of the juror, even the defendant who removed him might have standing to object to the strike. See *United States v. Huey*, 76 F.3d 638 (5th Cir. 1996).

39. To achieve this goal, the Court has extended *Batson* to cover challenges by the defense, *Georgia v. McColum*, 505 U.S. 42 (1992), all civil matters, *Edmonton v. Louisville Concrete Co.*, 500 U.S. 614 (1991), and gender discrimination. *JEB v. Alabama ex rel. T. B.*, 511 U.S. 127 (1994).

40. How does one show that a potential juror is (or is not) in the protected class? Under Jim Crow laws, "Negro" was statutorily defined as a person with 1/32 negroid blood. Should each juror have to show blood type and history? Are all African Americans "black"? Are all persons from South America "Hispanic"? "Latino"? "Spanish"? See *State v. Alen*, 616 So. 2d 452 (Fla. 1993).

1. The defendant shows a *prima facie* case of discrimination. Usually this is statistical: a showing that the prosecutor used a large percentage of his peremptories to strike, e.g., women, or a showing that a large percentage of the women on the venire were challenged.[41]
2. The prosecutor provides an explanation for the strikes.
3. The Court decides whether the prosecutor's explanation is race (or gender, or ethnic) neutral.[42]

i. Step One — The Prima Facie Case

If an attorney strikes 15 out of 15 women, and no men, from the venire, most would conclude that the statistics alone present a *prima facie* case. But that would be the rare case. What if the attorney has stricken five women (out of eight) and four men (out of 15)? In *Johnson v. California*, 545 U.S. 162 (2005), the Court made clear that a defendant meets the "first step" of a *Batson* challenge if he shows merely an "inference" of intentional discrimination. The Court said that California requirement that the defendant show that prejudice was "more likely than not" was an "inappropriate yardstick" by which to measure the sufficiency of a *prima facie* case.

ii. Step Two — The Neutral Explanation

No one — well, few — will admit to being a bigot, particularly if that means he will lose a case (or even have to start all over), so an attorney is likely to suggest some reason — however fanciful — for striking those 15 women. Attorneys have explained their peremptories on, among others, the following:

- body language
- eye movement
- religious beliefs
- marital status
- residence
- occupation

In *Purkette v. Elem*, 514 U.S. 765 (1995), the Court held that a prosecutor who struck all jurors with "facial hair" was not violating *Batson*, even though all those jurors happened to be African Americans. *Elem*, said one author, "converted *Batson* into a charade." Brian W. Wais, Actions Speak Louder Than Words: Revisions to the Batson Doctrine and Peremptory Challenges in the

---

41. Courts, of course, differ on what percentage of strikes would create a *prima facie* case.
42. See José F. Anderson, Catch Me If You Can! Resolving the Ethical Tragedy in the Brave New World of Jury Selection, 32 New Eng. L. Rev. 343, 376 (1998).

Wake of Johnson v. California and *Miller-El v. Dretke*, 45 Brandeis L.J. 437, 448 (2007). Ten years later, however, the tide seems to have turned. In *Miller-El v. Dretke*, 545 U.S. 231 (2005), the Court declared: "[I]f any facially neutral reason sufficed to answer a *Batson* challenge, then *Batson* would not amount to much more than *Swain*. . . . A *Batson* challenge does not call for a mere exercise in thinking up any rational basis for a peremptory."

Even with a deferential standard, however, the discriminatory strike of one juror may violate *Batson*. In *Snyder v. Louisiana*, 552 U.S. 472 (2008), the prosecutor gave two reasons for striking an African-American juror: (1) he looked nervous; and (2) he was a student teacher who was concerned about missing classes and might convict the defendant of a noncapital homicide so as to avoid the time involved in a (capital) sentencing hearing. The trial court called the dean of the school, who indicated that it would not be a problem if the juror missed a week of classes. The Supreme Court, after rejecting the "demeanor" reason because there was no basis in the record for it, compared the prosecutor's nonuse of peremptories with regard to similarly situated white jurors and had little trouble in finding a *Batson* violation based on the purported second reason.

iii. Step Three — Assessing the Claim

In assessing the truth of the proffered explanation, lower courts had used a "comparative analysis" method. In *Miller-El*, the Court embraced that approach wholeheartedly, comparing every explanation given by the prosecutor with regard to the stricken jurors with other jurors who were not removed (or even who were removed, but later in the process). It is not too much to suggest that the comparative method is now the technique to be employed in future challenges.

In *Foster v. Chatman*, 195 L. Ed. 2d 1, 13 (2016), the Court held that, in reviewing a *Batson* claim, "all of the circumstances that bear on racial animosity must be consulted." Foster was convicted and sentenced to death after the prosecutor struck all four prospective black jurors. Foster's habeas attorneys reviewed the prosecutors' trial file. In the file they discovered a number of references to race. For instance, the race of black jurors was circled on their questionnaires, a letter "B" appeared next to each black prospective juror's name and a document listing all prospective black jurors as definite no's was discovered. The prosecution argued that these notes should not be considered in determining whether the prosecution committed a *Batson* violation. The Court disagreed. In the Court's opinion, the "focus on race in the file demonstrates a concerted effort to keep black prospective jurors off the jury." Id. at 21. Foster's significance is in the Court's insistence that lower courts should look beyond the prosecution's explanation in assessing a *Batson* challenge. Other evidence of racial animus also should be considered, such as prior *Batson* violations by the same prosecutor or the same prosecutor's office.

Foster, *Johnson* and *Miller-El* may resuscitate *Batson*, which, prior to those decisions, was viewed by most attorneys and scholars as a valiant but vain attempt to lessen, if not eradicate, racial intolerance from this small corner of the criminal justice system. Prior to *Purkette*, one study[43] found that *Batson* challenges succeed about 16 percent of the time. Is that glass one-sixth full, or five-sixths empty? That may depend on (a) how frequently one believes that attorneys rely on racial or gender stereotypes and (b) how efficacious the *Batson* process is at ferreting out such discrimination. Whether these two new decisions will actually impact practice remains to be seen.

Thus, if Hana claims that she removed Juancinto, a Hispanic, because he reads the *New York Times* (hardly a vicious offense, but a sufficient "hunch" that Clarence Darrow would have regarded as a basis for employing a challenge), the court will attempt to determine whether Hana also removed non-Hispanic jurors who read the *New York Times*. This is not an illogical methodology, but it ignores the psychology of peremptory strikes: that a lawyer may use his peremptories more liberally at the beginning of the process than at the end, thus allowing someone to stay whom he would have stricken earlier, if given the chance.

Because it is based upon the equal protection clause, *Batson* reaches only "suspect" ("protected") classes under that doctrine's traditional decisions. Sixth Amendment doctrine, however, protects any "cognizable" group from being precluded from the jury wheel. The difference between *Batson* and *Taylor*, between the parameters of the Fourteenth and the Sixth Amendment challenges, is seen in the so-called dual motivation cases. In *Hernandez v. New York*, 500 U.S. 352 (1991), the Court held that peremptory challenges to Spanish-speaking jurors who expressed some hesitancy about relying on an in-court English translator were sustainable even though the persons removed would be disproportionately Hispanic. If defendant had only to show disparate impact, the claim might be successful; but since it is an equal protection claim, disparate impact is not enough — the defendant must show intent to discriminate.[44]

---

43. Kenneth J. Melilli, Batson in Practice: What We Have Learned about Batson and Peremptory Challenges, 71 Notre Dame L. Rev. 447 (1996).

44. Another aspect of the Fourteenth Amendment basis of *Batson* is that it is the juror — and not the defendant — whose rights have been infringed. In *United States v. Huey*, 76 F.3d 638 (5th Cir. 1996), Huey's attorney used his five peremptory challenges to remove African Americans from the jury on the ground that tape recordings that the government intended to introduce contained racial slurs by the defendant. Both the government and Huey's codefendant objected to the strikes on *Batson* grounds, which the trial court denied without explanation. The Fifth Circuit found *Batson* error and ordered a new trial *for both defendants*. The court justified granting the transgressor a remedy by asserting that "only by repudiating all results from such a trial can public confidence in the integrity of this system be preserved, even when it means reversing the conviction of the very defendant who exercised the discriminatory challenges."

iv. Step Four — Remedy

When a *Batson* violation occurs, the question then becomes one of remedy. A trial judge who agrees with the challenge may (a) order the jurors (re)seated, *People v. Stiff,* 206 A.D.2d 235, 620 N.Y.S.2d 87 (N.Y. App. Div. 1994); (b) order a new venire; (c) preclude the offending party from using more peremptories; (d) hold the offending attorney in contempt; or (e) refer to the Bar for possible disciplinary sanctions. None of these remedies is without cost. A (reseated) juror who knows the removal was because of race or gender may find it difficult thereafter to be unbiased in assessing the case of the side who removed him. Striking the entire panel and beginning again, seems excessively time-consuming and wasteful, not to mention injurious to the other jurors. If, as suggested above, *Batson* is based primarily on the rights of prospective jurors, and not of the defendant, then restarting the jury selection process is consistent with protecting the defendant, while reseating the juror (if that is possible) is more consistent with protecting the juror. Of course, if a defense counsel misuses peremptories, and the jury acquits, the only remedy is a sanction against the lawyer.

These difficulties, however, pale beside those presented when the trial judge accepts the neutral explanation, but an appellate court disagrees. At that point, the most obvious remedy is to overturn the conviction, and to find *Batson* errors harmful *per se*. But some courts have refused to take that path, as they have in dealing with most trial errors (see Chapter 12). After all, the rudimentary question is whether the defendant received a fair trial by an unbiased jury; unless there is some showing that the juror who replaced the stricken one was biased, it seems difficult for the defendant to succeed on that claim. A more fitting remedy for discriminatory use of peremptories, perhaps, is disciplinary action against the offending attorney.[45] (See Chapter 14.)

e. Abolish Peremptories?

These questions lead to the critical one: Should peremptories be abolished? The Supreme Court has consistently said they are not constitutionally required. *Rivera v. Illinois,* 556 U.S. 148 (2009). States, and even Congress, are free to eliminate them entirely. But only law professors, and an occasional outside observer, seem to think they should do so.[46] Why? Perhaps

---

45. In *People v. Muhammad,* 108 Cal. App. 4th 313, 133 Cal. Rptr. 2d 308 (2003), the trial judge fined the prosecutor $1,500 for discriminatory use of peremptories. The appellate court upheld the *power* of the court to take such action, but because no order had been issued prohibiting such action beforehand, the actual sanction was reversed.

46. Jeffrey Abramson, Abolishing the Peremptory But Enlarging the Challenge for Cause, 96 Amer. Phil. Ass'n Newsletter 59 (Fall 1996); Morris B. Hoffman, Peremptory Challenges Should Be Abolished: A Trial Judge's Perspective, 64 U. Chi. L. Rev. 809 (1997). Mr. Justice Marshall, concurring in *Batson,* declared that "only by banning peremptories entirely can such

because there is an intuitive "sense" that there *are* differences among these groups;[47] indeed, one might argue that the entire cross-section requirement is premised on that view, and that *Taylor* and *Batson* are therefore irreconcilably at odds. But another view is possible:[48] "Although they derive from separate constitutional sources, the 'fair cross-section' and equal protection requirements combine to serve a single goal — insuring that juries reflect the diversity of the American people." Or perhaps it is because there is "a tremendous psychological pressure for lawyers on both sides to exercise some peremptory challenges . . . if they do not [use all their challenges] in most jurisdictions they lose any appellate argument regarding erroneous rulings on challenges for cause."[49]

One (pen)ultimate point: peremptories show that, while we generally speak of "selecting a jury," that is a misnomer. Instead, we "de-select" a jury, removing what each side thinks is the "worst" jurors for its case. One (impish) law professor suggested that we should allow each side to have affirmative selection instead, in which each side may prevent the other from removing, on a peremptory basis, any juror who has not been found challengeable for cause.[50]

In the end, unless courts are more vigorous in assessing grounds for cause, peremptories may be an inevitable evil.[51] And, circularly, so long as

---

discrimination be ended." 476 U.S. at 108. The court in *Minetos v. City University of New York*, 925 F. Supp. 177 (S.D.N.Y. 1996), reviewing the "ten frustrating years" since *Batson*, declared that "All peremptory challenges should now be banned as an unnecessary waste of time and an obvious corruption of the judicial process." Justice Breyer, concurring in *Miller-El*, agreed; but he was the sole Justice to do so. Peremptories have been abolished in a number of other countries, including England and Ireland.

47. Thus, in note 11 in *J. E. B. v. Alabama ex rel. T. B.*, 511 U.S. 127 (1994), the Court declared that even if there were some statistical evidence that women decide differently, "gender classifications that rest on impermissible stereotypes violate the Equal Protection Clause . . . a shred of truth may be contained in some stereotypes, but (that) requires that state actors look beyond the surface before making judgments about people that are likely to stigmatize as well as to perpetuate historical patterns of discrimination." And Justice O'Connor, also in J.E.B., observed: "[T]he import of our holding is that any correlation between a juror's gender and attitudes is irrelevant as a matter of constitutional law. But to say that gender makes no difference as a matter of law is not to say that gender makes no difference as a matter of fact."

48. See R.J. Allen, W.J. Stuntz, J.L. Hoffmann and D,A, Livingston, Comprehensive Criminal Procedure, 1200.

49. Allen et al., *supra* note 48, at fn. 199.

50. Richard Singer, Peremptory Holds — A Suggestion (Only Half Specious) of A Solution to the Discriminatory Use of Peremptory Challenges, 62 U. Det. L. Rev. 301 (1986). For a case of simultaneous invention, see T.L. Altman, Affirmative Selection: A New Response to Peremptory Challenge Abuse, 38 Stan. L. Rev. 781 (1986). But see Hans Zeisel, Affirmative Peremptory Juror Selection, 39 Stan. L. Rev. 1165 (1987).

51. C. Whitebread and C. Slobogin, Criminal Procedure 746 (2000): "The Court's reluctance to allow individualized questions during voir dire, combined with its unwillingness to imply bias from circumstances, means that . . . peremptory challenge . . . may be the only way a defendant can remove from the venire, individuals strongly suspected of bias. Unless the ground for challenges for cause . . . are relaxed considerably, some entitlement to peremptories may be necessary."

courts know that attorneys have peremptories, judges are likely to deny a motion to remove a juror for cause, rather than invite appealable (and reversible) error, expecting that the attorney will use a peremptory to remove that juror.

6. A Quick Summary

Some have argued that the recent spate of cases, noted above, which seem to deny "cognizable status" to all groups *except* those already in "suspect" classes erases the overlap between the Sixth and Fourteenth Amendments.[52] On the other hand, to the extent that they do *not* overlap, they seem to contradict each other: *Batson* proposes that racial and gender differences are irrelevant, while *Taylor* claims that they are definitive. A doctrinal explanation is possible: the equal protection cases aim at protecting the juror, while the Sixth Amendment cases aim at protecting the *defendant*.

8.1

	Equal Protection	Sixth Amendment
Areas Covered	Grand Jury Composition; Peremptory Challenges	Construction of the Wheel
Items to Be Proved	Impact and Discriminatory Intent	Impact Only
Persons Covered	Suspect or Semisuspect Classes	Cognizable, "Distinct" Group
Person Protected	Potential Juror	Defendant

Examples

1. Horace, who killed his wife after catching her in flagrante delicto, wants the judge to ask each of the jurors whether they have ever had an affair, or discovered that their spouse was having an affair. (a) Should the judge ask

52. Laurie Maguid, Challenges to Jury Composition: Purging the Sixth Amendment Analysis of Equal Protection Concepts, 24 San Diego L. Rev. 1081 (1987). See also Sara S. Beale, et al., Grand Jury Practice 3:13 (Callaghan 1997). In *Batson* itself, the appellant had relied solely on the Sixth Amendment argument, but the Court relied on the equal protection clause, rather than the Sixth Amendment.

the question? (b) If the judge asks the question, may the jurors refuse to answer?

2. Jeremiah Jefferson is prosecuting Courtney Bellows for "illegal possession of a gun by an ex-felon." In response to a questionnaire asking jurors their views on guns, and whether they owned a gun, Juror # 8, James Bogus, has indicated that he belongs to the National Rifle Association. Should Jeremiah ask the other potential jurors how they feel about guns? Should he challenge Bogus for cause, or wait until peremptories, and then remove him from the venire?

3. (a) Suppose that statistics show that, in a specific district, the poor, the (very) young, and the elderly fail to register to vote at least 20 percent below the norm for other age and population groups. The jurisdiction relies only upon voter registration lists. Would a challenge to the jury wheel be successful?

   (b) Suppose the jurisdiction relied exclusively on drivers' registration lists?

4. Martha, a 58-year-old chief executive, is being tried for stock fraud. She notes that the state statute provides that "persons over 55" need not serve on juries, and are allowed to serve only if they sought to serve. What are her chances if she challenges that statute, and the composition of the wheel?

5. Sabrina, a white Anglo-Saxon woman, urges Kunstler, her defense counsel, to use a peremptory challenge to strike Jerome, the only African American on the jury venire. "I can't do that," he replies. "He's the only minority member available." After Sabrina is convicted, what are the chances of a successful appeal based upon a *Batson* violation? (See Chapter 10 for whether this would be ineffective assistance of counsel.)

6. During jury selection, prospective juror Edith revealed that a cousin to whom she had been close had been murdered but, through the grace of her church, she had learned to forgive the slayer. Another juror, Martin, acknowledged that he spent 20-30 hours per week at his church or reading religious works. He declared his belief that all people were in a state of grace with God. The prosecutor struck both with peremptory challenges. Defense counsel objected. What should the trial court do?

7. A federal district court, following the Jury Selection and Service Act, establishes a computer program which randomly selects persons from a "resident list." There is no debate that the list is representative of the demographics in the population. However, when summonses are sent to a randomly selected group on that list, no women respond.

The defendant, Darryl, argues that he cannot be tried by the resulting all-male jury. Is he right?

8. Defendant, an African American, is charged with murder. He objected to the prosecutor's strikes against three African-American prospective jurors. The prosecutor justified the strikes of these jurors on the grounds that they agreed with the verdict in the highly publicized O.J. Simpson case (Simpson was acquitted of killing his Caucasian ex-wife; most African Americans supported the acquittal, most Caucasians did not). The defense claims that the prosecutor's explanation is pretextual, that it was just an attempt by the prosecutor to remove African Americans from the jury. How should trial judge rule?

Explanations

1. (a) There is little case law on this subject. In *Brandborg v. Lucas*, 891 F. Supp. 352 (E.D. Tex. 1995), a prospective juror refused to answer questions about her income, religious preference, TV and reading habits, memberships in organizations, political affiliation, or income. She was held in contempt by the state court, but the conviction was overturned on federal habeas corpus. The answer might depend on whether the asserted purpose is to establish a cause challenge, rather than peremptory one. Horace's best argument for asking the question, after all, is that it may be relevant in ascertaining a challenge for cause: whether the juror could follow the law — a juror who has forgiven a philandering spouse might find it difficult to follow the law of "heat of passion," reducing a killing to manslaughter. And the prosecutor might wish to exclude such jurors peremptorily, lest they be sympathetic to the defendant. Can it be said that each side has an "interest" in the answer to the question, or merely that each side is "interested" in the answer? And even if there is an "interest," does that outweigh the juror's right to privacy? Or does the juror waive any such right when he submits himself to jury duty?

An empirical study of jurors' reactions to such questions shows that questions far less invasive than the one suggested here are felt by jurors to be unnecessary. Thus, questions about whether a juror owns a gun, or relating to hobbies, were felt to violate a sense of privacy, even though most jurors answered them. See Mary R. Rose, Expectations of Privacy, 85 Judicature 10 (July-August 2001). And in *United States v. McDade*, 929 F. Supp. 815 (E.D. Penn. 1996), the trial court, sua sponte, restricted inquiries into the jurors' state of health, deeming some questions too intrusive, and totally struck questions regarding television shows watched, newspapers read, or organizational memberships.

(b) Again, judicial discretion generally controls. But if the question is sensitive, the court should offer (at least) the option of discussing this issue in camera. See *Press-Enterprise Co. v. Superior Court*, 464 U.S. 501, 512 (1984); *Brandborg v. Lucas*, 891 F. Supp. 352 (E.D. Tex. 1995).

2. Hold your fire, Jeremiah. Membership in the NRA is not grounds for cause removal, even where the crime relates to firearms. *United States v. Salamone*, 800 F.2d 1216 (3d Cir. 1986). The question is one of strategy, not law. If the judge allows jurors to be questioned about guns, will other gun-owning (or gun-favoring) jurors feel pressured, and hence react negatively toward Jeremiah and the government, particularly since they did not provide any information on this issue on the questionnaire? On the other hand, will they feel that way regardless, so that such a question is relatively harmless? If Jeremiah waits until peremptories, he can surely remove Bogus.

3. (a) The first question here is whether these groups are "cognizable" groups. That usually requires some showing that they are coherent enough, either through experiential facts, or otherwise, to have some "perspective" that other groups can't replicate. Courts have disagreed over whether blue-collar workers (*Anaya v. Hansen*, 781 F.2d 1 (1st Cir. 1986)); college students (*United States v. Fletcher*, 965 F.2d 781 (9th Cir. 1992)); people between the ages of 18 and 34 (*Barber v. Ponte*, 772 F.2d 982 (1st Cir. 1985)); those under the age of 25 (*Johnson v. McCaughtry*, 92 F.3d 585 (7th Cir. 1996)); those over 65 (*Brewer v. Nix*, 963 F.2d 1111 (8th Cir. 1992)); or over 70 (*People v. McCoy*, 40 Cal. App. 4th 778, 47 Cal. Rptr. 2d 599 (1995)); and the "politically alienated," *United States v. Dellinger*, 472 F.2d 340 (7th Cir. 1973), are distinct groups, with distinct perspectives.

As noted in the text, one factor is whether these potential jurors will "change" their characteristics over time. Gender and race are not likely to alter; youth is. But once there is a "cognizable group," the defense has shown a prima facie case; under the Sixth Amendment, it need not show that the process was established to discriminate against these groups — impact is enough. The burden now shifts to the state to show that there are good reasons to use (exclusively) the voter registration lists. Administrative ease would be one such reason; indeed, all challenges to the exclusive use of the list have thus far failed. The state may also argue that it is not the state, but persons (or groups) unwilling to register to vote, who are self-selecting themselves out of the jury process. Moreover, the state can argue that (exclusive use of) many other lists — property tax rolls, drivers' licenses, telephone listings, etc. — will discriminate against some of these groups (certainly "the poor") and perhaps others (urban dwellers who do not need to own cars — except in Los Angeles). Since the state is not charged with an affirmative duty to "force" the wheel to be representative, the challenge will fail.

(b) Same result. In *State v. Mann*, 959 S.W.2d 503 (Tenn. 1997), the court declared that using driver's registration was not unconstitutional, even though the defendants argued that voter registration lists should be used. The court declared: "We note that the statistics provided by the Dyer County circuit court clerk reveal that licensed drivers in Dyer County constitute 73.68 percent of the entire population of the county. Thus, it is readily apparent that the list of licensed drivers provide[s] a large and easily accessible source of names, to which all potential jurors have equal access and which disqualifies jurors solely on the basis of objective criteria."

4. Very poor. One might argue that most "old" people have a unique perspective on social questions, and are therefore a "cognizable group." However, courts are unanimous that "the young" (however defined) are not a cognizable group. And other courts have held that people "over 65" are not a cognizable group either. *State v. Johnson*, 2003 WL 22999449, 2003 Tenn. Crim. App. Lexis 1074 (Tenn. Crim. App. 2003). Thus, the state could remove them at will. On the other hand, old age is an immutable characteristic; while you can cease being "young," you cannot cease being "old," at least not if you can still do jury duty. Thus, there is an argument under that approach to "cognizability" that at some point the "old" become a cognizable group. Of course, there still might be a "significant state interest" under Duren for allowing the state to exclude this group—fear of senility.

5. Surprise. Although *Batson* appears to preclude consideration of race in employing peremptories, and although defense counsel did exactly that, the court in *United States v. Angel*, 355 F.3d 462 (6th Cir. 2004), held that a "failure to act" (that is, strike) could not be equated with *Batson*'s prohibition of an "act." Moreover, the defendant's argument that his counsel struck an "otherwise qualified white juror to make room for the minority juror" was treated as describing a "hypothetical" rather than an actual event reflected in the record. Said the court: "We find no support for the proposition that a defense attorney's failure to challenge a juror, even if motivated by race, implicates the equal protection rights of either the juror or the defendant . . . Lawyers do not select jurors, after all; they only remove prospective jurors."

6. Start the trial. Do not strike the jurors, or provide any other remedy to the defense. At the moment, whether Batson precludes strikes based upon religion has not been resolved by the Supreme Court, although most courts prohibit such a strike. In *United States v. Stafford*, 136 F.3d 1109 (7th Cir. 1998), the court summarized the law as it stands even today: "It is necessary to distinguish among religious affiliation, a religion's general tenets, and a specific religious belief. It would be improper

and perhaps unconstitutional to strike a juror on the basis of his being a Catholic, a Jew, a Muslim, etc. It would be proper to strike him on the basis of a belief that would prevent him from basing his decision on the evidence and instructions, even if the belief had a religious backing; suppose, for example, that his religion taught that crimes should be left entirely to the justice of God. In between and most difficult to evaluate from the standpoint of Batson is a religious outlook that might make the prospective juror unusually reluctant, or unusually eager, to convict a criminal defendant. That appears to be this case." Accord: *United States v. DeJesus*, 347 F.3d 500 (3d Cir. 2003). Compare *State v. Davis*, 50 N.W.2d 767 (Minn. 1993), cert. denied, 511 U.S. 1115 (1994) with *People v. Wheeler*, 22 Cal. 3d 258, 583 P.2d 748 (1978).

In dissenting from the denial of certiorari in Davis, Justices Thomas and Scalia argued that "It is at least not obvious . . . why peremptory strikes based on religious affiliation would survive equal protection analysis." See generally Annot. 63 A.L.R.5th 375 (1998). Religion is not an immutable characteristic, so that approach would not help the defense; on the other hand, religious affiliation is surely a "cognizable" group and would fall under the Sixth Amendment, were a statute to preclude religious persons from being placed on the wheel. Whether it violates the equal protection clause remains to be seen. Three dissenters in *J.E.B. v. Alabama ex rel. T.B.*, 511 U.S. 127 (1994), opined that Batson would inevitably declare such strikes unconstitutional, but the rest of the Court has not yet taken that step.

7. No. Darryl's just going to have to put up with all those men. Although nationally only 40 percent of those summoned report for jury duty, there is no requirement that the government take affirmative steps to remedy this situation. See Arthur L. Burnett, Sr., Jury Reform for the 21st Century: A Judge's Perspective, 20 Crim. Justice 1 (Spring 2005), pp.32 and 34. In *United States v. Green*, 389 F. Supp. 2d 29 (D. Mass. 2005), the returns from summonses by minority residents were less than those from non-minorities, resulting in a 3 percent actual disparity, and a 50 percent comparative disparity in their appearance on the wheel. Judge Nancy Gertner, who has written much about juries and sentencing, published an opinion finding that the plan violated the Federal Jury Reform Act (but not the Constitution). The government argued that the failure to return a summons was not "caused" by the government, but by the individuals. Judge Gertner, however, found that there were more "bad addresses" for certain zip codes which happened to be significantly minority. She then ordered the jury administrator to target a second-round mailing of summonses to those zip codes. On appeal, the First Circuit overruled her determination, finding that the process she ordered was incompatible with the Act, because it would violate the requirement of the statute that

there be "equal odds" for every resident on the list to serve. In re United States, 426 F.3d 1 (2005). On remand, the district court, in its administrative capacity, adopted much of Judge Gertner's affirmative selection process in an effort to assure that there would be more minorities on the wheel. On the other hand, one can sometimes find news reports that judges in small towns have ordered their clerk to "find people at the grocery store" and give them summonses. Is that action any "less affirmative" than Judge Gertner's order?

8. The trial judge denied the *Batson* challenge. The appellate court upheld the trial judge and rejected the claim that the striking of these jurors was motivated by race. See *Shelling v. State*, 52 S.W.3d 213 (Tex. Ct. App. 2001). This case illustrates the court's willingness to accept the prosecution stated justification as long as it's not contradicted by a comparative analysis or by other evidence of the prosecutor's racial animus.

C. THE PASSIVE JURY — AND JURY REFORM

Imagine taking a law school course and being forbidden to ask any questions or take any notes throughout the entire semester, and having to review for the exam without any materials relating to the course. Until recently jurors were in this situation — most jurisdictions forbade them to take notes, or to ask questions, throughout the process. Allowing jurors to ask questions, even through the trial judge, would, it was thought, override the strategy of the attorneys and possibly conflict with the rules of evidence (a juror might ask for example, about hearsay, and be unhappy when told that the law does not allow that question to be asked).[53]

That, however, has changed dramatically in the past 20 years: virtually all federal circuits, and the vast majority of states, now permit the trial judge to allow jurors to provide questions to the judge, who will decide whether to ask them at all, or in an edited form. *State v. Doleszny*, 844 A.2d 773 (Vt. 2004) (collecting cases, statutes, and articles on the subject). On the other hand, a few states have concluded the process would be unconstitutional under state statutes. *State v. Costello*, 646 N.W.2d 204 (Minn. 2002); see also *State v. Glidden*, 144 Ohio App. 3d 69, 759 N.E.2d 468 (Ohio Ct. App. 2001). A growing number of states permit jurors to take notes as well. *State v. Rose*, 748 A.2d 1283 (R.I. 2000). The concern is that taking notes would distract jurors from listening (do you find that a problem as a student in class?) and

---

53. See P. Tiersma, Jury Questions: An Update to Kalven and Zeisel, 39 Crim. L. Bull. 10 (2003); Sarah E. West, "The Blindfold Is Not a Gag": The Case for Allowing Controlled Questions of Witnesses by Jurors, 38 Tulsa L. Rev. 529 (2003).

that disputes would erupt in the jury room over whose notes are more accurate. (Of course, with 12 sets of notes, there is likely to be some form of consensus.) Moreover, in many jurisdictions, jurors in the past received no written set of jury instructions, and no copy of the indictment. This has also changed.

D. THE JURY — ALTERNATE JURORS

Because jurors can become sick, or otherwise unable to proceed, virtually all states provide for the selection, at the time of voir dire, of alternate jurors. In some instances, the alternates are identified as alternates at the time, in other jurisdictions, the "real" jury is determined only after the case has been heard. As a general matter, whether a juror should be replaced by an alternate prior to deliberations is within the full discretion of the trial judge. *United States v. Fajardo*, 787 F.2d 1253 (11th Cir. 1986). In most jurisdictions, alternates may replace regular jurors only before the jury begins deliberating. There is a dramatic split as to the procedure to be followed if an alternate is needed once deliberations begin. In some jurisdictions, when deliberations begin, the alternates are sent to the jury room, but instructed not to participate in deliberations. In others, the (potential) substitutes are held in abeyance during deliberations; if events necessitate replacing a juror, deliberations are to begin again. The former procedure, which is obviously more efficient, has nevertheless been criticized on the basis that it invades the secrecy of jury deliberations. Some jurisdictions now allow for deliberations by the remaining 11 jurors, assuming that both parties agree.

E. IMPEACHING JURY VERDICTS

Juries are black boxes. Jurors do all sorts of things inside that black box. They:

- conduct experiments, such as simulating the crime[54]

---

54. In *People v. Collins*, 49 Cal. 4th 175, 232 P.3d 32, 110 Cal. Rptr. 3d 384 (2010) one juror, convinced from his own experience that the gunshot that killed the victim must have been from an execution-style killing, performed on his home computer "what can only be described as a simulation model." He then brought into the jury room a protractor, and the jury recreated several possible methods and angles of killing. The opinion discusses many cases involving experiments by juries.

- reveal possibly racist views[55]
- receive threats from the outside
- obtain information from outside sources — increasingly the Internet and similar sites[56]
- rely on their own "expertise" (or their own experience)
- fall asleep, take drugs, etc.[57]
- ask for outside guidance — from God,[58] a Ouija board,[59] Facebook members,[60]
- or a coin[61] look for information about the legal system[62] or legal terms[63]

---

55. One juror said to another, "I've got a rope," to which the other responded, "I've got a tree." *State v. Johnson*, 630 N.W.2d 79 (S.D. 2001). In *United States v. Benally*, 546 F.3d 1230 (10th Cir. 2008), one juror expressly declared that "American Indians get drunk when they get near alcohol," and another spoke of "sending a message back to the reservation." See Lee Goldman, Post-verdict Challenges to Racial Comments Made During Juror Deliberations, 61 Syracuse L. Rev. 1 (2010); Andrew C. Helman, Racism, Juries, and Justice: Addressing Post-verdict Juror Testimony of Racial Prejudice During Deliberations, 62 Me. L. Rev. 327 (2010).

56. The use of Google, Facebook, and the Internet has become so widespread that many courts have promulgated rules to explicitly deal with these sources. For example, in Michigan, jurors are instructed not to use any handheld devices, such as iPhones or BlackBerrys, and Connecticut expressly prohibits use of "internet maps of Google Earth, internet chat rooms, blogs, and social websites." See, generally, Judicial Conference Committee on Court Administration and Case Management, Proposed Model Jury Instructions: The Use of Electronic Technology to Conduct Research on or Communicate about a Case, available at www.uscourts.gov/ newsroom/2010/DIR10-018.pdf); G. Blum, Prejudicial Effect of Juror Misconduct Arising from Internet Usage, 48 A.L.R 6th 135 (2009); Amanda McGee, Juror Misconduct in the Twenty-first Century: The Prevalence of the Internet and its Effect on American Courtrooms, 30 Loy. L.A. Ent. L. Rev. 301 (2010). In one instance, a judge learned that a juror was conducting outside research about the case on the Internet. He questioned the rest of the jury and found that eight other jurors had been doing the same thing. McGee, at notes 57–59.

57. *Smith v. State*, 284 Ga. 17, 663 S.E.2d 142 (2008); *Tanner v. United States*, 483 U.S. 107 (1987).

58. *State v. Young*, 710 N.W.2d 272 (Minn. 2006). Where jurors actually bring Bibles into the jury room, courts have usually held this is not prejudicial. E.g. *People v. Williams*, 40 Cal.4th 287 (2006) (not prejudicial). But see *McNair v. State*, 706 So.23d 8282 (Ala. Crim. App. 1997) (prejudicial).

59. R v. *Young*, [1995] 2 Crim. App. R. 379.

60. McGee, *supra*, note 56, cites (at note 66) Urmee Khan, Juror Dismissed From a Trial After Using Facebook to Help Make a Decision, Telegraph.co.uk, Nov. 24, 2008, www.telegraph.co.uk/news/newstopics/lawreports/3510926/Juror-dismissed-from-a-trial-after-using-Facebook-to-help-make-a-decision/html. In that case, a juror in a child abuse trial posted confidential details on Facebook and then held an online poll asking her readers to vote on the defendant's guilt. She was dismissed.

61. *Vaise v. Delaval*, 99 Eng. Rep. 944 (K.B. 1785).

62. Juries are not entitled to know what the sentences are for the charges against the defendant. In *United States v. Polizzi*, 549 F. Supp. 2d 308 (E.D.N.Y. 2008), Judge Jack Weinstein — who was a professor at Columbia Law School before he became a judge — delivered a 174-page opinion in which, among other things, he held that the defendant had a Sixth Amendment right to a jury informed of the 5-year minimum if he were convicted of a specific crime. The Second Circuit reversed, 564 F.3d 142 (2d Cir. 2009).

63. See Caren Myers Morrison, Can the Jury Trial Survive Google?, 25 Crim. Justice 4 (WTR 2011) (collecting cases where the jurors have gone to the Internet to find legal definitions of words such as "attempt," "aggravating," and "great bodily injury," among others).

There are two separate issues here — (2) was the defendant prejudiced; (1) may the court hear the evidence?

1. Hearing the Evidence

a. The "External" versus "Internal" Dichotomy

The adversary system depends on jurors relying only on the evidence adduced at trial. When they seek evidence from the "outside," courts are likely to find that the defendant has been prejudiced. Jurors, for example, have gone to the Internet to obtain definitions of legal terms, or to determine what the possible sentence might be, or to "check" the accuracy of a witness; in such cases, they are clearly going beyond the record and beyond the testimony. In other instances, however, deciding whether information is "extraneous" or "internal" can be difficult. The most obvious case of "external" pressure is a threat made to a juror to "acquit or else." But most cases are more nuanced.

Thus, in *State v. Mann*, 131 N.M. 59, 39 P.3d 124 (2002), a juror gave to other jurors his expert views on the probability that an injury could have occurred the way the defendant claimed. In *People v. Maragh*, 94 N.Y.3d 569, 729 N.E.2d 701 (2000), a conviction was overturned when two nurse jurors answered questions relating to the way in which injuries could heal. Obviously, where a juror goes out of her way to obtain the information — such as conducting an experiment to test one party's theory, or going on the Internet to obtain the "legal" definition of "malice" — this constitutes an "extraneous" event, and the juror may reveal it. See Michael Mushlin, Bound and Gagged: The Peculiar Predicament of Professional Jurors, 5 Yale L. & Pol'y Rev. 239 (2007).

In *Meyer v. State*, 119 Nev. 554, 80 P.3d 447 (Nev. 2003), a juror, who had some medical background, had given her views about the effects of Accutane, and had then gone home, referred to the Physician's Desk Reference, and reported her findings to the jury. The court said that she could rely on her own experience, but that resorting to the PDR was prejudicial.[64]

b. Inside versus Outside the Jury

For centuries, the general rule has been that jurors are not allowed to "impeach" their own verdict — they may not "testify" about anything that went on in the jury deliberations. More than two hundred years ago,

---

64. For another case rehearsing in great detail the problems this causes, see *Kenrick v. Pippin*, 252 P.3d 1052 (Colo. 2011) (civil case).

in the "coin-toss" case referred to above, Judge Mansfield set out this rule, which has been followed assiduously ever since. Thus, in *Tanner v. United States*, 483 U.S. 107 (1987), the defendant alleged, on the basis of information conveyed to his attorney after conviction, by two of the 12 jurors who convicted the defendant, that several of the jurors drank, causing them to sleep through the afternoon sessions of the trial. One affidavit, signed by a juror, alleged that:

- seven of the jurors drank alcohol during lunch;
- four drank from one to three pitchers of beer at lunch;
- other jurors consumed mixed drinks;
- four smoked marijuana regularly during the trial;
- one juror ingested cocaine five times, and another did so one or two times;
- one juror sold one-quarter pound of marijuana to another during the trial.

The Court held that none of this information could be officially brought before the judge. Under Federal Rule of Evidence 606 (emulated by virtually every state), no juror could testify about what occurred in the jury room. (If, of course, the elevator operator in the courthouse is willing to testify, that would present a different issue.) The operative verb in this discussion is "testify." A juror is not prohibited from telling everyone he knows about what happened in the jury room; indeed, many jurors write books about it. The question is whether the law will listen.

Jury secrecy is a virtue. It:

- protects the finality of jury verdicts;
- guards the frankness and candor of jury room discussion;
- prevents post-verdict harassment of jurors.

There is one exception to this general rule. If the jurors have been affected by "outside" or "extraneous" influences, courts may both hear the information and take action. The most obvious "extraneous" matter is a threat to one or more of the jurors.

In the "Ouija board" case, the Court stretched to find that the "seance" had occurred not during deliberations, but during a "break," and therefore the prohibition on testimony about "deliberations" was not violated.

The general rule is quite different if the "misconduct" is unveiled before the verdict is entered. In such instances, the judge will call in the jurors (one by one), inquire about the alleged problem, and take whatever actions (including removing a juror) the judge deems necessary. As a general rule, trial courts are reversed only for "abuse of discretion." *United States v.*

Sababu, 891 F.2d 1308 (7th Cir. 1989). In cases involving racism, courts seem more willing to overturn convictions.

2. Prejudice to the Defendant

When a court does listen to evidence of "extraneous" information, it is not clear who carries the burden of proof. Most courts have actually held that the defendant carries only the burden of proving some "likelihood of prejudice," after which the government must prove harmlessness. See *State* v. *Andersen*, 252 Neb. 6759, 564 N.W.2d 581 (1997). Moreover, the usual rule is that a court cannot ask jurors whether they were actually influenced by that information; that would tread on the rule of secrecy. Instead, the test *is whether an average, reasonable juror would have been affected by this information.* If so, it's time for a new trial.

Examples

1. Your client, Michael Milkcan, has been convicted on 47 counts of fraud. Several months after the verdict, you visit the bar in which the jurors had dinner every night. The bartender, recognizing you, says: "Boy, was your jury soused. I'm surprised they could count to 47 after the way they drank. And they really didn't have a clue about the judge's fraud instruction. Before I became a bartender, I went to law school, and passed the bar, and I know — they were really in the dark about that." You've read *Tanner*, *supra*, 483 U.S. 107. Do you have another drink? Or do you call the judge?

2. At the outset of Domingo's trial for stock fraud, the judge provides the jurors with the names of witnesses, and asks them whether they know any of the witnesses. No one responds. In the middle of the trial, defense counsel calls Emilio, a newly discovered witness; the trial judge permits this, giving the prosecution time to investigate Emilio. During deliberations, juror Crooner points to Emilio's testimony as exculpating Domingo. At that point Lucille Sphere, another juror, declares: "Emilio's a liar. He wouldn't know the truth in a crowded phone booth. I ought to know — I dated the jerk for three years. If he says Domingo's innocent, I say he's guilty." Domingo learns of this (don't ask how) only after the jury convicts. What chance has Domingo of obtaining a new trial?

3. Defendant, charged with arson of a building, calls an expert who testifies that the building was wired with Zemmadem, which he claims is a flammable substance, and that Zemmadem was the cause of the fire. During deliberations, (a) Hernando, an art dealer, declares "I do metal sculpture as a hobby, and that Zemmadem may be new, but it's

wonderful, and it's not flammable"; (b) he makes the same statement, but Albus challenges him: "Are you sure it was the same stuff?" The next day Hernando brings with him a book on wiring, which declares that Zemmadem is not flammable; (c) he comes back the next morning and announces that he bought some Zemmadem the night before and tried to ignite it, but was unable to do so, except when he used a blow torch. You are the defense attorney. What do you do?

Explanations

1. Put down that Chivas and get to the phone. Although the law is always cautious about investigating what occurred during deliberations, *Tanner* was based on Rule 606, which precludes a juror from providing evidence about jury competence. If you can find enough witnesses (the bartender alone will probably not suffice) to testify about enough occasions (particularly during the deliberative process itself) on which a substantial part of the jury appeared incompetent, you might at least get a hearing. And that's a start. But such testimony is incredibly subjective, and you've got to show that the verdict was truly influenced by the drunken stupor (if that's what it was). Can you prove that the misunderstanding continued in the jury room and that it prejudiced Milkcan?

2. Not very good. Clearly, Lucille should have informed the judge of her relationship with Emilio as soon as he was called to the stand. The judge almost certainly would have conducted an in camera hearing with Lucille. Had he found her incapable of deciding the case fairly, he might have declared a mistrial (assuming the parties could not, or would not, agree to a trial by the remaining 11), or replaced Lucille with an alternate juror. The same might have occurred if the relationship had been revealed during deliberations. Once the verdict is in, however, the burden shifts to the defendant to show prejudice; and, remember, the courts are divided on this issue. Moreover, he cannot bring on evidence about what occurred in the jury room itself, nor can other jurors testify to Lucille's comments. The goal of finality outweighs the goal of assuring Domingo of a fair trial. Can the court take action against Lucille? It is possible that she is guilty of contempt of court. But she will claim surprise about Emilio's appearance. Most courts tend to find such mistakes, even glaring ones like this, not sufficient to warrant a sanction of contempt unless intentional and spiteful. If, of course, Lucille had known at the start of the trial that Emilio would testify, that might be a different matter. See, e.g., Ark. Stat. Ann. §16-31-107.

3. (a) This is the Maragh problem, but magnified. In Maragh itself, voir dire disclosed the two juror-nurses' vocation, and hence possible knowledge.

The defendant may have waived his right to complain when they used their knowledge. Here, however, it would have been highly unusual for the defendant to ask on voir dire whether anyone on the venire had experience with Zemmadem. Still, "[w]hile the goal is utter impartiality, each juror inevitably brings to the jury room a lifetime of experience that will necessarily inform her assessments of the witnesses and the evidence. It is precisely such experience that enables a jury to evaluate the credibility of witnesses and the strength of arguments." *State v. Arnold*, 96 N.Y.3d 358, 753 N.E.2d 846 (2001). Defendant is likely to lose on a motion for a new trial.

(b) Now it becomes more difficult, for two reasons. In (a), jurors might have simply ignored Hernando, or thought to themselves that he was misremembering his experience. More doctrinally, he has now brought to the jury room an "extraneous" source of information. In several recent cases, jurors have relied upon the Bible in deciding whether to impose the death penalty. Some of the courts have literally determined these cases on whether the juror brought in the actual book, or merely "relied upon his memory." See *People v. Harlan*, 109 P.3d 616 (Colo. 2005); *Lenz v. True*, 370 F. Supp. 2d 446 (W.D. Va. 2005); Dean Sanderford, The Sixth Amendment, Rule 606(B) and the Intrusion in Jury Deliberations of Religious Principles of Decision, 74 Tenn. L. Rev. 167 (2007). In this instance, it is highly likely that a new trial will be granted.

(c) This is easy. Clearly, Hernando has conducted an "experiment" and we have no way of knowing (and neither did the other jurors) whether the conditions were remotely like those under which the fire occurred. This is about as "extraneous" as you can get. New trial.

Double Jeopardy

> ... the State with all its resources and power should not be allowed to make repeated attempts to convict an individual for an alleged offense, thereby subjecting him to embarrassment, expense and ordeal and compelling him to live in a continuing state of anxiety and insecurity as well as enhancing the possibility that even though innocent he may be found guilty.
>
> Green v. United States, 355 U.S. 184 (1957)[1]

> [T]he double jeopardy clause has produced some of the most confusing and seemingly contradictory decisions in recent Supreme Court history.
>
> Allen, Stuntz, Hoffmann, Livingston,
> Comprehensive Criminal Procedure 1354 (2001)

A. THE GENERAL ISSUE

1. The Purpose of Double Jeopardy

The Double Jeopardy Clause of the Fifth Amendment declares that:[2]

---

1. The Court was more expansive on this last point in Burks v. United States, 437 U.S. 1 (1978), protesting against the "test run" which would result if the state had an "opportunity to supply evidence which it failed to use in the first proceeding."

2. See, generally, George C. Thomas III, Double Jeopardy: The History, The Law (N.Y.U. Press 1998).

no person shall be subject for the same offense to be twice put in jeopardy of life or limb

It protects against (1) a second prosecution for the same offense after acquittal (autrefois acquit); (2) a second prosecution for the same offense after conviction (autrefois convict); and (3) multiple punishments for the same offense. *North Carolina v. Pearce*, 395 U.S. 711 (1969).

Protection against successive prosecutions really forms the heart of the Double Jeopardy Clause. The fundamental idea is to prevent the state from "wearing down" the defendant through multiple successive litigations. With many trials, either the defendant might lose hope (or resources), or the state will use earlier trials to learn both the weaknesses in its own case and the strengths in the defendant's case. In effect, without the double jeopardy protection, the motto for the state could be "if at first you don't succeed, try, try, try, try, try again."[3] This autrefois acquit rule can also be seen as assuring the nullifying power of juries.[4]

The prohibition is so strong that a defendant who has been acquitted may confess his guilt as he leaves the courthouse, and never be touched by the state again. Indeed, this very scenario recently occurred in England. There, after an acquitted defendant boasted that he had in fact killed his 22-year-old victim, there was such outrage that Parliament passed the Criminal Justice Act of 2003, c. 44, which provides for possible reprosecution in several instances where the crime carries a possible sentence of life imprisonment. There are several procedural requirements — and several layers of approval, which ultimately may involve approval by the House of Lords (not in its judicial capacity) — before the successive prosecution may occur.[5] And the frustration caused by the autrefois acquit doctrine has been seen once or twice in this country. In *Aleman v. Illinois*, 313 Ill. App. 3d 51, 729 N.E.2d 20 (Ill. App. Ct. 2000), the court held that the defendant acquitted at his first homicide trial because he had bribed the trial judge had never been in jeopardy at his first trial, thus there was no "double" jeopardy when he was retried for the homicide. While the sentiment that drove that

---

3. Even in the absence of a double jeopardy clause, there might be a due process limitation on how many successive prosecutions the state could bring, but courts are usually unreceptive to such an argument.

4. *See* Peter Westen, The Three Faces of Double Jeopardy: Reflections on Government Appeals of Criminal Sentences, 78 Mich. L. Rev. 1011 (1980).

5. For an exhaustive discussion of this case and this topic, see David Rudstein, Retrying the Acquitted in England, Part I: The Exception to the Rule Against Double Jeopardy for "New and Compelling Evidence," 8 San Diego Int'l L.J. 387 (2007) and Part II: The Exception to the Rule for "Tainted Acquittals," 9 San Diego Int'l L.J. 217 (2008). See also Kyden Creekpaum, What's Wrong with a Little More Double Jeopardy? A 21st Century Recalibration of an Ancient Individual Right, 44 Am. Crim. L. Rev. 1179 (2007); Andrea Koklys, Second Chance for Justice: Reevaluation of the United States Double Jeopardy Standard, 40 J. Marshall L. Rev. 371 (2006).

decision is certainly understandable, *Aleman* is the exception: The recourse is to prosecute the defendant for bribery, or jury tampering; the bulwark of double jeopardy stands firm.[6]

Similarly, a defendant who has been convicted of a crime may not be later (re)tried and punished again for that offense ("autrefois convict"). Here, the explanation is not so obvious. If the defendant has been found guilty, why not allow the state to prosecute him twice, or even 20 times? The concern must be simply the exhaustion point, as there is no worry that we are convicting, in a second trial, a person already "found" to be innocent.

The third part of the *Pearce* triumvirate — protection against multiple punishments — would seem to encompass some notion of proportionality. It has been severely weakened in the last two decades. As we will see, it may actually be a relatively unimportant protection as the twenty-first century begins.

Although the words of the Fifth Amendment restrict the protection to cases of "life and limb," today, when few felonies are capital, these words, if taken literally, would turn the clause into a dead letter. Instead, the courts have applied it consistently to any crime, even those not involving prison terms. *Ex Parte Lang*, 85 U.S. 163 (1873).

2. When Does Jeopardy Begin?

By definition, the *Double* Jeopardy Clause only applies if the defendant has previously been "in jeopardy." Many of the reasons articulated in *Green v. United States*, 355 U.S. 184 (1957), for the clause are activated almost immediately when the defendant is indicted: He may lose his job, and (if the offense is bailless, or he cannot make bail) freedom; he will certainly suffer ignominy; and begin to suffer financial loss, not the least from hiring an attorney. His psychological resources will also be at risk after a true bill is returned. One might, then, say that his jeopardy begins at that point.

Nevertheless, the case law is clear that the defendant is not considered to have been placed *in jeopardy* until after a jury has been sworn and impaneled or, in a trial to a judge, the first witness has been sworn. Indeed, the line is so bright that at least one court has held that a defendant acquitted of homicide by a jury that was never properly sworn cannot claim double jeopardy if he is tried again and convicted for that same offense. *Spencer v. Georgia*, 281 Ga. 533, 640 S.E.2d 267 (2007). On the other side of this fine line stands *Downum v. United States*, 372 U.S. 734 (1963). The jury was selected, and sworn, and then dismissed for the day. The next day, the prosecution's

---

6. Anne Bowen Poulin, Double Jeopardy and Judicial Accountability. When Is an Acquittal Not an Acquittal?, 27 Ariz. St. L.J. 953 (1995).

key witness became unavailable, and the court granted a mistrial. When the defendant was later prosecuted, he argued double jeopardy. The Supreme Court agreed — although no witness had been called, the swearing of the jury was the bright line. Whether the swearing in of the jury should actually carry such magical powers, the rule at least establishes a clear event, which neither side is likely to seek to manipulate (in contrast, for example, to a rule that would set the bar when the indictment is signed, which would be in the control of the prosecution).

In *Martinez v. Illinois*, 134 S. Ct. 2070 (2014), the Supreme Court reaffirmed that jeopardy attaches once a jury is sworn. On the day that Martinez's trial was to begin, Martinez was ready for trial but the State was not ready because its two witnesses did not appear. The State previously had been granted numerous continuances in order to obtain the appearances of their witnesses. On the day of trial the State sought another continuance. The trial court denied the motion for a continuance, allowed a jury to be sworn, and then directed the state to make an opening statement and to call its first witness. The prosecution failed to make an opening statement and rested without calling any witnesses. The defendant moved for a directed verdict on the grounds of insufficient evidence. The trial court granted the motion and dismissed the charges. The State subsequently appealed the trial court's denial of its motion for continuance. The Supreme Court held that double jeopardy attached as a result of the jury being sworn. The Court also held that double jeopardy barred the State's appeal because the trial court's directed verdict ruling was "a textbook acquittal: a finding that the State's evidence cannot support a conviction." Id. at 2076.

In a plea of guilty or nolo contendere, jeopardy does not attach until the plea is accepted. In *Ohio v. Johnson*, 467 U.S. 493 (1984), the defendant, at arraignment, and over the objections of the prosecution, pled guilty to two lesser counts, but not to two greater counts. The trial court then dismissed the greater counts. The Supreme Court held that the defendant was never in jeopardy on the greater counts. When a defendant "conditionally" pleads guilty, but the plea is thereafter withdrawn or rejected, jeopardy has not attached, and the Double Jeopardy Clause does not prevent a conviction of an offense greater than that to which the defendant initially pled. *United States v. Patterson*, 381 F.3d 859 (9th Cir. 2004). Similarly, if the first court did not have jurisdiction to try the defendant for the crime charged in the second proceeding, double jeopardy does not apply. *State v. Perkins*, 276 Va. 621 (2003).

3. When Is a Defendant "Acquitted"?

The "autrefois acquit" doctrine precludes reprosecution of a defendant for a crime of which he has been acquitted. *United States v. Ball*, 163 U.S. 662

(1896). Usually, determining whether the defendant has been acquitted is straightforward. But not always. In *Green v. United States*, 355 U.S. 184 (1957), defendant was tried for first degree murder; the jury returned a verdict convicting him of second degree murder. After Green successfully appealed that conviction, the prosecutor sought to reprosecute for first degree murder, but the Court held that the jury's verdict had "impliedly acquitted" Green of first degree murder, and the Double Jeopardy Clause precluded a second prosecution for that offense.

A judicial statement of acquittal, however, must be very clear. In *Price v. Vincent*, 538 U.S. 634 (2003), the defendant moved for a directed verdict on first degree murder, and the trial judge declared: "My impression is that there has not been shown premeditation or planning . . . what we have at the very best is second degree murder." The next day, after hearing argument from the prosecution, the judge reversed himself and decided to send the first degree charge to the jury, which returned that verdict. The state supreme court affirmed the conviction. On a habeas corpus challenge by the defense that the trial and judge had effectively granted its motion for a directed verdict as to first degree murder, the Supreme Court held that the state supreme court's decision was not "contrary to" and did not involve an "unreasonable application" of clearly established federal law, as is required by the habeas statute (see Chapter 12).

A jury acquittal must also be very clear. In *Blueford v. Arkansas*, 566 U.S. 599 (2012), the jury foreperson reported that the jury was unanimous against guilt on charges of capital murder and first-degree murder, was deadlocked on the manslaughter charge, and had not yet voted on the negligent homicide charge. The trial court instructed the jury to continue to deliberate. The jury continued its deliberations but could not reach a verdict. The trial court then declared a mistrial. The prosecutor filed new charges which included all the charges from the previous trial, including the capital murder and first-degree murder charges which the foreperson reported that the jury was unanimous in rejecting. Both parties agreed that the defendant could be retried on the manslaughter and negligent homicide charges. The defendant, however, moved to dismiss the capital murder and first degree murder charges on double jeopardy grounds. The Supreme Court held that because no formal judgment of acquittal had been entered, the defendant could be retried on the capital murder and first-degree murder charges. The Court held that the jury foreperson's report was not a final resolution of anything since the jurors continued to deliberate after this report and could have revised its earlier vote rejecting the capital murder and first-degree murder charges.

However, in *Smith v. Massachusetts*, 543 U.S. 462 (2005), in a similar setting, the Court held that double jeopardy did apply because the trial court, at the end of the prosecutor's case, had granted a defense motion to enter a not guilty finding on one count of the indictment. After closing arguments, the prosecution presented case law to the judge that persuaded her to rescind her earlier decision, and to submit the count to the jury, which convicted the defendant. Because state law did not provide for a "conditional" decision of acquittal, or for a reconsideration of such an action, the Supreme Court, 5-4, held that the defendant had been acquitted on the one count, and it was error to submit it to the jury. See Note, 41 Gonz. L. Rev. 391 (2005-2006). Thus, the double jeopardy protection, as stated in *Smith*, turns on fact-specific conditions, and on state law. Thus, in *Curry v. State*, 930 So. 2d 849 (Fla. App. 2006), for example, there was no double jeopardy where the trial judge first orally granted a motion for acquittal, but reversed himself before the bench conference had concluded.

On the other hand, *Smith* makes clear that a trial court error as to the law, as well as to the facts, will create jeopardy. Thus, in *Carter v. State*, 365 Ark. 224, 227 S.W.3d 895 (2006), the trial judge erroneously believed that aggravated robbery required that a gun be used as a gun, rather than as a bludgeon, and acquitted the defendant on the aggravated robbery charge. Although the trial judge was wrong, a subsequent prosecution for aggravated robbery was barred by the Double Jeopardy Clause. Similarly, in *Evans v. Michigan*, 568 U.S. 313 (2013), the trial court granted defendant's directed verdict motion after erroneously adding an element to the arson statute with which Evans had been charged. The Court held that double jeopardy attached whenever the trial court's decision to grant a directed verdict resulted either from it erroneously adding a statutory element to a crime or from it misconstruing the elements in a statute. Thus, Evans could not be retried even though he received a windfall as a result of the judicial error.

When a conviction is overturned on the grounds of insufficient evidence of guilt, the Double Jeopardy Clause precludes a second trial. *Burks v. United States*, 437 U.S. 1 (1978). In *United States v. Alvarez*, 351 F.3d 126 (4th Cir. 2003), the district court entered a "Judgment of Acquittal" after the jury deadlocked. But that, said the Court of Appeals for the Fourth Circuit, could not preclude a reprosecution unless it were shown that the trial judge had considered the sufficiency of the evidence. On the other hand, in *Yeager v. United States*, 557 U.S. 110 (2009), defendant, senior vice president of an Enron subsidiary, was charged with 126 counts of various federal crimes, all related to economic fraud and insider trading. The jury acquitted him on the fraud counts but hung on the insider trading counts. After the government reindicted defendant on the "hung counts," he moved to dismiss. On the basis of *Ashe* (see pp. 215-216, *infra.*), the Supreme Court held that the hung counts could not be considered in attempting to determine what had "necessarily" been decided for purposes of collateral estoppel: "Because a jury speaks only through its verdict, its failure to reach a verdict cannot—by negative implication—yield a piece of information that helps put together the trial puzzle." The Court remanded the case for the court of appeals to consider, if it wished, the government's argument that even with this clarification the acquittal did not actually reflect a jury finding that precluded the renewed insider trading prosecution.

4. Double Jeopardy and Sentencing

It appears that the Double Jeopardy Clause does not apply in sentencing at all. The Court has held that a failure of proof in a sentencing proceeding simply does not have the "qualities of constitutional finality that attend an acquittal," *Monge v. California*, 524 U.S. 721 (1998), except where the first proceeding was the sentencing phase of a capital case. *Bullington v. Missouri*, 451 U.S. 430 (1981). In *Sattazahn v. Pennsylvania*, 537 U.S. 101 (2002), the jury had "hung" on the death penalty issue, and state law had required the imposition of a life imprisonment sentence. After defendant successfully appealed his conviction, the state sought, and obtained, the death penalty in a second trial. The Supreme Court held that this did not violate the Double Jeopardy Clause because the entry of the life imprisonment sentence in the first trial had not been an "acquittal" of the death penalty.[7]

B. THE "SAME OFFENSE" DOCTRINE

I. "Punishment" for "Offenses"

The Double Jeopardy Clause protects only against "punishment" for an "offense." Many government restrictions, even severe ones, are not punishment if the legislative intent is not to punish, but to achieve some other, regulatory, goal. Thus, lifetime "civil" imprisonment for sexually violent offenders,[8] lifetime registration for sex offenders,[9] administrative monetary penalties and occupation debarment,[10] and "civil" forfeiture of "instrumentalities of crime,"[11] among many governmental actions, are not "punishment" and hence not affected by the Double Jeopardy Clause. Recently, an expelled congressman learned that, because expulsion from Congress is not a punishment for an offense, he could be criminally prosecuted for the same acts that caused his expulsion. See *United States v. Traficant*, 368 F.3d 646 (6th Cir. 2004).

---

7. For critiques of *Sattazahn*, see Comment, 94 J. Crim. L. & Criminology 587 (2004); Comment, 38 Suffolk U.L. Rev. 245 (2004).
8. *Kansas v. Hendricks*, 521 U.S. 346 (1997).
9. *Smith v. Doe*, 538 U.S. 84 (2003).
10. *Hudson v. United States*, 522 U.S. 93 (1997).
11. *Bennis v. Michigan*, 516 U.S. 442 (1996).

2. The "Same Offense" — An Overview

Thirty-five years ago, the Court itself declared that its double jeopardy decisions were "a veritable Sargasso Sea which could not fail to challenge the most intrepid judicial navigator." *Albernaz v. United States*, 450 U.S. 333, 343 (1981). That statement continues to apply today. In two separate instances, the Court in double jeopardy cases overruled three-year-old precedents,[12] and in one more instance, overruled an eight-year-old precedent.[13] So get ready for a rousing adventure at sea. The first shoal — the "same offense" language of the clause.

The Double Jeopardy Clause protects against two jeopardies for the "same offense." Sounds fairly clear, right? Robbery is robbery, mail fraud is mail fraud. Not so quick. If Mortimer is prosecuted for robbing the First National Bank at 3:00 on Monday, it would seem from the words of the clause that whether he is acquitted or convicted he cannot be reprosecuted for robbing the First National Bank at 3:00 on Monday. But suppose the second indictment alleges that the robbery was done with a rifle, and seeks a conviction for *armed* robbery. Does the first verdict preclude reprosecution? The courts have used several different tests to answer that question:

- the "same elements" test;
- the "same conduct" (or "same transaction" or "same event") test;
- the "same evidence" test.

3. The "Same Elements" Test —
Blockburger v. United States

In *Blockburger v. United States*, 284 U.S. 299 (1932), the Court adopted the "same elements" test to determine whether the defendant has been punished or convicted twice for the "same offense":

> Where the same act or transaction constitutes a violation of two distinct statutory provisions, the test to be applied . . . is whether each provision requires proof of an additional fact which the other does not.

This formula provides a very bright line. The court need only look at the words of the statute(s) involved. If the words are identical, it is the "same

---

12. *United States v. Scott*, 437 U.S. 82 (1978), overruling *United States v. Jenkins*, 420 U.S. 348 (1975); *United States v. Dixon*, 509 U.S. 688 (1993), overruling *Grady v. Corbin*, 495 U.S. 508 (1990).
13. See *Hudson v. United States*, 522 U.S. 93 (1997), effectively overruling *United States v. Halper*, 490 U.S. 435 (1989).

offense." If not, they are different offenses. Thus, if one statute prohibits "robbery by violence" and the other prohibits "robbery on a sidewalk," they are different offenses, and double jeopardy does not prevent conviction and punishment for both. There is one exception — if one statute prohibits "robbery by violence" and the other prohibits "robbery by violence on a sidewalk," the first is a "lesser included offense" of the second, and *is* a "same offense."

In *Harris v. Oklahoma*, 433 U.S. 682 (1977), the defendant, in the first trial, was prosecuted for murder, based solely on the theory that the death was a felony murder, occurring during a robbery. After the murder trial, the state sought to prosecute on the robbery itself. The statutes were clearly different; there were many different "elements." But the Court appeared to take a major step away from *Blockburger*, and held the second prosecution barred, although the felony murder statute did not restrict itself to homicides occurring during robbery. This view meant that the statutory words were not *always* the magic test: In some circumstances, the Court was willing to look at the way in which the crimes had been committed, rather than solely at the statutes involved.

In *Grady v. Corbin*, 495 U.S. 508 (1990), the Court appeared to take this view to heart. In *Grady*, the Court held that the Double Jeopardy Clause would be violated if the state prosecuted, for homicide, a driver of a car who had already pled guilty to traffic offenses which were based upon the poor driving which had caused the accident from which the victim died. Clearly the two offenses (a traffic offense; homicide) each contained unique elements, and therefore were not the "same offense" under *Blockburger*. Nevertheless, the Court focused not on the statutory elements, but on both the *conduct* which was proved in the traffic offense, and the *evidence* which the prosecutor had used in the first proceeding, and would use in the second proceeding. The Court noted that the "time, place, and circumstances" for the two offenses were virtually identical, although they obviously were composed of different elements. Even if the statutes were substantially differently worded, said the Court, and a second prosecution therefore not barred by *Blockburger*, a more expansive reading of the Double Jeopardy Clause should prevail. The precise test laid out by *Grady* was ambiguous. But it seemed clear that the Court was abandoning, or at least supplementing, *Blockburger*.

Three years later, however, the Court, badly divided about both its rationale and about the application of its rationale, overruled *Grady*. In *United States v. Dixon*, 509 U.S. 688 (1993), the Court declared that the *Grady* test had proved (in three years???) to be "unworkable," as well as not grounded in historical double jeopardy concerns. It (re)embraced *Blockburger* as the "one and only" test of a "same offense" within the Double Jeopardy Clause.

Before *Grady*, and obviously since *Dixon*, there were still exceptions to the *Blockburger* rule. Consistent with the purpose of the clause to prevent a prosecutor from "sandbagging" a first proceeding, successive prosecutions would be allowed if there were facts that either had not yet occurred, or could not have reasonably been discovered to have occurred, at the time of the first prosecution. *Brown v. Ohio*, 432 U.S. 161 (1977). For example, in *Grady*, the victim of the traffic accident died almost instantly at the crash. But if the traffic prosecution had occurred prior to his death, such that the prosecution could not have "joined" that crime (see below), neither *Blockburger* nor, hypothetically, *Grady*, would bar a successive prosecution for homicide.

4. The "Same Conduct" and the "Same Evidence" Tests

Many commentators, and a number of state courts, see *Blockburger* as too narrow. After all, if Mortimer (our bank robber) took the money from three tellers and two customers, are there *five* crimes (one for each individual victim) or *three* (the two customers, and the bank)? In either instance, it means that a prosecutor could essentially turn Mortimer's "one robbery" into a multitude of offenses, for which he could be separately and successively prosecuted, ostensibly wearing down the defendant and eviscerating the double jeopardy protection.[14]

These concerns led a number of state courts to adopt different approaches. The terms ("same transaction," "same episode," "single impulse," "same evidence," "same conduct"), and therefore the results, are somewhat diverse, but the thrust is the same — to look beyond the *Blockburger* statutory elements of the offense in the abstract approach, and to the actual "event."[15] There are, of course, many difficulties in deciding when an "event" began, and when it ended. Suppose that Mortimer kidnaps one of the customers to use as a hostage, and releases the customer unhurt several miles away. Obviously, kidnapping has very different statutory "elements" than bank robbery. Just as obviously, the two crimes are intimately connected in this specific course of conduct. But many states require, or encourage, joinder of the claims in order to avoid the need for multiple prosecutions, the heavy drain on the defendant's resources, and the strong likelihood of prosecutorial advantage gained during the first trial.

---

14. For a case allowing multiple prosecution in just such an instance, see *People v. Borghesi*, 66 P.3d 93 (Colo. 2003). If there were any limitation on that notion at all, it would appear to lie not in the Double Jeopardy Clause, but in the cruel and unusual punishment clause — and those who have studied the law of proportionality know that there is only limited help there. See *Ewing v. California*, 538 U.S. 11 (2003); *Harmelin v. Michigan*, 501 U.S. 957 (1991).

15. See, e.g., *People v. White*, 390 Mich. 245, 212 N.W.2d 222 (1973); *Commw. v. Campana*, 455 Pa. 622, 314 A.2d 854 (1974); Hawaii R. Pen. P. 8; N.R.R.Ct. 3:15-1.

Under the "same evidence" test, the defendant must demonstrate a reasonable possibility that the evidentiary facts used by the fact finder to establish the essential elements of one offense may also be (or have been) used to establish the essential elements of a second challenged offense. In *Lamagna v. State*, 776 N.E.2d 955 (Ind. Ct. App. 2002), for example, the court precluded convictions for both possession and conspiracy to possess cocaine: "It is apparent that the evidence relied on by the jury to find defendant guilty of dealing in cocaine was the evidence that D delivered to X a bag containing a white powder. The overt act in the conspiracy was the possession of cocaine."

The "same conduct (transaction, event)" test may clash with the "same evidence" approach. In *Taylor v. Commw.*, 995 S.W.2d 355 (Ky. 1999), the defendant was indicted for assaulting the victim with a .38 caliber pistol, and of robbing him with a rifle. At trial, however, the evidence indicated that both crimes were committed with the rifle. A court looking at the indictment might well decide that the two crimes were different, while a court looking at the evidence at trial might conclude, at least under a "conduct" approach, the two were the same.

C. "MULTIPLICITY"

Another problem, often termed the *unit of prosecution* issue, concerns prosecutorial discretion (in criminal procedure, this is a pervasive issue). Suppose the state punishes the sale of 10 grams of cocaine with 10 years in prison. A separate statute punishes the sale of 100 grams of cocaine with 25 years in prison. If Guido sells Maximilian one block of cocaine weighing 100 grams, he is facing 25 years in prison. But suppose Guido sells Maximilian 10 bags of 10 grams each. Now the prosecutor may have a choice between a single 25-year penalty or 100 years (10 bags of 10 grams each). Yet the "transaction" is the same. The problem of multiplicity is hardly new. In *Crepps v. Durden*, 2 Cowp. 640 (K.B. 1777), the court held that four sales of bread on Sunday, in violation of a "blue law," should nevertheless be construed as a single offense; otherwise, said the court, "if a tailor sews on the Lord's day, every stitch he takes is a separate offense." But *see State v. Broeder*, 90 Mo. App. 169 (Mo. App. 1901), holding that a defendant who sells 1,800 bottles of beer without a license can be prosecuted for 1,800 separate offenses.

It seems unduly harsh to send Guido away for life depending on how the prosecutor chooses to charge the "crime." Yet, if we hold the prosecutor to the "single event," does that mean that Mortimer's three robberies of the three customers must be boiled down to one robbery, thus making the other two robberies "freebies"? The problem may be one of sentencing — whether sentences in this situation should be concurrent or consecutive;

but it can also be seen as a double jeopardy problem, particularly if the prosecutor attempts seriatim trials.[16]

In *United States v. Universal C.I.T. Credit Corp.*, 344 U.S. 218 (1952), the Court appeared to be moving away from *Blockburger*. There, it held that 32 violations of the Fair Labor Standards Act stated only three offenses, treating as one offense "all violations that arise from that singleness of thought, purpose, or action, which may be deemed a single 'impulse.'" And the Court later declared that: "The Double Jeopardy Clause is not such a fragile guarantee that prosecutors can avoid its limitations by the simple expedient of dividing a single crime into a series of temporal or spatial units." *Brown v. Ohio*, 432 U.S. 1621 (1977).

A conclusion that two acts are (or are not) the "same offense" has obvious implications for successive trials and, as discussed below, for multiple punishments. But the impact may go beyond that. For example, undocumented individuals may be deported if convicted of two (but not one) drug charges. See 8 U.S.C. §1227(a)(2)(B)(I). And "three-strike" laws (discussed in Chapter 12) usually require two prior separate offenses. Because of these and other severe effects of multiple convictions, decisions allowing states (or individual prosecutors) effortlessly to establish multiple offenses seem to jar with the general import of the rule of lenity.

One area in which the "same offense" doctrine seems particularly unhelpful is that of the relatively new "compound crimes," where a defendant is subjected to a greater exposure once convicted of several predicate offenses. For example, in the Racketeer Influenced and Corrupt Organizations Act (RICO), 18 U.S.C. §§1961 *et seq.*, a defendant who commits two predicate crimes may be sentenced for them *and* for the fact that those crimes were committed as a part of an eligible "enterprise." The Court has upheld the use of the predicates against challenges that these "second" prosecutions violated the Double Jeopardy Clause. R.J. Allen et al., *supra*, Comprehensive Crim. Pro. at 1385, conclude that "the Supreme Court has . . . thrown up its hands and admitted that current double jeopardy doctrine is inadequate to deal with (such) complex crimes."

1. Collateral Estoppel (Issue Preclusion)

Even if the offense is not "the same," there is the possibility that a subsequent prosecution will be barred by "collateral estoppel." Students who have wrestled with the civil concept of collateral estoppel will be overjoyed to learn that this concept has also made its way into criminal

---

16. *Blockburger* itself involved multiple punishments, and could have been so limited. However, in *Brown v. Ohio*, 432 U.S. 161(1977), the Court relied on the *Blockburger* rule in deciding when separate prosecutions for related offenses are permissible.

prosecution. In *Ashe v. Swenson*, 397 U.S. 436 (1970), the defendant was prosecuted and acquitted for robbery of one of six victims. The trial record reflected that the defendant's prime claim was that he was not present and hence not the perpetrator. The prosecutor then sought to try the defendant for robbing victim number two. The Supreme Court held that the second proceeding was barred, even though the victim was different: the first acquittal, said the Court, clearly rested upon the jury's determination that the defendant was not the perpetrator. That factual determination would preclude a finding of guilt in the second prosecution, which was therefore barred by the Double Jeopardy Clause. Similarly, where the defendant had been found not guilty by reason of insanity in an earlier proceeding, the verdict established his insanity for all arson-related acts within the pertinent time frame and the prosecution was collaterally estopped from pursuing a second arson claim against the defendant. *United States v. Carbullido*, 307 F.3d 957 (9th Cir. 2002).

Ashe supplements *Blockburger* as a means for determining whether successive prosecutions are permissible under the Double Jeopardy Clause. But that may be little help — applying collateral estoppel in criminal cases is no easier than in civil cases. If, for example, the defendant's only argument in *Ashe* had been that no one robbed victim number one, and the jury had acquitted, that would not have precluded a prosecution for another victim. And if the defense had raised *both* claims (victim number one had not been robbed at all, and if he had, it was not by the defendant) the Court would have to determine (if possible) which of those two predicates had been the basis of the first acquittal. The dilemma is reflected in *Standefer v. United States*, 447 U.S. 10 (1980), where the Court held that defendant *A*'s acquittal on a bribery charge did not preclude a later prosecution of defendant B for aiding and abetting the same bribery.

The Court's most recent foray into this quagmire has not been definitively more helpful. In *Yeager* (discussed *supra*, p.209), the Court held that where a jury acquits on some counts and hangs on some other (apparently closely related) counts, the analysis under *Ashe* can only ask whether the *acquittals* necessarily involved a determination on a fact crucial to the hung counts; the reviewing court could not consider the implications one might draw from the jury's inability to reach a verdict on the "hung" counts.

D. MULTIPLE PUNISHMENTS

Although some Supreme Court language declares that the Double Jeopardy Clause protects against multiple punishments for the same crime, more recent decisions seem virtually to eliminate that protection. In *Missouri v. Hunter*, 459 U.S. 359 (1983), the defendant was tried — in a single proceeding — for two offenses, which, although proscribed by two separate statutes *were*, everyone agreed, the "same offense." The defendant argued that he could not be punished twice for the "same offense." But the Missouri legislature had expressly provided for two different punishments for the two different provisions. The trial court sentenced Hunter to *consecutive* terms for the two statutory offenses. The United States Supreme Court declared that the prohibition against multiple punishments was essentially subject to legislative overruling, so long as the legislature made clear that it wished to impose multiple punishments.[17]

One could distinguish between multiple punishments for the same offense imposed because of two convictions during the same trial, and for two convictions occurring in two different, successive, trials. In the first instance, courts are likely to say that the issue is one of legislative intent as, after all, the legislature could have made the punishment for "each" offense zero to life. Professor Poulin has put it bluntly:[18]

> The assertion that double jeopardy protects against multiple punishment imposed in a single proceeding . . . rests on a long history of tangled reasoning. . . . [T]he Court has never struck down as a violation of double jeopardy any legislatively-authorized criminal penalty imposed in a single proceeding.

Multiple punishments are a creature of the legislature. So long as two statutes under which a defendant is charged protect different social goals, multiple punishments do not violate the Double Jeopardy Clause. Professor Poulin argues that the real concern is not multiple punishment but multiple prosecutions for what appears to be the "same offense." Thus, if Pam is convicted of crimes *A* and *B*, which are essentially the "same offense," in the same proceeding, and punished consecutively for them, Poulin argues that there is no double jeopardy problem, and no other problem except proportionality. After all, if the legislature can constitutionally provide a 20-year sentence for crime Z, it would seem to be relatively insignificant if the sentence is imposed for one offense (with 20 years) or two offenses (each with 10 years). Nancy J. King, Portioning Punishment: Constitutional Limits on Successive and Excessive Penalties, 144 U. Pa. L. Rev. 103 (1995). See also Jacqueline E. Ross, Damned Under Many Headings: The Problem of Multiple Punishment, 29 Am. J. Crim. Law 245 (2002), a powerful argument that the issue is one of sentencing, particularly under structured sentencing schemes such as the Federal Sentencing Guidelines (see Chapter 12). But if

---

17. In some, perhaps most, instances where there is no clear legislative intent to allow the imposition of both punishments, the courts will apply the more specific — or the most recent — statute. They may also apply the less harsh punishment. This, however, is a matter of state law, and of statutory interpretation.

18. Anne Bowen Poulin, Double Jeopardy and Multiple Punishment: Cutting the Gordian Knot, 77 U. Colo. L. Rev. 595, 627-28 (2006).

Pam is prosecuted first for *A* and punished for *A*, and then prosecuted for B and punished for B, the real problem is not multiple punishments for the same offense, but multiple prosecutions, which wear down the defendant.

Several courts have concluded that *Hunter* says that the sentences are not "multiple" but "cumulative" (even if the defendant receives consecutive sentences). Justice Marshall, dissenting in *Hunter*, viewed the opinion as saying that these were not the "same offense," and that the term "same offense" should be interpreted the same way for both multiple prosecutions and multiple punishments.

Whether *Hunter* applies to more than multiple punishments is unclear. In *Brown v. Ohio*, 432 U.S. 1621 (1977), predating *Hunter*, the Court declared that "Where the judge is forbidden to impose cumulative punishment for two crimes at the end of a single proceeding, the prosecutor is forbidden to strive for the same result in successive proceedings." This language might suggest that, after *Hunter*, successive prosecutions *could* be entertained where multiple (or cumulative) sentences could be imposed in one trial. Indeed, this analysis might draw some support from Justice Scalia's opinion in *United States v. Dixon*, 509 U.S. 688, 704 (1993), which argued that the successive *prosecution* strand of the Double Jeopardy Clause cannot have a meaning different from the multiple *punishment* strand because it would be "embarrassing to assert that the single term 'same offense' has two different meanings." Justice Scalia has directly challenged the orthodoxy, arguing that the clause "prohibits not multiple punishment, but only multiple prosecutions."

Hunter makes the legislature the ultimate determiner of constitutional rights.[19] If *Hunter* holds the legislature can authorize cumulative punishments for the "same offense," could it also specifically authorize, even mandate, successive prosecutions on lesser included offenses? Could the state mandate nonjoinder of claims? Finally, could the state mandate that any acquitted defendant be tried again for the same offense? Ostensibly, such legislation would be invalid; but that would mean that *Hunter* allows the legislature to decide what a "same offense" is, but not how that same offense may be prosecuted.

E. JOINDER AND SEVERANCE — THE "KISSING COUSINS" OF DOUBLE JEOPARDY

Some of the issues generated by the doctrines just discussed might be addressed, if not fully resolved, by rules relating to joinder. Joinder of

---

19. "[D]ouble jeopardy analysis turns on whether Congress has authorized the result at issue. If Congress has enacted statutes that separately punish the same conduct, there is no double jeopardy violation." *United States v. Smith*, 354 F.3d 390 (5th Cir. 2003) (citing *Hunter*). See also *State v. Marlowe*, 277 Ga. 383, 589 S.E.2d 69 (2003).

claims, or defendants, has some obvious benefits — it is more economical, reduces inconvenience to witnesses, jurors, and attorneys, and lowers the possibility of conflicting verdicts. A majority of jurisdictions emulate the federal criminal rules, which provide that:

> The indictment or information *may* charge a defendant in separate counts if . . . the offenses charged are . . . based on the same act or transaction or are connected with, or constitute parts of, a common scheme or plan.

Fed. R. Crim. P. 8(a) (emphasis added).

Clearly, these words *permit, but do not require,* joinder of related claims, and go beyond the *Blockburger* "same elements" test. A handful of jurisdictions, however, *require* mandatory joinder of all claims arising from the "same transaction"; for example, W. Va. R. Crim. P. 8(a) provides:

> Two or more offenses may be charged in the same indictment or information. . . . All offenses based on the same act or transaction or on two or more acts or transactions connected together or constituting parts of a common scheme or plan *shall be charged in the same indictment or information.* . . .

In those jurisdictions, the joinder rules supplant the *Blockburger* test — while the Double Jeopardy Clause would allow a second trial on a separate act, the joinder rules do not. There is a close relationship between the "same transaction" test and mandatory joinder. As Justice Scalia argued in *Grady v. Corbin,* 495 U.S. 508, 527 (1990):

> The majority's holding will require prosecutors to observe a rule we have explicitly rejected in principle: that all charges arising out of a single occurrence must be joined in a single indictment.

Contrarily, to the extent that the separate crimes were parts of a "common plan," the efficiencies may dissipate if the charged offenses were committed at different times and in different places.

The rule thus places the initial decision as to joinder in the hands of the prosecution — if Hana wishes to try Dan on eight related "counts," but is worried about her proofs, she can ask the grand jury to return eight separate indictments each of one count. She may then try the first case on one count. Unless *Ashe* collateral estoppel would apply to subsequent proceedings, an acquittal on count one would not preclude a later prosecution for count two. A defendant who believes that the counts or charges have been *misjoined,* may move (in the federal system under Rule 13) on that basis. Since the joinder is by definition illegal, the defendant need not show prejudice. On the other hand, even a misjoinder may not result in defendant's ultimate victory; if the defendant is convicted and then appeals, the misjoinder is subject to harmless error analysis. *United States v. Lane*, 474 U.S. 438 (1986) (see Chapter 13).

On the other hand, Hana may ask the grand jury to hand down one indictment, with eight counts, fearing that while the petit jury may see each of the eight counts as separately weak, it may well conclude that Dan is a criminal at heart ("where there's enough smoke, there must be some fire"). Thus, the multiple counts may support each other. Moreover, evidence which would be inadmissible on one count, but admissible on another, may be allowed in a joint trial; the question then will be whether the instruction to the jury to use the evidence as to only one count will suffice to prevent prejudice. *Drew v. United States*, 331 F.2d 85 (D.C. Cir. 1964). See Arthur Best, Evidence: Examples and Explanations (6th ed. 2010). Here, too, the prosecutor has the choice.[20]

Dan may be willing to testify as to one count, but be concerned when there are counts which are clearly distinct in time, place, and evidence. He then may move to *sever* the charges under Rule 14 (which is again emulated by many jurisdictions):

> If the joinder of offenses or defendants . . . appears to prejudice a defendant or the government, the court may order separate trials of counts, sever the defendants' trial, or provide any other relief that justice requires. (Emphasis added.)

A motion for severance is different from a motion based upon misjoinder. A motion for severance agrees that the counts *may* be joined but argues that prejudice to the defendant should persuade the judge to sever the counts. *Zafiro v. United States*, 506 U.S. 534 (1993), while a misjoinder motion contends that the counts *cannot* be joined.

Generally, trial judges who are, after all, not familiar with the case, are loathe to overrule the prosecutorial decision, and to order joinder, or severance, once the indictments have been filed. And since the standard of review on either severance or joinder is "abuse of discretion" (*Johnson v. United States*, 356 F.2d 680 (8th Cir. 1966)), a defendant is unlikely to prevail on either motion.

Prosecutors may also seek to join *defendants* as well as counts. In addition to all the other benefits (economy, single use of witnesses, etc.) inherent in the joinder of claims, the prosecution is almost sure to benefit from the "birds of a feather" pastiche when several (up to 25?) defendants appear together in the courtroom, as well as from the possibility of conflicting defenses.

---

20. "[T]he empirical data show that a defendant faces a greater likelihood of conviction if he faces a single trial with joined offenses than if he is tried separately on all offenses, although the studies do not agree on exactly why this is so." James Farrin, Rethinking Criminal Joinder: An Analysis of the Empirical Research and Its Implications for Justice, 52 L. & Contemp. Probs. 325 (1989).

Other provisions of the constitution may limit joinder — or at least what evidence can be used in a joint trial. *Bruton v. United States*, 391 U.S. 123 (1968), held that in a joint trial of *A* and *B*, the admission of *A*'s confession, particularly where it mentioned *B*, violated *B*'s confrontation rights when *A* did not testify. Merely substituting a "blank" or the word "deleted" whenever *B* was mentioned in *A*'s confession is an insufficient remedy, *Gary v. Maryland*, 523 U.S. 185 (1998), although a more careful redaction, which does not lead to the inference that the "blank" refers to *B*, may be adequate. *Richardson v. Marsh*, 481 U.S. 200 (1987).

Examples

1. Indicted for six counts of mail fraud, in a case which would stretch the limits of that statute, Adolph is informed that the case has been assigned to Judge Sabatini, who is generally hostile to such charges. Adolph elects to waive a jury and be tried by the Judge. Two days before the trial, Judge Sabatini is taken ill; the prognosis is that he will recover in three weeks. Thereupon the assignment judge assigns the case to Judge Combs, who has always favored expansion of the mail fraud statute. After his motion for a continuance of the trial date, until Judge Sabatini is better, is denied, Adolph moves to bar Judge Combs from hearing the case, arguing double jeopardy. What result?

2. Sergio is being prosecuted for possession of drugs within 1,000 feet of a school facility; that is the only count — there is no lesser count of possession of drugs. His counsel has made numerous pleas for discovery, in particular for the names of the expert witnesses who will testify that the event happened within 1,000 feet of the building, which he acknowledges to be a school facility. Nick, the prosecutor, has not responded. On the day of trial, the defendant moves for sanctions for the failure to provide discovery. Nick immediately says he will offer the expert's name, and his report. The trial judge refuses to allow this, and instead, as a sanction for non-discovery, precludes the witness from testifying, and the report from being entered. Nick asks for a continuance, but this is denied. Nick then says he has no further evidence. Sergio then moves for acquittal. The trial judge declares that "in a non-jury trial, acquittals cannot be granted until at least one witness has testified." Defense counsel then calls Sergio, who gives his name and address, and denies he had drugs, much less that he was anywhere near a school facility. Defense rests, and moves again for acquittal, which the trial judge grants. Three weeks later, Nick summons Sergio for trial. Sergio claims double jeopardy. What result?

3. Pablo, an ardent art lover, visits the Museum of Modern Art when it has a touring exhibition of van Gogh, and removes "Starry Night." He is

charged with breach of the peace, and convicted. Thereafter, he is charged with grand larceny. Double jeopardy?

4. Sigmund believes (erroneously, as it later turns out) that his wife has been cheating on him. He drives to her office, where he throws her against the wall. When a co-worker intervenes, he throws the co-worker against the wall, and threatens her with a pair of scissors which he picks up off his wife's desk. He then drags his wife, at scissors point, to her Jeep, which he drives to a remote location, at speeds well over the limit. At one point, he makes her exit the Jeep, which he then ignites. Ultimately, he and his wife reconcile. But the police are not so readily forgiving. Sigmund is charged with: (1) assault on his wife; (2) assault on the co-worker; (3) terroristic threats; (4) family abuse; (5) unlawful imprisonment; (6) kidnaping; (7) destruction of property; and (8) arson. At a family court proceeding, he pleads guilty to the abuse charge; the prosecutor details all of the above facts. Thereafter, a different prosecutor, but from the same office, indicts Sigmund in a criminal trial court for the remaining counts. If Sigmund pleads double jeopardy, what result?

5. Bertram arranges for his niece to take his car and destroy it. He then calls the police and tells them his car has been stolen; during this conversation, he lies about: (a) where the car was "stolen"; (b) when the car was last used; (c) the value of the car; (d) what was in the car; (e) the fact that he did not own any other cars. He then telephones his insurance company with the same story. Several days later, he fills out a police report with the same facts. A state statute provides that insurance fraud is punishable by a maximum of five years in prison. If there are five "acts" of fraud, however, the penalty is increased to 10 years for each count. How many years is Bertram facing?

6. Paris, a basketball icon, was charged with the forcible rape of Helen Troy, a 15-year-old part-time worker at a spa where Paris was relaxing. At the trial, Ms. Troy indicated that she did not want to have sex, but she was unsure whether she made that clear to Paris; Paris argued that he was not the person involved; that he was shooting baskets in the hotel's gym at that time. The jury acquitted. The prosecutor then filed charges of statutory rape (the age in the jurisdiction is 18). Paris's counsel moved to bar the second prosecution, because of double jeopardy. What result?

7. Rolanda robs a bank, and kills a teller. She is first prosecuted and convicted for first degree murder. Thereafter the prosecution seeks to prosecute her for the robbery. She pleads double jeopardy. How will things go for Rolanda?

8. Arnold, a lawyer, pleads guilty to a charge of stealing funds from a client. The state bar association now seeks to disbar him for life. Arnold argues that this is double jeopardy. What result?

9. Harriet is convicted in her first trial of Armed Criminal Action defined as "commission of a felony with a firearm," and sentenced to the maximum permissible punishment (20 years). She is thereafter prosecuted for first degree robbery, defined as "taking of property from the presence of another by use of a firearm," and sentenced to 40 years. Is one of these prosecutions barred? If so, which one?

10. Police seize Scott's computer and find 46 pornographic images of children in sexually explicit conduct. Scott is charged with 46 counts of possession of pornography. Scott moves to have the counts consolidated, arguing multiplicitous pleading by the prosecution. What result?

11. Dale was acquitted of manslaughter while intoxicated; the evidence was that he had been high on marijuana. The prosecution then reindicted, charging the intoxicant was alcohol. What should the court do when the defendant moves, on double jeopardy grounds, to bar the second prosecution?

12. The police arrested Josh as he was emerging from the Ungerliter's house, carrying a DVD, a set of golf clubs, and $5,000 in pearls. The modus operandi was similar to that used in five other burglaries in the same area over a period of six months. Further investigation strongly supports the inference that Josh is the perpetrator of all six. A search of Josh's house also turned up 50 grams of cocaine. (a) Which of these offenses *may* be joined in a single indictment? (b) Would your answer be different in a mandatory joinder jurisdiction? (c) If the prosecutor elects to have Josh tried, seriatim, on each of the burglaries and the cocaine charge, would there be a double jeopardy problem? (d) Assuming the prosecutor seeks to join all the burglaries, is Josh likely to succeed on a motion to sever?

13. In the movie *Fracture*, starring Sir Anthony Hopkins, defendant (we'll call him Sir to show reverence) discovers that his wife is cheating on him. One night, he shoots her three times. Miraculously, she does not die, but goes into a coma. Sir confesses to John, at the scene of the crime. Sir is then prosecuted for the attempted murder of his wife. For many reasons which form the heart of the film, he persuades the trial judge that John, the key witness, is lying. Moreover, the murder weapon cannot be found, and the "fatal" bullet lies in the body of the wife. The court thereupon finds Sir not guilty. Thereafter, Sir, having his wife's power of attorney and her living will, pulls the plug (in front of many witnesses, including a clergyman). Sir then gives John the

murder weapon, and John further obtains the bullet, whereupon John tries to charge Sir with the homicide of Sir's wife. As the film ends, John explains to Sir that he could not have tried Sir for the homicide at the time of the first trial, because there was no death. Hence, he says, double jeopardy does not apply. Sir winces, gives a small wink and nod of appreciation, and offers his hands for handcuffs. What should Sir do now?

14. In 1981, John Hinckley tried to assassinate President Ronald Reagan. Hinckley was unsuccessful in his assassination attempt but he did wound both President Reagan and the President's press secretary, James Brady. Hinckley was tried for his attempt to assassinate President Reagan but the jury found that he was not guilty by reason of insanity. Brady never fully recovered and was never able to again assume his press secretary duties. In 2014, Brady died and his death was ruled a homicide, caused by the gunshot wound he received in 1981. Since there's no statute of limitations for murder, what result if Hinckley is charged and tried for murder of Brady?

Explanations

1. This example draws the distinction between when jeopardy attaches in a jury trial and a bench trial. In the former, once the trier of fact has been determined and sworn, jeopardy attaches; any change in that trier, thereafter, may raise double jeopardy issues. As noted in the text, the courts have vigorously protected the defendant's right to be tried in one sitting, by the originally selected trier. In a bench trial, however, there is no jeopardy until the first witness is sworn. Adolph's motion to bar the prosecution is bound to lose. But Adolph might argue that the reason for the reassignment is suspect: borrowing a test from other double jeopardy situations, he might argue that there was no "manifest necessity" to reassign the case; the court simply could have waited until Judge Sabatini had recovered. If there is any indication that the reassignment was "vindictive," that is, an attempt to convict Adolph under a broad view of the statute, it is possible that there would be a due process violation. Since there was no jury here, there was no question of whether the jurors could return at the relevant time (indeed, as we saw earlier, if a single juror becomes ill, there is always the possibility of replacing him with an alternate). The example here could also be distinguished from one where the first judge died, or retired, since his return would be impossible, and the necessity to find a different judge "manifest." But, as a matter of doctrine, the "manifest necessity" test applies only after a finding that the defendant was in jeopardy, and the

courts have not generally brought the language from one area of double jeopardy into another. Adolph is unlikely to get Combs out of his hair (or vice versa).

2. This, of course, is a real case. Well, almost a real case. In the actual case, the defense counsel called the defendant's daughter, whose total testimony was "That's my dad." The problems, however, are numerous. First, the judge is correct — in a bench trial, there must be at least one witness before "jeopardy" attaches. His hint was correct. Second, was the trial judge's order precluding the expert and his report "proper," or should he have given Nick his continuance? Or, in the alternative, declared a mistrial (in which case no double jeopardy)? When courts have taken the latter course, at the urging of an unprepared prosecutor, the answer has generally been that there is "manifest necessity." Third, and more to the point for our current purposes, was Sergio in jeopardy in the first trial? Was the first proceeding even a "trial"? As we have suggested, the Double Jeopardy Clause usually employs very bright lines — if the jury is sworn, jeopardy attaches; if not, even if there is a whole trial, jeopardy never attached. Nevertheless, the First Circuit, citing *Aleman* (see p. 206) and a number of other Illinois decisions,[21] concluded that the trial court's "acquittal" was a "sham," and that the defendant was never in jeopardy.[22] Hence, *double* jeopardy was not applicable. *Gonzalez v. Justices of the Municipal Court of Boston*, 382 F.3d 1 (1st Cir. 2004).

3. Although every theft breaches somebody's peace of mind (at least), the two crimes have different elements. Under *Blockburger*, there is no double jeopardy. Under the "same conduct," "same transaction," or "single impulse," however, the second prosecution appears banned. If, on the other hand, Pablo made a great deal of noise after the theft was noticed, and while he was trying to escape, maybe. . . . Modern art is so confusing. By the way, in a New Jersey case on which this example is based, the court, employing a "same conduct" test, barred the larceny prosecution.

---

21. It does seem strange that the court found no case from other jurisdictions. Maybe there's something in the Illinois water.

22. Citing, e.g., *People v. Rudi*, 103 Ill. 2d 216, 469 N.E.2d 580 (1984) (discerning no double jeopardy bar when the prosecution had refused to present evidence after its request for a continuance had been denied, the defendant was sworn, and the judge entered a finding of not guilty without taking any testimony); *People v. Verstat*, 112 Ill. App. 3d 90, 444 N.E.2d 1374 (Ill. App. 1983) (deciding that acquittals amounted to appealable dismissals when the trial judge denied the prosecution's requests for a continuance, swore in the defendants, asked only their names and addresses, and found them not guilty); *People v. Edwards*, 97 Ill. App. 3d 407, 422 N.E.2d 1117 (Ill. App. 1981) (similar).

4. These are basically the facts (with a little poetic license) in *State v. Lessary*, 865 P.2d 150 (Haw. 1994). First things first — the unlawful imprisonment and the kidnaping charges might be the "same offense" under *Blockburger*, although it is possible to unlawfully imprison someone without taking them anywhere, and kidnaping generally requires the use of force. Intriguingly, the state conceded that the imprisonment charge was barred by the abuse conviction. Similarly, if the charge of assault on his wife is based on the scissors, it might be precluded by the family abuse charge. Beyond that, however, each of these offenses seems clearly not to be the "same offense" as the one pled to in family court. In *Lessary*, the defendant sought to have the court adopt a "same episode" approach, and argued that this entire series of events was one "episode." Whether the events in the office would be separable from the events in the Jeep thus constituting two "episodes" is unclear, but the court did not dwell on that. Instead, it adopted the "same conduct" approach adopted by the United States Supreme Court in *Grady v. Corbin*, 495 U.S. 508 (1990), and abandoned three years later in *United States v. Dixon*, 509 U.S. 688 (1993). The Court said that the test was met when "[t]he conduct was so closely related in time, place, and circumstances that a complete account of one charge cannot be related without referring to details of the other charge." On that basis, the scissors threats were separate from the rest of the events, said the Court; even if they were the same episode, they were not the same conduct. This is simply a good instance of where the various tests might well lead to different results.

   Remember that this case arose in a "successive prosecution" context. But had the charges all been joined, multiple punishments would most likely not have been permissible under *Missouri v. Hunter*, 459 U.S. 359 (1983), because there was no indication that the Hawaii State Legislature so intended. Thus, those crimes that "merged" could only be punished with the more severe of the penalties. *CAVEAT:* Do not confuse this with consecutive-concurrent sentences, which will be discussed in Chapter 12.

5. Here's the rub of multiplicity. If every time he lied to anyone, Bertram committed insurance fraud, he's up the river for many years. On the other hand, if every *document* is one "act," he's likely to return before he's Methusaleh. So held the court in *State v. Fleischman*, 189 N.J. 539, 917 A.2d 732 (2007).

6. *Quel dommage*, Paris, you lose. Even though the charges stem from the same conduct, the two crimes are not the "same offense" under *Blockburger* — rape requires sex by force, whereas statutory rape can occur even where there is consent, as long as the victim is under a specific age. Collateral estoppel might apply, but it is possible that the first jury

believed that Ms. Troy still consented (or at least that Paris could reasonably believe she did). Her consent, of course, is irrelevant in statutory rape. If the jury acquitted because it believed Paris was indeed more interested in free throws, and in the gym, there would be collateral estoppel, but we can't be sure — that's one of the reasons that *Ashe v. Swenson* is not as important as it might otherwise be. Paris is simply going to have to go into overtime.

7. Clearly, under a straight *Blockburger* approach, there would be no problem with a second prosecution — robbery and homicide are not even minimally the "same offense," and have numerous diverse elements. Nevertheless, in *Harris v. Oklahoma*, 433 U.S. 682 (1977), the Court held that, because the homicide case had been premised on a felony-murder theory, which required proof (and effectively conviction) of the robbery, the autrefois conviction doctrine precluded the robbery prosecution. However, if the first prosecution was not based upon the robbery, but upon premeditation, deliberation, and willfulness, then there will be no bar to the robbery proceeding.

8. Arnold should have taken criminal procedure when he was in law school. Disbarment, as well as a myriad of other professional disciplinary actions, are not "punishment" for "crime" — they are regulatory decisions taken for a nonpunitive purpose. Arnold's just going to have to become a movie star.

9. This tests the applicability of *Blockburger* after *Missouri v. Hunter*, 459 U.S.359 (1983). These two offenses are obviously "the same offense" — the armed action statute is a lesser offense of armed robbery. But *Hunter* said that a clear legislative intent would allow multiple punishments. Could it be possible that the prosecution can rely on collateral estoppel, and then have Harriet punished for armed robbery under *Hunter*? Or will *Blockburger's* rule preclude the prosecution? Remember — *Blockburger* was itself a multiple punishment, rather than a multiple prosecution, case. Allen et al. conclude that "the Court has apparently used different tests for determining the same offense in the successive-prosecution and multiple-punishment contexts." This "test case" would decide whether the Double Jeopardy Clause allows legislatures to define offense and punishments, even if they were tried in separate trials.

10. Scott will lose. We employ a two-prong test when analyzing a multiplicity challenge: (1) whether the charged offenses are identical in law and fact; and (2) whether the legislature intended multiple offenses to be charged as a single count. *State v. Schaeffer*, 266 Wis. 2d 719, 668 N.W.2d 760 (2003). In the *Schaeffer* case, upon which this example is based, the court held that even though all the pornographic photos were

on a single computer Zip disk, each file was identified by a different name, and could be prosecuted as a different count. The court noted that there was no evidence as to how the photos had been downloaded (one by one, or in a group). Absent such evidence, the court said a "reasonable inference could be that they were downloaded separately."

11. Ask the prosecutor what he's been smoking. The kind of intoxicant was clearly not an "element" of the crime; the jury's acquittal concludes that the defendant was not intoxicated — on anything. *See Ex parte Taylor*, 101 S.W.3d 434 (Tex. Crim. App. 2002).

12. Preface — the cocaine charge is so different from the burglary charges that they cannot be joined. So we deal here only with the burglaries.

    (a) Given the words of Federal Rule 8(a), the burglaries are "of the same or similar character" and *may be* joined. But the prosecutor need not join all of them; she may join some, and leave others for separate indictment.

    (b) Even in most mandatory joinder jurisdictions, it is unlikely that the burglaries will meet the test; the burglaries are not "based on the same act or transaction" nor, so far as we know from these facts, are they "parts of a common scheme or plan."

    (c) Since *Blockburger* would only bar successive prosecutions of the "same act," the failure to join any or all of these counts would not present a *Blockburger* problem.

    (d) To avoid joinder, Josh will have to prove that the consolidation results in prejudice. Since the burglaries happened in different places, etc., the efficiencies often associated with joinder would seem to be minimal. Nevertheless, Josh's main argument for prejudice will turn on the premise that a jury seeing so many charges may well think that at least some of them must be accurate. A trial court is unlikely to consider that sufficient "prejudice." And if Josh appeals the denial of his severance motion, he's almost certain to lose; it would not be an abuse of discretion to allow the prosecutor to join the burglary counts.

13. Get a plane ticket, read a book, sit back and relax. While John is partially correct, he should have considered more carefully. Read on. This movie generated much discussion on the servers of criminal law professors across the country. After much debate about whether the actual killing of the wife was "authorized" or "justified," and whether the bullet found in her body after her death constituted "new evidence," the general conclusion was that a subsequent prosecution would, contrary to the satisfying end of the movie, be barred by *collateral estoppel*, and Hopkins could not be (re)tried. The first trial concluded that Sir did not kill, or intend to kill, his wife. The actual death in the hospital was "justified." But there may yet be justice — if

John can persuade a court that there was deceit in the use of the power of attorney, perhaps Sir will be barred from claiming justification, in which case he may be prosecuted *not* for the act which caused the coma, but for the pulling of the plug. See — law professors *do* go to the movies once in a while.

14. Because the jury found that Brady was insane at the time of the shooting in 1981, the government will be precluded from relitigating the case. The finding that Brady was insane at the time he shot President Reagan means that he was also insane at the time he shot Brady, since both shootings occurred during the same incident.

F. HUNG JURIES, MISTRIALS, AND MANIFEST NECESSITY

I. Mistrials

No trial ever runs as smoothly as either side anticipates. There are always glitches, some of which may turn into insurmountable impediments for one of the parties. A major witness (or attorney, or juror) may become sick, disappear, or die. New evidence may suddenly disrupt a trial plan. Inadmissible evidence (e.g., the defendant's criminal record) may inadvertently be seen by the jury or referred to in testimony. In instances like these, the adversely affected party may seek some remedy, including a judicial declaration that the problem is so severe that the trial should be stopped, and a "*mistrial*" declared. A mistrial occurs when the court, during the trial, decides to abort the procedure. The decision may be made (1) upon request of either party, or (2) *sua sponte* by the judge. A mistrial undermines what the Supreme Court has called the defendant's "valued right to have his trial completed by a particular tribunal," *Wade v. Hunter*, 336 U.S. 684 (1949). It is not quite clear whether the major concern here is the defendant's psychological well-being, or his financial resources. In *Downum v. United States*, 372 U.S. 734 (1963), the Court spoke of the possible "harassment of an accused by successive prosecution," and in *Arizona v. Washington*, 434 U.S. 497 (1978), focused on the "increased financial and emotional burden" which the accused would bear. If the mistrial has been granted over the defendant's objection, and upon the prosecutor's request, or if the trial judge acted on her own, a reprosecution will be allowed only if there was a *manifest necessity* to declare the mistrial. *Oregon v. Kennedy*, 456 U.S. 667 (1982).

a. Hung Juries

The classic "manifest necessity" is when a jury is "hung" — unable to reach a verdict, even after a judge has given them a "dynamite" charge urging them to reconsider their differences.[23] One might think, since the prosecution has not proved its case beyond a reasonable doubt, that a hung jury should be treated like an acquittal, but the Supreme Court has held otherwise, saying that the rule "accords recognition to society's interest in giving the prosecution one complete opportunity to convict. . . ." *Richardson v. United States*, 468 U.S. 317 (1984). More realistically, "If retrial . . . were barred whenever an appellate court viewed the 'necessity' for a mistrial differently from the trial judge, there would be a danger that the latter, cognizant of the serious societal consequences of an erroneous ruling, would employ coercive means to break the apparent deadlock." *Arizona v. Washington*, 434 U.S. 497 (1978). If the defendant concurs, a trial judge has broad discretion as to whether a jury is hung. See *Renico v. Lett*, 559 U.S. 766 (2010).

b. Trial Errors

There are four factors in considering whether a mistrial will bar a retrial declared because of a trial error:

1. who asked for the mistrial;
2. whether the requesting party had an improper motivation;
3. whether the defendant suffered special prejudice;
4. whether meaningful alternatives existed, and were considered.

Although almost any trial error COULD be considered grounds for a mistrial, here are some that may be considered circumstances that justify a mistrial based on "manifest necessity":

- violating the rape shield laws in questioning a witness;
- exposing the factfinder to illegal or otherwise inadmissible evidence;
- where events may require closure of the trial court indefinitely (such as after the Sept. 11, 2001 attacks);
- where both counsel express concern about possible juror bias;
- prejudicial opening statements.

On the other hand, the following will usually NOT constitute manifest necessity:

---

23. Hung juries are an American invention; in earlier times the jury was to be kept, without food and drink, until they reached a verdict.

- arrest of a witness during recess in trial;
- impatience of the trial court with counsel's behavior;
- where trial court ordered mistrial in belief that a witness was bullied into telling his story a certain way;
- defendant's nervousness and breathing problems;
- single juror's illness, at least where court did not consider a continuance;
- remediable misconduct by jurors (see Chapter 8);
- revelation that a juror had sat on a grand jury that had returned an earlier indictment against the defendant for the same offense.

Granting a mistrial requires starting over again from scratch. Courts are therefore wary of endorsing such an action. In *United States v. Jorn*, 400 U.S. 470 (1971), the trial judge, over the protest of the prosecutor, declared a mistrial after concluding that prosecution witnesses had not been sufficiently warned of their Fifth Amendment rights. The Supreme Court concluded that the trial court should have considered a less drastic alternative and held a subsequent prosecution barred by double jeopardy. A nonexhaustive list might include:

1. permitting a continuance;
2. ordering a severance of defendants (for example, because the prosecutor inadvertently disclosed that the co-defendant had threatened a complaining witness);
3. permitting defense counsel to examine a witness about a conversation he had had with the counsel;
4. determining whether the defense objected to the mistrial as well;
5. issuing curative instructions;
6. removing obstreperous counsel from the case;[24]
7. continuing with 11 jurors.[25]

Where there appears to be a reasonable alternative to a mistrial, a trial judge's discretionary actions will be scrutinized more carefully. As one court put it:

The doctrine . . . stands as a *command* to trial judges not to declare a mistrial without the defendant's consent until a scrupulous exercise of judicial

---

24. *Rubenfeld ex rel. Walters v. Appelman*, 230 A.D.2d 911, 646 N.Y.S.2d 79 (N.Y. App. Div. 1996).
25. In those states where a jury may proceed with 11 jurors, declaring a mistrial when one juror becomes disabled is not manifestly necessary, and a subsequent prosecution will be barred. *Hill v. State*, 90 S.W.3d 308 (Tex. Crim. App. 2002). On the other hand, if both parties must agree to 11 jurors, the prosecutor's refusal to agree requires a mistrial, and a second prosecution is not barred. *Zanone v. Comm.*, 40 Va. App. 364, 579 S.E.2d 634 (Va. Ct. App. 2003).

discretion leads to the conclusion that a termination of the trial is manifestly necessary.

Commw. v. Balog, 395 Pa. Super. 158, 576 A.2d 1092 (Pa. Super. 1990) (emphasis added).

In *Arizona v. Washington*, 434 U.S. 497 (1978), the Court declared that:

[I]t is manifest that the key word "necessity" cannot be interpreted literally; . . . we assume that there are degrees of necessity and we require a "high degree" before concluding that the mistrial is appropriate . . . [T]he prosecutor must shoulder the burden of justifying the mistrial. . . . His burden is a heavy one.

For example, where a trial judge, personally frustrated with the manner in which the case was being tried by the state, declared a mistrial because he feared that his anger over the "bombastic" style of the prosecutor would affect the jury and skew the result, there was no manifest necessity, and a second prosecution was barred by double jeopardy. *Commw. v. Kelly*, 797 A.2d 325 (Pa. Super. 2002).[26] In part, the appellate court feared that the trial judge, unconsciously, was concerned that the state would lose the case not because of the merits, but because of the prosecutor's style.

Where there is no readily apparent alternative, however, the judge's decision may be given more weight. Thus, in *Illinois v. Somerville*, 410 U.S. 458 (1973), when the prosecutor noted (after the jury was sworn but before trial testimony began) that the indictment did not meet state law requirements, the trial court declared a mistrial. Agreeing that this was a "manifest necessity," the Supreme Court emphasized that, had the case gone through to verdict, the defense would have easily won an appeal. There was no alternative, said the Court, to the mistrial declaration. *Somerville* also seems to demonstrate the Court will not be overly concerned with who is "at fault" for the necessity. Clearly, the prosecutor was negligent for not obtaining a proper indictment, but the Court did not use that negligence to damage the state's chance at a conviction.[27]

---

26. Where, during a 13-day delay in the trial, two jurors lost a parent and the prosecutor was unable to appear (because, as she told the judge, she had an irreversible vacation planned for that time) and the trial judge *sua sponte* declared a mistrial, there was no manifest necessity. *State v. Georges*, 345 N.J. Super. 538, 786 A.2d 107 (N.J. Super. 2001).

27. It is also possible that defense counsel was attempting to "sandbag." By not challenging the indictment, defense counsel might have been hoping that, if defendant were convicted, there would be a successfully appealable issue. Had defense counsel raised that issue directly, particularly prior to the swearing of the jury, the prosecutor might have obtained a new indictment, or filed a new information. Moreover, the prosecutor's motion came before the start of trial, so there was no possibility that the prosecutor was attempting to "salvage" a case

One factor which courts weigh heavily in assessing the "manifestness" of the necessity is the degree to which the trial judge consulted with the adversely affected counsel before declaring a mistrial. Indeed, there were so many hastily declared mistrials that Federal Rule 26.3 was amended in 1993 to require the judge to discuss the issue with both counsel before declaring a mistrial and to consider alternatives.

Where the defendant asks for a mistrial (for example, after the prosecution has introduced highly prejudicial inadmissible evidence), and then seeks to bar reprosecution, the courts almost invariably reject the motion to bar a second prosecution. The common explanation is that the defendant has waived his double jeopardy protection to avoid an (almost inevitable) conviction. *United States v. Dinitz*, 424 U.S. 600 (1976). There is one exception to this general rule: If the defendant can show that the prosecutor has intentionally "*goaded*" the defendant into making such a motion, retrial may be barred. This standard may be impossible for the defendant to meet; as Justice Stevens, concurring in *Oregon v. Kennedy*, 456 U.S. 667 (1982), observed: "It is almost inconceivable that a defendant could prove that the prosecutor's deliberate misconduct was motivated by an intent to provoke a mistrial instead of an intent simply to prejudice the defendant." He advocated a more flexible approach, based on overreaching and egregious prosecutorial misconduct. A substantial number of state courts find the *Kennedy* standard far too restrictive, and have used Justice Stevens's approach. See *State v. Kennedy*, 295 Or. 260, 666 P.2d 1316 (1983) (on remand from *Oregon v. Kennedy, supra*);[28] *Commw. v. Simons*, 514 Pa. 10, 522 A.2d 537 (1987). On the other hand, the *Dinitz* Court, 424 U.S. at 610 note 12 (quotations omitted), argued that a rule that focused on impact, and not on prosecutorial intent, might ultimately redound to defendants' detriment saying that such a rule would:

> give rise to much reluctance in granting mistrials because [the] trial courts will understand that society will be better served by completing a trial, even after clear error has arisen and the defendant seeks the mistrial, than the alternative of a mistrial and the possible bar of double jeopardy based on the error.

---

that was going badly. Had *the prosecutor* waited until late in the trial, it is possible that *he or she* might have been accused of sandbagging.

28. It is difficult to distinguish "simple prosecutorial error, such as an isolated misstatement or loss of temper," from "misconduct that is so egregious that it raises concerns over the integrity and fundamental fairness of the trial itself." *State v. Jorgenson*, 198 Ariz. 390 (2000). Some states, acknowledging the difficulty of proving that the prosecutor "intentionally" provoked a mistrial motion, hold that the defense need merely demonstrate that the prosecutor's actions were "reckless." *Ex parte Lewis*, 219 S.W.3d 335 (Tex. Crim. App. 2007).

See, generally, Cynthia C. Person, Note, Prosecutorial Misconduct and Double Jeopardy: Should States Broaden Double Jeopardy Protection in Light of *Oregon v. Kennedy*?, 37 Wayne L. Rev. 1699 (1991).

Another way to think of this is as follows:

Did Defendant Consent to the Mistrial?

Yes — then no bar to retrial.

Exception: Unless the prosecutor *intentionally* "goaded" the motion or acquiescence.

No —

Then ask: Did the trial Court consider options (continuance, preclusion of witnesses) and discuss them with counsel?

If *Yes* — Then standard is abuse of discretion.

If *No* — Then subject to rigorous scrutiny.

Finally, if the judge *dismisses* the case on the merits, the Court views it as an acquittal which bars retrial, unless (a) defendant consented or (b) there was "manifest necessity." *United States v. Bonas,* 344 F.3d 945 (9th Cir. 2003).[29] On the other hand, most dismissals occur before jeopardy attaches and are not on the merits; and thus, the prosecution may appeal and, if successful, (re)prosecute.

G. SUCCESSFUL APPEALS: DOUBLE JEOPARDY AND VINDICTIVENESS

It has long been settled that the Double Jeopardy Clause does not bar reprosecution if the defendant successfully appeals his conviction. But the explanation for this rule has altered several times over the years: (1) defendant has waived his right to the protection of double jeopardy; (2) the jeopardy "continues" until there is a "legitimate" final verdict;[30] (3) without such a rule, courts would be reluctant to find errors and overturn convictions.[31]

---

29. The issue has created one of the "flips-flops" in double jeopardy law. In *United States v. Jenkins,* 240 U.S. 358 (1975), the Court applied the double jeopardy bar in such a setting, but a scant three years later, it overruled *Jenkins. United States v. Scott,* 437 U.S. 81 (1978). *Scott* may be restricted to cases where the defendant seeks and obtains a dismissal on grounds not relating to the sufficiency of the government's case. The Court in *Scott* said that the critical question was whether the trial court's ruling was based on a failure of proof in establishing the "factual elements of the offense."

30. *United States v. Ball,* 163 U.S. 662 (1896). As Justice Holmes, dissenting in *Kepner v. United States,* 195 U.S. 100, 134(1904), explained: "[L]ogically and rationally, a man cannot be said to be more than once in jeopardy on the same cause, however often he may be tried. The jeopardy is one continuing jeopardy from its beginning to the end of the cause."

31. As Justice Harlan noted in *United States v. Tateo,* 377 U.S. 463, 466 (1964): "[I]t is at least doubtful that appellate courts would be as zealous as they are now in protecting against the effects of improprieties at the trial or pre-trial state if they knew that reversal of a conviction would put the accused irrevocably beyond the reach of further prosecution."

There are two exceptions to the "right to retry" rule. First, if the reversal is based on the appellate court's judgment that the evidence at trial was legally insufficient to sustain the conviction, the state has had its one fair chance at conviction, and a new prosecution is prohibited. *Burks v. United States*, 437 U.S. 1 (1978). Where the reversal is based on the *weight* of the evidence rather than its sufficiency, however, retrial is not barred. *Tibbs v. Florida*, 457 U.S. 31 (1982).

Second, if the second prosecution appears "vindictive," it will be barred, not by double jeopardy, but by due process. In the past three decades, the Supreme Court, in a series of decisions, has prevented "vindictive" reprosecution of a defendant who successfully appeals a conviction. The Court has declared that a prosecutor who increases the charges on a second prosecution must demonstrate that the increase is based on the merits, and not cemented in vindictiveness because of the successful appeal. *North Carolina v. Pearce, supra,* 395 U.S. 711 (see p. 46); *Blackledge v. Perry,* 417 U.S. 21 (1974).

H. THE DUAL SOVEREIGNTY DOCTRINE

The dual sovereignty doctrine allows two states, or the federal government and a state, each to prosecute a defendant successively for the "same offense." It is palpably fictitious — the states are not "sovereign" (at least as regards the federal government) and it is difficult to say they are "sovereign" even vis-á-vis each other.[32] It is, however, now a major fixture of double jeopardy law. There are several "explanations," none of them overly convincing, for the doctrine.

One possible explanation is that the dual prosecutions do not involve "the same offense." Remember Mortimer, who was tried in state court for bank robbery (p. 213)? If he were later tried in a federal court for robbing a *federally insured* bank, that element would be a "new" element. Since every offense carries with it an implicit element "against sovereign A," it is plausible to argue that an offense in state B, even premised on exactly the same transaction, is nevertheless a different offense. Thus under *Blockburger*, he may be retried by a second sovereign because there is a new element in the second crime — the new victim. The difficulty with this explanation is that it stretches *Blockburger* to its breaking point. Surely if nothing is different

---

32. The doctrine was first applied in *United States v. Lanza,* 260 U.S. 377, 385 (1922), where the Court allowed the federal government to prosecute a group of defendants under the National Prohibition Act, even though the defendants had been previously tried, based on the same conduct, for violating state liquor laws.

except the name of the prosecuting sovereign, the rule seems to outstrip the reason for double jeopardy protection.

A more defensible explanation is that each sovereign has a different interest in prosecuting the offense. If the state's interest was in protecting banks against robbery, the federal government's interest was in avoiding insurable losses. This explanation, however, ultimately explains little, for under that view, the town officials where the bank was located have yet a different interest than the state; yet these political entities are viewed as the "same" sovereign, and double jeopardy applies.

Still another explanation is that each sovereign fears that the other sovereign will prosecute the first case incompetently (possibly even intentionally so); if a first prosecution, no matter how incompetent or sham, precluded a second prosecution by another sovereign, there would be a "race to the courthouse."[33] *Bartkus v. Illinois*, 359 U.S. 121 (1959). It may be that it is "unseemly" to have the court of the second sovereign determine whether there was incompetence or collusion in the first prosecution. The dual sovereignty doctrine avoids that investigation.

Nearly all of the controversial aspects of the dual sovereign doctrine were activated by the so-called Rodney King case. After a long and dangerous car chase, King, a black man, was finally stopped by a large contingent of Los Angeles police (virtually all of whom were white), who thereupon subdued him, using batons, fists, feet, and other such weapons (many had their guns drawn throughout the arrest). A passing motorist happened to catch the entire arrest and subsequent events on videotape. That tape appeared to show a massive use of excessive force; it was played and replayed on both national and international television literally thousands of times. In the state trial of the police officers indicted for beating King, the jury acquitted the defendants of virtually all counts. Outraged by the verdict, blacks in Los Angeles rioted, causing hundreds of millions of dollars of damage. Thereupon the federal government prosecuted four of those same officers, in federal court, for violating King's civil rights; they were convicted of many of the charges.

The King prosecutions exemplified more than the theoretical debate over the dual sovereignty doctrine. The federal prosecution demonstrated exactly how a second prosecution could learn from an unsuccessful

---

33. In *Bartkus*, Justice Frankfurter cited to the infamous case of *Screws v. United States*, 325 U.S. 91 (1945), where a white sheriff had fatally beaten a handcuffed black prisoner. The sheriff had never been prosecuted by the state; indeed, he was later elected to the state legislature. Were there no "dual sovereignty" doctrine, declared Frankfurter, the "trivial" one- and two-year sentences that sheriff Screws actually received in federal court could result in a "shocking and untoward deprivation of the historic right and obligation of the State" to prosecute Screws. Of course, the Court was well aware of the irony — if there were no dual sovereignty doctrine, a sham prosecution by the state in *Screws* would have prevented even the minimal sentences he received in the federal prosecution.

prosecution and obtain a conviction — precisely one of the concerns of the double jeopardy rule. During the first trial, the state, not surprisingly, had relied extensively on the videotape which appeared to demonstrate totally unwarranted use of force. The defense, however, slowed the film down and attempted to show the jury how, frame by frame, cell by cell, the police had been justified in using the force they used. The prosecution seemed stunned by the trial tactic. While no one believed that the state prosecutors had purposely lost the case, a number of critics of the acquittal argued that the state had relied too heavily on the videotape, had not fought a change of venue with sufficient vigor,[34] and had not put the strongest case forward, overconfident that the jury would reflect the same outrage that had greeted the nationally televised tape. The federal prosecutors were ready for the defense approach, and were (apparently) able to neutralize it. The dual sovereignty doctrine permitted the federal prosecution without requiring such a finding.

The doctrine is very controversial. It is obviously contrary to the interests the Double Jeopardy Clause is designed to protect: (1) the second prosecuting sovereign can learn from the first's presentation (whether successful or not); (2) the defendant's resources (and resilience) may be worn down by the second prosecution.[35] The Executive Board of the American Civil Liberties Union, for example, divided almost exactly down the middle as to whether to oppose the second King prosecution; a significant number of members of that Board resigned over the decision to oppose the federal intervention. A majority of states, by statute or even by constitution, preclude prosecution once another sovereign has tried the defendant.[36] Even here, however, state courts disagree. If the statute or constitutional provision

---

34. The King event highlighted one more aspect of American justice. The first trial, initially set for Los Angeles, in which the jury would likely have been heavily minority, was transferred to Simi Valley, a substantially white suburb of Los Angeles. Many argued that the white jurors of Simi Valley identified more with the police than with the black victim. The second (federal) trial occurred inside Los Angeles, and the jury was much more interracial.

35. In England, a foreign government's prosecution of a defendant would bar reprosecution in an English court. Professor Akhil R. Amar, Reconstructing Double Jeopardy: Some Thoughts on the Rodney King Case, 26 Cumb. L. Rev. 1, 5 (1995), observes England would give more respect to the adjudication of another Nation than the dual sovereignty doctrine requires in this country.

36. Statutes restricting the application of the doctrine are in place in 24 states. These statutes fall generally into two groups: (a) statutes which bar successive prosecution based on the same "offense" (Arkansas, Delaware, Hawaii, Minnesota, Mississippi, New Jersey, Pennsylvania, and Wisconsin); and (b) the 16 other states, which bar successive prosecution based on the same "act." Section 21 of the Uniform Narcotic Drug Act applies the doctrine to drug offenses: "If a violation of this article is a violation of a federal law or the law of another state, a conviction or acquittal under federal law or the law of another state for the same act is a bar to prosecution in this state." A number of states have adopted this provision, in addition to a general bar on subsequent prosecutions. But see People v. Zubke, 496 Mich. 80, 664 N.W.2d 751 (2003), where the court found that an act giving rise to a federal drug conspiracy conviction was not the "same act" underlying a charge of possession with intent to deliver.

precludes prosecution for an "act" which has already been the subject of prosecution, some courts will apply *Blockburger*, and conclude that the second prosecution is for a different "act," while others will note that *Blockburger* applies only to the same "offense" and not the same "act."[37]

Although the United States Supreme Court has constantly adhered to the doctrine, allowing subsequent prosecutions, the Department of Justice has, for more than 50 years, voluntarily applied the so-called *Petite policy*, named after *Petite v. United States*, 361 U.S. 529 (1960), the case in which it was first noted.[38] That policy establishes a presumption against federal prosecution subsequent to a state trial; only in rare cases will such a prosecution be authorized, and then only if the Attorney General signs the authorization documents. Thus, while this action may exacerbate relations with the state executive, it avoids the scenario where a federal court would be determining whether the state prosecution was "weak," arguably even a greater strain on federal–state relations. Supporters of this policy argue that there is a need to avoid sham or incompetent state prosecutions; critics of the policy argue that the King prosecution demonstrates that the policy is subject to unprincipled political pressures. Critics also point out that the many states that preclude second prosecutions do not appear to be concerned with sham or incompetent proceedings by the same states that ostensibly worry the federal government.

Even if most states will not prosecute after another sovereign has sought to convict the defendant, so long as the federal government is restrained only by the *Petite* policy, the dialogue will continue. Indeed, given the rapid expansion of federal criminal law over the past three decades, it is likely that virtually every state offense will soon have its federal counterpart, thereby potentially testing the application of the doctrine in numerous settings.

Examples

1. Mary's husband, having embezzled her sizable trust fund, fakes his murder and frames her for it. She is convicted in Washington. When she escapes, she tracks him down to New Orleans and kills him there. Can she plead double jeopardy if she is prosecuted in the Big Easy?

So far as appears from the opinion, the same drugs were involved in both prosecutions. This is a good example of how a general statutory prohibition against successive prosecutions can be narrowly interpreted. The majority looked at the words of the statute which related to the "same act," while the dissent focused on the conduct which "gave rise to" the federal conviction. See Christina G. Woods, The Dual Sovereignty Exception to Double Jeopardy: An Unnecessary Loophole, 24 U. Balt. L. Rev. 177 (1994).

37. See, e.g., *State v. Hansen*, 243 Wis. 2d 328, 627 N.W.2d 195 (2001) "Our initial inclination is to conclude that Hansen's interpretation of 'same act' as meaning 'same conduct' is more consistent with the plain and ordinary meaning of the term."

38. The policy was announced one week after the *Bartkus* decision.

2. Malcolm, an African American, is charged with beating a white female. The jury venire is 85 percent African American, although the general population is only 36 percent African American. During voir dire, the prosecutor strikes every African American, male or female. After four strikes, the trial court warns the prosecutor that he is facing a *Batson* violation (see Chapter 8). The prosecutor ignores the court, and strikes three more. The court warns him again. The prosecutor continues to use peremptoriness in this fashion. Finally, the judge dismisses the proceeding. When Malcolm's attorney receives notice of a retrial, he moves to bar the trial on double jeopardy grounds. He also shows that the new venire, from which any jury for the new trial would be chosen, is only 27 percent African American. What result?

3. (a) At Bob's trial for fraud, the prosecutor asks a witness about other arguably fraudulent transactions, for which Bob has not been indicted. Upon objection from defense counsel, the judge admonishes the prosecutor. The prosecutor continues, and obtains another warning. The prosecutor continues. The defendant then moves for a mistrial, which is granted. Thereafter, Bob moves to bar reprosecution on the grounds of double jeopardy. What result? Would it make any difference if the trial judge had acted on her own, without waiting for defense counsel to move for a mistrial?

   (b) Suppose that the trial judge denies the prosecutor's motion. At the end of the trial, he gives a precautionary instruction to the jury about the prosecutor's references to the (inadmissible) evidence. Bob is convicted, but the conviction is reversed because of the prosecutorial misconduct. What result if the prosecutor now seeks to retry the defendant?

4. At the first day of Rodney's jury trial for driving while intoxicated, Ahmad, the prosecutor, appears with a videotape of defendant's arrest, which should have been disclosed prior to trial. The prosecutor explains that the arresting officer had locked the tape in his filing cabinet, and that the police department evidence technician had reported that the tape was not in the evidence room. Ahmad was unaware of the tape's location until the officer arrived in court to testify during the trial. Defense counsel, Esmerelda, moves to exclude the evidence, or for a continuance of several days. The court immediately declares a mistrial. When Ahmad seeks a second trial, Rodney raises a double jeopardy bar. What result?

5. During Zeke's trial for aggravated incest, Henry, the lead investigator in the case, was being vigorously cross-examined by defense counsel. Suddenly, Henry, who knew that there was a pre-trial order precluding any reference to a polygraph which Zeke had taken, blurted out a reference to the test. The court declared a mistrial. (a) Can Zeke be retried? (b) Suppose the outburst had occurred during the victim's testimony?

6. After a long and bitter trial, jury deliberations are in their tenth day. Judge Roy Bean receives a note from the jury foreperson suggesting that one juror was "corrupt." Bean immediately calls a mistrial. If the prosecution seeks to retry the defendant, what result?

7. During opening argument in Jodie's trial for assault, Jodie's defense counsel goes into great detail about what Jodie will say when she takes the stand, including that the victim had attacked her, and that the victim had changed his story on several occasions, while Jodie had given one consistent explanation of the events in question. At the end of the prosecution's case, defense rests without putting Jodie on the stand. The court grants a prosecution motion for a mistrial, on the grounds that the defendant had given the jury his "explanation," without being subjected to cross-examination, and that the jury cannot be expected to forget defense counsel's "story." If Jodie is thereafter tried for the assault, and raises a double jeopardy objection, what result?

8. Lolita is convicted of aggravated burglary and felony murder. On appeal, the felony murder conviction was reversed on the grounds of an improper jury instruction, but the burglary conviction was affirmed. On retrial, the prosecutor asks the trial court to prevent the defendant from contesting her guilt of the aggravated burglary. What should the trial court do?

9. Mitt's wife, Sarah, disappeared on January 1, 2010. The police were convinced that Mitt had killed her, but after a year's search for the body, they found nothing. Nevertheless, the prosecutor decided to move ahead with a homicide case. On the second day of trial, Sarah's body was found in another state. The prosecution asked for a continuance. Over Mitt's objection, the trial court, opining that it would take two months to do a total examination of the body, declared a mistrial, stating that testing on the body might help either side. Was there manifest necessity?

Explanations

1. Movie buffs will recognize this as the plot in Double Jeopardy. In the film, Mary was advised by a fellow prisoner, that, having been (unjustly) convicted of killing her husband, Mary could actually kill him with impunity "in Times Square at noon." As you well know, that is *dead wrong*. Under the dual sovereignty doctrine, New York could easily prosecute Mary for a crime (killing her husband in New York) because it offended a different sovereign. (Don't worry, in the movie, Mary does not follow the legal advice she got; she actually kills her husband in self-defense.) Perhaps someone should have killed the legal consultants to the

movie. Some observers have suggested that even if both killings occurred in the same state, such that dual sovereignty could not apply, the proper way to deal with this hypothetical is to vacate the first murder conviction, give Mary credit for time served, and convict her of the actual murder.

2. Sorry. There's no double jeopardy issue here, because jeopardy never attached — the general rule is that the jury must be sworn. Does that mean that the prosecutor (or defense counsel, in a different situation) can simply abuse the peremptory system? Not necessarily. First, there are possible disciplinary sanctions to be used against an attorney who misuses peremptory challenges, or who baits the opponent (or the court). Moreover, in the scenario here, the court could find the prosecutor in contempt of court. But those remedies do nothing for Malcolm. Is he helpless here? Not necessarily. The Supreme Court has intimated, in several double jeopardy settings, that even if the specific case does not violate double jeopardy protections, other protections might be available. Thus, even if multiple punishments do not violate double jeopardy, they might violate the Eighth Amendment. Here, using an analogue to the mistrial cases, the second court might find that the judge's actions were not "manifestly necessary" and a new prosecution would violate (substantive) due process. Aside from the remedies already suggested, the trial court might have started out with a new venire, or even reinstated the removed jurors (as the discussion in Chapter 8 suggests, remedies for *Batson* violations are flexible, if nothing else). On the other hand, if we assume that black jurors would be favorable to Malcolm, then the prosecutor has gained "something" by the mistrial; the new venire is (stereotypically) less friendly to Malcolm than the first one was assumed to be. But the venire's percentages are insufficiently disparate from the population to raise a jury-selection-process challenge. And certainly Malcolm has been unduly put upon. On the other hand, it may be hard to argue that he has suffered "that much more" than he would have had the trial gone forward. (Does that suggest why the Court has drawn the jeopardy line where it has?)

3. (a) Not clear. The appellate court has concluded that the prosecutor crossed the line at trial. Had the trial judge ruled properly on the motion, a retrial would be precluded under *Kennedy*, and subjecting defendant to a second trial gives the state a second bite at the apple, which it clearly does not deserve. Should the state benefit because the trial judge erred in its favor after this misconduct? Since the defendant asked for the retrial, the normal rule would allow the reprosecution. But if the judge hearing the motion determines that Bob's counsel was "goaded into" asking for a mistrial, double jeopardy may apply. In most instances, however, a defendant is required to show not merely that he reacted to improper behavior by the prosecutor,

but that the prosecutor *intentionally* misbehaved in order to obtain a defense motion for a mistrial. It will be the rare situation in which a trial judge will make such a finding with regard to either counsel, preferring to think that the outburst was simply done in the "heat of the moment." The trial judge should have recognized that the defense counsel was acting impetuously, and should not have granted the mistrial. Perhaps she should have considered other alternatives, such as curative instruction. Nevertheless, Bob, unhappily, is likely to have to go through a second trial.

4. This is a close call. In *People v. Bagley*, 338 Ill. App. 3d 978, 789 N.E.2d 860 (Ill. App. Ct. 2003), the court held that the prosecutor's failure to disclose was merely negligent, and not done in bad faith. Therefore, the exclusion of the tape would have been an excessive sanction. Given that the defendant wanted a long continuance, the appellate court concluded that the granting of a mistrial was manifestly necessary. Hence, there was no double jeopardy bar. However, the trial court appeared not to have conversed with both counsel over what might be done, usually a *sine qua non* before actually imposing a mistrial. Moreover, even if Ahmad sincerely did not know where the tape was, he should have — that he called the officer to testify suggests that he prepared him for testimony beforehand, at which time he should have pursued the matter of the videotape. If he had not called that officer, perhaps Ahmad's surprise when the officer appeared with the tape would be more justified.

5. (a) Probably. *State v. Wittsell*, 275 Kan. 442, 66 P.3d 831 (Kan. 2003). Although the prosecutor is not responsible for the conduct of all the state's witnesses, a court hearing in this case led the trial court to conclude that Henry had deliberately torpedoed the trial because he thought it was going poorly. An appellate court thought this sufficient to hold the prosecutor responsible for the outburst, and applied the Double Jeopardy Clause. The Kansas Supreme Court, however, disagreed, holding that once the prosecutor informed the witnesses of the ban on the testimony, he had discharged his responsibilities, and the defendant might have a claim only if it were clear that the prosecutor had elicited the reference to the polygraph. The court explicitly rejected an analogy to the discovery cases (see *Brady* and *Kyles*, Chapter 6) and held that the *bad faith* of the detective could not be imputed to the prosecutor. This is a dubious result. After all, Henry is a professional and an agent of the state. Holding the "state" (if not "the prosecutor") responsible here avoids investigating whether the prosecutor's warnings to Henry were sufficient. Moreover, had the prosecutor asked the witness whether Zeke had taken a polygraph, at least some state courts would ask whether the prosecutor had overreached. The *Kennedy* test focuses solely on the prosecutor, and not on

the effect which a second trial has upon the defendant (or upon his chances of being convicted).

(b) Retrial is more likely. If there was no double jeopardy bar in the actual *Wittsell* case, there would certainly seem to be no bar here. But even if *Wittsell* is problematic, or just plain wrong, here the witness is not an officer of the state. It is more plausible that the conduct, while clearly grounds for a mistrial, was an emotional reaction to the trial, rather than an attempt to have the trial start again.

6. Bean was off his bean — his action was much too precipitous. Even if the trial had been much shorter, he should have explored with the two counsel possible options. In the first place, it is not clear what the note meant — to say that a juror is "corrupt" could mean that: (1) he's been bribed; and/or (2) the foreperson (and/or other jurors) thinks he's been bribed; and/or (3) the foreperson (and/or other jurors) and this juror disagree about some matter, large or small. In the actual case on which this is based, the court held that the Double Jeopardy Clause precluded a subsequent trial for the same crime. *Ross v. Petro*, 382 F. Supp. 2d 967 (N.D. Ohio 2005). Thus, because the judge was too quick on the trigger, the "state" is precluded from prosecuting an arguably guilty defendant. Perhaps, here also, remedies against the judge, not the state, should be considered. See Chapter 14.

7. The question here is whether there was a "manifest necessity" for the mistrial. On the one hand, the trial court might have considered a "curative" instruction to the effect that defense counsel's opening statement was not evidence and the jury should decide the case only on the evidence. On the other hand, any such instruction might come dangerously close to commenting on the defendant's right to remain silent, which would result in a reversal of any conviction. Moreover, finding a double jeopardy violation might encourage future defense counsel to do exactly what was done here, thus "sandbagging" the prosecution. Nevertheless, a closely divided court found that in these circumstances a mistrial was not "necessary," and the subsequent trial prohibited by double jeopardy. *State v. Moeck*, 280 Wis. 2d 777, 696 N.W.2d 280 (Wis. Ct. App. 2005).

8. Give the prosecutor an A for effort. The theory here is collateral estoppel — that the earlier conviction prevents the defendant from challenging that decision as "law of the case." But that would mean that the defendant has to "concede" the burglary, which is the basis of the felony murder charge. He would then have to argue (to the jury?) that the burglary can't serve as the basis for a felony murder charge (perhaps because the felony had ended, or because it was not a "dangerous felony in the abstract" or some other notion of substantive criminal law). Some

courts have held that the use of collateral estoppel by the prosecution to establish an essential element of the charged offense — here, felony murder — violates the defendant's right to jury trial. See *State v. Scarbrough*, 181 S.W.3d 650 (Tenn. 2005) (discussing other cases as well).

9. A state court found manifest necessity, and a federal court, on a federal habeas corpus petition, concurred. *Baum v. Rushton*, 572 F.3d 198 (4th Cir. 2009). The court found that the state court's opinion that the judge had acted cautiously was not clearly erroneous. Surely this is debatable — the mere fact of the discovery of the body would significantly help the prosecutor's case, and a year's interval between the homicide and the discovery might suggest that there was little evidence available (as turned out to be the case). A dissent argued that a continuance of four to five days would have been sufficient to determine whether the body would produce any useful evidence. In fact, the actual coroner's report was ready the afternoon the mistrial was declared. The majority held that the trial judge did not act precipitously and that his conclusion of manifest necessity was not clearly wrong. (Note: the majority indicated that the procedural posture of the case may have been critical: "Although we might consider manifest necessity a closer call than the state court of appeals apparently did, we cannot say that its determination was objectively unreasonable" (which is the habeas corpus standard — see Chapter 13).)

Speedy Trial

10

Justice Delayed is Justice Denied.

William Gladstone, British politician (1809–1892)
(Four times British Prime Minister)

Too great haste leads us to error.

Molière (1622-1673), Sganarelle (I, 12)

A. INTRODUCTION

The Sixth Amendment to the Constitution, and virtually every state's constitution, provides for a speedy trial:[1] "In all criminal prosecutions, the accused shall enjoy the right to a speedy trial." The reason for this guarantee appears self-evident. As Chief Justice Warren noted:

> The pendency of the indictment may subject [a defendant] to public scorn and deprive him of employment, and almost certainly will force curtailment of his speech, associations and participation in unpopular causes.[2]

1. The notion is at least as old as the Magna Carta: "We will not deny or defer to any man either justice or right."
2. *Klopfer v. North Carolina*, 386 U.S. 213, 221 (1967).

A defendant in custody almost always wants a speedy trial, either because he may be found innocent, or because he may be placed on probation after conviction.[3] Even if he is sent to prison, the physical conditions there may be better than those in the jail. Strategic reasons also urge speedy resolution, particularly for the prosecution. Evidence in a criminal investigation may deteriorate or disappear. Memories dim; witnesses move (or die). Thus, both sides would seem to have an interest in having the case resolved quickly (although the defendant who thinks he will be convicted if he goes to trial may wish for delay, hoping that witnesses or documents "disappear").

On the other hand, hasty prosecution can also result in mistaken verdicts. Thus the need for accuracy conflicts with the need for speed.

1. Pre-Indictment Delay

Because the Sixth Amendment speaks only of the right of an "accused"[4] to a speedy "trial," the courts have held that it does not apply until there is a formal charge of crime; there is no "right" to a "speedy indictment." *United States v. Marion*, 404 U.S. 307 (1971). The one exception to this doctrine occurs if the prosecutor delays the indictment for the sole purpose of disadvantaging the defendant; in those instances, courts may find a due process (but not a speedy trial) violation. The courts look at two factors: (1) the reason for the delay and (2) the prejudice to the defendant. In deciding whether the delay was unreasonable, the most important factor is the state's explanation for delaying the indictment. A majority of federal circuits require the defendant to show that the delay was tactical, made in order to weaken the defendant's ability to defend. A minority of circuits holds that "reckless or even negligence may satisfy, if actual prejudice to the defendant is shown." *United States v. Mays*, 549 F.2d 670 (9th Cir. 1977); *State v. Stokes*, 350 Or. 44, 57, 248 P.3d 953 (2011). The most common explanation for delay is that the prosecutor needs more information — if, as we have previously discussed, even being indicted fractures the defendant's life, we don't want the prosecutor to rush to indictment if she or he is not sure that there is probable cause (or more) to indict. *United States v. Lovasco*, 431 U.S. 783 (1977). Other reasons include the: (1) prosecutor's reasonable doubt that the accused is in fact guilty; (2) extent of the harm caused by the offense; (3) disproportion of the authorized punishment in relation to the particular offense or the offender; (4) possible improper motives of a complainant; (5) reluctance of the victim to testify;

---

3. Since it is possible that the defendant, even if convicted, will not be thereafter imprisoned, the state also has the less noble, but nevertheless realistic, hope of avoiding the costs of keeping the defendant in jail.

4. The argument that this term merely articulates who has standing to complain, rather than requiring him to be formally charged, has been rejected by the Court.

(6) cooperation of the accused in the apprehension or conviction of others; and (7) availability and likelihood of prosecution by another jurisdiction.

As in other areas where the prosecutor's mental state is relevant,[5] most defendants fail to leap this hurdle, particularly since it requires the court to find that the prosecutor is not seeking justice, but a conviction at all costs. Courts differ as to who has the burden of proof of (bad) intent; some courts require the defendant to show that the delay was intentional,[6] while others require the government to prove a valid reason for the delay. In *United States v. Lovasco,*[7] the Supreme Court appeared to embrace the former view, at least for federal criminal prosecutions.

Even if the court doubts the validity of the prosecutor's reasons for delay, the defendant must still show that he was prejudiced. In many white collar cases a defendant may be aware his (or his company's) activities are being subjected to public scrutiny, and probably should have at least prepared for the possibility of criminal charges.[8] In *United States v. Marion,* 404 U.S. 307 (1971), for example, the FTC entered a cease and desist order against the defendants' company in February 1967. In October, a series of newspaper articles detailed the FTC's investigation. Although the defendants were not indicted until April 1970, the Court found no violation of due process. Even if, the Court noted, the "government" was on notice as of the FTC order, so were the defendants. Similarly, a subpoena of documents will certainly alert a defendant that the government is at least interested in his acts, as would the fact that friends or employees of the defendant are being questioned by the grand jury.

Thus, the best protection a defendant has against a dilatory indictment is the statute of limitations — the legislatively enacted time within which the prosecutor must act once the crime has occurred. These periods range dramatically from state to state, and from crime to crime. Most states provide no limitation for serious crimes such as homicide.

2. Post-Indictment Delay

a. What Constitutes "Speedy"?

Defining "speedy" is not easy: One person's "due deliberation" is another's "tardiness." Because this line is so vague, virtually all jurisdictions, in

---

5. For example, selective prosecution (see Chapter 3), alleged discriminatory use of peremptories (Chapter 8), causing a mistrial (Chapter 9), and destruction of evidence (Chapter 6).

6. See *State v. Lacey,* 187 Ariz. 340, 929 P.2d 1288 (Ariz. 1996).

7. 431 U.S. 783 (1977).

8. As noted in Chapter 4, many prosecutors will send a letter to a grand jury witness indicating whether she is a "target," a "suspect," or merely a "witness." While not binding on the prosecution, such a letter is critical information about the current status of the prosecutor's view of the evidence.

addition to the statute of limitations, requiring indictment within a time certain after the crime has occurred, also have a statute which creates a time frame within which trial must begin after indictment (or, in some cases, arrest). The Federal Speedy Trial Act, for example, requires trial within 70 days of the publication[9] of the indictment; in the states, the range is wide, but no state allows more than a year. These statutes, however, all provide for periods of time during which the stated time period is "tolled."[10] Some statutes enunciate in great detail the events that will have this effect, while others simply provide that "for good cause shown," the court may extend the statutory time.

b. The *Barker* Test

The seminal United States Supreme Court case deciding the constitutionality of delays in bringing an indicted defendant to trial is *Barker v. Wingo*, 407 U.S. 514 (1972). Willie Barker and Silas Manning were arrested and charged with homicide. Barker's trial was initially set for one month after his indictment. The prosecutor, however, proceeded against Manning first, believing that he could not convict Barker without first securing Manning's conviction (and possible testimony at Barker's trial). The state therefore sought a continuance of Barker's trial. But it took the state five trials — and more than four years — to successfully convict Manning. The state then prosecuted Barker, who claimed a speedy trial violation. Seven Justices found no violation of the speedy trial provision. Noting that the "speedy trial" provision was "more vague a concept than other procedural rights," the Court established a four-pronged balancing test for determining whether that right had been violated:

i. The Length of the Delay

The first prong requires that the delay be "long enough" to warrant examination of the other factors. This "threshold" time is fluid — while a delay of one week would never trigger the provision, the courts seem to view delays approaching one year as presumptively sufficient to require inquiry into the other factors.[11] If the defendant crosses this threshold, the court proceeds to the remaining three factors. In *Barker*, the four-year delay clearly met this requirement.

---

9. Where an indictment is "sealed" by the court for some reason, the clock does not begin.
10. In *United States v. Tinklenberg*, 563 U.S. 647 (2011), the Court parsed several provisions of the federal act, determining that "the filing of a pretrial motion falls within (a provision excluding time spent on pretrial motions) irrespective of whether it actually causes, or is expected to cause, delay in starting a trial."
11. *Doggett v. United States*, 505 U.S. 647 (1992).

ii. The Reasons for the Delay

All definitions of "speedy" carry "exceptions," either created by courts, or articulated in the statute. The court first attributes the delay to the proper party. Requests for continuance are "counted" for that side, regardless of the reason for that request. A defense request for a continuance tolls the statute — a defendant who asks for a delay before trial begins cannot thereafter complain that his request was granted. (Whether one views this as an "exception," or as a "waiver" of the Sixth Amendment right, the result is clear.[12]) This may seem unfair to the defendant. After all, if the prosecutor has (legitimately) investigated the defendant for (say) three years before indicting, it is unlikely that the defendant is going to be ready for trial in 70 days. Attributing the "delay" to his request so that he can build a legitimate defense seems dubious. The reason for the prosecutor's delay, therefore, may become relevant in determining whether the defendant's request for a continuance is a "voluntary" "waiver" of his right to a speedy trial.

Once the times are "attributed" to the responsible side, the court must decide how much "weight" to give to the factor *in this case*. The absence of a trial judge because she has to preside over another trial, even if attributable to the state, may be given "little weight" in a jurisdiction with no alternate judges available, whereas in a jurisdiction with some judicial time available, the state might be required to "reassign" one of the judges; its failure to do so might weigh "heavily" against it. For example, in *State v. Magnusen*, 646 So. 2d 1275 (Miss. 1994), a "rape kit" sent to the state's crime laboratory was not even opened for 15 months, while defendant waited (in jail) to be tried. The court nevertheless found that the delay, while the responsibility of the state, should be given little weight because there was only one serologist in the entire lab. This "weighing" approach is certainly open to criticism — while the individual prosecutor is surely not to "blame" if there are insufficient judges, or serologists, to allow the defendant a speedier trial, the fact remains that the defendant's trial becomes less "speedy" because the "state" as a whole has allotted insufficient funds to provide a faster trial. Most defendants are represented by "assigned counsel" — that is, by public defenders, or lawyers paid by the state pursuant to *Gideon v. Wainwright* (see Chapter 11). In *Vermont v. Brillon*, 556 U.S. 81 (2009), the Court held that delays caused by such an attorney, even though paid by the state, should be attributed to the defendant, not the state. The court recognized one possible exception: if the delays were due to such inadequate funding for counsel that there was a "systemic breakdown" in the state's representation process.[13]

---

12. *State v. Brazell*, 325 S.C. 65, 480 S.E.2d 64 (1997).

13. Many states stand on the brink of "breakdown." (See Chapter 11.) In *Brillon* itself, much of the delay was because Brillon's various defense counsel (he had five, seriatim), asked for continuances because of their heavy caseload (Brillon's final lawyer's caseload had been

iii. The Defendant's Assertion of His Right

Even if the prosecution is responsible for much of the delay, the defendant's right to a "speedy" trial is activated only when he invokes that right. Then he must consistently with his declared desire for speedy resolution; if his subsequent actions are inconsistent (i.e., by proceeding in a manner that prevents the government from trying his case expeditiously), he may then be found to have waived his right, or at least forfeited his right to complain of that part of the delay. In *Barker*, for example, the defendant did not complain about the lethargy of the state for the first three and one-half years after his indictment, even though he had spent the first 10 months of that time in jail.

iv. The Prejudice to the Defendant

Even long delays supported by weak reasons, attributable to the prosecution, and objected to by the defendant, do not establish a constitutional violation if the defendant has not suffered *actual* prejudice. The *Barker* Court articulated its analysis here around three subfactors:

- preventing oppressive incarceration;
- minimizing the anxiety and concern of the accused;
- limiting potential impairment of the defense.

Pre-trial incarceration has, as we have seen in Chapter 2, many impacts; the longer the time spent in jail, the more oppressive the delay and the greater the likelihood that the defendant has been prejudiced by an inability to consolidate a firm defense.

The second factor is patent, but virtually unmeasurable. Most courts will simply have to "surmise" how much angst the threat of conviction and imprisonment visited upon the defendant.

It is the third interest — impairment of the defense — that the *Barker* Court viewed as the most important: "[T]he inability of a defendant to adequately prepare his case skews the fairness of the entire system."[14]

Attempting to balance the last three *Barker* factors, including the "subfactors" of prejudice, is obviously difficult, particularly if some delays are "weightier" than others. Yet the Court's approach seems correct — the polyphony of facts that should be assessed before a court dismisses a case due to infringement of this right does not permit a Plimsoll line.

In *Barker* itself, the defendant was unable to make a showing of actual prejudice. In fact, the Court noted that Barker did not *want* a speedy trial and

---

"reduced" to 174 defendants). The Vermont Supreme Court had not found that there was a "breakdown."

14. *Barker, supra,* 407 U.S. at 532.

was, in fact, hoping that Manning would be acquitted. Indeed, Justices White and Brennan, concurring, would have concluded that there *was* a speedy trial violation (despite the lack of prejudice and non-excessive incarceration) "had Barker not so clearly acquiesced in the major delays in this case."

While the *Barker* factor-test established guidelines for determining whether a defendant's right to a speedy trial has been violated, none of these four factors was "either a necessary or sufficient condition. Rather, they are related factors and must be considered together."[15] In addition, the four *Barker* factors should not be applied to the exclusion of other relevant factors — the totality of the circumstances is to be considered.

One reason courts are reluctant to find a violation of the constitutional speedy trial right is that the Supreme Court has made clear that the remedy is a permanent bar to prosecution.

3. Delay in Sentencing

Can a defendant assert the right to a speedy trial after having been convicted but before having been sentenced? The Supreme Court addressed this question in *Betterman v. Montana*, 136 S.Ct. 1609 (2016). In *Betterman*, there was a 14-month gap between the defendant's conviction and his sentencing. The delay in sentencing was totally attributable to the state: the pre-sentence report took nearly five months to complete; the trial court took several months to deny two pre-sentence motions; and the trial court was slow in setting a date for the sentencing hearing. The defendant was ultimately sentenced to seven years imprisonment. The defendant claimed that the 14-month delay in sentencing violated his speedy trial right. The Supreme Court held that the speedy trial right only protects defendants from the time of arrest or indictment until conviction. The right is inapplicable after the defendant has been convicted or has pleaded guilty. The Court held that the right to speedy trial is designed to protect the presumption of innocence but once convicted, defendant no longer has a presumption of innocence. The Court indicated that in the event of an inordinate delay in sentencing, the defendant may have recourse under the due process clause and under statutes and rules prescribing time periods for sentencing such as Fed. Rule Crim. Proc. 32(b)(1) which directs courts to "impose sentence without delay."

Examples

1. Aileen transports several kilograms of cocaine inside state A, hoping to make some quick cash. After Anika, the prosecutor, learns that Aileen has

---

15. Id. at 533.

flown down to Rio, to enjoy that cash, Anika does not pursue her prosecution. Aileen enjoys the pleasures of the Copacabana for two years abroad before returning to the United States, where she subsequently finishes college, earns a graduate degree, marries and has children. Nineteen years after her alleged offense, the state arrests Aileen for her earlier drug offense. She is indicted and tried within the statutory time frame. The state has a 25-year statute of limitations on drug crimes. Have Aileen's rights been violated?

2. Noah, the prosecutor, believes that Vick, 16 years old, has sexually abused a younger victim. He knows that if he files charges now, the case will be heard in juvenile court, and Vick will receive what Noah considers a "light" punishment (or "treatment" in a juvenile facility). If he waits until Vick's 18th birthday to file an indictment (the adult charge carries a term of 25 years in prison) and Vick moves to dismiss the indictment, what result?

3. Jeffrey is indicted for bank robbery. A state statute requires that he be tried within 120 days; if not the case may be dismissed "with or without" prejudice for the government to reindict and retry within the statute of limitations. One hundred days after indictment, the government is ready for trial, but Jeff skips the jurisdiction. Seven months later, he is brought back, but the government now takes 45 days to begin his trial. He moves for dismissal on the basis of (a) the statute and (b) the Speedy Trial provision of the United States Constitution. What should the trial court do?

4. Dimitri is arrested and charged with possessing counterfeit money in Smallo, a remote village in the easternmost part of the county. His trial is to take place in Grando, a large metropolis in the westernmost part of the state. He is transported to Grando on the last day of the statutorily established period to try a case, and the government van transporting him gets tied up in traffic, so much so that his trial cannot begin until the next day. He now moves to preclude the trial on the basis of the state speedy trial provision. What result?

5. Al Libido is charged in Oregon with sexual assault, but the grand jury refuses to indict him. Thereafter, Libido is convicted in California for totally unrelated charges and receives a sentence of 15 years to life. The Oregon prosecutor puts the case folder in the "dead letter" file. Eight years later, Libido is about to be released from California as a result of good time calculations and so on. As he leaves the prison, he is immediately arrested by Oregon officials, who show him an indictment, authorized by a new grand jury in Oregon, called by a new prosecutor. The indictment is within the Oregon statute of limitations. Al moves to preclude the trial. Is he likely to succeed?

6. Skvarla is charged with receipt and distribution of child pornography and possession of child pornography. He elects to be tried by a judge. After the parties rest their cases and the trial is completed, the judge does not render a verdict for 30 months ultimately finding the defendant guilty. Defendant appeals, claiming that his right to a speedy trial was violated as a result of the 30-month delay between the conclusion of the bench trial and the judge's verdict. Is he likely to succeed?

Explanations

1. These facts show the dissonance between the Court's views on pre- and post-indictment delay. Even if Aileen had not been indicted until her children were grown, she would be entitled to no relief (even if prejudiced) unless she could show that Anika delayed the indictment for the purpose of putting her at a disadvantage at trial. The only protection she might have would be the statute of limitations, and her departure for South America might have tolled that statute at least until she became tired of Carnival. On the other hand, if she had been indicted before her departure, she would have a speedy trial claim. In *Doggett v. United States*, 505 U.S. 647 (1992), on similar facts (trial nine years after indictment), the Court found a violation of the speedy trial right.

2. Although most defendants will lose such a motion, the defendant in this case did not. *State v. Trompeter*, 555 N.W.2d 468 (Iowa 1996). Usually, a prosecutorial attempt to "disadvantage" a defendant focuses on the possible loss of evidence. Here, the disadvantage was the greater sentence which the prosecutor *thought* the defendant would receive. This purpose was sufficient to allow the court to invalidate the pre-indictment delay on due process grounds. Consider also that the prosecutor did not *have to* delay the indictment in order to have the adult punishment imposed on Vick. He might have asked the juvenile court to "waive" the 16-year-old Vick to adult court, and avoided the pre-indictment delay.

3. Try Jeffrey. In a parallel case involving the federal speedy trial *statute*, the Court interpreted that act to urge trial courts to dismiss "without," rather than "with" prejudice. *United States v. Taylor*, 487 U.S. 326 (1988). But see *Strunk v. United States*, 412 U.S. 434 (1973), where the Court held that dismissal of the prosecution was the only remedy for a violation of the constitutional right to speedy trial. Here, without a showing of prejudice, Jeffrey won't have a winnable *Barker* claim, and his self-help vacation is unlikely to make the government responsible for any prejudice he might be able to show. Thus, Jeffrey has a losing constitutional claim, and his statutory claim is also very weak (although requiring the prosecution to seek a new indictment might deter future

delays of 44 days (the "extra" delay the government caused once Jeff was back in its clutches).

4. In *People v. Hajjaj*, 50 Cal. 4th 1184, 214 P.3d 828, 117 Cal. Rptr. 3d 327 (2010), the court held that court administrators should plan for travel contingencies, and that "the neglect of the state in not providing resources adequate to enable the (court) to bring cases to trial in a timely manner in the face of these routine, consistent, predictable obstacles (was attributable to the state)." Defendant wins. While this decision involved interpretation of a state statute, consider the contrary approach taken by the United States Supreme Court in Brillon.

5. *State v. Stokes*, 350 Or. 44, 248 P.3d 953 (2011). Al did not succeed. Under the majority view, pre-indictment delay only violates due process if the delay was a tactical move by the prosecutor to disadvantage the defendant. Even applying the minority test for pre-indictment delay, the first prosecutor was neither reckless nor negligent in not resubmitting the case to the original grand jury. After all, it appeared that Libido would be controlled for the rest of his life in another state.

6. *United States v. Skarvla*, 673 Fed. Appx. 111, 2016 U.S. App. LEXIS 23185 (2d Cir. 2016), the Court rejected Skarvla's argument. The Court held that Skarvla suffered no prejudice as a result of the 30-month delay. During the 30-month interval, he was not incarcerated. Furthermore, defendant failed to assert his right during the 30-month delay. For instance, he could have but did not file a motion for a verdict during the delay. According to the Court, the lack of prejudice to defendant is also demonstrated by his failure to assert the right during the delay.

11

Assistance of Counsel

A lawyer in a criminal trial is a necessity, not a luxury.

Gideon v. Wainwright, 372 U.S. 335 (1963)

No constitutional right is celebrated so much in the abstract and observed so little in reality as the right to counsel.

Bright, Gideon's Reality: After Four Decades, Where Are We,
Crim. Just. (Summer 2003), p.5

A. THE RIGHT TO COUNSEL

At his initial appearance, if not before, Dan will be informed of his right to counsel. It was not always so. In fact, until the beginning of the nineteenth century, lawyers in England — even those retained by the defendant — were prohibited from appearing in court in a felony case, unless the charge was treason. This may have been due, in part, to the fact that non-treason criminal prosecutions were often brought by the injured party (or survivors), rather than "the Crown." On the other hand, counsel was allowed in misdemeanor trials.

In early colonial times, lawyers were similarly eschewed. An article in the Fundamental Constitution of the Carolinas declared that "it shall be a base and vile thing to plead for money and reward"; a similar document for East Jersey (1683) provided that "[i]n all courts persons of all perswasions may freely appear in their own way . . . and there personally plead their own causes themselves, or if unable, by their friends, no person being allowed to take money for pleading or advice in such cases."[1] This animosity rapidly dissolved. The Declaration of Independence expressly complained about the denial of counsel, and 12 of the original 13 states guaranteed in their constitutions a right to counsel for felony cases. As a result, the right to have counsel present was embodied in the Sixth Amendment, which provides:

> In all criminal prosecutions the accused shall enjoy the right . . . to have the Assistance of Counsel for his defense.

Today, counsel are *allowed* in virtually every process in which the government pits itself against an individual.[2] The question today, as we will see below, is whether the state must *appoint* counsel for a given proceeding. Here, the first four words of the Sixth Amendment — "In all criminal prosecutions" — are critical. Not every proceeding in which a citizen can suffer serious harm at the behest of the government is a *criminal* prosecution. Nor is every part of the criminal *process* necessarily a criminal *prosecution*.

There may be a *Fifth* Amendment right to have counsel present even in noncriminal proceedings. In *Hamdi v. Rumsfeld*, 542 U.S. 507 (2004), the Supreme Court held that citizens held by the United States military had a right to a rudimentary hearing to challenge the government's conclusion that they were "enemy combatants." The Court noted that Hamdi had recently obtained counsel, and declared that "[h]e unquestionably has the right to access to counsel in connection with the proceedings on remand." Id. at 539.

B. THE RIGHT TO COUNSEL

Because roughly 90 percent of all defendants are represented by state-paid attorneys, the focus of the caselaw, particularly in the past 50 years, has been on appointed counsel. But as we go through these materials, keep in mind that the defendant is entitled to *effective* counsel even from a paid attorney. Moreover, a defendant is generally entitled to be represented by any attorney he can afford, and an erroneous deprivation of the right to counsel of one's

---

1. Francis H. Heller, The Sixth Amendment to the Constitution of the United States, 17-19 (1951).
2. But see *United States v. Ash*, 413 U.S. 300 (1973) (no right to have defense counsel present at a pre-trial photographic display to a witness). Several states preclude counsel even at a post-presentment search warrant application to obtain DNA. *State v. Blye*, 130 S.W.3d 776 (Tenn. 2004) (citing several other states with the same rule).

choice is a *per se* violation of the Sixth Amendment; that is, the defendant need not show prejudice. *U.S. v. Gonzalez-Lopez*, 548 U.S. 140 (2006). That right is still subject to the issue of conflict of interest (see *infra*), so the court must ensure that the trial was not plagued by such conflict.

Moreover, while a paying client may hire (subject to the above) any attorney who will accept the fee, a defendant whose counsel is paid by the state is entitled to "adequate" representation — but not necessarily by the attorney he wants. So long as the representation is effective, the Constitution is satisfied, even if the defendant sometimes is not.

1. The Right to Counsel — To What Does It Apply?

a. What Is a "Criminal Prosecution"?

The government may take many actions against a person which will have dramatic and possibly lifelong effects upon that person, and in which the assistance of an attorney might therefore be helpful if not crucial. But under the words of the Sixth Amendment, unless these proceedings can be characterized as "criminal prosecutions," there is no right to counsel. Among those proceedings held not to be a "criminal prosecution" are:

- civil proceedings;
- forfeiture proceedings;
- deportation proceedings; or
- civil commitment proceedings.

b. What Constitutes Part of a "Criminal Prosecution"?

Even when the criminal process machinery is underway, the Sixth Amendment protections apply only to *critical stages* of a criminal case. The following *do not* constitute part of the criminal prosecution; hence there is no *Sixth Amendment* right to appointed counsel for these proceedings:

- pre-indictment lineup;
- grand jury (see Chapter 4);
- forfeiture;
- probation or parole revocation;
- post-conviction proceedings, including:
  - motions for a new trial based on new evidence;
  - appeal from conviction, whether discretionary or mandatory (see Chapter 13);[3]

---

3. *Ross v. Moffitt*, 417 U.S. 600 (1974).

- collateral relief (see Chapter 13);[4]
- federal habeas corpus (see Chapter 13);[5]
- evaluation of defendant as a sexually violent predator;[6]
- a hearing to consolidate several co-defendants' cases;[7]
- interview with probation officer in preparation for pre-sentence report;
- discretionary reviews, including certiorari to the United States Supreme Court;[8]
- motion to reconsider sentencing.

The Court has used different words to define "critical stage." In *Gerstein v. Pugh*, 420 U.S. 103, 122 (1975) (discussed in Chapter 2), it was defined as "those pretrial procedures that would impair defense on the merits if the accused is required to proceed without counsel." In *United States v. Wade*, 388 U.S. 218, 226 (1957), involving line-ups, the Court defined it as "any stage of the prosecution, formal or informal, in court or out, when counsel's absence might derogate from the accused's right to a fair trial."[9] But even those definitions may be insufficient for current purposes. In *Rothgery v. Gillespie County*, 554 U.S. 191 (2008), the Court held that the right to counsel attached even at a proceeding which was *not* a "critical stage." Rothgery was arrested as a felon in possession of a weapon. Appearing before a magistrate at an initial hearing, who informed him of the charges and set bail, he asked

---

4. *Pennsylvania v. Finley*, 481 U.S. 551 (1987).

5. Congress has provided for the appointment of counsel to assist indigents seeking collateral relief in federal court. Those challenging capital sentences or conviction in federal court, and those who are granted evidentiary hearings in federal habeas corpus, are entitled to counsel. Other petitioners may be appointed counsel when "the interests of justice so require." These latter statutes, however, have had only limited effect: After the first appeal, most prisoner habeas corpus petitions are prepared without outside legal assistance; however, in 1996, Congress provided expedited federal habeas review of petitions filed by capital defendants if the state of conviction provided a mechanism for the "appointment, compensation, and payment of reasonable litigation expenses" in post-conviction proceedings. A decade later, no state had had its procedures certified (as required by statute) by the federal circuit court in the region. Congress thereupon amended the statute, giving the Attorney General the power to determine whether a state's procedures were satisfactory. See Chapter 13.

6. In re *Detention of Kistenmacher*, 134 Wash. App. 72, 138 P.3d 648 (2006), *aff'd on other grounds*, 163 Wash. 2d 166, 178 P.3d 949 (2008).

7. This was allowed because state rules allowed counsel to file a motion to sever later on. *Van v. Jones*, 475 F.3d 282 (6th Cir. 2007).

8. The Court has explained that there is no constitutional right to counsel in these proceedings, because the brief and other papers filed by counsel on the first (as of right) appeal will form the basis of any later proceedings; hence the legal issues will have been assessed by counsel, and available for all succeeding courts. This same analysis was applied in *Halbert v. Michigan*, 545 U.S. 605 (2005), where the Court held that the Constitution mandates appointment of counsel for indigents who have pled guilty but who seek to appeal, not as of right, but as a discretionary matter.

9. See Pamela R. Metzger, Beyond the Bright Line: A Contemporary Right-to-Counsel Doctrine, 97 Nw. U.L. Rev. 1635 (2003).

for counsel, but the magistrate ignored the request. Rothgery did make bail, but several months later he was indicted on the basic charge brought by the police and rearrested. Unable this time to make bail, he spent three weeks in the county jail. Finally, he was assigned an appointed attorney, who rapidly demonstrated to the prosecutor that Rothgery had never been convicted of a felony. The charges were then dropped. Rothgery then sued the county under 42 U.S.C. §1983 for a "constitutional tort." In an 8-1 decision, the Supreme Court held that Rothgery had a constitutional right to counsel at the initial hearing because it was the "initiation of adversarial criminal proceedings." The Court did not expressly hold that Rothgery was entitled to *appointed* counsel at this appearance. Nor did it expressly hold that the bail determination alone constituted a "critical stage." Indeed, some commentators have argued that the Court stopped short of holding that the pre-indictment period was a "critical stage" altogether. But it did say that this was the "first judicial proceeding."

The precise impact of *Rothgery* is not clear. It probably does not apply to "station house" bail proceedings (because those are not "judicial" proceedings), and it may or may not result in a requirement for appointing a lawyer even at a magistrate's proceeding. But the emphasis on the "adversary nature" of the process might be seen as reaching some of those processes listed above as not entitling one to representation by a lawyer. Indeed, the state had argued that because there was no prosecutor present (or required) at Rothgery's first appearance, there was no right to counsel. The Court's rejection of that position may expand the right to counsel in the future.

Whether Fifth Amendment due process requires appointment in such instances is another matter. Although *Murray v. Giarratano*, 492 U.S. 1 (1989), is thought to hold that, since defendants are not constitutionally entitled to post-conviction proceedings, and hence are not entitled to counsel at those proceedings, they are not entitled to *effective* counsel at those proceedings. One critic points out that, while the Court denied relief in that case, there were actually five Justices who believed that the state was obligated to provide counsel — and effective counsel — in these proceedings. Eric M. Freedman, *Giarratano* Is a Scarecrow: The Right to State Capital Postconviction Proceedings, 91 Cornell L. Rev. 1079 (2006).

On the other hand, the Sixth Amendment *does* apply in the following:

- preliminary hearing (see Chapter 5);
- post-indictment lineup;
- plea-bargaining discussions;
- sentencing;
- on a motion for a new trial immediately after conviction;
- probation revocation which also includes sentencing;
- presentence discussions with prosecutor over cooperation;

- post-indictment psychiatric interview to determine competency to stand trial.

As these lists may suggest, usually the official initiation of proceedings, (commonly deemed to occur when there is an indictment, preliminary hearing, or information) activates the Sixth Amendment. Thus, for example, if state law deems waived defenses not raised at this proceeding, there is a right to counsel. *Hamilton v. Alabama*, 368 U.S. 52 (1961). Similarly, because normally a plea of guilty at the first appearance could be withdrawn later, this would not be a critical stage — but if the state can use the plea against a defendant at trial, the hearing is transformed into a critical stage where a lawyer must be present. *White v. Maryland*, 373 U.S. 59 (1963).

The "criminal prosecution" ceases once the defendant has been convicted and sentenced. Although appeal is not constitutionally required (see Chapter 13), once the state has created such a procedure, it may not, *consistent with due process*, structure that procedure so that it is basically a "meaningless ritual." Thus, there is no Sixth Amendment right to appointed counsel in any post-conviction process, including appeal, state post-conviction relief, or federal habeas corpus. The Supreme Court has held that *equal protection* required that the state provide counsel if the appeal was a matter of right. *Douglas v. California*, 372 U.S. 353 (1963). But *Ross v. Moffitt*, 417 U.S. 600 (1974), held that there was neither an equal protection nor a due process right to counsel on *discretionary* appeal. Similarly, while there is no Sixth Amendment right to counsel in a probation revocation proceeding, the Sixth Amendment does apply if the defendant will be sentenced at that hearing. *Mempa v. Rhay*, 389 U.S. 128 (1967).

That there is no federal constitutional right to assistance of appointed counsel does not, of course, preclude the state from providing such counsel, either as a state constitutional or statutory matter, or even by court rule. Thus, while many states do not provide counsel to indigent inmates seeking collateral review, all but one state provide counsel to inmates on death row for that purpose. Several states and the federal system provide counsel for bail hearings, and virtually all states actually provide appointed counsel in parole revocation hearings and discretionary appeals.

The Court has held that any right to effective counsel on a first appeal of right stems from the Fifth (Fourteenth) Amendment due process clause rather than the Sixth Amendment. *Evitts v. Lucey*, 469 U.S. 387 (1985). There is no right to effective assistance of counsel — based on either Amendment — in later proceedings. Id. at 396 n.7; *Pennsylvania v. Finley*, 481 U.S. 551 (1987); *Murray v. Giarranto*, 492 U.S. 1 (1989). Thus while an attorney who slept through a trial would have rendered inadequate assistance under the Sixth Amendment (see discussion below), he could sleep with impunity through a probation or parole revocation.

C. THE RIGHT TO APPOINTED COUNSEL

1. *Gideon* and *Argersinger*

Until 1963, the Sixth Amendment was not held applicable to the states; defendants seeking the appointment of counsel had to rely upon the due process clauses of the Fifth (and Fourteenth) Amendments.

In *Powell v. Alabama*, 287 U.S. 45 (1932), the Supreme Court held, for the first time, that Fifth Amendment due process—not the Sixth Amendment—required the "guiding hand of counsel" at a capital criminal proceeding. If the defendant could not afford counsel, the due process clause required the state to provide one.

Powell involved the infamous Scottsboro trial, in which nine young black men were charged with raping a white woman. The trial judge appointed "the entire bar" of Scottsboro to represent the defendants. But only one local attorney, and one out-of-state attorney, even appeared for the defendants.[10] The Supreme Court held that appointing *all* attorneys was the equivalent of appointing *no* attorney.

Powell was a capital case. Soon thereafter, although it had required appointment of counsel in all felonies tried in *federal* court, the Court rejected an attempt to apply *Powell* to other felonies in *state* courts. *Betts v. Brady*, 316 U.S. 455 (1942). After *Betts*, only if the case demonstrated "special circumstances"—illiteracy, mental incapacity, possible bias in the courtroom—would the noncapital state defendant be entitled to an appointed attorney.

For nearly 20 years after *Betts*, the Supreme Court rendered a series of opinions vainly attempting to define "special circumstances." Finally, in 1963, in *Gideon v. Wainwright*, 372 U.S. 335 (1963), the Court cut the Gordian knot, holding that the due process clause required appointment of counsel for all indigent[11] persons charged with any felony.[12]

---

10. The Tennessee lawyer announced he was retained to assist the defendants, but, as one chronicler put it, his "modest legal abilities were further limited by his inability to remain sober." Gerald F. Uelman, A Train Ride: A Guided Tour of the Sixth Amendment Right to Counsel, 58 Law & Contemp. Probs. 13, 15 (Wtr. 1995) citing Dan T. Carter, Scottsboro: A Tragedy of American South 19 (1969).

11. Although the Court did not define "indigency," statutes, administrative regulations, and court rules have filled that gap. See, e.g., 18 U.S.C.A. §3006(A); Ky. Rev. Stat. §31.120; Me. R. Crim. P. 44. See Helen Anderson, Penalizing Poverty: Making Criminal Defendants Pay for Their Court-Appointed Counsel Through Recoupment and Contribution, 42 U. Mich. J.L. Reform 323 (2009).

12. Clarence Gideon, a poor drifter with a record of minor offenses (including several burglaries) was charged with burglarizing a pool hall for approximately $25 and some alcohol. His request for appointed counsel was denied, and he was convicted and sentenced to five years. His in *forma pauperis* petition for certiorari was granted by the Supreme Court,

Almost a decade later, the Court expanded that requirement to all misdemeanors in which any amount of incarceration — even one hour — *was actually imposed*. *Argersinger v. Hamlin*, 407 U.S. 25 (1972). *Argersinger* refused to follow the rule for juries that the Sixth Amendment only required a jury trial where the defendant *could* be imprisoned for more than six months (see Chapter 8). The *Argersinger* rule requires a judge to determine, prior to trial, whether the defendant might be sentenced to incarceration; if so, counsel must be appointed. If no counsel is appointed, the defendant cannot be sentenced to jail, whatever the facts may show about him, or his crime.

In *Alabama v. Shelton*, 535 U.S. 654 (2002), the Court held that for a person to be incarcerated for violating the terms of a suspended sentence, counsel must have been provided for the underlying offense, even if defendant was not facing incarceration at the time of conviction.

Of course, while the Court would never declare that "Beggars can't be choosers," it has said: "[An indigent] defendant may not insist on representation by an attorney he cannot afford or who for other reasons declines to represent the defendant." *Wheat v. United States*, 486 U.S. 153, 159 (1988). Still, as discussed below, any attorney must be "effective."

2. The Right to Appointed Counsel — Systems of Providing Counsel

Today, the major issue is whether the promise of *Gideon* and *Argersinger* — that every defendant would receive proper representation before being incarcerated (or executed) — has been met. There is much bleak evidence that in many parts of this country many defendants are not adequately represented at trials, including capital trials. Every year, reports are filed by various state bar associations and by national organizations, documenting the abysmal underfunding of legal services. See, e.g., Bruce A. Green, Criminal Neglect: Indigent Defense From a Legal Ethics Perspective, 52 Emory L.J. 1169, 1183-84 nn. 57-73 (2003), citing a number of such reports. American Bar Association, Gideon's Broken Promise (2004), available at www.abanet.org/legalservices/sclaid/defender/brokenpromise/fullreport.pdf;

---

which appointed Abe Fortas, a prominent Washington attorney, to represent him. The Court held, 9-0, that the failure to appoint counsel violated the Sixth Amendment. On retrial, Gideon was represented by a local attorney appointed by the court, and was acquitted. Abe Fortas went on to become a member of the United States Supreme Court. Gideon's performance at his first trial, however, was quite respectable. One commentator has opined that "If a lawyer had done what Gideon did, it is doubtful that Gideon could later have successfully demonstrated that but for what the lawyer did not do there was a reasonable probability that the outcome would have been different." William S. Geimer, A Decade of Strickland's Tin Horn: Doctrinal and Practical Undermining of the Right to Counsel, 4 Wm. & Mary Bill of Rts. J. 91, 108 (1995).

Constitution Project, Justice Denied: America's Continuing Neglect of Our Constitutional Right to Counsel (2006). See also Mary Sue Backus and Paul Marcus, The Right to Counsel in Criminal Cases: A National Crisis, 57 Hastings L.J. 1031 (2006); Anne B. Poulin, Strengthening the Criminal Defendant's Right to Counsel, 28 Cardozo L. Rev. 1213 (2006). Former federal Circuit Judge Richard Posner, who is also formerly a law professor, has announced: "I can confirm from my own experience as a judge that criminal defendants are generally poorly represented," and Justice Ruth Bader Ginsburg, also a former law professor, has declared: "I have yet to see a death case, among the dozens coming to the Supreme Court, even on the eve of execution petitions, in which the defendant was well represented at trial."[13]

In one sense the aspirations of *Gideon*, 50 years after the decision, have been realized. Nationally, over three-quarters of criminal defendants are represented by appointed counsel. These attorneys are generally provided through one of three methods. The most well known (handling about 80 percent of the cases) is a *public defender's* office — a salaried staff of full- or part-time attorneys — that renders service either through a public or private nonprofit organization or as direct government-paid employees. The second method is through *contract services*. In this method, the responsible government unit (usually the county) contracts with a group of private attorneys to handle all cases arising in that area for a period of time (usually one year, but sometimes longer). These contracts may provide for a lump-sum payment for the year, without regard to the caseload, or for payment per case.[14] Over the past few years, the number of jurisdictions providing some portion of their indigent defense through a contract system has increased dramatically. Finally, an *assigned counsel plan* appoints private attorneys on a *case-by-case basis*. Where either of the first two systems operates, and there is a conflict (for example, when co-defendants each need an appointed attorney) the assigned-counsel method will normally be used.

In 30 states, public defender systems are funded entirely by state appropriated funds. Nat'l Legal Aid & Defender Ass'n, A Race to the Bottom, Speed and Savings over Due Process: A Constitutional Crisis, at 5 n.8 (2008), See www.mynlada.org/michigan/michigan_report.pdf. In other states, the state coverage of all expenses runs from over 90 percent (Arkansas, Kentucky, Tennessee) to less than 10 percent (Arizona, California, District of Columbia, Michigan, Nebraska, Nevada, Pennsylvania, Utah, and

---

13. Ruth Bader Ginsburg, In Pursuit of the Public Good: Lawyers Who Care, a lecture delivered on April 9, 2001. Available at http://www.supremecourtus.gov/publicinfo/speeches/sp_04-09-01a.ht.

14. There are six kinds of contracts used across the nation: (1) fixed fee, all cases; (2) fixed fee, specific type of case; (3) flat fee, specific number of cases; (4) flat fee per case; (5) hourly fee with caps; (6) hourly fee without caps. U.S. Dept. of Justice, Contracting for Indigent Defense Services: A Special Report 4 (2000).

Washington).[15] Many states employ public defenders in some parts of the state, and either contract or assigned counsel in other parts.

No institution ever believes it has sufficient funding. Surely every prosecutorial office would claim underfunding,[16] but virtually all observers agree that, however measured, most defender programs are drastically underpaid and overworked. Even before the great recession of 2008, states have consistently struggled to fund these programs. Some states have elicited special fees from attorneys, or established filing fees that help pay for counsel for indigents. In Minnesota, public defenders were no longer furnished free; the state attempted to require defendants to pay $50 or more for their services. The state supreme court, on expedited review, held that experiment unconstitutional. *State v. Tennin,* 674 N.W.2d 403 (Minn. 2004).[17] On the other hand:

> [i]n Oregon, where the Courts say they've run out of money to appoint lawyers, the prosecutors . . . brought suit to guarantee every criminal defendant the right to appointed counsel . . . In three Oregon counties, the elected district attorneys have filed writs of mandamus in state court and a federal sec. 1983 action to ensure court-appointed lawyers . . . In Wisconsin, 25 elected district attorneys just offered to cut their own wages because the state is going to force layoffs of state-paid assistant prosecutors.

Joshua Marquis, Astoria, Oregon, District Attorney, letter to the New Jersey Law Journal, June 23, 2003.

As might be expected, conditions deteriorated during the Great Recession of 2008. In Minnesota, the public defender's office shrank from 86 full-time attorneys to about 50, leaving each lawyer with a caseload of approximately 740. In Missouri, the state public advocate filed a lawsuit that would allow defenders to turn down cases they could not handle. In Florida, a trial judge allowed public defenders to refuse to represent defendants arrested on lesser felony charges so they could provide a better defense for those charged with more serious crimes. NY Times, Nov. 21, 2008, at A34. In November 2008, public defenders offices from seven states either refused to take on

---

15. The Spangenberg Group, State and County Expenditures for Indigent Defense Services in Fiscal Year 2005 (2006) (prepared for the American Bar Association).

16. In 1999, surveyed counties spent an estimated $1.1 billion on indigent criminal defense, compared to the approximately $1.9 billion spent by prosecutors. But the latter figure does not include law enforcement resources (police, investigators) or forensic laboratory work, or expert witnesses, most of whom already work for the state.

17. The purpose of counsel is to assure that the innocent defendant is not improperly convicted. But once the defendant has been found guilty, many states allow the state to recoup the cost of appointed counsel. Of course, if the defendant was really indigent *before* trial, she's unlikely to earn millions while in prison; but if the lottery comes through, the state will be there. Such provisions have been upheld as constitutional. *Fuller v. Oregon,* 417 U.S. 40 (1974). See Anderson, *supra* note 11.

new cases or sued to limit them. Laura Appleman, The Plea Jury, 85 Ind. L.J. 731, 769 n.249 (2010), citing Erik Eckholm, Citing Workload, Public Lawyers Reject New Cases, N.Y. Times, Nov. 9, 2008, at A1. These are obviously mere examples, which could be multiplied around the country.

Assessing the "adequacy" of resources is incredibly complicated. Caseload limits are often employed as one standard, but one major murder case may take more time than 500 misdemeanor or even minor felony cases. In 2003, the President of the National Association of Criminal Defense Lawyers contended that "part-time public defenders in Lake Charles, La. have 600 felony cases and, on average, do not meet clients until nine months after their arrest." Letter to the New Jersey Law Journal, June 23, 2003. In Miranda v. Clark County, Nevada, 391 F.3d 465 (9th Cir. 2003), a civil case, plaintiffs alleged that the county public defender (a) gave limited resources to clients who either refused to take, or "failed" a polygraph; and (b) assigned the least-experienced attorneys to capital cases without providing any training.[18] Obviously, the public defender was attempting to "triage" a heavy caseload by removing resources from those defendants least likely to be acquitted. The court held that, if proved, these allegations could establish an unconstitutional deprivation of counsel.

In most assigned-counsel systems, either by statute or other regulation, the amount to be paid per case, or per hour, is "capped" at a figure well below that which most attorneys would consider minimal, much less adequate. In Colorado and Delaware, the maximum allocated for a non-capital, serious, trial is $15,000; in Florida, $2,500; Kansas, $1,600; Mississippi, $1,000. In 2007, the hourly rates for non-capital cases for court-appointed counsel fees varied significantly, sometimes in apparent relation to general cost of living in the state, sometimes not. Generally, the rates ranged from below $50 hourly (Alabama, Georgia, Idaho, Kentucky, Mississippi, Missouri, New Jersey, Oklahoma, Oregon, South Carolina, Tennessee, Vermont, West Virginia, and Wisconsin) to highs between $90 and $100 (California, Hawaii, Kansas, Massachusetts, Nevada, Rhode Island, Virginia, and the United States Government).[19] In early 2000, Mississippi spent less per case on public defense than any other state in the region ($3.19 per defendant). Florida spent an average of $11.70, and Texas, an average of $4.65. Kimberly H. Zelnick, In Gideon's Shadow: The Loss of Defendant Autonomy and the Growing Scope of Attorney Discretion, 30 Am. J. Crim L.

---

18. As the dissent pointed out, the public defender argued that it provided experienced "back up" for the new lawyers. The County argued that "as a matter of law, attorneys who have graduated from law school and passed the bar should be considered adequately trained to handle capital murder cases."

19. The Spangenberg Group, Rates of Compensation for Court-Appointed Counsel in Non-Capital Felonies at Trial, 2007 (2007).

363, 375 n.64 (2003), citing NAACP Legal Defense and Education Fund, Inc., Assembly Line Justice: Mississippi's Indigent Defense Crisis.

The figures are even more appalling for capital cases. While many states put no cap on expenditures in capital cases, in Phoenix, Arizona, for example, attorneys were paid a flat fee of $10,000 per capital case, and an additional $10,000 if the case went to trial. In Tucson, Arizona, however, there was a $15,000 maximum, even if the case went to trial. In Los Angeles, total payments ranged from $67,000-$200,000 per attorney. Ohio had a $50,000 cap, but it could be waived.[20]

In 2008, Congress increased the hourly rate for private attorneys in federal cases to $100 for non-death-penalty cases and $170 for death penalty cases.

Not surprisingly, defendants and the attorneys representing them have sought creative litigation methods to force increased funding. In State v. Smith, 140 Ariz. 355 (1984), the Arizona Supreme Court struck down Mohave County's contract defense system, which assigned contracts to the low bidder. The Oklahoma Supreme Court found that inadequate compensation for court-appointed counsel constituted an illegal taking of the lawyer's property. State v. Lynch, 796 P.2d 1150 (Okla. 1990). And in New York, the court decreed, "The pusillanimous posturing and procrastination of the executive and legislative branches have created the assigned counsel crisis impairing the judiciary's ability to function . . . Equal access to justice should not be a ceremonial platitude, but a perpetual pledge vigilantly guarded." New York County Lawyers' Association v. State of New York, 196 Misc. 2d 761, 763 N.Y.S.2d 397 (Sup. Ct., N.Y. Cty. 2003). The New York State Legislature thereupon raised the per hour figure to $75.00.[21]

Publicly financed counsel are often demeaned as providing ineffective service; a commonly repeated comment, allegedly made by convicted defendants who, when asked whether they had a lawyer, is: "No, I had a public defender." Statistics belie this widespread libel; public defenders perform the same functions every bit as well as the typical private attorney.[22] In 1998, 92 percent of defendants with public counsel and 91 percent with

---

20. The Spangenberg Group, Rates of Compensation for Court-Appointed Counsel in Capital Cases at Trial, 2002 (2003).

21. For other litigation involving the validity of compensation to counsel, see In re Order on Prosecution of Criminal Appeals by the Tenth Judicial Circuit Public Defender, 561 So.2d 1130 (Fla. 1990); State v. Robinson, 123 N.H. 665, 465 A. 2d 1214 (1983); Arnold v. Kemp, 306 Ark. 294, 813 S.W.2d 770 (1991); State ex rel. Stephan v. Smith, 242 Kan. 336 (1987). See generally Richard Klein, The Eleventh Commandment: Thou Shalt Not Be Compelled to Render the Ineffective Assistance of Counsel, 68 Ind. L.J. 363 (1993), arguing that many such suits have been unsuccessful or that public defendant officers are intimidated by threats of local governments. See, more generally, Darryl K. Brown, Rationing Criminal Defense Entitlements: An Argument from Institutional Design, 104 Colum. L. Rev. 801 (2004).

22. According to Radha Ieyngar, An Analysis of the Performance of Federal Indigent Defense Counsel, NBRER Working Paper No. 13187 (June 2007), public defenders perform

private counsel either pleaded guilty or were found guilty at trial.[23] However, of those found guilty, 88 percent with public counsel, and 77 percent with private counsel received jail or prison sentences, and the difference was greater in "large state courts" (71 percent versus 54 percent).

Individual defendants have also sought to demonstrate that this lack of resources violates not only their right to "adequate counsel" (see below) but other rights as well. Thus, in Brillon (see Chapter 9), defendant argued that the Vermont defender system had broken down so as to violate his right to a speedy trial. As discussed there, the Supreme Court rejected that view, holding that much of the delay in the case was due to defense counsel and not attributable to the state. Of course, defendant's position was that this was essentially blaming the victim—the reason defense counsel delayed was the overwhelming caseload, caused by insufficient funding for the program.[24]

D. THE RIGHT TO EFFECTIVE COUNSEL

The right to be represented assumes that the representation must be "effective."[25] But effectiveness cannot be assessed on the basis of result—guilty criminal defendants who complain about the level of their representation know (or should know) that not even Clarence Darrow won every case. How, then, can an appellate court, looking at a cold record, determine whether the defendant received "adequately effective" help from her attorney?

---

significantly better than panel attorneys when compared in percentage of conviction rates and sentence length. Available at ssrn.com/abstract-994235.

23. U.S. Dept. of Justice, Bureau of Justice Statistics, Defense Counsel in Criminal Cases, NCJ 179023 (2000).

24. See also *Weis v. State*, 287 Ga. 46, 694 S.E.2d 350 (2010). Weis, facing the death penalty, had originally been provided a contract attorney, but when the legislature refused further appropriations, the contract attorney was replaced by a public defender, who then asked to be removed because he had neither the resources nor expertise to defend the case. The trial court then reappointed the original contract attorneys, who refused to go forward when they still had not been paid. The state supreme court held that none of these delays violated Weis's speedy trial rights. After the state supreme court's decision, a petition for certiorari was filed, and an amici brief, signed by the past Chief Justice of Georgia and supported by many officials previously connected with the Georgia State system, declared that "Petitioner Weis can no more be faulted either for the trial court's abrupt, prosecutor-driven removal of his long-standing appointed counsel, nor for the delay occasioned by a complete lack of funding for defense services in his case for over two years than can the hundreds of indigent defendants across the State of Georgia who are facing the effects of a systemic crisis." The petition for certiorari was denied. *Weis v. State*, 562 U.S. 850 (2010).

25. David L. Bazelon, The Realities of Gideon and Argersinger, 64 Geo. L.J. 811, 819 (1976): "The Sixth Amendment demands more than placing a warm body with a legal pedigree next to an indigent defendant."

1. The "Three Prongs" of Ineffectiveness

Courts and commentators alike have divided analysis of the effectiveness of counsel into three "types" of claims:

1. instances of so-called state interference;
2. claims that counsel had a conflict of interest and should not have handled the case;
3. claims that counsel failed to provide "effective" assistance.

a. State Interference

The most obvious instance where the state has "interfered" with defendant's right to representation occurs when the state refuses to appoint an attorney at all. In essence, this is what the Supreme Court found to be the case in *Powell* — that although there were warm bodies with law degrees present in the courtroom, the circumstances of their appointment and the way in which the case was tried essentially prevented them from acting as knowledgeable counsel. Even if the state appoints counsel, there may be barriers to making that representation effective. Thus, for example, the Supreme Court has found violations of either the Fifth or Sixth Amendments when states: (1) banned an attorney-client consultation overnight, *Geders v. United States*, 425 U.S. 80 (1976) (but forbidding such communication during the lunch recess is okay, *Serrano v. Fischer*, 412 F.3d 292 (2d Cir. 2005), cert denied, 546 U.S. 1182 (2006)); (2) forbade defense counsel from giving a summation at a bench trial, *Herring v. New York*, 422 U.S. 53, 57 (1975); (3) required the defendant to testify first, or not at all, *Brooks v. Tennessee*, 406 U.S. 60 (1972); or (4) precluded the defendant from testifying under oath, allowing him only to give an unsworn statement to the jury. *Ferguson v. Georgia*, 365 U.S. 570 (1961).[26]

While these decisions have focused primarily on interference during trial, the court in *United States v. Stein*, 435 F. Supp. 2d 330 (S.D.N.Y. 2006), moved the focus to *pre-trial* activities when it held that the Justice Department's policy of considering, while deciding whether to indict a company, whether the company paid for its employees' attorney's fees effectively chilled the *employees'* right to counsel. And one commentator has suggested that restrictive discovery rules, or rules which allow for late discovery, may be seen as interfering with counsel. Jenny Roberts, Too Little, Too Late:

---

26. This is not quite as anomalous as it may now seem in the twenty-first century. Well into the late nineteenth century, it was thought that defendants should not be tempted to risk eternal damnation by providing perjurious testimony in an attempt to avoid the gallows. But they were allowed to make *unsworn* statements to the jury.

Ineffective Assistance of Counsel, the Duty to Investigate, and Pretrial Discovery in Criminal Cases, 31 Fordham Urb. L.J. 1097 (2004).

Where the court concludes that the state *has* actively interfered with counsel's ability to represent the defendant, as in *Powell, reversal is automatic*; the defendant need not show how the state's rule undermined the specific presentation in the specific case. This stands in stark contrast to the *Strickland* rule, discussed below, where the defendant must show not only that counsel was ineffective, but that the ineffectiveness prejudiced his case.

It is not surprising that a defendant will try to argue that his case is "like" *Powell* — where counsel is assigned, but is either unfamiliar with criminal proceedings, or with the facts of the case. In *Cronic v. United States*, 466 U.S. 648 (1984), the trial court appointed a relatively young and inexperienced real estate attorney, who did no criminal work, to represent a defendant charged with 13 counts of mail fraud amounting to $9 million. The appointment was made 25 days before trial; the government had taken almost five years to prepare its case. Defendant, convicted and sentenced to 25 years, argued that these factors combined to make the case "like" *Powell* — although there was a lawyer present, he could not possibly deal with the intricacies of a complex, criminal case. The Supreme Court rejected the parallel to *Powell*, concluding that a good attorney could become acquainted with the materials of the case. The defendant, therefore, would have to demonstrate specific prejudice (which was defined in *Strickland v. Washington*, decided the same day, and discussed in detail below).

b. Conflict of Interest

Attorneys owe their clients undiluted loyalty. If Henry, a lawyer who is on retainer from the First National Bank in civil matters, is appointed to represent Amy, charged with robbing that very bank, there is real concern whether Henry can ardently represent her. Because Henry may wish (even subconsciously) to assure that future bank robbers are deterred, he may not be able to give Amy the 100 percent zealous advocacy she deserves, and to which she is constitutionally entitled. The general rule is that counsel should be Caesar's spouse — there should not be even the slightest possibility of conflict. The standard applies equally to retained and appointed counsel.

Conflicts may arise between or among lawyers if those lawyers representing conflicting interests belong to the same law firm. While "fire walls" may alleviate the problem, the fear that the wall will be breached moves most courts (and most attorneys) to avoid even the possibility by finding counsel outside the firm to represent "conflicted" defendants. The concern may become acute, of course, when "the firm" is a public defender's office, particularly if that office handles most (if not all) criminal defense work in the vicinity.

The first problem is determining whether there is a conflict, either actual or potential. Generally, *actual conflicts* obtain where there is a present and obvious difference between two defendants, both of whom are represented by the same lawyer; most other conflicts are not "actual" but only *potential*. Various state and nationally promulgated ethical standards, including but certainly not limited to, the Code of Professional Responsibility, will assist courts, and lawyers, in determining whether there is a potential conflict. Some potential conflicts are evident; when one lawyer represents multiple co-defendants, there is always a danger that loyalty to one will undercut loyalty to the other(s). If zealous representation of Hermine requires that counsel suggest that Dianne really committed the crime, counsel who represents both, even in severed trials, faces an impossible dilemma. See *Holloway v. Arkansas*, 435 U.S. 475 (1978), *McFarland v. Yukins*, 356 F.3d 688 (6th Cir. 2003).

Beyond that, however, the waters are murkier. For example, if the representation is successive, not simultaneous, or of a witness, and not a co-defendant, the problems are compounded. For example, in *Eisemann v. Herbert*, 274 F. Supp. 2d 283 (E.D.N.Y. 2003), counsel represented two defendants who were not actually co-defendants in a single trial, but who were subjects of parallel investigations, arrests, interrogation, and indictments. Even though an associate had handled most of the actual trial of one defendant, the court found that the conflict still existed. At the very least, said the court, the trial court should have made the defendant aware of the danger that he might face as a result of these conflicting interests: "The question is not whether or not the attorney did, in fact, pursue a sound trial strategy. Rather, it is whether or not the attorney was forced to forego a reasonable [though not necessarily better] strategy because of the conflict." Id. at 303.

Some (potential) conflicts involve counsel and money. In *Commw. v. Perkins*, 450 Mass. 834, 883 N.E.2d 230 (2008), defense counsel arranged with a television company to wear a wireless microphone during the trial. The court held this was a conflict but that it could be waived (see below). Again, where counsel appears to have a monetary interest in not pursuing the case too hard, there may be problems. Of course, counsel who charge a "flat fee" may always be tempted to "skim" the edges of adequate representation, but there are instances where the temptation seems "too" great. In *People v. Doolin*, 45 Cal. 4th 390, 198 P.3d 11, 87 Cal. Rptr. 209 (2009), the defendant argued that his appointed, state-contract counsel did not vigorously represent him because he received an $80,000 flat fee under the contract that included $60,000 for defense expenses; however, counsel was allowed to keep any of the money not spent. The court found no actual conflict, and no "adverse effect," but two justices dissented.[27] Where the conflict is "personal," the courts tend to find a conflict. Thus, in *Barentine v.*

---

27. Should the defendant have argued state interference with his counsel (*supra*)?

United States, 728 F. Supp. 1241 (W.D.N.C. 1990), defendant's lawyer, who was having an affair with the defendant's fiancee, never communicated a plea offer, hoping that the defendant would be convicted and sentenced to a long prison sentence.[28] The court found a conflict.

One final "conflict" is virtually omnipresent: where he will face the same prosecutor, or appear in front of the same judge in other cases, defense counsel may decide not to make motions that should be made. Surely one of the most stunning instances of this is *Ex Parte Hood*,[29] 2009 WL 2963845 (Tex. Crim. App. 2009), where the defense counsel knew that the prosecutor and judge had been previously involved in an affair but did not move to recuse the judge because he wished to "avoid angering" the judge.[30] The appellate court found that the defendant had not met the statutory requirements and dismissed his petition as an abuse of the writ. While defendant contended that he had not received a fair trial, he did not directly argue that his counsel was ineffective because of the decision not to challenge the judge.

A defendant who shows a conflict is not required to demonstrate actual *prejudice*, as required by *Strickland, infra*, p.273 but merely that the conflict had *adversely affected* his counsel's performance. *Cuyler v. Sullivan*, 446 U.S. 335 (1980). The standards may seem the same, but they are not. Suppose, for example, Ezekial represents Joseph in a criminal matter. Marietta is a possible witness for the defense, but because he has previously represented Marietta in noncriminal matters, and is concerned that the stress might be too great for her, Ezekial does not call Marietta in Joseph's trial. Even if the court concludes that Marietta's testimony would not have altered the outcome of the trial (i.e., *prejudiced* it) (see below), it may well determine that Ezekial's performance was "adversely affected" by his conflict.

When an attorney specifically informs the court that a conflict, actual or potential, exists, and he or she thinks it best to appoint a separate counsel for a co-defendant, the court should (a) honor that request without more inquiry; or (b) at the very least, conduct a very searching inquiry before denying the motion. *Holloway v. Arkansas*, 435 U.S. 475 (1978). But where there is no open request for a second attorney, it now appears that the trial

---

28. Where defense counsel threatened to punch defendant in the face and declared that he was the absolute worst client he had ever represented, the court's failure to probe more thoroughly resulted in ineffective assistance of counsel. *People v. McClam*, 60 A.D.3d 968, 875 N.Y.S.2d 568 (N.Y. App. Div. 2009).

29. The *Hood* case, which gained national publicity, is discussed in Mark White, Affair Between Prosecutor and Judge Calls for New Trial in Capital Case, 200 N.J.L.J.19, April 5, 2010; and Steven Seidenberg, Too Close for Comfort, ABA J., July 2010, p.24. Mr. White was governor of Texas from 1983-1987 and Attorney General from 1979-1983. He filed an amicus brief in support of Hood's petition for certiorari, but on April 19, 2010, the Court refused to grant cert. 559 U.S. 1072. See James C. McKinley, Jr., Judge and Prosecutor Admit to Affair, Lawyer Says, N.Y. Times, Sept. 10, 2008, at A17.

30. *Ibid.*, Dissent of Cochran, J., citing Francis Aff., dated August 1, 1996; Haynes Aff., dated March 6, 2009.

court need not conduct such an inquiry, even where it knows, or should know, that there is a potential conflict. In *Mickens v. Taylor*, 535 U.S. 162 (2002), the trial court had appointed Bryan Saunders as counsel to represent Timothy Hall. Ten days later, after Hall was killed, the same judge appointed Saunders to represent Walter Mickens, who was accused of murdering Hall. In speaking for the five-person majority, Justice Scalia, *starting from the assumption that the potential conflict did not affect counsel's performance*, declared that "automatic reversal (is not) an appropriate means of enforcing (a) mandate of inquiry." The Court then concluded that, even if the trial judge should have conducted such an inquiry, petitioner still had to show an "adverse effect" upon counsel's performance, which he had not done.[31]

The requirement of active inquiry (and the possibility of a *per se* reversal if there is no such inquiry) where a trial judge does not, but "should" know of a possible conflict, now appears to be limited to "multiple representation" settings.[32] All other cases are to be assessed under *Strickland* standards, set out below. Some state courts, however, do not agree with *Mickens*, and continue to follow a *per se* rule of reversal. In *People v. Daly*, 341 Ill. App. 3d 372, 792 N.E.2d 446 (Ill. App. 2003), for example, the key witness against the defendant was a confidential informant whom defense counsel had represented only weeks before the defendant's trial. Finding that the prior representation might have affected counsel's performance "in ways difficult to detect and demonstrate," the court reversed the conviction.

i. Waiving Conflict

The right to conflict-free counsel may be waived, at least generally; standards governing waiver vary with the timing and nature of the proceeding.

---

31. For example, the panel of the Fourth Circuit had noted that Saunders was ethically prevented from using information he had gained in his representation of Hall to impugn Hall's character for Mickens's benefit, and that Saunders was precluded from investigating, and bringing to court, evidence of Hall's relationship with his mother. *Mickens v. Taylor*, 227 F.3d 203 (4th Cir. 2000), opinion vacated, 240 F.3d 348 (4th Cir. 2001). See Note, 13 Cap. Def. J. 393 (2001); Scott A. Levin, An Open Question? The Effect of *Cuyler v. Sullivan* on Successive Representation after *Mickens v. Taylor*, 39 Crim. L. Bull. 55 (2003).

32. For example, in *Mickens*, the Court noted that the Federal Rules of Criminal Procedure treat concurrent and successive representation differently. That, of course, was irrelevant in *Mickens* itself, since it was a state, not a federal prosecution. But the attempt to distinguish the two situations may indicate that the *Cuyler* rule (see *Cuyler v. Sullivan*, 446 U.S. 335 (1980)), that failure to inquire in a *multirepresentation setting* results in *per se* reversal still obtains. Professor Allen et al., *supra*, suggest that there should be no *per se* rule even in multirepresentation cases, because that approach may persuade the defendant (and defense counsel) to "sandbag" the trial court. If the defendant is acquitted, the defendant wins, and if the defendant is convicted, the trial court's failure to inquire — even though not actually notified by counsel of the multirepresentation problem — will result in a new trial. Obviously, such behavior by defense counsel may be unethical, and, if unearthed, subject him to disciplinary sanctions. Is it likely that defense counsel would risk such discipline?

A defendant seeking to waive such conflict immediately before the trial must ordinarily demonstrate more awareness of the potential harm than one seeking to waive during the course of police investigatory procedures. *Von Moltke v. Gillies*, 332 U.S. 708, 723-24 (1948) ("a judge must investigate [a request to waive a conflict] as long and as thoroughly as the circumstances of the case before him demand").[33] As a general matter, because we wish to protect each defendant's autonomy, the Court will allow the waiver of a conflict. But because nonlawyers may not fully appreciate the nuances of potential conflict, a trial court may determine, in extreme circumstances, that no such waiver can be allowed, and override the waiver. *Wheat v. United States*, 486 U.S. 153 (1988).[34]

Do not confuse the ability of the court to override a defendant's choice of counsel in the context of a conflict of interest, with other settings. In *United States v. Gonzalez-Lopez*, 548 U.S. 140, 150 (2006), the Court, per Justice Scalia, held that the trial court's action in erroneously disqualifying defendant's counsel of choice gave rise to a *per se* constitutional violation requiring no proof of prejudice. It was, he said, a "structural" error, not subject to "harmless error" analysis (see Chapter 13 for more on this point):

> [T]he erroneous denial of counsel bears directly on the framework within which the trial proceeds. . . . It is impossible to know what different choices the rejected counsel would have made, and then to quantify the impact of those different choices on the outcome of the proceedings. . . . Harmless error analysis in such a context would be a speculative inquiry into what might have occurred in an alternate universe.

c. Effectiveness of Representation — *Strickland v. Washington*

The third, and by far the most litigated, prong of effective representation goes to the actual performance of trial counsel during the representation

33. In *Von Moltke*, Justice Black provided a long list of inquiries a trial court should make before accepting a waiver of conflict. Because it was only a plurality opinion, however, *Von Moltke* has been modified by lower courts. See, e.g., *Hsu v. United States*, 392 A.2d 972 (D.C. App. 1978); *United States v. Harris*, 683 F.2d 322, 325 (9th Cir. 1982) (The real inquiry is "what the defendant understood—not what the court said."). It is clear that the defendant must understand the charges, and possible defenses to the charges. Various lower courts have characterized a defendant's awareness of possible defenses as a basic element of an acceptable waiver. However, other courts have virtually discarded that portion of the *Von Moltke* opinion. They focus on the charges and the range of punishment. Indeed, some courts have said that it is not clear that defendant need understand the specific elements of the crime for waiver of counsel, though it is obviously needed for a guilty plea.

34. A notorious case holding that a conflict could not be waived, even after an intense pre-trial court inquiry establishing defendant's clear awareness of many permutations of the conflict, is *United States v. Schwarz*, 283 F.3d 76 (2d Cir. 2002), involving the prosecution of several police officers for a brutal attack, inside a police station, upon Abner Louima. The Court of Appeals for the Second Circuit required each officer to be represented by a different attorney.

period. The law here is confused and confusing, and is so fact-specific as to make virtually any articulation of standards suspect. The rule in the abstract is, however, very clear; as usual, the devil is in the details. As articulated by the Supreme Court in *Strickland v. Washington*, 466 U.S. 668 (1984), the effectiveness inquiry has two parts:

1. Did counsel perform effectively? (The performance issue.)
2. If not, did that ineffective performance actually injure the defendant? (The prejudice issue.)

i. The Standard of Performance

Lawyers (like judges and other human beings) make mistakes. But not every mistake means that a defendant was ineffectively represented. As observers have noted, a defendant is entitled to a "fair" trial, but not a "perfect" one. *Delaware v. Van Arsdall*, 475 U.S. 673, 681 (1986).

Until 50 years ago, most of the lower courts, both federal and state, had held that counsel was ineffective only if the representation was so poor as to make the trial a "farce and mockery." After *Gideon*, however, the courts increasingly rejected this basement-level norm and took one of two approaches in assessing performance: (1) use of ethical and nationally promulgated standards, such as those of the American Bar Association, which had promulgated its first set of standards relating to the defense function;[35] (2) a "reasonableness" test.[36] The latter approach sometimes echoed the malpractice test in torts, namely, whether the attorney had acted with the level of performance in his local community; the former used national standards, sometimes enhanced by local practice.

The procedural posture of *Strickland* is important. Defendant, convicted of capital murder, did not claim that his attorney's performance at trial was ineffective. Rather, the complaint concerned the capital sentencing hearing. Thus, *Strickland* appears to: (1) establish a rule for all "critical stages" of a criminal prosecution; and (2) allow assessment of the performance of

---

35. A number of organizations have promulgated rules or standards of conduct, but by far the most important are those established by the American Bar Association (ABA). There are, of course, the general Model Code of Professional Responsibility and the Model Rules of Professional Conduct. But the ABA has, over the last 35 years, published an entire series of Standards of Criminal Justice. They are all available at http://www.abanet.org/crimjust/standards/. Several of those volumes, however, are of particular relevance to the question here: Defense Function, available at http://www.abanet.org/crimjust/standards/dfunc_toc.html; Providing Defense Services, available at http://www.abanet.org/crimjust/standards/defsvcs_toc.html; and Prosecution Function, available at http://www.abanet.org/crimjust/standards/pfunctoc.html.

36. A court can now also consider, besides the ABA model rules and code, the American Lawyer's Code of Conduct and the standards promulgated by the National Association of Criminal Defense Lawyers.

counsel at each critical stage, rather than combining all such stages and the overall performance. The habeas corpus petition alleged that defendant's attorney had failed to:

1. move for a continuance to prepare for sentencing;
2. request a psychiatric report;
3. investigate and present character witnesses;
4. seek a presentence report;
5. present meaningful arguments to the sentencing judge;
6. investigate the medical examiner's report.

The Eleventh Circuit had (1) formulated some specific guidelines to define counsel's duty to investigate; and (2) had ruled that if a defendant shows that counsel's failing worked to the defendant's actual and substantial disadvantage, the writ of habeas corpus must be granted unless (3) the state proved counsel's ineffectiveness was harmless beyond a reasonable doubt. The Supreme Court, in an opinion by Justice O'Connor, reversed, rejecting each of those approaches.[37]

The Court's opinion began by emphatically rejecting any attempt to employ national standards as anything more than guides. The Court explicitly declared that "[m]ore specific guidelines [than reasonableness] are not appropriate," that "the basic duties" do not "form a checklist"; and that "[p]revailing norms of practice as reflected in [ABA standards] are guides . . . but they are only guides." Indeed, added the Court: "[a]ny such set of rules would interfere with the constitutionally protected independence of Counsel and . . . could distract counsel from the overriding mission of vigorous advocacy of the defendant's cause."[38]

The Court then turned to what would constitute deficient performance. The critical inquiry, said the Court, was "*whether counsel's assistance was reasonable considering all the circumstances.*" The "circumstances faced by defense counsel . . ." were so varied, said the Court, that only a broad standard such as reasonableness could be employed. The Court observed that "it is all too tempting for a defendant to second-guess counsel's assistance . . . [E]very effort [must] be made to eliminate the distorting effects of hindsight." To reduce this possibility:

---

37. In the same year she wrote *Strickland*, Justice O'Connor had remarked that "ineffective assistance of counsel claims are becoming as much a part of state and federal habeas corpus proceedings as the bailiff's call to order in these courts." *McKaskle v. Vela*, 464 U.S. 1053 (1984) (O'Connor, J., dissenting from denial of certiorari).

38. The same day as its decision in *Strickland*, the Court decided *United States v. Cronic*, 466 U.S. 648 (1984). In *Cronic*, the lower court had used five factors in assessing the adequacy of performance of a real estate attorney appointed as defense counsel 25 days before a major mail fraud prosecution. Like the *Strickland* opinion, the *Cronic* opinion rejected the use of any such factors as "determinative" of the issue.

1. courts should indulge a *"strong presumption"* that counsel's conduct falls within the wide range of reasonable professional assistance;[39]
2. *defendant* would carry the burden of demonstrating that the assistance was deficient, although that burden would be less than the typical "preponderance" standard;
3. tactical decisions are "virtually unchallengeable."

Strickland's approach is certainly understandable, particularly as it applies to decisions regarding trial tactics, and, even more acutely, to those decisions made during the trial itself. Two attorneys faced with the same problem might well decide on two wholly different approaches, each of which is not "unreasonable." One counsel might choose to cross-examine an adverse witness at length, hoping to demonstrate bias. A second attorney, perceiving that the witness has not done major damage to the defendant's case, might decide not to cross-examine at all, or to tread lightly, lest the witness do more damage, or win the jury's empathy. That the defendant was convicted does not itself demonstrate that the strategy was "wrong," or that a different strategy was either "better" or "might have worked."

Even if trial judgments made in the heat of the moment are difficult to assess, strategic judgments made outside the courtroom, with more time for reflection, are more subject to analysis. An incomplete investigation may well mean that the "tactical decision" was uninformed, and hence not "unchallengeable." Thus, counsel has been held ineffective, for example, for failing to investigate evidence of the defendant's brain impairment, *Frazier v. Huffman*, 343 F.3d 780 (6th Cir. 2003), or failing to interview and call witnesses who would have helped impeach the government's two key witnesses, *Cargle v. Mullin*, 317 F.3d 1196 (10th Cir. 2003). Given five possible courses of defense, or ten possible witnesses to interview, an attorney is forced to decide among them, and allocate time accordingly.

Strickland itself reflects this dilemma. Justice O'Connor concluded, on the basis of the record developed in the habeas proceeding, that each of the defendant's allegations of inadequate performance could be explained as a reasonable strategic decision. Defense counsel, said the Court, 466 U.S. 668, 699 (emphasis added) had:

> made a strategic choice to argue for the extreme emotional distress mitigating circumstance and to rely as fully as possible on respondent's acceptance of responsibility for his own crimes. . . . Trial Counsel could reasonably surmise

---

39. Some have questioned the notion of a "presumption" here, pointing out that even in tort cases, other professions — including lawyers — are not given such a benefit. See Richard D. Klein, The Emperor Gideon Has No Clothes: The Empty Promise of the Constitutional Right to Effective Assistance of Counsel, 13 Hastings Const. L.Q. 625 (1986).

from his conversation that character and psychological evidence would be of little help . . . Restricting testimony on respondent's character to what had come in at the plea colloquy ensured that contrary character and psychological evidence and respondent's criminal history . . . would not come in. *On these facts, there can be little question . . . that trial counsel's defense, though unsuccessful, was the result of reasonable professional judgment.*

Justice Marshall, dissenting, argued that the reasonableness standard "is so malleable that, in practice, it will either have no grip at all or will yield excessive variation in the manner in which the Sixth Amendment is interpreted. . . . To tell lawyers and the lower courts that counsel for a criminal defendant must behave 'reasonably' . . . is to tell them almost nothing."[40] Id. at 707-708.

The debate has not subsided over the years since *Strickland*. For example, any nonlawyer would be stunned to learn that a series of cases has debated whether *Strickland* is violated when the defense counsel appears intoxicated,[41] or distracted, or even sleeping during trial testimony. But to a lawyer, particularly to an attorney whose conduct is called into question, and who fears disciplinary sanctions, there may be many explanations for the apparent conduct. First, there is the challenge that the counsel may not have been intoxicated or sleeping; he simply may have had his eyes shut. Only counsel knows with certainty, and he is likely to say he was not asleep. In addition, a counsel who closes his eyes may be entertaining a strategy to demonstrate how unimportant the testimony was.[42] Finally, even a few seconds napping in a long trial, some judges have concluded, is not sufficient in itself to demonstrate unequivocally ineffective representation.[43] After much travail,

---

40. Amy R. Murphy, The Constitutional Failure of the Strickland Standard in Capital Cases Under the Eighth Amendment, 63 Law & Contemp. Probs. 179 (2000) (*Strickland* "made unmistakably clear that bright line rules for representation were not part of the Sixth Amendment"). As the Court said in *Strickland*, 466 U.S. 668, 693: "Representation is an art and an act or omission that is unprofessional in one case may be sound or even brilliant in another." *Strickland,*, *supra*, 466 U.S. at 693.

41. Thus, in *People v. Garrison*, 47 Cal. 3d 746, 765 P.2d 419, 254 Cal. Rptr. 257 (Cal. 1989), defendant's attorney, an alcoholic who was arrested while driving to the courthouse, was not proven to be ineffective. Shortly after the trial, the attorney died of alcoholism. The court, however, concluded that "a review of the acts indicates that the attorney did a fine job in this case." Jeffrey L. Kirchmeier, Drink, Drugs, and Drowsiness: The Constitutional Right to Effective Assistance of Counsel and the Strickland Prejudice Requirement, 45 Neb. L. Rev. 425 (1996).

42. Although Clarence Darrow was never accused of sleeping at trial, he was known to use various techniques to distract the jury — or to suggest to them that he found the (possibly devastating) testimony boring. A classic "distraction" was to light up a massive cigar during prosecution testimony and have the jury watch to see when the ashes from the cigar would fall into the ashtray. Darrow, however, had placed wires in the cigar before trial, making it difficult, if not impossible, for the ashes to actually fall.

43. E.g., *McFarland v. Texas*, 928 S.W.2d 481 (Tex. Crim. App. 1996), *cert. denied*, 519 U.S. 1119 (1997). See also *United States v. Katz*, 425 F.2d 928, 931 (2d Cir. 1970) ("the testimony during

the Fifth Circuit established a "presumption" that counsel who were perceived as sleeping had not performed effectively. *Burdine v. Johnson*, 262 F.3d 336, *cert. denied, sub nom. Cockrell v. Burdine*, 535 U.S. 1120 (2002) (mem).[44]

(Allegedly) sleeping counsel are merely the tip of the iceberg. There is virtually no action that a lawyer has taken—or not taken—that has not been found to be (in)effective or not (in)effective. Each decision is fact specific. But some generalizations are possible. *Failure to investigate* has often been the key to a finding of ineffectiveness.[45] In death penalty cases, discussed more fully below, where the issue is not guilt but punishment, the investigation should consider the "social background" of the defendant, as well as anything relating to the defendant's mental status—brain injuries, past mental problems, and so on. In noncapital cases, investigation of witnesses, particularly those named by the defendant, is crucial. Of course, before a decision not to investigate (further) can be deemed "strategic," there must be at least some investigation of the facts on which that decision was based.[46]

A *mistake or ignorance of law* is almost surely deficient performance. Lower court cases have found ineffective performance caused by an attorney's legal error. Thus, attorney error has been found when counsel:

- did not challenge the legality of a search because he was unaware of the rule that allowed him to do so;

---

the period of counsel's somnolence was not central to the accused's case and . . . if it had been [the trial judge] would have awakened him rather than waiting for the luncheon recess to warn him."). As those who may have catnapped during a class may attest, a few somnolent seconds may not affect one's ability to understand the process, and power naps do not necessarily affect ultimate performance. The problem, however, is that the critical questions—Was he asleep? Did it affect performance?—can be fairly answered only by the attorney. The witnesses in a hearing involving such a matter—jurors, or possibly court personnel—are unlikely to be keeping minute details of the duration, or precise occurrence, of counsel's siestas. Indeed, if the jurors were watching the defense counsel rather than the witness, we would have other concerns. The judge, similarly, may be concerned with the testimony, or other matters, paying little attention to defense counsel. The person most likely to be sufficiently interested to keep notes is the defendant—who will perhaps nudge his attorney, but who will hesitate before "waking" him, or before complaining to the judge.

44. Some two decades earlier, the Ninth Circuit had created an identical presumption in another sleeping counsel case. *Javor v. United States*, 724 F.2d 831 (9th Cir. 1984). Plus que ça change. . . . The same lawyer who slept during Burdine's trial, slept during the trial of Carl Johnson, but both the Texas Court of Criminal Appeals and the Fifth Circuit upheld the conviction and death sentence. Neither court published its opinion. David R. Dow, The State, the Death Penalty and Carl Johnson, 37 B.C.L. Rev. 691, 711 (1996).

45. See, e.g., *Ard v. State*, 372 S.C. 318, 642 S.E.2d 590 (2007) (failure to hire expert to examine the absence of gun residue on defendant's hands).

46. *Wiggins v. Smith*, 539 U.S. 510 (2003) ("[S]trategic choices made after less than complete investigation are reasonable" only to the extent that "reasonable professional judgments support the limitations on investigation").

- failed to object to illegally seized evidence because he misread the leading case on the issue;
- advised a plea of guilty to the charge of forgery, unaware that there was a statute which carried a lighter penalty, and which applied more directly;
- "induced" the defendant to plead guilty on the "patently erroneous advice that he may be subject to a sentence six times more severe than that which the law would really allow";
- requested a jury instruction that (wrongfully) placed upon the defendant the burden of proving an element of the crime;
- failed to contest the trial court's decision, notwithstanding a probation recommendation to the contrary, not to group certain charges, thereby increasing the sentencing range from 63-78 months to 78-97 months;
- failed to ascertain that defendant was not a persistent violent felony offender, which both the prosecutor and the trial court thought to be the case.[47]
- The Supreme Court has also found deficient performance caused by an attorney's legal error.

In *Hinton v. Alabama*, 134 S.Ct. 1081 (2014), trial counsel mistakenly believed that he was only entitled to $1,000 to retain an expert. Alabama law in fact allowed him to be reimbursed for any reasonable expenses that he incurred. As a result of the mistaken belief that he only had $1,000 available to hire an expert, he hired an expert whose trial testimony was weak and largely discredited. The additional funding that was available to him would have allowed him to hire a more qualified expert. Hinton claimed trial counsel was ineffective as a result of his misreading of the law. The Supreme Court found that trial counsel's performance had been deficient: "An attorney's ignorance of a point of law that is fundamental to his case combined with his failure to perform basic research on that point is a quintessential example of unreasonable performance under *Strickland*." Id. at 1089. The Court stressed that it was counsel's inexcusable mistake of law that was deficient, not his choice of an expert, which is typically a strategic choice entitled to deference.

The impact of *Padilla* (discussed in Chapter 7) is not yet clear, but it may portend that counsel has to become familiar with various consequences of a guilty plea (or conviction) and warn the client of these risks; failure to know the law here might become "per se" ineffective representation. On a similar note, failure to meet a clear statutory or rule deadline for action is likely to be

---

47. E.g., Counsel did not understand state law as to modicum of evidence required for instruction. *McCree v. Secretary, Dept. of Corrections*, 63 F. Supp. 2d 1316 (M.D. Fla. 2009).

ineffective representation. United States v. Shedrick, 493 F.3d 292 (3rd Cir. 2007); Cave v. Singletary, 971 F.2d 1513 (11th Cir. 1992). Recently, in Holland v. Florida, 560 U.S. 631 (2010), the Court, in an analogous setting, held that the one-year statute of limitations on petitions for federal habeas corpus could be tolled where defendant's counsel simply had been lethargic in following defendant's admonitions to be sure not to miss the filing deadline.

The reason for this equivocation is Strickland's view — almost certainly reflecting reality — that virtually any decision by counsel can be characterized as "strategic." Thus, in Florida v. Nixon, 543 U.S. 175 (2004), a death penalty case, defense counsel began his opening by conceding that his defendant had committed the crime. The Court held that that was not necessarily ineffective representation: The evidence of guilt was so overwhelming that counsel's decision not to alienate the jury by feigning innocence, but to build a rapport so as to persuade them not to impose the death penalty, was a strategic decision. Even if it was "wrong" (and in this case the jury did impose death), the decision was not unreasonable. If conceding the guilt of a defendant in a capital case can be considered not unreasonable, given the circumstances of the case, there is virtually no decision that, without considering the circumstances, "must be" unreasonable. Similarly, persuading a client to plead guilty and hope for a light sentence, is not necessarily ineffective assistance. Hodges v. Bell, 548 F. Supp. 2d 485 (M.D. Tenn. 2008). However, an attorney's performance is deficient when he fails to inform a client of a plea offer, Missouri v. Frye, 566 U.S. 134 (2012); and when erroneous legal advice is given which causes a client to reject a favorable plea offer. Lafler v. Cooper, 566 U.S. 156 (2012).

Indeed, because the focus is on defense counsel performance in this case, not even pending disciplinary proceedings, even if they result in disbarment, are sufficient to create a per se presumption of poor performance. Young v. Runnels, 435 F.3d 1038 (9th Cir. 2006).[48]

Justice O'Connor's view that the test of due process was whether the result was fair, whether the error "undermined confidence in the outcome of the proceeding," effectively adopted the Brady-Kyles approach (discussed in Chapter 6) that requires a reviewing court to assess each possible error of defense counsel both singly and cumulatively. Thus, Strickland requires a detailed, retrospective fact-specific investigation into the entire record, into defense counsel's mental state at the time of the trial, and the ways in which a "competent" attorney might have handled the trial, absent the

---

48. See Sanjay K. Chhablani, Chronically Stricken: A Continuing Legacy of Ineffective Assistance of Counsel, 28 St. Louis U. Pub. L. Rev. 351 (2009) (citing studies of disciplined attorneys who represented clients; specifically that the percentage of counsel disbarred either before or after capital cases were: Illinois (12%); Kentucky (25%); Louisiana (66%)). Laurie L. Levenson, Just Give Me a Real Lawyer, Nat'l L.J. 10, August 9, 2010.

error. As we saw in *Kyles*, any attorney, much less those on appellate courts both state and federal, is liable to disagree vehemently about the effect that a "good" lawyer might have had in a hypothetically errorless trial. At the very least, this test leads to unfettered speculation, well after the fact. As with *Brady*, this approach has led judges to consider not only the impact of the evidence which defense counsel did not find, or the argument he did not make, but the counter-counter factual of what the prosecutor might then have responded.[49] If this sounds like high level speculation, that is not necessarily an "unreasonable" interpretation of the case law.

As Justice Marshall said, dissenting in *Strickland*: "Seemingly impregnable cases can sometimes be dismantled by a good defense counsel. On the basis of a cold record, it may be impossible for a reviewing court confidently to ascertain how the government's evidence and argument would have stood up against rebuttal and cross examination by a shrewd, well-prepared lawyer."[50] *Strickland, supra*, 466 U.S. at 710. In most cases, a single mistake by counsel, even a significant one, will not meet *Strickland* standards. Instead, defendant will normally attempt to show a series of errors, which should be considered cumulatively. See *Miller v. Senkowski*, 268 F. Supp. 2d 296 (E.D.N.Y. 2003).

As already suggested, one theme running through these cases, both in the Supreme Court and in lower courts, is the relevance of the ABA Standards, both those of general and specific import. In *Strickland*, the Court appeared to use them (if at all) only as "guidelines." In a series of cases in the early 2000s, the Standards appeared to be more important.[51] In recent decisions, the standards have become, if anything, less than "guidelines." Indeed, in *Bobby v. Van Hook*, 558 U.S. 4, 14 (2009), Justice Alito specially concurred for the express purpose to:

> emphasize my understanding that the opinion in no way suggests that the American Bar Association's Guidelines for the Appointment and Performance of Defense Counsel in Death Penalty Cases (rev. ed. 2003) (2003 Guidelines or ABA Guidelines) have special relevance in determining whether an attorney's performance meets the standard required by the Sixth Amendment. The ABA is a venerable organization with a history of service to the bar, but it is, after all, a

---

49. In *Wong v. Belmontes*, 558 U.S. 15 (2009), the Court, per curiam, held that counsel's failure to adduce specific evidence was not clearly ineffective because had counsel offered it, it "would have invited the strongest possible evidence in rebuttal."

50. Certainly, many would attribute to masterful defense lawyering the acquittals in the O.J. Simpson murder trial and the state prosecution of the police officers involved in beating Rodney King, two cases which, on their face, appeared to be "slam dunks" for the state.

51. See, e.g., *Wiggins v. Smith*, 539 U.S. 510 (2003); *Williams v. Taylor*, 529 U.S. 3652 (2000); *Rompilla v. Beard*, 545 U.S. 374 (2005); *Porter v. McCollum*, 558 U.S. 30 (2009); Robert T. Rigg, The T-Rex Without Teeth: Evolving Strickland v. Washington and the Test for Ineffective Assistance of Counsel, 35 Pepperdine L. Rev. 77 (2007); Stephen Smith, Taking Strickland Claims Seriously, 93 Marq. L. Rev. 515, 540 (2009).

private group with limited membership. The views of the association's members, not to mention the views of the members of the advisory committee that formulated the 2003 Guidelines, do not necessarily reflect the views of the American bar as a whole. It is the responsibility of the courts to determine the nature of the work that a defense attorney must do in a capital case in order to meet the obligations imposed by the Constitution, and I see no reason why the ABA Guidelines should be given a privileged position in making that determination.

Beyond the question of whether standards can be enunciated, much less adopted, is the question of the burden and standard of proof. One could, after all, require the defendant to allege specific errors in representation, and to meet a burden of production, but require the state to demonstrate that the representation was adequate (or not inadequate). Instead, *Strickland* put the burden of proof on the defendant, and then added the "strong presumption" that the representation was effective. Although Justice O'Connor clearly announced that the standard only required the defendant to prove ineffectiveness by a "reasonable probability," and explicitly rejected higher standards of proof, as the Court observed in *Kimmelman v. Morris*, 477 U.S. 3655 (1986), the strong presumption of competence makes the defendant's task "though . . . not insurmountable . . . a heavy one."

ii. Demonstrating Prejudice

Even if the defendant overcomes the presumption that trial counsel's stumbling was actually trial strategy and proves ineffective representation, *Strickland* holds that the reviewing court should not grant relief unless, as well, the defendant demonstrates that the result would have been different. The purpose of counsel, said Justice O'Connor, was "to ensure a fair trial . . . a trial whose result is reliable . . . [one which did not show] a breakdown in the adversary process that renders the result unreliable."[52]

Justice Marshall, dissenting in *Strickland*, argued that focus on the result vitiated the purpose of both counsel and other Sixth Amendment guarantees. Even the guiltiest defendant, argued Marshall, was entitled to a fair trial; concern with a "reliable result" would mean that an obviously guilty defendant could never obtain relief even after a trial which was a "farce and mockery."[53] *Strickland*, *supra*, 466 U.S. at 714.

Strickland made prejudice relevant. Justice O'Connor placed upon the defendant the burden of proving that there was a "reasonable probability"

---

52. *supra*.
53. Some states, such as New York, have taken Marshall's approach, focusing not on the outcome, but "on the fairness of the process as a whole, rather than any particular impact on the outcome of the case." *People v. Henry*, 95 N.Y.2d 563, 144 N.E.2d 112 (2000).

that he had been prejudiced. While, as Justice O'Connor indicated, this was not the most difficult hurdle the Court could have erected, it was more stringent than some. Earlier lower court decisions (and the Eleventh Circuit in *Strickland*) had placed upon the prosecution the burden of demonstrating that the (proven) ineffective assistance had not harmed the defendant.[54] The chart below suggests the span of positions one might take in this regard.

11.1

Lowest Burden on Defendant			Highest Burden on Defendant	
Automatic Reversal (Nonrebuttable)	Presume Prejudice (Gov't may rebut)	*D* Must Show Reason Prob *Strickland*	*D* Carries by Preponderance	*D* Carries BRD ("Farce")

The prejudice standard must also be read in tandem with the performance standard. Justice O'Connor's opinion made clear that a reviewing court need not assess counsel's performance if the defendant did not carry the proof on prejudice. This holding provided courts a method by which they could avoid the unpleasant task of "grading" performance at all.[55]

2. Is Death Different?

Of course it is. Aside from the obvious irreversibility of the sanction, capital cases are the only cases where there is a sentencing hearing before a jury. And even in non-capital cases, the issues are not ones of "law," but of philosophy and practicality. Even though (perhaps, because) the jury has been "death qualified," defense counsel must "seek to make the defendant a human being" so that jurors willing to impose the death sentence in the abstract will decide not to impose it in this case.

The *timing* of the sentencing process in capital cases is also unique, and calls for substantial planning. In non-capital cases, sentencing may occur

---

54. See the discussion in Chapter 12 of the *Chapman* "harmless error" rule that "[p]roof of a constitutional error . . . casts on someone other than the person prejudiced by it, a burden to show that it was harmless . . . . [T]he original common law harmless error rule put the burden on the beneficiary of the error either to prove that there was no injury or to suffer a reversal of his erroneously obtained judgment." *Chapman v. California*, 386 U.S. 18, 24 (1967).

55. Cf. *White v. Singletary*, 972 F.2d 1218 (11th Cir. 1992): "We are not interested in grading lawyers' performance; we are interested in whether the adversarial process at trial, in fact, worked adequately."

weeks after the verdict. In that time, at least theoretically, counsel can investigate the defendant's background. In capital cases, because the same jury decides the sentencing issue, the process begins immediately after the verdict (in some cases as quickly as half an hour after). This fact has significant implications for attorneys. It means that prior to trial, they must have completed virtually all of the investigation for information they will present to the jury if the defendant is convicted. Thus, counsel must decide, weeks or months before trial, how to allocate resources between efforts to obtain an acquittal and efforts to find sufficient mitigating information to prevent a death sentence after conviction.

Of course, even in non-capital cases, defense counsel should prepare for sentencing. But because the stakes are so high in capital cases, the investigation into the defendant's background must be much more intense and thorough. And it has been upon the investigation aspect of these cases that the Supreme Court has focused.

From 1984-2000, the Court, applying only the *Strickland* standards (remember that *Strickland* itself was a capital sentencing case), found no capital counsel constitutionally ineffective. That has now been dramatically altered. In the space of seven years, the Court overturned several death sentences on the basis of ineffectiveness, all focusing on the inadequate investigation of information for the sentencing phase. In *Williams (Terry) v. Taylor*, 529 U.S. 362 (2000) and *Williams (Michael) v. Taylor*, 529 U.S. 420 (2000), the Court concluded that effectiveness in a death sentencing case required intense assessment of the defendant's background, including: (1) medical records (particularly if there were mental illness or physical brain damage); (2) school records (to determine whether defendant's violent behavior had begun early in life); (3) addiction to alcohol or drugs; and (4) numerous other aspects of defendant's early life. In *Wiggins v. Smith*, 539 U.S. 510 (2003), the Court held that counsel's reliance upon the information contained in the defendant's presentence report was not "reasonable."

Capital defense attorneys saw *Wiggins* as a potential turning point. "*Wiggins* will have a profound effect on the way capital sentences are reviewed. It will no longer be possible for courts to dismiss claims of ineffectiveness lightly by characterizing the failure to present mitigation as a 'strategy'."[56]

That assessment turns out to have been more hopeful than warranted. In a subsequent series of cases, the Court upheld some ineffectiveness challenges, while rejecting others. It is hard to assess, much less reconcile, these cases, in part because several of them (going each way) were relatively short per curiam opinions. In *Rompilla v. Beard*, 545 U.S. 374 (2005), for example, defense counsel had spoken to three mental health professionals and five

---

56. Ira Mickenberg, Criminal Cases, Ineffective Counsel, The National Law Journal, August 4, 2003.

members of the defendant's family in an attempt to discover mitigation. Moreover, Rompilla did not assist them, and his family suggested that there was no mitigating evidence. Nevertheless, the Court held that this investigation was ineffective because defendant's criminal file (which was available in the courthouse) contained evidence regarding his traumatic childhood, organic brain damage, mental retardation, and alcoholism.[57] Neither was the counsel's decision not to probe further into defendant's mental state totally without basis — some of this evidence might have presented a "double edged sword," suggesting to the jury that the defendant would be unable to control his future behavior.[58]

The next five years demonstrated a schism — perhaps a schizophrenia — in the Court's decisions. In *Schriro v. Landrigan*, 550 U.S. 465 (2007), the Court relied primarily on the ground that defendant has asked that there be no mitigation evidence presented at the penalty phase.[59] Where counsel failed to find any mitigating evidence, including defendant's war heroism, the Court found counsel ineffective at the death penalty stage. *Porter v. McCollum*, 558 U.S. 30 (2009). But in *Cullen v. Pinholster*, 559 U.S. 314 (2011), a majority held that counsel who had prepared only 6.5 hours and presented only one witness at the penalty phase had not been ineffective.[60]

Although the Court's precedents give counsel a lot of leeway in deciding how to defend his client, counsel cannot present evidence that makes it more likely that a jury will sentence his client to death. *Buck v. Davis*, 137 S.Ct. 759 (2017). In Texas, in order to sentence a defendant to death, a jury must determine that he will continue to be dangerous in prison. Duane Buck's attorney presented the testimony of an expert that it hired. His attorney elicited from the expert that Buck was more likely to be dangerous in prison

---

57. Death row inmates have higher levels of "intellectual limitations, poor academic achievement, learning disability, psychological disorders, family of origin histories of child maltreatment and abuse, parental substance dependence, and pre-confinement substance dependence." M.D. Cunningham and T.J. Reidy, A Matter of Life and Death: Special Considerations and Heightened Practice Standards in Capital Sentencing Evaluations, 19 Behav. Sci. & L. 473, 477 (2001). See, e.g., *Anderson v. Simmons*, 493 F.3d 1131 (10th Cir. 2007), where defendant was held to be deprived of effective assistance at the sentencing phase where trial counsel did not adduce evidence that defendant suffered from brain damage, was borderline mentally defective, only completed the eighth grade, and functioned below the bottom 2 percent of the general population.

58. Even if the potentially available mitigating evidence appears likely to be double-edged, the attorney . . . should conduct a full investigation and . . . introduce at least some of the mitigating evidence at the penalty trial. . . ." Welsh S. White, A Deadly Dilemma: Choices by Attorneys Representing "Innocent" Capital Defendants, 102 Mich. L. Rev. 2001 (2004).

59. The dissent disagreed with this assessment, concluding that Landrigan had only forbidden trial counsel to call his relatives for mitigation; the ban, said the dissent, would not have reached other witnesses.

60. See, e.g., *Smith v. Spisak*, 558 U.S. 139 (2010); *Knowles v. Mirzayance*, 556 U.S. 111 (2009); *Jefferson v. Upton*, 564 U.S. 284 (2010), all finding ineffectiveness. But in *Wood v. Allen*, 558 U.S. 290 (2010), *Wong v. Belmonts*, 558 U.S. 15 (2009), and *Bobby v. Van Hook*, 558 U.S. 4 (2009), the Court declined to find ineffectiveness. See, generally, Annot., 31 A.L.R. Fed. 211.

because of his race (African American). The attorney also entered into evidence the expert's report, which included his conclusions about race. The Court found that the attorney was deficient and that Buck had been prejudiced by the expert's testimony.

These cases, standing alone, would themselves suggest that the Court may have poured new wine into the *Strickland* bottle. This view may be heightened by the fact that the Court in *Rompilla* and *Wiggins* referred repeatedly to the ABA Guidelines for the Appointment and Performance of Defense Counsel in Death Penalty Cases (2d ed. 2003).[61] The Guidelines, written specifically for capital cases, are specific and detailed, and recognize the significantly greater duties placed upon counsel in these cases. For example, the Guidelines call for a "team," including a minimum of two counsel and a mitigation expert, to handle every death case. While many public defender offices follow these standards, many cannot.[62] Some courts have held that a failure to consider using a mitigation specialist is itself ineffective assistance. *Jells v. Mitchell*, 538 F.3d 478 (6th Cir. 2008). But see the discussion, *supra*, p.281 and Justice Alito's comments therein.

The Court's recent decisions must be read in the context of the increased scrutiny of the death penalty, and of representation in those cases.[63] Project Innocence, which, often on the basis of DNA evidence, has obtained exoneration of over 200 prisoners, many of them on death row, has generated new debate over the penalty. The American Bar Association's call for a moratorium on the penalty, which has been followed by several states, has also had an impact. Moreover, the level of representation, even at this

---

61. Reprinted in 31 Hofstra L. Rev. 913 (2003).

62. Thus, Laurence A. Benner, The Presumption of Guilt: Systemic Factors That Contribute to Ineffective Assistance of Counsel in California, 45 Cal. West. L. Rev. 263, 296 (2009) found that California offices were significantly below this level:

> Only nine offices, however, had staff personnel with a Masters degree in social work (MSW) to assist in such investigations. Even fewer offices (four) had a full-time death penalty mitigation specialist on staff. Nine offices, that had represented collectively thirty-three death penalty clients, had no such staff assistance at all. While one of these offices was in a metropolitan county (over 1 million population), the majority were in counties having a population ranging from 100,000 to 500,000. Only twelve offices had personnel specifically assigned to develop sentencing alternatives for clients in non-capital cases. While a bare majority (53%) of offices had paralegals on staff, fourteen offices had no such staff assistance.

See Leona D. Jochnowitz, Missed Mitigation: Counsel's Evolving Duty to Assess and Present Mitigation at Death Penalty Sentencing, 43 Crim. L. Bull. 3 (2007).

63. In the span of 23 years, 68 percent of capital judgments reviewed by the courts were overturned due to serious error, most commonly because of grossly incompetent defense lawyering. James S. Liebman, Jeffrey Fagan & Valerie West, A Broken System: Error Rates in Capital Cases, 1973-1995 (Columbia Law Sch. Pub. Law Research Paper, Working Paper. No. 15, 2000), available at http://www.thejusticeproject.org/press/reports/pdfs/Error-Rates-in-Capital-Cases.

level, has been "breathtakingly low in many jurisdictions."[64] Professor Bright found that one-third of the lawyers who represented people sentenced to death in Illinois had been disbarred or suspended. One of the lawyers, a convicted felon and the only lawyer to be disbarred twice, represented four men who were sentenced to death.[65]

Whether the string of cases discussed here affects non-capital cases or not, clearly counsel's actions in capital cases will be examined microscopically, and measured against not only the ABA Guidelines, but other such standards as well.

3. The Right to Effective Assistance — Expert Witnesses

Lawyers, even the best of lawyers, are only lawyers; they are not experts in psychiatry, medical technology, or firearms. It is sometimes argued that for counsel to be "effective" and for a trial to be "fair," the state must appoint not merely an attorney, but an expert witness. In *Ake v. Oklahoma*, 470 U.S. 68 (1985), the trial court had, *sua sponte*, ordered the defendant, charged with a capital offense, to be examined for competency to stand trial. When the trial actually occurred, appointed defense counsel asked for funding to hire a psychiatrist to support a claim of insanity. The Supreme Court held that, in these circumstances, the state was obligated, as a matter of due process (not the Sixth Amendment) to provide the assistance of one competent psychiatrist, which was a "basic tool" in this case. The Court noted that most states would provide such assistance in similar circumstances, so long as the defendant points to "substantive supporting facts" that could make such a plea feasible. In *McWilliams v. Dunn*, 137 S. Ct. 1790 (2017), the Court clarified that *Ake* requires that the state must provide an indigent defendant whose mental state is a possible issue in the case with access to a mental health expert who is sufficiently available to the defense and *independent* from the prosecution to examine and evaluate the defendant and to assist the defense in the preparation and presentation of a mental defense. The obligation, therefore, is not met by appointing an expert who is available to assist both the prosecution and the defense, as was done by the trial court in *McWilliams*.

Federal and state courts are divided on whether *Ake* applies outside the psychiatric realm. Courts have concluded that, depending on the precise

---

64. Erica J. Hashimoto, Defending the Right of Self-Representation: An Empirical Look at the Pro Se Felony Defendant, 85 N.C. L. Rev. 423, 467 (2007).
65. Stephen B. Bright, Gideon's Reality, Crim. Just. (Summer 2003), p.5. See also Stephen B. Bright, Counsel for the Poor: The Death Sentence Not for the Worst Crime, But for the Worst Lawyer, 103 Yale L.J. 1835 (1994).

factual setting, due process may require providing a forensic expert, a hypnotist, and an investigator to find critical evidence.

Because the state is paying for this assistance, the defendant must make a compelling showing that the expert is necessary. While nonindigent defendants may hire (and present) as many experts as they wish (subject to problems of multiplicity, etc.), indigent defendants must show that the issue in the case is "pivotal" and of "critical importance." Even then, as *Ake* itself declared, the indigent defendant is limited to one expert per issue, and that expert *may* be designated by the court.

Since 1964, a federal statute has provided for paid expert witnesses for indigent defendants and that statute has been interpreted rather beneficently. A sizable number of states, through decisions, statutes, or court rules, provide such assistance, but they may be limited to specific issues, or specific charges (e.g., Ariz. Rev. Stat. sec. 13-4013(B) (capital cases)). For recent commentary, see Cara H. Drinan, The Revitalization of Ake: A Capital Defendant's Right to Expert Assistance, 60 Okla. L. Rev. 283 (2007); Emily J. Groendyke, Ake v. Oklahoma: Proposals for Making the Right a Reality, 10 N.Y.U.J. Legis. & Pub. Pol'y 367 (2006-2007); Aimee Kumer, Reconsidering Ake v. Oklahoma: What Ancillary Defense Services Must States Provide to Indigent Defendants Represented by Private or Pro Bono Counsel?, 18 Temp. Pol. & Civ. Rts. L. Rev. 783 (2009).

4. Raising the Right to Effective Counsel

In most instances, the same counsel who handled the trial will represent the defendant on appeal. It is therefore unlikely that any claim of ineffective assistance will be raised on direct appeal. Moreover, even if it were raised, the record of the trial would be unlikely to reflect even trial errors (such as inadvertence, sleeping, etc.), and would certainly be devoid of any reference to out-of-court events. On rare occasions, the appellate court might be able to decide at least some parts of the claim, but in most cases, some extra-record evidence will be necessary. This leaves the appellate court (even assuming the issue is raised) with two options: (1) to remand for a hearing at that time; or (2) to ignore the claim, rule on the other issues, and suggest to the defendant that he or she try another procedural route to have the claim heard. As a result, virtually all claims of inadequate representation are raised on collateral attack, and usually generate a hearing, at which the trial counsel is examined by defendant (or defendant's new counsel in those states that provide counsel in these proceedings). If the appellate process is lengthy, however, these hearings may occur several years after the trial, when memories have dimmed, witnesses have died, and the paper trail has grown cold (not to mention that defendant has been imprisoned for this time). Each of these factors, combined with the fact that trial counsel is seeking to protect his or her reputation, make more difficult the process of a true assessment of counsel's representation.

5. The Right to Effective Assistance — Limits

The Sixth Amendment only applies to "criminal proceedings," and the right to counsel on first appeal is covered only by the Fifth Amendment, not the Sixth. Thus, although many states provide for appointed counsel in post-conviction relief, and all states except one provide for such counsel in all steps of death penalty cases, there is no right to *effective* lawyering in these proceedings. Indeed, a number of states have expressed this view statuto-rily;:[66] for example, Ohio Stat. Ann. §2953.32(H)(I)(2) (1998), provides:

> The ineffectiveness or incompetence of counsel during proceedings under this section does not constitute grounds for relief in a proceeding under this section, in an appeal of any action under this section, or in an application to reopen a direct appeal.

6. Frivolous Appeals

Counsel at trial (or during plea bargaining) are enjoined by ethical standards to be "fierce advocates." This may allow, or even require, that defense counsel proffer even the most extreme of claims. Once there is a conviction, however, the lawyer has an ethical obligation as an officer of the court not to assert frivolous claims. In *Anders v. California*, 386 U.S. 738 (1967), the Supreme Court agreed that a defense counsel could withdraw from representing the defendant on appeal if he thought the appeal frivolous, so long as the defense counsel provided a brief referring to anything in the record that might support the appeal. The obligations of counsel with regard to frivolous issues on appeal were reduced even further in *Smith v. Robbins*, 528 U.S. 259 (2000), where the Court found "adequate" a California rule requiring merely that counsel file a brief summarizing the case and attest that he had reviewed the record, explained the case to his client, and given the client a copy of the brief. In *McCoy v. Court of Appeals of Wisconsin*, 486 U.S. 429 (1988), the Court upheld a procedure which required the defense counsel to explain why the lawyer thought the contentions

---

66. Some state courts have held that when a state statute grants a mandatory right to the assistance of capital postconviction counsel, it satisfies the requirements of the Due Process Clause only if it also grants the right to effective assistance from that counsel. See *McKague v. Warden*, 112 Nev. 159, 912 P.2d 255 n.5 (Nev. 1996). But this is a state-based, not consti-tutionally based, decision. Moreover, AEDPA (see Chapter 13) prohibits defendants from challenging the effectiveness of state and federal habeas counsel during federal habeas corpus review.

were frivolous. The Court reasoned that this would ensure that counsel had researched the relevant issues. Several states require counsel to follow through on appeal, even if the lawyer thinks the appeal is frivolous.

In Jones v. Barnes, 463 U.S. 745 (1983), the Court held that appellate counsel did not have to present a nonfrivolous claim that his client wished to press if the attorney believed that the better strategy was to limit his argument. Jones, however, did not resolve whether a strategic decision not to raise a claim urged by defendant would bar consideration of that claim on collateral attack, but many other cases have strongly suggested that review would be barred.

E. DEFENDANT AUTONOMY

1. Self-Representation

It is often said that "the lawyer who represents himself has a fool for a client." Perhaps. But the Constitution protects the right to be a fool, even in capital cases. Our concern for the defendant's autonomy and dignity is so strong that we allow such a choice. The right of self-representation was specifically noted in various colonial and state constitutions and statutory provisions that established a right to counsel. In Faretta v. California, 422 U.S. 806 (1975), the Supreme Court, in holding that the trial court had improperly denied Faretta the right to represent himself, made clear that the Constitution protected this right (which has been declared by one commentator the "right to shoot oneself in the foot").[67] The Court in Faretta relied heavily on the "structure of the Sixth Amendment," in particular, pointing out that the Amendment refers to the defendant's right to the "assistance" of counsel. This indicated a desire to make counsel "like the other defense tools guaranteed . . . in aid to a willing defendant, not an organ of the State interposed between an unwilling defendant and his right to defend himself personally." At least seven times in the opinion, the Court spoke of protecting defendants from having counsel "forced" upon them.[68]

---

67. John F. Decker, The Sixth Amendment Right to Shoot Oneself in the Foot: An Assessment of the Guarantee of Self-Representation Twenty Years After Faretta, 6 Seton Hall Const. L.J. 483 (1996); Martin Sabelli and Stacey Leyton, Train Wrecks and Freeway Crashes: An Argument for Fairness and Against Self-Representation in the Criminal Justice System, 91 J. Crim. L. & Criminology 161 (2001); Robert E. Toone, The Incoherence of Defendant Autonomy, 83 N.C.L. Rev. 621 (2005). Chief Justice Burger, dissenting in Faretta, decried the result: "The system of criminal justice should not be available as an instrument of self-destruction." 422 U.S. at 840.

68. 422 U.S. 806, 815, 817, 820, 825, 833, and 834. Many of the Justices who aggressively expanded the right to counsel in Gideon and other cases also supported, in Faretta, the right of any defendant to waive counsel and proceed pro se.

Just as an improper refusal to allow defendant the right to choose the (retained) attorney of his choice requires automatic reversal (see *United States v. Gonzales-Lopez*, supra, p.257), so does the improper denial of a request for self-representation. *McKaskle v. Wiggins*, 465 U.S. 177, 186 n.8 (1984).

The waiver of the right to counsel, however, like all other waivers of constitutional rights, must be "voluntary and knowing." The courts have employed the general competency standard — whether the defendant has "sufficient present ability to consult with his lawyer with a reasonable degree of rational understanding." *Dusky v. United States*, 362 U.S. 402 (1960); *Godinez v. Moran*, 509 U.S. 389 (1993).[69] In *Indiana v. Edwards*, 554 U.S. 164 (2008), however, the Court held that "the Constitution permits States to insist upon representation by counsel for those competent enough to stand trial under *Dusky* but who still suffer from severe mental illness to the point where they are not competent to conduct trial proceedings by themselves."

In *Iowa v. Tovar*, 541 U.S. 77 (2004), the Supreme Court addressed the question of what a trial court should do when a defendant indicated he wishes to waive counsel and plead guilty. Tovar had appeared at several hearings in connection with a driving while intoxicated charge. On each occasion, the trial court explained that if Tovar pleaded not guilty, he would be entitled to be represented by an appointed attorney who could "help him select a jury, question and cross-examine the State's witnesses, present evidence, if any, on his behalf, and make arguments to the judge and jury on his behalf." Tovar chose to represent himself.

The Iowa Supreme Court found these admonitions insufficient to make Tovar's self-representation knowing, and instead required that every trial judge explicitly advise the defendant (a) that there are defenses to criminal charges that may not be known by laypersons and that the danger in waiving the assistance of counsel in deciding whether to plead guilty is the risk that a viable defense will be overlooked; (b) that by waiving his right to an attorney he will lose the opportunity to obtain an independent opinion on whether, "under the facts and applicable law, it is wise to plead guilty." The Supreme Court unanimously held that those two, specific, "rigid," admonitions were not required by the Sixth Amendment. The Court distinguished earlier cases concerned with self-representation at trial, on the ground that "the full dangers and disadvantages of self-representation . . . are less substantial and more obvious to an accused than they are at trial" (quoting *Patterson v. Illinois*, 487 U.S. 285, 299 (1988)).

The opinion in *Tovar* was short, and the unanimity suggests that its holding really should be construed merely as rejecting the explicit and "rigid" guidelines set out by the Iowa Supreme Court.

---

69. Anne Bowen Poulin, Strengthening the Criminal Defendant's Right to Counsel, 28 Cardozo L. Rev. 1213 (2006).

Even if there are no *Miranda* warnings which a judge must expressly and rigidly provide during either a guilty plea decision or before a defendant represents herself at trial, good policy at least requires that a trial court should:[70]

- take special care to advise the defendant as to the pitfalls of self-representation;
- inform defendant that "presenting a defense is not a simple matter of telling one's story," but requires adherence to various "technical rules";
- be sure defendant understands that a lawyer has substantial experience and training in trial procedure and that the prosecution will be represented by an experienced attorney, and that a person unfamiliar with legal procedures may allow the prosecutor an advantage by failing to make objections to inadmissible evidence;
- be sure that defendant understands that there may be possible defenses of which counsel would be aware;
- emphasize that a defendant proceeding *pro se* will not be allowed to complain on appeal about the competency of his representation;
- inform the defendant that the dual role of attorney and accused may undercut his defenses.

There are three possible grounds for denying the request for self-representation:

1. *Timing.* The request in *Faretta* was made "well before the date of trial"; a late request might be so disruptive of orderly proceedings that it would be disallowed.
2. *Defendant's behavior.* If the defendant has been, or becomes, obstreperous and obstructionist, counsel, or standby counsel, may be appointed to return civility to the trial process.
3. *Lack of intelligence.* If the trial judge finds that the defendant truly is not able to make a knowing waiver, there might be a question as to the defendant's competence to assist in his or her own defense.

There is some indication that the Court's imprimatur on the right of self-representation may have recently waned. In *Martinez v. Court of Appeals of California*, 528 U.S. 152 (2000), the Court held, unanimously, that the *Faretta* right does not extend to appeals. Much of the Court's language reflected diminished enthusiasm for *Faretta*.

---

70. For a list of specific, suggested questions, as well as an analysis of pre-*Tovar* law, see Myron Moskovitz, Advising the *Pro Se* Defendant: The Trial Court's Duties under *Faretta*, 42 Brandeis L.J. 329, esp. 344-345 and n.52 (2003-2004).

In *Edwards*, however, the court explicitly declined to overrule *Faretta*, citing the Hashimoto article (*supra*) and noting that few defendants actually choose to represent themselves. But see Robert E. Toone, The Incoherence of Defendant Autonomy, 83 N.C. L. Rev. 621 (2005).

Justice Breyer, in *Martinez*, proclaimed that "there is no empirical research . . . that might help determine whether, in general, the right to represent oneself furthers, or inhibits, the Constitution's basic guarantee of fairness." A recent initial foray into that area, attempting to fill that gap, has found:

> [T]he outcomes for pro se defendants in [state court] were at least as good as, and perhaps even better than, the outcomes for their represented counterparts. A total of 234 defendants were pro se at case termination. Approximately 50% . . . were not convicted of any charge. Of the 50% who were convicted, just over 50% (or 26% of the total number . . .) were convicted of felonies. For represented state court defendants, a total of 75% were convicted of some crime, and 85% were convicted of felonies. Thus, 26% of the pro se defendants ended up with felony convictions, while 63% of their represented counterparts were convicted of felonies. Pro se federal felony defendants were just as likely to be acquitted as their represented counterparts. . . .

Erica J. Hashimoto, Defending the Right of Self-Representation: An Empirical Look at the Pro Se Felony Defendant, 85 N.C. L. Rev. 423, 445-48 (2007). While there are many questions about the limitations of this study (which the author recognized), it at least throws some doubt on the almost universally accepted view that it is foolish to represent oneself.

Even if a trial judge feels compelled to recognize the *Faretta* right, she or he is not totally powerless to leave the arrogant, but clearly capable, defendant totally in the lurch. The judge may appoint a "standby counsel" to assist the self-representing defendant; although these counsel are to be "advisors" only, and may not "direct" the defendant, they may provide legal, or even tactical, advice if requested to do so by the defendant.[71] A variation of the "standby counsel" is "hybrid representation," with defendant or the attorney speaking for the defense during different phases of the trial. Courts have been leery of allowing this kind of procedure, in part because it becomes unclear whether the defendant is in fact representing herself, or being represented by counsel. See Joseph A. Colquitt, Hybrid

---

71. Anne Bowen Poulin, The Role of Standby Counsel in Criminal Cases: In the Twilight Zone of the Criminal Justice System, 75 N.Y.U. L. Rev. 676 (2000). There is no right to standby counsel, although better practice is to appoint one. See, e.g., Minn. R. Crim. P. 5.02. There is, indeed, no right to standby counsel even in death penalty cases, although some courts have found failure to appoint such counsel to be an abuse of discretion. See *People v. Bigelow*, 37 Cal. 3d 731, 691 P.2d 994, 209 Cal. Rptr. 388 (Cal. 1984); *People v. Gibson*, 136 Ill. 362, 556 N.E.2d 226 (Ill. 1990).

Representation: Standing the Two-Sided Coin on Its Edge, 38 Wake Forest L. Rev. 55 (2003). This reticence is not unreasonable, but it does seem inconsistent with the fairly persuasive semantic argument that the Sixth Amendment protects the defendant's right to "assistance" of counsel. But where standby counsel interjects himself unsolicited, there is not necessarily a violation of defendant's *Faretta* rights. *McKaskle v. Wiggins*, 465 U.S. 168 (1984).

2. The Larger Question

The tension in the self-representation cases is only a reflection of a larger issue — defendant autonomy in a criminal case. If, as *Faretta* determines, there is at least a *prima facie* right to totally control one's criminal defense by self-representation, is there equally a right to control each decision during the process? The answer, as it is so many times to a legal question, is "it depends." The key tension here is that, as the Court recognized in *Faretta*, "The defendant, and not his lawyer or the State, will bear the personal consequences of a conviction." Yet, it is a well-accepted principle that, except in a few carefully defined circumstances, a criminal defendant is bound by his attorney's tactical decisions. *Florida v. Nixon, supra*, p.279.

The "well-defined exceptions" include:[72]

- whether to plead guilty;
- whether to forego a jury trial;
- whether to testify in his own behalf;
- whether to appeal.

On the other hand, it is clear that defense counsel may, without consulting with the client, decide what witnesses to call and which jurors to challenge. *Taylor v. Illinois*, 484 U.S. 400, 418 (1988).[73] Indeed, as the Nixon

---

72. Richard Uviller, Calling the Shots: The Allocation of Choice Between the Accused and Counsel in the Defense of a Criminal Case, 52 Rutgers L. Rev. 719 (2000).

73. "Numerous choices affecting conduct of the trial, including the objections to make, the witnesses to call, and the arguments to advance, depend not only upon what is permissible under the rules of evidence and procedure but also upon tactical considerations of the moment and the larger strategic plan for the trial. These matters can be difficult to explain to a layperson; and to require in all instances that they be approved by the client could risk compromising the efficiencies and fairness that the trial process is designed to promote. In exercising professional judgment, moreover, the attorney draws upon the expertise and experience that members of the bar should bring to the trial process. In most instances, the attorney will have a better understanding of the procedural choices than the client; or at least the law should so assume." *Gonzalez v. United States*, 553 U.S. 242, 250 (2008), citing *Jones v. Barnes*, 463 U.S. 745 (1983).

case (*supra*, p.279) shows, counsel may decide to concede the client's guilt in the attempt to save his or her life.

One part of this rule is inextricably intertwined with *Strickland's* general premise — counsel must make reasonable (if not always correct) judgments. Particularly in the middle of a trial (but remember how few cases go to trial), defense counsel cannot "call a time-out" while attempting to explain to the client the (assumed) intricacies of a decision. Even on questions that arise pre- or post-trial, lawyers must make "quick" (though hopefully not "snap") decisions without detailing their thinking.

Another concern that has led to this "general principle" is "sandbagging" — allowing counsel to make what appear to be reasonable decisions and then raising ineffectiveness issues if the decision turns out to be wrong. The timing aspect here is almost completely opposite that of the first concern — it focuses on decisions that counsel could have and might have (and perhaps should have) discussed with the client in private and with significant time to discuss the matter.

The issue of autonomy attains its apogee where the defendant orders his counsel not to present mitigating evidence in the penalty phase of a death case. In this situation, where the question is literally one of life and death, not surprisingly, the courts have proven reluctant to allow that determination and have even placed upon counsel an affirmative duty to disregard his client's wishes. See, e.g., *Muhammad v. State*, 782 So. 2d 343 (Fla. 2001); *Morrison v. State*, 258 Ga. 683, 373 S.E.2d 506 (Ga. 1988); Kamela Nelan, Restricting Waivers of the Presentation of Mitigating Evidence by Incompetent Death Penalty Volunteers, 27 Dev. Mental Health L. 24 (2008); Daniel R. Williams, Mitigation and the Capital Defendant Who Wants to Die: A Study in the Rhetoric of Autonomy and the Hidden Discourse of Collective Responsibility, 57 Hastings L.J. 693 (2006). But see *Allen v. McNeil*, 611 F.3d 740 (11th Cir. 2010). (Where a defendant orders his or her counsel not to present mitigating evidence at the sentencing phase of a capital murder trial, counsel is not ineffective in following that order.)

The United States Supreme Court's *Schriro* decision may have foreclosed that argument. The Court held that "it was not objectively unreasonable for that [state] court to conclude that a defendant who refused to allow the presentation of any mitigating evidence could not establish *Strickland* prejudice based on his counsel's failure to investigate further possible mitigating evidence." *Schriro*, 550 U.S. at 478. Caution: *Schriro* is a habeas corpus case, and the standard for overturning a decision on ineffectiveness is very, very strict (see Chapter 13). Nevertheless . . .

Examples

1. After a jury trial, in which the defendant's background and child abuse was highlighted, defense counsel presents no evidence at the capital sentencing stage; his only summation is as follows:

   > Ladies and Gentlemen; I appreciate the time you took deliberating; the thought you put into this. I'm going to be extremely brief. I have a reputation for not being brief. Jesse, stand up.
   >
   > The Defendant: Sir?
   >
   > Counsel: Stand up. You are an extremely intelligent jury. You've got that man's life in your hand. You can take it or not. That's all I have to say.

   Is this ineffective counsel?

2. Gerry, charged with grand larceny, hires Dudley to represent him. He gives Dudley a $10,000 "up front" retainer, with a promise of $30,000 more. By the middle of the trial, and at the start of what promised to be a two-week defense presentation of witnesses, Dudley has asked Gerry on three separate occasions to pay his bill. Gerry keeps postponing the due date. Dudley asks the judge to allow him to withdraw, but his request is denied. Thereafter, Dudley calls three witnesses, who testify in one day. Gerry ultimately brings a claim of ineffective assistance of counsel during collateral attack. What standard should be used by the collateral attack court?

3. Dominique's conviction of burglary was affirmed on appeal. At that point, she was appointed a new counsel, Gustav, who immediately filed papers for state post-conviction review. Unhappily, Gustav's cocaine addiction got the best of him, and he never met any of the subsequent deadlines for filing. A year later, the state post-conviction court denied any relief. Dominique's new (third) lawyer wants to re-open the state post-conviction process, claiming ineffective assistance of counsel. Does she have a case?

4. Glenna Near was convicted of killing a bunny rabbit belonging to her lover's child. Her appointed counsel, Mike Kirk, remained silent as the prosecutor removed all nonparents off the jury with eight peremptory challenges. Can Glenna win a claim of ineffective assistance?

5. After he was convicted of embezzlement, Muffasa learned that his lawyer, Scar, had been placed in pre-trial intervention (see Chapter 3) for stalking. Scar never revealed this to him. After Muffasa was convicted, Scar, who had successfully completed his PTI, was nevertheless suspended for one year by the bar association. Was Muffasa deprived of effective counsel?

6. Martha, a vice president in a stock brokerage firm, has been involved in a conspiracy with other executives to artificially inflate the price of

certain stocks. At a cocktail party, a junior associate warns her that "the feds have been sniffing around." The next day, Martha contacts Ramin, the U.S. Attorney, who offers to indict her for one count, carrying a five-year maximum, on the condition that Martha cooperates fully. Ramin assures her that this is a good deal, but urges her to consult counsel. Martha does so. The lawyer, Jonathan Periwinkle III, fails to call Ramin, or investigate in any way the facts of the charges. He advises Martha not to accept the offer. Later, Martha is indicted on 35 counts of securities fraud, and receives a 20-year sentence. Ineffective assistance of counsel?

7. Georgia has been indicted on 10 counts of drug possession. When she was arrested, her retained counsel, Burger Kemp, was in her office, and accompanied her to the police station, where she was booked. The police officers at the station were not authorized to set bail, and because the courts were closed, Georgia spent the evening as the guest of the state. The next morning she arrived at her initial appearance. But Burger was nowhere to be seen. She asked the judge to delay her case until Burger arrived. She even tried, twice, to reach Burger on her cell phone. She was told he was "on his way." "Time, tide, and this court wait for no one," bellowed the judge, who proceeded to set bail at $5,000,000, noting that Georgia had her own private jet, and was facing a possible 50 years imprisonment. Rather than arguing that she was not a flight risk, Georgia merely protested her innocence of the charges, believing that that was the issue before the court. She didn't make the $5,000,000, and spent the next week in jail, before Burger was able to move (successfully) for a lower bail, which she made. Was Georgia ineffectively represented at the bail hearing, such that she could raise such a claim if she's convicted?

8. Harvey, an ardent Chicago Cubs fan, is returning from yet another dismal baseball game when he runs into a total stranger, who is wearing a New York Mets hat. Harvey, carrying a baseball bat that was given away that night at Wrigley field, pummels the stranger. He is charged with attempted murder. Ray, Harvey's attorney, has Harvey visited by a psychiatrist, who tells Ray that, while Harvey is clearly obsessed with baseball, and has very poor judgment, he is not insane. The psychiatrist further informs Ray that Harvey may suffer from frontal lobe dysfunction, and that his inability to control his behavior may be physically linked. Assume that Illinois does not recognize diminished capacity as a defense to a specific intent crime. If Ray doesn't pursue the issue more, has he provided effective counsel?

9. Rashad, a Turkish student here on a student visa, is charged with four counts of fraud in connection with his application for student loans. His

attorney, Stuart Appleby III, tells him that the prosecutor will accept a plea to one count of attempted larceny, which is unlikely to result in any jail time. Rashad asks whether he'll be deported if he pleads. Stuart, hardly an immigration expert, replies: "This is a trivial matter. It's possible, but I wouldn't worry if I were you. Take the deal." Rashad does. At sentencing, the trial judge does not mention that she will be sending a letter to the INS. Rashad (of course) finds himself scheduled to be put on the next plane to Turkey. Before he goes, he asks you (his new counsel) whether he can attack his plea as "involuntary." What do you tell him?

10. Burt has pled guilty to several drug offenses. He is contacted by the probation officer, Meredith Wilson, for an interview to establish facts which will be communicated in Wilson's "presentence report" to the judge (see Chapter 11). Burt asks his lawyer, Jackie Moran, to accompany him, but Jackie does not show up. Is this ineffective assistance of counsel?

11. (a) Remo, a first-time homebuyer, goes to Fabian, an attorney, for some legal advice on how to finance the transaction. He follows Fabian's advice, which not only turns out to be wrong, but results in charges of fraud. Nevertheless, not understanding the connection between the advice and the criminal charges, Remo hires Fabian to represent him. The case law provides for a defense to fraud charges of "reliance on advice of counsel." Fabian urges Remo to plead guilty. Nothing is said at the allocution about Fabian's advice. If Fabian is aware of this defense, but does not tell Remo, can Remo successfully claim ineffective representation if convicted?

(b) Same facts, but Fabian is unaware of the possible defense.

12. Ludwig discovers, after he has been convicted of burglary in a jury trial presided over by Judge Marvin Atwater, that his appointed counsel had, several months previously, testified against Judge Atwater in an ethics investigation, and that a preliminary report sustaining the charges against the judge had issued only a week prior to Ludwig's trial. Ineffective assistance?

13. Harlow is charged with shoplifting, a misdemeanor that carries a maximum penalty of one year. The judge tells him that, even if convicted, as a first offender he will not be sentenced to jail. Nevertheless, concerned that, if convicted, he could lose his job and benefits, he hires Moishe. After he is convicted, Harlow discovers that there was a video recording of him at his workstation, at the exact time the shoplifting occurred. Harlow told Moishe that he was at work, and that several people saw him there. May he successfully claim ineffective assistance? (Harlow was sentenced to probation.)

14. On the day of trial, the defendant, Miller Azinger, complains that he cannot communicate with his counsel, and asks you, the judge, to appoint a new attorney. Otherwise, he says, he will defend himself. What do you do?

15. After Raoul was convicted, his counsel immediately indicated that he would appeal. The judge said, in open court and on the record, "Just remember, you've only got 17 days to file a notice of appeal." In fact, the rule allowed only 14 days. Counsel filed on the sixteenth day and was told he was out of luck. Is this ineffective assistance?

16. Rudolph grabbed Boris's watch. When Boris resisted, Rudolph hit him in the eye. Boris suffered from severe headaches for months thereafter. There was no clear determination of how badly the eye had been damaged. Meanwhile, Rudolph, represented by Ornesto, pled guilty to a charge of first degree robbery, defined as "robbery with serious physical injury." At the plea colloquy, the judge had asked Rudolph whether he had inflicted such injury, and Rudolph said he had. Two months later, at the sentencing hearing, the judge sentenced Rudolph to 10 years in prison, the mandatory minimum for first degree robbery. (Second degree robbery, which does not have a mandatory minimum, is punishable by 5 to 20 years). During the time of the appeal, Rudolph's newly assigned counsel, Myra, learns two things: (1) "physical serious injury" is defined as "bodily injury which creates a substantial risk of death or which causes serious permanent disfigurement, or protracted loss or impairment of the function of any bodily member or organ;" (2) Boris's eyesight was perfect three months before Rudolph pled guilty. Was Ornesto "ineffective" within the meaning of the Sixth Amendment? Was there prejudice?

17. (a) Vince, counsel for Danielle, who has just been convicted of first degree murder, presents several witnesses at the penalty hearing who attest to the defendant's stability, as well as her middle-class background. The family witnesses contend that imposing the death penalty would "devastate" their family. Vince had also learned that Danielle had been sexually abused as a child, had suffered frontal lobe injury to her brain, and had abused a number of substances. He had discussed Danielle with two psychological experts who told him she had substantial problems in mental cognition and reasoning and that she scored at or below the first tenth percentile in several categories of cognitive function. Vince decided to try the "middle class" argument. The jury imposes death. Ineffective Assistance?

(b) Suppose Vince had not uncovered the evidence relating to Danielle's mental stability?

18. Client has been charged with assault and battery on a child resulting in death. The prosecution's expert testified that the baby died as a result of "shaken baby syndrome" and that the injuries could not have been caused by the baby falling off a couch onto the floor as the defendant claimed. Defendant was indigent but trial counsel was retained by defendant's father. Counsel asked the defendant's father for the necessary funds for an expert to advise him regarding the medical evidence and shaken baby syndrome and to counter the state's expert but defendant's father refused to provide funds for the expert. After he was convicted, defendant has raised a claim of ineffective assistance of counsel as a result of counsel's failure to seek funds from the trial court. How should the appeals court rule?

Explanations

1. Not in the Fifth Circuit. In *Romero v. Lynaugh*, 884 F.2d 871 (5th Cir. 1989), the appellate court reversed a district court conclusion that "the decision not to present any argument at the sentencing phase" was so "patently unreasonable" as to "constitute a deficiency. . . ." The court considered the summation a "dramatic ploy" which did not "fall off the constitutional range." Perhaps. But perhaps before such a "dramatic ploy," counsel should have reminded the jury, if not through argument, then through witnesses, of the possible mitigating factors. The prosecutor will surely raise the *Nixon* case, in which defense counsel, in essence, admitted defendant's guilt in his opening at trial, and the Court held that not to constitute ineffective assistance. But in *Nixon* the defense counsel then presented, at the sentencing phase, a number of mitigation witnesses, and argued vigorously against execution.

2. This would seem like the prototypical case where an attorney has a conflict of interest. He wishes to be paid, his client hasn't paid, and he thereafter "walks through" the case. It might appear that this should apply the *Cuyler* standard on the presumption of prejudice, and that the state will have to demonstrate no "adverse effect." But a number of courts have held that some personal interests of counsel should be judged not by the "automatic" prejudice approach of *Cuyler*, but by the looser standards of *Strickland*. See, e.g., *United States v. O'Neil*, 118 F.3d 65 (2d Cir. 1997). In that event, Dudley is entitled to a "strong presumption" that he acted not from a conflict, but from Gerry's best interest. Gerry will have to carry the burden of proof on both poor performance and on prejudice. If Dudley can explain his change of trial strategy, perhaps by arguing that he thought the prosecution case so

weak that he did not wish to give the prosecution more opportunities than necessary, Gerry will be hard-pressed to win his claim.

3. Not under the Sixth Amendment. Once Dominque's conviction was complete, she had no Sixth Amendment right to competent counsel. And once she lost her appeal, it was all over. Since postconviction processes are not "criminal," her only relief may be under state statutes or state case law; the Sixth Amendment passed her by long ago. See *Wainwright v. Torna*, 455 U.S. 586 (1982). However, she may have a remedy in federal court based on *Martinez v. Ryan*, discussed in more detail in Chapter 13.

4. In cases where the error has resulted in a "structural" effect upon the trial, such as a wrongful denial of a change of venue, or a rejection of a challenge to jury composition, appellate courts, somewhat along the lines of the harmless error doctrine (see Chapter 13), have imposed a *"per se"* automatic reversal rule, because it is simply impossible to know what would have happened in a different (proper) venue or a properly representative jury. Moreover, while the prosecutor's tactic is obvious, parents are not a "cognizable group" under the Sixth Amendment, much less a "suspect class" under the Fourteenth. (See Chapter 8.) If, by some chance, all the parents had been males, Kirk might have had a *Batson* claim. In short, since there was no legal basis to protest the prosecution's actions, then there was no ineffective assistance.

5. Courts have held that even the threat of prosecution or disciplinary action was insufficient, in and of itself, to demonstrate an actual conflict or ineffectiveness. Instead, they looked to the way in which counsel actually represented the client at trial. Here, there are no facts on which you could base an opinion. But in *State v. Cottle*, 194 N.J. 449, 946 A.2d 550 (2008), the Court, using a parallel to dual representation cases, adopted a per se rule of conflict and ineffectiveness. (The decision, however, was based on state law. Nothing in the federal constitution establishes a per se rule of ineffectiveness merely for dual representation — though a hearing may be required in such a situation.) See, however: "As is regularly the case when a lawyer is disbarred after a defendant's trial, the burden is on the defendant to show that his lawyer at the time of trial made mistakes that prejudiced the outcome of the case." *People v. Taussi-Casucci*, 57 A.D.3d 209, 868 N.Y.S.2d 53 (N.Y. App. Div. 2008).

6. The right to *effective* assistance of counsel begins only when the right to counsel begins, when there is a formal initiation of judicial proceedings. This is a bright line test. Thus, no matter how ineffective Jonathan was, his ineffectiveness is irrelevant under the Sixth Amendment. He may be the subject of disciplinary proceedings, and possibly even a legal

malpractice suit, but Martha is going to spend many long years decorating her jail cell.

7. This is almost — now — an easy case. *Rothgery* held that even at an "initial appearance," there is a right to counsel. But remember — *Rothgery* was a civil suit against the county, not an attempt to have the charges reduced or thrown out (the prosecutor did that once he was contacted by Rothgery appointed counsel). Nevertheless, it is inconceivable that *Rothgery* does not actually apply to Georgia's inquiry. The question here is remedy — besides suing the county (which the decision in *Rothgery* clearly allows) and suing her attorney for breach of contract or malpractice (governed by tort law), Georgia's victory may be Pyrrhic.

8. This is a trick — or at least a tricky — question. Since Harvey's mental condition will not provide a defense to the crime, Ray's decision can easily be explained as tactical. But on sentencing, the judge may well be persuaded to impose a lower sentence, or even put Harvey on probation subject to psychiatric counseling. One way to approach this problem, then, is to ask whether the duty to investigate mitigating circumstances, which has now clearly been embraced in death cases by the Supreme Court, might be expanded to non-capital sentencing procedures.

9. When this example appeared in the second edition, the answer was "Tell him to enjoy Ankara." Although some courts had held information as to how deportation was "direct," it did not serve as the basis for vacating a guilty plea. Now, after *Padilla, supra*, 559 U.S. 356 (see Chapter 7), that is clearly not the case. The law *does* change, and sometimes swiftly. Rashad's guilty plea will be erased, and he may try again.

10. No. Most courts hold that an interview such as this is not a "critical stage" of the criminal process, in large part because the proceeding is not seen as adversarial. If it is not a critical stage, there is no right to effective assistance; Meredith's absence may be unethical, but it does not render her assistance ineffective.

11. (a) This is clearly a case of conflict of interest. Aside from possibly ending up in a malpractice law suit, or a disciplinary hearing, Fabian is simply not likely to want anyone to know of the (mis)advice he has given the client. And since there are few instances where advice of counsel is a relevant claim (see Richard Singer and Lafond, Criminal Law Examples and Explanations, Chapter 5 (4th ed. 2007) for a more detailed analysis), it might never occur to the court, at allocution, that this would be a possible avenue to pursue. Twenty years ago, this case would have been assessed under *Cronic*, perhaps resulting in an automatic reversal, or at least a hearing. See *United States v. Taylor*, 139

F.3d 924 (D.C. Cir. 1998). But after *Mickens*, it is possible that the court will apply *Strickland*. Even if Fabian's failure is ill-motivated and is poor practice, the court might decide that Fabian's overall performance did not sink below the *Strickland* norm. This leaves aside entirely whether, after *Mickens*, the new standard for "harm" is still whether the conflict "adversely affected" the presentation of the case (which it almost surely did) or whether defendant must now show that it reached the level of prejudice.

(b) Extraordinarily enough, Remo may have a better case here than in the first example. Courts have generally treated lack of knowledge of the law as much more serious than most other errors. And many have shown a greater willingness to find prejudice where a possible legal argument was not made because counsel was unaware of the law.

12. Apparently not—at least in New York. In *Frase v. McCary*, 2003 WL 57919 (N.D.N.Y. 2003), the court held that defendant had not articulated any plausible alternative defense strategy that his counsel might have pursued. There is nothing in the opinion that considers the possibility that counsel's "alternative strategy" might have been asking the judge to recuse himself, or have the case reassigned, or ask the judge to replace counsel.

13. Not successfully. Since there was no possibility of jail, there was no right to be represented by counsel. And if there was no right to counsel, there was no right to effective assistance of counsel. And any Fifth Amendment right to effective counsel argument that, even though there was no right to counsel, he sufficiently relied upon counsel, who was empowered by the state to represent him, that the state should not gain by Moishe's reliance, will fall on deaf ears. If, on the other hand, the trial judge had observed clearly incompetent conduct by Moishe, perhaps the complaint *now* would be that the trial judge should have interceded. But that is not this case. Too bad, Harlow. Hope you find a good job.

14. Pray. Defendants in high profile trials often want to represent themselves. In the case of the Unabomber, Ted Kaczynski, the trial court found that at least six weeks in advance of the trial, Kaczynski had known that he had an irreconcilable conflict with his attorneys about whether to claim mental instability. Since Kaczynski waited until the first day of trial to move for their removal, and to represent himself, the trial court concluded the only reason for the request was to delay the proceedings. *United States v. Kaczynski*, 239 F.3d 1108 (2000), *reh'g denied*, 262 F.3d 1034 (9th Cir. 2001), *cert. denied*, 535 U.S. 933 (2002). Kaczynski ultimately pled guilty. But as the trial judge here, you may not get that luxury. You will have to assess whether Miller is competent to

defend himself. And if you find that he is, you must allow him to do so. Although there is no magic list of questions you should ask, you should try some suggested in the text, or in the Moskovitz article, cited in footnote 70. Remember that *Tovar* may not apply here at all, because this is a trial, not a guilty plea. Miller may be running into a hornet's nest, but assuming your inquiry is sufficiently probing, you must, under *Faretta*, recognize his right to eschew lawyers. You should, however, also appoint a standby counsel. This may create headaches for you, but it's better than having a conviction reversed at a later time.

15. This case came to the United States Supreme Court not on the question of ineffectiveness, but as to whether the trial court had in fact lost jurisdiction. *Bowles v. Russell*, 551 U.S. 205 (2007). The Court, 5-4, held that it had; the rule was the rule was the rule. In fact, the Court went further: It held that it would no longer recognize the "unique circumstances" exception to excuse an untimely filing of a notice of appeal, overruling *Harris Truck Lines, Inc. v. Cherry Meat Packers, Inc.*, 371 U.S. 215 (1962), and *Thompson v. INS*, 375 U.S. 384 (1964). Four Justices dissented, calling this an "intolerable" "bait and switch." But here's the ineffectiveness issue: was trial counsel's reliance on the words of the judge "reasonable"?

Usually a mistake of law is not "reasonable," and there is ineffectiveness. Raoul should be able to obtain state postconviction (or federal habeas) review on that basis. But if both counsel and the judge made the same mistake of law, what result? Would the answer be different if this had been a long holiday weekend and the mistake was based upon the court's (and attorney's) understanding that weekends and holidays don't "count" in the 14 days? Probably not.

16. First, although it's not asked in this question, could Rudolph successfully move to vacate his plea? Remember (Chapter 7) that he must show a "manifest injustice" to accomplish that, and that's a very rigorous standard. The question here is ineffectiveness. This was clearly a mistake of law. Ornesto should have known the statutory definition and then determined whether Boris's injury met that standard. Under the facts here, it does not appear to do so, so there's ineffectiveness. The harder question is prejudice. The judge could have sentenced Rudolph to 10 years even for second-degree robbery, and the presumption is that not even ineffective assistance is prejudicial. Rudolph will have to "prove" that the sentencing judge would have given him a lighter sentence in the absence of a statutory constraint. On the other hand, the Court in *Glover v. United States*, 531 U.S. 198 (2001), declared that counsel who did not object to a legal error that affected the calculation of a prison sentence was clearly prejudicial: "[A]ny amount of actual jail time has Sixth

Amendment significance." Since Ornesto's mistake was one of law, and not of fact, Rudolph may have a claim.

17. (a) The choice between the two arguments — (1) that Danielle was from a middle-class family that would be "devastated" by the death penalty and (2) that she had substantial diminished capacity — is one for counsel to make. Many attorneys choose the middle-class argument, and it has been successful in some cases. Strategic decisions like this are well within the bounds of *Strickland*, so no ineffectiveness

(b) Now things have changed. In *Sears v. Upton*, 561 U.S. 945 (2010), the Court concluded that this was ineffective counsel. The growing case law has made it imperative that counsel look for any and all possible evidence regarding mental ability. The Supreme Court concluded that on the prejudice issue, the state court, which had declared that it was "just not possible to know what effect a different mitigation theory would have had," had applied the wrong standard. The Court remanded for further proceedings. When the question is, literally, between life and death, shouldn't the question of prejudice be reversed — that the state should show that the jury would still have unanimously imposed death?

18. Counsel's conduct was deficient because he failed to seek funds from the court to retain an expert witness for his indigent client. "Where, as here, the defendant was indigent and the family member who was otherwise furnishing funds for the defense refused to pay for an expert witness, it was manifestly unreasonable for defense counsel not to apply to the judge for the funds needed to retain an expert witness." *Common. v. Millien*, 474 Mass. 417, 50 N.E.3d 808 (Mass 2016). Defendant was also prejudiced because a defense expert would have "called into question whether shaken baby syndrome is a valid and scientifically supported medical diagnosis."

Sentencing

CHAPTER 12

A. THE IMPORTANCE OF SENTENCING LAW — AN INTRODUCTION

Few things are more important to the defendant — even before conviction — than the possible length of incarceration she faces if convicted.[1] But, far less obviously, the sentencing structure of a jurisdiction is also crucial in ascertaining the real impact of substantive criminal law.[2]

1. "Multiple Discretions"

Although we commonly refer to a judge as "sentencing" a defendant, at least five separate institutions may be involved in making actual determinations of sentence duration: (1) the legislature; (2) the prosecutor; (3) the fact finders; (4) the sentence imposer (usually but not always a judge); and (5) corrections officials. Any sentencing scheme, therefore, may be one of "multiple discretions." Franklin E. Zimring, Making the Punishment

_____

1. For everything you ever wanted to know about sentencing, but were afraid to ask, see Professor Douglas Berman's extraordinary blog at www.sentencing.typepad.com.
2. For example, if the sentences for murder and manslaughter are exactly the same, the careful parsing of homicide doctrines, which so preoccupies first-year law students, becomes suspect, if not irrelevant, in the real world.

Fit the Crime: A Consumer's Guide to Sentencing Reform, 12 Occasional Papers of the University of Chicago Law School (1977).

The legislature defines crimes, and the punishment structure as well. Depending on the structure chosen, one or more of the other actors will play an important role in the process. As seen in Chapter 3, unless the legislature mandates prosecution of all crimes, and forbids plea bargaining, the prosecutor chooses among the possible crimes and thereby affects the sentence which the defendant confronts. If, for example, the prosecution charges assault, and only assault, in what appears to be a first degree murder, the defendant's exposure is limited to the potential sentence for assault. This, of course, is the grist of the plea bargaining mill. (See Chapter 7.) Since the charging decision is essentially unreviewable by a court in the common law, not even the most "determinate" system of sentencing restricts this discretion.

The fact finder may refuse to find aggravating (or mitigating) circumstances, thus convicting the defendant of a lesser (or greater) crime, in an attempt to manipulate the facts to accord with what it anticipates will be the sentence it thinks is "right."[3] After the fact finder has resolved this question, the sentencer will impose a sentence allowed (or dictated) by the sentencing scheme. Judges may have the power to choose a sentence within wide ranges set by the legislature (or the legislature may mandate a specific "flat" sentence for a specific crime). Corrections officials may affect "good time," and parole boards will determine whether the offender will be released prior to the expiration of his sentence.

2. Types of Punishments

For most offenses, punishments may range from an admonition through fines, community service, restitution to the injured party, probation, incarceration, and death.

---

3. Except in capital sentencing, juries are not entitled to be informed, and usually are not informed, of sentencing consequences of a particular conviction. That often does not prevent them from speculating on what the sentences might be, not only for the charged crime, but also for various lesser included offenses. In *United States v. Polizzi*, 549 F. Supp. 2d 308 (E.D.N.Y. 2008), Judge Jack Weinstein — who was a professor at Columbia Law School before he became a judge — delivered a 174-page opinion in which he held that the defendant had a Sixth Amendment right to a jury informed of the 5-year minimum if he were convicted of a specific crime. The Second Circuit reversed. 564 F. 3d 142 (2d Cir. 2009). Some juries have used the Internet to obtain statutory sentences (see Chapter 8). Judges have felt compelled to grant mistrials. See Karen Nelson, Judges Say Technology in Jurors' Hands Threatens Courts Cases, Biloxi Sun Herald, April 25, 2010, 2010 WLNR 8530803; Keren Rivas, Jury's Conduct Leads to Mistrial; Foreman Brought in Copy of Law, Discussed It with Jurors, Times-News (Burlington, N.C.) April 23, 2010, 2010 WLNR 8452132. See *United States v. Polizzi, supra,* p.118, n.61.

Probation — release after conviction without having incarcerative punishment — is extremely discretionary: a sentencer may impose virtually any and all conditions, except those which would violate the defendant's constitutional rights (e.g., a condition that one not attend church would be unconstitutional). Even conditions which would otherwise impinge on quasi-constitutional rights (e.g., submission to nonprobable cause searches, abstaining from liquor) are upheld if connected — even tangentially — to the defendant's crime or his character. Public shaming conditions — wearing placards, writing letters, or giving speeches expressing remorse for one's offense — have recently been reinstituted in some instances. Probation is *not* parole. The latter occurs when a prisoner is released after having been incarcerated; probation occurs before incarceration.

Most sentences are nonincarcerative. Nevertheless, in part because it is easier, in part because we often speak in terms of incarceration, we will speak here of "years" in prison, rather than in other terms. But keep in mind that such sentences are, in the larger vision, a minority of punishments. This is true even though the American prison population has increased tenfold in the past 40 years, and America has the highest per capita imprisonment rate in the world.[4]

3. Indeterminate and Determinate Sentencing Structures

a. Indeterminate Systems

At one end of the sentencing structure spectrum lies the *totally indeterminate* system. This structure establishes legislative punishments (1-5 years for larceny and 6-10 for robbery). The judge has no power to affect either the minimum or maximum sentence; the minimum is mandatory, and the release date is determined solely by a releasing authority (parole board). These schemes are associated primarily with the philosophies of rehabilitation and incapacitation (discussed below) because we simply cannot tell when a prisoner will be rehabilitated or, conversely, whether he will need to be incapacitated for many years to come. A *totally* indeterminate system (0-life for all crimes, however defined) would, on its face, remove *all* discretion, as to both the prosecutor and the sentence imposer.

Beyond this point, there is still much variation. In some so-called indeterminate systems, the sentence imposer has discretion either to impose a

---

4. Between 1974 and 2005, the number of inmates in federal and state prisons jumped from approximately 216,000 to 2,186,230. In the same period, the *rate* of imprisonment more than tripled, from 149 inmates to 488 inmates per 100,000 people. From 1977 to 2004, the number of *federal* inmates increased sixfold, from 32,088 to 180,328.

determinate point within the range (e.g., three years for larceny in the above system), or to establish a shorter *range* (2-4 years) within the larger legislative range; in others there is no such discretion. Regardless of whether the judge has discretion, someone must decide when to release the prisoner. Moreover, a correctional authority, by giving the prisoner good time credits (of which there may be several variations), may also affect the actual eligibility date for parole or the maximum sentence he will serve, whether or not he is paroled.

Cumulatively, these variations of parole eligibility, good time credits, and other administrative processes may mean that a sentence with a 10-year maximum may turn out to have a one- or two-year minimum.

b. Determinate Systems

At first glance, the "determinate" sentence is diametrically opposed to the "indeterminate" sentence — the term of imprisonment is legislatively set. For example: "Robbery shall be punished by six years in prison." Once the defendant is convicted, no other institution may affect the sentence; the judge must impose a six-year sentence, and that is what the defendant will serve; there is no parole, and no good time. In a *totally determinate* sentencing scheme, therefore, the prosecutor sets the sentence, by establishing the (only) charge available, subject only to the jury's power of fact finding. But few systems actually operate that way — parole release and good time credits change the determinate sentence into one almost as indeterminate as that in the first system.

Suppose Edwina is sentenced to a "determinate" sentence of "10 years." If Edwina is scheduled to receive 20 months off her sentence for "good behavior," then Edwina's effective maximum sentence would be reduced to eight years, four months (assuming she receives the maximum good time). If the system also has parole, and fixes eligibility at one-half of the maximum, her "real sentence" would appear to be reduced to five (earliest parole eligibility) to eight and one-third years (5-$8\frac{1}{3}$) (maximum sentence less good time, even if she is not paroled). If, in addition, her parole eligibility is *also* reduced by good time (even though, of course, it has not yet been "earned" by actual good behavior), and the "one-half sentence" rule of parole eligibility still applies, we reduce her parole eligibility by the same 20 months, and Edwina's sentence has now morphed into three years, two months to eight and one-third years (3.2-8.4).[5]

---

5. Of course, as one number changes, so do the rest. In many states, the earliest parole eligibility is one-third of the maximum. If the "maximum" is calculated as eight and one-third years (10 years less good time), her earliest release date is two and two-thirds years, etc., etc., etc.

To many observers this sounded like a shell game; in the past 20 years or so, under a title something like the "Truth in Sentencing Act," 12 states (and the federal system) have either abolished parole, or severely limited parole eligibility (particularly for violent offenders).[6]

Whether one agrees with that criticism or not, the point is that, while in theory determinate and indeterminate sentence systems are polar opposites, most systems have aspects of the other. The critical questions are: Who has discretion, and what is the degree to which that discretion is subject to alteration by some institution later in the chain? As we examine the sweeping changes that appear to have occurred in the past two decades in the sentencing systems in this country, keep looking for that hidden needle of discretion.

B. THEORIES OF PUNISHMENT AND SENTENCING

1. Utilitarian Theories of Punishment

If you don't know what you're trying to achieve, you can't determine whether you're succeeding. Assessing sentencing schemes, therefore, requires at least a quick review of the purposes of punishment.[7] Utilitarian goals seek to reduce the crime level. The goal of *rehabilitation* is to reform the offender, and persuade him not to act criminally (immorally) upon release. *Incapacitation* proposes to make it impossible for the offender to commit more crimes. The death penalty, of course, is the ultimate incapacitation, but since we reject all other corporal punishments, incapacitative theory requires incarceration until we predict that the defendant will no longer commit crimes if released.

Either of these two goals is achievable only if the criminal is held until the goal has been achieved. Thus, a full blown system of either of these would have a truly indeterminate sentence — 0 to life — for virtually every crime. Some method of assessing the prisoner's progress would be required.

General deterrence theory, on the other hand, focuses not on the actual prisoner, but upon the effect that punishing one offender has on other possible criminals. As one reported colloquy put it:

> [It] is very hard, my lord, said a convicted felon at the bar to the late excellent Judge Burnet, to hang a poor man for stealing a horse. You are not to be

---

6. These statutes are often known as NERA — No Early Release Acts.
7. For a longer discussion, see Richard G. Singer and John Q. LaFond, Criminal Law: Examples and Explanations, Chapter 2 (4th ed. 2007).

hanged, sir, answered my ever honoured and beloved friend, for stealing a horse, but you are to be hanged that horses may not be stolen.[8]

The punishment threatened (discounted by the possibility of not being captured) must be sufficiently severe to deter the future crime. In theory at least, this cost-benefit analysis could be resolved mathematically, and there would be no need for anyone — judge or other official — to vary from a legislatively pre-set sentence. (A threat of 20 years in prison might deter even the most ardent jaywalker.)

2. Retribution as a Theory of Punishment

Retribution focuses on the (im)moral choice which the offender has made. It is concerned both with the harm which that choice has caused, and the mental culpability with which that harm was inflicted. (An intentional killing is perceived as more "immoral" than a reckless one, though the harm is the same in both.) The punishment inflicted must be proportionate to those factors. Assuming an ability to define properly the requisite harm and culpability levels, retributive sentencing schemes, like deterrent systems, could also be totally determinate.

3. Proportionality

Although neither incapacitation nor rehabilitation requires proportionality as a restriction on sentencing, both deterrent and retributivist approaches to sentencing require that the punishment imposed be "proportionate" to the crime, though for different reasons. Proportionality is required for a deterrence theorist only insofar as we wish to deter criminals from committing greater crimes to avoid capture (punishing theft with death might encourage thieves to kill their pursuers). A retributivist, by definition, may impose no more harm than the offender's act caused society; while this may be difficult to assess, it sets a limit on punishment which the other three do not. After several attempts, a majority of the Supreme Court appears now to have concluded that proportionality is required by the Eighth Amendment, but it has applied that concept narrowly. In its most recent decision on this point,[9] the Court held that a sentence of 25 years to life was not unconstitutionally

---

8. As quoted in L. Radzinowicz, A History of English Criminal Law 411, n.40 (1957).
9. A later case, *not* involving aspects of federalism, held that a forfeiture of $357,144 for failing to report that the defendant was carrying that amount of money outside the country was an excessive fine. *United States v. Bajakajian*, 524 U.S. 321 (1998).

disproportionate for a person whose third offense was shoplifting several golf clubs worth less than $1,200. *Ewing v. California*, 538 U.S. 11 (2003).

Table 12.1 reflects these different purposes and likely sentencing structures:

12.1

Purpose	Typical Sentence	Sentence Determiner
Rehabilitation	Highly indeterminate. 0-life would be best, but some cap or minimum sentence might be tolerable.	Experts in human behavior; parole board.
Incapacitation	Same as Rehabilitation.	Same as Rehabilitation.
Deterrence	Proportionate sentences, but limited and channeled by scientific understanding of how much threat is needed to deter from this specific crime. Determinate.	Legislature, as aided by experts on deterrence.
Retribution	Proportionate sentences based on harm and mental state. Determinate.	Legislature or other body reflecting community standards.

C. A SHORT HISTORY OF SENTENCING IN THE UNITED STATES

Few sentencing schemes in history, and certainly none in the United States, have been "pure" systems of any of these theories, but each of these theories has been dominant at different times in our history. Even when rehabilitation was the dominant theory of punishment, for example, legislatures placed maximum caps upon the duration of punishment — recidivist jaywalkers, or even burglars, would rarely be subjected to a possible life sentence. Similarly, when retribution was the dominant theory, there were still possible methods by which a defendant could avoid the determinate sentence (e.g., probation).

Prior to the American Revolution, incapacitation seemed to be the primary goal of punishment for felonies — the death penalty, the common sanction for any felony, assured that the defendant would not offend again. The only discretion lay in the jury's fact-finding ability. English juries early in the nineteenth century commonly engaged in "pious perjury" so as to avoid imposing the death penalty upon many defendants. Thus, many juries determined the value of objects stolen to be 39 pence — because the distinction between grand (capital) larceny and petit (non-capital) larceny was 40 pence.

Almost immediately after the American Revolution, Quakers in Pennsylvania created a new form of punishment — incarceration. Not only did this limit the death penalty (to which the Quakers were opposed), but it provided the defendant with an opportunity to become penitent (hence the name penitentiary). Legislatures began enacting statutes with wide sentence ranges, so that the penitentiary could have time to work its magic. Within those ranges, in a substantial number of states, juries, and not judges, set the sentence.[10]

By the end of the nineteenth century, jury sentencing declined, as criminal jurisprudence embraced a modified rehabilitative model of sentencing. If pure rehabilitative and individualized sentencing had been embraced, judges would simply have imposed an established legislative indeterminate range, allowing experts in the corrections system to determine when to release the prisoner. In practice, however, judges were usually empowered to establish the "first cut" — first (for many offenses) by deciding whether to place a defendant on probation, and second by setting, within the indeterminate range, either a determinate term, or a shorter indeterminate range.

A system which allows at least some discretion to some institutional authority to consider variations in how crimes are actually committed is very appealing; other systems may be attacked as "mechanical" or "rigid." As Aristotle noted more than two millenia ago, legislatures must, by definition, speak in terms of universals — they cannot (because language cannot) describe every detail which might be relevant in determining the "precisely right" punishment for a specific crime. As many critics have argued, the

---

10. This is a slight overgeneralization. The prospect of a revival of jury sentencing has generated significant revision of the story of jury sentencing in America. The most detailed examination thus far is Erik Lillquist, The Puzzling Return of Jury Sentencing: Misgivings About *Apprendi*, 82 N.C.L. Rev. 621 (2004). Other outstanding works are Jenia Iontcheva, Jury Sentencing As Democratic Practice, 89 Va. L. Rev. 311, 317 (2003); Ronald F. Wright, Book Review, 108 Yale L.J. 1355 (1999); Frank O. Bowman, III, Fear of Law: Thoughts on Fear of Judging and the State of the Federal Sentencing Guidelines, 44 St. Louis L.J. 299, 311 (2000); Adriaan Lanni, Jury Sentencing in Non-Capital Cases: An Idea Whose Time Has Come (Again), 108 Yale L.J. 1775, 1790 n. 651875, 1899 (1999); Morris B. Hoffman, The Case for Jury Sentencing, 52 Duke L.J. 951 (2003). According to Benjamin J. Priester, The Canine Metaphor and the Future of Sentencing Reform: Dogs, Tails, and the Constitutional Law of Wagging, 60 S.M.U.L. Rev. 209, n.127 (2007), citing Lanni, 108 Yale L.J. at 1790 n. 65, five states continue to have jury sentencing in noncapital cases.

thug who threatens a victim with a crow bar and the playground bully who obtains lunch money from a cowering third grader have both committed "robbery," but the circumstances of the two crimes seem relevant to assessing punishment. Only those who deal with the individual instances of the defined crime will see those nuances. This, at heart, was the engine behind the individualization movement.

Systems which seek either to rehabilitate or to incapacitate are essentially predictive, and based on a minute and complex assessment of the character of the defendant — whether he "needs" treatment, and if so what kind, and how long that treatment is "likely" to take. No information (not even the rankest hearsay) is necessarily irrelevant — the defendant's criminal record, charges against him which have not been pursued (or of which he has been acquitted), his employment record, and even whether he kicks cats, are all grist for the individualization mill. This information was provided by a "pre-sentence report," prepared by a probation officer, trained in obtaining such information.

The high water mark of the rehabilitation-individualization movement, and hence of judicial sentencing authority, was *Williams v. New York*, 337 U.S. 241 (1949). A jury convicted Williams of first degree murder during a burglary, but recommended a life sentence. The judge, rejecting that recommendation, imposed the death penalty, relying upon information in the pre-sentence report (which was never disclosed to the defendant — see below), which asserted "many material facts concerning appellant's background which . . . could not properly have been brought to the attention of the jury," including 30 other burglaries which the police attributed to the defendant (although the defendant had not been convicted of any of these). The report also indicated that the appellant possessed "a morbid sexuality." The United States Supreme Court upheld the death sentence, and the process, declaring:

> A sentencing judge . . . is not confined to the narrow issue of guilt. His task . . . is to determine the type and extent of punishment after the issue of guilt has been determined. Highly relevant — if not essential — to his selection of an appropriate sentence is the possession of the fullest information possible concerning the defendant's life and characteristics. . . . [He should not be] denied an opportunity to obtain pertinent information by a requirement of rigid adherence to restrictive rules of evidence properly applicable to the trial. . . . To deprive sentencing judges of this kind of information would undermine modern penalogical policies that have been cautiously adopted throughout the nation after careful consideration and experimentation.

Williams reflects the general assumption, both for incapacitation and rehabilitation theories, that every piece of information about a defendant, including any past bad conduct, whether or not a possible crime, and whether or not resulting in conviction, is relevant in determining the sentence. Even if the defendant had been acquitted of the alleged crime, sentencers were still allowed to consider such conduct. The rationale here is that the standard of proof in a criminal case — beyond a reasonable doubt — does not apply in sentencing procedures, and hence the conduct, if proved by a preponderance of the evidence, may still be considered by the sentencing judge.

D. PROCEDURES AT SENTENCING

1. Rules of Evidence

In a system that focuses on rehabilitation (or incapacitation), the sentencer should "know everything" about the individual[11] there is to know — "individualization" of the sentence is crucial to the enterprise.[12] As a doctrinal matter, the "rules of evidence" do not apply at sentencing.[13] Since the character of the defendant is the focus, a judge may consider *any* information that she considers relevant to a character assessment — whether the defendant has lied in the past, been a hero, or kicked cats may demonstrate some aspect of character crucial to determining whether he needs rehabilitation (or incarceration) and how long that process might take.

Moreover, the judge may consider suppressed evidence because the purpose of suppression — control of bad police conduct — has already been served by excluding that evidence at trial.[14] Evidence of conduct which was not criminal, or with which the defendant has not been charged, is also admissible, since it may still bear upon his character. United States v. Witte, 515 U.S. 389 (1995). Even conduct for which the defendant has been charged and acquitted is relevant: the jury's verdict only means that the government has not proved beyond a reasonable

---

11. For a tour de force examining all these questions in detail, see Alan Michaels, Trial Rights at Sentencing, 81 N.C. L. Rev. 1771 (2003).

12. As a matter of pure logic, *sentencing* should be individualized — if at all — only for the "in-out" decision: whether the defendant "needs to be" dealt with in a confined setting. Since the determination of whether a defendant has been rehabilitated (or must still be incapacitated) can best be made while that person is confined, that aspect of individualization should be left to later authorities (such as the parole board). As indicated in the text, however, legislatures placed caps on virtually all sentences, thereby tacitly undercutting the rehabilitative or incapacitative justifications for sentencing. But that is a story for another day.

13. This is not unusual. For virtually all administrative proceedings, the rules are either relaxed or ignored; the fact finder may listen to hearsay, excited utterances, and so on, and consider them "for what they are worth."

14. But remember: less than 10% of all cases go to trial.

doubt, that defendant engaged in the conduct that was the subject of the trial; it does imply in any way that the conduct has or has not been proved by a lesser standard as that was not the job of the jury. *United States v. Watts*, 519 U.S. 148 (1997).

2. Confidentiality of Information

Until the 1970s, because some of the information relied upon could only be obtained upon promises of confidentiality, defendants were not entitled to see that information. *United States v. Dockery*, 447 F.2d 1178 (D.C. Cir. 1971).[15] Moreover, since this information was collected after conviction, the judge, rather than the jury, was to decide the proper sentence.

In recent years, courts, in both their rule-making and adjudicatory functions, have begun to change these views. Thus, in *Gardner v. Florida*, 430 U.S. 349 (1977), the Court, effectively overruling the narrow holding of *Williams*, held that a defendant in the sentencing phase of a *capital* case was constitutionally entitled to see the prosecution's evidence. Although the Court explicitly restricted *Gardner* to capital cases, it has, in its supervisory function, provided in Rule 32(e)(2) and 32 (I)(A) for virtually full discovery of the pre-sentence report in all federal cases, not merely capital ones.[16] Virtually all states now provide that the defendant may see the report, although some portions may be restricted as "confidential." And in *Mitchell v. United States*, 526 U.S. 314 (1999), the Court affirmed that the defendant retained the right to remain silent at sentencing, and that no adverse implications could be drawn from her silence.

3. Burden of Proof

In assessing one's "character," every item may be relevant. But must every item be "proved"? Can it be? Because there was no judicial review of

---

15. In *State v. Pohlabel*, 61 N.J. Super. 242, 160 A.2d 647 (N.J. Super Ct. App. Div. 1960), the defendant, convicted of stealing a checkbook and passing checks totaling approximately $1,500, was given seven consecutive 3–5-year sentences. After eight years in prison, he learned that the probation officer had described him in the pre-sentence report as a "master of deception" who had "spent the greater part of his life in penal institutions." In fact, the defendant had previously been convicted only once, as a juvenile. His case was remanded for re-sentencing.

16. One stated explanation for this was that it was impossible to articulate reasons for a specific sentence. See, e.g., *State v. Douglas*, 87 Ariz. 182, 349 P.2d 622 (1960). If sentencing was indeed "individualized" and "subjective," this explanation has some plausibility. In *Burns v. United States*, 501 U.S. 129 (1991), the Court hinted that this right might be grounded in the due process clause, but because of Rule 32 it did not have to reach this issue.

sentences, that question was moot for many decades. In *McMillan v. Pennsylvania*, 477 U.S. 79 (1986), the Court originated the term *sentencing factor* and concluded that the state need prove any such "factor" only by a preponderance of the evidence, not by the usual beyond a reasonable doubt test. The Court has reaffirmed the "preponderance standard" test. *Harris v. United States*, 536 U.S. 545 (2002).

4. Non-Jury Proceedings

As a doctrinal matter, the Sixth Amendment jury right only applies to "criminal proceedings." For that right at least, sentencing is *not* a "criminal proceeding," although the Court in *Mitchell v. United States*, supra, declared that "to maintain that sentencing procedures are not part of 'any criminal case' is contrary to law and to common sense."[17] This is also a practical necessity — in non-capital cases, the information relevant to sentencing is not accumulated by the state before conviction. (Why obtain information that will become moot if the defendant is acquitted?) Unless a different jury were to decide the sentence, the current jury would have to be reconvened at a (much?) later date. Finally, juries are not likely to be experts in sentencing, while judges, who will preside over many sentences, and see many presentence reports, are or will become so.

5. Nonreview of Sentences

Determination of character must be done in person — it is virtually impossible using only a cold record to assess a person's sincerity, dangerousness, remorse, and so on. Only the sentencing judge — who spoke directly to and with the defendant — is in a position to render those judgments. Consequently, courts held that sentences were not subject to appellate review unless the sentence was not within the legislatively set parameters.

In summary, while there are few definitive holdings, the following list of "trial rights at sentencing" reflects the likely situation today and for the immediate future:

---

17. This same dichotomy has already been seen: the Court has established different triggers for the right to jury (more than six months incarceration possible) (Chapter 8) and right to appointed counsel (One day in prison) (Chapter 10), even though they are both in the Sixth Amendment. Moreover, the Court held in *Mempa v. Rhay*, 389 U.S. 128 (1967), that for purposes of the Sixth Amendment right to counsel, a hearing combining probation revocation and sentencing was a "critical stage" of a "criminal proceeding." Remember (again) Holmes: "the life of the law has been not logic, but experience."

12.2　Trial Rights at Sentencing

Clearly Applicable	Likely to Apply	Clearly Inapplicable or Unlikely to Apply
right to counsel and appointed counsel	discovery	right to jury trial[*]
	speedy hearing	
	right to confrontation	
right to present evidence	right to see relevant evidence	rules of evidence (the court may consider suppressed evidence, hearsay, acquitted conduct, and conduct which has not been charged)
right to remain silent		standard of beyond a reasonable doubt[*]
right to public resolution		double jeopardy clause[18]
right to allocution		

[*] But see *Apprendi* and *Blakely, infra.*

E. A REVOLUTION IN SENTENCING — STRUCTURED SENTENCING

1. First Caveat

The majority of states today retain mostly indeterminate systems. Discretionary judgments by individual sentencers, combined with release mechanisms such as parole and a significant amount of "good time," continue to dominate the American landscape. Nevertheless, the detailed discussion of structured sentencing which follows is warranted for several reasons: (1) the debate over structuring begins a substantive discussion of what factors are relevant in sentencing and reflects, as well, the renewed interest in the purposes of punishment; (2) national organizations,

---

18. *Monge v. California,* 524 U.S. 721 (1998).

such as the American Bar Association and the American Law Institute, have embraced some form of structured sentencing; (3) the developing case law raises at least some question about the constitutionality of the indeterminate system as it occurs in most states; (4) 16 states have, in one form or another, moved toward structured sentencing;[19] and — probably most critical to law students — (5) most casebooks also spend a significant amount of time discussing structured sentencing.

2. The Move Away from Individualized Sentences

The perceived problem with such a widely discretionary system was that the ranges were so broad that individual judges were implementing their own view of what was important in sentencing and why sentences were imposed. One judge could use deterrence as a determining philosophy, while one in the next court might use rehabilitation. Moreover, two judges might view the same facts through entirely different philosophical eyes: one judge might see in a 20-year-old ghetto dweller with a long juvenile history a threat of a long and increasingly violent future, and sentence him to 20 years, whereas another might see the defendant as much a victim as a perpetrator, and provide probation, or a "relatively short" period of incarceration for the same crime.

Individualization and rehabilitation were discarded as operative philosophies by many legislatures during the 1970s and 80s. Studies of rehabilitation programs were — accurately or not — interpreted to say "nothing works." The notion of rehabilitation as a determining factor in the length of imprisonment was attacked by the original creators of the idea, the Quakers, who also argued that "unfettered discretion" in the hands of sentencing judges had led to blatant racial and economic discrimination. American Friends Service Committee, Struggle for Justice (1972). The Quakers recommended that equality of sentencing could best be assured by a determinate sentencing scheme, in which the crime, and not the defendant, was the focus. Four years after the AFSC report came a well-received call for a return to retribution as the key purpose of sentencing. A. von Hirsch, Doing Justice (1976). At the same time, many who thought that individualized sentencing had been too lenient, resulting in the premature release of convicts who thereafter recidivated, called for longer, incapacitative sentences, which could not be shortened by correctional officials. Finally, the entire notion of unreviewable judicial sentencing discretion was eloquently attacked by

---

19. As of 2007, 16 states, the District of Columbia, and the federal system were operating with sentencing guidelines promulgated by a sentencing commission. American Law Institute Model Penal Code: Sentencing, Tentative Draft No. 1 (April 9, 2007), p.xxxii.

United States District Court Judge Marvin Frankel, in his book entitled Criminal Sentences:[20]

> The almost wholly unchecked and sweeping powers we give to judges in the fashioning of sentences are terrifying and intolerable for a society that professes devotion to the rule of law.

This dramatic alteration in theory and practice has undercut at least one premise of the traditional, indeterminate system — that it is not possible, within some limits and accepting some variations, to articulate the relevant factors that most actors in the system (legislators, judges, experts, etc.) believe relevant, and to avoid the kind of disparity which wide indeterminacy allowed. Most systems now articulate the factors which most persons would concede are potentially relevant in determining punishment. Among these are: (1) whether a weapon was used (brandished, possessed); (2) the defendant's degree of involvement in the commission of the crime (e.g., an accomplice or the actual killer, see n. 52, *infra*); (3) the amount of harm inflicted, measured by loss of money or amount of drugs; (4) the degree of trust betrayed; and (5) factors reducing, but not removing, moral culpability, such as age, influence by a superior, etc. Whether these factors seem relevant, the structured sentencing movement has brought the debate into the open. Once these factors — and their impact upon sentencing — have been agreed upon by a legislative body, the actual sentencer can fill in interstices within narrowly drawn ranges. For example, a legislature might declare that an assault carries a punishment of X, plus or minus two months, leaving for the jury or judge the precise sentence, depending on whether there are variations on the facts which have not been clearly eliminated by the legislature.

a. Mandatory Minimum Sentences

There are many ways to remove or reduce discretion in sentencing. A full ban on plea bargaining (see Chapter 7), coupled with a fully determinate sentencing structure, and no parole or good time, would fully remove all discretion. But no state has yet adopted anything approaching such a sweeping rejection of discretion throughout the process. Virtually all states, however, have adopted at least one restriction on sentencing discretion — mandatory minimum sentences.[21]

---

20. M. Frankel, Criminal Sentences, p.5 (1973).
21. There are now over 60 federal criminal statutes that contain mandatory minimum penalties. However, between 2010-2016 there has been a decline in the number of federal inmates sentenced under mandatory minimum laws. See http://www.uscourts.gov/news/2017/07/25/mandatory-minimum-sentences-decline-sentencing-commission-says.

Most commentators (not to mention judges) oppose these statutes, not only because they severely reduce the power of judges to individualize sentences, but because (opponents argue) these statutes provide the prosecutor with greater bargaining power, by engaging in "fact bargaining" in which the prosecutor "ignores" a fact (e.g., that the defendant was carrying a weapon) in exchange for a plea to the same (or lesser) "base offense." Proponents of these statutes contend that individualization must yield to a need for deterrence, and that persons contemplating crime who think they can otherwise obtain a light sentence (or probation) will rethink their possible crime if they know they face a definite term of imprisonment. Retributivists can also support these statutes, assuming the minimum length of sentence is proportionate.

If mandatory minimum laws are primarily incapacitative, even more obviously aimed at incapacitation are statutes which provide a very long sentence for "recidivists." Recidivist (or "habitual offender") laws have existed since 1928: today a sizeable number of states have enacted so-called "three strikes" laws, which usually provide that a defendant who is now being convicted of a third predicate felony[22] will serve a specified minimum amount of incarcerative time (frequently 25 years) before being considered for parole.

b. The Disappearance of Parole Release

The reaction to parole release, and good time, which often resulted in an offender serving less than one-fifth of his sentence in incarceration (See p. 308, *supra*), generated a move to abolish, or restrict, parole. This movement, dubbed "Truth in Sentencing," reflects the perceived public animosity toward a "bark and bite" system of criminal justice. Today seven states have abolished parole entirely, while a much larger number effectively restrict it to non-violent offenders. The impact of good time, including in those states retaining parole, has also been dramatically transfigured. Virtually all states have adopted statutes providing that violent offenders (variously defined) must serve 85 percent of their sentence before being released even conditionally. A number of states which have abolished or restricted "early parole release" still provide for "post-incarceration community supervision," which is thought to assist prisoners in acclimating upon their return to society. Thus, while "parole release" has been

---

22. The statutes differ significantly. In California, for example, at least one of the two prior felonies must be violent, but the third may be non-violent, as in *Ewing v. California*, 538 U.S. 11 (2003), where the Court held not disproportionate, because he had two prior felony convictions, a 25-to-life sentence for a defendant who had stolen three golf clubs worth $1200. In other states, the current felony must be violent, but the earlier ones need not be. Of course, there are also widespread differences in the definition of which crimes qualify as "violent" in those states where that is necessary to activate the "three strikes" legislation.

abandoned, "community supervision" remains; the major difference is that the defendant has served most or all of her sentence before being supervised in the community.

c. Presumptive Sentences

Under indeterminate sentencing the ranges were so wide (e.g., 2-20 years) that individual judges, using their individual punishment philosophies, could settle on any possible sentence. Judge shopping was the order of the day. In response, several states have adopted a "presumptive" sentencing scheme, in which the judge is given a range within which to sentence, but told explicitly to begin at a "presumed" sentence (usually in the middle), which may be varied only if the judge finds specific aggravating or mitigating facts.

3. State Sentencing Commissions

These statutes constitute one very important part of the structured sentencing movement. But the most important part of that movement is the creation of "sentencing commissions," first proposed by Judge Marvin Frankel as an ingenious solution to unlimited judicial sentencing discretion. Judge Frankel suggested that the legislature place the basic decision about what factors would be relevant in sentencing not in the hands of individual judges, but an administrative agency which would create "guidelines" to be used by judges in imposing individual sentences. The extent to which these guidelines would "bind" the judge, or merely "assist" her, was left to later development.

A growing number of states have adopted this approach, which is now endorsed by the ABA and the Tentative Draft of the American Law Institute, Model Penal Code: Sentencing (2007). In most such states, the Commission establishes presumptive sentences, using a combination of the crime of conviction and the offender's past criminal record. Although the rough outlines of state and federal commissions are similar, in many details they are extraordinarily different. We will, therefore, discuss state commissions separately from the federal system.

a. Guideline Systems

As of 1996, 16 states had adopted guideline systems; nine were determinate while seven adhered to the indeterminate mode. While these vary in some significant ways, the heart of the process is to establish guidelines, like those proposed by Judge Frankel, which will curtail judicial discretion. Few of these systems abolish such discretion entirely, and six make compliance with their guidelines only "voluntary." Nevertheless, many of these systems share some salient characteristics:

- an administrative agency sets and reviews the guidelines;
- the guidelines set "presumptive" sentences or sentence ranges, within which a judge may sentence; most list "aggravating and mitigating" circumstances which may increase or decrease that range, to a specified degree;
- a judge may "depart" from the guidelines entirely (as opposed to varying within the guidelines) only after giving written reasons;
- either side may appeal on the grounds that the guidelines were ignored or improperly applied;
- the guidelines either prohibit many of the factors which "individualizing" judges would have considered in earlier systems, or create narrow sentencing "ranges" in which the judge may use these factors;
- all of the systems consider past criminal record, even if the defendant is not eligible for the recidivist statute of the jurisdiction;
- seven states require the commission to consider "resources" (i.e., prison capacity) in setting guidelines;
- many systems abolish, or severely restrict, early release upon parole.

i. The "Commission"

Guideline systems generally establish a commission, which has a permanent staff, but whose members are only part-time. The ideal is to have representatives from every side of the criminal justice system (e.g., judges, prosecutors, defense counsel, victims, and prisoners) as well as "citizen members." The guidelines are to reflect the experiences — and interests — of all sides in the system, so that the guidelines will be acceptable to most (institutional) actors in the process. The commission staff also collects and analyzes data regarding actual sentences, to determine whether the guidelines are being followed by sentencing judges and to assess whether reasons given for departing from the presumptive sentence should be incorporated into later versions of the guidelines. The record on revision is mixed: Some commissions have been quite active in revising the guidelines, while other commissions have been relatively quiescent.

ii. "Presumptive" Sentencing

Most guideline systems establish a presumptive sentence. The guidelines establish a "*heartland*" of sentences, in which the vast majority of sentencing decisions should fall. If the judge finds certain legislatively specified facts, she may increase or decrease the sentence, but again, usually by a specified amount or within a specific range. If the judge wishes to "depart" from the guidelines entirely, essentially ignoring the guidelines, she must provide a written reason; there may be a presumption that such a departure is unwarranted. Minnesota, for example, requires that the judge demonstrate through "clear and convincing evidence" that a departure is warranted.

Commissions have employed several methods of determining the "heartland." Minnesota, the first commission, developed its guidelines only after heated debate about the purposes of sentencing. Its initial guidelines adopted a normative framework based primarily on retribution, but also reflected the significant impact that the defendant's criminal history was to have on the sentence to be imposed. This "prescriptive" approach, which has been adopted by a majority of state commissions, may clash with the hierarchy of seriousness levels established by the legislature; if so, to the extent that there is no legislative participation in the process, the guidelines might be attacked as anti-democratic. In contrast, states which have adopted a "descriptive" approach, have guidelines that seek to reflect current sentencing practices, to the degree they can be ascertained. Because these guidelines will emulate current judicial practice, there is likely to be less judicial resistance; however, to the extent that the guidelines capture, as a "fly in amber," the precise problems with the existing judicial practice they were designed to remedy, they will fail to achieve that objective.

iii. Offense-Based Sentencing; Criminal Record

Every state which has adopted a structured sentencing scheme has opted for "offense-based" sentencing. The seriousness of the offense of conviction is the primary factor.[23] Of secondary, but still substantial, importance, is the defendant's past criminal record. Although variously defined (some states include all offenses, including misdemeanors; some states provide "sunset" clauses, while others do not), this reflects the view that past conduct is relevant in assessing a current sentence. Most states restrict the use of uncharged or acquitted conduct.

Most states adopt a "grid" approach which incorporates these two factors as the two axes of the grid. The complexity of the grid varies; the number of "offense gravity score levels" ranges between 9 and 15. Within each "box," the ranges in which the judge may choose a sentence may be broad or narrow — but in virtually all cases they are much narrower than those embraced in the pre-guidelines era. Thus, a single grid cell may provide the judge a choice of, e.g., 15-28 months; in virtually no case would a guideline read "24-240 months," which was often the situation in pre-guideline statutes. An early version of the Minnesota grid is typical:

---

23. A few states, such as Florida, have separate guidelines for different categories of offenses (e.g., drugs). Most states, however, rank all offenses on a single scale of seriousness.

12.3 Minnesota Sentencing Grid
(Terms to be served are indicated in *months*, not years.)

Criminal History Score

	0	0	1	2	3	4	5	6 or more
1 Unauthorized use of motor vehicle Possession of marijuana	N	N	N	N	N	N	19 18-20
2 Theft-related crimes	N	N	N	N	N	N	21 20-22
3 Theft crimes	N	N	N	N	19 18-20	22 21-23	25 24-26
4 Nonresidential burglary Theft crimes (over $2,500)	N	N	N	N	25 24-26	32 30-34	41 37-45
5 Residential burglary Simple robbery	N	N	N	30 29-31	38 36-40	46 43-49	54 50-58
6 Criminal sexual conduct, 2nd degree	N	N	N	34 33-35	44 42-46	54 50-58	65 60-70
7 Aggravated robbery	24 23-25	32 30-34	41 38-44	49 45-53	65 60-70	81 75-87	97 90-104
8 Criminal sexual conduct, 1st degree; Assault, 1st degree	43 41-45	54 50-58	65 60-70	76 71-81	95 89-101	113 106-120	132 124-140
9 Murder, 3rd degree; Murder, 2nd degree (felony murder)	105 102-108	119 116-122	127 124-130	149 143-155	176 168-184	205 195-215	230 218-242
10 Murder, 2nd degree (with intent)	120 116-124	140 133-147	162 153-171	203 192-214	243 231-255	284 270-298	324 309-339

Note: "N" denotes a presumption of a non-imprisonment sentence.

(Column header S E R I O U S N E S S O F O F F E N S E runs vertically on the left side of the grid.)

This grid allows us to distinguish three important terms. Using residential burglary (offense level 5) as an example:

1. The *statutory maximum sentence*, which is not reflected on the grid itself, is 10 years. The longest sentence that a court, using the grid, could

impose for a residential burglary upon an offender with a criminal history score of 6 or more is 50-58 months, less than half the statutory maximum.

2. The *range* for residential burglary is probation to 58 months, depending on the defendant's past criminal history. Within a particular "box," the judge has discretion, although the range is very narrow inside a given "box" (e.g., 43-49 months for residential burglary by a person with a "5" criminal history).

3. If the judge wishes to go "outside the box" — i.e., to *"depart"* from whichever grid box the defendant's criminal history requires, she must provide reasons. That *departure* can be at any level, up to but not exceeding the 10-year *statutory maximum*, or down to probation.

iv. Institutional Resources

A number of states, following Minnesota's lead, caution the commission to adjust its guidelines to take into consideration "correctional resources," assuring that prisons do not fill beyond their capacity. The requirement has had some effect in some jurisdictions (although, as a nation, the United States continues to have the highest per-capita rate of incarceration in the world). In those commissions taking this exhortation seriously, legislatively prescribed longer terms for some offenses must mean lower terms for other crimes. Some commission guidelines also incorporate non-custodial and intermediary sanctions.

v. Appellate Review

Prior to the advent of presumptive sentences and guidelines, there was no meaningful review of trial court sentences; the only restriction was that the sentence fall somewhere within the statutory minimum and maximum. *Stanford v. State*, 110 So. 2d 1 (Fla. 1959). This may have been understandable when judges had "unfettered" discretion, did not have to give reasons or find facts, and could rely on any factor to warrant "individualization." But in the new guideline systems which articulate factors that should be considered in sentencing, and sometimes mandate findings on those factors, either side may now appeal sentences which vary from the guideline sentence.

Proponents of appellate review anticipate that the effect will be to create a "common law" of sentencing which will supplement the legislature's initial attempt to rationalize sentencing. Although the experiment has been extant for several decades, it is not clear whether that goal has been achieved; one can read the opinions of the Supreme Court of Minnesota (the state with the oldest guideline system) as either clarifying or muddying the guidelines.

Even if appellate review does not result in clearer reasons for sentencing, it may have one other unseen benefit. Some commentators argue that before appellate review was formally allowed, appellate courts upset with the sentence imposed might stretch the substantive rules of criminal law or criminal procedure, to overturn the conviction. As Holmes said, "hard cases make bad law." Now at least, where an appellate court believes the conviction is valid, but questions the sentence, it can do so directly.

4. Second Caveat

Only 5 percent of all crimes — and all criminals — are sentenced under the federal system, so whatever sentencing structure it embraces would seem to be peripheral to this discussion. But for several reasons, that is not so. First, the rollercoaster ride that has been the fate of the federal guidelines over the past quarter-century may hold lessons for future attempts to structure sentencing. Second, while most decisions of the United States Supreme Court are matters of statutory interpretation and thus relevant only to the federal code, the Court's five-year excursus, beginning with *Apprendi* and ending with *Booker* (both discussed below), into constitutional aspects of sentencing may ultimately carry a stealth weapon aimed at indeterminate, fully discretionary sentencing. Third, and again solely as a pragmatic matter, virtually all of the academic commentary — and many pages of most casebooks — focus on the federal guidelines, either because they are more accessible or because the Supreme Court's decisions relating to them may carry truths beyond the federal venue.

Beware: the discussion in this subsection describes the guidelines as they operated prior to the Court's decision in *Booker*. The Court's post-*Booker* decisions may totally change the guidelines, and hence sentencing under them, so that most of what follows in this section is history, not current reality. The trend certainly seems that way, but the "trend" is less than five years old. Post-*Booker* developments are discussed below as well.

5. Federal Sentencing Commission

a. Guidelines

While the federal guidelines look similar to the states', closer inspection shows that they are starkly different in many aspects from the state processes. The federal guidelines have been the target of unrelenting criticism since their adoption, unlike the state processes, which often have been hailed by commentators and judges alike. We will briefly examine below some of the main differences, and the criticisms of the federal guidelines.

i. The Commission

Unlike almost all state analogues, the federal Commission is housed in the judicial branch of government. A United States Supreme Court decision upheld this placement against a challenge that it breached the separation of powers. *Mistretta v. United States*, 488 U.S. 361 (1989). In contrast to state commissions, which are often quite large, the federal Commission consists of seven members. The initial statute required that at least three of these must be federal judges; the statute has now been amended so that no more than three may be on the federal judiciary. There is no statutory requirement that any of the remaining members have any experience in the actual practice of criminal justice.

ii. The Basis of the Grid

The federal Commission opted to follow a "descriptive" approach in establishing the initial guidelines. Perhaps because of its empowering legislation,[24] the Commission explicitly refused to choose among sentencing goals. Instead, it drew upon an empirical assessment of over 10,000 federal sentences which had been handed down by federal judges in the year preceding the guidelines.[25] In explaining this decision, the Commission declared:

> Such a choice [among purposes of sentencing] would be profoundly difficult. The relevant literature is vast, the arguments deep, and each point of view has much to be said in its favor. A clear-cut Commission decision in favor of one of these approaches would diminish the chance that the guidelines would find the widespread acceptance they need for effective implementation.

Federal Sentencing Guidelines Manual, ch. 1, pt. A, introductory cmt., reprinted in 52 Fed. Reg. 18, 046-138 (1987).

Critics have argued that this leads to no sturdy foundation on which to sentence.[26]

---

24. The Senate Report creating the Commission specifically declared that it "has not shown a preference for one purpose of sentencing over another in the belief that different purposes may play greater or lesser roles in sentencing for different types of offenses committed by different types of defendants." Senate Judiciary Committee's Report on the Sentencing Reform Act, S. Rep. No. 98-225, p. 77 (1983).

25. Jeffrey S. Parker and Michael K. Block, The Limits of Federal Criminal Sentencing Policy; Or, Confessions of Two Reformed Reformers, 9 Geo. Mason L. Rev. 1001, 1010 (2001). (Prof. Block was an original member of the federal Sentencing Commission.)

26. See Mark Osler, Must Have Got Lost: Traditional Sentencing Goals, the False Trail of Uniformity and Process, and the Way Back Home, 54 S.C.L. Rev. 649 (2003): "By simply replicating past patterns, the Commission passed on this opportunity . . . no underlying principle other than uniformity was the functional basis for the Guidelines as written." Id. at 655.

iii. Real Offense Sentencing

The federal guidelines, unlike any of the state systems, adopt a "real offense" sentencing scheme. This allows the judge to sentence the offender based not solely on the offense of which the defendant has been convicted (or pled), but upon his "real offense," so long as the sentence is within the maximum permissible penalty for the offense of conviction.

Suppose Herbert, a first-time offender,[27] was convicted of mail fraud. Although the statute imposes a five-year maximum, under the guidelines, Herbert's crime is a "base level" 13. The federal grid (p. 330) tells us that he would receive a guidelines sentence between 12 and 18 months. (The X axis is "I," the Y axis is 13.) This level may increase, depending on the amount of money stolen or a number of other "specific offense characteristics." If the court determines Herbert "abused a position of trust" in committing the fraud, there will be an increase in the base level. This is "real offense" sentencing. If there are enough "specific offense characteristics," the base level might be increased to, e.g., 30 (97 to 121 months). But the statutory limit (60 months) would preclude a sentence of more than five years.

Chapter Two of the Guidelines, which provide "real offense" sentencing factors for literally hundreds of federal offenses, is extraordinarily detailed (some would characterize this as "nuanced"). Thus, the guidelines on robbery list six different ways in which a weapon might be employed, and prescribe a different level of sentence enhancement for each one of the six. This complexity, reflected by 258 boxes within the sentencing grid (in contrast to most states, which have significantly fewer boxes) (see pages 324, *supra*, and 330 *infra*), has caused many to criticize the guidelines as arcane and unduly byzantine. Kevin R. Reitz, The Federal Role in Sentencing Law and Policy, 543 The Annals 116, 121 (1996); Kyron Huigens, *Harris*, *Ring*, and the Future of Relevant Conduct Sentencing, 15 Fed. Sent. Rept. 88 (2003).

Proponents of "real offense" sentencing argue that the "crime of conviction" approach used by the states, which bases its sentences exclusively on the charges to which the defendant pleads, places the dominant power in the hands of the prosecutor during plea bargaining — whatever charge is settled upon will dictate the sentence to be imposed. Under a "real offense" approach, these supporters argue, the judge will be empowered to consider such facts, thereby lessening the power of the prosecutor. As one commentator has put it:[28]

> The Commission created the relevant conduct provisions primarily to ensure that the discretion withdrawn from judges was not merely transferred to prosecutors.

---

27. See the discussion that follows of the role of criminal history.
28. Bowman, Fear of Law, *supra* n.10, 44 St. Louis L.J. at 339.

Critics, however, argue that plea bargaining continues, (Ilene H. Nagel and Stephen J. Schulhofer, A Tale of Three Cities: An Empirical Study of Charge and Bargaining Practices Under the Federal Sentencing Guidelines, 66 S. Cal. L. Rev. 501 (1992)), and that bargaining now concerns not merely the charges, but the various sentencing factors which permeate the federal guidelines (fact bargaining).

Again in contrast to state systems, federal judges may consider both uncharged criminal conduct and conduct for which the defendant has been acquitted in setting the "real offense" offense level. The Supreme Court has upheld this process against both due process and double jeopardy challenges. *United States v. Watts*, 519 U.S. 148 (1997); *Witte v. United States*, 515 U.S. 389 (1995).

The impact of the "real offense characteristics" can be substantial, even devastating. In *United States v. Ibanga*, 454 F. Supp. 2d 532 (E.D. Va. 2006), the jury convicted Ibanga of conspiracy to launder money but acquitted him of actual money laundering, conspiracy to distribute methamphetamine, and distributing methamphetamine. Nevertheless, the court found (by a preponderance of the evidence) that the defendant was responsible for distributing 124.03 grams of methamphetamine, the very charge of which the jury had acquitted the defendant. Under the guidelines, this resulted in a 10-level increase of "offense severity" and a sentence of 151 to 188 months instead of 51 to 63 months — a difference of about 10 years.

iv. Past Criminal Conduct

Like the state systems, the federal Commission gives criminal history (including misdemeanors) a substantial role in ascertaining the presumptive sentence. As in state systems, the guidelines assign various "points" for different "levels" of past convictions, and provide for sunset time lines for some past crimes. But the federal system is much more intricate than any state approach.

v. Departures

Few aspects of guideline systems in general, and the federal system in particular, have been as contentious as the ability of judges to "depart" from the guidelines. This power must be distinguished from the right, within the guidelines, to move within the grid, based upon particular findings of fact. "Departures" occur when the judge simply ignores the guideline structure and sentences the defendant within the statutory range, based upon whatever factors the judge feels relevant.

Prior to 2003, the federal guidelines permitted judges to depart in two instances: (a) where the government moved for a "substantial assistance"

12.4 Federal Sentencing Guidelines Table in Months of Imprisonment

			Criminal History Category (Criminal History Points)			
	Offense Level	I (0 or 1)	II (2 or 3)	III (4, 5, 6)	IV (7, 8, 9)	V (10, 11, 12)	VI (13 or more)

Zone	Offense Level	I (0 or 1)	II (2 or 3)	III (4, 5, 6)	IV (7, 8, 9)	V (10, 11, 12)	VI (13 or more)
Zone A	1	0-6	0-6	0-6	0-6	0-6	0-6
	2	0-6	0-6	0-6	0-6	0-6	1-7
	3	0-6	0-6	0-6	0-6	2-8	3-9
	4	0-6	0-6	0-6	2-8	4-10	6-12
	5	0-6	0-6	1-7	4-10	6-12	9-15
	6	0-6	1-7	2-8	6-12	9-15	12-18
	7	0-6	2-8	4-10	8-14	12-18	15-21
	8	0-6	4-10	6-12	10-16	15-21	18-24
Zone B	9	4-10	6-12	8-14	12-18	18-24	21-27
	10	6-12	8-14	10-16	15-21	21-27	24-30
Zone C	11	8-14	10-16	12-18	18-24	24-30	27-33
	12	10-16	12-18	15-21	21-27	27-33	30-37
	13	12-18	15-21	18-24	24-30	30-37	33-41
	14	15-21	18-24	21-27	27-33	33-41	37-46
	15	18-24	21-27	24-30	30-37	37-46	41-51
	16	21-27	24-30	27-33	33-41	41-51	46-57
	17	24-30	27-33	30-37	37-46	46-57	51-63
	18	27-33	30-37	33-41	41-51	51-63	57-71
	19	30-37	33-41	37-46	46-57	57-71	63-78
	20	33-41	37-46	41-51	51-63	63-78	70-87
	21	37-46	41-51	46-57	57-71	70-87	77-96
	22	41-51	46-57	51-63	63-78	77-96	84-105
	23	46-57	51-63	57-71	70-87	84-105	92-115
	24	51-63	57-71	63-78	77-96	92-115	100-125
	25	57-71	63-78	70-87	84-105	100-125	110-137
	26	63-78	70-87	78-97	92-115	110-137	120-150
	27	70-87	78-97	87-108	100-125	120-150	130-162
Zone D	28	78-97	87-108	97-121	110-137	130-162	140-175
	29	87-108	97-121	108-135	121-151	140-175	151-188
	30	97-121	108-135	121-151	135-168	151-188	168-210
	31	108-135	121-151	135-168	151-188	168-210	188-235
	32	121-151	135-168	151-188	168-210	188-235	210-262
	33	135-168	151-188	168-210	188-235	210-262	235-293
	34	151-188	168-210	188-235	210-262	235-293	262-327
	35	168-210	188-235	210-262	235-293	262-327	292-365
	36	188-235	210-262	235-293	262-327	292-365	324-405
	37	210-262	235-293	262-327	292-365	324-405	360-life
	38	235-293	262-327	292-365	324-405	360-life	360-life
	39	262-327	292-365	324-405	360-life	360-life	360-life
	40	292-365	324-405	360-life	360-life	360-life	360-life
	41	324-405	360-life	360-life	360-life	360-life	360-life
	42	360-life	360-life	360-life	360-life	360-life	360-life
	43	life	life	life	life	life	life

departure; (b) where the departure was based upon "an aggravating or mitigating circumstance of a king, to a degree, not adequately taken into consideration" by the Sentencing Commission.

The obvious intent of the substantial assistance provision is to encourage defendants to "turn state's evidence" on higher defendants.[29] A substantial assistance departure is based on one defendant's having provided substantial assistance in the investigation or prosecution of another person who has committed an offense. Substantial assistance departures are, under Section 5K1 of the guidelines themselves, allowed only "upon motion of the government." *Wade v. United States*, 504 U.S. 181 (1992), held that this provision precluded a judge, *sua sponte*, from recognizing such assistance. Thus, the discretion as to whether even to consider the defendant's cooperation is placed solely in the prosecutor's hands. There is only one exception—if the defendant can demonstrate that the prosecutor's refusal to move for such a reduction is based upon *constitutionally* infirm grounds (race, political activism, etc.), the court may grant relief.[30]

In *Koon v. United States*, 518 U.S. 81 (1996), it appeared that the Court had decided that federal sentencing judges could "depart" for many of the reasons that they would have employed preguidelines, but which were arguably prohibited under the guidelines. (Among these factors in *Koon* were (1) the victim significantly provoked the crime; (2) defendants were subjected to successive state and federal prosecutions; (3) defendants would lose their jobs.) The Court also interpreted the statute and guidelines as allowing trial judges to "continue" much of their traditional sentencing "discretion" and a narrow standard of appellate review. While some District Court Judges—and Circuit Courts—interpreted *Koon* as "liberating" federal judges, others read it narrowly. Nevertheless, some in Congress were annoyed, or even outraged. In 2003, Congress enacted the "Feeny Amendment," which precluded departure in all but "substantial assistance cases" and a few other "extraordinary" situations. The statute also created a de novo standard for appellate review. In addition, the amendment required the Commission to keep data on individual judge's rates of

---

29. Some states also expressly recognize this factor. See, e.g., *Brugman v. State*, 255 Ga., 497, 339 S.E.2d 244 (Ga. 1986), interpreting Ga. Code Ann. §16-13-31(e)(2).

30. A study in 2003 by the General Accounting Office found that three-quarters of the downward departures in drug cases were (1) substantial assistance departures; (2) pursuant to a plea agreement; or (3) "fast track" departures. GAO, Federal Drug Offenses; Departures from Sentencing Guidelines and Mandatory Minimum Sentences, Fiscal Years 1999-2001 (GAO-04-105). Moreover, there were wide differences among the circuits. Offenders sentenced in the Third Circuit were over three times more likely to have received a substantial assistance departure than offenders sentenced in the First Circuit. And offenders in the Ninth Circuit were over 18 times more likely to have received a non-substantial assistance departure than those sentenced in the Fourth Circuit.

departure.[31] Within weeks, the Attorney General had announced that the Department of Justice would also keep data on departures, and expressly warned all federal attorneys not to "stand silently by" while a defendant moved for a downward departure. This was also part of the Attorney General's broader declaration severely restricting the ability of individual prosecutors to engage in plea bargaining. The statute resulted in a firestorm of criticism, and in late September 2003, the Judicial Conference of the United States, headed by the Chief Justice, voted unanimously to ask Congress to repeal the law. This background may help explain the Court's decision in *Booker* and post-*Booker* cases. See Kate Stith, The Arc of the Pendulum: Judges, Prosecutors, and the Exercise of Discretion, 117 Yale L.J. 1420 (2008).

vi. How It Really Worked

There are four basic steps:

- determine the "base offense" level, as established by the Commission;
- increase the base level by "specific offense characteristics." For example, if the crime was robbery, a characteristic is the amount of money stolen;
- increase (or decrease) the base offense level again by "adjustments." These factors may relate to any crime—for example, a defendant, whether charged with robbery or mail fraud, may have his "base offense level" increased if he was a "manager" (as opposed to merely a "participant") in the event;
- find the defendant's "criminal history."

The difference between a "real offense" system, such as the federal government's, and an "offense of conviction" system such as Minnesota's (and all other guideline states), can be seen in the following example. Suppose Ronald, who has previously been convicted of three felonies, none of them involving violence, has robbed a federally insured bank at gun point.

a. He points the gun at three different customers.
b. His take is $75,000.
c. He is a recovering alcoholic.
d. He has a fourth-grade education.

---

31. Representative Feeney explained these provisions as follows: "The Sentencing Commission must, upon request, provide any data. . . . This disclosed information includes the name of the sentencing judge. Such information helps ensure that federal judges are properly accountable for their sentencing decisions comporting with the law. . . . America is not going to return to the days of unfettered power resting in the hands of a single district judge." Feeney, Reaffirming the Rule of Law in Federal Sentencing, Crim. Just. Ethics 2, 72-73 (Winter/Spring 2003).

If Ronald is prosecuted in Minnesota, his "offense level" is 7 ("aggravated robbery"). Let us assume his three priors were severity level IV; the guidelines make his criminal history score a 3. Thus, under the grid on page 328, he will be facing a possible 45-53-month sentence. The judge may consider the amount stolen as a reason for going toward 53 as opposed to 45 months, but if the judge wishes to go beyond 53 months on the basis of this information, she must "depart" and give a written set of reasons for doing so. On the other hand, she may consider Ronald's low level of education or his attempt to rehabilitate himself as moving him toward the 45-month sentence. (The Minnesota guidelines expressly forbid "departing" based upon social factors or educational attainment, but allow a judge to consider these items *within* the sentencing range.)

In the federal system, Ronald's "base offense" level (on the Y axis) is 20 (p.334). By specific guidelines language, the "pointing" of the gun, which is the equivalent of "brandishing," raises that by five levels. (If a dangerous weapon other than a gun was brandished, there is an increase of four levels.) The guidelines also distinguish offenses by the amount of money involved; a loss of $75,000 raises the offense by two levels; a loss of $800,000 by four levels. Thus, Ronald now has an offense level of 27 (20 + 7). With three prior felonies, his criminal history score (the X axis) is likely to be IV, and his "base sentence" would be 51-63 months. Based on the "real offense" factors, however, he is facing a sentence, on the grid, of 100-125 months (more than double the initial sentence). Now the judge has discretion *within this range*, and may consider Ronald's alcoholism or his education level as mitigating factors. (Again, the judge may not "depart" from the guideline range on the basis of these factors.)

The critical point here is that while the Minnesota judge *may* consider the gun, or the amount taken, the federal judge *must* do so — each of these factors has a specific increase in base offense level that removes much of the discretionary judgment of the judge and which substantially increases the defendant's potential incarceration.

6. Structured Sentencing — An Assessment

Notwithstanding the diversity among the state and federal provisions, the structured sentencing movement has demonstrated several important facts:

- it is possible, even if difficult, to prioritize purposes of sentencing, and to establish a system which reflects those purposes;
- it is possible, within limits, to articulate the specific factors which judges (or other sentencers) consider relevant, and then to assess those factors in light of the purposes discovered above;

- while actors in the system will seek ways to avoid what they perceive as overregulation of their power, they also will often recognize the need for some uniformity and regularization of the results of their actions, particularly if their representatives are included in the process of initial establishment of this regularization.

12.5

	Federal Guidelines	State Guidelines	Traditional Sentencing
Commission composition	Seven members; not more than three federal judges*	{Sixteen states} Wide range; many require "roles" of criminal justice system (prosecutor, defense counsel)	Judges appointed or elected
Basis of original "guidelines"	Past practice; now often altered by normative decisions or Congress	Past practice *or* re-examination of normative purposes	Not applicable
"Base" of sentencing decision	Relevant conduct; real offense	Charge of conviction	Charge of conviction
How guidelines may be altered	New guidelines effective 180 days after promulgation unless Congress affirmatively negates	*Same* as federal *or* need affirmative legislative approval	Not applicable
Binding or voluntary?	Binding	Ten binding, six voluntary	Not applicable
Range of sentences	Narrow within each grid box, but many grid boxes	Narrow within grid boxes, many fewer than federal grid	Usually wide range
Movement from box to box?	Controlled by highly detailed set of "relevant conduct" factors; given quantified impact on sentence	Aggravated and mitigating circumstances listed, but generally no specific quantitative effect for specific factor	Not applicable

12.5 Continued

	Federal Guidelines	State Guidelines	Traditional Sentencing
Departures	Downward departures for cooperation, only on motion of government; otherwise, as allowed under *Koon*	Allowed in "extraordinary cases"	Court typically considers factors which would be allowed under guideline systems, but many others as well
Personal facts? (Age, employment, family, health, etc.)	Typically discouraged or explicitly forbidden	Often allowed, if not encouraged	Always considered
Criminal history	Forms one axis of grid; specific restriction on what may be considered; quantifiable impact on "offense level"	Typically same as federal, but impact may vary from federal, as may past offenses which may be considered	In non-recidivist setting, always considered. No specific quantitative effect; no limits on what past offense may or may not be considered
Appellate review	Yes, for both sides	Yes, for both sides	No
Incarceration constraints?	In statute, but Commission has not implemented	Varies, but many states have such restrictions, and follow them	No

* Originally, "at least three" had to be federal judges.

F. UNDOING THE REVOLUTION? OR REFRAMING IT? *BLAKELY, BOOKER,* AND THE FUTURE OF SENTENCING (STRUCTURED AND UNSTRUCTURED) IN THE UNITED STATES

I. Third Caveat — And an Apology

Everything that has been said in the last few pages about the federal guidelines may be wrong, or at least no longer applicable. In a dramatic set of opinions delivered in the last five years, the Court has appeared to reinstitute totally discretionary sentencing in the federal system, while purporting to retain the guidelines. The story of how this has happened is instructive and chastening.

2. *Blakely* and *Booker* — Undoing the Federal Guidelines

As mentioned earlier, in 1986 the Court had created the concept of a "sentencing factor," which could be decided upon by a judge using a "preponderance of the evidence" standard. In *Jones v. United States*, 526 U.S. 227 (1999), a federal statute provided for a sentence of 15 years for carjacking but established a 25-year maximum; if there had been "serious" injury, the sentence could be 25 years, and if death had occurred, life imprisonment. The Court held that as *a matter of statutory interpretation*, a jury, not a judge, had to determine those last two factors (serious harm or death). In a footnote, however, the Court indicated that the Sixth Amendment might be involved; it was not inclined to turn the jury into a "mere gatekeeper" while the truly important facts were left to a judge.

One year later that footnote became law. In *Apprendi v. New Jersey*, 530 U.S. 466 (2000), a defendant convicted of illegally possessing a firearm, a crime which carried a maximum sentence of 10 years, was sentenced to 12 years because the trial judge, using a *preponderance* standard, concluded that the defendant had acted with a racial bias. The Supreme Court reversed, holding that any factor which "increased the maximum sentence" must be submitted to the jury and assessed by the *beyond a reasonable doubt* standard. Justice Thomas, casting the fifth and decisive vote, argued that any increase, whether or not it went beyond the maximum, should be submitted to the jury.

The dissenters (Justices O'Connor, Rehnquist, Kennedy, and Breyer), argued that *Apprendi* was entirely formalistic. If New Jersey had merely enacted a statute punishing illegal possession of a firearm by 0-20, but required a finding that the defendant had acted from racial motive before a sentence of more than 10 years could be imposed, the statute would survive the actual words of the plurality, since the maximum sentence (20 years) was not being increased by a finding of racial animus. Constitutional guarantees should not be so fragile, the dissenters argued. The majority response was, essentially, "not so long as this Court sits."

Neither *Jones* nor *Apprendi* was argued as a "sentencing" case — the gravamen of each decision was protection of the power of the jury.[32] But their impact was soon to be felt on the structured sentencing schemes discussed above.

---

32. Full disclosure. The author was a counsel of record in *Apprendi*. I hope the following discussion will be evenhanded; if not, my bias is at least revealed.

Four years after *Apprendi*, the Court applied it to a structured sentencing system. In *Blakely v. Washington*, 542 U.S. 296 (2004), defendant, convicted of kidnapping, was exposed to a "structured sentencing grid" of 49 to 53 months, although the statutory limit was 10 years. The sentencing judge, however, concluded that Blakely had acted with "deliberate cruelty," a statutory ground for departure in these cases, and imposed a sentence of 90 months. The Court, per Justice Scalia, held that the "maximum" referred to in *Apprendi* was not the statutorily established maximum sentence, but the sentence the judge could impose solely on the basis of the facts reflected in the jury verdict or admitted by the defendant.

Although Justice Scalia declared that this was a case about the jury, and not about sentencing, Justice O'Connor in dissent lamented that "Congress will either trim or eliminate altogether their sentencing guidelines schemes and, with them, 20 years of sentencing reform."

Justice Breyer, an original member of the United States Sentencing Commission, also read *Blakely* as invalidating all structured sentencing schemes. He posited three options for legislatures to take in response to the majority's view:

1. Create a simple, pure or nearly pure, charge offense system;
2. Return to indeterminate sentencing schemes;
3. Retain a structured scheme, but allow the judge only to depart downward, not upward.

He rejected all three: "Whatever the faults of guidelines systems — and there are many — they are more likely to find their cure in legislation emerging from the experience of, and discussion among, all elements of the criminal justice community, than in a virtually unchangeable constitutional decision of this Court." Moreover, he argued that any of these systems would enhance plea bargaining, and hence increase reliance on a system "in which punishment is set not by judges or juries but by advocates acting under bargaining constraints. . . . I am unaware of any variation that does not involve the shift of power to the prosecutor . . . inherent in the charge offense system. . . ." *Blakely, supra*, 542 U.S. at 338 and 340.

Blakely created chaos in the federal system: District courts were uncertain of the validity of guideline sentencing. The Supreme Court took the unusual step of ordering expedited hearings in a case, raising the applicability of *Blakely* to the federal guidelines, and heard argument on the Court's first day of the new session, an extremely unusual occasion. Less than six months later, the shoe dropped. In *United States v. Booker*, 543 U.S. 22 (2005), the Court held that *Blakely* invalidated the federal mandatory sentencing guidelines because it removed those issues from the jury (the "merits" holding). Then, in a startling move, the Court announced a "remedy" for the unconstitutionality of the guidelines: It held that the guidelines were no longer mandatory, but advisory. As a consequence of this remedy, a federal judge no longer "had to" alter a sentence based upon a finding of an "offense characteristic" or an "adjustment." *Blakely* did not apply to "advisory" guidelines because these facts would not inevitably alter a sentence. The Court also invalidated the "Feeney Amendment" as inconsistent with advisory guidelines, and it reasserted that appellate federal courts should uphold any "reasonable" sentence imposed by a federal judge.

The *Booker* remedy created by Justice Breyer was either a coup d'etat or a tour de force, depending on one's perspective. It "saved" the federal guidelines process from the *Blakely* requirement of jury determinations of fact, but retained "restricted" judicial sentencing discretion by imposing some, but not *de novo*, appellate review. Moreover, it was a stunning surprise; not even Justice Breyer, in his dissent in *Blakely* six months earlier, had posited this approach as a viable alternative.

In the (few) years since *Booker*, the Court has (re)established discretionary sentencing in the federal courts. Although it has warned that federal judges must "begin" by "considering" the guidelines, it has made clear that the guidelines are "advisory." It has held[33] that an appellate court may (but need not) create a presumption of validity to a sentence *within* the guidelines, and a sentence *outside* the guidelines should not be presumptively invalid.[34] Moreover, it has made pellucid that even if a circuit adopts a presumption, district courts should feel free to ignore it and sentence wherever they wish — the presumption is "an appellate" one, not meant to limit district court discretion. It has gone much further, however: Having initially held that a district court judge, when sentencing a defendant, might impose a sentence notwithstanding clearly articulated Commission policies (*Kimbrough v. United States*, 552 U.S. 85 (2007)), the Court has now held that a judge may totally disagree with an entire sentencing policy and ignore it.[35] In *Spears v. United States*, 555 U.S. 261 (2009), the Court upheld, without briefs or arguments, a sentence imposed by a judge who disagreed with the so-called "10/1 ratio"

---

33. *Rita v. United States*, 551 U.S. 338 (2007).
34. *Gall v. United States*, 552 U.S. 38 (2007).
35. The circuit courts are divided on whether *Kimbrough* — or *Spears* — is restricted to the crack cocaine issue. They have split on whether sentencing judges may consider the fact that some defendants, in some districts, are entitled to lower sentences because of the "fast-track" plea bargaining policies in those districts (see Chapter 7). Compare *United States v. Reyes-Hernandez*, 624 F.3d 405 (7th Cir. 2010) (may consider) with *United States v. Vega-Castillo*, 540 F.3d 1235 (11th Cir. 2008) (may not consider). See, generally, Katherine Arnold McCurry, Rejecting Consideration of the "Fast-Track Disparity" in a Post-*Kimbrough* World, 45 Wake Forest L. Rev. 1401 (2010); Thomas E. Gorman, Fast-Track Sentencing Disparity: Rereading Congressional Intent to Resolve the Circuit Split, 77 U. Chi. L. Rev. 479 (2010). There are even some cases declaring judicial disenchantment with the guidelines on sentencing persons possessing child pornography. See Carissa Byrne Hessick, Appellate Review of Sentencing Policy Decisions after *Kimbrough*, 93 Marq. L. Rev. 717, 731 (2009).

for crack versus noncrack cocaine and who had adopted his own personal ratio for sentencing cases. That Congress and the Commission had (at that point in time) imposed a substantially large ratio, was ignored by the judge—and by the Supreme Court.[36] Perhaps even more indicative of the Court's swift race back to discretionary sentencing is *Pepper v. United States*, 562 U.S. 476 (2011), where the Court held that at a resentencing,[37] a court could consider the defendant's postsentence rehabilitation, a factor which had been expressly precluded in the guidelines when they were mandatory. The court was not hesitant—a sentencer should have "the widest possible breadth of information about a defendant" before sentencing. Finally, the Court held in *Oregon v. Ice*, 555 U.S. 160 (2009), that *Apprendi-Blakely* did not preclude a state from allowing a sentencing judge to impose sentences so that they must be served consecutively, rather than concurrently, even though the statute allowed the judge to do this only if the judge made specific findings of fact in addition to those made by the jury.

3. *Blakely* (and *Booker*) in the States

The *Booker* remedy, of course, did not apply directly to the states, since it interpreted the federal sentencing statutes.[38] The question, then, is what impact *Blakely* and *Booker* will have upon the structured sentencing schemes adopted in the states. There are several possibilities:

(a) "*Blakelyize*" *the system*, by requiring juries to ascertain whether factors which will, or even may, affect the sentence are present.[39] At least six states, including Minnesota[40] and Alaska,[41] have adopted this approach. Even before *Blakely* was decided, Kansas had gone even further, and "bifurcated" its procedure, putting these questions in the hands of the jury.[42] Opponents of this idea argue that, given the number of factors which could affect a sentence, jury trials would become impossibly lengthy. Proponents argue

---

36. In what one critic has characterized as a "cranky" opinion, the Court declared: "[W]e now clarify that district courts are entitled to reject and vary categorically from the crack-cocaine guidelines based on a policy disagreement with those guidelines. The guidelines no longer have mandatory and binding effect and the sentencing court may not presume them correct or reasonable when it considers an individual sentence."

37. But not in a sentencing "modification." See *Dillon v. United States*, 560 U.S. 817 (2010).

38. For a meticulous state-by-state study of how *Blakely* affected states by 2008, see Stephanos Bibas and Susan Klein, The Sixth Amendment and Criminal Sentencing, 30 Cardozo L. Rev. 775 (2008).

39. See Kyron Huigens, Solving the Apprendi Puzzle, 90 Geo. L.J. 387 (2002).

40. Kevin S. Burke, State v. Dettman: The End of the Sentencing Revolution or Just the Beginning?, 33 Wm. Mitchell L. Rev. 1331 (2007); Richard S. Frase, Blakely in Minnesota, Two Years Out: Guidelines Sentencing Is Alive and Well, 4 Ohio St. J. Crim. L. 73 (2006).

41. Teresa W. Carns, Alaska's Responses to the Blakely Case, 24 Alaska L. Rev. 1 (2007).

42. Kan. Stat. Ann. §21-4716 et seq.

that (1) the proliferation of "factors" could be significantly reduced; (2) in fact, few such factors are actually involved in a single case; and (3) the states which have adopted this approach appear to handle the problem.

(b) *"Bookerize" the system*, either by legislatively amending the statute (as in California and Indiana)[43] or reinterpreting the statute (as in New Jersey and Ohio)[44], to make guidelines voluntary and reinstate judicial discretion. Opponents of this approach argue that it marginalizes the jury and ignores the essence of *Blakely* and *Apprendi*, while returning to a judicial discretionary system, the original target of guidelines.

(c) *Impose jury sentencing directly*. As indicated earlier in this chapter, jury sentencing was widespread in the nineteenth century in this country, and six states continue to rely on jury sentencing in virtually all cases. Some observers argue that jury sentencing is undesirable, because it is both time-consuming and erratic. Supporters of jury sentencing contend, however, that to the extent jury sentences are more random, because each one is imposed by a "newcomer" to sentencing, the solution is to provide the jury with information about sentencing, particularly information reflecting how other juries have treated similarly situated defendants, to resolve some of that discrepancy. The information would be a condensed version of the research on which the "descriptive" guidelines were built. Currently, "[N]o state provides juries with anywhere near the amount of sentence-related information that is currently provided to judges."[45] Finally, proponents of jury sentencing point out that every state leaves the decision of life or death to juries (see below). If juries can be trusted with that critical decision, they urge, they can be similarly trusted with lesser determinations. It is unlikely that *Blakely* would require jury sentencing as envisioned by these observers, but *Blakely* is certainly a major reinvigorator of the Sixth Amendment.

(d) *Create a simple "charge offense" system*, in which no "relevant conduct" or aggravating and mitigating factors are considered at all.

(e) *Repudiate structured sentencing entirely and return to totally discretionary sentencing*. As already noted, most states still have wide indeterminate range sentencing, with "unfettered" judicial discretion. This approach appeals to those who believe that individualizing sentences is more important than even rough

---

43. California at first argued that its structured system was distinguishable from *Blakely*'s. The United States Supreme Court rejected that view in *Cunningham v. California*, 549 U.S. 470 (2007). Within 10 weeks, California had legislatively reinstituted sentencing discretion. Cal. S.B. 40, amending Cal. Penal Code §1170 (b) (enacted March 30, 2007). The Indiana Supreme Court held in *Smylie v. State*, 823 N.E.2d 679 (Ind. 2005), that *Blakely* applied to its sentencing scheme. According to Limrick, Senate Bill 96: How General Assembly Returned Problem of Uniform Sentencing to Indiana's Appellate Courts, 49-Feb. Res Gestae 18 (2006), the Indiana legislature was poised to ratify that view but, in a stunning turnaround, suddenly "Bookerized" its legislation.

44. E.g., *State v. Natale*, 184 N.J. 458, 878 A.2d 724 (2006); *State v. Foster*, 109 Ohio St. 3d 1, 845 N.E.2d 470 (2006).

45. Jenia Iontcheva, *supra*, n.10 at 367.

equality among defendants, and that only each judge, facing each individual defendant, can assess the "right" sentence. All nine Justices in *Blakely* and *Booker* appeared to assume that full indeterminacy was constitutional, although this seems somewhat inconsistent with the statement in *Blakely* that *Apprendi* "ensur[es] that the judge's authority to sentence derives *wholly* from the jury's verdict" (emphasis added). As many commentators have noted, a judge who, even in a totally indeterminate, totally discretionary system, adopts *any* sentence must do so on the basis of facts beyond those explicitly found by the jury — otherwise, there would be no basis for the sentencing decision.[46] It is possible, however, that articulation by sentencing commissions, legislatures, or others, of the most important sentencing factors, and the impact they may have, has undercut, at least in part, the notion that it is not possible to discern those factors which actually affect sentences.

On a doctrinal level the very premise of *Williams*, and of individualization, was that the purpose of sentencing was rehabilitation. Few systems now articulate that as a goal, so *Williams's* viability is doubtful (although the Supreme Court has several times cited it favorably in recent opinions). As one critic has put it, "I remain at a loss to understand why unexplained, indeterminate decision-making is constitutionally permissible, but explained, reasoned decision-making is not."[47]

4. Final Thoughts

In substantive criminal law, courts and writers have debated for centuries about whether certain claims (self-defense, necessity, etc.) "negated *mens rea*" (and therefore had to be rebutted by the prosecution) or were "stand alone" claims on which the defendant could be made to carry the burden of proof, (and not merely production) (see Richard G. Singer and John Q. LaFond, Criminal Law: Examples and Explanations, Chapter 15). The debate over whether a particular item is an "element" of the crime or a "sentencing factor" is equally deep and perhaps unanswerable here. When the Court in *McMillan* coined the term *sentencing factor*, it was probably only a matter of time before that concept was questioned. After all, was the crime "robbery," or was it "(1) robbery (2) with a gun which was (3) brandished (but not fired)" (4) wearing a mask, and netting between (5) $X and $Y?. Each of the five "factors" might be considered relevant in determining a sentence, and if

---

46. See, e.g., Frank O. Bowman, III, "The Question Is Which Is to Be Master — That's All": *Cunningham, Claiborne, Rita* and the Sixth Amendment Muddle, 19 Fed. Sent. Rep. 155 (2007); Katie M. McVoy, "What I Have Feared Most Has Now Come to Pass": *Blakely, Booker* and the Future of Sentencing, 80 Notre Dame L. Rev. 1613 (2005).
47. Rosenzweig, Testimony before the United States Sentencing Commission, November 17, 2004.

they were only sentencing factors, then the risk was that the jury might become, as the Court in *Jones* feared, a "gatekeeper," while all the "important" decisions were made by a judge. The McMillan Court, *McMillan v. Pennsylvania*, 477 U.S. 79, 88 (1986) spoke of the "tail" (the sentencing factor) that: "wags" the "dog of the substantive offense."

Apprendi and its progeny were careful to speak of issues that "worked like" elements of the crime, but that language is still with us. Subsequently, in *United States v. O'Brien*, 560 U.S. 218 (2010), the Court held unanimously that under the specific federal statute involved there, whether the firearm was a machine gun (which increased the mandatory minimum to 30 years) was an element to be determined by the jury. While noting that the question was largely one of legislative intent, the Court delineated five criteria it might use: (1) language and structure, (2) tradition, (3) risk of unfairness, (4) severity of the sentence, and (5) legislative history. From an earlier decision,[48] the Court declared, 560 U.S. at 227, that

> Sentencing factors traditionally involve characteristics of the offender — such as recidivism, cooperation with law enforcement, or acceptance of responsibility. Id., at 126, 120 S. Ct. 2090. Characteristics of the offense itself are traditionally treated as elements, and the use of a machine gun under §924(c) lies "closest to the heart of the crime at issue."

United States v. O'Brien, 130 S. Ct. 2169 (2010)[49]

Some have suggested that *Apprendi-Blakely* concerns "facts," while leaving "judgments" about those facts (and the defendant's character) and issues of rehabilitation, deterrence, retribution, and so on, to sentencers. That distinction, too, has been criticized. See *Villagarcia v. Warden, Noble Correctional Institution*, 599 F.3d 529 (6th Cir. 2010).

The fact seems to be that while this is a Sixth Amendment issue of diluting the impact of the jury, it is *also* a battle between judges and prosecutors. As Professor Bowman has put it:[50]

> [W]e have watched the Court decide a series of cases nominally about the Sixth Amendment right to a jury trial that have had virtually no practical effect on how many cases are decided by juries or even on the issues decided by juries in those cases that go to trial. . . . The jury trial rate in federal courts is now lower than it was before *Booker*. And in those cases that go to trial, juries decided no more facts related to sentencing than they did before *Booker*. The entire debate

---

48. *Castillo v. United States*, 530 U.S. 120 (2002).
49. On the other hand, the Court in *Dean v. United States*, 566 U.S. 568 (2009) held that, under the same statute, the way in which the gun was handled (possessed, carried, used, brandished, or discharged, each of which required a different mandatory minimum) was a sentencing factor to be found by the judge.
50. Bowman, *supra*, n.46 at 163.

about the post-*Booker* federal sentencing world has had nothing to do with juries, and everything to do with the allocation of sentencing power between the judiciary, . . . Congress, and federal prosecutors.

The tension reflected in the two majority opinions in *Booker* has been present in sentencing for decades, if not centuries. The desire to individualize sentences, particularly premised on rehabilitation, is strong. But the fear that individual sentencers will hold very different goals and perceive the same facts very differently informs the need to restrain that discretion. It is not so much a need for "uniformity" in sentencing as it is a fear of "disuniformity" that sparked the move toward structured sentencing. After all, each of us believes that she could hand down the "right" sentence in every instance — but that her neighbor is less enlightened and influenced by irrelevancies (such as deterrence or retribution).[51] Since *Blakely* was decided, there have been hundreds of judicial decisions attempting to determine its limits and applications. Literally scores — and possibly hundreds — of law review articles have been written on the subject generally, and on the cases specifically. The debate is not over; indeed, it has probably just begun.[52]

G. SENTENCING AND DEATH

The death penalty has always been controversial. In recent years, with the uncovering of a number of defendants who, though actually innocent, were convicted of capital offenses, and an even larger number of defendants who were inadequately represented at trial or at the capital sentencing process (see Chapter 11), a growing cry for a moratorium on the death penalty has emerged. There has been, as well, a growing consensus that no death penalty should be imposed unless the jury — the cross section of the community — concludes that there are sufficient facts to impose death.

But the jury which decides the life-death issue is not fully representative of that community. As noted in Chapter 8, prosecutors are able to "death qualify" a jury — to remove, for cause, any potential juror who acknowledges that he could not impose the death penalty under any circumstances. The Court in *Utrecht v. Brown*, 551 U.S. 1 (2007), appeared to make it easier

---

51. This same concern lives in law school faculties. Some schools adopt a "mandatory" grading curve, concerned that students' grades will be (drastically) affected by the (harsh or easy) professors to which they are arbitrarily assigned during first year. Other faculty defend to the death their "academic freedom" to grade as they will, notwithstanding that they are below (or above) the class average by a full point or more.

52. For those interested in the topic, there are many sources. This book could expand by at least 40 pages just by listing all the law review pieces on the subject. For those interested in the federal sentencing guidelines, the best source is the Federal Sentencing Reporter.

for a prosecutor to "death qualify" a jury. This process is hotly debated for several reasons. First, one might argue that death should be imposed only if all members of the community — including those staunchly opposed to the death penalty in the abstract — believe the facts to be so gruesome as to warrant death. This argument has not been successful. Second, there is some evidence that "death-qualified" jurors are more prone to convict. If so, one might argue that the guilt jury should not be death qualified, and that only if the defendant is convicted should persons opposed to the penalty be removed and replaced by others not so opposed. Again, this argument has been unsuccessful. Third, opposition to the death penalty surely lies across a spectrum of persuasion; many persons who believe themselves to be opposed to the penalty might be persuaded, in a particularly heinous offense, to impose the penalty. The precise wording of the voir dire question, and the precise depth of questioning about the potential juror's beliefs, are therefore critical to assuring the state and the defendant that the jury is "as" representative as possible.

Prior to 1972, the decision between life and death was left almost exclusively to juries, without any instructions about when the death penalty might be imposed. Most states allowed the death penalty to be imposed on those convicted of "first degree" murder, which was commonly defined as "premeditated, deliberate and willful." Beyond that, the jury was left to its own devices. In *McGautha v. California*, 402 U.S. 183 (1971), the Supreme Court rejected a challenge, based upon the due process clause, that capital juries were "standardless" concerning whether to impose the penalty. Echoing the view that individualization precludes rationalization, Justice Harlan, speaking for the Court, declared:

> To identify before the fact those characteristics of criminal homicides and their perpetrators which call for the death penalty and to express these characteristics in language which can fairly be understood and applied by the sentencing authority [is] beyond present human ability.

Nevertheless, one year later, the Court, by a vote of 5-4, with each of the nine Justices writing an opinion, held that the death penalty, *as then implemented*, violated not the due process clause but the Eighth Amendment. While at least two of the majority Justices concluded that the death penalty would never be constitutionally acceptable, the thrust of the other three was that the penalty was arbitrarily imposed: as "freakish as being hit by lightning." *Furman v. Georgia*, 408 U.S. 238 (1972).

The states immediately rewrote their death penalty provisions. Four years after *Furman*, the Court decided that a statute seeking to avoid the "freakishness" of the death penalty by mandatorily imposing the death penalty upon all persons convicted of "capitally eligible" offenses also violated the Eighth Amendment. *Woodson v. North Carolina*, 428 U.S. 280 (1976).

On the other hand, statutorily enacted aggravating and mitigating factors (most of which were copied from the Model Penal Code) gave sufficient structure to the sentencer to overcome *Furman's* concern of freakishness. *Gregg v. Georgia*, 428 U.S. 153 (1976). Among the common aggravating factors are that:

- the method of death was particularly heinous or cruel;
- the defendant's criminal history;
- statements from the victim's family and others describing the impact of the victim's death.

Among the common mitigating factors are that:

- there was a plausible defensive claim, such as duress or necessity, though not rising to the level of a total defense;
- the perpetrator was particularly young, or influenced by another;
- the victim "provoked" the killing in some way;
- the defendant suffered abuse as a child;
- the defendant suffers from mental illness;
- the defendant's role was "relatively minor" or he did not actually kill.[53]

Thirty-five years have passed, and the jurisprudence of death is indeed complex. For our purposes, however, the decisions can be easily summarized: While the state may be limited in what evidence it presents to persuade the sentencer that death should be imposed, the defendant is entitled to present any evidence regarding the defendant's character, background or circumstances of the offense, whether or not consistent with statutorily enunciated mitigating factors. In effect, the defendant may plead for mercy based upon facts which are statutorily irrelevant — the sentencer may be freakish in granting mercy, but not in imposing death.[54] The death penalty decision, then, is to be intensely individualized, and no goal of normal sentencing is necessarily dominant.

---

53. The Virginia statute under which John Muhammad was prosecuted for the "sniper" killings in the Washington, D.C. area in 2002 allowed the death penalty only for the actual shooter. Thus, Muhammad's attorneys sought to show that, if he was guilty at all, it was only as an accomplice who drove the car, and that Lee Malvo was the actual sniper.

54. See, e.g., *Skipper v. South Carolina*, 476 U.S. 1 (1986), allowing the defendant to show good behavior in prison (which theoretically has nothing to do with deterrence or retribution for the offense); *Lockett v. Ohio*, 438 U.S. 586 (1978); and *Eddings v. Oklahoma*, 455 U.S. 104 (1982) (defendant must be allowed to offer any evidence regarding his background, character, or circumstances of the offense); Scott E. Sundby, The *Lockett* Paradox: Reconciling Guided Discretion and Unguided Mitigation in Capital Sentencing, 38 UCLA L. Rev. 1147 (1991). See generally Susan R. Klein and Jordan M. Steiker, The Search for Equality in Criminal Sentencing, 2002 Sup. Ct. Rev. 223.

The process of deciding the death issue is virtually uniform throughout the country. A second hearing is held at which the jury that convicted the defendant determines the penalty. The death-eligible defendant has a constitutionally protected right to see the pre-sentence report, which, as we have already seen, is not clearly guaranteed to a non-death defendant. *Gardner v. Florida*, 430 U.S. 349 (1977). Moreover, the defendant has the right to present evidence (including hearsay), subject only to typical rules on cumulative evidence. On the other hand, hearsay evidence is allowed, as it is in non-capital sentencing.

The decision whether the facts suffice to impose death is now the sole province of the jury. Prior to *Apprendi*, the Court had upheld a system by which a judge could make that decision, either acting alone, or even after a contrary recommendation from the jury. In *Ring v. Arizona*, 536 U.S. 584 (2002), the trial judge had concluded, after a sentencing hearing, that the murder in question had been committed "in an especially heinous, cruel or depraved manner" and in pursuit of something of "pecuniary value." The United States Supreme Court overturned the death sentence, holding that *Apprendi* applied, and required such a fact, which increased the maximum sentence from life to death, to be found by a jury. A similar result was reached in *Hurst v. Florida*, 136 S.Ct. 616 (2016). Although Florida law allowed jurors to render an advisory verdict, the final decision as to whether the defendant would be sentenced to death was made by the trial judge. The trial judge was required to hold a hearing and decide whether sufficient aggravating circumstances existed which warranted the death penalty. The Supreme Court found that as in *Ring*, this scheme violated the defendant's right to jury trial because the judge had the sole responsibility for finding facts which would increase the defendant's sentence from life imprisonment to death.

The constitutionalization of capital sentencing procedures has been called a "dismal failure."[55] It might be argued that Justice Harlan was correct — that it is not possible to individualize death sentences and still regularize the process. While individualizing non-capital sentences clearly does not involve as dramatic a question, the lesson may be important for policy determination, even if it does not constitutionally require structured sentencing.

Examples

1. (a) The following appears in the pre-sentence report on Herbert Wooldridge, who is convicted of 20 counts of indecent exposure, mostly to prepubescent girls: "Wooldridge's former wife Delores recounts a story

---

55. Klein and Steiker, *supra*, n.54.

in which he appeared at their front door at 4 a.m. wearing a mask and screaming in some foreign language. He banged on the door until she admitted him. She said it left her hair white; she doubts whether he has all his marbles." The judge relies on this information, but does not disclose it to Herb. Does Herb have a complaint?

(b) The judge discloses the pre-sentence report, including this incident, to Herb, who disputes the story, and says that his ex-wife is vengeful. At the sentencing hearing can he: (i) require Delores to be present and cross-examine her; (ii) require the probation officer to be present and cross-examine him; (iii) give his own version of the story, and a recounting of Delores' alleged animosity toward him?

2. (a) Sally, charged with possessing 50 grams of cocaine, successfully moved to suppress 40 grams of that cocaine because the search violated the Fourth Amendment. She was still convicted of possessing the 10 grams. At her sentencing, the judge declared: "You've only been convicted of 10 grams, which carries a sentence of 3-10 years. Since you're a first offender, I'd normally impose the three-year minimum. But you really had 50 grams, which carries a sentence of 10-30. Your sentence is 10 years. And consider yourself lucky that the cops violated your Fourth Amendment Rights." May Sally complain — successfully — that the judge considered the illegally seized coke?

(b) Suppose Sally had been charged with 50 grams and there had been no suppression, but the jury had returned a verdict of acquittal on the 40 grams. Could the judge use the 40 grams in assessing Sally's sentence?

3. (a) Lenny was convicted of 40 counts of mail fraud, each count of which carries a five-year maximum term. Lenny swore on the stand that he was totally unaware of any fraud in the thousands of brochures he mailed to particularly vulnerable victims. At the sentencing hearing, the judge, Roy Bean, told Lenny that, while he would normally sentence him to only two years, "You lied on the stand, and that, sir, is perjury." He gave Lenny the full five years on each count, to run concurrently. Has Lenny been deprived of any constitutional right?

(b) Same facts, except that the judge now imposes consecutive sentences on three of the counts, the rest to run concurrently, so that Lenny might now serve 15 years.

4. Bonnie and Clyde rob the First National Bank, a federally insured institution. Each is a first offender; each has a similar background. Bonnie is convicted in state court and sentenced to two years probation. Clyde is convicted in federal court. The federal guidelines call for a 10-year sentence. The trial judge "departs" from the guidelines, announcing that, if anything, Bonnie was more blameworthy than Clyde, and

"concepts of equity, as well as equal protection, forbid these wildly disparate sentences upon similarly situated accomplices." The federal prosecutor appeals the sentence. What result?

5. Section 101 of the relevant penal code provides: "It is a felony to possess a controlled dangerous substance" (CDS). Section 102 provides a long list of penalties for violating section 101, depending on the kind of drug involved and the amount possessed. Constantine is indicted for "possessing a controlled dangerous substance." The evidence at the trial shows that he grew marijuana in his backyard. There is substantial dispute about how many pot plants there were. The judge instructs the jury not to consider the amount of marijuana involved. The pre-sentence report, which both Constantine and his lawyer see, concludes that Constantine had 5,000 plants, which, by statute, requires a sentence of 10 years. Had he possessed only one plant, the statute would permit probation. Constantine argues that (a) the type of CDS and (b) the amount should have been submitted to the jury. Is he correct?

6. In a state having an indeterminate sentencing scheme, Antonin is convicted of a crime carrying a 2-30 year sentence. Susan B., the judge, relies upon all the kinds of evidence laid out in examples 1-5 above (assessment of defendant's mental capacity, perjury, illegally obtained evidence, possible other crimes, victim declarations, and acquitted conduct) and gives Antonin the maximum sentence. What now?

7. Leonid was convicted in 2003 of the federal offense of robbing a bank. He had two prior convictions, each for assault, each stemming from separate barroom brawls. The federal sentencing guidelines provided that a career offender's "offense level" must be increased significantly. The trial judge imposed the lowest sentence possible under the career offender guideline, saying "I don't agree with this — you're really not the kind of guy the guidelines had in mind. But you do qualify, and my hands are tied." In 2007, Leonid moves for reconsideration of his sentence. What result?

8. Kadzimir, facing a charge of kidnapping with a maximum sentence of 25 years, was offered a plea bargain of five years, but he went to trial and was convicted. The system is unstructured. At his sentencing, the trial judge says, "You took the court's time, I'll take some of yours. Twenty-five years." Kadzimir asks you whether he has any recourse.

9. Barbarino enters a plea agreement that the prosecutor would advocate for no more than a five-year sentence. At the plea colloquy, the judge said to Barbarino, "I've read the agreement, and this looks likely. Are you ready

to plead?" Barbarino does so. Thereafter, he receives a pre-sentenced report in which John Breitbart is reported as having told the probation officer that Barbarino is one of the mob's most active and dangerous members. At the sentencing hearing, Barbarino declares, "I saw what this rat said, your honor. I'd like to have him here in court to show you what a scumbagging liar he is." The judge denies the request and says, "In light of this evidence, I can't abide by the five-year sentence. Twenty years." "At least let me examine the probation officer." Again, no. What can Barbarino do now?

Explanations

1. (a) As a matter of federal constitutional law, Herb has no right to see any of the pre-sentence report. But virtually every state — and the federal courts — have provided by rule or decision for disclosure of the report generally. However, a judge may deem some information so confidential that she may refuse to disclose it to the defendant. The purpose of the confidentiality pledge is to obtain information now and in future pre-sentence reports. This is solely in the discretion of the judge, and will not be overturned unless the judge has abused that discretion.

    (b) Herb has no *right* to have Delores at the hearing, much less to cross-examine her. The Sixth Amendment confrontation clause only applies at a "criminal prosecution" and, for these purposes, sentencing is not such a proceeding. Nor would due process require either compulsory process or cross-examination. Nor, perhaps more surprisingly, does Herb have a right to have present, or to cross-examine, the probation officer who wrote the report. Although these officers are almost always present during sentencing, they are only rarely subjected to cross-examination. Herb's best path is simply to contest the report, and to persuade the judge that she shouldn't rely on that episode, or on Delores' assessment of him. He might also argue that the story, even if true, is simply irrelevant to both his crime and his possible sentence. But since "everything is relevant" in an individualizing jurisdiction, that argument is unlikely to succeed. And — biggest surprise — although virtually all courts allow the defendant to allocute, there is at least some doubt as to whether it is constitutionally required. See *Hill v. United States*, 368 U.S. 424 (1962); *Specht v. Patterson*, 386 U.S. 605 (1967).

2. (a) There's an easy answer to this one. No. Although the Supreme Court has never held unequivocally that the exclusionary rule of the Fourth Amendment does not apply *at sentencing*, both the lower courts and analogous decisions from the Court itself support this conclusion. E.g., *United*

States v. Brimah, 214 F.3d 854 (7th Cir. 2000); *United States v. Tauil-Hernandez,* 88 F.3d 576 (8th Cir. 1996); *United States v. Montoya-Ortiz,* 7 F.3d 1171, 1181-1182 (5th Cir. 1993). In *United States v. Calandra,* 414 U.S. 338 (1974), the Court held that illegally seized evidence could be admitted and relied upon in grand jury proceedings. If it appears, however, that the police seized the evidence for *the purpose* of influencing sentencing, courts are inclined to preclude its use. *United States v. Kim,* 25 F.3d 1426, 1435 & n.8 (9th Cir. 1994); *State v. Habbena,* 372 N.W.2d 450 (S.D. 1985). On the other hand, confessions obtained in violation of the Fifth Amendment must be suppressed even at a sentencing hearing. *Estelle v. Smith,* 451 U.S. 454 (1981).

(b) Yes. Well, maybe. As noted in the text, in *United States v. Watts,* 519 U.S. 148 (1997), the Court upheld the use, in sentencing, of conduct of which the defendant had been acquitted. The Court explained this conclusion by noting that, while the jury had not found the defendant guilty beyond a reasonable doubt, this did not preclude the trial judge from concluding, by the lower standard of preponderance of the evidence, that the defendant had acted as charged.

3. (a) No. No???!!! How can that be? The judge decided, using some unarticulated standard of proof, that Lenny had committed a crime. There was no cross-examination, no specific chance to rebut that conclusion. Yet no violation of due process, or *Winship,* has occurred because the judge did not sentence Lenny for perjury — he merely used this one conclusion (that Lenny had abused the trial process) as a factor in deciding what the penalty for mail fraud should be. This is simply another variation of *Williams,* which allows the trial judge to rely on any information, while assessing the penalty. The Supreme Court has held this to be perfectly proper. See *United States v. Grayson,* 438 U.S. 41 (1978). Indeed, in *Grayson,* the Court noted that courts had almost without exception concluded that "a defendant's truthfulness or mendacity while testifying . . . is probative of his attitudes toward society and prospects for rehabilitation. . . ." However, in footnote 11 in *Blakely,* Justice Scalia threw significant doubt upon the continued viability of *Grayson,* suggesting that the proper approach was to indict and prosecute such a defendant for perjury.

(b) Most states allow the judge discretion to impose either concurrent or consecutive sentences, but a majority also provide that concurrent sentences are presumed, unless the court finds a specific reason to run the sentences consecutively. A handful of states presume that sentences should be consecutive. See Erin E. Goffette, Sovereignty in Sentencing: Concurrent and Consecutive Sentencing of a Defendant Subject to Simultaneous State and Federal Jurisdiction, 37 Val. U.L.

Rev. 1035, 1050-1051 (2003). But even then, the sentences are not reviewable at all, or only for "abuse of discretion," which is highly unlikely here.

4. Clyde should pack everything he has; he's off to prison for a long time. The federal appellate courts have consistently held that wide disparities between state sentences and federal sentences are not grounds to depart from the federal guidelines. *United States v. Vilchez*, 967 F.2d 1351 (9th Cir. 1992). In part, the courts view the necessity for *intra* jurisdictional uniformity as more important (and more in their control) than *inter* jurisdictional uniformity. In part, as well, these decisions are driven by a respect for the prosecutorial discretion which chose to prosecute Clyde in federal court and leave Bonnie to the state. (See Chapter 3.) After *Gall v. United States*, 552 U.S. 38 (2007), however, this may change. Stay tuned.

5. Yes. Before *Apprendi*, Constantine's argument was rejected by every federal court that confronted it. The "crime," said those courts, was possession of *any* controlled dangerous substance, of *any* amount. After *Apprendi*, however, the courts agreed that, since the maximum sentences were increased depending on the type and amount of drug, those issues would have to be submitted to the jury. Virtually all states had submitted both issues to juries long before *Apprendi*. *Blakely* reaffirms this entire approach. The larger issue focuses on how one decides what the "crime" is. A charge of "assault with a deadly weapon" could be said to be a charge of "assault" only, and that "with a deadly weapon" is not an element of the offense, but a "sentencing factor." Intuitively we reject that analysis because we have become accustomed to "assault with a deadly weapon" as a single "phrase" and hence as a single "offense." It is more difficult to see "possession of 30 grams of cocaine, while acting as a supervisor of a drug trade, and armed with a firearm" as a single "phrase" or "offense," even if each of those added factors adds years to the potential sentence. The crucial question in this area is how to determine which facts must be determined (1) beyond a reasonable doubt, and (2) by the jury. As to this specific statute, the resolution is now clear — both of these facts are jury facts because they increase the potential maximum.

Irrelevant caveat — and a straw in the wind? The wording in the paragraph above (and that of the Supreme Court in both *Apprendi* and *Blakely*) seeks to avoid saying that the type and weight of drug are "elements" of the crime, although that is often the language used by courts. If these are elements of the crime, the next question (not for *this* course, but for substantive criminal law purposes) is whether the government must not only prove them beyond a reasonable doubt, but also show a *mens rea* with regard to these facts (i.e., that the defendant "knew" — or was reckless with regard to — the type or amount of drug he took). Some courts, to avoid this implication, have noted that in *Apprendi* itself, the Court sometimes used the phrase "functional equivalent of an element," in discussing "*Apprendi/Blakely* facts" rather than the phrase "element of the crime."

6. This may be the $64 billion question. Since *Blakely*, many have contended that the states will return to a totally indeterminate sentencing scheme, in which nothing constrains a judge's discretion within wide ranges. (That is to say, nothing requires the judge to find "deliberate cruelty" before sentencing, nor does anything require that, if she finds "deliberate cruelty," she must affect the sentence.) All nine Justices in *Blakely* appeared to assume that, if the states did so, there would be no constitutional impediment to that action, particularly if the state systems did not require a judge to articulate why she imposed the sentence in question. Yet an argument surely can be made that (a) the Constitution requires articulation of the reasons for the sentence — particularly now that structured sentencing systems have demonstrated that it is possible to do so; (b) those reasons should be subject to appellate scrutiny; and (c) once there are articulable grounds for increasing a sentence, they are subject to *Blakely*. That is far in the future (10 years???), but it is something upon which to muse. Happy musing.

7. Although Leonid's application would otherwise be untimely, he relies on the notion that the Supreme Court in *Booker* made the guidelines voluntary and that the court in *Kimbrough* allowed a district court judge to impose a lower sentence because of disagreement with any policy of the guidelines. But *Kimbrough* involved the crack cocaine–cocaine disparity, which both the Sentencing Commission and Congress had considered unduly harsh. The Court expressly made a distinction between the Guidelines' disparate treatment of crack and powder cocaine offenses — where Congress did not direct the Sentencing Commission to create this disparity — and the Guideline's punishment of career offenders, which was explicitly directed by Congress. Because *Kimbrough* highlights this distinction, it is less likely that the Supreme Court would apply *Kimbrough* to the career offender statute. On the other hand, several Circuit courts have so held that trial courts may ignore the career guidelines as well in sentencing (see, e.g., *United States v. Corner*, 698 F.3d 411 (7th Cir. 2009); *United States v. Clay*, 524 F.3d 877, 878-879 (8th Cir. 2008); *United States v. Herrera-Zuniga*, 571 F.3d 568 (6th Cir. 2009); *United States v. Jimenez*, 512 F.3d 1, 9 (1st Cir. 2007)). In at least two cases, the Court has remanded cases where a trial court expressly disagreed with the policy underlying the career offender guidelines. E.g., *Ryals v. United States*, 561 U.S. 1003 (2010). Together, these opinions seem to stand for the proposition that district court

judges are now free to reject any *guideline* with impunity.[56] So if Leonid were being sentenced today, he could argue vociferously for a "departure" from the career guidelines. Timing really is everything.

8. Easy: no. Indeed, See Chapter 7. Indeterminate, wide-range sentence structures allow a court to decide on any sentence for any reason. Were he pressed, the judge would no doubt point to the "trouble and expense" that the trial cost, Kadzimir's apparent lack of remorse (as demonstrated by his going to trial), and the need to deter kidnapping of this particularly heinous sort. (All kidnappings might be characterized as heinous, so this is probably easy to do.)

9. He could seek to vacate his plea, but that would require a demonstration that refusing to do so would constitute "manifest injustice" (see Chapter 7). (Indeed, under the federal system, he would have to seek post-conviction relief.) He can't win a claim about the hearsay that the probation officer reported — the rules of evidence don't apply at sentencing. And he'll also lose a claim of confrontation rights — they don't apply at sentencing either. He might try to argue ineffective counsel, but on the meager facts here, he'll lose as well. Sentencing just isn't a trial, Barbarino.

---

56. Professor Benjamin Priester has argued that these cases suggest that the Court is moving in the direction of holding that judges are constitutionally entitled to disagree not only with commission guidelines, but with legislatively established guidelines. See Apprendi Land Becomes Bizarro World: "Policy Nullifications" and Other Surreal Doctrines in the New Constitutional Law of Sentencing, 51 Santa Clara L. Rev. 1 (2011).

Appeals and Collateral Attack

13

"If at first you don't succeed, try, try again."

"Enough already!!!"

A. A GENERAL OVERVIEW OF REVIEW

Just because Dan has been convicted doesn't mean he'll go gently into that good night. Guilty or not, Dan will certainly want some institution other than the jury (or judge) to determine whether he's been treated fairly. In modern America, Dan has three[1] separate, and very distinct, routes to follow:

- (direct) appeal;
- collateral attack in the state courts;
- federal habeas corpus.

We will discuss these seriatim. But there are some overarching questions that will apply to each of these processes:

1. Why allow review of any decision at all?
2. What should be the scope of review?

_____

1. If Dan has been convicted of a federal crime, the second and third processes merge.

3. What effect should a reversal have (a) upon the party seeking review; and (b) upon other persons?

1. Why Allow Review at All?

It is easy to see why Dan wants review, but what advantages does the state see in allowing him to seek such review? Several benefits may be suggested:

- *A perception of justice.* Others assessing the system might perceive that some method of review, removed from the moment of the events, and therefore not as likely to be consumed by possible prejudice or vengeance, gives Dan (and other citizens) a surer sense of impartiality.
- *Uniform application of the law.* Ensuring that the lower courts are indeed enforcing the laws, both statutory and common law, that apply to the case.
- *A review of the facts.* Particularly if fact finders are viewed warily.
- *Reconsideration of existing law.* An opportunity to assess the principles actually applied in the trial and determine whether those principles should continue to be applied.

In England, there was no review of a trial jury's verdict of guilt. Hanging often occurred *tout de suite* after the verdict. (Remember that felons were not entitled even to retained counsel, so there was no one who could have pursued an appeal, even if one had been provided.) In fact, for most criminal cases, appellate processes came to England only at the end of the nineteenth century. In large part, this was driven by ideology; if the court (King) is always right, there is no need for appeal.

On the other hand, if government is distrusted, or thought to be fallible, appeal becomes appealing. In most of the American colonies, therefore, defendants had a statutory right to appeal their convictions to an "appellate court," which usually meant the state's supreme court; there were few, if any, intermediate appellate state courts prior to the middle of the twentieth century. By the middle of the nineteenth century, appeal was universally available in the states; the federal government adopted appeals in 1879.

Even so, for over a century, the rule has been clear: *There is no federal constitutional right to state appellate review of a criminal conviction. McKane v. Durston,* 153 U.S. 684 (1894). But every state provides statutorily for at least one appeal "as of right," and the Supreme Court has surrounded *that* appeal with several ancillary rights, including the right to appointed (and competent) counsel, and the right to a transcript.

2. What Is the "Scope of Review"?

Although review could be *de novo* — hearing the witnesses again and deciding the case as though no proceeding had occurred below — that virtually never[2] happens in either civil or criminal processes. As students of civil procedure are aware, over the centuries, courts have divided questions below into three categories: (1) purely legal questions; (2) purely factual questions; and (3) "mixed" questions of law and fact. Courts are generally agreed that *purely legal* questions should be assessed *de novo*, because a decision from a higher court will bind all lower courts within the jurisdiction. At the other end of the spectrum, significant (but not total) deference is given to the fact finder concerning *factual* questions, in large part because the resolution often turns on credibility.

The real thorny issue has been "mixed questions." In recent years, the United States Supreme Court, rather than address this question directly, has simply moved toward allowing *de novo* review of issues which previously would have been called "mixed." State supreme courts appear to have pursued the same path.

3. What Remedy? Retroactivity and Finality; Herein of Legal Realism and Other Relevant Irrelevancies

Every judicial decision is influenced by concepts of law (jurisprudence). Often, the influence is unspoken, but in evaluating the question of retroactivity, philosophical questions as to the nature of law leap to the forefront. Until the twentieth century, most lawyers, including law professors, believed (or at least said) that the common law (as opposed to legislatively established law) was "natural," so that judges "found" rather than "made" law. In such a setting, courts would always apply any decision they reached to any person who had been, or could be, affected by application of the "wrong" law. After all, the earlier decisions announcing a different rule had been *wrong* — the law had always been X (as we now discovered) and X should have been applied to every possible case.

In the twentieth century that view was rejected, perhaps most famously by Justice Holmes's aphorism that "The common law is not a brooding omnipresence in the sky." Judges who believe (or recognize) that they "make" law may also determine whether to make the "new" law retroactive. Note the double-edged sword aspect of each perception: Judges who feel

---

2. In many states, a person charged with a petty misdemeanor, or a traffic offense, can opt to be tried first before a magistrate and then may seek *de novo* review in a higher level tribunal. But this is not true for felonies.

duty-bound to apply any "newly discovered" law to all past cases may be highly reluctant to "find" new law, particularly if there are many persons who could legitimately ask to have the new law applied to their already settled cases. On the other hand, judges who believe they "make" new law and are therefore not *required* to give it retroactive effect may be more willing to "craft" new rules for future application.

A court seeking to determine the impact of its "new rule" may take any one of at least the following possible paths:

1. *Total non-retroactivity.* Apply it only to defendants who are tried after the announcement of the rule; do not apply it even to the defendant who obtained the "new rule";

2. *Almost total non-retroactivity.* Apply it only to the specific defendant whose case resulted in the new rule (and those in the future);

3. *Pipeline or partial retroactivity.* Apply it to all defendants who, while tried under the "old" rule, have still not had their judgments of convictions affirmed by an appellate court;

4. *Total retroactivity.* Apply it to all defendants who, while tried and convicted under the old rule, are still in some way being affected by that conviction, and are in that sense, injured.

The first of these approaches implicitly asserts that the primary, and, perhaps, the only, function of appellate review is to announce new rules, and not to assure the fairest trials for earlier defendants. So long as the trial courts accurately applied the "old" rule, the conviction stands, because that trial was "fair" as "fair" was then defined and understood. But this approach would probably discourage defendants from appealing; while their dedication to truth and justice might be very strong, the knowledge that even a new rule would not accrue to them personally might dissuade them from appealing, and the law might then stagnate.

The second approach provides a "finder's fee" for the defendant whose attorney was sufficiently persuasive to convince the court to jettison an old rule and adopt a new one. This approach encourages defense counsel to argue for new rules. But, assuming either that judges "look" for opportunities to change rules, or that all lawyers on appeal would be equally persuasive, this approach seems too random, particularly where an appellate court has discretion to take any case, and simply "opts" to choose one of 10 cases raising the same legal question.

Therefore, the third approach, applying the rule to everyone in the pipeline and who "could" have been the engine of the new rule, appears sensible and more equitable.

If the third approach makes sense, then the fourth approach seems even fairer. Suppose, for example, an appellate court (or the United States Supreme Court) decides that due process requires that prosecutors open their files (subject to confidentiality and other such concerns) to defendants. Not only prisoners who are in the pipeline, but all those languishing in prison (including those whose convictions became final one day before the announcement of the "new rule") have suffered the same deprivation. How can the right to due process depend on which day one's conviction became "final"?

Those who support limited retroactivity argue that whether anyone (including the defendant whose appeal resulted in the new rule) was deprived of a fair trial depends on how one defines the term. Dan, and all others, by hypothesis, received what, at the time of their trial, was considered due process (or equal protection, etc.). If the purpose of review is solely to assure whether lower courts were following "the law" (statute or rule, state or federal constitution), they were — and that should be the end of that. But if the purpose is to assure an "accurate" verdict, then *perhaps* review should be allowed. The resolution of that question, discussed in more detail below, might rest on the degree to which the old process might have unfairly affected what would have been considered a fair trial.

At this point the state's interest in finality becomes even more relevant than it was in determining the timing of review in the first instance. Applying a "new" rule to *everyone* who might be affected, including the thousands of prisoners currently incarcerated (and possibly thousands more who, while no longer in prison, are suffering "collateral consequences" of their convictions), would raise the risk that the state might be inundated with new trials. And since this approach might cover persons convicted decades earlier, the state may be unable to provide a new trial, and a defendant who actually may be guilty, and who was provided a fair trial as that term was defined at the time of the proceeding, will be unconditionally freed. Some would call this a "windfall" to such defendants, and the damage to the state (and its citizenry) might be extensive.

Moreover, there is simply an interest in finality in and of itself ("If I've told you once, I've told you a hundred times. Don't ask again"). The state, and its citizens, must also, at some point, enjoy the protection of repose. There is also the crass, but not totally irrelevant, question of administrability and costs; assuming that the new trial would come to the "right" conclusion, should economic considerations matter? Finally, if full retroactivity were embraced, "new rules" could be applied *ad infinitum*; finality would never be assured, even decades after a conviction had been "settled."

Each of these concerns will be present in every step of any review process. Never lose sight of these overarching questions. They will appear and reappear in slightly different guises, but they will always be there.

If there was error in the court below, the typical remedy is a retrial of the defendant, unless that is precluded by the Double Jeopardy Clause. As a general rule, a reversal of the conviction does not signify that the defendant was not guilty, only that there was a flaw in the process by which he was found guilty. A new trial, where that error does not occur, may well result in another conviction. This is also true if the appellate court concludes that, weighing the prosecution's case against the defendants, the conviction was "against the weight of the evidence." If, however, the grounds upon which the conviction is reversed is that there was insufficient evidence to convict (i.e., that the government did not even make out a *prima facie* case), then retrial is barred.

When the United States Supreme Court, in the 1960s, began enlarging the scope of constitutional rights of defendants, it initially tried each of these approaches—some rules were said to be totally retroactive, while others would only be prospective (except that they would include the defendant who had actually won the case announcing the new rule). *Linkletter v. Walker*, 381 U.S. 618 (1965). Confusion ensued. In *Griffith v. Kentucky*, 479 U.S. 314 (1987), the Court cut the Gordian knot and adopted the "pipeline" approach to retroactivity. Most states have the same rule.

B. APPEALS

> Errors are the insects in the world of law, traveling through it in swarms, often unnoticed in their endless procession. Many are plainly harmless; some appear ominously harmful. Some, for all the benign appearance of their spindly traces, mark the way for a plague of followers that deplete trials of fairness.
>
> Judge Roger Traynor, *The Riddle of Harmless Error*

1. Plain Error—The "Contemporaneous Objection" Rule

If an error occurs at trial, but no one notices, is it error? This is not a deep philosophical question, but an intensely practical one. As the quotation from Judge Traynor suggests, errors, big and little, permeate trials as well as pre-trial proceedings—not because lawyers, or jurors, or witnesses are malevolent, but because they are human, and the law is often complex.

One method of reducing the number of errors, and therefore the appealable issues, is to be sure that the trial court has had an opportunity to correct any mistakes.[3] Thus, in earlier times, appellate courts generally required that

---

3. Another method is to restrict the remedy. While England applied the "Exchequer" rule—that any error, no matter how small, would require reversal (and no new trial)—American courts did not apply such a rule, both (a) finding some errors not to require reversal at all; and (b) allowing subsequent proceedings if reversal was required. (See Chapter 9 for a discussion of the double jeopardy issues.)

the defendant make a "contemporaneous objection" to any purported error; failure to raise the objection waived the right to appeal the ruling.[4]

This doctrine, however, was seen as excessively harsh. While it is lawyers, prosecutors, judges, and defense counsel who make such errors, defendants pay the ultimate price — conviction and punishment. Courts therefore adopted the concept of "plain error" to ameliorate the rigidity of the "contemporaneous objection" rule. The heart of a "plain error" rule is that if the error was *really* significant, the appellate court may reverse the conviction notwithstanding the absence of a contemporaneous objection. The federal approach is typical.[5] In *United States v. Olano*, 507 U.S. 725 (1995), the Court announced that a federal appellate court would have to find four criteria before reversing on the basis of an unobjected-to error:

1. there must be error;
2. the error must be plain;
3. the error must affect the substantial rights of the defendant;
4. failure to correct the error could bring the criminal justice system (especially the courts) into disrepute.

The first criterion clearly goes to verdict accuracy. The second appears to be concerned with monitoring trial courts. But in *Olano*, the Court explained that the "plainness" of the rule is assessed not at the time of trial, but at the time of appeal. Thus, even if the trial court (and the lawyers) were following the law as it applied at the time, *Olano* allows reversal if, in the interim, a higher court has determined that the process of which the appellant complains has now been determined to be illegal. The focus is on the fairness and accuracy of the conviction, rather than on monitoring trial courts.

The third prong of the "plain error" rule is concerned primarily with the effect of a violation of the legal rules. The prosecutor's failure to turn over a police report may violate state discovery rules, but it may not be clear that,

---

4. This rule also prevents "sandbagging" — when a defense lawyer, believing that an error has been made, sits silently, hoping that his client will be acquitted (in which case the error has done him no harm) but also hoping that the appellate court will reverse on the basis of the error. The degree to which courts are concerned about sandbagging is reflected by the "plain error" rules.

5. Some states, however, use a broader mix of factors: "[I]n deciding whether to exercise its discretion to consider an error of law apparent on the face of the record, among the factors that a court may consider are: the competing interests of the parties; the nature of the case; the gravity of the error; the ends of justice in the particular case; how the error came to the court's attention; and whether the policies behind the general rule requiring preservation of error have been served in the case in another way, i.e., whether the trial court was, in some manner, presented with both sides of the issue and given an opportunity to correct any error. Those factors do not comprise a necessary or complete checklist; they merely are some of the permissible considerations." *Ailes v. Portland Meadows, Inc.*, 312 Or. 376, 382 n.6, 823 P.2d 956 (1991).

either in the abstract or the specific case, the defendant actually suffered harm. On the other hand, failure to turn over *Brady* material, or striking all minority venire members (even if not objected to) may so undermine the values of a fair trial that remedy is required. In *United States v. Marcus*, 560 U.S. 258 (2010), the Court rejected the notion that "any possibility" of prejudice was too low a standard; a "tiny risk" of prejudice, said the court, was insufficient to meet the *Olano* standard.

If the defendant's substantive rights were impinged, some would argue that reversal should be automatic. But remember that we are discussing errors *to which the defense counsel did not object*. In that context, the fourth prong asks an institutional question, that is, whether the trial court's failure to notice the error was so egregious that appellate failure to upbraid the trial court would weaken the "public reputation of judicial proceedings." In the end, the fourth prong usually turns on whether there is "overwhelming" evidence that the defendant is guilty — the "guilty as sin" rule. Perhaps this reflects the understanding that reversing the conviction of a person who is "obviously" guilty would taint the reputation of the courts more than failing to chastise the trial court for allowing an error which affected that defendant's "substantial rights."

Because the defendant did not object to the error at trial, and thereby helped "create" the error, most appellate courts have placed upon the defendant the burden of meeting each of the four prongs of the "plain error" rule. But see *State v. Ramey*, 721 N.W.2d 294 (Minn. 2006) (once defendant shows plain error, prosecutor must prove no prejudice).

2. "Harmless" Error

Even in the "harmless" error context where the defense counsel has objected at trial,[6] the federal courts as well as most state courts, distinguish between mistakes of (federal) constitutional law and all other law (state constitutions, statutes, court rules, etc.) for the purpose of determining what standard to apply in assessing error.

a. Non-Constitutional Mistakes

Where the defendant *has* objected, and the trial court has nevertheless committed error, albeit one that does not violate the United States Constitution, the equities are significantly different, and most states now place the burden upon the state, not the defendant, to show that the error did not cause

---

6. See Annotation, What Constitutes Harmless or Plain Error Under Rule 52 of the Federal Rules of Criminal Procedure — Supreme Court Cases, 157 A.L.R. Fed. 521.

substantial harm. Courts have used terms such as "miscarriage of justice," which suggests a concern with the accuracy of the verdict, rather than solely with the fairness of the process.[7] Some courts distinguish between "structural" and "nonstructural" non-constitutional errors (for example, a wrong instruction to the jury), asking whether the defendant was denied a substantive right. If the non-constitutional error is characterized as a "trial error" (for example, a ruling on admissibility of evidence), the miscarriage-of-justice language is more frequently employed.[8]

On the other hand, it is certainly tempting to ignore, or severely discount, an error, even a large one, where the *"other"* evidence of the defendant's guilt appears irrefutable. In *Kotteakos v. United States*, 328 U.S. 750 (1946), the Supreme Court held that an error is harmless unless it "had substantial and injurious effect or influence in determining the jury's verdict." This has been seen as a very rigorous test for defendants to overcome.

Many state courts follow a similar approach. Even failure to follow Rule 11 in accepting a guilty plea (see Chapter 7) is subject to the harmless error analysis, *United States v. Bonn*, 535 U.S. 44 (2002), though a failure to obtain the critical information, or to provide the requisite warnings, would almost surely be harmful.

b. Constitutional Errors

The *Kotteakos* approach applies in federal cases (and in many state courts) so long as the violation is "merely" one involving a statute, rule, or common law doctrine. If the error violates the United States Constitution, the *standard* is raised significantly. Prior to 1967, the federal courts consistently held that *any* violation of *any* constitutional provision resulted in automatic, *per se*, reversal. No constitutional error could be "harmless." But such a rule, much like the Exchequer's rule (see n.3 above) had the effect of dissuading courts from articulating new constitutional doctrines. A court, such as the Warren Supreme Court, willing to establish new constitutional protections, could not ignore the pressures of the Exchequer rule's tension. Thus, in *Chapman v. California*, 386 U.S. 18 (1967), the Court held that while a prosecutor's comment, during summation, on the defendant's failure to testify violated the defendant's Fifth Amendment right against self-incrimination, reversal was not required if the prosecutor demonstrated that the error was "harmless" "beyond a reasonable doubt." This sea change in assessing constitutional error has been called "the most far-reaching doctrinal change

---

7. Cf. the discussion of *Strickland v. Washington*, 466 U.S. 668 (1984), Chapter 10.

8. Commentators have not been kind to the harmless error rule. Bennett Gershman, The New Prosecutors, 53 U. Pitt. L. Rev. 393, 425 (1992) has called it a "jurisprudential fiasco," and Harvey Weissbard has argued that "No more pernicious doctrine has infected the legal system in the past century . . ." The Harm in Harmless Error, 195 N.J.L.J., March 2, 2009, p.19.

in American procedural jurisprudence since its inception." Childress and Davis, Federal Standards of Review, §7.01 (2d ed. 1986).

But, as it turns out, not all constitutional errors are equal. While most constitutional errors are now subject to *Chapman* analysis, some constitutional errors (such as the total absence of counsel) simply result in immediate reversal. As the Court explained in *Arizona v. Fulminante*, 499 U.S. 279 (1991), these errors "deprive defendants of basic protections without which a criminal trial cannot reliably serve its function as a vehicle for determination of guilt or innocence." In these cases, there is an irrebuttable presumption of harm.

How, then, does one distinguish between those constitutional errors which require reversal (*per se* errors, in which the prejudice is irrebuttably presumed) and those which merely allow, but do not require, reversal? The Court has listed the following as requiring automatic reversal:

- biased judge;
- denial of a speedy trial;
- racial discrimination in the selection of the grand or petit jury;
- denial of consultation between defendant and his counsel;
- denial of a public trial, including voir dire;
- erroneous reasonable doubt instructions;
- denial of the right to self-representation;
- denial of counsel entirely;
- denial of retained counsel of one's choice (absent a finding of conflict).

In at least two instances, the Court has reversed without expressly deciding whether reversal would be automatic — where defendant was forced to wear prison garb at trial and where the trial court refused to ask prospective jurors about their racial bias.

The Court has found most constitutional errors are subject to the harmless error analysis, including:

- admission of evidence obtained in violation of the Fourth Amendment;
- admission of evidence obtained in violation of the defendant's right to counsel;
- admission of an out-of-court statement in violation of the confrontation clause;
- a jury instruction containing an unconstitutional rebuttable presumption;
- *Blakely* errors (see Chapter 12);
- most sentencing errors;
- prosecutorial breach of a plea bargain;

- failure of indictment to include an *"Apprendi* element"
- submission of an invalid aggravating factor to a capital sentencing jury;
- a misdescription of an element of the offense;
- violations of the confrontation clause;
- violations of the Sixth Amendment right to have a jury determine all the facts upon which a sentence can be predicated.

In *Fulminante v. Arizona*, 499 U.S. 279 (1991), the Court suggested that the line between these groups of errors could be seen as involving, on the one hand, trial errors which could, in some metaphysical sense, be "quantified" and measured against the other evidence in the case and, on the other hand, indeterminate, structural errors whose impact could not be easily assessed, and which had a pervasive influence on the entire trial. The Court has also spoken of errors which affect the "framework" of the trial versus those which simply occur "during" trial. In its most recent statement in this regard, the Court has identified three grounds, apparently separate, for determining if a constitutional error is structural: (1) the process is rendered fundamentally unfair; (2) it is difficult to assess the effect of the error; (3) the "irrelevance of harmlessness." *United States v. Gonzalez-Lopez*, 548 U.S. 489, n.4 (2006). Thus, in *Williams v. Pennsylvania*, 136 S.Ct. 1899 (2016), the Court, applying these three grounds, held that the participation of an appellate judge in a death penalty appeal after he had given his official approval to seek the death penalty against the defendant as a prosecutor was a violation of due process and was "not amendable to harmless-error review regardless of whether the judge's vote was dispositive." Id. at 1909. According to the Court, there was no way to determine the impact that the judge might have had on his colleagues during their deliberations about the case since these deliberations are secret and protected from disclosure.

The distinction drawn by *Fulminante* is remarkably similar to the approach taken by state courts assessing non-constitutional trial errors. Even if, as critics of *Chapman-Fulminante* argue,[9] it is difficult to assess the actual damage which *any* error, no matter how "trivial," might have in actual jury deliberations, a return to the Exchequer rule is not only unrealistic but counterproductive. As unsatisfying as current law may be on where to draw the line between errors that require automatic reversal and those that allow a weighing of the facts (and law) adduced at trial, it is probably inevitable that that line will be drawn somewhere. See Steven M. Shepard, The Case Against Automatic Reversal of Structural Errors, 117 Yale L.J. 1180 (2008).

The Supreme Court has not been extremely clear as to how one measures the "harmlessness" of a constitutional error. Some decisions appear to

---

9. *Chapman v. California*, 386 U.S. 18 (1967).

focus on the possible impact of the error on the trial, and determine whether the error might have "contributed" to the conviction (even looking at the other evidence in the trial), while other opinions speak of assessing the degree of harm which the constitutional error wreaked in light of the "overwhelming" (or less than overwhelming) evidence of guilt. The profusion of standards for assessing the degree of harm necessary in plain versus harmless error cases, and distinguishing direct appeal from collateral review, may be overnice. In *United States v. Benitez*, 542 U.S. 74, 86-87 (2004), Justice Scalia, concurring, observed that "By my count, this Court has adopted no fewer than four assertedly different standards of probability relating to the assessment of whether the outcome of trial *would* have been different if error had not occurred, or if omitted evidence had been included. . . . Such an enterprise is not fact finding, but closer to divination." (Emphasis in original.) Indeed, Justice Souter, in the same decision, noted that even the United States Courts of Appeal appeared to confuse the tests, and when to apply them. 542 U.S. 74 n.8.

Table 13.1 summarizes these rules:

13.1   Direct Appeal

	Not Objected To (Plain)	Objected To (Harmless)		
		Non-Constitutional	Constitutional Structural	Trial
Burden of Proof	Defendant Carries	Prosecutor Carries (by Preponderance)	Prosecutor Loses, Automatic Reversal	Prosecutor Carries Burden
Standard of Proof	Miscarriage of Justice; Varied	Likely to Produce Guilt; Tendency to Produce Guilt		BRD Did Not Contribute to Verdict

Examples

1. When Curtis was indicted for unlawful possession of a weapon, he was given *Miranda* warnings, but nothing more. At trial, he unsuccessfully objected to the admissibility of the confession he gave immediately after those warnings. While his case was pending on appeal, the state supreme court in another case (*Sanchez*) determined, as a matter of state, not federal, constitutional law that any interrogation outside the presence

of counsel after a defendant had been indicted was invalid. May Curtis take advantage of the intervening *Sanchez* decision to have his conviction reversed?

2. In Alan's trial for murder, he raised self-defense. The trial judge instructed the jury that Alan carried the burden of proof that the killing occurred in self-defense. He did not instruct the jury on the standard of proof on that particular issue. State law actually requires the prosecution to carry the burden of proof once the defendant "adequately" raises the issue (meets the burden of production). What result on appeal if (a) Alan's counsel did not object or (b) if Alan's counsel did object?

3. Dimitrius, convicted of bribery involving $3,000, is sent to prison while his appeal is taken to the state supreme court. His cellmate, Ivanovich, was convicted of bribery involving $500 three years ago. One day, Dimitrius tells Ivanovich that he's appealing on the ground that, under the state statutory scheme, only bribes of more than $5,000 should be considered felonies (and hence punishable by a sentence to prison). Ivanovich grins. "I tried that two years ago, but the state supreme court told me to pound sand. Lots of luck. I've still got four years in here." The next day, Alexander (a jailhouse lawyer) runs into their cell, exclaiming: "The state supreme court has just held that bribery under $5,000 isn't punishable as a felony." Who's grinning now?

4. At Diesel's trial for robbing a convenience store, the clerk, Clark, identified him as the culprit. The prosecution also introduced a video tape showing Diesel taking the money. After trial, Diesel's attorney discovers that the prosecutor promised Clark he would drop two pending (unrelated) charges against Clark if he testified truthfully. Reversible error?

Explanations

1. Yes. First, Curtis is "in the pipeline" — if the new *Sanchez* rule is to apply to anyone beyond *Sanchez*, it should reach Curtis as well. Most courts agree that the decision should be given retroactive effect. *Griffith v. Kentucky*, 479 U.S. 314 (1987); *State v. Waters*, 296 Mont. 101, 987 P.2d 1142 (Mont. 1999). Other state courts, applying an approach previously endorsed in *Linkletter v. Walker*, 381 U.S. 618 (1965), use various factors, but they generally include: (1) the purpose of the rule; (2) the degree of reliance placed on the old rule by those who administered it; (3) the effect a retroactive application would have on the administration of justice. Under this approach, the purpose of the *Sanchez* rule is to assure reliable confessions, but also to discourage police interrogation of indicted, unrepresented defendants. As to the second and third prongs, police

policy, even before *Sanchez*, actively discouraged interrogations of an *indicted* defendant in the absence of counsel. Thus, police had not in fact relied upon a prior, more generous interrogation rule, which also meant that there would unlikely be a sea of cases currently pending that would require retrial if *Sanchez* was made retroactive. *State v. Knight*, 145 N.J. 233, 678 A.2d 642 (1996).

2. (a) In both instances, Alan is likely to prevail, although the analysis is likely to be differently articulated. Where there was no objection, the analysis will be done under the "plain error" rule. Here, there is no question but that there was error, and it was plain. Moreover, it obviously affected Alan's rights. Note, however, the issue is not one of federal constitutional right; the Supreme Court has decided that the state may put the burden of proving self-defense on the defendant. The remaining question under *Olano*, which some state courts do not undertake, is whether the failure to correct this plain error would cast the judiciary (both trial and appellate) in a poor light. Since the law (by hypothesis) was clear at the time of the trial, and dramatically shifted the burden of proof, the answer is almost surely yes.

(b) Absolutely. Since counsel objected, the court employs the "harmless error" rather than the "plain error" approach. Here, the state must prove beyond a reasonable doubt that the error had no impact on the jury. While many errors in jury instructions may not be so severe, this one surely is. Unless there was absolutely no evidence beyond Alan's protestation, and (as well) substantial evidence that the victim was not aggressive, etc., the likelihood that the error was manifestly harmless would be virtually infinitesimal.

3. Only Dimitrius. He's still "in the pipeline," and can use the new decision. But Ivanovich is stuck, at least in terms of appeals. As we will discuss in the next sections, he may find relief on collateral attack, on the ground of a "new rule" that his class of conduct is no longer a crime (or at least not a felony). The example demonstrates the fine (and arbitrary) line that the pipeline rule establishes. Drawing bright lines makes decisions easier — but there is always someone "just on the other side" of the line. While Dimitrius walks, Ivanovich, who under this hypo arguably committed a "less serious" crime (because less money was involved), will be fortunate indeed if he is released before his four years are up. In a parole system, of course, it is possible — though not necessary — that the parole board might consider the apparent inequities here. On the other hand, when Ivanovich committed his bribe, he "knew" (or should have known) that he was risking a very long prison sentence, since that's what the statute promised.

4. No. You may read (even in court opinions) that *Brady* (and *Strickland*) errors require automatic reversal. But that is only because they incorporate a requirement of prejudice in their *prima facie* criteria. Thus, no matter which way you analyze this, there is no reversible error. First, under *Brady*, even if the prosecutor had to disclose the potentially impeaching promises, there was no "substantial prejudice," given the video. Thus, under that approach, there is no constitutional error to begin with. But even assuming that there was error, it was not "harmful" because Diesel's guilt is overwhelmingly demonstrated by the tape.

C. COLLATERAL ATTACK

Once Dan has unsuccessfully gone through the state's appellate procedure, he may still pursue "collateral" remedies, either because of what occurred during trial, or what he has discovered since. For example, suppose that Dan learns that (a) his counsel (contrary to Dan's explicit instructions) did not interview any of the witnesses about which Dan told him, did not research the law, and was unaware that the search that led to the incriminating gun was palpably illegal; (b) Gulliver, an inmate in another state, has confessed to the crime for which Dan was convicted; (c) Esteban, the prosecutor, now admits suppressing certain evidence from Dan's trial, some of which was arguably covered by *Brady*, some of which was required to be disclosed by state statute or court rule; and (d) the state supreme court, shortly after Dan's appeal was final, changed its mind about an issue which he had raised and on which he had lost.

1. State Collateral Review

Prior to the middle of the twentieth century, Dan would have been unable to raise almost any of these claims in most states (and in federal tribunals as well, but let's take one step at a time). Final was final was final. One bite at the apple (appeal) was all that was allowed. In the mid-1960s, however, the United States Supreme Court seemed poised to consider whether the Constitution required the states to provide "collateral processes,"[10] by which a prisoner

---

10. *Case v. Nebraska*, 381 U.S. 336 (1965). Such a holding, of course, would have been stunning in light of the view that the Constitution did not require even direct appellate processes. But all states provided those processes, while many did not have collateral attack mechanisms in place even as late as 1965. See D. Wilkes, Federal and State Postconviction Remedies and Relief 216 (1983). Indeed, the Court has since declared, in dictum, that the Constitution imposes no such duty upon the states. See *United States v. MacCollum*, 426 U.S. 317 (1976). See also *Felker v. Turpin*, 518 U.S. 651 (1996).

who had already lost his state appeals could nevertheless attack his conviction on at least federal constitution grounds. Before the Court could reach that point, however, the case was mooted; since then, fearing the handwriting on the wall, the states have responded by establishing such procedures.

As with appeals, most collateral relief statutes establish some procedural barriers before the claim may even be considered. Typically:

1. a prisoner may not raise a claim which was already adjudicated during the appeals process;
2. the claim must be filed within a specified time period after the occurrence of a specific event (such as the entry of final judgment by the state's highest appellate court, or a denial of certiorari from the United States Supreme Court)[11] unless the delay is excused;
3. a claim must be "new," which means that the claim:
   (a) could not have been raised on appeal; or
   (b) could have been raised on appeal, but was not, due to an "excusable" failure.
   (c) Parallel to the "contemporaneous objection" rule at trial, the failure to raise an issue on direct appeal will usually preclude a prisoner from raising that issue during collateral attack, for reasons similar to those on appeal: (1) the desire to bring all claims to the attention of a single court at one time, reflecting a fear that prisoners would continue to raise issues seriatim simply to exhaust the process; and (2) the concern that prisoners would wait until proof had dissipated in the hope that the state would face significant difficulties in retrying the case.

But some failures to raise an issue may be beyond the control of the defendant. As with the "plain error" doctrine of appeal, there is concern that a defendant should not be penalized because her attorney was negligent (or worse). Thus, some failures to raise issues on appeal may be excused.

The most obvious of these is a claim of ineffective assistance of (trial) counsel. In most instances, trial counsel also handles the original appeal. Because it is unlikely that the attorney will raise her own negligence as an issue for consideration by the court of appeals, states generally allow a prisoner to raise this issue on collateral attack.[12] Moreover, the trial record is unlikely to contain all the facts necessary to assess the efforts of trial

---

11. E.g., Nev. Rev. Stat. §34.726 (setting the time to file to "within one year of the decision of the state supreme court . . . unless good cause is shown for delay").
12. One writer, noting that several years usually pass between a conviction and the defendant's collateral attack, has urged that new counsel be appointed to pursue the appeal and that the record be opened to obtain possible evidence of ineffectiveness before the evidence becomes stale. Eve Brensike Primus, *Structural Reform in Criminal Defense: Relocating Ineffective Assistance of Counsel Claims*, 92 Cornell L. Rev. 679 (2007).

counsel. See *Trevino v. Thaler*, 133 S.Ct. 1911, 1921 (2013). Indeed, in a parallel case involving a federal prisoner, the court held that even if a defendant "could" raise a claim of ineffective assistance on direct appeal, if he did not he would not be precluded from raising the issue on collateral attack. *Massaro v. United States*, 538 U.S. 500 (2003).

Even if Dan's counsel was not so poor as to be "inadequate," in some states his counsel's failure to raise a specific issue may be excused, and he may be allowed to raise that issue on collateral attack. In determining whether to allow the issue to be raised, state courts have applied several different approaches, but the most common are the *deliberate bypass* rule and the *cause and prejudice* rule. Each of these tests originated in United States Supreme Court decisions on federal habeas corpus. The deliberate bypass rule, enunciated in *Fay v. Noia*, 372 U.S. 391 (1963), held that a prisoner should not be precluded from raising a complaint which his counsel had failed to raise on appeal unless the defendant had *personally* agreed to the attorney's decision. The rule was premised on the view that attorneys often make decisions without consulting the client, but that the client pays the price if the decision is incorrect. The Fay Court analyzed the decision not to pursue a particular issue as a "waiver" of that issue, which had to be done personally by the defendant in a knowing and intelligent way. The Fay rule, however, was shortlived. It was overturned only 14 years later in *Wainwright v. Sykes*, 433 U.S. 72 (1977). *Sykes* declared that the Fay rule had proved unworkable because it was impossible to determine whether a defendant had been informed of, and, if informed of, understood, the nuances of foregoing a particular legal challenge. The Court there adopted a new standard that the petitioner carried the burden of demonstrating a *cause* for her counsel's failure at trial, and of showing actual *prejudice*.[13] Virtually all states have now abandoned the "deliberate bypass" approach, and moved in the direction of (if not actually adopting) the much stricter *Sykes* test. See, e.g., *Younger v. State*, 580 A.2d 552 (Del. 1990). Several state statutes or rules speak of counsel's "reasonable" or "due" diligence. E.g., Colo. Rev. Stat. §16-12-206(1)(c); Idaho Code §19-4901.

Measuring Dan's claims under the "cause and prejudice" standard, or even under the "due diligence" approach, will be tricky. His claim of new evidence in (b) above, even a confession such as Gulliver's, will face difficult times. First, a defendant's failure to discover the "newly discovered" evidence, if not due to ineffective counsel, may not be excusable. Gulliver, after all, might have been a witness known to Dan, or Dan's counsel, or discoverable through a more thorough investigation (we're back to ineffectiveness now). Even if that were not true, the "new" evidence may not be subject to real testing, either because it is stale, or for some other reason.

---

13. Compare this rule to that of the *Strickland* case, discussed in Chapter 11.

Herrera v. Collins, 506 U.S. 390 (1993). Even where claims of new evidence are allowed and considered, the defendant carries an extremely heavy burden of demonstrating a reasonable excuse for not discovering the evidence earlier.

Dan's complaint about Esteban's discovery violations in (c) above, whether based on state law or on *Brady*, raises similar questions of cause and staleness. It may be years before these violations come to light, and it may be extremely difficult for Dan to show actual prejudice from those violations. But he may raise these issues on collateral attack, assuming that he can show a "cause" for not having learned of the violations earlier.

Claims that the law, whether statutory, court rule, or constitutional (state or federal), was violated are generally cognizable on collateral review, particularly where the evidence supporting them was not available at the time of trial or appeal. Thus, Dan's complaint in (d) above, that the law has changed since he was convicted, raises both the problem of *retroactivity* and the issue of *cause*. In our discussion of retroactivity, we noted that most states apply new interpretations to those "in the pipeline"; but that was defined as those whose convictions had not been affirmed by the state's highest court of appeal. Under that definition, Dan is out of time, and luck. The bite of those rules on retroactivity now becomes apparent. Assuming that Dan's trial was fair as "fair" was defined at the time of his trial, the need for finality appears to outweigh the concern that Dan's trial might have been "unfair" (as we *now* define unfairness). Here, more than in any of the other claims, the question comes down to the purpose of allowing collateral review. If it is to monitor erring trial (or appellate) courts, these courts were not errant in their application of the then extant law. If, on the other hand, the concern is with the accuracy and fairness of the proceedings as we now understand fairness, Dan *may* have a claim. Remember that it was for that reason that even under the "plain error" rule, the "plainness" of the error was assessed by the law at the time of the appeal, rather than at the time of the trial. If that same approach were taken here, all prisoners who would benefit by the new rule would be entitled to at least raise the issue on collateral review. The tension between fairness and efficiency, between justice and administrative feasibility, is manifest.

But it's not over yet. Dan must still demonstrate that his counsel's failure to anticipate the new rule was itself not a lack of "due diligence." Here, the state collateral relief court will review the precedents upon which the appellate court announced the "new rule," and ascertain whether a diligent counsel would have *anticipated* the new rule. If so, the failure to raise the legal issue at the original trial will mean that Dan could not avail himself of the new rule even if it were otherwise given retroactive effect to prisoners like him.

If Dan convinces the state collateral relief court that his claims are not barred by procedural lapses, the court will assess the claims on their merits. As to some claims, the already existing trial record will be sufficient for resolution. But as to other claims, particularly an ineffective assistance of counsel claim, that record will have to be supplemented, which may, in turn, necessitate a hearing.

Of course, simply because the state collateral relief court will listen to Dan's complaint(s) does not mean that he will succeed. The court may also conclude that the new evidence is either unbelievable, or, even if believed, is insufficient to warrant relief. On all claims, Dan will carry the burden of persuasion. For example, as we saw in Chapter 10, his claim of ineffective counsel, at least under *Strickland*, will require him to prove both ineffective performance and "prejudice," and the *Brady* claim will confront the latter test as well. In short, once his conviction and appeal are final, Dan has a very long road ahead of him.

2. Federal Habeas Corpus

Hope springs eternal. Even if Dan has unsuccessfully pursued his appeal through both the intermediate appellate court and the state supreme court, and tried collateral review in the state courts, he won't give up. One last opportunity remains — federal review, in the form of a writ of "habeas corpus." Here, however, the prisoner may only raise claims that the proceedings in state court violated his *federal constitutional rights*; decisions on state law matters are solely within the state courts' jurisdiction. *Coleman v. Thompson* 501 U.S. 722 (1991); *Warthout v. Cooke*, 562 U.S. 216 (2011).

a. A (Very) Short History of the "Great Writ" of Habeas Corpus
i. Generally

The "Great Writ" of habeas corpus originated with the Magna Carta. Ever since, it has been seen as preventing the abuse of royal authority and protecting the freedoms of subjects. In *Bushell's Case*, discussed in Chapter 8, the jurors invoked habeas corpus, pled their case, and were released, thus establishing the right of the jury to nullify. When President Thomas Jefferson tried to prevent those charged, along with Aaron Burr, for conspiracy to commit treason, from using the writ of habeas corpus, he failed. During the Civil War, President Lincoln suspended the writ, but Chief Justice Taney issued an order stating that only Congress could suspend the writ. More recently, the United States Supreme Court held that prisoners in Guantanamo Bay, Cuba, could file in federal court for habeas corpus (*Hamdi v. Rumsfeld*, 542 U.S. 507 (2004); *Rasul v. Bush*, 542 U.S. 466 (2004); *Hamdan v. Rumsfeld*, 548 U.S. 557 (2006)) because there was no clear unequivocal declaration by Congress that the writ was *not* available to them. In the *Hamdi* case, the Court explicitly referred to the historical roots of the writ:

"Executive imprisonment has been considered oppressive and lawless since John, at Runnymede, pledged that no free man should be imprisoned, dispossessed, outlawed, or exiled except by the judgment of his peers or by the law of the land. The judges of England developed the writ of habeas corpus largely to preserve these immunities from executive restraint." That view was echoed in *Rasul*: "Habeas corpus is . . . a writ antecedent to statute . . . throwing its roots deep in to the genius of our common law."

The (apparently) final word was written in *Boumedienne v. Bush*, 553 U.S. 723 (2008). Congress had precluded habeas corpus applications by prisoners in Guantanamo, providing instead another process by which they could have determinations of the Military Commission reviewed. The Court struck this statute as an unconstitutional suspension of the writ, holding that essential to habeas corpus was the ability to bring to the attention of a reviewing court evidence not allowed by, or discovered after the decision of, the trial court.

As a doctrinal matter the Guantanamo cases are not immediately relevant for this book, because even if the "writ" is being suspended, it is not being suspended in "criminal" prosecutions. Nevertheless, the perceived historic and symbolic importance of having the writ available to *all* who claim that their detention violates the Constitution may hang in the balance.

ii. Federal Habeas and the States — Federalism versus Fairness

The history of *federal* habeas corpus and state courts has been rocky, to say the least. During Reconstruction, federal courts began tentatively applying a federal habeas statute to provide relief for state prisoners as well. By the 1940s, they were entertaining habeas petitions from state prisoners who argued that they were being held in custody on the basis of convictions obtained in violation of specific federal procedural requirements. In 1948, Congress, in a new "codification" of the earlier law, provided that a petition could not be entertained unless: the prisoner had "exhausted the remedies available in the state courts"; or there was "an absence of available State corrective process or the existence of circumstances rendering such process ineffective to protect the rights of the prisoner." The prisoner would not be "deemed to have exhausted" remedies if he had "the right under the law of the State to raise, by any available procedure, the question presented."

In the landmark decision of *Brown v. Allen*, 344 U.S. 443 (1953), however, the Court read the statute only to codify the exhaustion doctrine that the Court itself had established in an earlier case.[14] Once prisoners gave state courts one opportunity to address federal claims, they were free to file petitions for the writ in federal court. Moreover, a previous state court

---

14. *Ex parte Royall*, 117 U.S. 241 (1886).

decision on the merits of a federal claim was not *res judicata*, but was entitled only to the weight the federal court would give to the conclusion of a court of last resort of another jurisdiction on federal constitutional issues.

As the Warren Court expanded the application of constitutional provisions to the states, and as the embryonic civil rights movement grew, the Court, in a trilogy of cases,[15] expanded the writ to ensure that virtually every state prisoner could obtain one *federal* court interpretation of federal constitutional law as it applied to his state court criminal conviction. For the next 30 years, the Court first broadened, then narrowed, the availability of federal habeas corpus for state prisoners. Then in 1996, in response to the Oklahoma City bombings, Congress enacted the Antiterrorism and Effective Death Penalty Act (AEDPA), amending 28 U.S.C. §2241 et seq., which has been called "the most significant change to the habeas statute since the Civil War."[16] Many of the provisions, adopted without much debate or discussion, sought to limit the conditions under which state prisoners could obtain federal habeas relief. Merely construing the language of AEDPA, much of which is quoted below, would be difficult enough; as Justice Souter has declared: "[I]n a world of silk purses and pigs' ears, the Act is not a silk purse of the art of statutory drafting." *Lindh v. Murphy*, 521 U.S. 320 (1997). But there is another problem: how to read the (restrictive) language of AEDPA, however interpreted, against the common law doctrines the Court had established in the decades preceding AEDPA. One could have argued, after all, that statutory language supersedes common law doctrines, and that only AEDPA applied. The Court, however, has now clearly rejected that view; instead, the state prisoner must satisfy both the common law hurdles and the AEDPA hurdles. *Horn v. Banks*, 536 U.S. 266, 272 (2002).

An overarching policy question permeates this — and the following — debate about federal habeas corpus: Why should a *state* prisoner *ever* have a right to have a *federal* court review his *federal* constitutional claims? Two primary explanations for federal review of state court decisions, with very different perspectives, have been offered:

1. federal court judges are more "expert" in federal constitutional law than state court judges, who might inadvertently misunderstand the federal decisions;

---

15. *Fay v. Noia*, 372 U.S. 391 (1963); *Sanders v. United States*, 373 U.S. 1 (1963); *Townsend v. Sain*, 372 U.S. 293 (1963).

16. Lyn S. Entzeroth, Reflections on Fifteen Years of the Teague v. Lane Retroactivity Paradigm: A Study of the Persistence, the Pervasiveness, and the Perversity of the Court's Doctrine, 35 N.M. L. Rev. 161, 173 (2005). On the other hand, Professor Blume suggests that AEDPA merely echoes, rather than changes, limitations which the Supreme Court had already put in place. John H. Blume, AEDPA: The "Hype" and the "Bite," 91 Cornell L. Rev. 259 (2006).

2. state court judges fully understand federal constitutional decisions, but simply will not apply them.

Whichever view one takes, the mere "oversight" of state courts by federal court judges creates tension in a federalist system. If one believes that state court judges are as competent as federal court judges in assessing constitutional rights and that they will not purposefully undermine those rights, then the case for federal "oversight" is problematic indeed. That is the dilemma faced by federal courts construing not only AEDPA, but the pre-AEDPA case law as well.

b. Federal Habeas Corpus — Common Law and AEDPA

Federal courts will not oversee state trials unless the prisoner has previously presented his federal claim to the state court. Thus, the prisoner seeking federal review of his or her state court conviction must show that:

- the petition is timely filed;
- the petitioner has exhausted his or her (available) state remedies; and
- the petitioner is not precluded from relief by procedural default.

As we attempt to navigate the maze of common law and statutory requirements, consider that defendants are not constitutionally entitled to appointed counsel after their first state appeal and that because federal habeas proceedings occur long after the original trial, prisoners may confront difficulties of memory, loss of evidence, and so on.[17] During their state collateral review proceedings, they may have to grapple with these matters pro se. They are entitled, however, as a federal statutory matter, to appointed counsel once they have filed their habeas corpus petitions, but failure to file in a timely fashion may mean they are without federal review.[18] All but one state provides for appointed counsel in capital cases, including post-conviction and federal habeas proceedings. AEDPA initially provided that a state could provide speedy and adequate resolution of capital cases, and if the federal circuit court approved of the plan, it would expedite federal habeas review. Nine years after AEDPA became effective, not a single state had successfully opted in to these provisions. Congress thereupon amended the statute to provide for certification by the United States

---

17. Professor Yackle has suggested the federal courts should review decisions of state supreme courts directly, without state collateral proceedings, lest the record go stale. Larry W. Yackle, State Convicts and Federal Courts: Reopening the Habeas Corpus Debate, 91 Cornell L. Rev. 541 (2006).

18. Note that since there is no constitutional right to counsel, there is also no constitutional right to effective counsel in habeas proceedings.

Attorney General, 28 U.S.C. §2261(b) (2006). There has yet to be such a certification.

i. Timeliness

AEDPA establishes, for the first time, a deadline by which a petition must be filed. Prior to AEDPA, the question of timeliness was one of reasonableness in the district court's equitable discretion.[19] Now, a state prisoner must file within one year after:

1. the date on which the state court judgment becomes "final" by the conclusion of direct review; or
2. the date on which an unlawful state "impediment" is removed; or
3. the date on which the constitutional right asserted is "initially recognized by the Supreme Court," provided that the Supreme Court has explicitly made it retroactive to cases on collateral review; or
4. the date on which the factual predicate of a claim is discoverable through the exercise of due diligence.

Attempting to decide the proper time frame has created much confusion. As of 2005, the Supreme Court had granted review in nine cases involving AEDPA's statute of limitations. Yackle, supra note 16 at 552.[20]

The courts have applied these limits rigorously. An extreme case (perhaps) is Rouse v. Lee, 339 F.3d 238 (4th Cir. 2003). Defendant, an African American, was convicted and sentenced to death by an all-Caucasian jury for the murder of an elderly Caucasian female. One juror allegedly intentionally failed to disclose that his mother had been murdered by an African-American male (who was executed for the offense). The court of appeals dismissed the petition as time-barred because his attorneys filed the habeas petition one day late. The court also refused to find equitable tolling,

_____

19. "[P]rior to the enactment of AEDPA, we affirmatively rejected the notion that habeas courts' traditionally broad discretionary powers would support their imposition of a time bar. We repeatedly asserted that the passage of time alone could not extinguish the habeas corpus rights of a person subject to unconstitutional incarceration. . . . [T]his doctrine was so well entrenched that the lower courts regularly entertained petitions filed after even extraordinary delays." (Scalia, J., dissenting in Day v. McDonough, 547 U.S. 198, 210 (2006).)
20. E.g., Clay v. United States, 537 U.S. 522 (2003) (judgment becomes "final" when the time expires for filing a petition for certiorari); Dodd v. United States, 545 U.S. 353 (2005) (time-frame begins on the date on which the Supreme Court initially recognized the right, not the date on which that right was made retroactive); Woodford v. Garceau, 538 U.S. 202 (2003) (motion for appointment of counsel in a federal habeas petition does not toll the statute of limitations). The decisions continue: Lawrence v. Florida, 549 U.S. 327 (2007) (time for seeking review of a denial of postconviction relief is not tolled while defendant seeks certiorari); Wall v. Kholi, 562 U.S. 545 (2011) (state's prisoner's motion in state court to reduce sentence tolls the AEDPA statute of limitations). For a thorough discussion, see Lee Kovarsky, AEDPA's Wrecks: Comity, Finality and Federalism, 82 Tul. L. Rev. 443 (2007).

concluding that neither the severity of his death sentence nor the strength of the claim presented was relevant to the equitable tolling analysis.[21] State court decisions issued under "flexible" timeliness requirements may serve as "adequate and independent state ground" for denying federal habeas relief. *Walker v. Martin*, 562 U.S. 307 (2011). On the other hand, where the untimeliness is due to counsel's dilatoriness, the test may be less rigid because there is no issue of overriding state procedural rules. *Holland v. Florida*, 560 U.S. 631 (2010).

The Court has held that AEDPA's time deadlines can be overcome by a showing of actual innocence that satisfies the standard announced in *Schlup v. Delo*, 513 U.S. 298, 327 (1995) (In light of new evidence "it is more likely than not that no reasonable juror would have found petitioner guilty beyond a reasonable doubt."). In *McQuiggin v. Perkins*, 133 S.Ct. 1924 (2013) Perkins filed his federal habeas petition six years after the one-year statute of limitations had expired. In his petition he provided affidavits pointing to someone else as the killer and claimed that his trial counsel was ineffective in failing to discover and present this evidence. The Supreme Court held that AEDPA's statute of limitations is not an absolute barrier to having an untimely petition considered on the merits provided a petitioner can meet the rigorous *Schlup* standard. The defendant can overcome the timeliness requirement even if he had not been diligent in discovering the new evidence. However, the Court did hold that an unexplained delay would undermine the credibility of the actual innocence claim and can be considered by the courts in determining whether the claim is credible.

ii. Exhaustion of Remedies

More than a century ago, in the seminal case of *Ex Parte Royall*, 117 U.S. 241 (1886), the Court articulated the notion that it should not "review" a state decision until all relevant state authorities had been afforded the opportunity to do so first. The salient notion is to provide the state court a real opportunity to assess the federal claim. AEDPA protects the interests of the state in exhaustion by explicitly providing that "a State shall not be deemed to have waived the exhaustion requirement or be stopped from reliance upon the requirement unless the State, through counsel, expressly waives the requirement." 28 U.S.C. §2254(b)(3). The exhaustion requirement is not a

21. The Court has reached an equivalent conclusion with regard to a federal prisoner who sought to use the equivalent process. In *Bowles v. Russell*, 551 U.S. 205 (2007), the trial judge (mis)informed the defendant and counsel that he had 17 days to file an appeal. In fact, the Rules had a 14-day limit. When defense counsel filed on the sixteenth day, the Court, 5-4, affirmed a finding that the 14-day limit was jurisdictional, and hence the petition was untimely. Four Justices dissented. Justice Souter declared, "It is intolerable for the judicial system to treat people this way, and there is not even a technical justification for condoning this 'bait and switch.'" Would Bowles have a claim of ineffective counsel?

jurisdictional prerequisite, but rests on the comity that federal courts owe to the states and state court. *Branberry v. Greer*, 481 U.S. 129 (1987). When a petitioner fails to satisfy the exhaustion requirement, the federal court *postpones, but does not lose*, the exercise of jurisdiction. The importance of the filing deadline is primarily formal — to alert all concerned that the prisoner intends to seek federal review if state procedures prove unfruitful.

Using the state appellate process does not complete the exhaustion requirement. If the state provides other processes (such as state collateral relief, discussed above), the prisoner must present through those channels all claims which she wishes the federal court to consider should state processes not result in a new trial. AEDPA's language is similar — exhaustion has not occurred if the prisoner "has the right . . . to raise, *by any available procedure*, the question presented" (emphasis added).

Under case law, futile or uncertain remedies were not "effective" avenues of relief, and did not need to be exhausted. *Duckworth v. Serrano*, 454 U.S. 1 (1981). AEDPA similarly provides that the state prisoner need not exhaust a process "if circumstances exist that render such process ineffective to protect the rights of the applicant."

Exhaustion requires that the prisoner has "fairly present[ed]" the issue to the state court; if he has not done so, the federal court may refuse to consider the habeas petition. In *Baldwin v. Reese*, 541 U.S. 27 (2004), the brief in the state collateral relief proceeding merely complained that defendant's appellate counsel provided "ineffective assistance," but did not expressly cite or rely upon federal (as opposed to state) standards. The Court held that this was not a "fair presentation" and petitioner had therefore not exhausted his state remedies. On the other hand, if the substance of a claim is presented to the state courts, even if additional facts are included in the federal claim, it has been exhausted. Thus, in *Conner v. Quarterman*, 477 F.3d 287, 292 (5th Cir. 2007), defendant claimed in his state petition that a foot injury made it impossible for him to have been the gunman who fled by foot in a botched robbery-murder and that his trial counsel had been ineffective in failing to make this argument to the jury. After his claim was rejected in state court, he made the same claim in federal court, but he supplemented the claim with his medical records documenting that he had a serious foot injury at the time of the crime. The additional evidence presented in support of his claim in federal court did not change the nature of the claim that he presented in state court.

If the prisoner files his habeas petition timely, but must exhaust state remedies, the filing "tolls" the one-year statute of limitations. State prisoners, of course, are not constitutionally entitled to counsel on any collateral review — state or federal (see Chapter 10, *supra*) — and may not be aware that they must "exhaust their remedies." The Court has explained that even poor lawyering cannot excuse a litigant's failure to exhaust because "the costs associated with an ignorant or inadvertent procedural default are no less than where the failure to raise a claim is a deliberate strategy: it deprives the state courts of the opportunity to review trial errors." *Coleman v. Thompson*, 501 U.S. 722, 752 (1991). Before *Rhines v. Weber*, 544 U.S. 69 (2005), a prisoner who filed a habeas petition in federal court, but whose petition was dismissed for lack of exhaustion, found himself, upon return to the federal court, now barred because his (new) petition had been filed more than a year after the "final" judgment of conviction. In *Rhines*, however, the Court encouraged district courts to "stay and abey" the petition, thus effectively tolling the time during which the exhaustion occurred, even where some of the claims had been presented to the state courts, but others had not.

iii. Procedural Default

A requirement that the prisoner "exhaust state remedies" simply delays federal assessment of the prisoner's trial. If, however, he has *procedurally defaulted* the claim, he has lost all hope that a federal court will consider his claim.

Over time, the court has vacillated on how severely to apply state procedural default rules. Before the 1960s, a state defendant (or his counsel) who failed to comply with state procedural rules was rigorously barred from federal relief.[22] For about 20 years, however, the Court ameliorated that rule and required that the defendant have participated personally in a decision not to raise an issue or objection. *Fay v. Noia*, 372 U.S. 391 (1963). In *Wainwright v. Sykes*, 433 U.S. 72 (1977), the Court jettisoned *Fay* and adopted the current standard, which requires a prisoner who has not followed state procedural rules to show that:

1. there was a "cause" for his failure to do so; and
2. the procedural default has prejudiced his case.

Although AEDPA does not explicitly set out standards for assessing the effect of procedural default, the Court appears to apply the *Sykes* approach.

The requirement that a prisoner provide the state court system with at least one opportunity to correct any possible federal or constitutional errors makes obvious sense if the purpose of federal habeas corpus is to assure that state courts are properly applying federal constitutional decisions. On the other hand, the procedural default rule ironically grants a second review to

---

22. In *Daniels v. Allen*, 344 U.S. 443 (1953), a state rule required that an appeal on a jury composition issue had to be "filed" within 60 days of the judgment. Mailing on the 60th day would have met the deadline, but counsel decided instead to file the papers by hand on the 61st day; had he mailed the papers on the 60th day, they would not have arrived earlier than they did when he brought them to the clerk's office. Nevertheless, the state appellate court refused to hear the appeal, and the United States Supreme Court held this was a procedural default which precluded review of the jury claim. Daniels was later executed.

defendants who have had a claim considered (and rejected) by state courts, but no review to defendants who have not raised the issue in state court.

(a) Overcoming Procedural Default — Cause

The Supreme Court has identified five circumstances that could excuse default, that is, that rise to the level of "cause":

1. the legal or factual basis for the claim was not reasonably apparent at the time it should have been presented to the state courts and there are now no state processes available, *Murray v. Carrier*, 477 U.S. 478 (1986);
2. the state has prevented a defendant from presenting the claim;
3. the defendant's attorney abandoned him;
4. defendant's representation was ineffective;
5. the defendant can demonstrate actual innocence through new evidence.

The first circumstance, involving a "new" "unanticipated" rule, will be discussed below. Here, it is sufficient to note that if the claim is "really" so new that counsel be faulted for not having raised it, the federal court is likely to be barred from applying it, under other rules.

The second circumstance parallels the earlier inquiry into state intervention. For example, in *Amado v. Zant*, 486 U.S. 214 (1988), the prosecutor ex parte requested jury commissioners to underrepresent African-American women on the wheel. The Court held this constituted "impairment" sufficient to excuse the prisoner from having raised the jury issue in a timely fashion. In *Banks v. Dretke*, 540 U.S. 668 (2004), a prosecutor's nearly 20-year refusal to disclose *Brady* material but instead telling defense counsel that "you have everything we have" constituted cause.

The third circumstance occurred in *Maples v. Thomas*, 565 U.S. 266 (2012). After Maples was sentenced to death by an Alabama jury, he filed a petition for state post-conviction relief, alleging that his trial counsel had been ineffective. He was represented pro bono in this matter by two New York associates of the Sullivan & Cromwell firm since Alabama does not provide death-sentenced defendants with the assistance of counsel in state post-conviction proceedings. While Maples's state petition was still pending, both attorneys left Sullivan & Cromwell for jobs in which they could no longer represent Maples. They failed to withdraw as attorneys of record and they also failed to notify Maples that they could no longer represent him. After the attorneys left the firm, Maples's petition was denied. The clerk of court mailed a notice of the denial to Sullivan & Cromwell but an employee in the mailroom returned the notice unopened. The clerk did nothing further. There was no attempt to reach the attorneys of record and no notice was sent to Maples. The time to appeal the denial of his post-conviction writ expired without Maples having filed a notice of appeal. Maples filed a federal writ which was denied by both the district court and the court of appeals on procedural default grounds. The Supreme Court held that the default should be excused since Maples missed the deadline to appeal the denial of his writ through no fault of his own. The Court found that Maples's attorneys abandoned him without giving notice either to the court or to Maples and therefore the client could not be charged with the acts of an attorney who had abandoned him. Because the circumstances causing the procedural default were beyond Maples's control, there was ample cause to excuse the procedural default.

The fourth circumstance ("cause") is essentially a claim of ineffective assistance of both trial counsel and state habeas counsel. This situation arises when a defendant's state post-conviction counsel fails to raise a meritorious claim of ineffective assistance of trial counsel. In most states, the post-conviction proceeding is a defendant's only opportunity to raise a claim of ineffectiveness of trial counsel. *Trevino v. Thaler*, 133 S.Ct. 1911, 1921 (2013). Previously, the failure of post-conviction counsel to raise the claim meant that it was procedurally defaulted and the federal courts had no means by which it could consider the merits of the claim. Therefore, even an egregiously substandard representation would never be adjudicated. In *Martinez v. Ryan*, 566 U.S. 1 (2012), the Supreme Court expressed its equitable judgment that state prisoners must be afforded access to at least one court to meaningfully challenge their convictions and sentences on the ground that their trial counsel were ineffective under the Sixth Amendment. It therefore designated the federal courts as the appropriate venue for initial review of defaulted trial counsel ineffectiveness claims. *Martinez* allows a petitioner to overcome the procedural default of his ineffectiveness of trial counsel claim by demonstrating both cause and prejudice. A petitioner proves cause by demonstrating either that there was no counsel in the state proceeding or that counsel in that proceeding was ineffective. The Court indicated that in determining whether state post-conviction counsel was ineffective, the lower courts should apply *Strickland*. In order to prove prejudice as a result of the default, a petitioner must demonstrate that the ineffective assistance of trial counsel claim is substantial. The Supreme Court defined the "substantiality" standard as requiring that the underlying trial counsel ineffectiveness claim has some merit. However, a petitioner who successfully demonstrates both that state post-conviction counsel was ineffective in failing to raise a claim *and* that the claim has some merit, does not automatically prevail on his or her underlying ineffectiveness of trial counsel claim. Rather, doing so simply entitles the petitioner to have the underlying ineffective assistance of trial counsel claim adjudicated on the merits in federal court.

In *Davila v. Davis*, the Court refused to extend *Martinez* to procedurally defaulted claims that the direct appeal counsel was ineffective. In *Davila*, appellate counsel failed ro raise a claim regarding jury instruction on direct appeal. The state post-conviction counsel also failed to raise the claim in the state post-conviction proceeding. The petitioner argued that *Martinez* allowed the federal courts to adjudicate the ineffective assistance of appellate counsel claim. The Supreme Court disagreed. The Court created the *Martinez* exception out of concern that a meritorious claim of ineffective assistance of trial counsel may never be considered on the merits by either a state or appellate court. The Court, however, did not have the same concern about an ineffective assistance of appellate counsel claim since at least one judge, the trial judge, would have reviewed the claimed error.

However, because there are federalism issues present, the state court's determination of effectiveness is due "double deference"—once under *Strickland* (which affords broad discretion to trial lawyers and courts assessing their conduct) and once under the comity notions of federalism. *Premo v. Moore*, 131 S. Ct. 733 (2011); *Knowles v. Mirzayance*, 129 S. Ct. 1411 (2009). But the Court has been uneven and confusing in applying this view. In *Sears v. Upton*, 130 S. Ct. 3259 (2010), the Court declared that there should be a "probing and fact-specific analysis" when a *Strickland* claim was raised. And in *Porter v. McCollum*, 130 S. Ct. 447 (2009), the Court found the state court's decision that counsel was not ineffective an "unreasonable application of federal law."

The fifth circumstance ("cause,") that can excuse default—when the petitioner demonstrates his or her actual innocence of the crime for which he or she has been convicted through new evidence—is discussed in more detail in Section 4, Actual Innocence.

The mere fact that a state court had held that a federal constitutional claim procedurally barred by its own rules does not preclude a federal court from holding an evidentiary hearing to broaden the record to determine whether the claim is in fact barred. *Cone v. Bell*, 556 U.S. 449 (2009). An extraordinary case is *Wellons v. Hall*, 558 U.S. 220 (2010). Defendant was charged in a rape-murder. He had learned, after trial, that the jurors had given to the judge chocolate shaped as male genitalia and to the bailiff chocolate shaped as female breasts and that the jurors and the bailiff were planning a reunion. Although the petitioner had attempted to raise the question of juror misconduct on direct appeal and during state collateral proceedings, the state courts refused to consider the claim on the ground that it was procedurally barred. The Supreme Court in *Hall*, *supra*, 558 U.S. at 223 n.3, said a hearing was required to determine the record, declaring:

[I]t would be bizarre if a federal court had to defer to state-court factual findings, made without any evidentiary record, in order to decide whether it could create an evidentiary record to decide whether the factual findings were erroneous. If that were the case, then almost no habeas petitioner could ever get an evidentiary hearing. So long as the state court found a fact that the petitioner was trying to disprove through the presentation of evidence, then there could be no hearing. AEDPA does not require such a crabbed and illogical approach to habeas procedures.

(b) Overcoming Procedural Default — Prejudice   It is difficult enough for a prisoner to show cause under the *Sykes* standard. But beyond that, she or he must also demonstrate that the failure to raise the issue in a timely manner resulted in prejudice. As suggested above in the discussion of appeals and waivers, the decisions are unclear, but it appears that the prejudice test here is similar to, if not identical with, the *Strickland-Brady* criterion: that there is a "reasonable probability" that the outcome would have been different, which undermines confidence in the verdict. In assessing the "harmlessness" of any error, however, the standard is clear: In *Brecht v. Abrahamson*, 507 U.S. 619 (1993), the Court held that the *Kotteakos* standard, which requires the defendant to show an error had a "substantial and injurious effect on the verdict," should be applied to assessing the harmless(ness) of even a constitutional error in a state trial. The Court explicitly rejected applying the *Chapman* standard, which places the burden on the prosecution to show harmlessness beyond a reasonable doubt. The Court recently reaffirmed that approach. *Fry v. Pliler*, 551 U.S. 112 (2007). For an in-depth treatment, see Jeffrey S. Jacobi, Mostly Harmless: An Analysis of Post-AEDPA Federal Habeas Corpus Review of State Harmless Error Determinations, 105 Mich. L. Rev. 805 (2007).

(c) The Merits of the Claim

(i) Pure Legal Issues

If Dan has not procedurally defaulted on the claim and has exhausted his state processes, will the federal court consider that claim?

a) Pre-AEDPA   If Dan's claim is one of law (that some action in the state court violated a rule of constitutional law), the first question is: *Was the constitutional rule of law extant at the time of the state proceeding?* If so, then Dan's sole claim is that the state court improperly applied a fixed rule of federal constitutional law. Ostensibly, this was *precisely* the reason for the Warren court's expansion of the writ — to assure that states were not avoiding federal constitutional doctrines, particularly in an era when constitutional rights were being established in rapid order.

In *Brown v. Allen*, 344 U.S. 443 (1953), the Court, per Justice Frankfurter, held that federal courts were to "independently apply the correct constitutional standard" "no matter how fair and completely the claim had been litigated in state courts." This reflected the view that federal courts were simply more knowledgeable about constitutional standards than state courts. In an era when few provisions of the Bill of Rights applied to the states, and few constitutional issues would therefore be argued in the state courts, that might well have been the case. By the 1980s, however, states were daily dealing with the nuances of the Fourth, Fifth, and Sixth Amendments in state criminal trials; the only claim federal courts then could make was not greater knowledge but possibly greater impartiality. But such a claim flew in the face of the notions of federalism and comity.

b) AEDPA   Congress addressed the question in AEDPA. That statute provides that habeas shall not be granted unless the adjudication of a claim:

> resulted in a decision that was contrary to, or involved an unreasonable application of, clearly established Federal law, as determined by the Supreme Court of the United States.

28 U.S.C. §2254(d)(1).

What do these phrases mean? The Court has been clear, as the statutory language declares, that the "federal law" that the state court has gotten "wrong" must be an opinion from the United States Supreme Court, not from a lower court. *Tyler v. Cain*, 533 U.S. 656 (2001). Prior to AEDPA, federal district and circuit courts would often articulate constitutional rules, which they would then apply to state court convictions. This was done in part in the belief that the Supreme Court could handle only a few direct appeals, and therefore the lower federal courts could — indeed, had to — establish constitutional principles. However, only seven years prior to AEDPA, the Court, in *Teague v. Lane*, 489 U.S. 288 (1989), had essentially declared that the purpose of federal habeas was simply to oversee state courts. *Teague* held that a federal district court could neither (a) announce, nor (b) apply, a "new rule" of constitutional breadth. Thus, a petitioner had to show that his state court conviction had, essentially, been in violation of a (United States Supreme Court) decision already then existing. Under *Teague*, the federal habeas court should:

1. determine when the defendant's conviction became final;
2. ascertain the "legal landscape as it then existed";
3. ask whether the earlier decisions rule *compelled* the new rule sought to be applied; if prior precedent "compelled" the rule, then it is not new, and may be applied by a habeas court. If it is new, it may not be so applied.

Thus, a circuit court opinion, even one with a holding directly on point, does not "clearly establish" federal law for AEDPA purposes. *Renico v. Lett*, 559 U.S. 766 (2010). Many have argued that this "debases" the lower federal courts, who must wait for a decision from the United States Supreme Court, rather than "finding" new constitutional rules themselves.

Second, the Supreme Court decision involved must "clearly establish" the constitutional right allegedly infringed. Law students well know that opinions and decisions can be "narrowed" so that they only apply to the exact facts before them. Dictum, and strong arguments in dissent or concurring opinions, will not suffice. *Abdul-Kabir v. Quarterman*, 550 U.S. 233 (2007); *Carey v. Musladin*, 549 U.S. 70 (2006). A good example is *Lockyer v. Andrade*, 538 U.S. 63 (2003). Defendant was sentenced, under California's three-strikes law, to a minimum term of 25 years for stealing videotapes worth $154.54. Because, as the Court admitted, its earlier opinions on proportionality "have not been a model of clarity," the California Supreme Court's decision that the sentence was not constitutionally disproportionate had to be upheld. Again, in *Berghuis v. Smith*, 130 S. Ct. 1382 (2010), the Court in a *Taylor* challenge (see Chapter 8) held that it had never "clearly established" a methodology for assessing minority underpresentation on a jury wheel, and therefore the state court was not required to use a specific methodology. (The Court expressly refused to embrace a methodology for future cases — leaving the law still "unclear".)[23] And the Supreme Court decision has to have been settled at the time the petitioner's state court conviction became final.

Third, a state court decision can be overturned by a federal court if it is "contrary to" clearly established federal law. To be "contrary to" the Supreme Court's precedent, the state decision must not be merely "somewhat" wrong. In *(Terry) Williams v. Taylor*, 529 U.S. 362 (2000) (see infra, note 29), a very fractured Court held that a state court decision must be "opposite to" or "diametrically opposed to" the relevant precedent of the Court. Moreover, there was a suggestion that the facts of the case under review had to be "materially indistinguishable" from those in the guiding precedent.

Finally, the federal court can also reverse a state court decision that is "unreasonable." This means that if the state court decision was "wrong," and a misreading of a (fairly clear?) precedent, relief can be granted under AEDPA. *Schriro, supra.* However, the decision is not "unreasonable" if the specific legal rule has not been squarely established by the Supreme Court. *Knowles v. Mirzayance*, 556 U.S. 111 (2009).

If the state court has not reached the merits of a defendant's constitutional claim and there is no procedural default or exhaustion requirement, federal habeas review is de novo. *Cone v. Bell*, 556 U.S. 449 (2009). On the other hand, there need not be an *opinion* from the state court to activate the deference due its judgment; the federal court should consider what "might have been" the state court's reason, and may grant the petition only if those putative reasons were invalid under AEDPA. *Harrington v. Richter*, 562 U.S. 86 (2011).[24]

---

23. See Ursula Bentele, The Not So Great Writ: Trapped in the Narrow Holdings of Supreme Court Precedents, 14 Lewis & Clark L. Rev. 741 (2010); Melissa M. Berry, Seeking Clarity in the Federal Habeas Fog: Determining What Constitutes "Clearly Established" Law under the Antiterrorism and Effective Death Penalty Act, 54 Cath. U.L. Rev. 747 (2005); Padraic Foran, Unreasonably Wrong: The Supreme Court's Supremacy, The AEDPA Standard, and *Carey v. Musladin*, 81 S. Cal. L. Rev. 571 (2008).

24. Professor Kovarsky (*supra*, n 19) refers to this kind of state court decision as a "postcard denial."

In *Teague*, the Court suggested that a new Supreme Court decision might nevertheless be applied by a federal habeas court, even if the state court had had no opportunity to act on that decision under either of two circumstances:

1. The decision established a "watershed" rule implicating "fundamental fairness" and "central to an accurate determination of innocence or guilt." However, as the Court acknowledged in *Schriro v. Summerlin*, 542 U.S. 349, 353 (2004), "We have yet to find a new rule" that is a "watershed."
2. If the new rule were "substantive," federal district courts could apply them in habeas proceedings. But in *Schriro*, the Court narrowly defined the kind of substantive rule that might be applied (for the first time) on habeas:

> A rule is substantive rather than procedural if it alters the range of conduct or the class of person that the law punishes. . . . In contrast, rules that regulate only the manner of determining the defendant's culpability are procedural.

It would now appear that only new decisions deciding that the state could not punish anyone for the conduct, or could not punish anyone like the *defendant* for the conduct, are "substantive" within the meaning of this distinction. For example, the Court's decisions that no mentally retarded person[25] and that no juvenile[26] can be executed for their crimes would fall within the reach of *Teague*'s definition of "substantive." But decisions as to who sentences, even for death, are procedural. Thus, in *Schriro*, the defendant had been sentenced to death by a judge.[27] After that decision was final, the Court held that the Sixth Amendment precluded judges from making that determination. Nevertheless, because "who decides the death penalty" was procedural rather than substantive, Summerlin could not avail himself of the "new" rule.[28]

---

25. *Atkins v. Virginia*, 536 U.S. 304 (2002).

26. *Roper v. Simmons*, 543 U.S. 551 (2005).

27. The defense attorney had an affair with the prosecutor, and the judge was later disbarred for use of marijuana, including during the period he sentenced Summerlin. (There was no evidence, however, that he was smoking while trying Summerlin's case.) *See* C. Ryan Russell, Death Anyways: Federal Habeas Corpus Retroactivity Law and the Decision in *Schriro v. Summerlin*, 83 Or. L. Rev. 1389 (2004). Might there be a later due process issue on collateral review?

28. As might be expected, the decision has been roundly criticized. *See, e.g.,* Matthew R. Doherty, The Reluctance Towards Retroactivity: The Retroactive Application of Laws in Death Penalty Collateral Review Cases, 39 Val. U.L. Rev. 445 (2004); Katharine A. Ferguson, The Clash of *Ring v. Arizona* and *Teague v. Lane*: An Illustration of the Inapplicability of Modern Habeas Retroactivity Jurisprudence in the Capital Sentencing Context, 85 B.U. L. Rev. 1017 (2005).

(ii) "Issues of Fact" or "Mixed Questions of Fact and Law"

Many petitioners argue that the state court erred not only in the way it applied a legal rule, but in the facts it found to which it applied that rule. Suppose, for example, that the defendant claims that during police interrogation he said "I want a lawyer," but the state court finds, after a hearing, that he said no such thing. The finding is critical, at least in terms of a *Miranda* challenge to a confession admitted into the state trial. Or suppose a state court collateral review court has concluded that defense counsel *did* interview 15 witnesses named by the defendant, but the defendant contests this finding, which might be crucial to a claim of ineffective assistance. How much weight should a federal habeas court accord to these findings?

In an earlier time, federal district courts were authorized, and in some instances urged, to hold evidentiary hearings at which a defendant might challenge many, if not all, of the factual conclusions reached by the state courts. Some, but little, deference was to be given to those findings.

Although the Supreme Court had already substantially altered its view before AEDPA, but AEDPA has rewritten the framework concerning the resolution of factual issues, and the hearings to allow challenges to them. First, the statute provides that any actual factual finding by a state court "shall be presumed to be correct" and that "the applicant shall have the burden of rebutting the presumption . . . by clear and convincing evidence." 28 U.S.C. §2254(e)(1); *Schriro v. Landrigan, supra,* 550 U.S. 465. On the basis of the record developed in the state courts, it is unlikely that a defendant will be able to meet that burden. So he will seek an evidentiary hearing at which he can "supplement" the state court record. But he has a heavy burden of persuasion before that may occur.

The defendant may run directly into Section (3e)(2) of AEDPA, which provides that if he has "failed to develop the factual basis" of a claim, the federal court "shall not" hold a hearing unless the applicant shows:

> (A) the claim relies on
>
>   (i) new rule of constitutional law, made retroactive to cases on collateral review by the Supreme Court, that was previously unavailable; OR[29]
>
>   (ii) a factual predicate that could not have been previously discovered through the exercise of due diligence; AND
>
> (B) the facts underlying the claim would be sufficient to establish by clear and convincing evidence that but for constitutional error, no reasonable fact finder would have found the applicant guilty of the underlying offense.

---

29. Emphasis and capitalization added.

The prisoner must meet these standards *before* the evidentiary hearing can be held. In *(Michael) Williams v. Taylor*, 529 U.S. 420 (2000)[30] the Court seemed to interpret the AEDPA language ("could not have been previously discovered . . .") to apply primarily to evidence that truly "could not have been" discovered, such as new scientific tests, or recanting witnesses. Otherwise, said the Court, a prisoner (or his attorney) did not exercise "diligence" when he had an opportunity to pursue a claim in state court.

At any hearing, the petitioner will carry the burden "by clear and convincing evidence" that the state court determination is incorrect. A good example is *Schriro v. Landrigan*. Landrigan argued in his habeas corpus petition that his counsel had been ineffective, by failing to present mitigating evidence at his capital sentencing. As we have seen (see Chapter 11), the Court in recent years had been somewhat receptive to that claim. Here, however, the state court had found that Landrigan had instructed his counsel *not* to present mitigating evidence. There was a substantial dispute as to whether that instruction went to all mitigating evidence, or only that supplied by Landrigan's family. The federal district court, finding the state court's factual conclusions not unreasonable, denied Landrigan's motion for an evidentiary hearing, but the Ninth Circuit reversed, saying that Landrigan's instructions had been sufficiently ambiguous as to warrant further inquiry. The Supreme Court, 550 U.S. at 481, reversed the Ninth Circuit, reinstating the decision of the district court:

> Even assuming the truth of all the facts Landrigan sought to prove at the evidentiary hearing, he still could not be granted federal habeas relief because the state court's factual determination that Landrigan would not have allowed counsel to present any mitigating evidence at sentencing is not an unreasonable determination of the facts under [AEDPA] and the mitigating evidence he seeks to introduce would not have changed the result. In such circumstances, a District Court has discretion to deny an evidentiary hearing.

In *Cullen v. Pinholster*, 563 U.S. 170 (2011), the Court appears to have further limited the importance of evidentiary hearings. After having discouraged federal courts from holding an evidentiary hearing, *McDaniel v. Brown*, 558 U.S. 120 (2010), the *Cullen* Court held that even if the federal court were to hold such a hearing, it could not use any "new" facts to assess the "unreasonableness" of the state court's legal conclusions — federal habeas review was limited to the record before the state court, and new evidence could not be considered in deciding claims that were not

---

30. Incredibly, the Supreme Court decided two cases, each involving a capital habeas corpus petitioner named Williams, each from Virginia, in back-to-back decisions. When citing *Williams v. Taylor*, be sure to distinguish between "Michael" and "Terry" Williams.

adjudicated on the merits in state court.[31] Moreover, in *Harrington v. Richter*, 562 U.S. 86 (2011), the Court appeared to extend the "double deference" for assistance of counsel cases to all state court findings of fact. These cases again confirm the current view that federal habeas corpus is to assure that state courts did not misapply already existing law, rather than considering the defendant's actual innocence (see below). See, generally, Justin F. Marceau, Deference and Doubt: The Interaction of AEDPA section 2254(d)(2) and (e)(1), 82 Tul. L. Rev. 385 (2007).

That makes it very unlikely that Dan's going to succeed on a factual claim. What, then, about "mixed" questions of law and fact? The standard for review of "mixed" questions has always been important, and murky. And even on direct review, it is not yet clear what the standard, either constitutional or otherwise, is. But on habeas corpus under AEDPA, that distinction may literally mean the difference both between obtaining a hearing and not, and the standard (if not the burden) of proof involved in the subsequent proceeding.

The Court has always been sensitive to the "factual" or "mixed" distinction; but it has taken a wide-ranging policy approach to deciding how to characterize each issue. See *Miller v. Fenton*, 474 U.S. 104 (1985). This distinction would seem to retain its importance even under AEDPA.

If a district court dismisses the habeas petition, §2253(c)(1) requires a petitioner to obtain a "certificate of appealability" from the relevant circuit court of appeals in order to have the merits of his appeal considered. This process, which could be quite cumbersome if followed assiduously, was enacted to relieve circuit courts of habeas cases. In order to obtain a certificate of appealability, an applicant must make a substantial showing of the denial of a constitutional right. An applicant makes a substantial showing if jurists of reason could disagree with the district court's resolution of his constitutional claims. Thus, if the district court's decision was debatable, the applicant is entitled to a certificate of appealability and thus to have the merits of his or her appeal considered by the court of appeals. *Buck v. Davis*, 137 S.Ct. 759, 773-74 (2017).

iv. A Short Assessment

What is one to make of these developments? One objection to the narrowing of federal habeas corpus, sometimes called the "percolation" argument, is that by precluding federal district courts from announcing new constitutional rights on habeas corpus, *Teague* (and AEDPA) interferes

---

31. The Court left open the possibility, however, that a district court could rely upon "new evidence" obtained during an evidentiary hearing in assessing a "new claim," which for some reason had been neither forfeited nor waived in prior proceedings, and which could now not be presented to the state courts.

with the ability of issues to "percolate up" to the Supreme Court. Thus, prior to *Teague* and AEDPA, both district and circuit courts were able to grapple with the constitutional issue over a period of time before the Supreme Court "had to" take a case to resolve the issue. Another aspect of this argument is that, prior to *Teague* and AEDPA, federal and state courts would engage in a "dialogue" concerning the proper scope of federal constitutional protections, but that this dialogue is now threatened (if not stopped cold) by the restrictions engendered by *Teague* and AEDPA.

v. Federal Habeas Corpus — Successive Petitions

Even after Dan has been through state appeals, state collateral relief, and federal collateral relief, and has lost every time, hope keeps springing eternal. Prior to AEDPA, district courts decided whether a second habeas petition was an "abuse of the writ," using approaches similar to those of the "deliberate bypass" rules of *Fay v. Noia*, or even the "cause and prejudice" rules of *Wainwright v. Sykes*. AEDPA adopts a much more stringent approach. New claims raised in second petitions are assessed by virtually the same standards established for evidentiary hearings where the applicant had failed to develop a factual basis for the claim.[32] A hearing may be granted only if the new claim relies upon

A: (1) a new rule (2) of constitutional law (3) explicitly made retroactively applicable to collateral review (4) by a Supreme Court holding[33]

OR

B: a "factual predicate" which (1) could not have been discovered earlier (2) by the exercise of *due diligence.*

Even if these latter tests are met, the applicant must show "by clear and convincing evidence" that "no reasonable fact finder" would have found the applicant guilty of the underlying offense. The effect is likely to make second petitions, even based upon new decisions of the Supreme Court, virtually a waste of the prisoner's (and the court's) time.

On the other hand, there may be some leeway in determining whether the defendant is filing a "second" petition. In *Magwood v. Patterson*, 561 U.S. 320 (2010), the Court held that defendant's habeas petition challenging his re-sentencing to death after the federal district court had remanded for

---

32. 28 U.S.C. §2244(b)(2).
33. In *Tyler v. Cain*, 533 U.S. 656 (2001), the Court implicitly rejected the view that merely announcing the principle of determining a question might activate this provision of AEDPA. That, in turn, would have allowed lower federal courts, after deciding that a rule of constitutional law was "new," to further decide whether the "new" rule fell within the two exceptions of *Teague*. After *Tyler*, it would appear that only the United States Supreme Court can decide that question.

re-sentencing was not a "successive petition" challenging a state "judgment" under AEDPA, and was therefore not precluded by that statute.[34] See Mark T. Pavrov, Does "Second" Mean Second?: Examining the Split among the Circuit Courts of Appeals in Interpreting AEDPA's "Second or Successive" Limitations on Habeas Corpus Petitions, 57 Case W. Res. L. Rev. 1007 (2007). And in Cone v. Bell, 556 U.S. 449 (2009), the Court, showing impatience with the Sixth Circuit, decided the case for the third time — surely a record.

Further, AEDPA requires that the Circuit Court of Appeals, not the district court, decide whether the second petition falls within AEDPA's narrow rules. Leaving aside any other considerations, the difference in numbers of circuit court judges (179) versus district court judges (680) makes it less likely that the circuit courts will be able seriously to consider second petitions.

Finally, a petition that raises the *same* claim that an earlier petition raised "shall be dismissed." This statutory language seems unequivocal, but there is a possibility that, if the petitioner showed evidence of "actual innocence," discussed below, the court might allow such a claim to be considered a "new" claim (thus subject to the standard set out just above) or even in an original petition to the Supreme Court. These arguments, however, are highly speculative; at this point the law seems clear: A defendant should not actually pursue the habeas route until he (and the state courts) have carefully considered all the possible claims, at which time he or she should put them all in the same basket. Two bites will not be allowed at the federal apple.

3. Original Supreme Court Jurisdiction

In *In re Davis*, 557 U.S. 952 (2009), the Supreme Court, in a virtually unique action, exercised its original jurisdiction to review the habeas corpus petition of Troy Davis. Davis's petition alleged that seven of the key trial witnesses had recanted their testimony and that others had implicated the state's key witness as the shooter. Davis, having exhausted all his state remedies, and having been denied federal habeas relief, had filed a second petition for habeas corpus in the United States District Court, which denied the writ, and the Court of Appeals denied a certificate of appealability. Davis then took the extraordinary step of filing an original habeas corpus petition directly in the Supreme Court, which transferred the case back to the District Court, ordering it to hold an evidentiary hearing. The District Court did so, and in a 70-page opinion concluded that Davis had failed to show actual

---

34. See also *Panetti v. Quarterman*, 551 U.S. 930 (2007), holding that a defendant who had been found competent to stand trial could nevertheless file a new petition to stop his execution on the grounds that he was not competent to be executed.

innocence of his murder conviction. The Circuit Court then held that Davis had to appeal that decision directly to the Supreme Court, rather than to the Circuit Court. *Davis v. Terry*, 625 F.3d 716 (11th Cir. 2010). The Supreme Court denied certiorari. *Davis v. Humphrey*, 563 U.S. 904 (2011). Davis was later executed. It is unlikely that the Court will again allow its original jurisdiction to be invoked, but the case shows that ingenuity may find other paths to federal review.

4. Actual Innocence

Appeals and collateral attacks are not concerned with the defendant's actual innocence; they focus on whether the process by which the defendant was convicted was valid. On the other hand, recent events, especially DNA tests and the perseverance of the Innocence Project,[35] have demonstrated that some defendants really are innocent, even after all the possible avenues have examined their case. (The Project itself has proved 272 case of actual innocence.)[36] Where, then, does a claim of actual innocence stand in the second decade of the twenty-first century?

a. Innocence Commissions

Lawyers most commonly think of litigation and court hearings as the preferred method of resolving such claims — indeed, of resolving any claims of any nature. But there are other processes. In 2006, North Carolina became the first state to establish an "Innocence Commission," to hear claims from those who promised "real evidence" of actual innocence.[37] See www.innocencecommission-nc.gov/; Jerome Maiatico, All Eyes on Us: A Comparative Critique of the North Carolina Innocence Inquiry Commission, 56 Duke L.J. 1345 (2007).

---

35. For information about the Project, and about the cases they have won, see www.innocenceproject.org.

36. This is not a new phenomenon. Eighty years ago, Professor Edwin Borchard found 65 cases in which defendants had been wrongfully convicted of crimes. At that point, the primary relief mechanism was clemency. E. Borchard, Convicting the Innocent (1932) (as cited in *Herrera v. Collins*, 506 U.S. 390 (1993).

37. Canada and the United Kingdom also have such commissions. Brandon Garrett, Aggregation in Criminal Law, 95 Cal. L. Rev. 383, 435-446 (2007), describes such commissions in several other states. See also Jon Gould, The Innocence Commission: Preventing Wrongful Conviction and Restoring the Criminal Justice System (2008); Brandon Garrett, Claiming Innocence, 92 Minn. L. Rev. 1629 (2008); Kent Roach, The Role of Innocence Commission: Error Discovery, Systemic Reform or Both, 85 Chi. Kent L. Rev. 89 (2010); Stephanie Roberts and Lynne Weathered, Assisting the Factually Innocent: The Contradictions and Compatibility of Innocence Projects and the Criminal Cases Review Commission, 29 Oxford J. Legal Studies 43 (2009) (discussing England's Commission); Barry Scheck and Peter Neufeld, Toward the Formation of "Innocence Commissions" in America, 86 Judicature 98 (2002).

b. Actual Innocence in the Courts

Most prisoners maintain their claims of innocence throughout their incarcerations. Simply allowing any such claim to "reactivate" any process — state or federal — would surely lead to significant abuse. On the other hand, the mere thought that someone might actually be innocent of the crime for which he was convicted creates a moral conundrum.

Initially, in addition to, or even before, allowing post-conviction review of the defendant's trial, states provided for defendants who raised a claim of "new evidence," that is, evidence which had become available only after conviction. The statutes vary widely but generally establish a time limit (from 30 days to a few years, or "in the interests of justice"). On rare occasions, such claims result in a hearing, a new trial, and exoneration, but the hurdles are substantial.[38] The advent of increasingly sophisticated DNA testing has created a separate category for this kind of "new evidence." All but four states now provide for post-conviction access to material for DNA testing, but each has some requirements that must be met. As noted earlier (see Chapter 6), the United States Supreme Court has twice recently considered the proper federal avenue by which prisoners can raise claims seeking more DNA testing.

Slowly the Supreme Court has recognized that some final mechanism might be created to provide for such claims of actual innocence. In *Herrera v. Collins*, 506 U.S. 391, 416-417 (1993), a very divided court, in five opinions, concluded that a mere assertion of innocence, even based upon alleged new evidence, was insufficient, in itself, to support a writ for federal habeas corpus:

> Our federal habeas cases have treated claims of "actual innocence," not as an independent constitutional claim, but as a basis upon which a habeas petitioner may have an independent constitutional claim considered on the merits, even though his habeas petition would otherwise be regarded as successive or abusive.

In *Schlup v. Delo*, 513 U.S. 298, 327 (1995), the Court elaborated, holding that prisoners asserting innocence as a "gateway" to defaulted claims must establish that, in light of new evidence, "it is more likely than not that *no reasonable* juror would have found petitioner guilty beyond a reasonable doubt" (emphasis added). Although this hurdle is a high one, it was not as high as the "clear and convincing" standard of earlier cases. Nevertheless, for 10 years, the Court declined to find for any prisoner. In *House v. Bell*, 547

---

38. For one case in which a claim of new DNA testing resulted in exoneration, see *Ex Parte Thompson*, 153 S.W.3d 416 (Tex. Crim. App. 2005). But see *Moeller v. Weber*, 689 N.W.2d 1, 7 (S.D. 2004) (noting that "newly discovered evidence is not a sufficient ground for habeas relief where no deprivation of a constitutionally protected right is involved").

U.S. 518, 537 (2006), the first case in the Supreme Court dealing with DNA testing, the Court applied this pre-AEDPAstandard and found that a state prisoner had raised on a habeas corpus petition sufficient new evidence of actual innocence that he was entitled to a full evidentiary hearing in the District Court on claims that were procedurally barred under state law:

> A petitioner's burden at the gateway stage is to demonstrate that more likely than not, in light of the new evidence, no reasonable juror would find him guilty beyond a reasonable doubt or, to remove the double negative, that more likely than not any reasonable juror would have reasonable doubt.

Even after *House*, however, a convicted prisoner must present evidence of actual innocence *and* claim that some aspect of his trial[39] was constitutionally infirm. Thus, the claim of innocence is only a "gateway" that allows the defendant to overcome earlier defaults or appellate decisions. Brandon Garrett, while recognizing the narrow nature of this view, nevertheless argues that it points to the "groundwork for an innocence-based regime." Claiming Innocence, *supra*, n.36.

In its most recent declaration on the subject, the Supreme Court, in *District Attorney's Office for Third Judicial Dist. v. Osborne*, 557 U.S. 52 (2009), declared that:

> Whether such a federal right exists is an open question. We have struggled with it over the years, in some cases assuming, arguendo, that it exists while also noting the difficult questions such a right would pose and the high standard any claimant would have to meet

Examples

1. Sheba, convicted of possessing cocaine, has lost her appeals to the state appellate and supreme courts. She thinks her lawyer at trial and on direct appeal was incompetent, and she files a federal habeas corpus petition alleging that as the sole ground. What should the district court do?

2. Febrezio was convicted in state court of securities fraud. While his appeal was pending in state court, the United States Supreme Court decided *Batson*. The state supreme court remanded for reconsideration in light of the new decision, but the state trial court found against the defendant concluding that the prosecutor's explanations were race neutral. The United States Supreme Court denied certiorari. For the next five years, Febrezio sought collateral relief from the state court,

---

39. There is a likelihood that a defendant who attempts to show "actual innocence" of aggravating factors resulting in the death penalty would also be covered by *Schlup-House*. See *Dretke v. Haley*, 541 U.S. 386 (2004).

but ultimately lost. He files a petition for habeas corpus. The state argues that the U.S. District Court should not entertain the petition because there was no constitutional violation at his trial. Should the court deny the petition?

3. Remember Curtis? (See example 1, *supra*, p.366.) Suppose the *Sanchez* decision was rendered after his conviction became final and was affirmed by the state supreme court. Could he still take advantage of *Sanchez* (a) on collateral review; (b) on federal habeas corpus?

4. Assume that the Fourteenth Circuit has decided that the Fourth Amendment requires that police officers must obtain a signed permission slip from the owner before searching a car or truck, under any and all circumstances. Lionel was tried in a state court in the Fourteenth Circuit where the trial judge refused to follow that rule. The state supreme court affirmed the conviction, announcing that the defendant's claim, while plausible, does not comport with its own reading of the precedent for the United States Supreme Court. What should the district court do on Lionel's habeas petition?

5. On the day she planned to call three alibi witnesses to testify for her client, Maya discovered that those witnesses were absent from the courtroom. She asked for time to find them, but the trial court refused. Maya was convicted. On appeal to state court, the government argued, for the first time, that Maya had not put her request for a continuance in writing, as required by state court rule. The appellate court therefore concluded that the claim had been forfeited. Assume that the case finally gets to federal court. Will the federal court hear the complaint?

6. (a) Cleopatra was convicted of capital homicide in 1982, under a state statute which used the term, "especially heinous, atrocious, or cruel (HAC)." On appeal, however, her attorney focused on other concerns, and did not attack the phrase as vague. The state appellate court upheld the conviction and death penalty in 1984. Cleopatra filed her first state post-conviction petition in the state trial court on June 22, 1984, attaching the conviction and death sentence. The trial court held a hearing and denied the petition. The state court of criminal appeals affirmed the denial and the state supreme court declined her request to appeal. Five years later, in June 1989, Cleo filed a second state post-conviction petition. In her second petition, Cleo alleged numerous constitutional violations including, for the first time, an Eighth Amendment claim that the language of the aggravator considered by the jury in the sentencing phase was unconstitutionally vague. The trial court dismissed the second petition as barred by the successive petition restrictions of the state's post-conviction statute, holding that all the grounds raised in the second petition were barred either because they had been previously

determined or because the had been waived. The judgment was affirmed by the court of criminal appeals and the state supreme court denied the application for permission to appeal. The United States Supreme Court denied Cleo's petition for a writ of certiorari. She now seeks federal habeas corpus. The state has moved to dismiss, on the ground that the claim is procedurally barred. What should you, as the district court judge, do?

(b) Assume you, as the district judge, have decided that the state supreme court did decide that claim on the merits. You must now determine whether Cleo's death penalty was legal. Your research reveals the following: (1) In *Godfrey v. Georgia*, 446 U.S. 420 (1980), the Supreme Court held that a state statute which considered, as an aggravating factor in determining the death penalty, whether the homicide was "outrageously or wantonly vile, horrible or inhuman," standing alone, was unconstitutionally vague. (2) Later, in *Maynard v. Cartwright*, 486 U.S. 356 (1988), the Court held that the "especially heinous, atrocious, or cruel" aggravating circumstance (HAC) of another statute was unconstitutionally vague, as it did not offer sufficient guidance to the jury in deciding whether to impose the death penalty. Although Cleo's trial court did instruct the jury in terms of HAC, it also gave a limiting instruction, which defined some of the terms of the aggravating factor as follows: "Heinous" means extremely wicked or shockingly evil. "Atrocious" means outrageously wicked and vile. "Cruel" means designed to inflict a high degree of pain, utter indifference to, or enjoyment of, the suffering of others, pitiless. The state courts, through a long series of appeals and post-conviction petitions, upheld the death penalty. (3) In *Proffitt v. Florida*, 428 U.S. 242 (1976), decided eight years before Cleo's conviction became final, the Court held that Florida's HAC aggravator was not unconstitutionally vague in light of the Florida courts' narrowing construction that the term "heinous, atrocious, or cruel" means a "conscienceless, or pitiless crime which is unnecessarily torturous to the victim." *Id.* at 255-56. The narrowing language is the identical language the state supreme court used in narrowing the state's aggravator. (4) However, in *Shell v. Mississippi*, 498 U.S. 1 (1990) (per curiam), the Supreme Court announced that the "heinous, atrocious, or cruel" language, along with the same "limiting" definitions as were provided to the jury in Cleo's case, was unconstitutional. (5) Finally, in *Stringer v. Black*, 503 U.S. 222 (1992), the Court declared that "the language [in *Maynard* ("especially heinous, atrocious or cruel")] gave no more guidance than did the statute in *Godfrey* [("outrageously or wantonly vile, horrible or inhuman")] . . . *Godfrey* and *Maynard* did indeed involve somewhat different language. But it would be a mistake to conclude that the vagueness ruling of *Godfrey* was limited to the precise language before us in the case." What do you do now?

7. Juanita is convicted in state court. Her counsel on appeal does not raise certain issues. New counsel files a claim asserting that Juanita's first appellate counsel was inadequate, in the appropriate state court, one hundred days after the judgment affirming Juanita's conviction. State rules required the filing to be within 90 days "unless the applicant shows good cause of filing at a later time." The state court dismisses the inadequate counsel claim, on the grounds that it was untimely filed. What should the federal habeas court do?

8. A jury convicted John of murder. The trial had been watched by several members of the victim's family who wore buttons featuring a photo of the victim. John's lawyer, Sadie, objected to the presence of the photo buttons at the outset of the trial, but the trial court denied the motion, stating that it saw "no possible prejudice to the defendant." John appealed his conviction to the state court of appeals, and to the state supreme court, unsuccessfully raising in each court the issue of the buttons. The state supreme court's opinion discussed, *inter alia*, two United States Supreme Court decisions. In *Estelle v. Williams*, 425 U.S. 501 (1976), the Supreme Court held that a defendant who was compelled to wear identifiable prison clothing at his trial was denied due process. In *Holbrook v. Flynn*, 475 U.S. 560 (1986), the Court held that the seating of four uniformed state troopers immediately behind the defendant was not so inherently prejudicial that it denied the defendant a fair trial. The state supreme court concluded that the *Flynn* decision, rather than *Williams*, applied, and denied John's constitutional claims.

    At the conclusion of the state process, John filed an application for a writ of habeas corpus in federal district court. The district court granted the writ, saying that both *Williams* and *Flynn* clearly established the test for inherent prejudice applicable to spectators' courtroom conduct, and that the state supreme court's application was "contrary to clearly established federal law and constituted an unreasonable application of that law" under AEDPA. The circuit court affirmed, and the state now appeals to the United States Supreme Court. What is the likely result?

9. In Elvira's trial for larceny, the voir dire of jurors was held before Judge Major, but when Major became ill, Judge Kenyon replaced him and heard peremptory challenges. When Elvira argued that the prosecutor had dismissed two female jurors in violation of *Batson*, the prosecutor argued that one of the jurors had been "somewhat humorous" and another "not serious." Kenyon denied the claim. Both state appellate courts and state post-conviction courts also denied the claim. Elvira then went to federal court, arguing that the state courts had all given

Kenyon's decisions "deference" that was undeserved. *Batson* suggested such deference, she argued, because the trial judge had seen the voir dire. But Judge Kenyon had not seen the voir dire, and the state court's deference violated both her Sixth Amendment rights and the equal protection rights of the two jurors. What should the District Judge do?

10. While Tom Crews's appeal is pending before the Missouri Supreme Court, the United States Court of Appeals for the Eighth Circuit (which sits in St. Louis) holds, in a case from Iowa with a fact pattern identical to that involved in *Crews*, that Iowa violated the defendant's *Miranda* federal constitutional rights. The Missouri Supreme Court rejects Crews's claim, saying (inter alia): "We are aware of the recent decision by the Eighth Circuit on facts identical to these. Suffice to say that we disagree with that court as to the reach of *Miranda*." Crews now seeks federal habeas corpus, citing the conflict. Should the federal District Court grant the writ?

11. Albert Albrecht's wife died in a fire in their house. Al was prosecuted for arson and murder. Al argued that the fire had been started by a smoldering cigarette and that somehow the fire had spread to the rest of the house. The prosecution expert (Trooper York) testified at length (and was cross-examined for three days) that there was clear evidence of accelerant and that the pattern of burns left no doubt that the fire was set. After exhausting his state appeals and filing a federal habeas corpus petition (which was denied), Al files a second petition, contending that a new expert would testify that new advances in fire science have provided evidence that directly contradicted the prosecution's expert. The expert submits an affidavit that the fire was most likely accidental, and the spreading was caused by "flashover," a phenomenon only recently studied by such experts. Al argues that this information proves his actual innocence and that he should not be barred from bringing this petition because this information could not have been presented at trial, or even during his state court processes. What result?

12. At his murder trial, Guillermo was represented by Paul, who was licensed to practice in the state. Guillermo was convicted and sentenced to death. Paul also handled Guillermo's appeal. When those failed, Guillermo's new counsel, Maurice, contacted the law firm of Dewey and Howe (DH), a large out-of-state law firm which provided pro bono representation in capital cases. That firm assigned Jebediah to handle the post-conviction proceedings. Maurice appeared at the post-conviction proceeding solely for the purpose of moving the pro hac vice admission of Jebediah. He did not further participate in the case. Among the post-conviction claims were that (1) Paul had provided ineffective assistance at trial, because Paul had failed to ask for an instruction on the lesser

included offense of manslaughter. (2) Paul had failed to find, and present at the penalty phase, substantial mitigating evidence. Two years later, the state trial court denied post-conviction relief, finding no ineffective assistance. A copy of the judgement was sent to Maurice, and to Jebediah at DH. State law required that any appeal from the denial of post-conviction relief be filed within 42 days. Maurice did not respond. Unhappily, Jebediah had left the firm, and the postal clerk in the firm's office did not forward the court notice to Miriam, who had been assigned by DH to the matter. Instead, the postal clerk returned the notice to the state court, unopened. It was stamped "Return to Sender — Attempted — No Longer at Firm." Miriam later sought to obtain relief from the state Supreme Court, which denied her motion for an out-of-time appeal of the denial of post-conviction relief. Thereafter, when Guillermo sought relief in federal habeas corpus, the federal district court found that his failure to file an appeal within 42 days was a procedural default, and that he was precluded from raising the issues he had sought to raise in the post-conviction proceeding. On appeal, what result?

13. Defendant was serving a life sentence when he killed a prison guard and an inmate. The jury sentenced him to death. Trial counsel failed to investigate defendant's background. Had he done so, he would have learned that defendant suffered from Fetal Alcohol Spectrum Disorder, which had resulted from his mother's use of drugs and alcohol while she was pregnant with defendant and that this condition contributed to defendant's impulsiveness and impacted his judgment. State habeas counsel fails to assert a claim regarding trial counsel's ineffectiveness due to counsel's mistaken belief that funding was capped. Defendant raises the claim for the first time in federal court. What should the federal court respond?

14. Defendant's trial counsel challenged the admission of incriminating evidence on Fourth Amendment grounds, claiming that the evidence should have been suppressed. The challenge was unsuccessful and defendant was convicted. Defendant appeals his conviction. Defendant's new appellate attorney fails to assert a claim challenging the admission of this evidence due to a misreading of Supreme Court precedents. Defendant subsequently files a writ of habeas corpus in state court. In the writ he fails to claim that his appellate attorney was ineffective for failing to assert the Fourth Amendment claim. After his state writ is denied he files a federal writ in which for the first time he claims ineffective assistance of appellate counsel. Should the federal court consider the merits of the claim?

Explanations

1. We start off with an easy one — don't touch the claim; instead tell Sheba to exhaust her state remedies. Whether the policy behind federal habeas corpus is to assure a fair trial, or to be sure that state courts were accurately applying federal law (in this case *Strickland*) the state courts have had no chance to act on this claim.

2. In *Miller-El v. Cockrel*, 537 U.S. 322 (2003), the Court held that since defendant's federal claim had never been decided by a federal court, his procedural posture was that he had a right to assert the new rule because his case was still on direct review when *Batson* was decided. *Teague* was intended to prevent federal courts from applying a "new rule" to a situation in which the state courts had never had an opportunity to apply the rule. Here, there was such an opportunity. The Court remanded for a decision on the merits of the federal claim.

3. (a) Possibly, but not likely. Many states either refuse totally or are at least reluctant to review again any issue which was, or could have been, raised on appeal. Had Curtis raised the question on appeal, the leading case might be *State v. Curtis* rather than *State v. Sanchez*. The serious point here is that we want to encourage defendants to raise every possible argument on appeal, not wait to see whether the law develops in their favor and then become a free rider. Collateral attacks are frequently limited to those issues which were not, and "could not" have been raised on appeal (such as ineffective assistance of counsel) e.g., Okla. Stat. tit. 22, §1089(c), or those on which more evidence would be necessary to resolve a factual issue. Most state statutes also allow raising an issue if a "manifest injustice" would be done if the claim were not allowed to be raised. See, e.g., 42 Penn. Cons. Stat. §9453(a). Even in a state allowing broader collateral review, the application of a newly announced decision may depend on whether the new decision is seen as announcing a "new rule" which the trial court could not have anticipated. This position, which is the state analogue of *Teague*, focuses on supervising trial courts rather than on a retrospective view of whether the trial was "fair" as we now understand it.

   (b) No. Absolutely not. As the problem is written, the *Sanchez* case is not based on the United States Constitution. The first predicate of federal jurisdiction is a federal constitutional issue. There is none here. Case over.

4. Deny the petition and affirm the conviction. Even though the circuit court has declared its view of the Constitution, under AEDPA, so long as the state court's interpretation of the law is not "contrary" to "established *Supreme Court* precedent," the decision is to be upheld, even if the

district judge thinks it is incorrect. AEDPA makes clear that in these circumstances, the petition "shall not be granted." The result would be the same even if *all* circuit courts agreed with the Fourteenth Circuit. It is true that state courts have never been "bound" by federal circuit court opinions, even from circuit courts in their own circuit. But AEDPA makes clear that the state courts may effectively ignore those courts, as well as district courts.

5. Probably not. The general rule is that failure to comply with a state procedural rule bars federal review. *Stewart v. Smith*, 534 U.S. 157 (2002). This, after all, is a legitimate state procedural rule, and the issue was precluded. There is no "cause" for Maya's failing to put it in writing. However, in *Lee v. Kemna*, 534 U.S. 362 (2002), the Court found that the defense attorney's strenuous oral objections to the judge's refusal to grant the continuance, coupled with (a) the state trial court's reason for not allowing the continuance (he had a personal matter the following day), and (b) the fact that the trial court knew that the witnesses had been present throughout the trial, sufficed to show that the purpose of the state rule — to make the trial court fully aware of the dilemma — had been fulfilled. Therefore, the district court should not have precluded further inquiry into the matter. As it turned out, the three witnesses later filed affidavits that they had been told, by court officers, that they would not be called until the following day. *Kemna* seems extremely fact-specific; but it also reflects the Court's impatience with restrictive application of the procedural default rules. By the way, the *Kemna* Court barely cited AEDPA, or its limiting language.

6. (a) This example reflects the complicated nature of timing in habeas cases. If this were not a death penalty case, Cleo's claim would almost surely be procedurally barred. She, or her counsel, appears not to have clearly and unequivocally put the issue to the state courts. Even on a "deliberate bypass" test, the failure to raise the claim would preclude federal review. To overcome the default under the more restrictive "cause and prejudice" test of *Sykes*, Cleo would have to show that her counsel excusably did not focus on the language of the statute. As a general rule, on habeas review, federal courts may not consider procedurally defaulted claims. *Seymour v. Walker*, 224 F.3d 542, 549-50 (6th Cir. 2000). Thus, if the prisoner has forfeited the claim, such forfeiture will constitute a procedural default and will serve as an adequate and independent state ground barring habeas review in the court. On the other hand, if the state courts "previously determined" the claim, the federal court may consider the merits. You, as the district judge, must determine which one actually describes the status of Cleo's constitutional claim in the state courts. If she is not barred, you may move on to the merits (whether the state court's determination

"resulted in a decision that was contrary to, or involved an unreasonable application of, clearly established federal law, as determined by the Supreme Court of the United States"), which, of course, is still a high hurdle for her to vault. To reach your conclusion on this, you'd have to review the precise wording of state court precedents to determine whether this state court carries out "implicit review" in death penalty cases. Some federal courts frequently hold that a state court reviewing a death penalty appeal "implicitly" reviews all issues that could arguably be considered as raised within the wording of the petition or other moving papers.

(b) Under AEDPA, when a petitioner's claim has been adjudicated on the merits in a state court, a federal court may not grant a writ of habeas corpus with respect to such claim, unless the state court's determination resulted in a decision that was contrary to, or involved an unreasonable application of, clearly established federal law, as determined by the Supreme Court of the United States. A state court's decision must be evaluated against the clearly established Supreme Court precedent *at the time the petitioner's conviction became final.* Therefore, as a normal matter, only the *Godfrey* and *Profitt* decisions would be relevant. But in *Cone v. Bell*, 359 F.3d 785 (6th Cir. 2004), the case upon which this example is based, the Sixth Circuit found that the language of the Supreme Court in *Stringer* clearly set the "tone" for interpreting language of the kind involved in the death penalty aggravator here. Any such vague wording, whether explicitly addressed by the Supreme Court or not, was palpably unconstitutional after *Godfrey*, and before *Maynard*. Thus, at the time of Cleo's trial (1982), the use of that aggravator was contrary to "clearly established federal law." The example demonstrates how carefully a federal habeas court must parse earlier opinions, particularly Supreme Court opinions, particularly in light of AEDPA's limiting language. The Supreme Court reversed, 543 U.S. 447 (2005), finding that the state supreme court had applied its own law and, moreover, that the state court decision was not contrary to "clearly" established federal law, after a thorough dissection of the precise language used in many of those earlier Supreme Court opinions.

7. After *Edwards v. Carpenter*, 529 U.S. 446 (2000), the federal court should dismiss the application for habeas corpus because the inadequate counsel claim has been procedurally defaulted by procedural default in raising the claim. (Does this sound like Rod Serling to you?) What happened to the argument (see Chapter 10) that recognized that it is the defendant, not the attorney, who suffers when the attorney makes a mistake? Two mistakes? Two attorneys? Note, however, that the Court in *Carpenter* did recognize that if the defendant could demonstrate a "sufficient" probability that failure to review his federal claim "will

result in a fundamental miscarriage of justice," the federal claim could be heard, notwithstanding the default of the claim. On the other hand, as the Court in *Carpenter* noted, if there were no procedural default rule, "habeas petitioners would be able to avoid the exhaustion requirement by defaulting their federal claims in state court."

8. The district court found the right part of AEDPA — but it probably reached the wrong result. At least that's what the United States Supreme Court held in *Carey v. Musladin*, 549 U.S. 70 (2006). The Court actually said that neither *Flynn* nor *Williams* was directly on point, since in each of those cases there had been "state-sponsored" courtroom conduct, whereas "this Court has never addressed a claim that . . . private-actor courtroom conduct" was so inherently prejudicial that it deprived a defendant of a fair trial. The Court reviewed a "wide divergence" of decisions from federal and state courts, attempting to interpret *Williams* and *Flynn*. "Given the lack of holding from this Court . . . it cannot be said that the state court 'unreasonably applied clearly established' Federal law. No *holding* of this Court required [the state] to apply the test of *Williams* and *Flynn* to the spectators' conduct here" (emphasis added). The *Carey* decision reflects the view of at least some commentators that it is extremely difficult for habeas petitioners to show that there is a United States Supreme Court case that establishes a particular holding so "clearly" — and is so close to the facts of the case at bar — as not to be barred by AEDPA.

9. In *Thaler v. Haynes*, 559 U.S. 43 (2010), the Court, per curiam, concluded that while earlier opinions had spoken about giving deference because of personal observation, no earlier decision had "clearly established" that as a basis of *Batson* challenges. Therefore the state court decisions did not misconstrue "clearly established" federal law: "No decision of this Court clearly establishes the categorical rule" defendant sought.

10. No. Crews will bring his claim under AEDPA, which provides habeas corpus relief only if the state court decision is contrary to Supreme Court rulings. Even a direct conflict with a federal circuit court — including one sitting in the same region as the state court — will not be sufficient for habeas relief. *Renico v. Lett*, 559 U.S. 766 (2010). In essence, AEDPA recognizes that only the United States Supreme Court can issue constitutional decisions that "bind" the states.

11. In *Albrecht v. Horn*, 485 F.3d 103 (3d Cir. 2007), the court denied relief, finding that there was insufficient evidence of actual innocence and that the expert evidence was not "clear enough" to warrant allowing the second petition. The court meticulously compared the actual facts of the *House* case (where the Supreme Court found sufficient evidence of actual innocence in a DNA matter) with the facts in *Albrecht*, and concluded that

"[e]ven if we assume that Trooper York's testimony has been discredited . . . the new evidence raised questions about the alleged incendiary nature of the fire, while identity and motive (implicating Albrecht) were established by the other evidence." Thus, there was still sufficient evidence — without York's testimony — upon which the jury could have concluded that Albrecht wanted to kill his wife. "Because (the new defense expert) did not conclude that the fire was accidental, and because there was ample other evidence of guilt, Albrecht's new evidence falls short of showing that he is actually innocent under the *Herrera* standards." But (at least in non-DNA cases) few experts will give an "unequivocal" opinion. If that is what *Herrera-House* requires, virtually no defendants will obtain relief on a claim of actual innocence.

12. In *Maples v. Allen*, 586 F.3d 879 (llth Cir. 2009) the Eleventh Circuit concluded that Jebediah's failure to timely appeal did not constitute cause for excusing Guillermo's default, and that he could not argue Jebediah's ineffective assistance of counsel as cause for failing to file timely, because there was no constitutional right to effective assistance on post-conviction relief, and hence no constitutionally recognizable "cause." One judge of the panel dissented, arguing that (1) the 42 day time limit was not an adequate and independent state ground, in part because the statute had not been regularly followed; (2) the interest of justice required review of the claim of ineffective assistance of trial counsel..

In *Maples v. Thomas*, 565 U.S 266 (2012), the case on appeal from the Eleventh Circuit, the Court held that because defendant in similar circumstances had been abandoned by his post-conviction counsel, there was cause for the default and resulting prejudice.

13. The claim was procedurally defaulted as a result of state habeas counsel's failure to raise it in state court. However, *Martinez v. Ryan* allows the federal court to consider the claim on the merits if defendant can demonstrate the claim is substantial and that post-conviction counsel was ineffective in failing to raise it. The Supreme Court has recognized that this type of mitigation evidence is useful to defendants in the sentencing phase of a capital case because it diminishes their blameworthiness. The federal court will apply *Strickland* in determining whether state habeas counsel was ineffective. Trial counsel's performance certainly appears to have been deficient. A reasonable attorney would have known that his funding was not capped. The big question will be whether defendant suffered prejudice as a result of the failure to raise the claim. That will depend on the amount of aggravating evidence and other mitigating evidence that was presented during the sentencing hearing.

14. As a result of the Supreme Court's decision in *Davila v. Davis*, 137 S. Ct. 2058 (2017), the federal courts cannot consider the merits of the ineffective assistance of *appellate* counsel claim because it has been procedurally defaulted. According to the Court, the merits of the Fourth Amendment issue was considered by the trial court which ruled on the claim. The exception created in *Martinez v. Ryan* applies only to claims that were never considered in any state court.

Non-Criminal Remedies for Unacceptable Lawyering

Courts are reluctant to overturn convictions, even if one of the attorneys — prosecutor or defense counsel — has committed an error. As Judge (later Justice) Cardozo put it, it is not clear why "[t]he criminal is to go free because the [lawyer] has blundered." *People v. Defore*, 242 N.Y. 13, 21 (1926). As we have already noted, as the Warren Court both applied the Bill of Rights to the states and expanded the definitions of those rights, it simultaneously vitiated, in *Chapman v. California*, the view that all constitutional errors were harmful. And in the past half-century, fewer and fewer constitutional errors have been deemed automatic grounds for reversal. A constant refrain in these opinions was the view that the defendant was not entitled to a "windfall" just because the defense counsel was ineffective or the prosecutor (or the judge) had "blundered."[1] Moreover, in at least some of these areas (e.g., selective prosecution, prosecutorial "goading" of a defense motion for mistrial, or misuse of peremptory challenges), the defendant must demonstrate not merely that there *was* error of a constitutional level (e.g., that the prosecutor peremptorily struck all persons of a specific race), but that the prosecution *intended* to violate the Constitution. Bennett L. Gershman, Mental Culpability and Prosecutorial Misconduct, 26 Am. J. Crim. L. 121 (1998).

In the context of police conduct, the exclusionary rule appeared to be the only — or at least the most readily available — method by which the *courts* could deter future misconduct. In the case of prosecutors and defense counsel,

---

1. See, e.g., the comment of Justice Rehnquist: "[T]he touchstone of due process analysis is the fairness of the trial, not the culpability of the prosecutor." *Smith v. Phillips*, 455 U.S. 209, 219 (1982).

however, there are many other processes — many controlled or influenced by the judiciary — for dealing with such errors, and hopefully deterring attorney misconduct. In fact, a key explanation given by the Supreme Court for its holding in *Imbler v. Pachtman*, 442 U.S. 409 (1976), protecting prosecutors with absolute immunity from tort liability, was that there were other ways, short of reversing convictions of "clearly" guilty defendants, to deal with errant lawyers. This chapter explores some of those alternatives, and assesses their efficacy.

First, however, a caveat: The fact that there are cases demonstrating egregious conduct by prosecutors or defense counsel does not mean that more than a handful of lawyers violate the norms of acceptable behavior. Most attorneys, all the time, are both fair and competent.[2] Even those prosecutors or defense counsel who cross the line drawn by the Constitution (or court rules) do so mostly in the "heat of battle" or because of "cognitive bias."[3] The issue here is what steps, if any, may be taken by either the government or private individuals whose rights have been violated *even if the conviction stands*.

A. DEFINING — AND UNDERSTANDING — "MISCONDUCT"[4]

Misconduct, by either defense counsel[5] or prosecutor, can occur at any time — pre-trial, during trial, after trial. The wide varieties of decisions

---

2. Jonathan K. Van Patten, Suing the Prosecutor, 55 S.D.L. Rev. 214 (2010):

> The prosecutor at his or her best is indeed one of the most beneficent forces in our society. Whether it is the prosecution of small-time crooks or large-scale swindlers, the conviction of murderers, serial killers or terrorists, the prosecutor's diligence helps to ensure that no one is above the law. No diagnosis of the problem, nor prescription for cure, can ignore the indispensable role played by the prosecutor. It would be foolish to view the problem of the rogue prosecutor in isolation. Any diagnosis and prescription must take care not to jeopardize the independence and courage of the prosecutor who does the right thing.

3. In the past decade there has been an explosion of materials applying psychology and sociology to prosecutor (and defense counsel) decisions. See, e.g., Alafair Burke, Prosecutorial Passion, Cognitive Bias, and Plea Bargaining, 91 Marq. L. Rev. (2007); Alafair Burke, Neutralizing Cognitive Bias: An Invitation to Prosecutors, 2 N.Y.U. J.L. & Lib. 412 (2007); Daniel Medwed, The Zeal Deal: Prosecutorial Resistance to Post-Conviction Claims of Innocence, 84 B.U.L. Rev. 125 (2004); Dianne L. Martin, Lessons About Justice from the "Laboratory" of Wrongful Convictions: Tunnel Vision, the Construct of Guilt and Informer Evidence, 70 U.M.K.C. L. Rev. 847 (2002).
4. See, e.g., Randall D. Eliason, The Prosecutor's Role: A Response to Professor Davis, II Crim. L. Brief 15 (Fall 2006), arguing that even the term "prosecutorial [or defense — ED.] misconduct" is unfair, and should be replaced by the term "prosecutorial error."
5. Most ethical and professional standards apply to both defense and prosecuting counsel. However, the criminal defense attorney is exempt from the ethics provision that broadly prohibits "asserting or controverting an issue therein unless there is a basis in law and fact for

which can be found to be "error," or "ineffective" precludes an all-inclusive listing. But among commonly alleged violations are:

- abuse of the grand jury by the prosecutor;
- improper plea bargaining tactics (either side);
- failure to disclose information (either side);
- forensic misconduct in summation (either side);
- failing to investigate thoroughly, particularly where the lead might be helpful to the opponent;[6]
- ineffective assistance (defense counsel).

1. Abuse of the Grand Jury

A prosecutor might "abuse" the grand jury in many ways — issuing overly broad subpoenas, creating a "perjury trap," ignoring and/or not disclosing truly exculpatory information, etc. But, as discussed in Chapter 4, the Supreme Court has now effectively precluded relief in the criminal realm, at least by a convicted defendant, for such abuse. The *Mechanik* view that grand jury errors are "erased" by a petit jury conviction means that most such grand jury abuse, which is usually discovered after the trial, simply does not result in overturning a conviction.[7]

2. Investigative Issues

The number and sorts of ethical missteps that either side can make during the investigative process are legion. In 2008, the American Bar Association adopted its "Criminal Justice Standards of Prosecutorial Investigation." Among the chief abuses (in which defense counsel may also indulge) is

---

doing so." ABA Model Rules of Professional Conduct R. 3.1. Moreover, the Model Rules have a specific provision (3.8) covering only prosecutors.

6. "Prosecutors are under no obligation to conduct thorough investigations to ensure the veracity of each witness. Thus, they may engage in willful blindness, presenting a witness who helps their case without testing the truthfulness of his testimony." A. Davis, Arbitrary Justice 54 (2007).

7. *People v. Thorbourn*, 121 Cal. App. 4th 1083, 18 Cal. Rptr. 3d 77 (Cal. Ct. App. 2004). On the other hand, if the misuse is discovered before trial, courts have dismissed indictments, quashed subpoenas, issued protective orders, removed materials from the indictment, or excised testimony. See B. Gershman, Prosecutorial Misconduct, sec. 2:54; P. Henning, Prosecutorial Misconduct in Grand Jury Investigations, 51 S.C. L. Rev. 1 (1999). But see *State v. Vinegra*, 73 N.J. 484 (1977): "If the assignment judge was of the view that the prosecutor's conduct was so egregious as to call for disciplinary action, he might have referred the matter to the District Ethics Committee or the Administrative Director of the Courts. . . . Dismissal of the indictment was too drastic a remedy."

"trying the case in the press." The ABA Standards have been adopted by at least 24 states, virtually all of them since 2000. Niki Kuckes, The State of Rule 3.8: Prosecutorial Ethics Reform since Ethics 2000, 22 Geo. J. Legal Ethics 427 (2009).

3. Plea Bargaining Tactics

Because prosecutors have unreviewed charging discretion (see Chapter 3), it is common to begin the process with very serious charges. Similarly, in light of the double jeopardy jurisprudence which allows "double charging" for the same conduct, if covered by two separate statutes (see Chapter 9), prosecutors often start the negotiating stage from a position of enormous strength. As discussed in Chapter 7, prosecutors sometimes walk very close to the line in interpreting and applying plea agreements.[8] Moreover, in jurisdictions with structured sentencing systems, where judges have little or no discretion to affect the sentence of the crime of conviction, the prosecutor holds even greater cards in plea bargaining than was the case 20 years ago.

4. Discovery Violations

Failure to provide information required by discovery rules — whether by *Brady* or by court rules — is perhaps the single largest area of misconduct. As a constitutional matter, the prosecutor is required "only" to provide defense counsel with "exculpatory," "material" information. As detailed in Chapter 6, the Supreme Court has consistently narrowed the definition of "material" information so that a prosecutor who is not certain whether disclosure is required may well reasonably decide that the information is not "material." Even where court rules or decisions require broader disclosure, but fall short of "open file" disclosure, each side is likely to construe the rules so as to allow it not to disclose particularly harmful information. There are several plausible explanations for a non-disclosure decision by a prosecutor (or a defense attorney): (1) the prosecutor subjectively does not see the information as "exculpatory"; (2) the lawyer convinced of the defendant's guilt (or innocence), fears that disclosure would unjustifiably free (or convict) the defendant, so that the end (conviction or acquittal) justifies the means (non-disclosure). Prosecutors may also decide to have evidence

---

8. The court in *Herrera v. State*, 64 P.3d 724 (Wyo. 2003), excoriated the prosecutor who said she supported "with reluctance" a sentence agreed to in a plea bargain, warned her about playing "fast and loose" with such agreements, and reminded her of her ethical obligations under the state's rules of professional conduct.

destroyed. See *Wilkinson v. Ellis*, 484 F. Supp. 1072 (E.D. Pa. 1980). At least one court has held that such a decision is not protected by absolute immunity. *Yarris v. County of Delaware*, 465 F.3d 129 (3rd Cir. 2006).

Psychologists have, in the past several decades, labeled these explanations "cognitive bias"[9] and "noble cause."[10] Thus, in some instances, even where DNA evidence has exonerated a defendant, prosecutors have persisted in asserting the defendant's guilt.

5. Trial Problems

Prosecutors — and defense counsel — sometimes become so captured by the "cognitive bias" or the "noble cause"[11] of their position that, in the middle of trial, they present (or fail to prevent a state's witness from presenting) testimony that they know is perjurious,[12] harass witnesses, mischaracterize the evidence, or make improper closing remarks.

Trials are hectic events, filled with emotion and surprises. Most missteps at trial are impulsive, and often self-defeating. The age-old caution never to ask a question to which you don't know the answer stems from trials where the ardor of the moment may cause either attorney to "try too hard" and introduce evidence which obviously should be excluded, or to utter words which, in other contexts, she would never utter.[13] Still, even if most of these events may be inadvertent, there is always the possibility that the attorney planned the transgression, hoping to affect the verdict. Such unethical conduct, even if "harmless error" in the context of the criminal verdict, should be subject to some review.

---

9. See Rand, Understanding Why Good Lawyers Go Bad: Using Case Studies in Teaching Cognitive Bias in Legal Decision-Making, 9 Clinical L. Rev. 731 (2003); Donald C. Langevoort, Where Were the Lawyers? A Behavioral Inquiry into Lawyers' Responsibility for Clients' Fraud, 46 Vand. L. Rev. 75 (1993).
10. See Randall Grometstein, Prosecutorial Misconduct and Noble-Cause Corruption, 43 Crim. L. Bull. 63 (2007).
11. See R. Grometstein, *supra*, n.10. Although this article is limited to prosecutors, defense counsel, too, can be so persuaded that a client is innocent, or that the "system" is so corrupt, that "anything goes."
12. *Napue v. Illinois*, 360 U.S. 264 (1959) (intentional concealment of a plea bargain with prosecution witness, even when witness denied such an agreement on the stand).
13. Prosecutors are often judicially chastised for making either of two related arguments in death penalty cases: (1) "show the defendant as much mercy as he showed his victim"; (2) the "Golden Rule" argument — "do unto the defendant as he did unto the victim". See *Merck v. State*, 955 So. 2d 1054 (2007); *State v. Rice*, 375 S.C. 302 (2007). The reversals, however, are few. A. Alschuler, Courtroom Misconduct by Prosecutors and Trial Judges, 50 Tex. L. Rev. 629 (1972); Singer, Forensic Misconduct by Federal Prosecutors — and How It Grew, 20 Ala. L. Rev. 227 (1968).

6. Post Conviction (In) Action

As noted in Chapter 13, in 2008 the ABA amended section 3.8 of the Model Rules to require prosecutors to disclose post-conviction, new information that created a "reasonable likelihood" that the convicted defendant was innocent. While the Standards are not "law," they certainly suggest that prosecutors (and defense counsel) have post-conviction ethical obligations, which may soon be converted into legal obligations. See, generally, Laurie L. Levenson, Prosecutorial Sound Bites: When Do They Cross the Line, 44 Ga. L. Rev. 1021 (2010).

B. ALTERNATIVE REMEDIES

I. Internal Supervision

The most obvious, and least visible, process by which misconduct by a prosecutor (or public defender) may be monitored and corrected is inside the governmental agency for which he works. In most offices, senior attorneys will train, and assess, new lawyers. Whether there is formal training or not, managers inside the office will closely supervise the neophyte. In most instances, this will mean that a new attorney's "misconduct" is caught before it becomes "misconduct."

Supervision decreases, however, with seniority, which often means that attorneys who draw the more serious (or more difficult) cases will be less monitored than new attorneys. This means that unofficial pressures to walk near the line of unethical or unconstitutional conduct may be greatest here.

Internal chastisement, even when it occurs, is likely to be informal. If an attorney is substantially incompetent, particularly over a period of time, reassignment to less important cases, or notices to the file, may occur. It is not likely that the attorney will be fired directly.

These "internal" systems are "voluntary"; concerns may arise when a senior attorney views a less experienced lawyer's work product, or discusses the case with him, or sees her in court. Victims may file complaints with the office (see Chapter 15), but often do not have a "right" to have the matter pursued, much less to have the internal decision reviewed, either by a higher administrator, or by a court. In the military, supervising officers are criminally responsible for misconduct the commander "should have known" would occur. Were this standard (even in a civil, or even disciplinary) mode applied in criminal matters, it might have a significant effect upon supervision. See Geoffrey S. Corn and Adam M. Gershowitz, Imputed Liability for Supervising Prosecutors: Applying the Military Doctrine of Command

Responsibility to Reduce Prosecutorial Misconduct, 14 Berkeley J. Crim. L. 395 (2009).

In states which do not have "offices" of public defenders, but rely on "contract" lawyers, the likelihood of supervision is significantly less. Usually, it will only occur if the new lawyer seeks out more senior attorneys, in other firms, for guidance. This may well be inadequate.

2. Oversight by Attorneys

The ABA Model Rule of Professional Conduct 8.3 requires attorneys to notify local bar association disciplinary committees when they have "knowledge" that another lawyer has "committed a violation . . . that raises a substantial question as to that lawyer's honesty, trustworthiness or fitness as a lawyer in other respects. . . ." Yet studies show that this is rarely done, even when the opposing attorney's conduct is egregious. Obvious explanations for such reticence include: (1) empathy for the attorney ("there but for the grace . . ."); (2) reluctance to assume that misconduct in this one case epitomizes the conduct of the attorney generally; and (3) concern, particularly by defense attorneys, that their relationship with the individual prosecutor or the entire office of the prosecutor may be harmed if the complaint is seen as "unworthy" of formal action.

For practical reasons also, attorneys refrain from raising ethical complaints about their opponent's behavior. A particularly powerful and poignant example is given by Professor Vanessa Merton in her article, What Do You Do When You Meet a "Walking Violation of the Sixth Amendment" If You're Trying to Put That Lawyer's Client in Jail?, 69 Fordham L. Rev. 997 (2000). Previously having been an aggressive defense counsel, Professor Merton became the supervising attorney in a law school "prosecutorial" clinic. A defense attorney assigned to one of the cases handled by the law students was undoubtedly incompetent — not only in the specific case, but generally, as Merton discovered in discussions with other prosecutors. Nevertheless, as concerned as she was about the rights of the defendant, Professor Merton never raised with the trial judge the question of whether the defendant was receiving effective counsel. As she recognizes, this reticence may have violated commentary to the ABA Standards that declares that "[a] prosecutor may possess a natural and understandable interest in how vigorously that individual is being represented. . . . Prosecutors are often uniquely well situated to assess the quality of the defense bar and defense representation in their jurisdictions."[14] In part, her decision not to alert the court to what she perceived as totally inadequate representation was based

---

14. ABA Standards: Prosecution Function Standard 3-1.3(h) (Commentary).

on her fear that proceedings to show incompetence would consume hundreds of hours, which could result in less vigorous prosecution of other cases, and in less training for her student-prosecutors. In part, she was uncertain whether, even if defense counsel's incompetence were demonstrated, the court would remove him from the case, much less take further action. Thus, as a practical matter, Professor Merton's ethical concerns were outweighed by what she predicted the real-world impact would (or would not) be.[15]

3. Oversight by Courts[16]

Judges see the work product, and the actions, of attorneys on a daily basis. Again, informal "suggestions," or mild chastisement, will be aimed at "helping" the attorney, rather than actually disciplining him. When an attorney oversteps ethical or legal bounds, judges may informally alert the attorney's superiors (where there is such an office), or berate the attorney, usually in private, and demand "better" behavior.[17] In an extraordinary case, *United States v. Horn*, 811 F. Supp. 739 (D.N.H. 1992), the judge ordered the prosecutor removed from the case.

Studies have shown that judges are loathe to take steps to refer attorneys to disciplinary procedures unless the conduct is not "only" unethical, but palpably illegal.[18] The reasons, here as elsewhere, are complex. First, even a referral to a committee, however confidential the referral, may taint an

---

15. Steele, Unethical Prosecutors and Inadequate Discipline, 38 Sw. L.J. 965, 980 (1984), reported that, as of that time, "Only one reported case has been found . . . in which defense counsel reported a prosecutor to a bar grievance committee." Citing In re Burrows, 291 Or. 135, 629 P.2d 820 (1981).

16. See Judith McMorrow, Jackie A. Gardina & Salvatore Ricciardone, Judicial Attitudes Toward Confronting Attorney Misconduct: A View from the Reported Decisions, 32 Hofstra L. Rev. 1425 (2004). At one time, the rules of the Supreme Court of Hawaii provided that after a conviction was overturned because of ineffective counsel, a special master could be appointed who could recommend "corrective action" against the attorney, including remedial education, suspension of the attorney's license, or referral to the state legal ethics authorities. The provision was repealed in 1996. See also Yuema, A Comparative View of Judicial Supervision of Prosecutorial Discretion, 44 Crim. L. Bull. 2 (2008).

17. Several federal courts have suggested that they will report violations of the U.S. Atty. Manual to the Department of Justice Office of Professional Responsibility. *United States v. Gillespie*, 974 F.2d 976, 802 (7th Cir. 1992); *United States v. Pacheco-Ortiz*, 89 F.2d 310, 310-311 (1st Cir. 1989). Indeed, this is what happened in the case of Senator Stevens, discussed in Chapter 6, *supra*, pp. 107-108.

18. See, e.g., ABA Standing Comm. on Professional Discipline, ABA Center for Professional Responsibility, the Judicial Response to Lawyer Misconduct, I.3 (1984) (deploring failure of trial judges to refer cases of prosecutorial misconduct to disciplinary boards). For a rare case in which a federal court found state counsel ineffective, reversed the conviction, and directed the court clerk to send a copy of the opinion to the State Bar of Arizona, see *United States v. Swanson*, 943 F.2d 1070 (9th Cir. 1991).

attorney for years, if not for a whole career. Second, at least with regard to prosecutorial misconduct, many judges believe that judicial action may invade the separation of powers doctrine. This wariness of intervening in prosecutorial affairs is somewhat recent:[19]

> [P]rosecutors for over forty years recognized [supervisory power] as a limitation on their independence. Today prosecutors can and would be foolish to regard supervisory power as a serious threat to their autonomy.

On the other hand, consider the disheartened words of the court in *Johnnides v. Amoco Oil Co.*, 778 So. 2d 443 (Fla. Dist. Ct. App. 2001): "While . . . we feel duty bound . . . to report [the attorney] to the Florida Bar, we have no illusions that this will have any practical effect. . . . [O]f the many occasions in which members of this court reluctantly and usually only after agonizing . . . have found it appropriate to make such a referral about a lawyer's conduct in litigation . . . none has resulted in the public imposition of any discipline — not even a reprimand — whatever. . . ."

Of course, judicial creativity may occur at any time. Consider, for example, the instance, noted in Chapter 6, where a federal district judge, frustrated by federal prosecutors' discovery violations, arranged a "voluntary" program on discovery for all such attorneys.

4. Appellate Oversight — Naming Names

More than anything else, an attorney's reputation is critical to long-term success. As one federal prosecutor put it: "You would never want to be in that position . . . naming you by name by an appellate court. . . ."[20] However, appellate courts, even while finding error, even reversible (non-harmless) error, rarely name the individual prosecutor whose conduct required such a finding.[21] Indeed, a survey of hundreds of cases selected at random found few instances where the prosecutor was expressly named — the reference was almost always to "the prosecutor" or "the government."

---

19. Bennett L. Gershman, The New Prosecutors, 53 U. Pitt. L. Rev. 393, 433 (1992). The crucial decision was *United States v. Russell*, 411 U.S. 423 (1973).

20. Comments of Art Leach, Assistant United States Attorney, and Chief of the Organized Crime Strike Force, Georgia, in Panel Discussion: Criminal Discovery in Practice, 15 Ga. St. U. L. Rev. 781, 810 (1999).

21. "Appellate opinions that cite prosecutors for misconduct do not, for the most part, name the prosecutor who broke the rules. The Oklahoma Court of Criminal Appeal . . . [suggested that this] is tantamount to issuing a public censure without affording the prosecutor the due process protections to which they are entitled. . . ." Neil Gordon, Misconduct and Punishment: State Disciplinary Authorities Investigate Prosecutors Accused of Misconduct (The Center for Public Integrity), available at www.publicintegrity.org/pm/default .aspx?act=sidebarsb& aid=39#.

The reluctance to name prosecutors is demonstrated by *United States v. Horn*, 29 F.3d 754 (1st Cir. 1994). The prosecutor illegally obtained information which might have helped discern the defense's strategy. Thereafter, the prosecutor misled the trial court, "pour(ing) kerosene on a raging fire." Thereupon, the "lead prosecutor made a bad situation worse" when two pages "mysteriously disappeared" from documents requested by the court. The Circuit Court, although characterizing the prosecutor's misconduct as "unpardonable," noted that "[t]he district court made a deliberate decision to spare the lead prosecutor public humiliation . . . to delete any mention of the prosecutor's name. Although we, if writing on a pristine page, might not be so solicitous, we honor the district court's exercise of its discretion."[22] There are some exceptions, which manifest the frustration of the court involved. See, e.g., *United States v. Shaygan*, 661 F. Supp. 2d 1289 (S.D. Fla. 2009); *United States v. Jones*, 686 F. Supp. 2d 147 (D. Mass. 2010); *U.S. v. Isgro*, 751 F. Supp. 846 (C.D. Cal. 1990). An exhaustive study of this approach is Adam M. Gershowitz, Prosecutorial Shaming: Naming Attorneys to Reduce Prosecutorial Misconduct, 42 U.C. Davis L. Rev. 2059 (2009).[23] In contrast, virtually every case in which a claim of ineffective assistance is raised discloses the name of the defense counsel even when a court finds that defense counsel was well within the range of effective representation.

5. Disciplinary Sanctions[24]

For over a century, the American Bar Association has established guides by which to assess attorney conduct. Beginning with the Canons of Professional Ethics, generated in 1908, the ABA has promulgated ethical rules, the most

---

22. See also *United States v. Kojayan*, 8 F.3d 1315 (9th Cir. 1993), where the court held that the AUSA engaged in extensive and persistent misconduct; the slip opinion remanding the case named the offending attorney, but the final opinion deleted the name.

23. Among Gershowitz's findings: "In Montana, Vermont, Alaska, and Hawaii, courts reversed a total of 54 cases for prosecutorial misconduct, but not a single court in any of those states identified the prosecutor by name. By contrast, Missouri courts reversed 77 cases for prosecutorial misconduct and identified the prosecutor by name in 50 of those instances; North Carolina courts found 14 cases that merited reversal and named the prosecutor in almost all of them. The Missouri and North Carolina approach is certainly the exception and not the rule, however. The overwhelming majority of states named only a fraction of prosecutors when reversing cases for misconduct. These figures were determined by compiling information from The Center for Public Integrity, Harmful Error: Investigating America's Local Prosecutors, In Your State, www.publicintegrity.org/pm/states.aspx." ID., at fn.49.

24. The two leading scholars of this area are Fred C. Zacharias and Bruce A. Green. For a full bibliography visit Westlaw. For a few of their many articles, see Zacharias, The Professional Discipline of Prosecutors, 79 N.C.L. Rev. 721 (2001); Green and Zacharias, Regulating Federal Prosecutors' Ethics, 55 Vand. L. Rev. 381 (2002); Zacharias and Green, Federal Court Authority to Regulate Lawyers: A Practice in Search of a Theory, 56 Vand. L. Rev. 1301 (2002). See generally Annot., Disciplinary Action Against Attorney for Misconduct Related to Performance of Official Duties as Prosecuting Attorney, 10 A.L.R.4th 605.

recent of which are the 1969 Model Code of Professional Responsibility (Model Code) and the 1983 Model Rules of Professional Conduct (Model Rules). In addition to these documents, which were intended to serve as a model for disciplinary codes, the ABA has offered guidelines for attorney conduct in its multi-volume work Standards Relating to the Administration of Criminal Justice, of which two volumes are directly relevant here: (1) The Prosecution Function, and (2) The Defense Function. Prosecutors have been judged by "higher" standards than other lawyers from the beginning — Canon 5, adopted in 1908 provided, expressly, that:

> The primary duty of a lawyer engaged in public prosecution is not to convict, but to see that justice is done. The suppression of facts or the secreting of witnesses capable of establishing the innocence of the accused is highly reprehensible.

One hundred years later, Model Rule 3.8 provides much more detail, but continues to place upon prosecutors special ethical duties. The most recent amendment to rule 3.8 occurred in 2008. Spurred by the Innocence Project's results and the increasing availability and sophistication of DNA testing, the ABA confirmed a prosecutorial duty to disclose exculpatory evidence even post-conviction.[25]

Every state has adopted, with some variation, either the Model Code or the Model Rules as the basis for disciplinary action against attorneys. Sanctions can run from a mild rebuke, to a censure, to suspension, to disbarment. Nevertheless, studies have shown that, both in civil and criminal contexts, relatively few complaints about attorneys' conduct are referred to state bar associations; a small percentage of these — civil or criminal — result in sanctions.[26]

---

25. Niki Kuckes, *supra*, 22 Geo. J. Legal Ethics 427 (2009); Michele K. Mulhausen, A Second Chance at Justice: Why States Should Adopt ABA Model Rules of Professional Conduct 3.8(g) and (h), 81 U. Colo. L. Rev. 309 (2010).

26. It is hard to find empirical data relating to disciplinary sanctions. In 1996, state disciplinary agencies reported nearly 120,000 complaints (mostly from unhappy clients). Only 5 percent resulted in any sanction against the lawyer. Leslie C. Levin, The Emperor's Clothes and Other Tales About the Standards for Imposing Lawyer Discipline Sanctions, 48 Am. U. L. Rev. 1, 2 (1998). Jim Dwyer, Barry Scheck & Peter Neufeld, Actual Innocence: Five Days to Execution and Other Dispatches from the Wrongly Convicted, 265 (2000) present data on 62 cases of DNA exoneration, 26 of which involved prosecutorial misconduct. Forty-three percent consisted of suppression of exculpatory evidence. According to Kelly Gier, Prosecuting Injustice: Consequences of Misconduct, 33 Am. J. Crim. L. 191 (2006), the Center for Public Integrity cited nearly 600 Texas cases between 1970-2003 where defendants raised allegations of prosecutorial misconduct. "In 152 of those cases, a court held that the prosecutor's conduct prejudiced the defendant, resulting in a reversal and a remand of the conviction, sentence or indictment. Five of these defendants later proved their innocence. In another 36 cases, a dissenting or concurring judge thought the prosecutor's conduct was prejudicial," citing "Harmful Error," available at http://www.publicintegrity.org/pm/states.aspx?st=TX. Gier concludes that, of 173 total cases in this time frame, 23 (13 percent) were *Brady* cases.

6. Whose Ethics? The McDade Amendment[27]

State prosecutors are subject to state bar ethical standards. Federal prosecutors are subject to internal supervision and to sanctions by the Department's Office of Professional Responsibility,[28] and are now subject as well to state rules of conduct. The Federal Prosecutor Ethics Act (FPEA), known as the McDade Amendment, 28 U.S.C. §530B, provides that:[29]

> An attorney for the Government shall be subject to State laws and rules, and local Federal court rules, governing attorneys in each State where such attorney engages in that attorney's duties, to the same extent and in the same manner as other attorneys in that State.

7. "Show Me The Money" — Fines and Attorneys' Fees as Sanctions; Raises for Good Lawyering[30]

As strange as it may seem in a country where many actions are measured in money, courts generally have no power to fine the attorneys who appear before them except in contempt proceedings or when a specific statutory provision providing for fines exist. *McGuire v. State*, 677 P.2d 1060, 1065 (Nev. 1984) ($500 fine imposed on a prosecutor by the Nevada Supreme Court in a combined appeal of two defendants' convictions); *United States v. Prince*, 1994 WL 99231 (E.D.N.Y.) (Not otherwise reported) (court may not order jury costs, even for a *Brady-Giglio* violation); see also Leslie C. Levin, The Emperor's Clothes and Other Tales About the Standards for Imposing Lawyer Discipline Sanctions, 48 Am. U. L. Rev. 1, 17-18 & nn.77-81

---

27. See Jennifer Blair, The Regulation of Federal Prosecutorial Misconduct by State Bar Associations: 28 U.S.C. §530 B, and the Reality of Inaction, 49 UCLA L. Rev. 625 (2001); Ryan E. Mick, The Federal Prosecutors Ethics Act: Solution or Revolution?, 86 Iowa L. Rev. 1251 (2001).

28. Professor Podgor reports that, in 2000, the OPR opened 36 inquiries involving alleged misconduct for failure to comply with DOJ rules and regulations, but only 25 percent of that number actually resulted in actual investigations. Ellen S. Podgor, Department of Justice Guidelines: Balancing "Discretionary Justice," 13 Cornell J.L. & Pub. Pol'y 167 (2004).

29. Nevertheless, federal court judges rarely refer an attorney to a state disciplinary system, preferring the view that they are "responsible for cleaning their own house." McMorrow et al., *supra*, n.16 at 1443.

30. See, e.g., Lynn R. Singband, The Hyde Amendment and Prosecutorial Investigation: The Promise of Protections for Criminal Defendants, 28 Fordham Urb. L.J. 1967 (2001); Lawrence Judson Welle, Power, Policy and the Hyde Amendment: Ensuring Sound Judicial Interpretation of the Criminal Attorney's Fee Law, 41 Wm. & Mary L. Rev. 333 (1999).

(1998).[31] In 1997, Congress, responding to a number of court decisions finding that the federal government could not be required to provide compensation even for the most egregious kind of governmental misconduct, enacted the Hyde Amendment, which provides that if a defendant is "victorious" in a criminal prosecution and can show that the prosecution was "vexatious, frivolous or in bad faith," he may obtain counsel fees. 18 U.S.C. sec. 3006A. Professor Tracey L. Meares has suggested rather than fining prosecutors for bad behavior, one might consider financial rewards (among others) for "good behavior." Rewards for Good Behavior: Influencing Prosecutorial Discretion and Conduct with Financial Incentives, 64 Fordham L. Rev. 851 (1995).

8. Lawsuits, Damages, and Civil Liability

At common law, prosecutors were immune from suits for malicious prosecution and for defamation; this immunity extended to the knowing use of false testimony before the grand jury and at trial.[32] The United States Supreme Court has gone almost, but not quite, so far. In *Imbler v. Pachtman*, 424 U.S. 409 (1976), the Court granted *absolute* immunity to any prosecutor sued *under the federal Civil Rights Act* for violation of a defendant's *constitutional* rights. In so doing, the Court recognized that this immunity left the "genuinely wronged defendant without civil redress against a prosecutor whose malicious or dishonest action deprives him of liberty." Nevertheless, the Court concluded that the possibility that a damage suit might chill a prosecutor in his pursuit of any and all defendants had to be totally precluded.[33]

Fifteen years later, however, the Court held that a prosecutor who was acting in his "investigative" capacity, rather than his "prosecutorial" one, was entitled only to *qualified*, rather than *absolute* immunity. In contrast to absolute immunity, which protects even the most malevolent, intentional, purposeful violation of a person's rights, qualified immunity bars suits whenever the defendant's conduct "does not violate clearly established statutory or constitutional rights of which a reasonable person would have known." *Harlow v. Fitzgerald*, 457 U.S. 800 (1982). This definition is more severe than at the time of *Imbler*, when qualified immunity was thought of as "good-faith" immunity — if the prosecutor had not acted in good faith, he

---

31. On the other side of the spectrum, just barely half the states provide for compensation to those who have been unjustly convicted. See Joel Rudin, Suing for Prosecutorial Misconduct, 34-Mar Champion 242 (2010).

32. This immunity stems from the quasi-judicial character which prosecutors were thought to exercise; indeed, as indicated in Chapter 3, prosecutors were actually considered part of the judiciary in early American jurisprudence.

33. See Margaret Z. Johns, Reconsidering Absolute Prosecutorial Immunity, 2005 B.Y.U. L. Rev 53.

was liable for damages. In *Harlow*, however, the Court explicitly found the "good faith" test too easy to overcome: "The good faith defense has proved incompatible with our admonition . . . that insubstantial claims should not proceed to trial."

Today, the "investigative" "advocacy" distinction is the only way in which an abused defendant may sue under 42 U.S.C. §1983. Thus, while a prosecutor who gave misleading information to a judge in order to obtain a search warrant was acting as the "state's advocate," and hence totally immune, his actions in misadvising police concerning whether to conduct a search were not so protected. *Burns v. Reed*, 500 U.S. 478 (1991). In *Buckley v. Fitzsimmons*, 509 U.S. 259 (1993), a prosecutor who specifically looked for an expert who would link a suspect to a boot print at the crime scene, and who had made false statements at a press conference, was again only entitled to qualified, rather than absolute, immunity. *Reed* and *Buckley* seemed to hold that the determination of probable cause (by a grand jury or preliminary hearing) might constitute a "bright line" dividing qualified from absolute immunity, but that suggestion has been criticized as no more helpful than the "investigative-advocacy" line.[34]

The line between "investigative" and "advocacy" functions is obviously thin. In *Pottawattamie County v. Harrington*, 547 F.3d 922 (8th Cir. 2008), the prosecutor had violated the rights of another suspect (call him Jim) in order to obtain statements which were ultimately used in court to convict defendants (Tom and Huck), who were later (some 24 years later) released from prison. One of the defendants then entered an Alford plea; the other was never reprosecuted. The two then sued the prosecutor under Section 1983. Some courts in this situation had found no liability, on two grounds: (1) the violation of Jim's rights was not a violation of the defendants and hence they could not "piggyback" on that violation, even if it is not protected by absolute (but only qualified) immunity; (2) the subsequent use during trial of the otherwise illegally obtained statement, which would provide the prosecutor absolute immunity, retroactively provided him absolute immunity for the method by which he obtained the statement. The *Harrington* court rejected that analysis and held that absolute immunity protected the use in trial but that only qualified immunity applied to the violation of the suspect's rights.[35] The Supreme Court granted certiorari, but after oral argument in the Court, the lawyers announced a $12 million settlement, and the Court dismissed the case. According to Joel Rudin, Suing for Prosecutorial Misconduct, 34-Mar Champion 24 (2010), "during oral argument, several

---

34. Douglas J. McNamara, *Buckley, Imbler* and Stare Decisis: The Present Predicament of Prosecutorial Immunity and an End to Its Absolute Means, 59 Alb. L. Rev. 1135 (1996); Margaret Z. Johns, Reconsidering Absolute Prosecutorial Immunity, 2005 B.Y.U.L. Rev. 53 (2005).
35. For more details on the case, see Jonathan K. Van Paten, Suing the Prosecutor, 55 S.D. L. Rev. 214 (2010).

justices were openly troubled that a prosecutor might gain complete immunity from suit by *compounding* his initial wrongdoing in fabricating evidence by then utilizing it himself in a prosecution."

Absolute immunity only applies while there is a "prosecution." Once the defendant is convicted, if the prosecutor discovers exculpatory evidence and does not disclose it, assuming that *Brady* (or even due process) applies, he will be protected by qualified immunity only. *Houston v. Partee*, 978 F.2d 362 (7th Cir. 1992).

While prosecutors are therefore almost fully protected from civil suits in federal court, state-employed public defenders (and contracted counsel paid by the state) are not subject to federal liability at all, because they are not acting "under color of state law" as that statute requires. *Polk County v. Dodson*, 454 U.S. 312 (1981). On the other hand, private counsel actually hired by the defendant may be sued in tort for legal malpractice by their employers/defendants.[36]

Two recent cases appear to have strengthened immunity. In *VandeKamp v. Goldstein*, 129 S. Ct. 855 (2009), a unanimous court held that prosecutors were absolutely immune for failing to train deputy prosecutors about *Brady-Giglio* obligations and failing to institute a system of information sharing among deputy district attorneys about prosecutorial obligations to inform defense counsel of deals made with jailhouse informants. The Court held that these "kinds" of duties were "directly connected with the conduct of a trial" and were "unlike administrative duties concerning, for example, workplace hiring, payroll administration, the maintenance of physical facilities, and the like." This seems to have narrowed the kind of "administrative" duties which otherwise might have opened the prosecutor to liability.[37] In *Connick v. Thompson*, 563 U.S. 51 (2011), the Court further held that a municipality could not be sued under section 1983 for similar *Brady-Giglio* violations unless the plaintiff demonstrated that the municipality had a policy of purposely failing to train prosecutors about their legal obligations. Indeed, the Court's opinion seems to go further because it focuses not on the failure to train generally, but specifically on *Brady-Giglio* requirements. In effect, the Court requires the now-acquitted plaintiff to show a

---

36. In *Polk County*, the Court, in dictum, also suggested the possibility that the administrative-advocacy distinction might apply to individual public defenders also, but the case cited was (a) a suit for injunction rather than tort damages; and (b) brought against "the" head of the public defender's office "in his capacity as Public Defender."

37. One observer wryly noted: "The Court's ability to differentiate by function between prosecutorial and nonprosecutorial acts was tested in *VandeKamp* and the prosecutors won . . . ." Rudin, *supra*, n.31. Another opined that "the upshot of *VandeKamp* is that characterization of a prosecutor's actions as 'administrative' will not necessarily negate prosecutorial immunity." Martin A Schwartz, Wrongful Conviction Claim Barred by Prosecutorial Immunity, 241 N.Y. L.J. 3 (col. 1) (June 16, 2009).

"pattern and practice" of failing to train on specific legal doctrines, rather than a general failure to train.[38]

9. Prosecutor Review Boards

Several writers have suggested a "review board" that would either (a) act randomly or (b) investigate cases where appellate courts have found prosecutorial constitutional misconduct. Angela Davis, Arbitrary Justice: The Power of the American Prosecutor (2007); Lyn Morton, Seeking the Elusive Remedy for Prosecutorial Suppression, Dismissal or Discipline? 7 Geo. J. Leg. Ethics 1083 (1994); Ellen Yaroshefsky, Wrongful Convictions: It is Time to Take Prosecution Discipline Seriously, 8 U.D.C. L. Rev. 275 (2004). No state has yet adopted such an approach.

C. AN EXEMPLAR — THE DUKE LACROSSE CASE

Rather than include a *set* of examples here, we will use just one real example and explore it in some depth. It is a story which most readers believe they know, at least in part; but the entire tale is much more complicated. Even the facts given below are skeletal, but they are likely to be more detailed than many readers know. Their legal relevance will be examined in the "Explanation" immediately following. Many of the statements below are taken from the complaints filed by the Disciplinary Hearing Commission of the North Carolina State Bar (available at http://www.ncbar.com/); others are from materials found online (including many blogs — one such is durhamwonderland.blogspot.com), or from Stuart Taylor, Jr. and KC Johnson, Until Proven Innocent (2007).

The event has generated an extraordinary amount of comment. See, as well, Race to Injustice: Lessons Learned from the Duke Lacrosse Rape Case (Michael Siegel, ed., 2009); R. Michael Cassidy, The Prosecutor and the

---

38. Thompson was prosecuted and convicted of attempted armed robbery. The prosecutor did not disclose that a blood test of the robbery victim's pants showed that the blood was not Thompson's blood type. At a later trial for (an unrelated) murder, Thompson elected not to testify, fearful that the robbery conviction would be used to impeach him. Convicted of the homicide, he spent 18 years in prison, 14 on death row. One month before his scheduled execution, an investigator working for a new attorney discovered the blood test. After a full day's hearing, the reviewing court vacated Thompson's attempted robbery conviction. The district attorney nevertheless retried Thompson for murder; the jury acquitted. Note: this was the same prosecutorial office that prosecuted Mr. Kyles four times — when his conviction had been previously reversed on the basis of *Brady-Giglio* violations — before he was ultimately acquitted. See chapter 6.

Press: Lessons (Not) Learned from the Mike Nifong Debacle, 71 L. & Contemporary Probs. 67 (Fall 2008); Robert S. Mosteller, Exculpatory Evidence, Ethics, and the Road to the Disbarment of Mike Nifong: The Critical Importance of Full Open-File Discovery, 15 Geo. Mason L. Rev. 257 (2008).

In addition, consider the following North Carolina statutes:

15A-282. Copy of results to person involved

A person who has been the subject of nontestimonial identification procedures or his attorney must be provided with a copy of any reports of test results as soon as the reports are available.

15A-902. Discovery procedure

(a) A party seeking discovery under this Article must, before filing any motion before a judge, request in writing that the other party comply voluntarily with the discovery request. . . . Upon receiving a negative or unsatisfactory response, or upon the passage of seven days following the receipt of the request without response, the party requesting discovery may file a motion for discovery under the provisions of this Article concerning any matter as to which voluntary discovery was not made pursuant to request. . . .

(d) If a defendant is represented by counsel, the defendant may as a matter of right request voluntary discovery from the State under subsection (a) of this section not later than the tenth working day after either the probable-cause hearing or the date the defendant waives the hearing.

15A-903.

(a) Upon motion of the defendant, the court must order the State to:

(1) Make available to the defendant the complete files of all law enforcement and prosecutorial agencies involved in the investigation of the crimes committed or the prosecution of the defendant. The term "file" includes the defendant's statements, the codefendants' statements, witness statements, investigating officers' notes, results of tests and examinations, or any other matter or evidence obtained during the investigation of the offenses alleged to have been committed by the defendant. Oral statements shall be in written or recorded form. The defendant shall have the right to inspect and copy or photograph any materials contained therein and, under appropriate safeguards, to inspect, examine, and test any physical evidence or sample contained therein.

(2) Give notice to the defendant of any expert witnesses that the State reasonably expects to call as a witness at trial. Each such witness shall prepare, and the State shall furnish to the defendant, a report of the results of any examinations or tests conducted by the expert. The State shall also furnish to the defendant the expert's curriculum vitae, the expert's

opinion, and the underlying basis for that opinion. The State shall give the notice and furnish the materials required by this subsection within a reasonable time prior to trial, as specified by the court.

In addition, the North Carolina Bar Association's Rules of Professional Conduct provide:

3.3 (a) A lawyer shall not knowingly:

(1) make a false statement of material fact or law to a tribunal . . .

3.4 (d) A lawyer shall not . . .

fail to make (a) reasonably diligent effort to comply with a legally proper discovery request. . . .

3.8 Special Responsibilities of a Prosecutor . . .

(d) after reasonably diligent inquiry, make timely disclosure to the defense of all evidence or information required to be disclosed by applicable law, rules of procedure, or court opinion, including all evidence or information known to the prosecutor that tends to negate the guilt of the accused or mitigates the offense. . . .

(f) . . . refrain from making extrajudicial comments that have a substantial likelihood of heightening public condemnation of the accused. . . .

8.4 Misconduct. It is professional misconduct for a lawyer to . . .

(c) engage in conduct involving dishonesty, fraud, deceit or misrepresentation. . . .

I. The Example

In the early hours of March 14, 2006, a woman reported that she had been raped by three men during a party in Durham, North Carolina, attended by many members of the Duke lacrosse team. That night, the woman was physically examined and a "rape kit" was established. On March 16 and again on March 21, police presented a "photo lineup" to the victim, but she was unable to identify any of the people in the lineup as her assailants. In several interviews with the police over several days, the victim often gave conflicting statements regarding many aspects of the alleged rape.

On March 22, an investigator from the Durham police contacted the Durham District Attorney's office for assistance in obtaining a Nontestimonial Identification Order (NTO) which would compel all the partygoers to present themselves to be photographed and provide DNA samples. The District Attorney for Durham County, Michael Nifong, was then briefed on the case. In the application for the NTO, Nifong represented that "the DNA evidence requested will immediately rule out any innocent persons, and show conclusive evidence as to who the suspects are in the alleged violent attack. . . ." On March 24, Nifong assumed primary responsibility for prosecuting any criminal charges resulting from the investigation, and directed the police department to ask him how to conduct the investigation. Soon thereafter, he began making comments on local and national media concerning the "Duke lacrosse rape case," including clear assertions that a rape had occurred, and that forensic evidence would support that view. Many of those statements strongly suggested that several members of the lacrosse team either knew about the rape, or had participated in it, and had refused to make statements to law enforcement authorities.

At one point Nifong declared, "In this case, where you have the act of rape — especially a gang rape — is bad enough in and of itself, but when it's made with racial epithets against the victim, I mean it's just absolutely unconscionable." Nifong did not personally interview the victim until weeks after the allegations were made.

On March 31, Nifong instructed the police to conduct a third photo lineup, this time using only pictures of members of the Duke lacrosse team. This process violated both police regulations and guidelines, and the standards established by United States Supreme Court case law. The photo ID was held on April 4. The victim identified one of the players, but failed to recognize three other team members she had positively identified on March 16 as being at the party. She identified four players as her assailants.

The rape kit items were delivered to the State Bureau of Investigation (SBI) laboratory on March 27. On or about March 30, Nifong had a conversation with an agent in the DNA section of the SBI lab. A week later, the prosecutor's office obtained a court order allowing the transfer of the rape kit to a private laboratory (DSI) for more sophisticated testing. By April 10, 2006, DSI had analyzed the rape kit and excluded all of the lacrosse players as potential contributors of the DNA it had analyzed.

Although counsel for some of the suspects had asked Nifong to consider evidence that they contended provided an alibi or otherwise exonerated them, Nifong repeatedly refused those offers.

On April 17, the grand jury indicted two of the lacrosse players for first degree rape, first degree sex offense, and kidnaping. Two days later, one of those defendants served a motion for discovery material, including DNA analysis. By April 20, DSI had determined that all the lacrosse players could be excluded as contributors of the several DNA samples obtained from the victim; Nifong was so informed orally by Dr. Brian Meehan, DSI's president, on April 21. Nifong and Dr. Meehan agreed that, as earlier stated, the written report to be produced by DSI would only include tests for which

429

DNA found on specific evidence items matched or was consistent with DNA from known reference specimens. The final written report, provided on May 12 to Nifong, and later turned over by him to defense counsel on that same day, included only "positive results," and contained no statement indicating that DSI had discovered characteristics other than two "fingernail" matches which were "at least partially consistent" with the DNA profile of two unindicted lacrosse players. The report also mentioned one sperm fraction from the vaginal swab that was consistent with the DNA profile of the alleged victim's boyfriend. It did not memorialize Dr. Meehan's oral statements concerning the other results.

When he gave the defense counsel the DSI report, prosecutor Nifong filed written responses in which he stated that "[t]he State is not aware of any additional material or information which may be exculpatory in nature with respect to" the defendants. At a May 18, 2006 court hearing, he stated: "I've turned over everything I have." At a later court hearing, Nifong represented that no information beyond what was in DSI's report was discussed at the meeting with Dr. Meehan, stating: "We received the reports, which he [defense counsel] has received, and we talked about how we would likely use that, and that's what we did."

On May 15, 2006, the grand jury, relying on the fingernail DNA, indicted a third lacrosse player. A month later, the court required the disclosure of "results of tests and examination, or any other matter or evidence obtained during the investigation of the offenses" and "statements of any witnesses . . . a report of the results of any examination or tests conducted by any expert witness the State reasonably expected to call. . . ."

In September, at a court hearing, defense counsel specifically stated that they were seeking the results of any tests finding any additional DNA on the alleged victim, even if it did not match any of the defendants. Nifong responded that DSI's report encompassed all tests performed by DSI. The judge asked, "So you represent there are no other statements from Dr. Meehan?" Mr. Nifong replied, "No other statements. No other statements made to me."

In October, Nifong provided 1,844 pages of underlying documents and materials to the defendants, including materials relating to the DNA "nonmatch." Less than two months later, the bar association filed a complaint about his conduct, and the state attorney general removed Nifong from the case.

1. On the basis of these facts, what constitutional, statutory, or ethical violations might have occurred with regard to:
   (a) Nifong's failure to disclose, either to the grand jury or the defendants,
      (i) the DNA "non-matches,"
      (ii) the results of the photographic lineups,
      (iii) the arguably inconsistent statements made by the victim,

       (b) Nifong's statements in his various press conferences,

       (c) Nifong's statements to the court?

   2. What civil liability, if any, might Nifong face?

D. EXPLANATIONS

1. Non-Disclosure Questions

a. The DNA "Non-Matches"

Nifong knew that the State Bureau of Investigation crime lab had found no positive matches between the DNA provided by all the Duke lacrosse players and samples found in the "rape kit." Should Nifong have submitted this information to the grand jury? Should he have released it to defendants? Did he have a constitutional obligation to disclose the information from Dr. Meehan about the non-matches and, if so, when was that disclosure required?

i. Constitutional Questions

Under *Williams v. United States* (*supra*, Chapter 4), there is no constitutional requirement that the prosecutor present even obviously exculpatory evidence to the grand jury. Thus, Nifong violated no constitutional right of the defendants here. Under those jurisdictions (such as North Carolina) which require prosecutors to inform the grand jury of "exculpatory" information, the question is whether the non-matches were "exculpatory." In part this would depend on the precise wording of the court rule or case law with regard to discovery. But it also requires the prosecutor to know, at the time the case is presented, that the evidence meets the standard. Nifong argued, in his disciplinary proceedings (see below) that the lack of a match was *not* "exculpatory" but merely "not inculpatory." Moreover, in this case, Nifong believed the SBI results to be inconclusive, and therefore sent them to DSI for more sophisticated analysis.

    In its final report on the disciplinary hearings held on this case, the North Carolina Bar Association found that this information was exculpatory. But the issue in this book raises a broader question — whether the policy of asking the prosecutor to determine whether particular evidence is (or is not) exculpatory is sensible, particularly as it applies to this early stage of the proceedings. One need not characterize the prosecutor here as the fox in the chicken coop to suggest that many prosecutors would rationalize a determination that neither the SBI information nor the DSI information was exculpatory. As suggested in Chapter 4, few decisions have found that evidence *not* submitted to the grand jury was sufficiently "exculpatory" to require quashing the indictment.

Even assuming that the DNA "non-match" was not sufficiently exculpatory to require its disclosure to the grand jury, is it *Brady* material that must be disclosed pursuant to the defense request? The test, under *Kyles v. Whitley* (see Chapter 6) is whether there is a "reasonable probability" that the jury verdict would have been different had the jury been informed by defense counsel of this non-match. The first problem, of course, is that a prosecutor deciding whether *Brady-Kyles* requires disclosure is deciding that question *before* trial. Thus, the question she must ask is whether the jury verdict "would be" affected by the evidence. Prospectively, in the absence of what the evidence at trial might show (indeed in the absence of much evidence yet to be discovered), that question may be considerably more difficult for even the most fair-minded prosecutor to answer. Given cognitive bias, we would expect most prosecutors to answer that, in their reasonable judgment, the evidence is not sufficiently exculpatory. Moreover, *Brady* contains no time frame during which disclosure must occur. Many courts hold that disclosure even a few days before trial is sufficient to meet *Brady*'s constitutional imperative.

The (perhaps unhappy) conclusion, then, is that it may be very difficult for the plaintiffs to prove that Nifong's actions in suppressing this information from both the grand jury and from the defendants, at least to the point in time when he released them pursuant to court instruction, violated their constitutional rights.

ii. Statutory Issues

On the other hand, Nifong's failure to disclose the "non-match" DNA almost certainly violated the North Carolina discovery statutes. Clearly, the DNA tests are "NTOs", within the meaning of Section 15A-282, which requires disclosure "as soon as the reports are available." Nifong, however, *did* disclose the written report he received from DSI; he did *not* disclose the "non-inculpatory" "oral" statements from Meehan. While his acts are in direct conflict with the spirit of Section 282, it is arguable that his non-disclosure did not violate the actual wording of that section.

Section 903(a)(1) does not limit required disclosure to "exculpatory" evidence — it appears to relate to *all* "tests and examinations or any other matter or evidence." And under 903(d), this disclosure should be made within 10 days after a request. But (a)(2) deals expressly with expert reports, and requires only that the report and results of examinations by experts be furnished "within a reasonable time prior to trial, as specified by the court." Nifong could plausibly argue that, since the trial date was not set yet, he did not violate this subsection, which, because of its greater specificity, controls the timing of disclosure of the full contents of expert reports.

Moreover, case law had held that disclosure even as late as the trial itself might not violate the statute so long as the defendant was not prejudiced thereby. *State v. Pendleton*, 622 S.E.2d 708 (N.C. App. 2005); *State v. Love*, 568 S.E.2d 320 (N.C. App. 2002).

iii. Ethics Violations

The Bar Association's Rule of Professional Conduct 3.8 more arguably covers the DNA non-matches, since this is evidence which, even if not "exculpatory," "tends to negate the guilt of the accused or mitigates the offense." On the other hand, the rules require "timely" disclosure of the evidence, again specifying no time frame.

b. The Photographic Lineups

The facts of the example state that the photographic arrays, particularly that of March 31, violated the defendants' constitutional rights. Both because the defendants were not present at the array, and because they had not been indicted at that point, they were not deprived of the right to counsel at the lineup. (See Bloom and Brodin, Constitutional Criminal Procedure, Chapter 11.) The violation, then, would be a violation of due process. For that violation the usual remedy is suppression of the evidence. Since there has been (and had been) no trial at the time the case was dismissed, this might be an instance of a right without a remedy (except for civil liability, discussed below).

Under *Brady-Giglio*, the victim's failure to identify the defendants at the photographic lineup is surely impeachment evidence, and the prosecutor has to disclose it. Again, the United States Supreme Court has not established a time frame in which *constitutionally compelled* disclosure must occur. Many courts hold that disclosure even a few days before trial complies with *Brady*. Indeed, at his disciplinary hearing (see below), Nifong expressly argued that he had violated no rule or constitutional standard because the trial court had not even set a date for trial, and his failure to disclose some of this information could not, therefore, be "untimely," at least under *Brady*.

The argument made in Section A above with regard to the DNA non-matches—that the 10-day time frame specified by subsection (d) of the discovery statute does not apply to expert reports—is not relevant to the photo IDs, or the victim's statements. These are clearly governed by 903(a) and by section 3.8(d) of the Rules, which requires "timely" disclosure.

c. The Victim's Statements

Essentially the same analysis applied in the photo lineups applies here — the prosecutor had to disclose these statements at some point, but not necessarily until just before trial.

d. Nifong's Press Conferences

As discussed below, statements made by a prosecutor at press conferences may deprive the defendants of a fair trial and lead to federal civil tort liability. Moreover, the statements made here are clearly violative of sections 3.6 and 3.8(g) of the Rules, since they created a "substantial likelihood of heightening public condemnation of the accused. . . ."

e. Nifong's Statements to the Court

Many of Nifong's statements made to the court were, at best, misleading, and many were simply false.[39] In its disciplinary conclusions, the Bar Association found that many of the statements, in the words of the Rules, involved "dishonesty, fraud, deceit or misrepresentation in violation of 8.4(c)." None of these, of course, directly violated the defendants' rights except as more generally covered under a due process analysis; any effect which these might have had upon a jury could have been dealt with by a trial court, or even by a change of venue, had a trial occurred.[40]

2. Civil Liability

Since prosecutors are absolutely immune from a federal civil rights tort action for any actions they took during the "adjudication" phase of the process, but not for actions taken during the "investigative" phase, that dividing line is critical. In *Reed* and *Buckley*, the Supreme Court indicated that, once probable cause has been established (usually indicated by an indictment), there is little likelihood that a prosecutor's acts will be considered "investigative." The only such act here might be Nifong's instructions

---

39. For example, Nifong's statement that he had turned over all "reports" on the DNA was accurate; he simply did not disclose the oral statements made by Meehan which were not in the written report. This, of course, is too cute by half — but parsing words is often the task to which the lawyer is most attuned.

40. Again, the larger point. Since appellate courts only handle appealed cases, the traditional question is whether the defendants' *trial* rights have been infringed. Given the view that a plea essentially waives most (but not all) constitutional infirmities which have preceded the plea, an unscrupulous prosecutor (or defense counsel) might gamble that the violations will never be discovered or, if discovered, will be deemed waived, or harmless.

to the Durham police concerning the photographic lineup conducted on March 31. Usually, however, the remedy for an invalid lineup is to exclude the evidence of the lineup (and any fruit of that poisonous tree) at the trial. Since there was no trial, it may be argued that the defendants' constitutional rights were not infringed.

Many of Nifong's most inflammatory press conference statements, however, were made before the defendants were indicted. In *Buckley*, the Court held that such statements might well be considered part of the "investigative" phase of the process, in which case the prosecutor would be only qualifiedly, and not absolutely, immune from a federal tort suit. Moreover, the Bar Association complaint alleged, and later found, *inter alia*, that Nifong's statements were "improper commentary on the evidence and testimony expected to be presented in the trial of the case."

3. Overview of the Explanations

The "explanations" here are, by necessity, restricted by the facts detailed in the "example." These "explanations" are not intended to condone any of Nifong's actions, but to demonstrate the difficulty of proving, either for purposes of remedies at trial, or for purposes of civil liability, that constitutional violations occurred. *Brady*'s constitutional requirements are far from transparent, and the timing requirements opaque. Nifong's personal civil liability, if any, is likely to rest more on his press conference statements and the photographic lineup than upon the non-disclosure of the DNA material. Unless, therefore, significant changes occur in the law regarding discovery, the disciplinary actions of the Bar Association, premised on a more general assessment of a lawyer's obligations generally and a prosecutor's obligation specifically, may be the "best" remedy for actions like those of prosecutor Nifong. See, generally, Kenneth Williams, An Examination of the District Attorney's Alleged Unethical Conduct in Race to Injustice, *supra*, 265.

4. The "Result"

After he was removed from the case by the North Carolina Attorney General, Nifong was disbarred. The Final Order can be found at: http://www.ncbar.com/Nifong%20Final%20Order.pdf. The North Carolina Bar Commission found a vast variety of violations of the statutes and the Rules of Professional Conduct, many of them focusing on his press conference statements (in violation of Rule 3.8(f)) or his statements to the court (violating sec.

3.3(a)). The Bar also concluded that the failure to disclose the DNA non-matches violated the Rules of Professional Conduct, and that the oral statements from Dr. Meehan were covered by the Rules, and not the statute. The Bar found that Nifong's failure to make a reasonably diligent effort to comply with a legally proper discovery request did not violate section 3.4(d) of the Rules "at least to the extent that it is based upon the discovery statute at the time," because the Attorney General had previously taken the position that prosecutors did not have to provide such memorializations, and "there is a plausible reliance upon that position at the time." The chairman of the Commission concluded that:

> Nifong . . . out of self-interest, and self-deception, not necessarily out of an evil motive . . . lost sight of that and wandered off the path of justice. . . . There are very few deterrents upon prosecutorial misconduct. . . . [T]he only significant deterrent . . . is the possibility of disciplinary sanctions. And here the most severe sanction is warranted.

http://www.ncbar.com/Nifong%20Findings.pdf.

Following the disbarment, Nifong pled guilty to criminal contempt of court (for his misstatements to the court) and was sentenced to one day in jail.

Victim's Rights

In all cases, the crime includes an injury: every public offense is also a private wrong, and somewhat more; it affects the individual.

4 Wm. Blackstone Commentaries on the Law of England 5

A private citizen lacks a judicially cognizable interest in the prosecution or non-prosecution of another.

Linda R. S. v. Richard D., 410 U.S. 614, 619 (1973)

A. INTRODUCTION

A thousand years ago, in England, when tort and crime constituted a single proceeding, injured parties basically controlled whether a defendant would be criminally prosecuted, or simply pay damages for the injury. As English kings grew stronger, they resisted this encroachment on their power to control violence; moreover, such settlements could mean that the injury to the King (and therefore the state) would be unredressed. In addition, as criminal law began to require the prosecutor to demonstrate *mens rea*, and tort law continued to impose essentially strict liability, criminal proceedings diverged from those in tort law. Although the "criminal" proceeding in England often continued to be brought by, or at least in the name of, the injured party (or survivor),[1] by the time of the American Revolution, the general perception was that the victim of crime was the state, not the individual who had borne the brunt of the defendant's conduct.

By the late twentieth century, individual victims of crimes had increasingly won the right to participate in the criminal process. No longer limited to being the "witness for the prosecution," victims are now acknowledged by many state constitutions or statutes to have at least some of the following rights:[2]

- to be notified of proceedings;
- to attend proceedings;
- to be heard at proceedings;
- to be heard by the prosecutor before a plea bargain is entered;
- to read pre-sentence reports;
- to be notified of the defendant's sentence, escape, or release;
- to be given information by the prosecutor of the status of the case;
- to be informed when a suspect has been arrested;
- to have "input" for the bail decision;
- in a capital case, to present a "victim impact statement."

The reempowerment of victims may be seen as a response to plea bargaining, discretionary sentencing, and parole release. A victim who thought the perpetrator would receive a long (e.g., 20-year) sentence, was often aghast when the prosecutor supported, the two attorneys agreed upon, or the judge imposed, a three-year term, or when the parole board released the criminal after serving one-fifth of his sentence.

A common complaint from victims was that the plea-sentencing structure, which often shut out the victim entirely, failed to demonstrate to the defendant, or the government, the human trauma which the crime had inflicted. Often, survivors of homicide sought to "humanize the victim." This, for example, was obviously the spectators' motive in *Carey v. Musladin*, 549 U.S. 70 (2006), where the survivors' murder wore buttons bearing the murder victim's picture. Against a challenge that this violated the defendant's due process rights to a fair trial, the Court, noting that earlier cases had allowed similar practices, and especially observing that this was a *habeas corpus* petition, readily held that the decision of the state court allowing this practice had not "unreasonably applied clearly established Federal law" (see Chapter 13).

---

1. As noted earlier, ch. 3, the American colonies relied upon "public" prosecutors, and adhered to that practice after the Revolution.

2. For a complete listing of these states and their provisions, see National Victims' Constitutional Amendment Passage, www.nvcap.org.

If the victim is not provided the rights guaranteed, the only remedy is a post-conviction judgment, which may require vacating the plea bargain, or even the jury verdict. The federal statute expressly provides for an expedited (72 hour) appeal to the circuit court and allows the court to suspend criminal proceedings for up to five days while the issue is being debated.

B. THE VICTIM BEFORE TRIAL

As discussed in Chapter 3, most states continue to give full discretion to the public prosecutor as to whether, and if so how, to charge the defendant. Some states, however, require that the prosecutor confer with the victim before "finally" declining to prosecute. Arizona, for example, provides:

> If a prosecutor declines to proceed with a prosecution . . . the prosecutor shall, before the decision not to proceed is final, notify the victim and provide the victim with the reasons for declining to proceed.

Ariz. Rev. Stat. Ann. tit. 13, sec. 13-440.

Some statutes allow a victim to ask the state attorney general to review a local prosecutor's charging decision, but the power is rarely invoked.

In many states, a victim is entitled to be informed of developments in the case, including the possibility of a plea bargain. In Maryland, the Crime Victims' Resource Center, Inc., has established an automated Victim Information and Notification Everyday (VINE) system, which receives court and custody information from Maryland criminal courts, and alerts victims to events such as plea negotiations.

In none of these systems does the victim have a right to "veto" the plea bargain, or the declination of prosecution. But in nearly half the states victims must be given notification of proceedings, including bail and plea bargains. At those proceedings, victims are usually — but not always — allowed to speak against a particular course of action. In all of them, the victims may present written explanations of their opposition (it is usually opposition) to the move proposed by the district attorney.

C. THE VICTIM AT TRIAL

Obviously, the victim has a pivotal role at trial — she or he will testify and detail the way in which the defendant violated the law. But does the victim have any other role, either as witness or otherwise, during the trial process? Victims, after all, can be spectators — and after *Musladin* they are permitted to be present, at the trial, and to remind the jury (silently) of the true "victim" of the crime. As citizens, moreover, they may invoke their First Amendment (or other) constitutional rights, so long as they do not intimidate witnesses or jurors. These methods will, of course, be subject to the same limitations that might surround evidence generally (for example, those requiring sequestration of a witness until after he or she has testified).

In some states, victims may sit at the prosecutor's table. For example, Ala. Code §75-14-53 provides:

> . . . the victim of a criminal offense shall be entitled to be present in any court exercising any jurisdiction over such offense and therein to be seated at the counsel table of any prosecutor. . . .[3]

D. THE VICTIM AFTER TRIAL

The law is clearest here. After a number of ambiguous and contradictory opinions, the Supreme Court in *Payne v. Tennessee*, 501 U.S. 808 (1991), held that a state may allow the survivors of a victim in a capital case to prepare a "victims' impact statement," and to testify at the sentencing hearing about the effect the murder has had upon them individually and collectively. The Court rejected claims that allowing such evidence encouraged the imposition of the death penalty based on the jury's perceived "worth" of the victim, rather than upon statutorily enacted criteria, as well as an argument that the procedure violated the defendant's Fifth Amendment right to confront his "accuser." At least 30 states now allow such statements, with a diversity of limitations and restrictions.[4]

It is not clear whether *Payne* applies to non-capital cases. In other areas, the Court has been loathe to extend procedural rights for capital defendants to non-capital settings (e.g., a constitutional right to see the pre-sentence report; see Chapter 12). But, as Table 15.1 shows, four states provide that a victim may see the pre-sentence report in a non-capital case.

Many states require the prosecutor to notify a victim when the defendant is being considered for parole, and some allow the victim either to appear before the parole board or submit a statement. Some states even allow victim impact evidence at pardon proceedings.

---

3. Upheld in *Pierce v. State*, 576 So. 2d 236 (Ala. Crim. App. 1990).
4. John H. Blume, Ten Years of *Payne*: Victim Impact Evidence in Capital Cases, 88 Cornell L. Rev. 257, 268 (2003), finds only 33 states, but Carrie L. Mulholland, Sentencing Criminals: The Constitutionality of Victim Impact Statements, 60 Mo. L. Rev. 731, 742 n.74 (1995), lists 47.

15.1 Summary of State Constitutional Rights of Crime Victims

	To be Treated with Fairness and Respect	To be Informed of Rights	To Notification of Proceedings	To Notice of Sentence, Escape, or Release	To Attend Proceedings	To be Heard at Proceedings	To Confer with Prosecutor	To Speedy Disposition	To be Protected from Accused	To Refuse an Interview with the Defense	To Restitution	To Rights at the Juvenile Level	To Read Pre-Sentence Reports	TOTAL
Alabama			•		•									2
Alaska	•		•	•	•	•	•	•	•		•	•	•	11
Arizona	•	•	•	•	•	•	•		•	•	•			10
California											•			1
Colorado			•		•	•								3
Connecticut	•		•	•	•	•	•	•	•					9
Florida		•			•	•								3
Idaho	•		•	•	•	•			•	•	•	•	•	11
Illinois	•		•	•	•	•	•		•		•			9
Indiana	•		•		•	•								4
Kansas			•		•	•								3
Louisiana	•	•	•	•	•	•		•	•		•		•	11
Maryland	•	•	•		•						•			5
Michigan	•		•		•	•	•	•	•		•		•	9
Mississippi	•		•		•						•			4
Missouri		•	•	•	•	•		•	•		•	•		9
Nebraska			•	•	•	•								4
Nevada			•		•	•								3
New Jersey	•				•									2
New Mexico	•		•	•	•	•			•		•			9
North Carolina		•	•	•	•	•					•			7
Ohio	•	•	•					•						4
Oklahoma		•	•		•						•			5
Rhode Island	•				•						•			3
South Carolina	•	•	•	•	•	•	•	•			•	•	•	11
Tennessee	•	•	•	•	•	•	•		•		•			9
Texas	•		•	•	•		•	•			•			7
Utah	•		•		•	•					•			5
Virginia	•		•	•	•	•			•		•			7
Washington			•		•	•								3
Wisconsin	•		•	•	•	•	•	•			•			8
TOTAL	20	10	26	17	26	25	15	12	10	3	18	5	4	

Stearman, An Amendment to the Constitution of the United States to Protect the Rights of Criminal Victims: Exploring the Effectiveness of State Effects, 30.U. Balt. L.F. 63 (1999)

In sum, as Table 15.1 demonstrates, states have increasingly provided methods by which victims or their representatives are being "reintroduced" into the criminal process. While this trend is unlikely to take us "back to the future" where victims dominated the criminal process, it is certainly a process to keep in mind when assessing defendants' rights.

In the 1990s, an attempt was made to amend the United States Constitution to articulate victims' rights. While that statute did not pass, Congress enacted the Federal Victims' Rights Statute of 2004 — 18 U.S.C. §3771 — which provides many of the rights described in Table 15.1 above, and expressly provides that "[t]he prosecutor shall advise the crime victim that the crime victim can seek the advice of an attorney with respect to the rights described in subsection (a)." Victims' rights have clearly come a long way in the past century.

Examples

1. Hannibal is charged with the brutal murder of Jodie Dulles. Pursuant to state statute, Jodie's parents have been at the prosecutor's table every day of the trial. As the prosecutor begins summation, both parents stand up and unfurl large, color photographs of Jodie's body. The pictures are particularly gruesome. The defense counsel immediately calls for a mistrial. What result?

2. Kim was sexually assaulted by Bernard. When John, the prosecutor, told Kim that he was considering allowing Bernard to plead to simple assault, Kim objected, saying that she wanted to appear at the plea colloquy to voice her concerns. Kim was not present at the colloquy, and the plea was entered and accepted by the judge. Thereafter, Kim moved to set aside the plea, on the ground that state statute gave her the right to be present and speak at the colloquy. What should the judge do?

3. Sulejman Talovic, 15 years old, buys a gun from Hunter Heston. There is some discussion about a bank robbery. Heston is well aware that a federal statute prohibits selling a firearm to a minor. Two weeks later, Talovic walks into a crowded shopping mall and fires the weapon, killing five people, and wounding eight more. One of those injured is London Hilton. When Heston is prosecuted federally, London wants to be present at the plea hearing and sentencing. The federal statute defines "victim" as "a person directly and proximately harmed as a result of the commission of a Federal offense." The prosecutor says she is not a victim. Is she?

Explanations

1. Assume that the pictures are so graphic that, if presented by the prosecutor, they would be held inadmissible because they are too prejudicial. The first question is whether the actions of the parents can be attributed to the prosecutor (assuming she was as surprised as anyone else in the courtroom). Had the parents been merely "spectators," their use of the photographs would surely result in their being removed, and perhaps admonished by the judge. But they are not "mere" spectators — it is only by virtue of the statute that the parents were able to sit at the prosecutor's table. A court might find that, even if the prosecutor was unaware of the parents' plan, the "state" has embraced the plan. *Musladin* is unlikely to help either the state or the parents here. The pictures involved there were on small buttons and apparently only of the victim's face; the court expressly noted that the record did not reflect the precise nature of the photo. Second, the Court in *Musladin* distinguished between "spectator" and "state-sponsored" acts; the state statute here might well be seen as "sponsoring" the parents, even if not their specific actions. Third,

Musladin, a habeas corpus case, used the exceedingly narrow test of whether the state court's actions were a "clearly" "unreasonable" application of then-existing federal law. The test on direct appeal of a conviction would be much more rigorous.

Thus it is likely that the judge could — and would — grant a motion for a mistrial. But here's an even more perplexing question. As we saw in Chapter 9, if a *prosecutor* "goads" a defense counsel into moving for a mistrial, double jeopardy might preclude a second trial. Would that same analysis apply to a person "sponsored" by the state/prosecutor? (It's not likely, because the parents did not *intend* to have a mistrial declared. But it surely leaves a question open.)

2. What remedy should be provided victims if their rights are not protected is unclear. In the specific example here, at least two states expressly preclude reopening a plea, and most other state courts that have considered the issue agree. One reason is finality; another is that the defendant, having no obligation to the victim, has not violated any duty and therefore should not be "punished" for a failure to follow the statute. It is possible, though not likely, that some disciplinary action might be taken against John particularly if he purposely failed to notify Kim of the date of the colloquy. Even less likely (though there are cases differing) is disciplinary action against the judge, who may be under a duty to inquire as to the position of the victim. See generally, Beloof, Cassell & Twist, Victims in Criminal Procedure Chapter 11 (2d ed. 2006).

3. No, at least not according to In re *Antrobus*, 519 F.3d 1123 (10th Cir. 2008). While London is clearly a victim of Heston's actual shooting, the circuit court held that a trial court determination that London was not a victim was not so clearly wrong as to require a writ of mandamus (which is the remedy the act provides).

Table of Cases

Table of Cases

Table of Cases

Index

Index

Index

Index

Hyde Amendment of 1997, 423
Hydraulic theory of discretion, 7, 29

Idaho, assigned counsel in, 267
Identification, eyewitness, 116, 120, 128
Illinois, discovery in, 93
Immigration, 135, 136, 136n12, 300, 304
Immunity
  absolute immunity, 423-426
  clear and convincing evidence standard, 59
  grand juries, 59-60
  pocket immunity, 60
  qualified immunity, 423-426
  transactional immunity, 60, 72, 75
  use immunity, 59-60, 72, 75
Impeachment
  discovery of impeachment evidence, 97,
    102, 102n33
  exculpatory evidence, 120, 121, 125,
    127, 128
  of verdicts, 198-202
Implied bias, 181
Inadmissible evidence, 230, 294
Incapacitation, 311, 313, 315, 324
Incarceration
  Argersinger rule, 264
  bail as means to avoid, 11
  historical background, 315-318
  pretrial incarceration, 11, 22, 27, 132
  preventing oppressive incarceration, 252
  preventive detention. *See* Preventive detention
Incorporation
  generally, 3
  grand juries, inapplicable to, 56, 56n2
  right to jury trial, 169n6, 171
Independent counsel laws, 36
Independent discovery exception, 59
Indeterminate sentencing, 311-312,
    352, 356, 357
Indiana, state sentencing guidelines in, 344
Indictments
  by grand juries, 64-68
  post-indictment delay. *See* Post-indictment
    delay
  pre-indictment delay, 248-249, 255
  probable cause, 65
  right to speedy indictment, 248
  speedy trial. *See* Speedy trial
Indigent persons
  equal protection, 13, 260n5, 262
  right to counsel. *See* Right to counsel

Individualization in sentencing, 316-318,
    318n12, 345-347
Ineffective assistance of counsel, 269-292
  generally, 269
  appeals, 291-292, 298, 301, 303, 306, 410
  assertion of rights, 290-291
  burden of proof, 284
  in capital cases, 285-289, 301, 307
  collateral attack, 374-376
  commencement of right to counsel,
    303-304
  conflicts of interest, 271-275
  distraction, 279
  double deference, 387, 394
  excusing procedural default, 385-387
  expert witnesses, 281, 289-290, 302, 307
  failure to investigate, 280
  frivolous appeals, 291-292
  guilty pleas and, 136-137, 136n11
  intoxication, 279
  limitations, 291
  as misconduct, 413
  in misdemeanor cases, 300, 305
  mistake of law, 280-281, 306
  Model Code of Professional Responsibility,
    276n35
  Model Rules of Professional Conduct, 276n35
  per se, 281, 303
  plea bargaining, waiver of rights, 151
  post-conviction proceedings, applicability
    to, 291-292, 291n66
  prejudice requirement, 284-285, 288,
    306-307
  reasonableness standard, 277-279
  sandbagging, 297
  at sentencing, 298, 302
  sleeping during trial, 279-280, 279-280
    nn42-44
  standard of performance, 276-284
  state collateral review, 374-376
  state interference with representation,
    270-271
  strategic decisions, 282
  Strickland rule, 275-285
  structural error, 275, 303
Informations, 77
Initial appearance
  generally, 10
  failure to conduct, 24-25
  right to counsel at, 260-261, 299, 304
Innocence commissions, 397

471

Index